The MEDIEVAL RECORD

The

MEDIEVAL RECORD

SOURCES OF MEDIEVAL HISTORY

Alfred J. Andrea

University of Vermont

HOUGHTON MIFFLIN COMPANY   BOSTON   NEW YORK

Editor-in-Chief: Jean Woy
Assistant Editor: Keith A. Mahoney
Senior Project Editor: Janet Edmonds
Associate Production/Design Coordinator: Jennifer Meyer
Senior Manufacturing Coordinator: Marie Barnes

Cover design: Ron Kosciak, Dragonfly Design
Cover image: The Pierpont Morgan Library/Art Resource, NY

Source credits appear on pages 481–484.

Printed in the U.S.A.

Library of Congress Catalog Card Number: 96-76855

ISBN: 0-395-71862-7

56789-QF-07 06 05 04 03

Ingenia et artes maxime fovit.
To William M. Daly,
Professor Emeritus, Boston College,
who introduced a generation of students
to the challenge and pleasure
of reading medieval sources

Contents

Topical Contents

Women

Preface

The Medieval Record is based on the proposition that all students of history must meet the challenge of analyzing primary sources, thereby becoming active inquirers into the past, rather than passive recipients of historical facts. Involvement with primary-source evidence enables students to see that historical scholarship is principally the intellectual process of drawing inferences and perceiving patterns from clues yielded by the past, not of memorizing someone else's conclusions. Moreover, such analysis motivates students to learn by stimulating curiosity and imagination and helps them develop into critical thinkers who are comfortable with complex challenges.

Not only does primary-source evidence permit students of history to discover what people in the past thought and did, it also allows researchers to detect significant changes, as well as lines of continuity, in the institutions and ways of thought of given cultures. This, in turn, allows historians to divide the past into meaningful periods that highlight the historical turning points, as well as the constancies, that constitute the human story. In short, primary-source analysis is the essence of the historian's craft and the basis for all historical understanding.

In organizing this source book, I have attempted to arrange selections that fit together in such a way as to present an overview of medieval European history in mosaic form. It is my hope and intent that each source contributes to a single, large composition. I have tried to avoid isolated sources that provide a taste of some aspect of medieval European culture but, by their dissociation, shed no light on significant patterns of cultural creation, continuity, and change.

In selecting and placing the various pieces of this mosaic, I have sought to create a balanced picture of the emergence, efflorescence, and transformation of the First Europe. I have also attempted to give the readers and users of this book a collection of sources representing a wide variety of perspectives and experiences. Believing that the study of history properly concerns every aspect of past human activity and thought, I have tried to include sources that mirror the practices and concerns of a broad spectrum of representative persons and groups. Additionally, it has been my goal to include a wide variety of source genres, so that the book's users might better understand the various types of evidence that someone studying medieval European history might confront and should be acquainted with.

This dual quest for balance and comprehensiveness has also led me into the arena of unwritten evidence. Although most historians center their research on documents, the discipline requires us to consider *all* of the clues surrendered by the past, including its artifacts. Consequently, the book contains a number of illustrations of works of art and other artifacts that users can and should analyze as historical sources.

Source analysis is often a daunting exercise for students who have just begun studying history at an advanced level. To make these sources as accessible as possible, the book provides a variety of aids. First, there is the Prologue, in which I explain — initially in a theoretical manner and then through concrete examples — how a student of history goes about the task of interpreting written and artifactual sources. In the body of the book, there are chapter, section, and individual source introductions, all to help the reader place each selection into a meaningful context and understand its historical significance. Because *The Medieval Record* provides an interpretive overview of the broad outlines of medieval European history, these introductions are significantly fuller than those normally encountered in books of sources.

Suggested Questions for Analysis also precede each source; their purpose is to help the student make sense of each piece of evidence and wrest from it as much insight as possible. I firmly believe that a professor should not simply hand the novice student of history a document and ask, "Well, what do you make of it?" The questions that come so readily to professional historians are not obvious to most undergraduate students, who legitimately seek guidance in asking the right questions.

The Questions for Analysis are largely, but not inflexibly, presented in a three-tiered format, designed to resemble the historian's approach to source analysis and critical thinking. The first several questions are usually specific and ask the reader to pick out important pieces of information. These initial questions require the student to address two basic issues: What does this document or artifact say, and what meaningful facts can I garner from it? Addressing concrete questions of this sort prepares the student researcher for the next, more significant level of critical thinking and analysis — drawing inferences. Questions that demand inferential conclusions accompany every source and almost always follow the fact-oriented questions. Finally, whenever possible, a third tier of questions challenges the student to compare the individual, group, or phenomenon under present consideration with an individual, group, or phenomenon encountered earlier in the book. Drawing such comparisons is a natural and easy way of learning history.

Footnotes that explain terms and allusions that college students cannot reasonably be expected to know constitute another form of help. Some users might well find these sources overly annotated, but I prefer to err on the side of possibly providing too much information, rather than leaving readers uninformed. In that same spirit, the end of this book includes a Glossary of medieval terms that appear frequently throughout this text. Each word that is defined in the Glossary is indicated by an asterisk (*) at its initial occurrence in a source or introduction.

Some instructors might use *The Medieval Record* as their sole textbook. Most, however, will probably use it as a supplement to a standard narrative textbook, and many of them might not require their students to analyze every entry. To assist instructors (and students) in selecting sources that best suit their interests and needs, an analytical table of contents, which lists sources by topic, is provided in the front of the book. It is intended to suggest to professors and students alike the variety of material available within these pages, particularly as subjects for essays.

In summary, my major goal in putting together *The Medieval Record* has been to craft a text that sets up the student-reader for success — *success* being defined as comfort with historical analysis, proficiency in critical thinking, and deepened awareness of the dynamics of medieval European history. How well I have succeeded in that endeavor is for you to decide.

Acknowledgments

Whatever its merits, this book owes much to many colleagues and would be poorer without their contributions. The following historians and teachers reviewed all or portions of the evolving text and provided valuable critiques. Their comments helped me to refine both the sources selected and the editorial material: Blake R. Beattie, University of Louisville; Charles A. Frazee, California State University–Fullerton; Piotr Górecki, University of California–Riverside; Ellen E. Kittell, University of Idaho; and James M. Powell, Syracuse University.

Additionally, I must acknowledge and thank the following persons, who responded to my direct overtures for help: Blake R. Beattie (again) of the University of Louisville, who introduced me to the delights of Franco Sacchetti's wit and made available his translation of the novella that appears in these pages; James F. Powers of The College of the Holy Cross, who provided a translation of the *Fuero* of Cuenca; Joseph F. O'Callaghan of Fordham University, who shared his translations of several texts relating to representative government in Spain; Roswitha Dunlap of Louisville, Kentucky, whose insights into fifteenth-century German idioms proved so helpful; Nicole Yvette Brumsted of the University of Vermont, class of '96, who offered a student's perspective as the book evolved; and my dear friend and colleague, James H. Overfield of the University of Vermont, who critiqued the book's last two chapters from the perspective of a specialist in Renaissance-Reformation history. (He even manages to accept with good grace my quite tired jokes about the so-called Renaissance.)

I also owe special thanks to two master historians, who, so many years ago, laid the base for this book: my teachers, William M. Daly of Boston College, to whom the book is dedicated, and Brian Tierney of Cornell University. The only way in which I can ever repay them is to pass on the skills they taught and the passion for medieval history they communicated in and outside the classroom.

The person who has given me the greatest support and help is, of course, my dear wife, Juanita. She and our son and daughter, Peter and Kristina, have made all of this work possible and worthwhile.

A. J. A.

The
MEDIEVAL
RECORD

Prologue

▼▼▼

Primary Sources: What Are They, and How Do We Read Them?

What Is History?

Many students believe that the study of history involves simply memorizing dates, names, battles, treaties, and endless amounts of similar, usually uninteresting facts that seem to have no relevance whatsoever to their lives and concerns. After all, so they think, the past is over and done with. Historians have recorded what happened, and all that is left for students to do is to absorb this body of knowledge, for reasons known only to educators.

But these notions are wrong — totally wrong. History involves discovery and interpretation, and its content is vitally relevant to our lives. Our understanding of history is constantly changing and deepening, as historians continually learn more about the past and shed new light on its meaning. Just as significant, each person who studies the past brings to it a unique perspective and raises questions that are meaningful to him or her. Although there is certainly an objective past, which we all should endeavor to discover and understand as fully as possible, each of us must also explore a past that has personal meaning, in order to find in it insights and truths relevant to our own concerns. The drive to understand what has gone before us is innately human and springs from our need to know who we are. History serves this function of self-discovery in a special way because of its universality. Contrary to popular opinion, the study of history does not focus exclusively, or even primarily, on politics. It deals with all aspects of past human activity and belief, for there is no subject or concern that lacks a history. Therefore, each of us can explore the origins and historical evolution of whatever is most important to us.

No matter what our interests or questions, the study and interpretation of our complex and variegated historical heritage involves coming to grips with two fundamental issues: change and continuity. How and why do things change over time, and how and why do certain values and practices endure throughout a society's history? Answers to these basic questions, no matter how partial or tentative, reveal a culture's inner dynamics and also help us better understand the challenges that confront us in our own day.

The collection of sources in this book will help you discover some of the major lines of Europe's historical development from roughly A.D. 100 to 1500. As editor, I will not hand you answers; you will have to work for them, because hard work lies at the heart of historical study. The word *history,* which is Greek in origin, means "learning through inquiry," and that is precisely what historians do. They discover and interpret the past by asking questions and conducting research. Their inquiry revolves around an examination of evidence left by the past. For lack of a better term, historians call that evidence *primary source material.*

Primary Sources: Their Value and Limitations

Primary sources are records that, for the most part, have been passed on in written form, thereby preserving the memory of past events. These written sources include, but are not limited to, official records, private correspondence, literature, religious texts, merchants' account books, memoirs, and so on. No source by itself contains the unadulterated truth or the whole picture; each gives us only a glimpse of reality. It is the historians's task to fit these fragments of the past into a coherent picture.

Imagine, for a moment, that some historian in the late twenty-first century decides to write a history of your college class. Think about the primary sources this researcher would use: the school catalogue, the registrar's class lists, academic transcripts, and similar official documents; class lecture notes, course syllabi, examinations, term papers, and possibly even textbooks; diaries and private letters; school newspapers, yearbooks, and sports programs; handbills, posters, and even photographs of graffiti; and recollections written down or otherwise recorded by some of your classmates long after they have graduated. With a bit of thought, you could add other items to the list, among them some unwritten sources, such as recordings of popular music and photographs and videotapes of student life and activity. But let us confine ourselves, for now, to written records. What do all these documentary sources have in common?

Even this imposing list of sources does not and cannot present the past in its entirety. Where do we see evidence of long telephone calls home, all-night study groups, afternoons spent at the student union, or complaints shared among yourselves about professors and courses that never made any official record? Someone possibly recorded memories of some of these events and opinions, but how complete and trustworthy are those records? Also consider that all the documents available to this twenty-first-century historian will be fortunate survivors. As such, they will represent only a small percentage of the vast bulk of written material generated during your college career. Thanks to the wastebasket, the "delete" key, the disintegration of materials, and the inevitable loss of life's memorabilia as years slip by, the evidence available to the future historian will be fragmentary. This is always the case with historical evidence. We cannot preserve the records of the past in their total-ity. Clearly, the more remote the past, the more fragmentary our documentary evidence. Imagine the feeble chance any particular document from the twelfth century had of surviving the wars, worms, and wastebaskets of the past eight hundred years.

Now let us consider the many individual pieces of documentary evidence relating to your class's history that have survived. As we review the list, we see that no single primary source gives us a pure, unvarnished, and complete picture. Each has its perspective, value, and limitations.

You probably are aware of how every college catalogue presents an ideal-ized picture of campus life. Despite its flaws, however, that catalogue is an important piece of evidence, because it reflects the values of the faculty and administrators who composed it. In addition, it provides useful information by listing rules and regulations, courses, instructors, school organizations, and similar items. That information, however, is the raw material of history, not history itself, and certainly does not reflect the full historical reality of your class.

What is true of the catalogue is equally true of the student newspaper and every other piece of evidence generated by or pertinent to your class. Each primary source is part of a larger whole, but as we have already seen, we do not have all the pieces. Think of your historical evidence in terms of a jigsaw puzzle: Many of the pieces are missing, but it is possible to put most, though probably not all, of the remaining pieces together in a reasonable fashion to form a fairly accurate and coherent picture. The picture that emerges might not be complete, but it is useful and valid. The keys to fitting these pieces together are hard work and imagination. Each is absolutely necessary.

Examining the Sources

Hard work speaks for itself, but students are often unaware that a historian also needs an imagination to reconstruct the past. After all, many students ask, doesn't history consist of strictly defined and irrefutable dates, names, and facts? Where does imagination enter into the process of learning these facts?

Again, let us consider your class's history and its documentary sources. Many of those documents provide factual data — dates, names, grades, statistics. And while these data are important, individually and collectively, they have no historical meaning until they have been interpreted. Your college class is not a collection of statistics and facts. It is a group of individuals who, despite their differences, share and help mold a collective experience. It is a commu-nity evolving within a particular time and place. Influenced by its environ-ment, it is, in turn, an influence on that world. Any valid or useful history must reach beyond a mere list of dates, names, and facts and interpret the historical characteristics and role of your class. What were its values? How did it change and why? What impact did it have? These are some of the im-portant questions a historian asks of the evidence. The answers the historian arrives at help us gain insight into ourselves, our society, and our human nature.

In order to arrive at answers, the historian must examine each and every piece of evidence in its full context and wring from that evidence as many *inferences* as possible. Facts are the foundation stones of history, but inferences are its edifices. An inference is a logical conclusion drawn from evidence, and it is the heart and soul of historical inquiry.

Every American schoolchild learns that "In 1492 Columbus sailed the ocean blue." That fact is worthless, however, unless we understand the motives, causes, and significance of this late-fifteenth-century voyage. Certainly, a historian must know when Columbus sailed west. After all, time is history's framework. Yet the questions historians ask go far beyond simple chronology: Why did Columbus sail west? What factors made possible Spain's engagement in such enterprises at this time? Why were Europeans willing and able to exploit, as they did, the New World? What were the short- and long-term consequences of the European presence in the Americas? These are some of the significant questions to which historians seek inferential answers, and those answers can only be found in the evidence.

One noted historian, Robin Winks, has written a book entitled *The Historian as Detective,* and the image is appropriate, although inexact. Like the detective, the historian examines clues in order to reconstruct events. However, the detective is essentially interested in discovering what happened, who did it, and why, whereas the historian goes one step beyond and asks what it all means. In addressing that question, the historian transforms simple curiosity about past events into a humanistic discipline.

As a humanist, the historian seeks wisdom and insight into the human condition, but that wisdom cannot be based on theories spun out of fantasy, wishful thinking, and preconceived notions. It must be based on a methodical and probing investigation of the evidence. Like the detective interrogating witnesses, the historian also carefully examines the testimony of sources, and both investigators ask similar questions. First and foremost, the historian must evaluate the *validity* of the source: Is it what it purports to be? Artful forgeries have misled many historians. Even if the source is authentic (and most are), it still can mislead the historian. The possibility always exists that the source's author is lying or otherwise deliberately misrepresenting reality. Even if this is not the case, the historian can easily be led astray by not fully understanding the *perspective* reflected in the document. As any detective who has interviewed eyewitnesses to an event knows, what each person saw often differs radically, due to a number of factors. The police detective has the opportunity to reexamine witnesses and offer them the opportunity to change their testimony in the light of new evidence and deeper reflection. The historical researcher is usually not so fortunate. Even when the historian compares a piece of documentary evidence with other evidence in order to uncover its flaws, there is no way to cross-examine it in detail. What is written is written. Given this fact, it is absolutely necessary for the historian to understand, as fully as possible, the source's perspective. Thus, the historian must ask several key questions: *What* kind of document is this? *Who* wrote it? For *whom* and *why?* *Where* was it composed and *when?*

The *what* is important, because understanding the nature of a particular source can save the historian a great deal of frustration. Many historical sources simply do not address the questions a historian would like to ask of them. The twenty-first-century historian studying your class would be foolish to try to learn much about the academic quality of your school's courses from a study of the registrar's class lists and grade sheets. Student and faculty class notes, copies of old syllabi, examinations, papers, and textbooks would be far more fruitful sources.

Who, for whom, and *why* are equally important questions. The official school catalogue undoubtedly addresses some issues pertaining to student social life. But should this document, designed to attract potential students and to place the school in the best possible light, be read and accepted uncritically? Obviously not. It must be tested against student testimony, as recorded in such sources as private letters, memoirs, posters, student newspapers, and yearbooks.

Where and *when* are also important questions to ask of any primary source. As a general rule, distance in space and time from an event colors perceptions and can adversely affect the validity of a source's testimony. The recollections of a person celebrating a twenty-fifth class reunion could be quite insightful and valuable. Conceivably, this graduate now has a perspective and information that were absent a quarter-century earlier. Just as conceivably, that person's memory might be playing tricks. A source can be so close to or so distant from the event it deals with that its view is distorted or totally erroneous. Even so, the source is not necessarily worthless. Often, the blind spots and misinformation within a source reveal to the researcher quite a bit about the author's attitudes and sources of information.

The historical detective's task is not easy. In addition to constantly questioning the validity and particular perspectives of available sources, the historical researcher must often use whatever evidence is available in imaginative ways. The researcher must interpret these fragmentary and flawed glimpses of the past and piece together the resultant inferences and insights as well as possible. While recognizing that it is impossible to reconstruct a complete picture of the past, the historian assumes the responsibility of recreating a past that is valid and has meaning for the present.

You and the Sources

This book will actively involve you in the work of historical inquiry by asking you to draw inferences based on your careful analysis of primary source evidence. This is not an easy task, especially at first, but it is well within your capability. Moreover, your professor and I will be helping you along the way.

You realize by now that historians do not base their conclusions on analyses of single, isolated sources. Historical research consists of laborious sifting through mountains of documents. I have already done much of this work for you by selecting, paring down, and annotating important sources that individually allow you to gain some significant insight into a particular issue or moment in the long and complex history of medieval Europe. In doing this, I do not relieve you of the responsibility of recognizing that no single source, no matter how rich it might appear, offers a complete picture of the individual or culture that produced it. Each source that appears in this book is a piece of valuable evidence, but it is only partial evidence. This should never be forgotten.

You will analyze two types of evidence — *documents* and *artifacts*. Each source will be authentic, so you do not have to worry about validating it. I will also supply the information necessary for you to place each piece of evidence into its proper context and will suggest questions you legitimately can and should ask of each source. If you carefully read the introductions and notes, the suggested Questions for Analysis, and, most important of all, the sources themselves — and think about what you are doing — solid inferences will follow.

To illustrate how you should go about this task and what is expected of you, I will take you through a sample exercise, step by step. The exercise consists of our analyzing two sources: a document from the pen of Christopher Columbus and a reproduction of a late-fifteenth-century woodcut. The reason I have chosen the letter by Columbus is that you already know something about this man and his first voyage to the Americas, so you are not being thrown into a totally alien environment. I have chosen the woodcut because it has relevance to what you will read and discover in Columbus's letter. In this exercise, I will not try to draw every possible insight and inference from the two sources, nor will I try to address each of the Questions for Analysis. Rather, I hope to demonstrate how to go about answering several of the more important questions you should ask of these two sources. By the end of this exercise, if you have worked closely with me, you should be ready to begin interpreting sources on your own.

Now, let us begin our exercise by analyzing Columbus's letter of 1493. Turn to Chapter 13 and read the introduction to source 97 and the Questions for Analysis that follow that introduction. The former is intended to place the source into context; the latter should provide direction when it comes time to analyze that same source. One important point to keep in mind is that every historian approaches a source with at least one question in mind, even though it might be vaguely formulated. Very much like the detective, the historian wants to discover some particular truth or shed light on a certain issue. This requires asking specific questions of the witnesses or, in the historian's case, of the evidence. These questions, of course, should not be prejudgments. One of the worst errors a historian can make is setting out to prove a point or to defend an ideological position. Questions are simply starting points, nothing else, but they are essential. Therefore, as you approach a source, have your question or questions fixed in your mind and constantly remind yourself, as you work your way through a source, what issue or issues you are investigating. This book will provide you with a number of suggested questions for each source. Perhaps you or your professor will want to ask other questions. Whatever the case, keep focused on these questions and issues, and take notes as you read each source. Never rely on unaided memory; it almost inevitably leads us astray.

Needless to say, you must be honest and thorough as you study a source. Read each explanatory footnote carefully, lest you misunderstand a word or allusion. Try to understand exactly what the source is saying and its author's perspective. Be careful not to wrench items, words, or ideas out of context, thereby distorting them. Above all, read the entire source so that you understand, as fully as possible, what it says and, just as important, what it does not say.

Interpreting Columbus's Letter

Columbus's letter contains a number of interesting and potentially important facts. For example, the natives Columbus initially encountered were largely homogeneous and communicated with one another through interisland travel. Yet as fascinating and important as these facts are, knowing them does not necessarily make a person a historian. Similarly, garnering such isolated items from a source does not constitute full historical analysis. True historical analysis consists of drawing as much inferential insight as possible from a source and trying to answer, at least in part, the central question of historical study: What does it all mean? This document allows us to do just that.

Historians use no secret method or magic formula to draw historical insights from documentary evidence. All they need are attention to detail, thoroughness, common sense, and a willingness to enter imaginatively into the mind of the document's author as fully and honestly as possible, while trying to set aside momentarily personal values and perspectives. Anyone who is willing to work at it can profitably interpret written primary sources. To prove that point, let us address the core question: What evidence in this document allows us to judge Columbus's reliability as an objective reporter? By addressing this issue, we will essentially answer all of the Questions for Analysis, except number 7.

The researcher always has to evaluate the worth of each source, and this means understanding its point of view and reliability. In this letter, several things are obvious. Columbus believed he had reached Asian islands. John Mandeville's *Travels* and other accounts of Asia provided a number of reference points by which Columbus would have recognized the Orient, and he believed he had found many of them. Equally obvious is the fact that Columbus tried to present his discoveries in the best light possible. He sent this letter ahead to the court of Ferdinand and Isabella to ensure that when he arrived, he would be received with due honor.

Certainly, there is exaggeration, self-puffery, error, and possibly even deliberate distortion in Columbus's account. As the introduction informs us, he overestimated the size of several islands and, except for chilies, the spices he claimed to have discovered proved to be mirages. The admiral also failed to mention that the *Santa Maria* had been lost. There is no way he could have escaped informing his royal patrons of this unhappy incident, but apparently Columbus wanted to wait until he was at the court, where he could put his own spin on the facts surrounding the incident. Also not mentioned is a skirmish that he and his men had on January 13, 1493, with some bellicose natives, whom he incorrectly assumed were Caribs. Perhaps that incident, if reported without explanation, would have weakened the admiral's claim that Spain could easily subjugate these timid "Indians." Generally, however, despite Columbus's enthusiasm and understandable tendency to exaggerate, to conveniently neglect to mention anything negative, and to see what he wanted to see, he *seems* to have wanted to present an essentially factual account.

Columbus's reading of popular travel accounts had prepared him to encounter every sort of human monstrosity, and undoubtedly he would have enjoyed reporting such contacts. But he honestly reported that all the natives he encountered were quite unmonstrous in appearance and temperament. Of course, he reported stories of people with tails, of cannibals, and of warlike women who lived apart from men, but it is unlikely that the admiral deliberately tried to mislead anyone on this issue. The Carib cannibals were real enough. Rumors of tailed people and latter-day Amazons conceivably were nothing more than the natives' trying to please Columbus or simply the result of poor communication. It is not difficult to imagine the admiral inquiring after the locations of these various human curiosities whom Mandeville, Polo, and others had placed in the islands of the Indian Ocean. Likewise, it is not hard to imagine the Tainos' not knowing what Columbus was asking and agreeably pointing across the waters to other islands.

In fact, this raises one issue that has long vexed me and that goes straight to the heart of the question of this source's overall reliability: *How well was Columbus able to communicate with these people?* Columbus insisted that the Spaniards and Tainos were able to communicate with one another through gestures and learned words. Notwithstanding his assurances, I suspect that only the most primitive forms of communication were possible between Europeans and Native Americans in 1492–1493. Therefore, we should have a healthy skepticism about anything that Columbus reports about the Indians' beliefs and cosmological perspectives. Certainly, he seems to have missed the fact that the Tainos worshipped *cemis,* or spirit statues, in their ceremonial centers.

Still, all things considered, it seems reasonable to conclude that Columbus's letter can be accepted as a generally honest, if not totally accurate, account of his discoveries and experiences. That basic honesty, compromised to an extent by an understandable enthusiasm and desire to present his accomplishments in a positive and attractive manner, comes through in his attempt to describe the islands' physical qualities and the people he encountered there. The picture that emerges tells us a lot about the complex motives that underlaid his great adventure.

We notice that Columbus matter of factly took possession of the lands in the names of the monarchs of Spain and even renamed the islands, without once giving thought to anyone else's claims. He also thought nothing of seizing some natives as soon as he arrived and of carrying several Indians back to Spain. Moreover, Columbus noted toward the end of his letter that the monarchs of Spain could obtain as many *slaves* as they desired from among the islands' "idolaters." At the same time (and this might strike the modern student as curious), Columbus claimed that he had always acted kindly toward the native people, and his letter conveys a tone of admiration and even affection for the people whom he had encountered. Indeed, the admiral expressed a deep interest in protecting and winning over the native people of the "Indies," in an avowed hope that they might become Christians and loyal subjects of Ferdinand and Isabella. According to Columbus, the Indians' intelligence, timidity, naiveté, ignorance, sense of wonder at the Europeans, and ability to communicate freely among themselves made them prime candidates for conversion. It also made them ripe for subjugation, however.

The tone of this letter suggests that Columbus was concerned with the native people as humans and was genuinely interested in helping them achieve salvation through religious conversion. It is equally clear, however, that Columbus believed it to be his and Catholic Spain's right and duty to subjugate and exploit these same people. Here we see a tension that continued throughout the Spanish colonial experience in the Americas.

Subjugation of the Indians and their lands involved more than just a sense of divine mission and Christian altruism — as real as those motives were. Columbus, his royal patrons, and most other individuals who joined overseas adventures expected to gain in earthly wealth, as well. Even a superficial reading of Columbus's letter reveals the admiral's preoccupation with the riches of the islands. Gold, spices, cotton, aromatic mastic, and, of course, slaves were the material rewards that awaited Christian Europeans, and Columbus was fully interested in acquiring them.

Was he being cynical, hypocritical, or deliberately ironic when, in his closing words, Columbus claimed that Jesus Christ had provided this great victory to the Spanish monarchs (indeed, to all Christendom) and that from it would flow the dual benefits of converting so many people and obtaining such worldly riches? It does not seem likely. Columbus was a man who saw no contradiction between spreading the faith and benefiting materially from that action, even if doing so meant exploiting the converts.

Please note that in stating this, I am trying to avoid making any moral judgment. This does not mean that, as far as my own standards of right and wrong are concerned, I accept slavery as a justifiable human condition or that I believe it is proper to dispossess people of their lands and cultures. What it does mean is that I am trying to understand Columbus and his world view and not sit in judgment of a society whose values were, in some respects, radically different from my own. Passing moral judgment on a past society's actions might be emotionally satisfying, but it will not change what happened. Doing so also could conceivably blind the judge to the historical context in which those actions took place. As I suggested earlier, we study the past in order to gain insight and wisdom regarding the human condition. If that insight is to have any validity whatsoever, it must be based on as dispassionate a study of the evidence as possible.

Another point merits mention here: Perhaps you disagree with my conclusion that Columbus's letter is basically an honest and valuable source, despite its shortcomings. Well, if you do, you are in excellent company. Two eminent historians, William D. Phillips, Jr., and Carla Rahn Phillips, in their book *The Worlds of Christopher Columbus,* characterized this letter as "a tissue of exaggerations, misconceptions, and outright lies" (p. 185). We obviously disagree in our respective interpretations of the degree, nature, and extent of the letter's misstatements. Well, no historian is infallible, and I certainly do not claim that distinction. Moreover, no source is so patently clear in all respects that it presents no areas of potential disagreement for historians. That, in fact, is one of the exciting aspects of historical research. Despite all of the facts and conclusions that historians generally agree on, there are numerous areas in which they carry on spirited debate. The very nature of history's fragmentary, flawed evidence makes debate inevitable. Furthermore, no historian can possibly see everything there is to be seen in every source. What this means, so far as you are concerned, is that there is plenty of latitude in the sources that appear in this book for you to arrive at insights that are unique to you. In so doing, however, you must, at all times, attempt to divorce yourself of present mindedness and to enter imaginatively into the world of the author whose work you are analyzing. You will note that, as is the case with this letter from Columbus, I have endeavored to help you do this through suggested Questions for Analysis that often are quite leading — perhaps too leading. Do not be constrained by those questions. If you find a question misleading or wrong headed in its presumed assumptions, feel free to follow your own historical muse. Just be ready to defend the questions you have chosen to ask and the conclusions you have reached in answering them.

There are many other questions we could conceivably ask of Columbus's letter and other insights we could garner from it. Certainly, it tells us a lot about the Taino culture. Despite his cultural blinders, his naiveté, his tendency to see what he wanted to see, and his probably exaggerated belief in his ability to communicate with the native people, Columbus seems to have been a reasonably accurate and perceptive observer. Thus, anyone interested in the cultures of the Caribbean peoples before Europeans had much of a chance to influence them must necessarily look to this and similar accounts of first contacts. In fact, it would be good practice for you, right now, to try to answer question 7, which I have deliberately left unanswered. You will be surprised at how much you can learn about the Tainos from this brief description. As you do this exercise, however, do not forget to ask yourself constantly: How reliable does Columbus appear to be on this specific point, and why do I conclude this?

After you have tested your own powers of historical analysis by completing this exercise, it would be wise to put the letter aside for the present. By now, you have a good idea of how a student of history should examine and mine a documentary source, and it is time to turn to artifactual evidence.

Unwritten Sources

Historians distinguish between the prehistorical and historical pasts, with the chief defining feature of any *historical* culture being that it provides written records from which we can reconstruct its past. Without numerous and varied documentary sources, it is impossible to write any society's history in detail. This is not to say that the unwritten relics of the past are worthless. Archeology proves their value, and even historians use such sources. As a rule, however, no matter how extensive a culture's physical remains might be, if it has not left records we can read, its history largely remains a closed book.

Given the central role documents play in our reconstruction of the past, it should not surprise us to learn that most historians concentrate their research almost exclusively on written sources. Yet historians would be foolish to overlook any piece of evidence from the past. As suggested earlier, photographs could prove to be a rich source for anyone researching the history of your class. Our future historian might also want to study all of the extant souvenirs and supplies that were sold in your school's bookstore. Examined properly, they could help fill in some gaps in the story of your class's cultural history.

Artifacts can be illuminating, particularly when used in conjunction with written records. For instance, coins can tell us a lot about a society's ideals or its leaders' programs. Art, in its many forms, can reveal the interests, attitudes, and modes of perception of various segments of society, from the elites to the masses. More down-to-earth items, such as domestic utensils and tools, allow us to infer quite a bit about the lives of common individuals. In this book, we concentrate on written sources, for reasons already outlined, but it would be foolish to overlook artifacts. Therefore, let us see how to read a sample piece of artifactual evidence.

Look again at Chapter 13, this time at source 96. Read the introduction and Questions for Analysis, study the woodcut, try to answer the first three questions, and then compare your insights with mine. Chances are, you will see things that I missed.

Interpreting the Woodcut

Let us confine ourselves to addressing the first three Questions for Analysis. You can deal with question 4 later in the year, after you have read and studied Mandeville in Chapter 12.

Question 1 seems fairly straightforward, but it is a bit more challenging than it might first appear to be. I put the question in for two reasons: to make sure that you are developing the habit of paying attention to every detail and to provide an example of how images unaccompanied by text can defy interpretation.

Here we see depicted two of the many marvelous springs, or fountains, that Megenberg describes and nine varieties of marvelous people. In light of the explanatory remarks that precede this illustration, you should have little difficulty identifying one of the two fountains: the Arcadian well from which pregnant women drink to protect their fetuses. But would you really be sure that the other is a hot spring (such as those Europeans knew of from their contacts with Iceland) had I not given you the hint that in the original, hand-colored woodcut, the flames at the top were red — something you miss in our black-and-white reproduction? More than that, would you have been able to identify either of these wells without having read my introductory remarks? Would I have been able to identify them had I not read the German text? I think not.

Eight of the nine fabulous people are pretty easily identified, regardless of what you and I have read or not read. They are a man whose feet are on backward; a two-headed man; a one-legged man whose single foot is webbed; a headless man whose eyes are on his shoulders and whose mouth and nose are below his eyes, approximately where you would expect to find his nipples; a dog-headed man; a one-eyed man, or cyclops; a six-armed man; and, in the lower-left-hand corner, a bearded woman leading a panther on a leash. We skipped one person, the woman who appears between the bearded woman and the six-armed man. Her deformity is harder to identify from this wood-cut alone. When I studied the woodcut in an archive, I was stumped, until I took time to read the accompanying text (always a wise thing to do). There, as I note in a rather broad hint to you, Megenberg tells us that in certain regions — especially Burgundy — women develop goiters the size of pumpkins, which hang down to their navels. The discovery of this text, which solved my little mystery, just goes to show that sometimes a few dozen words are worth more than a single picture. At least, they can make the picture understandable.

The woman with the goiter stands apart from the other eight individuals because such ailments were common in iodine-deprived regions of Europe as recently as the early twentieth century. The other people, however, are constructs fashioned out of myths, fantasies, and garbled travelers' tales. As in the case of the cyclops, whom you possibly have encountered in Homer's *Odyssey,* many of these fabulous people had inhabited the Greco-Roman imagination and therefore were part of the body of natural science that medieval Europe received from antiquity. The wild, bearded woman was certainly also part of that heritage. Some of these fabulous people, however, seem to have been created out of misreadings of alien religious icons. For example, the dog-headed man could easily be the ancient Egyptian jackal-headed god of the dead, Anubis, whose features are prominently displayed in Egyptian tombs. The six-armed man is probably a vague reflection of numerous Hindu and Buddhist statues of multiarmed deities.

It is interesting to speculate on the mythological origins of these fantastic people, but we have not been asked to do so. Therefore, let us return to the Questions for Analysis. Regardless of whether you are able to identify the cyclops as a cyclops or the woman with a goiter as a person with a thyroid problem and regardless of whether you have ever heard of Anubis, you can provide insightful answers to questions 2 and 3.

Consider question 2. I can think of two major reasons why these men and women are portrayed without clothes. The first would be to present them as people who live in a state of innocence, by reason of not having inherited the consequences of Adam and Eve's Original Sin. The other would be to depict them as persons who are not fully (or even partially) civilized. Which do you think it is? Or are both answers correct? What implications are contained in your answer?

Question 3 is more difficult but not impossible to answer. As I read it, the overall message of this illustration is that great marvels and rewards await the intrepid explorer who ventures beyond Europe's frontier. There is something innately human in the attitude that the world is a mysterious place that houses all sorts of wonders that are yet to be seen or explained. We *want* to believe in the paranormal. What else can explain our own society's fascination with such phenomena as UFOs and the Loch Ness Monster? Medieval people were no different. Headless people and wild, bearded women of the forest were the counterparts of their day to the wonders that we today can read about in newspapers at supermarket checkout stands. Coupled with this belief in the reality of the abnormal is the hope that contact with these marvels will not only satisfy our need to encounter new experiences but will also bring us some tangible benefit. In the late fifteenth century, Bämler expressed that hope by portraying the woman drinking from the marvelous spring that prevents spontaneous miscarriage. Yes, as frightening as the world beyond Europe's frontiers might have been for the timid (uncivilized, dog-headed men are not to be taken lightly), it offered great promise of adventure and profit for the bold.

Have I read too much into the woodcut? It is arguable that I have allowed my imagination to get away from me. The historian always faces this problem when trying to analyze an isolated piece of evidence, particularly when it is an unwritten source. Yet as I suggested a few paragraphs above, this artifact is not completely isolated, because I brought to its analysis insight gained from documentary evidence — Megenberg's text and also, I must admit, Columbus's letter and the accounts of such writers as John Mandeville. In fact, this is how we generally read the artifacts of historical cultures: We attempt to place them in the context of what we have already learned or inferred from documentary sources. Documents illuminate artifacts, and artifacts make more vivid and tangible the often shadowy world of words.

As you attempt to analyze the unwritten sources in this book, keep in mind what you have learned from the documents you have already read as well as from your textbook and class lectures. Remember that these artifacts have been selected to illustrate broad themes and general trends. You should not find their messages overly subtle. As with the documents, always try to place each piece of nonverbal evidence into its proper context, and in that regard, read the introductions and Questions for Analysis very carefully. They supply all the information and clues you need.

A Final Word

My colleagues and I study history for many different reasons, but one thing we agree on is that research into the sources of the past is stimulating and satisfying. The word *fun* might even be appropriate. As you read and analyze these sources, I hope you experience some of that sense of discovery that keeps historians doing what they do.

Part One

▼▼▼

The Collapse of Roman Unity and the Emergence of Three Successor Civilizations: A.D. 100–1050

The decline and fall of the Roman Empire is one of the most vexing issues in Western history. Students and teachers often approach the question as they would a postmortem, examining the corpse of the Roman Empire to discover the time and cause of death. When did it die? Was it the year 410, when Visigoths sacked Rome, or was it 455, when Vandals did the same? Was it in 476, when the last western Roman emperor was deposed? Did it linger on a bit after 476, only to pass away quietly in its sleep? Did it die as a result of a long-term internal disorder? Was it the victim of a sudden disease from outside? Was it murdered? Did it commit unwitting suicide?

Many theories abound: Christianity weakened the empire's martial spirit and its ability to defend itself; Roman technology was inadequate to meet the demands of changing times; disease mortally weakened Roman society; an exhausted soil was incapable of supporting the empire's population; the empire's vitality was sapped when the Roman upper classes were submerged by rural, Eastern, and Germanic peoples. Some of these theories are blatantly wrong: Rome's Christian emperors and legions were no less vigorous in waging war than their pagan predecessors; there is no evidence of soil exhaustion; and the suggestion that Rome's supposedly superior upper classes were mongrelized by inferior outsiders is not supported by any objective evidence and is contemptible in its racism. Other theories, such as the view that plague and the incursions of Germanic and other fringe peoples weakened and battered an already overextended empire, contain a lot of truth, but they do not fully explain the passing away of Roman civilization.

The fact is, Rome did not fall in a single moment or pass away due to a single, isolated circumstance. Indeed, the notion that Rome *fell* is misleading. What happened was much more complex than simply the collapse of an empire. An entire Mediterranean-based civilization, which embraced the cultures of many diverse peoples other than just the Romans, was transformed over a period of centuries into three major successor civilizations: Byzantium; Islam; and Europe.

All of Eurasia's civilizations were battered and, in differing degrees, changed by forces that swept the entire landmass between roughly A.D. 200 and 700. The old equilibrium between seminomadic fringe peoples and their settled neighbors that had allowed the rise of great regional empires in China, India, Southwest Asia, and the Mediterranean during the first millennium B.C. had broken down, and with renewed assaults on these empires, the civilizations that they encompassed underwent change. The shift in balance between Eurasia's great empires of late antiquity and the fringe peoples was due to the weakening of the internal fabrics of these empires, their growing inability to defend swollen frontiers, and the greater aggressiveness of the so-called barbarians, especially mounted nomads.

On its part, the Roman Empire experienced serious invasions during the middle decades of the third century A.D. Fleets of Germanic pirates ravaged the Aegean, and various other Germanic invaders menaced the continent. So great was the threat to Italy, Emperor Aurelian (r. 270–275) deemed it necessary to construct massive defensive walls around the formerly unwalled city of Rome. Aurelian also found it necessary to shorten the empire's frontier by abandoning the province of Dacia (modern Romania) to the Goths. Such drastic measures, when combined with reorganization of the empire's frontier forces, eventually helped restabilize Rome's Rhine and Danubian borders toward the end of the third century.

A century later, however, Rome's barbarian problem once again reached crisis proportions. In 376 a Germanic people known as the Visigoths successfully petitioned the empire for permission to settle south of the Danube River in Roman-held areas of the Balkans. Abuse by Roman officials drove them to revolt, and in 378 they destroyed a Roman army and killed an emperor. Although Emperor Theodosius the Great (r. 378–395) saved the immediate situation, the late Roman Empire's political-military reverses had just begun.

The Visigoths were only the vanguard of the invaders. By the end of the fifth century, the western half of the empire, including Italy, was divided into a patchwork of independent Germanic kingdoms, and the eastern half of the empire, centered on Constantinople, was well on its way toward becoming the nucleus of a new civilization. The new invaders badly wounded the Roman Empire, and some historians argue that they cumulatively were the empire's assassins. This is true in a strictly political sense, so far as the western half of the empire was concerned. By the end of the sixth century, precious little of the western half of the Roman world was still ruled by imperial Roman authority. However, the collapse of imperial structures in the West was not the major story.

Empires in the ancient world were generally precarious entities, and many had risen and fallen over the previous three millennia. China's Han Empire (202 B.C.–A.D. 220), which was roughly as large and as old as the Roman Empire, disintegrated in the early third century against a background of plague, declining population, decreasing economic activity, invasion by various Turco-Mongol nomads, and the rise of local warlords. The end of empire occasioned over 350 years of disunity and dislocation, as well as some significant changes in Chinese life. What was more significant, however, was what did *not* change. In the late sixth century, China re-emerged from political chaos ready to create a new and even greater empire, and that new empire was an extension of a civilization firmly rooted in its remote past. In brief, the cultural continuities in China over the thousand-year period between 400 B.C. and A.D. 600 were far more significant than the differences. This was not true for Roman civilization, especially Roman civilization in the western half of the empire, where radical cultural changes took place.

Quite simply, Roman civilization did not suddenly collapse, fall, or die; it became something else. More correctly, it metamorphosed into several new civilizations.

Chapter 1

▾▾▾

Caesar and Christ

By the middle of the second century A.D., the Romans had carved out an empire that extended from the lowlands of Scotland to the northern regions of Arabia, from the forests of western Germany to the Sahara Desert, and from the Atlantic Ocean to Mesopotamia. The heart and soul of this three-thousand-mile-wide empire was the Mediterranean Sea, a richly diverse cultural region that had a long history well before Rome began its climb to greatness. More than just a political entity, the Roman Empire was late antiquity's most extensive and complex civilization. Borrowing heavily from their eastern Mediterranean subjects, especially the Greeks, the Romans fashioned a Mediterranean-wide community, in which an upper-class Greco-Roman culture flourished wherever Roman armies and officials exercised dominion. In the process of creating this synthesis, which bore its ripest fruits between the late first century B.C. and late second century A.D., Rome carried the ideas and institutions of several thousand years of civilization to a multitude of new recipients. Through the agency of Roman imperialism, civilization moved westward and northward, where it took shallow root among the elite classes of such Western peoples as the Celts of Gaul and Britain.

Ultimately, the most lasting impact that the Roman Empire had on history was its embracing of Christianity, a new religion out of Southwest Asia, and the creation of a Christian Roman Empire in the fourth century A.D. Long after the Roman state had passed out of existence and Roman civilization had metamorphosed into other, quite radically different forms of culture, Christian Roman empires and churches continued to flourish in both the eastern and western portions of the Mediterranean, with each claiming to be the sole heir of Roman legitimacy and authority. Without the several centuries of Christian-Roman synthesis that took place during the fourth and fifth centuries, the histories of Europe and the eastern Mediterranean would have been radically different.

▼▼▼

Remaking the Pax Romana

In the year A.D. 13 the aged Caesar Augustus (r. 30 B.C.–A.D. 14), Rome's first emperor, rendered a long account of his stewardship over the Roman state and in it boasted he had established a new era of peace. That claim had validity. The two centuries that span the period 30 B.C. to A.D. 180 are generally known as the age of the *Pax Romana,* or "Roman Peace," an age of general imperial prosperity and overall security. The key to maintaining the Pax Romana was imperial control of an army that became increasingly professional under Augustus and his successors.

Doubtless many subjects of the empire gloried in the peace and prosperity of the imperial system created by Augustus and brought to its peak by his second-century successors, but the Roman Peace had its systemic weaknesses, as the Crisis of the Third Century demonstrated. Between A.D. 180 and 284 the entire empire seemed to be on the verge of total disintegration. In the process of responding to the challenges of the third century, Rome's leaders changed forever the face and reality of the Pax Romana.

Imperial Reorganization
▼▼▼

1 ▼ *Lactantius,*
ON THE DEATHS OF THE PERSECUTORS

The third century A.D. witnessed the greatest concatenation of crises the Roman Empire had faced to date, as the Mediterranean world experienced invasions on every front, civil wars, economic collapse, social turmoil, massive epidemics, and numerous other natural disasters. The Crisis of the Third Century essentially ended with the imperial accession in 284 of the general Diocletian, who ruled until his voluntary abdication in 305. Although several of Diocletian's predecessors had anticipated some of his many reforms of the empire's military and civil structures and had even begun to restore order to a battered but still vital empire, Diocletian rightfully is accorded credit (and blame) for having initiated in a systematic manner the radical restructuring that enabled the Roman Empire to continue to exist for several more centuries. In the process of saving the empire, however, Diocletian and his immediate successors transformed it into an undisguised authoritarian state centered on a divine emperor.

One of the most important eyewitnesses to Diocletian's reign was L. Caecilius Firmianus Lactantius (ca. 250–325?). Born a pagan in North Africa, Lactantius became a celebrated master of Latin rhetoric* and was summoned to Nicomedia in Anatolia* by none other than Emperor Diocletian to teach rhetoric at this east-

---

*Please consult the Glossary whenever this sign accompanies a word.

ern center of imperial government and to supervise the Latinity of the imperial court's official documents. While in Nicomedia, Lactantius converted to Christianity and also witnessed the outbreak of the Great Persecution against the Christian Church in 303 (source 3). Evidence suggests that he lost his office and most of his pupils during this period but was not otherwise injured. The persecution ended, for the most part, in 311, and soon thereafter Lactantius completed the first edition of his *On the Deaths of the Persecutors,* which recounted in edifying detail the horrible ends suffered by the handful of emperors who had chosen to persecute Christians over the past 250 years.

Because Diocletian and his co-emperor, Maximian, fell into that category, we have the vivid portraits that follow. Even when we take into account Lactantius's obvious bias, whereby he judged emperors as good or bad on the basis of their policies toward Christians, we still have to regard this contemporary piece of evidence as a valuable source of information for what Diocletian attempted to accomplish during his reign.

QUESTIONS FOR ANALYSIS

1. What specific reforms and changes did Diocletian institute?
2. According to Lactantius, what were the consequences of these actions?
3. What do Diocletian's reforms, as enumerated here, suggest about some of the systemic problems in the empire — at least as Diocletian perceived them?
4. What appears to have been Diocletian's overall imperial policy?
5. Lactantius is obviously prejudiced against Diocletian and Maximian. Nevertheless, do any of his charges strike you as plausible? Which ones? Why?
6. Suppose that Diocletian wrote a rejoinder to Lactantius's critique. How would he answer those charges?

While Diocletian, that author of crimes and inventor of evils, was ruining everything, he could not even hold his hand back from God.[1] This man turned the whole world upside down by reason of his greed and timidity. He appointed three men to share his rule, having divided the world into four parts,[2] and he multiplied the armies, inasmuch as each individual co-regent strove to maintain a far larger number of troops than previous princes had when governing the

---

[1]This is a reference to the empirewide Great Persecution of the Christian Church, which officially lasted from February 303 to April 311, although it persisted a bit longer in some eastern regions. By imperial edict, all Christian churches were ordered destroyed and Christians were deprived of all legal rights. Anyone guilty of impeding enforcement of this policy was liable to execution, as was anyone who declined to sacrifice to the gods when requested to do so.

[2]This is a reference to the *Tetrarchy,* or "rule by four," a radically new way of governing the empire. Diocletian appointed a co-emperor, who bore, along with Diocletian, the title *Augustus* (plural: *Augusti*). Each emperor exercised sovereign authority over one-half of the empire. Moreover, each Augustus appointed a deputy emperor and heir-designate, who bore the title *Caesar.* Each Caesar received one-half of his Augustus's portion of the empire to govern. Thus, the empire was quartered so far as imperial civil and military authority was concerned.

state alone. The number of those who received sustenance from the government began to exceed the number of those who contributed by so much that, with farmers' resources exhausted by the enormous size of the imperial requisitions, farms were abandoned and cultivated land reverted to forest. To ensure complete terror, the provinces were divided into fragments;[3] many governors and even more officials were imposed on individual regions and almost on individual cities, and added to these were large numbers of accountants, controllers, and prefects' deputies.[4] All of these civil officials rarely acted with civility; rather, they engaged solely in frequent condemnations and proscriptions and exacted innumerable goods. The exactions were not simply frequent, they were unending, and by reason of these forced payments, unbearable damage was done. How also could the procedures for raising troops be endured?

Given his insatiable greed, this same Diocletian did not want the value of his treasury ever to be reduced. Rather, he constantly amassed extraordinary gifts and contributions[5] so that he could preserve, whole and inviolate, the wealth that he was storing up. When this same man created a huge price inflation by his various misdeeds, he tried to set by law the selling prices of commodities.[6] Then much blood was spilled over petty and trifling items. In the panic that ensued, nothing appeared for sale, and inflation raged worse than before until, after many had

lost their lives,[7] that law was repealed out of necessity.

On top of this, there was added a certain boundless passion for building, which resulted in a no less boundless demand that the provinces deliver workers, artisans, wagons, and whatever else was necessary for Diocletian's construction projects. Here he built basilicas,[8] there a circus, here a mint, there an arms factory, here a house for his wife, there one for his daughter. Suddenly a major portion of the city[9] had been destroyed, and all the citizens, accompanied by their wives and children, moved out, as if from a city that had been captured by the enemy. When these buildings had been completed (along with the ruin of the provinces), he would say: "They have not been built correctly. They must be done differently." They then would have to be torn apart and altered — perhaps only to undergo a second demolition. It was in this manner that he constantly raved, as he strove to make Nicomedia the equal of the city of Rome.

I pass over the many people who perished because of their property or wealth. As evil became commonplace, this became normal and almost legitimate. What was, however, peculiar to him was that whenever he saw a field that was cultivated in a superior manner or a building that was better decorated than most, a false accusation and capital punishment were straightway obtained against the owner, as though he could

---

[3]Ultimately, Diocletian's reorganization resulted in the creation of 120 provinces.

[4]As part of his grand restructuring plan, Diocletian distributed the empire's one hundred twenty new provinces among twelve *dioceses,** each of which was governed by a *vicar,* or prefect's deputy. Supervising the vicars were four *praetorian prefects,* each of whom was responsible for three such deputies and altogether about one-quarter of the empire's civil administration. These praetorian prefects, vicars, and governors exercised only civil authority and legally held no military power whatsoever. Thus, in the age of the Tetrarchy, the empire had two Augusti, two Caesars, four praetorian prefects, twelve vicars, one hundred twenty provincial governors, plus many more bureaucrats.

[5]That is, he extorted donations.

[6]The Edict on Prices of 301.

[7]The implication is that as goods fled the open market, they went into an illegal black market, accompanied by all of the violence and price gouging that such economies engender.

[8]*Basilicas* were long, rectangular-shaped public halls, covered by high, vaulted ceilings of concrete; they functioned primarily as law courts.

[9]Nicomedia, from where Diocletian ruled his portion of the empire.

not seize another's property without shedding blood.

What about his brother Maximian, who was called *Hercules*?[10] He was like Diocletian, for they could not be united in such loyal friendship if there were not in both men a single mind, a sameness of thought, a corresponding will, and a unanimity of judgment. They differed only in that Diocletian was greedier but more timid, whereas Maximian was less greedy but bolder — bolder not for doing good but for evil. Although he held Italy, the very seat of the empire,[11] and although very wealthy provinces, such as Africa or Spain, were subject to him, he was not especially diligent in holding onto the immense riches that were available to him. As the need arose, there was no shortage of extremely rich senators who, on the basis of perjured testimony, could be charged with having aspired to imperial power. The result was that the senate's luminaries were continually gouged out of that body, while Maximian's blood-gorged purse bulged with ill-gotten riches. . . . The only things in which he judged his happiness to lie and on which he believed the good fortune of his imperial power rested were the denial of nothing to his lust and evil desires.

---

[10]*Brother* in the sense of being his co-emperor. Maximian was proclaimed Caesar in 285 and was elevated to Augustus in 286. Diocletian took the name *Jove* to indicate his special relationship with Jupiter, chief deity of the Roman state. Maximian's assumption of the name *Hercules* indicated the relationship he enjoyed with this legendary hero who had arisen, by adoption, into the company of the gods.

[11]Actually, by this time Italy had ceased to be the center of the empire in anything other than a nostalgic sense. For that reason, Diocletian, the senior Augustus, had his capital in the East.

Late Roman Society
▼▼▼

2 ▼ *THE THEODOSIAN CODE*

Diocletian's autocratic state flourished and expanded under the control of Constantine (r. 306–337) and Constantine's immediate successors. The price of momentary stability, however, was that life became increasingly regimented, as all levels of society were marshaled to serve the state.

One of the best mirrors of late Roman society and its problems is *The Theodosian Code,* a collection of imperial proclamations that span the period from A.D. 313 to 437. The code, which was published in 438 and became law for the entire empire, exists largely because of the patronage of Theodosius II (r. 408–450), emperor of the eastern half of the Roman Empire; in 429 he commissioned a panel of jurists to arrange systematically all imperial edicts from the reign of Constantine I to his time, without attempting to resolve any contradictions. The result was more than 2,500 edicts divided among sixteen books, or chapters. Each book was divided into titles, or subjects, and the edicts under each title were arranged chronologically. For example, Title 1 of Book 12 is entitled "Decurions" and contains 192 edicts on the subject, dating from 313 to 436. The section regarding *decurions,* the municipal officials in charge of local administration, happens to be the lengthiest in the entire code, which is a good indication of the importance the emperors attached to the office and their consistent inability to solve the problems presented by the decurion system.

QUESTIONS FOR ANALYSIS

1. Exactly what was the status of coloni, and how, if at all, did they differ from slaves? What do the two edicts regarding coloni suggest about some of the problems that vexed the patrons of many coloni?
2. What do these edicts reveal about the military problems that the late Roman Empire faced? What measures did the emperors take to meet these problems? Judging from the evidence, how successful were these measures?
3. From the empire's perspective, what was the problem with its decurions? What measures did the empire institute to solve the problem? How successful do those measures appear to have been?
4. What does the decurion problem suggest about the systemic troubles that were plaguing the late Roman Empire?
5. How did the government attempt to regulate certain key crafts? Judging from the guilds that it regulated, what crafts did the government consider essential for the empire's prosperity? What do these guild regulations suggest about the fourth-century empire's economy? Based on the evidence, how successfully did the empire regulate its guilds and the economy?

COLONI[1] AND SLAVES

5.17.1

Any person in whose possession a colonus that belongs to another is found not only shall restore the aforesaid colonus to his birth status but also shall assume the capitation tax[2] for this man for the time that he was with him.

1. Coloni also who meditate flight must be bound with chains and reduced to a servile condition, so that by virtue of their condemnation to slavery, they shall be compelled to fulfill the duties that befit freemen.

   Given on . . . October 30, 332.

5.19.1

There is no doubt that coloni do not have the right to alienate the fields that they cultivate, to the extent that even if they have any belongings of their own, they may not transfer them to oth-ers without the advice and knowledge of their patrons.

   Given on . . . January 27, 365.

MILITARY AFFAIRS

7.1.5

We again call to the practice of war and to the camp the sons of those men who have continued steadfast in military service. We shall confer on these sons also the same advantages of terms of service as are enjoyed by those men of the second military rank[3] who perform especially salutary service to the State. 1. But if weakness of health or condition of body or smallness of stature should exempt some of them from the condition of armed imperial service, We order them to perform imperial service in other offices. 2. For if, after the age defined by Us,[4] they should

---

[1]*Coloni* (singular: *colonus*) were tenant farmers.
[2]A tax assessed on a head (*caput*), or person. In the case of a farmer, it was assessed on the amount of land that one able-bodied person could theoretically work.

[3]These recruits entered service with the same rank that ordinary soldiers enjoyed upon their first promotion.
[4]For the sons of veterans, the age of enlistment was sixteen; for other recruits, it was eighteen.

be addicted to a life of ignoble ease, they shall be bound to the municipal councils[5] without controversy, according to the quality of their resources and abilities. But if any such persons should be so weakened by fortuitous infirmity or diseases and broken physical health that they cannot be eligible for the service of camps or for any imperial service, they shall obtain perpetual exemption from imperial service, and they shall be freed from the duties of the compulsory public services of decurions.[6]

Given on . . . April 29, 364.

7.1.8

Your Authority shall announce to all veterans whatsoever that if any of them should not, of his own free will, offer his son who is entirely worthy of the honor of bearing arms, to the imperial service for which the veteran himself has toiled, he shall be involved in the toils of Our law.

Given on . . . September 24, 365. . . .

7.15.1

Whereas We have learned that the tracts of land which had been granted by a benevolent provision of the ancients to the barbarians[7] for the care and protection of the border and of the border fortifications are being held by some other persons, if such persons are holding these lands because of their cupidity or desire, they shall know that they must serve with zeal and labor in the care of the border fortifications and in the protection of the border, just as did those persons whom antiquity assigned to this task. Otherwise they shall know that these tracts of land must be transferred either to the barbarians if they can be found, or certainly to veterans,[8] not undeservedly, so that by the observance of this provision there may be no suggestion of fear in any portion of the border fortification and the border.

Given on . . . April 29, 409.

7.18.4

If any person should harbor a deserter, he shall be fined by the loss of the landholding on which the deserter was in hiding, and he shall have great fear of an even more severe sentence. Furthermore, he shall have no doubt that his overseer will be subjected to the flames, if, to the ruin of his master, the overseer should perchance either foster the crime by participation in it or disregard it by dissimulation. 1. But if a slave should surrender such deserter, he shall be given freedom. If a freeborn person of moderate status should surrender such deserter, he shall gain immunity.[9] . . .

Posted on . . . July 15, 380.

7.18.14

We grant by law to provincials the right to overpower deserters, and if the deserters should dare to resist, We order that punishment be swift everywhere. All persons shall know that, in defense of the common peace, they are granted this right to administer public vengeance against public brigands and deserters from military service. . . .

Given on . . . October 2, 403.

---

[5]Local municipalities were administered by councils (*curiae*), and the persons who sat on these councils came from the class known as *curiales* (singular: *curialis*). In theory, a curialis's wealth and property allowed him to serve in one of these unpaid positions. (See the next note.)

[6]An ancient title that originally meant one who was head of a tenth part of the assembly of Roman people. By the time of the Theodosian Code, it was a title borne by any member of a local municipal council, and the term was often interchangeable with *curialis* (see note 5). Over a stipulated period of time, a decurion would serve in a number of different administrative offices — all at his own expense. By the fourth century, the decurion's chief responsibility was to collect assessed imperial taxes.

[7]Whole tribes of barbarians would be settled along the frontiers as *foederati*, or allies. In return for land, these allies served under their own chieftains as auxiliary frontier troops, theoretically keeping their more troublesome cousins from penetrating the empire.

[8]Retired veterans also would be settled along Rome's borders, where they worked farms given them as pensions and also served as a reserve militia force.

[9]From all compulsory public service, including taxes.

7.18.17

We order that all the tribunes[10] who have assumed the duty of searching out vagrants and deserters throughout Africa shall be removed, that they may not devastate the province under a pretext of this kind. 1. In the future, moreover, We decree that this unholy title and office must not exist at all throughout Africa, and if any person should attempt to aspire to the forbidden rank of this office for the sake of plunder, he shall be subjected to the severity of capital punishment.

Given on . . . February 29, 412.

7.20.7

We learn that certain veterans, unworthy of that name, are committing brigandage. We command, therefore, that veterans of good character shall either till the fields or invest money in honorable business enterprises and buy and sell goods.[11] But capital punishment shall immediately rise up against those veterans who neither cultivate the land nor spend useful lives in business. For they must be stripped of all special privileges if they should disturb the public peace, and if they should commit the slightest delinquency, they shall be subjected to all the penalties.

Given on . . . August 11, 353(?).

DECURIONS

12.1.1

No judge shall attempt to grant exemption from compulsory municipal services to any decurion, nor shall he free anyone from the municipal council by his own judgment. For if any man should be impoverished by a misfortune of such kind that he needs to be assisted, his name must be referred to Our Wisdom,[12] so that an exemption from compulsory municipal services may be granted to him for a limited space of time.

Posted on . . . March 15, 313; 315; 326.[13]

12.1.7

We decree that the sons of decurions who have grown to the age of eighteen years shall be attached throughout the province of Carthage to compulsory municipal services. For We must not wait for them to be released from their family and freed from the sacred bonds of the paternal power, since the wishes of their fathers must not prejudice the interests of the municipalities.

Posted on . . . February 21, 320; 329.

12.1.13

Since We have learned that the municipal councils are being left desolate by those persons who are obligated to them through birth status and who are requesting imperial service for themselves through supplications to the Emperor and are running away to the legions and various governmental offices, We order all municipal councils to be admonished that if they should apprehend any persons with less than twenty terms of service in governmental offices, either in evading the duties that devolve upon their birth status or in insinuating themselves into the imperial service and holding in contempt the nomination to a municipal office, they shall drag such persons back to the municipal councils. . . .

Given on . . . May 17, 326.

12.1.62

If a decurion should steal into a guild of artisans[14] for the purpose of evading other duties, he shall be restored to his pristine status, and in the future no person who derives his birth status from decurions shall dare to aspire to the duties of such a guild.

Given on . . . December 10, 364.

---

[10]Commander of a cohort, which was anywhere from three hundred to six hundred soldiers at this time.

[11]Retired soldiers were often settled along the frontiers where they had previously served. In retirement, they worked small farms or engaged in minor border commerce and remained liable for call-up as reserve troops.

[12]The emperor.

[13]Note its reissue in 315 and 326.

[14]Known as *collegia* (singular: *collegium*), these craft associations were created and supervised by the state.

12.1.146

We observe that many men are hiding under the shadow of powerful men, in order that they may defraud their municipalities of the services which they owe. Therefore, a fine must be established to the effect that if any man should violate the general rule of the prescribed law, he shall be forced to pay to Our fisc[15] five pounds of gold for each decurion and one pound for each member of a guild. Therefore, they shall expel all such men whom they harbor, lest Our Clemency should be aroused to greater indignation on account of the contumacy of those who disregard Our law.

Given on . . . June 15, 395.

GUILDS

13.4.2

We command that artisans who dwell in each city and who practice the skills included in the appended list shall be free from all compulsory public services, since indeed their leisure should be spent in learning these skills whereby they may desire the more to become more proficient themselves and to instruct their children.

Given on . . . August 2, 337.

(Appended List.)

Architects, makers of paneled ceilings, plasterers, carpenters, physicians, stonecutters, silversmiths, builders, veterinarians, stone-masons, gilders of arms, step-makers, painters, sculptors, engravers, joiners, statuaries, workers in mosaics, coppersmiths, blacksmiths, marble-masons, gilders, founders, dyers in purple, layers of tes-

sellated stones, goldsmiths, mirror-makers, carriage-makers, directors of the distribution of the water supply, glassworkers, workers in ivory, fullers, potters, plumbers, furriers.

14.3.11

By this general sanction We proclaim that license shall be extended to no person whatever to take refuge in the Church[16] for the purpose of evading service as a breadmaker. But if any person should enter the Church, he shall know that the privileges attached to Christianity[17] have been abolished and that he can and must be recalled after any length of time to the association of breadmakers.

Given on . . . September 27, 365; 364.

14.3.14

If a daughter of a breadmaker should marry any man and afterward, when her fortune had been squandered, he should suppose that she may be released from the guild,[18] We command that he shall be bound to the compulsory duties and guild of breadmaking by the same law and reason as if he were held by the bond of birth status to such compulsory public service.

Given on . . . February 23, 372.

14.7.1

Competent judges shall assume the task of dragging back the guilds, that is, the guild members, and they shall order those who have departed to a distance to be dragged back, together with all their possessions, to their own municipalities. . . .

Given on . . . August 6, 365.

---

[15]The imperial treasury.
[16]As clerics.*
[17]Special clerical exemptions. Edict 16.2.2., a promulgation of October 21, 319, reads, "Clerics shall be exempt from all compulsory public services whatever, lest . . . they should be called away from divine services."

[18]The word is *consortium,* which can mean either *guild* or *marriage.* The double meaning is probably intentional.

▼▼▼

Early Christianity and the Roman World

As befit an empire containing so many different peoples and cultures, Roman authorities were generally tolerant of the diverse deities and religious practices of the empire's subjects. Normally all they required was that the various cults and their devotees not manifestly threaten public good order and morality and that each religion help guarantee the gods' continued favor toward the state. Yet as far as many Roman leaders were concerned, Christians violated those basic requirements because of their uncompromising monotheism and extreme sense of exclusivity. Therefore, Christianity ran afoul of Roman authorities early in its history.

Unyielding adherence to the Christian religion became a crime, at least theoretically punishable by death, from the age of Nero (r. 54–68) on. Despite this, persecution of Christians was sporadic, local, and often halfhearted until the mid third century. When persecutions did occur before A.D. 250, it was usually only when provincial governors found themselves forced to bow to local sentiment in order to keep a discontented populace quiet. Crop failures and other natural disasters often seemed to demand a few Christian victims as propitiation to the gods.

The first significant empirewide persecution of Christians occurred in 250 under Emperor Decius, who required every member of the empire to acquire a certificate attesting that the person had made an offering to some pagan deity. In the despair and confusion of the age, the empire was simultaneously seeking divine aid and searching for scapegoats. Pagan writers justified this attack on the Christians because their perceived failure to pray for the well-being of the empire, as well as their preaching of peace, was undermining Rome's defenses.

In 260 Emperor Gallienus halted persecution and extended de facto recognition to the Christian Church by returning confiscated property, but this was only a temporary reprieve. In 303 Diocletian launched the last and greatest persecution of Christians, probably under the influence Galerius, his Caesar, or deputy emperor; the attack was most bitter in the east and of only minor consequence in the west. It continued until 311 when Galerius, in the grips of a frightening disease, decided to strike a bargain with the Christian god. His edict of toleration granted Christians freedom of worship in exchange for their prayers for him. A few days after issuing the edict, Galerius was dead.

The following year, Constantine, son of the late emperor Constantius, was campaigning in Italy against his imperial rival, Maxentius. According to one Christian author, on the eve of battle, Constantine had a vision bidding him to mark his soldiers' shields with the Greek characters Chi (X) and Rho (P), which together comprised an ancient symbol of victory and the emblem of the Unconquered Sun, his father's personal god. To Christians, however, this was Christ's monogram, representing as it did the first two letters of the Greek word *Christos* — Christ, or the Anointed One. Constantine obeyed his vision, and shortly thereafter he won a decisive victory, thereby becoming uncontested emperor in the West. For whatever reason, Constantine ascribed his victory to Christ. In 313 he and his co-emperor, Licinius, met at Milan, in northern Italy, and there reached an agreement regarding freedom of worship for all persons in the empire and recognizing the full legal status of each local Christian church. Christianity had weathered the storm of Roman persecution.

After the meeting at Milan, Constantine never wavered in his patronage of Christianity, although it took him about a decade to wean himself fully away from residual attachment to the cult of the Unconquered Sun. Notwithstanding that, Christianity, a faith that commanded the belief of about ten percent of the empire's population in 313, was the emperor's favored religion, and the consequences were momentous for both the empire and Christianity, as study of the following three sources will suggest.

Persecution and Deliverance
▼▼▼

3 ▼ *Eusebius of Caesarea,*
ECCLESIASTICAL HISTORY

Eusebius (ca. 260–339 or 340), Greek bishop* of Caesarea in Palestine, was a prolific writer whose interests ranged over a broad spectrum of matters. His most enduring work is his *Ecclesiastical History,* which traces the fortunes of the Christian Church from its earliest days to the early fourth century. This history has rightly earned Eusebius the title *Father of Church history,* inasmuch as it is the most complete and coherent account that we possess of the early Church's first three centuries. More than that, Eusebius diligently incorporated into his text large amounts of documentary evidence that would otherwise be lost to us. Without the *Ecclesiastical History,* it would be exceedingly difficult, if not impossible, to reconstruct the history of the early Christian Church.

Eusebius's careful scholarship, however, did not obviate the apologetical tone and theological message of the *Ecclesiastical History.* Within its pages, history is a cosmic contest between the forces of God and those of the Devil. On the one side are the patriarchs,* prophets, and saints; on the other are pagans, persecutors, latter-day Jews, and heretics.* Although the Devil and his minions always lose, the righteous suffer considerably as they struggle against evil.

More than simply a scholar, Eusebius was quite active in the affairs of the early fourth-century Church and suffered in the process. He was imprisoned during the era of the Great Persecution (303–311) and saw many of his friends tortured and martyred. But he also lived to see the miracle of the Emperor Constantine's conversion to Christianity after his victory at the Milvian Bridge in 312. Following Eusebius's elevation to the episcopate around 313, the bishop came to enjoy this Christian emperor's patronage and friendship.

Earlier, before the onslaught of the Great Persecution, Eusebius had begun a detailed history of the Church to his own day, completing the work in seven volumes around 303. The events of 312 and following, however, necessitated that he update his history. Consequently, he enlarged the *Ecclesiastical History* to ten books in order to include the history of Christian fortunes down to 324, thereby demonstrating the manner in which Divine Providence had once again triumphed over the forces of evil.

The following excerpts come from Book 5, an appendix to Book 8 entitled "The Martyrs of Palestine," and Book 10. Note the significant differences in tone and message between the first two excerpts and the third, which deals with Constantine's victory in 324 over Licinius, his former co-emperor.

QUESTIONS FOR ANALYSIS

1. How did Eusebius distinguish between the history he wrote and the history the pagan Greeks and Romans wrote? Why did he make the distinction?
2. Consider the second excerpt. Why do you think Eusebius dwells on the punishments that Christian confessors* bore?
3. What does Eusebius's description of the heroism of the two female martyrs suggest about Christian notions of the place of women in the Church?
4. How does Eusebius's treatment of the conflict between Constantine and Licinius appear to contradict the message of the first excerpt? Does it really? If so, how? If not, why not?
5. Is there a new tone in the third excerpt? If so, what is it?
6. Does the third excerpt seem to hold out any promises? If so, what are they?
7. Consider questions 5 and 6 another way. Does this excerpt from Book 10 imply that human history has reached a new stage of development? If so, what is it?
8. What do you imagine might be the historical ramifications of this new Christian imperial system? Reconsider your answer after you have studied sources 4 and 5.

Other writers of history record the victories of war and trophies won from enemies, the skill of generals, and the manly bravery of soldiers, defiled with blood and with innumerable slaughters for the sake of children and country and other possessions. But our narrative of the government of God will record in ineffaceable letters the most peaceful wars waged in behalf of the peace of the soul, and will tell of men doing brave deeds for truth rather than country, and for piety rather than dearest friends. It will hand down to imperishable remembrance the discipline and the much-tried fortitude of the athletes of religion, the trophies won from demons, the victories over invisible enemies, and the crowns placed upon all their heads.

▼ ▼ ▼

Up to the sixth year[1] the storm had been incessantly raging against us. Before this time there had been a very large number of confessors[2] of religion in the so-called Porphyry quarry in Thebais,[3] which gets its name from the stone found there. Of these, one hundred men, lack-

---

[1] The sixth year of the persecution, which began in the spring of 303.

[2] Those who confess, or proclaim and live, the faith in a heroic manner.

[3] The region around Thebes in Egypt.

ing three, together with women and infants, were sent to the governor of Palestine. When they confessed the God of the universe and Christ, Firmilianus, who had been sent there as governor in the place of Urbanus, directed, in accordance with the imperial command, that they should be maimed by burning the sinews of the ankles of their left feet, and that their right eyes with the eyelids and pupils should first be cut out, and then destroyed by hot irons to the very roots. And he then sent them to the mines in the province to endure hardships with severe toil and suffering.[4]

But it was not sufficient that these only who suffered such miseries should be deprived of their eyes, but those natives of Palestine also, who were mentioned just above as condemned to pugilistic combat,[5] since they would neither receive food from the royal storehouse nor undergo the necessary preparatory exercises. Having been brought on this account not only before the overseers, but also before Maximinus himself,[6] and having manifested the noblest persistence in confession by the endurance of hunger and stripes, they received like punishment with those whom we have mentioned, and with them other confessors in the city of Caesarea. Immediately afterwards others who were gathered to hear the Scriptures read, were seized in Gaza;[7] and some endured the same sufferings in the feet and eyes; but others were afflicted with yet greater torments and with most terrible tortures in the sides. One of these, in body a woman, but in understanding a man, would not endure the threat of rape, and spoke directly against the tyrant who entrusted the government to such cruel judges. She was first scourged and then raised aloft on the stake, and her sides lacerated. As those appointed for this purpose applied the tortures incessantly and severely at the command of the judge, another, with mind fixed, like the former, on virginity as her aim, — a woman who was altogether mean in form and contemptible in appearance, but, on the other hand, strong in soul, and endowed with an understanding superior to her body, — being unable to bear the merciless and cruel and inhuman deeds, with a boldness beyond that of the combatants famed among the Greeks,[8] cried out to the judge from the midst of the crowd: "And how long will you thus cruelly torture my sister?" But he was greatly enraged, and ordered the woman to be immediately seized. Thereupon she was brought forward and having called herself by the august name of the Savior, she was first urged by words to sacrifice, and as she refused she was dragged by force to the altar. But her sister continued to maintain her former zeal, and with intrepid and resolute foot kicked the altar, and overturned it with the fire that was on it. Thereupon the judge, enraged like a wild beast, inflicted on her such tortures in her sides as he never had on any one before, striving almost to glut himself with her raw flesh. But when his madness was satiated, he bound them both together, this one and her whom she called sister, and condemned them to death by fire. It is said that the first of these was from the country of Gaza; the other, by name Valentina, was of Caesarea, and was well known to many.

▼ ▼ ▼

Thanks for all things be given unto God the Omnipotent Ruler and King of the universe, and the greatest thanks to Jesus Christ the Savior and Redeemer of our souls, through whom we pray that peace may be always preserved for us firm and undisturbed by external troubles and by troubles of the mind. Since in accordance with thy wishes, my most holy Paulinus,[9] we have added the tenth book of the Church History to those which have preceded, we will inscribe it

---

[4]Assignment to slave labor in stone quarries and mines, which usually ended in death, was a common criminal penalty.

[5]They were condemned to fight as boxing gladiators in the circus.

[6]Maximin Daia, emperor in the East from 305 to 313.

[7]The southern coastal region of Palestine.

[8]Professional wrestlers and boxers.

[9]The bishop of Tyre, whom Eusebius especially admired.

to thee, proclaiming thee as the seal of the whole work; and we will fitly add in a perfect number[10] the perfect panegyric upon the restoration of the churches, obeying the Divine Spirit which exhorts us in the following words: "Sing unto the Lord a new song, for he hath done marvelous things. His right hand and his holy arm hath saved him. The Lord hath made known his salvation, his righteousness hath he revealed in the presence of the nations."[11] And in accordance with the utterance which commands us to sing the new song, let us proceed to show that, after those terrible and gloomy spectacles which we have described, we are now permitted to see and celebrate such things as many truly righteous men and martyrs of God before us desired to see upon earth and did not see, and to hear and did not hear. But they, hastening on, obtained far better things, being carried to heaven and the paradise of divine pleasure. But, acknowledging that even these things are greater than we deserve, we have been astonished at the grace manifested by the author of the great gifts, and rightly do we admire him, worshiping him with the whole power of our souls, and testifying to the truth of those recorded utterances, in which it is said, "Come and see the works of the Lord, the wonders which he hath done upon the earth; he removeth wars to the ends of the world, he shall break the bow and snap the spear in sunder, and shall burn the shields with fire."[12] Rejoicing in these things which have been clearly fulfilled in our day, let us proceed with our account.

The whole race of God's enemies was destroyed in the manner indicated, and was thus suddenly swept from the sight of men. So that again a divine utterance had its fulfillment: "I have seen the impious highly exalted and raising himself like the cedars of Lebanon; and I have passed by, and behold, he was not; and I have sought his place, and it could not be found."[13] And finally a bright and splendid day, overshadowed by no cloud, illuminated with beams of heavenly light the churches of Christ throughout the entire world. And not even those outside our communion[14] were prevented from sharing in the same blessings, or at least from coming under their influence and enjoying a part of the benefits bestowed upon us by God.

All men, then, were freed from the oppression of the tyrants, and being released from the former ills, one in one way and another in another acknowledged the defender of the pious to be the only true God. And we especially who placed our hopes in the Christ of God had unspeakable gladness, and a certain inspired joy bloomed for all of us, when we saw every place which shortly before had been desolated by the impieties of the tyrants reviving as if from a long and death-fraught pestilence, and temples again rising from their foundations to an immense height, and receiving a splendor far greater than that of the old ones which had been destroyed. But the supreme rulers also confirmed to us still more extensively the munificence of God by repeated ordinances in behalf of the Christians; and personal letters of the emperor were sent to the bishops, with honors and gifts of money. It may not be unfitting to insert these documents, translated from the Roman into the Greek tongue, at the proper place in this book, as in a sacred tablet, that they may remain as a memorial to all who shall come after us. . . .

To him, therefore, God granted, from Heaven above, the deserved fruit of piety, the trophies of victory over the impious, and he cast the guilty

---

[10]According to Pythagorean numerology, *10* is the perfect number, because it is the sum of the four principal geometric numbers: *1, 2, 3,* and *4.*

[11]The Bible, Psalms 98:1–2.

[12]Psalms 46:8–9.

[13]Psalms 37:35–36.

[14]Non-Christians and Christian heretics.

one with all his counselors and friends prostrate at the feet of Constantine. For when Licinius[15] carried his madness to the last extreme, the emperor, the friend of God, thinking that he ought no longer to be tolerated, acting upon the basis of sound judgment, and mingling the firm principles of justice with humanity, gladly determined to come to the protection of those who were oppressed by the tyrant, and undertook, by putting a few destroyers out of the way, to save the greater part of the human race. For when he had formerly exercised humanity alone and had shown mercy to him who was not worthy of sympathy, nothing was accomplished; for Licinius did not renounce his wickedness, but rather increased his fury against the peoples that were subject to him, and there was left to the afflicted no hope of salvation, oppressed as they were by a savage beast. Wherefore, the protector of the virtuous, mingling hatred for evil with love for good, went forth with his son Crispus,[16] a most beneficent prince, and extended a saving right hand to all that were perishing. Both of them, father and son, under the protection, as it were, of God, the universal King, with the Son of God, the Savior of all, as their leader and ally, drew up their forces on all sides against the enemies of the Deity and won an easy victory; God having prospered them in the battle in all respects according to their wish. Thus, suddenly, and sooner than can be told, those who yesterday and the day before breathed death and threatening were no more, and not even their names were remembered, but their inscriptions and their honors suffered the merited disgrace. And the things

which Licinius with his own eyes had seen come upon the former impious tyrants he himself likewise suffered, because he did not receive instruction nor learn wisdom from the chastisements of his neighbors, but followed the same path of impiety which they had trod, and was justly hurled over the same precipice. Thus he lay prostrate.

But Constantine, the mightiest victor, adorned with every virtue of piety, together with his son Crispus, a most God-beloved prince, and in all respects like his father, recovered the East which belonged to them; and they formed one united Roman empire as of old, bringing under their peaceful sway the whole world from the rising of the sun to the opposite quarter, both north and south, even to the extremities of the declining day. All fear therefore of those who had formerly afflicted them was taken away from men, and they celebrated splendid and festive days. Everything was filled with light, and those who before were downcast beheld each other with smiling faces and beaming eyes. With dances and hymns, in city and country, they glorified first of all God the universal King, because they had been thus taught, and then the pious emperor with his God-beloved children. There was oblivion of past evils and forgetfulness of every deed of impiety; there was enjoyment of present benefits and expectation of those yet to come. Edicts full of clemency and laws containing tokens of benevolence and true piety were issued in every place by the victorious emperor. Thus after all tyranny had been purged away, the empire which belonged to them was preserved firm and with-

---

[15]Licinius had been co-emperor since 308. In 313 he and Constantine allied, with Constantine taking the western half of the empire, and in that same year they jointly issued an edict of religious toleration. In 316 Constantine attacked Licinius's lands, on the pretext that Licinius was persecuting Christians, and confiscated a major portion of the eastern half of the empire. In 324 Constantine returned to complete the job, on the same pretext. After capturing Licinius and uniting the entire empire under his control, Constantine had his former colleague murdered within a year. Circumstances thus forced Eusebius to excise earlier complimentary allusions to Licinius from the last edition of the *Ecclesiastical History.*

[16]Crispus was Constantine's eldest son and had held the title of *Caesar* since 317. He served with distinction in the war of 324, commanding Constantine's naval forces. For reasons unknown, Constantine ordered his execution in 326.

out a rival for Constantine and his sons alone. And having obliterated the godlessness of their predecessors, recognizing the benefits conferred upon them by God, they exhibited their love of virtue and their love of God, and their piety and gratitude to the Deity, by the deeds which they performed in the sight of all men.

The Peace of This World

▼▼▼

4 ▼ *Saint Augustine of Hippo, THE CITY OF GOD*

A century after his death, Eusebius's dream of a new age of peace under the authority of a God-ordained Christian Roman emperor was proving to be a phantasm in the chaos occasioned by barbarian incursions into the empire. Eternal Rome itself was captured and pillaged in 410 by *Christian* Visigoths, and in the midst of this catastrophe, numerous pagans asserted that Rome's misfortunes were due to its abandonment of the old gods and ancient virtues that had protected the empire for so many centuries.

In 413 Aurelius Augustine (354–430), bishop* of Hippo in North Africa and the dominant spiritual and intellectual figure of his age, began to compose a defense of Christianity. The project took thirteen years. Somehow, in the midst of all his other duties, St. Augustine of Hippo found time to dictate and publish serially the twenty-two books, or extended chapters, that comprise one of the theological masterpieces of the early Western Church — *The City of God.*

The City of God is a theology of world history. In its first ten books, Augustine outlined the calamities suffered by pre-Christian Rome and the dark and barbarous side of pagan life. His purpose was to show that the pagan world was not only as equally oppressive as the present but even more so, because it lacked the moderating influence of the true religion. All of this was prologue, however. Augustine refused to base his defense of Christianity on any promise of earthly peace or temporal benefits. The central argument of *The City of God* lay in its last twelve books. In a discursive survey of both sacred and profane history, Augustine divided all humanity into two mystical, invisible camps: the City of God and the Earthly City. According to Augustine, their differences are spiritual: those who love God as opposed to those who love self. One is a tiny minority of pilgrims* traveling as strangers through life toward a supernatural goal. Although they are *in* the world, they are not *of* the world. The other is the vast majority of humanity, wedded to the perishable things of this world. For Augustine, the whole course and meaning of history was nothing more or less than the spiritual voyage through time of the citizens of the City of God. Therefore, even though God's divine plan controls the destinies of everyone, mundane problems and earthly affairs do not really matter. Yet despite his emphasis on the absolute primacy of the City of God, Bishop Augustine acknowledged that earthly government did have a legitimate role in the course of human events.

The City of God served as the blueprint for Western Christian speculation on the correlation of faith and politics for the next eight hundred years and more. Not until Europe's thirteenth-century rediscovery of Aristotle's political thought would there be any strong challenger in the West to Augustine's vision of the nature and role of the peace offered by earthly government.

QUESTIONS FOR ANALYSIS

1. According to Augustine, how and why did earthly dominion (or the rule of one person over another) originate? What implications follow from Augustine's view of such origins?
2. According to Augustine, what positive impact can government have on the lives of people?
3. In what ways are the positive aspects of government limited?
4. To what extent should citizens of the City of God obey the laws of earthly governments?
5. How does Augustine justify the punishment meted out by the heads of households and, by extension, governments? Does he see this punishment as a positive or negative force?
6. Was Augustine, a loyal son of the Roman Empire, wedded to the idea that Christianity can only flourish under the rule of a Christian Roman emperor?
7. Based on your answers to all of the above questions, what do you conclude Augustine thought about the ideal and reality of a Christian Roman Empire?

CHAP. 15. — OF THE LIBERTY PROPER TO MAN'S NATURE, AND THE SERVITUDE INTRODUCED BY SIN — A SERVITUDE IN WHICH THE MAN WHOSE WILL IS WICKED IS THE SLAVE OF HIS OWN LUST, THOUGH HE IS FREE SO FAR AS REGARDS OTHER MEN.

This is prescribed by the order of nature: it is thus that God has created man. For "let them," He says, "have dominion over the fish of the sea, and over the fowl of the air, and over every creeping thing which creepeth on the earth."[1] He did not intend that His rational creature, who was made in His image, should have dominion over anything but the irrational creation — not man over man, but man over the beasts. And hence the righteous men in primitive times were made shepherds of cattle rather than kings of men, God intending thus to teach us what the relative position of the creatures is, and what the desert of sin; for it is with justice, we believe, that the condition of slavery is the result of sin. And this is why we do not find the word "slave" in any part of Scripture until righteous Noah branded the sin of his son with this name.[2] It is a name, therefore, introduced by sin and not by nature. The origin of the Latin word for slave is supposed to be found in the circumstance that those who by the law of war were liable to be killed were sometimes preserved by their victors, and were hence called servants.[3] And these circumstances could never have arisen save through sin. For even when we wage a just war, our adversaries must be sinning; and every victory, even though gained by wicked men, is a result of the

---

[1] The Bible, Genesis, 1:26.
[2] Genesis, 9:25–27.

[3] The Latin word for slave, *servus,* comes from *servare,* "to serve."

first judgment of God, who humbles the vanquished either for the sake of removing or of punishing their sins. Witness that man of God, Daniel, who, when he was in captivity, confessed to God his own sins and the sins of his people, and declares with pious grief that these were the cause of the captivity.[4] The prime cause, then, of slavery is sin, which brings man under the dominion of his fellow, — that which does not happen save by the judgment of God, with whom is no unrighteousness, and who knows how to award fit punishments to every variety of offence. But our Master in Heaven says, "Every one who doeth sin is the servant of sin."[5] And thus there are many wicked masters who have religious men as their slaves, and who are yet themselves in bondage; "for of whom a man is overcome, of the same is he brought in bondage."[6] And beyond question it is a happier thing to be the slave of a man than of a lust; for even this very lust of ruling, to mention no others, lays waste men's hearts with the most ruthless dominion. Moreover, when men are subjected to one another in a peaceful order, the lowly position does as much good to the servant as the proud position does harm to the master. But by nature, as God first created us, no one is the slave either of man or of sin. This servitude is, however, penal, and is appointed by that law which enjoins the preservation of the natural order and forbids its disturbance; for if nothing had been done in violation of that law, there would have been nothing to restrain by penal servitude. And therefore the apostle* admonishes slaves to be subject to their masters, and to serve them heartily and with good-will, so that, if they cannot be freed by their masters, they may themselves make their slavery in some sort free, by serving not in crafty fear, but in faithful love, until all unrighteousness pass

away, and all principality and every human power be brought to nothing, and God be all in all.[7]

CHAP. 16. — OF EQUITABLE RULE.

And therefore, although our righteous fathers[8] had slaves, and administered their domestic affairs so as to distinguish between the condition of slaves and the heirship of sons in regard to the blessings of this life, yet in regard to the worship of God, in whom we hope for eternal blessings, they took an equally loving oversight of all the members or their household. And this is so much in accordance with the natural order, that the head of the household was called *paterfamilias;*[9] and this name has been so generally accepted, that even those whose rule is unrighteous are glad to apply it to themselves. But those who are true fathers of their households desire and endeavor that all the members of their household, equally with their own children, should worship and win God, and should come to that heavenly home in which the duty of ruling men is no longer necessary, because the duty of caring for their everlasting happiness has also ceased; but, until they reach that home, masters ought to feel their position of authority a greater burden than servants their service. And if any member of the family interrupts the domestic peace by disobedience, he is corrected either by word or blow, or some kind of just and legitimate punishment, such as society permits, that he may himself be the better for it, and be readjusted to the family harmony from which he had dislocated himself. For as it is not benevolent to give a man help at the expense of some greater benefit he might receive, so it is not innocent to spare a man at the risk of his falling into graver sin. To be innocent, we must not only do harm

---

[4]Daniel, 9:3–20.
[5]The Gospel of John, 8:34.
[6]The Second Epistle of Peter 2:19.
[7]The Epistle to the Ephesians, 6:5–8.

[8]The patriarchs,* such as Abraham, Isaac, and Jacob.
[9]Literally, "the father of the family." The Roman family was extended to include all servants and slaves, and in Roman law, the *paterfamilias* had essentially the power of life and death over all members of his household. By extension, the emperor was perceived as the paterfamilias of the empire.

to no man, but also restrain him from sin or punish his sin, so that either the man himself who is punished may profit by his experience, or others be warned by his example. Since, then, the house ought to be the beginning or element of the city, and every beginning bears reference to some end of its own kind, and every element to the integrity of the whole of which it is an element, it follows plainly enough that domestic peace has a relation to civic peace — in other words, that the well-ordered concord of domestic obedience and domestic rule has a relation to the well-ordered concord of civic obedience and civic rule. And therefore it follows, further, that the father of the family ought to frame his domestic rule in accordance with the law of the city, so that the household may be in harmony with the civic order.

CHAP. 17. — WHAT PRODUCES PEACE, AND WHAT DISCORD, BETWEEN THE HEAVENLY AND EARTHLY CITIES.

But the families which do not live by faith seek their peace in the earthly advantages of this life; while the families which live by faith look for those eternal blessings which are promised, and use as pilgrims such advantages of time and of earth as do not fascinate and divert them from God, but rather aid them to endure with greater ease, and to keep down the number of those burdens of the corruptible body which weigh upon the soul. Thus the things necessary for this mortal life are used by both kinds of men and families alike, but each has its own peculiar and widely different aim in using them. The earthly city, which does not live by faith, seeks an earthly peace, and the end it proposes, in the well-ordered concord of civic obedience and rule, is the combination of men's wills to attain the things which are helpful to this life. The heavenly city, or rather the part of it which sojourns

on earth and lives by faith,[10] makes use of this peace only because it must, until this mortal condition which necessitates it shall pass away. Consequently, so long as it lives like a captive and a stranger in the earthly city, though it has already received the promise of redemption, and the gift of the Spirit as the earnest of it, it makes no scruple to obey the laws of the earthly city, whereby the things necessary for the maintenance of this mortal life are administered; and thus, as this life is common to both cities, so there is a harmony between them in regard to what belongs to it. But, as the earthly city has had some philosophers whose doctrine is condemned by the divine teaching, . . . and as the celestial city, on the other hand, knew that one God only was to be worshipped, . . . it has come to pass that the two cities could not have common laws of religion, and that the heavenly city has been compelled in this matter to dissent, and to become obnoxious to those who think differently, and to stand the brunt of their anger and hatred and persecutions, except in so far as the minds of their enemies have been alarmed by the multitude of the Christians and quelled by the manifest protection of God accorded to them. This heavenly city, then, while it sojourns on earth, calls citizens out of all nations, and gathers together a society of pilgrims of all languages, not scrupling about diversities in the manners, laws, and institutions whereby earthly peace is secured and maintained, but recognizing that, however various these are, they all tend to one and the same end of earthly peace. It therefore is so far from rescinding and abolishing these diversities, that it even preserves and adopts them, so long only as no hindrance to the worship of the one supreme and true God is thus introduced. Even the heavenly city, therefore, while in its state of pilgrimage, avails itself of the peace of earth, and, so far as it can without injuring faith and godliness, desires and maintains a common agreement among men regarding the acquisition of the necessaries of life, and makes this earthly peace bear

---

[10]As distinguished from those already in Heaven, who no longer have need of faith.

upon the peace of Heaven; for this alone can be truly called and esteemed the peace of the reasonable creatures, consisting as it does in the perfectly ordered and harmonious enjoyment of God and of one another in God. When we shall have reached that peace, this mortal life shall give place to one that is eternal, and our body shall be no more this animal body which by its corruption weighs down the soul, but a spiritual body feeling no want, and in all its members subjected to the will. In its pilgrim state the heavenly city possesses this peace by faith; and by this faith it lives righteously when it refers to the attainment of that peace every good action towards God and man; for the life of the city is a social life.

Christianity and the Imperial Culture
▼▼▼

5 ▼ *CHRIST TRIUMPHANT*

Early Christian artists generally depicted Jesus as either a lamb or as a youthful and beardless Good Shepherd. When Christianity became the emperor's religion, Christian artists had to create new iconographical symbols in order to incorporate Christ into the imperial culture. After all, the emperor was in theory neither a sacrificial lamb nor a humble and mild shepherd.

This *mosaic* (a mural composed of pieces of colored stone, glass, and precious metal), which dates from around the year 500, is located in the archbishops'' chapel at Ravenna, a city in northeast Italy that served as the western capital of the Roman Empire from 402 to 476 and thereafter continued to be Italy's most prominent political center into the eighth century. During the fifth century, the archbishops of Ravenna, often imperial appointees, rivaled the popes* of Rome in power and prestige.

Here Christ is dressed in the full military uniform of a Roman emperor: golden armor, a purple cloak with a shoulder clasp bearing three pendants to signify imperial rank, and campaign boots. Underneath his feet are a lion and a snake, representing two biblical quotations. The Book of Psalms declares, "You shall tread on the lion and the adder; the young lion and the dragon you shall trample under feet." In the Gospel* of Luke, Jesus tells his disciples, "Behold, I have given you power to tread on snakes and scorpions and to overcome all the power of the Enemy." The open book, symbolizing either the Gospels or the Book of Life, which contains the names of all the redeemed, reads, "I am the Way, the Truth, and Life," a statement of Jesus found in the Gospel of John.

QUESTIONS FOR ANALYSIS

1. Let us consider more fully the symbols in this mosaic. How does Christ carry his cross? Do you find any significance in that posture? If so, what? Describe Christ's facial expression. Again, do you find any significance here?

2. Based on your study of all of the mosaic's symbols, what do you conclude is the message of this piece of art?

3. Consider this mosaic in the light of Eusebius's *Ecclesiastical History* (source 3). Comparing the two, which strike you as more significant: the similarities or the differences in tone and message? What do you conclude from your answer?
4. What do you think would have been St. Augustine's commentary on this mosaic? Before answering, review source 4.

Christ Triumphant

Chapter 2

▾▾▾

Rome and Its Fringe Peoples

Since at least the late first century B.C., the Romans had conceived of their empire as one having no permanent boundaries or temporal limits. In the words of the poet Virgil, it was spatially and temporally "an empire without end." Rivers, deserts, and hostile neighbors were simply momentary obstacles to the eternal, divinely mandated power of Rome.

That faith was severely tested but not destroyed in the mid third century A.D. Between 230 and 285 both the Sassanian Persian Empire and a variety of seminomadic border peoples battered the Roman Empire. The empire, however, shored up its frontier defenses in the late third century and survived. Renewed military vigor, combined with drastic domestic measures, secured Rome's citizens an additional century of relative stability. Toward the end of the fourth century, however, the old frontier pressures again become intolerable, and the empire rapidly slid toward its unforeseen end. The empire would be defeated and transformed by "barbarian" fringe peoples, who came from beyond the borders of the Rhine and Danube Rivers.

The new invaders badly wounded the Roman Empire, and some historians argue that they cumulatively assassinated the empire. In a strictly political sense, this is true, at least so far as the western half of the empire was concerned. By the end of the sixth century, precious little of the western half of the Roman world was still ruled by imperial Roman authority. More profoundly, these newcomers played a key role in transforming culture in the West, thereby helping to usher out the old Greco-Roman order and to lay the basis for a new civilization that many historians call *The First Europe.*

The documents in the first section of this chapter illustrate some of the basic ways in which the Germans, who made up the vast majority of the fringe peoples migrating into the

Roman Empire, differed in values, organization, and overall culture from their Greco-Roman hosts. The sources in the second section shed light on some of the dreams and sobering realities regarding integration of the Germans into the world of the late Roman Empire.

▼▼▼

The Germans

One of the enduring clichés favored by writers of history textbooks is that medieval Europe emerged out of a fusion of three elements: the remnants of Greco-Roman civilization; Latin Christianity; and the culture and vigor of the fringe peoples who migrated into the western regions of the late Roman Empire. As is true of so many commonplace notions, there is a good deal of truth to this statement, but it does not tell the complete story. These three elements differed radically from one another in many essential ways, and it took many centuries for them to fuse into something resembling a coherent civilization. Even when they had achieved a level of integration, the differences among these elements continued to infuse into an emerging European civilization a number of tensions that became identifying characteristics of the new order developing in the West. One such characteristic was the stress between *Romanitas* — all the cultural and governmental elements associated with Roman civilization — and the cultures of the new fringe peoples, especially the Germans, who constituted the vast majority of the migrants and invaders entering the empire between the late fourth and late sixth centuries.

The Early Germans

▼▼▼

6 ▼ Tacitus, GERMANIA

As early as the first century A.D., the Romans were aware of the fact that the many Germanic tribes dwelling across the Rhine and Danube Rivers were a serious threat to the empire's security. In the year 9 an entire Roman army of about eighteen thousand soldiers was destroyed deep in the Teutoberg Forest as it unsuccessfully attempted to push Roman sovereignty all the way to the Elbe River in eastern Germany. The Germanic threat occasioned heightened Roman interest in these border barbarians, and one of Rome's most distinguished historians, Publius Cornelius Tacitus (ca. 55–120?), responded to this ready audience by composing a work of popular ethnography entitled *On the Origin, Location, Customs, and Inhabitants of Germany,* more commonly known as the *Germania,* in A.D. 98.

We know very little about Tacitus's life, other than that he was a high-placed aristocrat and civil official, but it appears unlikely that he ever traveled among the Germans. Most of the information that he recorded about these people came largely from now lost earlier written sources and secondhand oral reports. Moreover, Tacitus was a moralist who unabashedly advocated a return to the virtues of the old Roman Republic, a time when, so he believed, Romans possessed courage, love of liberty, and moral rectitude — qualities that he thought were sadly lacking among Romans in his own day. This social message permeates all of Tacitus's writings, including the *Germania.*

Despite these shortcomings, the *Germania* is a valuable source. It is the most detailed description of late-first-century Germanic society to survive from antiquity, and many of its details have been confirmed by modern archeological and historical scholarship. We can conclude, therefore, that this account contains a solid core of truth. However, some of the details that Tacitus presents and many of the judgments he makes are questionable at best. As you read this account, try to separate Tacitus's moral message and what appear to be simplistic stereotypes from evidence that appears to be more credible.

QUESTIONS FOR ANALYSIS

1. According to Tacitus, how do the border Germans differ from those of the interior? Why would this be so?
2. Ancient Germanic society has been characterized as "kin centered." It has also been characterized as a society that was bound together by personal relationships. What evidence in Tacitus's account supports or refutes these characterizations?
3. What does this account allow you to infer about the role and status of the warrior in first-century Germanic society? Does this appear to be a male-dominated culture?
4. Take the same question and apply it to women. What about their role (or roles) and status?
5. What does this account tell you about social divisions among the Germans? What were the bases of their social divisions? What do you infer from your answers?
6. In what ways does Tacitus use the *Germania* to point out the presumed shortcomings of his own society?
7. Which parts of this account appear to be most plausible? Which seem least plausible?
8. Based on your answers to question 7, what do you conclude we can say with a high degree of confidence about first-century Germanic society?

4. For my own part, I agree with those who think that the tribes of Germany are free from all taint of intermarriages with foreign nations, and that they appear as a distinct, unmixed race, like none but themselves. Hence, too, the same physical peculiarities throughout so vast a popu-

lation. All have fierce blue eyes, red hair, huge frames, fit only for a sudden exertion. They are less able to bear laborious work. Heat and thirst they cannot in the least endure; to cold and hunger their climate and their soil harden them.

5. Their country, though somewhat various in appearance, yet generally either bristles with forests or reeks with swamps. . . . It is productive of grain, but unfavorable to fruit-bearing trees; it is rich in flocks and herds, but these are for the most part undersized, and even the cattle have not their usual beauty or noble head. It is their number that is chiefly valued; they are in fact the most highly prized, indeed the only riches of the people. Silver and gold the gods have refused to them, whether in kindness or in anger I cannot say. I would not, however, affirm that no vein of German soil produces gold or silver, for who has ever made a search? They care but little to possess or use them.[1] You may see among them vessels of silver, which have been presented to their envoys and chieftains, held as cheap as those of clay. The border population, however, values gold and silver for their commercial utility, and are familiar with, and show preference for, some of our coins. The tribes of the interior use the simpler and more ancient practice of barter for commodities. They like the old and well-known money, coins milled, or showing a two-horse chariot. They likewise prefer silver to gold, not from any special liking, but because a large number of silver pieces is more convenient for use among dealers in cheap and common articles.

6. Even iron is not plentiful with them, as we infer from the character of their weapons.[2] But few use swords or long lances. They carry a spear (*framea* is their name for it), with a narrow and short head, but so sharp and easy to wield that the same weapon serves, according to circumstances, for close or distant conflict. As for the horse-soldier, he is satisfied with a shield and spear; the foot-soldiers also scatter showers of missiles, each man having several and hurling them to an immense distance, and being naked or lightly clad with a little cloak. . . . On the whole, one would say that their chief strength is in their infantry, which fights along with the cavalry; admirably adapted to the action of the latter is the swiftness of certain foot-soldiers, who are picked from the entire youth of their country, and stationed in front of the line. Their number is fixed, — a hundred from each *pagus;*[3] and from this they take their name among their countrymen, so that what was originally a mere number has now become a title of distinction.[4] Their line of battle is drawn up in a wedge-like formation. To give ground, provided you return to the attack, is considered prudence rather than cowardice. The bodies of their slain they carry off even in indecisive engagements. To abandon your shield is the basest of crimes;[5] nor may a man thus disgraced be present at the sacred rites, or enter their council; many, indeed, after escaping from battle, have ended their infamy with the halter.

7. They choose their kings[6] by birth, their generals for merit. These kings have not unlimited or arbitrary power, and the generals do more by example than by authority. If they are energetic, if they are conspicuous, if they fight in the front, they lead because they are admired. But to reprimand, to imprison, even to flog, is

[1]Jewelry and coins uncovered from the later burial mounds of Germanic warrior-leaders dating after A.D. 400 strongly suggest that this was not true in the Age of the Migrations (ca. 375–600). In Tacitus's day, the Germans cremated their dead.

[2]Iron ore is abundant in Germany, but it was not until several centuries after Tacitus's time that iron swords became common weapons among the Germans. The period ca. 400–800 is often called the *Germanic Iron Age.*

[3]Known to the Romans as a *pagus* and to the Germans as a *gau,* it was a regional division of a tribe's territory and consisted of a number of villages.

[4]Compare this with evidence from *The Salic Law* (see source 7).

[5]Compare this with *The Salic Law* (source 7).

[6]Many western tribes across the Rhine did not have kings at this time, but kingship seems to have been quite common among the tribes of eastern Germany that lay beyond the Danube.

permitted to the priests* alone, and that not as a punishment, or at the general's bidding, but, as it were, by the mandate of the god whom they believe to inspire the warrior. They also carry with them into battle certain figures and images taken from their sacred groves. And what most stimulates their courage is that their squadrons or battalions, instead of being formed by chance or by a fortuitous gathering, are composed of families and clans. Close by them, too, are those dearest to them, so, that they hear the shrieks of women, the cries of infants. They are to every man the most sacred witnesses of his bravery — they are his most generous applauders. The soldier brings his wounds to mother and wife, who shrink not from counting or even demanding them and who administer both food and encouragement to the combatants.

8. Tradition says that armies already wavering and giving way have been rallied by women who, with earnest entreaties and bosoms laid bare, have vividly represented the horrors of captivity, which the Germans fear with such extreme dread on behalf of their women, that the strongest tie by which a state can be bound is the requirement to give, among the number of hostages, maidens of noble birth. They even believe that the sex has a certain sanctity and prescience, and they do not despise their counsels, or make light of their answers. In Vespasian's days we saw Veleda,[7] long regarded by many as a divinity. In former times, too, they venerated Aurinia,[8] and many other women, but not with servile flatteries, or with sham deification.[9] . . .

11. About minor matters the chiefs deliberate, about the more important the whole tribe. Yet even when the final decision rests with the people, the affair is always thoroughly discussed by the chiefs. They assemble, except in the case of a sudden emergency, on certain fixed days, either at new or at full moon; for this they consider the most auspicious season for the transaction of business. . . . Their freedom has this disadvantage, that they do not meet simultaneously or as they are bidden, but two or three days are wasted in the delays of assembling. When the multitude think proper, they sit down armed. Silence is proclaimed by the priests, who have on these occasions the right of keeping order. Then the king or the chief, according to age, birth, distinction in war, or eloquence, is heard, more because he has influence to persuade than because he has power to command. If his sentiments displease them, they reject them with murmurs; if they are satisfied, they brandish their spears. The most complimentary form of assent is to express approbation with their weapons.

12. In their councils an accusation may be preferred or a capital crime prosecuted. Penalties are distinguished according to the offence. Traitors and deserters are hanged on trees, the coward, the unwarlike, the man stained with abominable vices, is plunged into the mire of the morass, with a hurdle put over him. This distinction in punishment means that crime, they think, ought, in being punished, to be exposed, while infamy ought to be buried out of sight. Lighter offences, too, have penalties proportioned to them; he who is convicted, is fined in a certain number of horses or of cattle. Half of the fine is paid to the king or to the state, half to the person whose wrongs are avenged and to his relatives.[10] In these same councils they also elect the chief magistrates, who administer law in the

---

[7]A priestess of the Germanic tribe known as the *Bructeri,* she ruled over a large area by virtue of her prophetic powers. In 69–70, the first two years of Emperor Vespasian's reign, she was involved in an unsuccessful rebellion against Roman authority.

[8]This is the only extant reference to this now unknown female leader, but Tacitus expected his readers to know who she was.

[9]As was done in regard to certain Roman women, especially within the imperial family.

[10]Compare this with *The Salic Law* (source 7).

pagi[11] and the towns. Each of these has a hundred associates chosen from the people, who support him with their advice and influence.

13. They transact no public or private business without being armed. It is not, however, usual for anyone to wear arms till the state has recognized his power to use them. Then in the presence of the council one of the chiefs, or the young man's father, or some kinsman, equips him with a shield and a spear. These arms are what the *toga*[12] is with us, the first honor with which youth is invested. Up to this time he is regarded as a member of a household, afterwards as a member of the commonwealth. Very noble birth or great services rendered by the father secure for lads the rank of a chief; such lads attach themselves to men of mature strength and of long approved valor. It is no shame to be seen among a chief's followers. Even in his escort there are gradations of rank, dependent on the choice of the man to whom they are attached. These followers vie keenly with each other as to who shall rank first with his chief, the chiefs as to who shall have the most numerous and the bravest followers. It is an honor as well as a source of strength to be thus always surrounded by a large body of picked youths; it is an ornament in peace and a defense in war. And not only in his own tribe but also in the neighboring states it is the renown and glory of a chief to be distinguished for the number and valor of his followers, for such a man is courted by embassies, is honored with presents, and the very prestige of his name often settles a war.

14. When they go into battle, it is a disgrace for the chief to be surpassed in valor, a disgrace for his followers not to equal the valor of the chief. And it is an infamy and a reproach for life to have survived the chief, and returned from the field. To defend, to protect him, to ascribe one's own brave deeds to his renown, is the height of loyalty. The chief fights for victory; his companions fight for their chief. If their native state sinks into the sloth of prolonged peace and repose, many of its noble youths voluntarily seek those tribes that are waging some war, both because inaction is odious to their race, and because they win renown more readily in the midst of peril, and cannot maintain a numerous following except by violence and war. Indeed, men look to the liberality of their chief for their warhorse and their blood-stained and victorious lance. Feasts and entertainments, which, though inelegant, are plentifully furnished, are their only pay. The means of this bounty come from war and rapine. Nor are they as easily persuaded to plough the earth and to wait for the year's produce as to challenge an enemy and earn the honor of wounds. Nay, they actually think it tame and stupid to acquire by the sweat of toil what they might win by their blood.

15. Whenever they are not fighting, they pass much of their time in the chase, and still more in idleness, giving themselves up to sleep and to feasting, the bravest and the most warlike doing nothing, and surrendering the management of the household, of the home, and of the land, to the women, the old men, and all the weakest members of the family. They themselves lie buried in sloth, a strange combination in their nature that the same men should be so fond of idleness, so averse to peace. It is the custom of the states to bestow by voluntary and individual contribution on the chiefs a present of cattle or of grain, which, while accepted as a compliment, supplies their wants. They are particularly delighted by gifts from neighboring tribes, which are sent not only by individuals but also by the state, such as choice steeds, heavy armor, trappings, and neck-chains. We have now taught them to accept money also. . . .

18. Their marriage code is strict, and indeed no part of their manners is more praiseworthy. Almost alone among barbarians they are content

---

[11]The plural of *pagus* (note 3).

[12]A garment that was the mark of manhood among the Romans.

with one wife, except a very few among them, and these not from sensuality, but because their noble birth procures for them many offers of alliance. The wife does not bring a dowry to the husband, but the husband to the wife. The parents and relatives are present, and pass judgment on the marriage-gifts, gifts not meant to suit a woman's taste, nor such as a bride would deck herself with, but oxen, a saddled steed, a shield, a lance, and a sword. With these presents the wife is espoused, and she herself in her turn brings her husband a gift of arms. This they count their strongest bond of union, these their sacred mysteries, these their gods of marriage. Lest the woman should think herself to stand apart from aspirations after noble deeds and from the perils of war, she is reminded by the ceremony which inaugurates marriage that she is her husband's partner in toil and danger, destined to suffer and to dare with him alike both in peace and in war. The yoked oxen, the harnessed steed, the gift of arms, proclaim this fact. She must live and die with the feeling that she is receiving what she must hand down to her children neither tarnished nor depreciated, what future daughters-in-law may receive, and may be so passed on to her grand-children.

19. Thus with their virtue protected they live uncorrupted by the allurements of public shows or the stimulant of feastings. Clandestine correspondence is equally unknown to men and women. Very rare for so numerous a population is adultery, the punishment for which is prompt, and in the husband's power. Having cut off the hair of the adulteress and stripped her naked, he expels her from the house in the presence of her kinsfolk, and then flogs her through the whole village. The loss of chastity meets with no indulgence; neither beauty, youth, nor wealth will procure the culprit a husband. No one in Germany laughs at vice, nor do they call it the fashion to corrupt and to be corrupted. Still better is the condition of those states in which only maidens are given in marriage, and where the hopes and expectations of a bride are then finally terminated. They receive one husband, as having

one body and one life, that they may have no thoughts beyond, no further-reaching desires, that they may love not so much the husband as the married state. To limit the number of their children or to destroy any of their subsequent offspring is accounted infamous, and good habits are here more effectual than good laws elsewhere.

20. In every household the children, naked and filthy, grow up with those stout frames and limbs which we so much admire. Every mother suckles her own offspring, and never entrusts it to servants and nurses. The master is not distinguished from the slave by being brought up with greater delicacy. Both live amid the same flocks and lie on the same ground till the freeborn are distinguished by age and recognised by merit. The young men marry late, and their vigor is thus unimpaired. Nor are the maidens hurried into marriage; the same age and a similar stature is required; well-matched and vigorous they wed, and the offspring reproduce the strength of the parents. Sister's sons are held in as much esteem by their uncles as by their fathers; indeed, some regard the relation as even more sacred and binding, and prefer it in receiving hostages, thinking thus to secure a stronger hold on the affections and a wider bond for the family. But every man's own children are his heirs and successors, and there are no wills. Should there be no issue, the next in succession to the property are his brothers and his uncles on either side. The more relatives he has, the more numerous his connections, the more honored is his old age; nor are there any advantages in childlessness.

21. It is a duty among them to adopt the feuds as well as the friendships of a father or a kinsman. These feuds are not implacable; even homicide is expiated by the payment of a certain number of cattle and of sheep, and the satisfaction is accepted by the entire family, greatly to the advantage of the state, since feuds are dangerous in proportion to a people's freedom. . . .

23. A liquor for drinking is made out of barley or other grain, and fermented into a certain resemblance to wine. The dwellers on the river-

bank[13] also buy wine. Their food is of a simple kind, consisting of wild-fruit, fresh game, and curdled milk. They satisfy their hunger without elaborate preparation and without delicacies. In quenching their thirst they are not equally moderate. If you indulge their love of drinking by supplying them with as much as they desire, they will be overcome by their own vices as easily as by the arms of an enemy. . . .

24. Strangely enough they make games of chance a serious occupation even when sober, and so venturesome are they about gaining or losing, that, when every other resource has failed, on the last and final throw they stake the freedom of their own persons. The loser goes into voluntary slavery; though the younger and stronger, he suffers himself to be bound and sold. Such is their stubborn persistency in a bad practice; they themselves call it honor. Slaves of this kind the owners part with in the way of commerce, and also to relieve themselves from the scandal of such a victory.

25. The other slaves[14] are not employed after our manner with distinct domestic duties assigned to them, but each one has the management of a house and home of his own. The master requires from the slave a certain quantity of grain, of cattle, and of clothing, as he would from a tenant, and this is the limit of subjection. All other household functions are discharged by the wife and children. To strike a slave or to punish him with bonds or with hard labor is a rare occurrence. They often kill them, not in enforcing strict discipline, but on the impulse of passion, as they would an enemy, only it is done with impunity. The freedmen[15] do not rank much above slaves, and are seldom of any weight in the family, never in the state, with the exception of those tribes which are ruled by kings. There indeed they rise above the freedborn and the noble; elsewhere the inferiority of the freedman marks the freedom of the state.

26. Of lending money on interest and increasing it by compound interest they know nothing, — a more effectual safeguard than if it were prohibited.

Land proportioned to the number of inhabitants is occupied by the whole community in turn, and afterwards divided among them according to rank. A wide expanse of plains makes the partition easy. They till fresh fields every year, and they have still more land than enough; with the richness and extent of their soil, they do not laboriously exert themselves in planting orchards, inclosing meadows, and watering gardens. Grain is the only produce required from the earth. . . .

27. In their funerals there is no pomp; they simply observe the custom of burning the bodies of illustrious men with certain kinds of wood. They do not heap garments or spices on the funeral pile. The arms of the dead man and in some cases his horse are consigned to the fire. A turf mound forms the tomb. Monuments with their lofty elaborate splendor they reject as oppressive to the dead. Tears and lamentations they soon dismiss; grief and sorrow but slowly. It is thought becoming for women to bewail, for men to remember, the dead.

Such on the whole is the account which I have received of the origin and manners of the entire German people.

---

[13]The Germans who lived alongside the Rhine and Danube Rivers.
[14]Usually, war captives or the offspring of war captives.

[15]A person who was freed from slavery (or whose forbearers had been freed). Such people were known as *leets*. See *The Salic Law* (source 7), note 5.

Frankish Law and Society
▼▼▼

7 ▼ *THE SALIC LAW*

Two of the chief glories of Roman civilization were its empirewide rule of law and its highly developed system of jurisprudence. The various archaic peoples who inhabited the regions on either side of the empire's borders were not as juridically sophisticated as their Greco-Roman neighbors, but they had laws. Originally, these "barbarian" laws were unwritten and committed to the memories of various tribal elders. Moreover, these early fringe peoples did not consider law to be a manifestation of the authority of some state or ruler. They also did not see their, or any other, body of laws as operative only within a particular political setting or geographic region. Rather, so far as they were concerned, laws were customary and, most significant of all, they were *personal.* That is, each tribe or people, by virtue of its common ancestry, shared laws peculiar to it, and those laws traveled with that people, collectively and individually. In the context of this vision, law was not something created by a legislator, it was inherited.

In the period of the great Germanic migrations of the fourth through sixth centuries, tribes that settled deeply within the borders of the Roman Empire underwent many changes, in large part as a consequence of their intensified contact with Roman society. One result was that a number of tribal laws were collected and written down, generally in Latin, thus recording the social values and relationships of cultures that were in the process of changing. One of the earliest of these new legal collections was *The Salic Law,* a codification of rules governing behavior within lands held by the Salian, or Salic, branch of the Frankish people. Most of the laws within the Salic code related only to the Franks, but surprisingly some concerned the Gallo-Roman majority that now found itself under Frankish control.

The initial codification of Salic law took place probably in the period 507–511, late in the reign of Clovis (r. 481–511), the man who united the Franks and carved out a substantial kingdom in Gaul (source 9). Although these laws were written down with the substantial assistance of Gallo-Roman jurists trained in the traditions of Roman law (Chapter 1, source 2), they undoubtedly reflect many Salian Frankish traditions that went back at least to the fourth century. At the same time, *The Salic Law* shows us how Frankish society was changing as a consequence of the rise of a king whose authority gave legitimacy to the code.

One important fact to keep in mind as you read these laws is that the fines mentioned in them were viewed as a means of reducing acts of private revenge and family feuds. To understand this more fully, review what Tacitus wrote about feuds and the expiation of guilt in Chapter 21 of his *Germania* (source 6).

QUESTIONS FOR ANALYSIS

1. What does the first title, or section, regarding court summonses allow you to infer about the power of early sixth-century Frankish kings? What other laws in this code give us hints about the extent and limits of the king's authority?

2. The scales of fines for injury and death allow us to infer a lot about the relative importance of various groups within the lands controlled by King Clovis. How well or poorly did this society value women? Children? Non-Franks? Free warriors? Friends and officers of the king?

3. While addressing question 2, ask yourself why Title XLI repeats fines contained in Title XXIV. (This is the only such repetition in the entire code.)

4. Another question regarding XLI: Why do you think a killer is fined more for concealing his or her crime?

5. Consider further the issue of the social value and position of women in the light of Title LIX. What were the Frankish laws of inheritance, and what do they suggest about the status and power of women relative to men?

6. This code allows us to see the different social levels that existed within Clovis's kingdom. What were they, and on what were they based?

7. Titles XIV and LIII tell us quite a lot about Frankish methods of adjudication. What were they, and what were the apparent reasons behind them?

8. Compare Tacitus's picture of Germanic society, its makeup and values, with that of Frankish society around 511, as mirrored in these laws. Which strike you as more significant, the differences or the similarities? What conclusions do you draw from that answer?

I. CONCERNING A SUMMONS TO COURT

1. If a man has been summoned to court[1] in accordance with the king's laws and does not come, and if a lawful excuse has not detained him, he shall be liable to pay six hundred denarii (i.e., fifteen solidi).[2] . . .

3. He who summons another man should go with witnesses to that man's house and summon him thus or, if the man summoned is not present, he should deliver the charge to that one's wife or to some other member of his family so he or she will make known to him [the accused] that he has been summoned to court.[3]

4. If a man is occupied in the king's service, he cannot be summoned to court.

---

[1]The court, or assembly of freemen, that met on a regular basis in the *hundred,* which was a division, or district, of the larger *county,* the old *pagus* mentioned by Tacitus (source 6, note 3). Originally, the hundred consisted of one hundred warriors, but by the year 500 that was probably no longer the case. (See Chapters 6 and 12 of Tacitus's *Germania.*)

[2]This is based on the Roman monetary system, which Clovis adopted as a means of integrating his people into Gallo-Roman society. A *solidus* (plural: *solidi*) was 1/72 of a pound of gold. The *denarius* (plural: *denarii*), or *denar,* was a small silver coin. Forty denarii equaled one solidus.

[3]Note that the victim or the victim's family, and not the king, was responsible for summoning an accused person to court.

XIII. CONCERNING THE ABDUCTION OF FREEMEN OR FREE WOMEN

1. If three men take a free girl from her house or workroom,[4] the three shall be liable to pay twelve hundred denarii (i.e., thirty solidi). . . .

6. If the girl who was seized had been placed in the king's protection, the fine to be exacted is twenty-five hundred denarii (i.e., sixty-two and one-half solidi).

7. If it was a servant of the king or a half-freeman[5] who abducted the free girl, he shall make composition with his life [i.e., he shall be given as a slave to the family of the girl].

8. But if the free girl voluntarily followed one of these she shall lose her freedom. . . .

12. He who takes a woman betrothed to someone else and joins her to himself in marriage shall be liable to pay twenty-five hundred denarii (i.e., sixty-two and one-half solidi) [to her family or guardian].

13. He shall be liable to pay fifteen solidi to the man to whom she was betrothed.

14. He who attacks on the road a betrothed girl with her bridal party being led to her husband and forcefully has intercourse with her [shall be liable to pay eight thousand denarii (i.e., two hundred solidi).[6]]

XIV. CONCERNING WAYLAYING OR PILLAGING

1. He who robs a freeman by waylaying him and it is proved against him shall be liable to pay twenty-five hundred denarii (i.e., sixty-two and one-half solidi) [plus return of the objects taken in addition to a payment for the time their use was lost].

2. If a Roman robs a Salic barbarian[7] and it is not certainly proved against him, he can clear himself with twenty-five oathhelpers,[8] half of whom he has chosen. If he cannot find the oathhelpers he shall go to the ordeal of boiling water[9] or it should be observed as in the case preceding [i.e., pay sixty-two and one-half solidi in addition to return of the objects taken or their value plus a payment for the time their use was lost].

3. If a Frank robs a Roman and it is not certainly proved, he shall clear himself with twenty oathhelpers, half of whom he has chosen. If he cannot find the oathhelpers, if it is proved, he shall be liable to pay twelve hundred denarii (i.e., thirty solidi) [in addition to return of the objects taken or their value plus a payment for the time their use was lost].

4. If anyone contrary to the king's command presumes to halt or attack a man who is trying

---

[4]The room set aside exclusively for women engaged in spinning wool.

[5]Known as a *leet,* this was someone who ranked midway between a free Frank and a slave. Nearly all Germanic tribes had such a class. (See Tacitus's *Germania,* Chapter 25.) Leets probably originated as the freed descendants of conquered people; hence, the word is often translated as *freedman* or *half freeman.* The status of a leet was similar to that of a Roman colonus (Chapter 1, source 2). Over time, coloni and leets intermarried, and the terms became interchangeable.

[6]It is unclear who gets the fine: the woman's family or her betrothed. Or did they share it?

[7]Note that the Salian Franks refer to themselves as *barbarians,* a common term for non-Romans who spoke little or no Latin or Greek.

[8]In many cases, a person could prove his or her innocence by taking a sacred oath and offering a requisite number of oathhelpers who supported the primary oath with formal, complicated oaths of their own. If they stumbled over their words or refused to act as oathhelpers, the person whom they were attempting to support was judged guilty.

[9]In this ordeal, the accused person reached in and took an object out of a pot of boiling water. The resultant wound was bound up and blessed. After a certain period of time, the wound was examined. If it was clean, the accused was innocent; if it was festering, the person was guilty.

to move somewhere and has a permit from the king [to do so] and can identify himself in public court, he shall be liable to pay eight thousand denarii (i.e., two hundred solidi) [to the man attacked].

XV. CONCERNING HOMICIDE OR THE MAN WHO TAKES ANOTHER MAN'S WIFE WHILE HER HUSBAND STILL LIVES

1. He who kills a freeman or takes another man's wife while her husband lives, and it is proved against him, shall be liable to pay eight thousand denarii (i.e., two hundred solidi).

2. He who rapes a free girl, and it is proved against him, shall be liable to pay twenty-five hundred denarii (i.e., sixty-two and one-half solidi).

3. He who secretly has intercourse with a free girl with the consent of both, and it is proved against him, shall be liable to pay eighteen hundred denarii (i.e., forty-five solidi).

XVII. CONCERNING WOUNDS

1. He who wounds or tries to kill another man and the blow misses him, and it is proved against him, shall be liable to pay twenty-five hundred denarii (i.e., sixty-two and one-half solidi).

2. He who tries to shoot another man with a poisoned arrow and the arrow misses him, and it is proved against him, shall be liable to pay twenty-five hundred denarii (i.e., sixty-two and one-half solidi).

3. He who hits another man on the head so that his blood falls to the ground, and it is proved against him, shall be liable to pay six hundred denarii (i.e., fifteen solidi).

4. He who strikes another man on the head so that the brain shows, and it is proved against him, shall be liable to pay six hundred denarii (i.e., fifteen solidi).

5. If the three bones that lie over the brain

protrude, he shall be liable to pay twelve hundred denarii (i.e., thirty solidi).

6. If the wound penetrates between the ribs or into the stomach so that it reaches the internal organs, he shall be liable to pay twelve hundred denarii (i.e., thirty solidi).

7. If the wound runs continuously and never heals, he shall be liable to pay twenty-five hundred denarii (i.e., sixty-two and one-half solidi). For the cost of medical attention, he shall pay three hundred sixty denarii (i.e., nine solidi).

XVIII. CONCERNING HIM WHO ACCUSES BEFORE THE KING AN INNOCENT MAN WHO IS ABSENT

He who accuses before the king an innocent man who is absent shall be liable to pay twenty-five hundred denarii (i.e., sixty-two and one-half solidi).

XX. CONCERNING THE MAN WHO TOUCHES THE HAND OR ARM OR FINGER OF A FREE WOMAN

1. The freeman who touches the hand or arm or finger of a free woman or of any other woman, and it is proved against him, shall be liable to pay six hundred denarii (i.e., fifteen solidi).

2. If he touches her arm [below the elbow], he shall be liable to pay twelve hundred denarii (i.e., thirty solidi).

3. But if he places his hand above her elbow, and it is proved against him, he shall be liable to pay fourteen hundred denarii (i.e., thirty-five solidi).

4. He who touches a woman's breast or cuts it so that the blood flows shall be liable to pay eighteen hundred denarii (i.e., forty-five solidi).

XXIV. ON KILLING CHILDREN AND WOMEN

1. He who kills a free boy less than twelve years old up to the end of his twelfth year, and it

is proved against him, shall be liable to pay twenty-four thousand denarii (i.e., six hundred solidi).

2. He who cuts the hair of a long-haired free boy[10] without the consent of his relatives, and it is proved against him, shall be liable to pay eighteen hundred denarii (i.e., forty-five solidi).

3. If he cuts the hair of a free girl without the consent of her relatives, and it is proved against him, he shall be liable to pay eighteen hundred denarii (i.e., forty-five solidi).

4. He who kills a long-haired boy, and it is proved against him, shall be liable to pay twenty-four thousand denarii (i.e., six hundred solidi).

5. He who strikes a pregnant free woman, and it is proved against him, shall be liable to pay twenty-eight thousand denarii (i.e., seven hundred solidi).

6. He who kills an infant in its mother's womb or within nine days of birth before it has a name, and it is proved against him, shall be liable to pay four thousand denarii (i.e., one hundred solidi).

7. If a boy under twelve years old commits some offense, a fine will not be required of him.

8. He who kills a free woman after she has begun to bear children, if it is proved against him, shall be liable to pay twenty-four thousand denarii (i.e., six hundred solidi).

9. He who kills a woman after she is no longer able to bear children, if it is proved against him, shall be liable to pay eight thousand denarii (i.e., two hundred solidi).

XXIX. CONCERNING DISABLING INJURIES

1. He who maims another man's hand or foot or gouges out or strikes out his eye or cuts off his

ear or nose, and it is proved against him, shall be liable to pay four thousand denarii (i.e., one hundred solidi).

2. If he has cut the hand and the hand remains hanging there, he shall be liable to pay twenty-five hundred denarii (i.e., sixty-two and one-half solidi). . . .

6. He who cuts off a man's second finger that is used to release arrows shall be liable to pay fourteen hundred denarii (i.e., thirty-five solidi).

7. He who cuts off the other remaining fingers — all three equally with one blow — shall be liable to pay eighteen hundred denarii (i.e., forty-five solidi). . . .

15. He who cuts out another man's tongue so that he is not able to speak shall be liable to pay four thousand denarii (i.e., one hundred solidi). . . .

17. He who castrates a freeman or cuts into his penis so that he is incapacitated shall be liable to pay one hundred solidi.

18. But if he takes the penis away entirely he shall be liable to pay eight thousand denarii (i.e., two hundred solidi) in addition to nine solidi for the doctor.

XXX. CONCERNING ABUSIVE TERMS

1. He who calls someone else a pederast shall be liable to pay six hundred denarii (i.e., fifteen solidi).

2. He who claims that someone else is covered in dung shall be liable to pay one hundred twenty denarii (i.e., three solidi).

3. He who calls a free woman or man a prostitute and cannot prove it shall be liable to pay eighteen hundred denarii (i.e., forty-five solidi). . . .

---

[10]All male children wore their hair long until they were twelve, the age of legal majority. When a child reached that age, the family would cut his hair in a ceremony that marked coming of age.

6. The freeman who accused another man of throwing down his shield and running away, and cannot prove it, shall be liable to pay one hundred twenty denarii (i.e., three solidi).

XLI. ON THE KILLING OF FREEMEN

1. He who kills a free Frank or other barbarian who lives by Salic law, and it is proved against him, shall be liable to pay eight thousand denarii (i.e., two hundred solidi).

2. If he throws him into a well or holds him under water, he shall be liable to pay twenty-four thousand denarii (i.e., six hundred solidi). And for concealing it, he shall be liable as we have said before.

3. If he does not conceal his crime, he shall be liable to pay eight thousand denarii (i.e., two hundred solidi). . . .

5. He who kills a man who is in the king's trust or a free woman,[11] and it is proved against him, shall be liable to pay twenty-four thousand denarii (i.e., six hundred solidi).

6. If he throws him into the water or into a well, he shall be liable to pay seventy-two thousand denarii (i.e., eighteen hundred solidi). . . .

8. He who kills a Roman who is a table companion of the king, and it is proved against him, shall be liable to pay twelve thousand denarii (i.e., three hundred solidi).

9. If a Roman landholder who is not a table companion of the king is killed, he who is proved to have killed him shall be liable to pay four thousand denarii (i.e., one hundred solidi). . . .

15. He who kills a free girl before she is able to bear children shall be liable to pay eight thousand denarii (i.e., two hundred solidi).

16. He who kills a free woman after she begins to bear children shall be liable to pay twenty-four thousand denarii (i.e., six hundred solidi).

17. He who kills her past middle age and no longer able to bear children shall be liable to pay eight thousand denarii (i.e., two hundred solidi).

18. He who kills a long-haired boy shall be liable to pay twenty-four thousand denarii (i.e., six hundred solidi).

19. He who kills a pregnant woman shall be liable to pay six hundred solidi.

20. He who kills an infant in its mother's womb or before it has a name shall be liable to pay one hundred solidi.

LIII. ON REDEEMING ONE'S HAND FROM THE HOT WATER ORDEAL

1. If a man has been sentenced to the hot water ordeal and it is agreed that he who was sentenced may redeem his hand and offer oathhelpers, then he may redeem his hand for one hundred twenty denarii (i.e., three solidi) if it were a case such that he would be liable to pay six hundred denarii (i.e., fifteen solidi) in composition.[12] . . .

3. If it is such a case that if he were proved guilty he would be liable to pay thirty-five solidi, and if it is agreed that he may redeem his hand and offer oathhelpers, he may redeem his hand for two hundred forty denarii (i.e., six solidi). . . .

5. If it is a more serious cause for which he can be judged liable to pay sixty-two and one-half solidi, and if it is agreed that he may redeem his hand, he may redeem his hand with fifteen solidi. . . .

7. If someone charges another man with a crime involving the payment of wergeld[13] and he has been sentenced to the ordeal, if it is agreed that he may offer oathhelpers and redeem his hand, he may redeem his hand with twelve hundred denarii (i.e., thirty solidi).

---

[11]Presumably, a free woman who was in the king's trust.
[12]*Composition* was the fine for a nonlethal injury.

[13]*Wergeld* (literally, "person money") was the fine imposed for homicide of any sort, including an unintentional killing.

LIV. ON THE KILLING OF A COUNT

1. He who kills a count[14] shall be liable to pay twenty-four thousand denarii (i.e., six hundred solidi).

LIX. CONCERNING ALLODIAL LANDS[15]

1. If a man dies and leaves no children, and if his father or mother survives him, this person shall succeed to the inheritance.

2. If there is no father or mother but he leaves a brother or sister, they shall succeed to the inheritance.

3. If none of these is living, then the sister of the mother shall succeed to the inheritance.

4. If none of the mother's sisters live, then the sisters of the father will succeed to the inheritance.

5. If there is no father's sister, after these kindred whoever is closest who comes from the father's kin shall succeed to the inheritance.

6. But concerning Salic land,[16] no portion or inheritance is for a woman but all the land belongs to members of the male sex who are brothers.

---

[14]As the chief judicial and military officer of a county (note 1), he answered directly to the king.
[15]Land held privately for which no service was owed anyone. (See the next note.)

[16]Land given out by the king for service to him, as opposed to allodial, or family, land.

▼▼▼

Invaders and Settlers

As was true of all ancient empires, Rome had an endemic barbarian problem. As early as 390 B.C., Celtic raiders captured most of the city before being beaten back. Despite such occasional and quite real threats to its security, however, Rome managed, for much of its history, to be more the attacker than the attacked, so far as its barbarian fringe peoples were concerned. The vast area of Roman Gaul, for example, was carved out at the expense of the indigenous peoples residing there.

Rome's relations with its border barbarians was not simply a case of incessant warfare and expansion. Quite often, tribes deliberately settled within a few miles of Roman frontier posts in order to enjoy the security and opportunities afforded by the presence of nearby imperial legions. Increasingly from the first century A.D. on, Germanic and other border peoples enrolled in the Roman armies. In some cases, they enlisted as entire tribes, serving as auxiliary troops under their own leaders and occupying lands within the frontier, where they could act as buffers against hostile fringe peoples. All things considered, the empire's borders tended to be fluid and reasonably open, so far as Rome's fringe peoples were concerned, and this was the way both sides generally liked it.

As we saw earlier, the third century A.D. witnessed a general breakdown of this symbiotic relationship, as the empire was attacked and penetrated on numerous fronts by aggressive Germanic confederations. Yet many of the Roman troops who eventually stabilized the frontiers in the late third century were themselves of barbarian stock. Increasingly, Rome's armies depended on Germanic and other noncitizen soldiers to shore up its defenses, and some of these warriors rose to the highest levels of military command.

For awhile, this increasingly Germanized Roman army managed to keep other Germans at bay, but by the last quarter of the fourth century, the system was failing. Rome's new barbarian problem began with the arrival of the Visigoths in 376 and continued with the coming of such peoples as the Ostrogoths (source 8) and the Franks (source 9). Most of these invaders came not to destroy the empire but to become part of it. The end of the Roman Empire was a concept unimaginable to most fourth- and fifth-century individuals, Roman and barbarian alike. In the process of settling within the empire's western provinces, however, the newcomers took over the reins of power and inevitably set in motion a process of cultural transformation. To be sure, the new Germanic lords of the West were a numerical minority, and many of them wished to emulate Roman society. Consequently, these German settlers became, to a degree, Romanized. Nevertheless, most of their basic values, customs, and ways of perceiving the world were generally so radically different from those of the people whom they had conquered that, despite the best of intentions, they did, in the end, serve as major agents of cultural metamorphosis in the West.

Civilitas in Theodoric the Ostrogoth's Kingdom

▼▼▼

8 ▼ *Cassiodorus, VARIAE*

Late in the fourth century A.D., the migrations of the Huns, a Turkic people out of Inner Asia, precipitated a series of events that placed tremendous pressure on Rome's Germanic neighbors and, ultimately, on the Roman Empire itself. The westward sweep of the Hunnish advance washed over the Ostrogoths no later than 375, and when the Ostrogoths entered the empire a few years later, they did so as subjects of the Huns. When Attila the Hun's horsemen were checked in 451 by a combined Roman and Germanic army on the Catalaunian Fields of Gaul, Ostrogothic warriors fought alongside the Huns against their Germanic cousins. The death of Attila only two years later, however, and the subsequent rapid breakup of the Huns as an identifiable force allowed the Ostrogoths to gain their independence. They were now on their own within the empire's borders.

Around midcentury, just about the time that the Ostrogoths gained their freedom from Hunnish control, the man who would lead this tribe to the heights of its power was born in the eastern Roman province of Pannonia. Known to history as *Theodoric the Ostrogoth* (ca. 453–526), this member of the Amali royal family went to Constantinople as a hostage at the age of eight and remained there as an imperial guest for a decade. During those ten years, he fell under the influence of the Greco-Roman civilization he found there. Forever after, he was committed to finding a legitimate and worthy place for his Gothic people within the Roman world.

In the early or mid-470s Theodoric became king of all the Ostrogoths. In 483 he was invested with the powers and title of a Roman general, and the following year this Gothic citizen of the empire was given the lofty but by then only honorific title of *consul.* Theodoric's titles and his reverence for Constantinople and the empire centered there did not preclude, however, his unsuccessfully marching against the city in 487 out of a sense that the empire was not providing properly for its Ostrogothic allies.

Emperor Zeno's fear of Theodoric led him to approve what must have seemed at the time a brilliant solution to two vexing problems. Italy was in the hands of the German adventurer *Odoacer* (also known as *Odovacar*), who in 476 had deposed and exiled the last Roman emperor in the West, Romulus Augustulus. In 488 Zeno commissioned Theodoric and his Ostrogoths to rewin Italy for the empire. In March of 493 Theodoric killed Odoacer and took over sole control of Italy and its neighboring territories. Although he acknowledged the overlordship of the emperor at Constantinople, Theodoric was now the king of Italy and the only effective ruler in the peninsula. Until his death in 526, he gave the people of Italy and adjacent lands conscientious government. That government was marred, however, by the fact that many of his subjects deeply resented being ruled by a Goth who subscribed to the *Arian* faith, a Christian heresy[*] that had arisen in early fourth-century Egypt and been carried to various East German tribes before their entry into the empire.

Not all Romans, however, resisted this heretic's[*] rule. One of Theodoric's chief ministers was Flavius Magnus Aurelius Cassiodorus Senator (ca. 490–ca. 583), an aristocrat, politician, educator, scholar, and later a monk.[*] Because Theodoric was illiterate, he depended greatly on secretary-ministers such as Cassiodorus to put into acceptable Latin prose his plans and decisions. In 538 Cassiodorus compiled the letters, edicts, and other official documents that he had written while functioning as a royal secretary. Known as the *Variae* (*The Potpourri*), the collection has survived and serves as one of our best sources for the reign and policies of Theodoric the Ostrogoth.

QUESTIONS FOR ANALYSIS

1. According to his letter to Emperor Anastasius, how did Theodoric view the empire and his relationship to it? Based on your study of Theodoric's other letters, does it appear that he was being truthful here? Explain your answer.
2. Consider Theodoric's next three letters, all of which concern the situation in Gaul. What do they suggest about Theodoric's view of his place among the German kings of the West and his role within the empire?
3. What do Theodoric's attempts to rebuild Rome suggest?
4. How did Theodoric, an Arian, treat the Catholic Church and the Jews?
5. What did Theodoric mean by *civilitas,* and what place did it play in his overall governmental policies?

6. What does Formula 3 allow you to infer about Theodoric's view of law and its place within his kingdom? What does it allow you to infer about his vision of the proper relationship that should exist between Romans and Goths?

7. According to these letters, what special qualities and functions did Theodoric, and presumably Cassiodorus, think the Goths brought to the empire?

8. In return, what did the empire offer the Goths and other Germans (at least as far as Theodoric was concerned)?

THEODORIC AND THE EMPIRE

King Theodoric to Emperor Anastasius.[1]
It is fitting for us, Most Clement Emperor, to seek peace, since there are no causes for anger between us.

Peace by which the nations profit; Peace the fair mother of all liberal arts, the softener of manners, the replenisher of the generations of humanity. Peace ought certainly to be an object of desire to every kingdom.

Therefore, most pious of princes, it accords with your power and your glory that we who have already profited by your affection should seek concord with your empire. You are the fairest ornament of all realms; you are the healthful defense of the whole world, to which all other rulers rightfully look up with reverence, because they know that there is in you something which is unlike all others: we above all, who by divine help learned in your republic the art of governing Romans with equity. Our royalty is an imitation of yours, modeled on your good purpose, a copy of the only empire; and in so far as we follow you do we excel all other nations.

OSTROGOTHS, VISIGOTHS, AND FRANKS

King Theodoric to Clovis,
King of the Franks.[2]
The affinities of kings ought to keep their subjects from the plague of war. We are grieved to hear of the paltry causes which are giving rise to rumors of war between you and our son Alaric,[3] rumors which gladden the hearts of the enemies of both of you. Let me say with all frankness, but with all affection, just what I think: "It is the act of a passionate man to get his troops ready for action at the first embassy which he sends." Instead of that refer the matter to our arbitration. It would be a delight to me to choose men capable of mediating between you. What would you yourselves think of me if I could hear unmoved of your murderous intentions towards one another? Away with this conflict, in which one of you will probably be utterly destroyed. Throw away the sword which you wield for *my* humiliation. By what right do I thus threaten you? By the right of a father and a friend. He who shall despise this advice of ours

---

[1] Anastasius I (r. 491–518).
[2] This letter was part of an unsuccessful attempt to prevent Clovis the Frank's invasion of the Visigothic kingdom of Toulouse in 507 and his conquest of southwest Gaul. (For more on Clovis and this war, see source 9.)

[3] Alaric II (r. 484–507), king of the Visigoths, whom Clovis killed in battle. Alaric was not a blood relative of Theodoric, but note the use of the term *son.*

will have to reckon us and our friends as his adversaries.

I send two ambassadors to you, as I have to my son Alaric, and hope that they may be able so to arrange matters that no alien malignity may sow the seeds of dissension between you, and that your nations, which under your fathers have long enjoyed the blessings of peace, may not now be laid waste by sudden collision. You ought to believe him who, as you know, has rejoiced in your prosperity. No true friend is he who launches his associates, unwarned, into the headlong dangers of war.

King Theodoric to All the Goths.[4]

To the Goths a hint of war rather than persuasion to the strife is needed, since a warlike race such as ours delights to prove its courage. In truth, he shuns no labor who hungers for the renown of valor. Therefore with the help of God, whose blessing alone brings prosperity, we design to send our army to the Gauls for the common benefit of all, that you may have an opportunity of promotion, and we the power of testing your merits; for in time of peace the courage which we admire lies hidden, and when men have no chance of showing what is in them, their relative merits are concealed. We have therefore given our Sajo,[5] Nandius, instructions to warn you that, on the eighth day before the kalends of next July,[6] you move forward to the campaign in the name of God, sufficiently equipped, according to your old custom, with horses, arms, and every requisite for war. Thus will you at the same time show that the old valor of your sires yet dwells in your hearts, and also successfully per-

form your king's command. Bring forth your young men for the discipline of Mars.[7] Let them see you do deeds which they may love to tell of to their children. For an art not learned in youth is an art missing in our riper years. The very hawk, whose food is plunder, thrusts her still weak and tender young ones out of the nest, that they may not become accustomed to soft repose. She strikes the lingerers with her wings; she forces her callow young to fly, that they may prove to be such in the future as her maternal fondness can be proud of. Do you therefore, lofty by nature, and stimulated yet more by the love of fame, study to leave such sons behind you as your fathers have left in leaving you.

King Theodoric to All the Gaulish Provinces.[8]

Obey the Roman customs. You are now by God's blessing restored to your ancient freedom; put off the barbarian; clothe yourselves with the morals of the toga;[9] unlearn cruelty, that you may not be unworthy to be our subjects. We are sending you Spectabilis[10] Gemellus as vicarius praefectorum,[11] a man of tried worth, who we trust will be guilty of no crime, because he knows he would thereby seriously displease us. Obey his commands therefore. Do not dislike the reign of law because it is new to you, after the aimless seethings of barbarism.[12]

You may now bring out your long-hidden treasures; the rich and the noble will again have a chance of suitable promotion. You may now enjoy what till now you have only heard of — the triumph of Public Right, the most certain solace of human life, the help of the weak, the curb of the strong. You may now understand that men

---

[4]Despite Theodoric's diplomatic efforts to prevent a Frankish attack on Visigothic Gaul, Frankish armies swept into the south, killing King Alaric II in the process of defeating the Visigothic army. This letter to all Ostrogoths dates from the summer of 508, when Theodoric was preparing to send troops into southeast Gaul in order to occupy the area around Arles and to deny the Franks access to the Mediterranean.

[5]A low-ranking Gothic officer who executed the king's mandates.

[6]June 24, 508.

[7]The Roman god of war.

[8]Written in 510 to the inhabitants of that portion of southeast Gaul that Theodoric managed to preserve from Frankish and Burgundian conquest.

[9]The garment worn by adult Roman male citizens.

[10]The *spectabiles* (notable men; plural of *spectabilis*) ranked second in the five-tiered hierarchy of the Roman civil administration, as restructured by Diocletian and his successors.

[11]See Chapter 1, source 1, note 4.

[12]The rule of the Visigoths and Franks.

are exalted not by their bodily strength, but by reason.

THE CITY OF ROME

King Theodoric to All the Goths and Romans.
Most worthy of royal attention is the rebuilding of ancient cities, an adornment in time of peace, a precaution for time of war.

Therefore, if anyone has in his fields stones suitable for the building of the walls, let him cheerfully and promptly produce them. Even though he should be paid at a low rate, he will have his reward as a member of the community, which will benefit thereby.

King Theodoric to Sura, Illustris.[13]
Let nothing lie useless which may redound to the beauty of the City. Let your Illustrious Magnificence therefore cause the blocks of marble which are everywhere lying about in ruins to be wrought up into the walls by the hands of the workmen whom I send herewith. Only take care to use only those stones which have really fallen from public buildings, as we do not wish to appropriate private property, even for the glorification of the City.

THEODORIC AND THE CHURCH

King Theodoric to Adila, Senator[14] and Comes.[15]
We wish to protect all our subjects, but especially the Church, because by so doing we earn the favor of Heaven. Therefore, in accordance with the petition of the blessed Eustorgius, bishop* of Milan, we desire you to accord all necessary protection to the men and farms belonging to the Milanese Church in Sicily: always

understanding, however, that they are not to refuse to plead in answer to any public or private suit that may be brought against them. They are to be protected from wrong, but are not themselves to deviate from the path of justice.

CIVILITAS

King Theodoric to All the Jews of Genoa.
The true mark of *civilitas* is the observance of law. It is this which makes life in communities possible, and which separates man from the brutes. We therefore gladly accede to your request that all the privileges which the foresight of antiquity conferred upon the Jewish customs shall be renewed to you, for in truth it is our great desire that the laws of the ancients shall be kept in force to secure the reverence due to us. Everything which has been found to conduce to *civilitas* should be held fast with enduring devotion.

King Theodoric to Unigis, the Sword-bearer.[16]
We delight to live after the law of the Romans, whom we seek to defend with our arms; and we are as much interested in the maintenance of morality as we can possibly be in war. For what profit is there in having removed the turmoil of the barbarians, unless we live according to law? Certain slaves, on our army's entry into Gaul, have run away from their old masters and betaken themselves to new ones. Let them be restored to their rightful owners. Rights must not be confounded under the rule of justice, nor ought the defender of liberty to favor recreant slaves. Let other kings desire the glory of battles won, of cities taken, of ruins made; our purpose is, God helping us, so to rule that our subjects shall grieve that they did not earlier acquire the blessing of our dominion.

---

[13]The top rank of the civil administration. The *illustres* (illustrious men; plural of *illustris*) were cabinet-level officers (see note 10).
[14]The name is Gothic, but he bears the rank of Roman senator.

[15]A *comes Gothorum,* or "count of the Goths," was a Goth who served as a regional military leader and judge and was answerable directly to the king. We saw Frankish counts mentioned in *The Salic Law* (source 7).
[16]A high-ranking Gothic officer in the royal household.

Formula 3.[17]

As we know that, by God's help, Goths are dwelling intermingled among you,[18] in order to prevent the trouble which is wont to arise among partners we have thought it right to send to you as count, _____ , a sublime person, a man already proved to be of high character, in order that he may terminate any contests arising between two Goths according to our edicts; but that, if any matter should arise between a Goth and a born Roman, he may, after associating with himself a Roman judge, decide the strife by fair reason. As between two Romans, let the decision rest with the Roman examiners, whom we appoint in the various provinces; that thus each may keep his own laws, and with various judges one justice may embrace the whole realm. Thus, sharing one common peace, may both nations, if God favor us, enjoy the sweets of tranquillity.

Know, however, that we view all [our subjects] with one impartial love; but he may commend himself more abundantly to our favor who subdues his own will into loving submission to the law. We like nothing that is disorderly; we detest wicked arrogance and all who have anything to do with it. Our principles lead us to execrate violent men. In a dispute let laws decide, not the strong arm. Why should men seek by choice violent remedies, when they know that the courts of justice are open to them? It is for this cause that we pay the judges their salaries, for this that we maintain such large official staffs with all their privileges, that we may not allow anything to grow up among you which may tend towards hatred. Since you see that one lordship[19] is over you, let there be also one desire in your hearts, to live in harmony.

Let both nations hear what we have at heart. You [oh Goths!] have the Romans as neighbors to your lands: even so let them be joined to you in affection. You too, oh Romans! ought dearly to love the Goths, who in peace swell the numbers of your people and in war defend the whole Republic. It is fitting therefore that you obey the judge whom we have appointed for you, that you may by all means accomplish all that he may ordain for the preservation of the laws; and thus you will be found to have promoted your own interests while obeying our command.

---

[17]This is a formulaic (or stock) letter to be sent to a region upon appointment of its new Gothic count (note 15).
[18]About one-third of the arable land of Theodoric's kingdom was confiscated for Ostrogothic settlements.

[19]The word used here is *imperium,* which technically means "Roman imperial power."

Clovis the Frank, Agent of God

▼▼▼

9 ▼ *Gregory of Tours, HISTORY OF THE FRANKS*

As the Ostrogoths moved into Italy, the Franks, a loose confederation of autonomous Germanic tribes united only by shared customs and language, spread slowly into Gaul from their ancestral lands along the northern and middle regions of the Rhine. Here they confronted other Germanic settlers — most notably the Alemanni, Burgundians, and Visigoths — and also some vestiges of Roman military and civic authority that had somehow managed to survive the Germanic invasions. Initially, these forces combined to block the Franks' penetration into the heartland of Gaul. A major turning point in Frankish fortunes occurred in 481, when Clovis (ca. 465–511) succeeded his father, Childeric, as leader of one of the several small groups that together made up the Salian branch of the Frankish people, so named because of its home on the Sala (Yssel) River in the central Netherlands. In 481 Clovis securely held only a small portion of northern Gaul and contiguous regions across the Rhine. Thirty years later, Clovis's four sons inherited and divided among themselves a kingdom that encompassed most of Gaul and significant portions of western Germany. Despite the vicissitudes of family intrigue and bloodletting in the generations that followed, Clovis's successors managed not only to hold onto but to expand his kingdom into the largest and most powerful of all the Germanic kingdoms of the West. Long after the Ostrogoths had passed out of history as an identifiable culture, the Franks were laying the base for the new Europe's first attempt at empire building.

Clovis's career was pivotal in the history of the Franks, because it was he who first united the Franks into a single kingdom and launched a series of successful campaigns of conquest against the Franks' Roman and Germanic neighbors. Just as significant, and inextricably intertwined with those two political-military accomplishments, was Clovis's conversion to Catholic Christianity. Whereas the Goths were Arian Christians and deeply hated by many native Roman clergy and laity for their heresy,* Clovis's Franks adopted the official faith of late Roman society in the West, thereby becoming more than acceptable to the Gallo-Roman clergy, the true shapers of opinion in the land of Gaul.

One of the most important sixth-century opinion shapers was St. Gregory of Tours (538–594), bishop* of the important see of Tours on the Loire. Without being conscious of it, Bishop Gregory represented, both in his person and his writings, the new synthesis that was taking shape between the ancient Mediterranean ways of thought and life that were withering away in the West and the bold and vigorous style of the conquering Germans. Although he was the offspring of a well-established Gallo-Roman aristocratic family, who had a long tradition of service both to the Gallican Church and the Roman state, Gregory's writings show him to be a man who was very much a part of a world in which social standards and values were radically changing.

Late in his busy life, Gregory took it upon himself to tell the story of the Franks, who had become the most important element in sixth-century Gaul. Most of the ten books of his *History of the Franks* center on Clovis's royal grandchildren, Gregory's own contemporaries, but Bishop Gregory also sketched the life and career of Clovis. Gregory's treatment of this early Frankish king gives us a fascinating glimpse of the process of cultural fusion that was taking place in fifth- and sixth-century Gaul. At the same time, we must use Gregory with caution for several reasons. First, there is the obvious fact that he composed his history almost a century after Clovis's death. Second, as a churchman, Bishop Gregory wrote his history from a religious position that undoubtedly colored his interpretation, and possibly even his presentation, of the events he narrated.

QUESTIONS FOR ANALYSIS

1. Review what Tacitus says about the Germanic kings in source 6, and study again the picture of early sixth-century Frankish royal authority that emerges from *The Salic Law* (source 7). Now consider the story of the vase at Soissons. What does it allow you to infer about the level of Clovis's authority around 486? Was it closer to what Tacitus described or to what we find in *The Salic Law*? What conclusion follows from your answer?

2. What do you make of Gregory's treatment of the conversion of Clovis and his Franks? Is the story believable? Could Gregory of Tours have had an artistic or other motive in telling the story this way? Explain your answer.

3. Consider the several baptismal scenes. What would have most impressed the Franks?

4. Consider the story of Clovis's campaign against the Visigoths. What does it suggest about his postconversion attitude toward the Church and its saints?

5. Based on the scanty evidence before you, why do you think Clovis converted, and when might he have begun entertaining such notions? In addressing these questions, do not overlook the story of the vase at Soissons and what Gregory tells us about St. Rémy. Consider also Clovis's postconversion actions.

6. What did Clovis's appointment to the consulship seem to mean to him? What do you infer from your answer?

7. What do these stories suggest about Clovis's character and policies?

8. Now that you have answered question 7, reconsider your answer in light of the fact that a scholar has recently argued that Clovis was fairly Romanized and nowhere near as barbaric as many textbooks portray him. If you use Clovis's Salic laws (source 7) as a possible corrective to Gregory's account, does your picture of Clovis change at all? Why or why not?

9. What picture does Gregory paint of Gallo-Frankish society? Were values and social standards changing? If so, which ones, and why?

10. One historian has written, "Bishop Gregory presented history as a compelling morality story revolving around constant combat between the forces of God and of the Devil." Does this statement seem to have any validity in light of what you have read in this excerpt?

With liberal culture on the wane, or rather perishing in the Gallic cities, there were many deeds being done both good and evil: the heathen were raging fiercely; kings were growing more cruel; the Church, attacked by heretics,* was defended by Catholics; while the Christian faith was in general devoutly cherished, among some it was growing cold; the churches also were enriched by the faithful or plundered by traitors — and no grammarian skilled in the dialectic* art could be found to describe these matters either in prose or verse; and many were lamenting and saying: "Woe to our day, since the pursuit of letters has perished from among us and no one can be found among the people who can set forth the deeds of the present on the written page." Hearing continually these complaints and others like them I [have undertaken] to commemorate the past, in order that it may come to the knowledge of the future; and although my speech is rude, I have been unable to be silent as to the struggles between the wicked and the upright; and I have been especially encouraged because, to my surprise, it has often been said by men of our day, that few understand the learned words of the rhetorician* but many the rude language of the common people. . . .

Childeric died and Clovis his son reigned in his stead. In the fifth year of his reign[1] Syagrius, king of the Romans,[2] son of Egidius,[3] had his seat in the city of Soissons which Egidius . . . once held. And Clovis came against him with Ragnachar, his kinsman, because he used to possess the kingdom, and demanded that they make ready a battle-field. And Syagrius did not delay nor was he afraid to resist. And so they fought against each other and Syagrius, seeing his army crushed, turned his back and fled swiftly to king Alaric at Toulouse.[4] And Clovis sent to Alaric to send him back, otherwise he was to know that Clovis would make war on him for his refusal. And Alaric was afraid that he would incur the anger of the Franks on account of Syagrius, seeing it is the fashion of the Goths to be terrified, and he surrendered him in chains to Clovis' envoys. And Clovis took him and gave orders to put him under guard, and when he had got his kingdom he directed that he be executed secretly. At that time many churches were despoiled by Clovis' army, since he was as yet involved in heathen error.

Now the army had taken from a certain church a vase of wonderful size and beauty, along with the remainder of the utensils for the service of the church. And the bishop of the church sent messengers to the king asking that the vase at least be returned, if he could not get back any more of the sacred dishes. On hearing this the king said to the messenger: "Follow us as far as Soissons, because all that has been taken is to be divided there and when the lot assigns me that dish I will do what the father[5] asks." Then when he came to Soissons and all the booty was set in their midst, the king said: "I ask of you, brave warriors, not to refuse to grant me in addition to my share, yonder dish," that is, he was speaking of the vase just mentioned. In answer to the speech of the king those of more sense replied: "Glorious king, all that we see is yours, and we ourselves are subject to your rule. Now do what seems well-pleasing to you; for no one is able to resist your power." When they said this a foolish, envious and excitable fellow lifted his battle-ax and struck the vase, and cried in a loud voice: "You shall get nothing here except what the lot fairly bestows on you." At this all were stupefied, but the king endured the insult with the gentleness of patience, and taking the vase he handed it over to the messenger of the church, nursing the wound deep in his heart. And at the end of the year he ordered the whole army to come with their equipment of armor, to show the brightness of their arms on the field of March.[6] And when he was reviewing them all carefully, he came to the man who struck the vase, and said to him: "No one has brought armor so carelessly kept as you; for neither your spear nor sword nor ax is in serviceable condition." And seizing his ax he cast it to the earth, and when the other had bent over somewhat to pick it up, the king raised his hands and drove his own ax into the man's head. "This," said he, "is what you did at Soissons to the vase." Upon the death of this man, he ordered the rest to depart, raising great dread of himself by this action. He made many wars and gained many

---

[1]In 486.
[2]This Gallo-Roman individual maintained an independent Roman enclave in Gaul.
[3]Egidius, a Gallo-Roman aristocrat and soldier, had actually been elected king of Childeric's tribe during a period in which Childeric was in exile.
[4]Alaric II, king of the Visigoths who had their capital at Toulouse in southern Gaul.

[5]*Papa,* which can be translated as *father* or *pope.* This term of respect was used widely for bishops at this time and was not yet reserved exclusively for the bishop of Rome.
[6]The field where they would normally assemble in the spring prior to campaigning.

victories. In the tenth year of his reign he made war on the Thuringi and brought them under his dominion.

Now the king of the Burgundians was Gundevech. . . . He had four sons; Gundobad, Godegisel, Chilperic and Godomar. Gundobad killed his brother Chilperic with the sword, and sank his wife in water with a stone tied to her neck. His two daughters[7] he condemned to exile; the older of these, who became a nun,* was called Chrona, and the younger Clotilda.[8] And as Clovis often sent embassies to Burgundy, the maiden Clotilda was found by his envoys. And when they saw that she was of good bearing and wise, and learned that she was of the family of the king, they reported this to king Clovis, and he sent an embassy to Gundobad without delay asking her in marriage. And Gundobad was afraid to refuse, and surrendered her to the men, and they took the girl and brought her swiftly to the king. The king was very glad when he saw her, and married her, having already by a concubine a son named Theodoric.

He had a first-born son by queen Clotilda, and as his wife wished to consecrate him in baptism,* she tried unceasingly to persuade her husband, saying: "The gods you worship are nothing, and they will be unable to help themselves or any one else. For they are graven out of stone or wood or some metal. . . . But he ought rather to be worshiped who created by his word heaven and earth, the sea and all that is in them out of a state of nothingness, who made the sun shine, and adorned the heavens with stars, who filled the waters with creeping things, the earth with living things and the air with creatures that fly, at whose nod the earth is decked with growing crops, the trees with fruit, the vines with grapes, by whose hand mankind was created, by whose generosity all that creation serves and helps man whom he created as his own." But though the

queen said this the spirit of the king was by no means moved to belief, and he said: "It was at the command of our gods that all things were created and came forth, and it is plain that your God has no power and, what is more, he is proven not to belong to the family of the gods." Meantime the faithful queen made her son ready for baptism; she gave command to adorn the church with hangings and curtains, in order that he who could not be moved by persuasion might be urged to belief by this mystery. The boy, whom they named Ingomer, died after being baptized, still wearing the white garments in which he became regenerate. At this the king was violently angry, and reproached the queen harshly, saying: "If the boy had been dedicated in the name of my gods he would certainly have lived; but as it is, since he was baptized in the name of your God, he could not live at all." To this the queen said: "I give thanks to the omnipotent God, creator of all, who has judged me not wholly unworthy, that he should deign to take to his kingdom one born from my womb. My soul is not stricken with grief for his sake, because I know that, summoned from this world as he was in his baptismal garments, he will be fed by the vision of God."

After this she bore another son, whom she named Chlodomer at baptism; and when he fell sick, the king said: "It is impossible that anything else should happen to him than happened to his brother, namely, that being baptized in the name of your Christ, he should die at once." But through the prayers of his mother, and the Lord's command, he became well.

The queen did not cease to urge him to recognize the true God and cease worshiping idols. But he could not be influenced in any way to this belief, until at last a war arose with the Alemanni,[9] in which he was driven by necessity to confess* what before he had of his free will

---

[7]Chilperic's two daughters.
[8]These two women were Catholics, even though most Burgundians were Arian Christians, whom Catholics considered to be heretics.

[9]Literally, "all people." Like the Franks, the Alemanni were a confederation of related tribes. They were settled in what is today French Alsace, southwest Germany, and Switzerland.

denied. It came about that as the two armies were fighting fiercely, there was much slaughter, and Clovis's army began to be in danger of destruction. He saw it and raised his eyes to heaven, and with remorse in his heart he burst into tears and cried: "Jesus Christ, whom Clotilda asserts to be the son of the living God, who art said to give aid to those in distress, and to bestow victory on those who hope in thee, I beseech the glory of thy aid, with the vow that if thou wilt grant me victory over these armies, and I shall know that power which she says that people dedicated in thy name have had from thee, I will believe in thee and be baptized in thy name. For I have invoked my own gods, but, as I find, they have withdrawn from aiding me; and therefore I believe that they possess no power, since they do not help those who obey them. I now call upon thee, I desire to believe thee, only let me be rescued from my adversaries." And when he said this, the Alemanni turned their backs, and began to disperse in flight. And when they saw that their king was killed, they submitted to the dominion of Clovis, saying: "Let not the people perish further, we pray; we are yours now." And he stopped the fighting, and after encouraging his men, retired in peace and told the queen how he had had merit to win the victory by calling on the name of Christ. This happened in the fifteenth year of his reign.[10]

Then the queen asked Saint Rémy, bishop of Rheims,[11] to summon Clovis secretly, urging him to introduce the king to the word of salvation. And the bishop sent for him secretly and began to urge him to believe in the true God, maker of heaven and earth, and to cease worshiping idols, which could help neither themselves nor any one else. But the king said: "I gladly hear you, most holy father; but there remains one thing: the people who follow me cannot endure to abandon their gods; but I shall go and speak to them according to your words." He met with his followers, but before he could speak the power of God anticipated him, and all the people cried out together: "O pious king, we reject our mortal gods, and we are ready to follow the immortal God whom Rémy preaches." This was reported to the bishop, who was greatly rejoiced, and bade them get ready the baptismal font.[12] The squares were shaded with tapestried canopies, the churches adorned with white curtains, the baptistery set in order, the aroma of incense spread, candles of fragrant odor burned brightly, and the whole shrine of the baptistery was filled with a divine fragrance: and the Lord gave such grace to those who stood by that they thought they were placed amid the odors of paradise. And the king was the first to ask to be baptized by the bishop. Another Constantine advanced to the baptismal font, to terminate the disease of ancient leprosy and wash away with fresh water the foul spots that had long been borne.[13] And when he entered to be baptized, the saint of God began with ready speech: "Gently bend your neck, Sigamber,[14] worship what you burned; burn what you worshiped." The holy bishop Rémy was a man of excellent wisdom and especially trained in rhetorical studies, and of such surpassing ho-

---

[10]This battle took place in 496.

[11]St. Remigius (ca. 434–530), known as Rémy in modern French, came from a rich, cultivated, and intensely pious Gallo-Roman family. His mother, Celina, was also recognized as a saint. Elected to the powerful bishopric of Rheims at age twenty-two, he presided over his see* for seventy-four years and was probably the most influential Gallican bishop of his day.

[12]Gregory wishes to give the impression that this happened in 496 (shortly after Clovis's victory over the Alemanni) in order to draw a close parallel with Emperor Constantine's fourth-century conversion (see the introduction to section 2 of Chapter 1); however, the baptism probably took place on December 25, 503 (or possibly 506).

[13]According to an ancient legend, which has no basis in fact, Emperor Constantine (Chapter 1, source 3) originally persecuted Christians and for that sin incurred leprosy, a deadly skin disease. When he entered the waters of baptism, the scales of the disease washed away and he was cured, just as the disease of paganism was washed from his soul.

[14]A reference to the fact that the early Salian Franks were also known as the *Sicambrians*.

liness that he equalled the miracles of Silvester.[15] For there is extant a book of his life which tells that he raised a dead man. And so the king confessed all-powerful God in the Trinity,* and was baptized in the name of the Father, Son and Holy Spirit,* and was anointed with the holy ointment with the sign of the cross of Christ. And of his army more than 3000 were baptized. . . .

Now when Alaric, king of the Goths, saw Clovis conquering nations steadily, he sent envoys to him saying: "If my brother consents, it is the desire of my heart that with God's favor we have a meeting." Clovis did not spurn this proposal but went to meet him.[16] They met in an island of the Loire which is near the village of Amboise in the territory of Tours, and they talked and ate and drank together, and plighted friendship and departed in peace. Even at that time many in the Gauls desired greatly to have the Franks as masters. . . .

Now Clovis the king said to his people: "I take it very hard that these Arians hold part of the Gauls.[17] Let us go with God's help and conquer them and bring the land under our control." Since these words pleased all, he set his army in motion and made for Poitiers where Alaric was at that time. But since part of the host was passing through Touraine, he issued an edict out of respect to the blessed Martin[18] that no one should take anything from that country except grass for fodder, and water. But one from the army found a poor man's hay and said: "Did not the king order grass only to be taken, nothing else? And this," said he, "is grass. We shall not be transgressing his command if we take it." And when he had done violence to the poor man and taken his hay by force, the deed came to the king. And quicker than speech the offender was slain by the sword, and the king said: "And where shall

our hope of victory be if we offend the blessed Martin? It would be better for the army to take nothing else from this country." The king himself sent envoys to the blessed church saying: "Go, and perhaps you will receive some omen of victory from the holy temple." Then giving them gifts to set up in the holy place, he said: "If thou, O Lord, art my helper, and hast determined to surrender this unbelieving nation, always striving against thee, into my hands, consent to reveal it propitiously at the entrance to the church of St. Martin, so that I may know that thou wilt deign to be favorable to thy servant." Clovis' servants went on their way according to the king's command, and drew near to the place, and when they were about to enter the holy church, the first singer, without any prearrangement, sang this response: "Thou hast girded me, O Lord, with strength unto the battle; thou hast subdued under me those that rose up against me, and hast made mine enemies turn their backs unto me, and thou hast utterly destroyed them that hated me." On hearing this singing they thanked the Lord, and paying their vow to the blessed confessor* they joyfully made their report to the king. Moreover, when he came to the river Vienne with his army, he did not know where he ought to cross. For the river had swollen from the rains. When he had prayed to the Lord in the night to show him a ford where he could cross, in the morning by God's will a deer of wonderful size entered the river before them, and when it passed over the people saw where they could cross. When the king came to the neighborhood of Poitiers and was encamped some distance off, he saw a ball of fire come out of the church of Saint Hilarius and pass, as it were, over him, to show that, aided by the light of the blessed confessor Hilarius, he should more boldly conquer the

---

[15]The Roman pope* whom legend mistakenly credited with having instructed and baptized Constantine.

[16]Alaric II (see note 4). It is possible that this encounter, if it actually took place, was arranged by Theodoric the Ostrogoth (see source 8).

[17]Alaric's Arian Visigoths. The Arian Burgundians held the Rhone Valley, but Clovis was temporarily allied with them against the Visigoths.

[18]St. Martin (ca. 316–397), former bishop and now saintly patron and protector of Tours, was the most popular saint in all of Gaul.

heretic armies, against which the same bishop had often fought for the faith.[19] And he made it known to all the army that neither there nor on the way should they spoil any one or take any one's property. . . .

King Clovis met with Alaric, king of the Goths, in the plain of Vouillé at the tenth milestone from Poitiers, and while the one army was for fighting at a distance the other tried to come to close combat. And when the Goths had fled as was their custom, king Clovis won the victory by God's aid.[20] He had to help him the son of Sigibert the lame, named Chloderic. This Sigibert was lame from a wound in the leg, received in a battle with the Alemanni near the town of Zülpich. Now when the king had put the Goths to flight and slain king Alaric, two of the enemy suddenly appeared and struck at him with their lances, one on each side. But he was saved from death by the help of his coat of mail, as well as by his fast horse. . . . When Clovis had spent the winter in Bordeaux and taken all the treasures of Alaric at Toulouse, he went to Angoulême. And the Lord gave him such grace that the walls fell down of their own accord when he gazed at them.[21] Then he drove the Goths out and brought the city under his own dominion. Thereupon after completing his victory he returned to Tours, bringing many gifts to the holy church of the blessed Martin.

Clovis received an appointment to the consulship from the emperor Anastasius,[22] and in the church of the blessed Martin he clad himself in the purple[23] tunic and chlamys,[24] and placed a diadem on his head. Then he mounted his horse, and in the most generous manner he gave gold and silver as he passed along the way which is between the gate of the entrance [of the church of St. Martin] and the church of the city, scattering it among the people who were there with his own hand, and from that day he was called *consul* or *Augustus*.[25] Leaving Tours he went to Paris and there he established the seat of his kingdom. . . .

When King Clovis was dwelling at Paris he sent secretly to the son of Sigibert[26] saying: "Behold your father has become an old man and limps in his weak foot. If he should die," said he, "of due right his kingdom would be yours together with our friendship." Led on by greed the son plotted to kill his father. And when his father went out from the city of Cologne and crossed the Rhine and was intending to journey through the wood Buchaw, as he slept at midday in his tent his son sent assassins in against him, and killed him there, in the idea that he would get his kingdom. But by God's judgment he walked into the pit that he had cruelly dug for his father. He sent messengers to king Clovis to tell about his father's death, and to say: "My father is dead, and I have his treasures in my possession, and also his kingdom. Send men to me, and I shall gladly transmit to you from his treasures whatever pleases you." And Clovis replied: "I thank you for your good will, and I ask that you show the treasures to my men who come, and after that you shall possess all yourself." When they came, he showed his father's treasures. And when they were looking at the different things he said: "It was in this little chest that my father used to put his gold coins."

---

[19]St. Hilary of Poitiers (ca. 315–367), patron saint and protector of Poitiers, was a fiercely anti-Arian theologian, who composed the first extensive Latin treatise on the Trinity. Contrary to the Catholic tradition, Arian Christians believed that the Son of God, the Second Person of the Holy Trinity, is a created being and, therefore, divine only by adoption.
[20]In 507 (see source 8).
[21]Compare this to the miracle of the walls of Jericho falling down before the Israelites (the Bible, Joshua, 6:20).
[22]Anastasius I (r. 491–518).
[23]Purple was the color worn by consuls and members of the imperial family.

[24]A short Greek mantle that fastened at the shoulders.
[25]Consuls were originally the two annually elected chief magistrates of the Roman Republic. In the age of the empire, the two annual consulships were only honorific titles of nobility. Perhaps even more significant, Clovis's name does not appear in Constantinople's official list of imperial consuls. Moreover, the title *Augustus* was not synonymous with *consul*, which was reserved exclusively for the emperor and could not have been awarded to Clovis.
[26]The same Sigibert who had been wounded while allied with Clovis against the Alemanni.

"Thrust in your hand," said they, "to the bottom, and uncover the whole." When he did so, and was much bent over, one of them lifted his hand and dashed his battle-ax against his head, and so in a shameful manner he incurred the death which he had brought on his father. Clovis heard that Sigibert and his son had been slain, and came to the place and summoned all the people, saying: "Hear what has happened. When I," said he, "was sailing down the river Scheldt Cloderic, son of my kinsman, was in pursuit of his own father, asserting that I wished him killed. And when his father was fleeing through the forest of Buchaw, he set highwaymen upon him, and gave him over to death, and slew him. And when he was opening the treasures, he was slain himself by some one or other. Now I know nothing at all of these matters. For I cannot shed the blood of my own kinsmen, which it is a crime to do. But since this has happened, I give you my advice, if it seems acceptable; turn to me, that you may be under my protection." They listened to this, and giving applause with both shields and voices, they raised him on a shield, and made him king over them. He received Sigibert's kingdom with his treasures, and placed the people, too, under his rule. For God was laying his enemies low every day under his hand, and was increasing his kingdom, because he walked with an upright heart before him, and did what was pleasing in his eyes.

Two Images of Christ in Majesty
▼▼▼

10 ▼ THE BARBERINI IVORY and THE ALTAR OF KING RATCHIS

Theodoric's dream of creating a new Roman *civilitas* out of the combined efforts of Italo-Romans and Ostrogoths proved empty. In the generation following Theodoric's death, imperial armies sent by Emperor Justinian I (r. 527–565) invaded and devastated the Italian peninsula (Chapter 3, source 11). After almost three decades of warfare, the Ostrogoths disappeared as a recognizable people, and a severely weakened, reconquered Italy was ripe for a new Germanic invasion from the north. Those invaders, the Lombards, appeared in 568.

The Lombards were one of the most destructive of all the invaders to enter what had once been the western regions of the Roman Empire. Initially, they looked upon Italy solely as a source of plunder. In time, however, they settled down, established several competing states, converted from Arianism to Roman Catholicism, and adopted many of the other attitudes and habits of the people of Italy. Although the Lombards never managed to conquer the entire peninsula, they were a major political-military force in Italy down to the late eighth century. They were also artists, and much of the artwork they created is extant today in the cities they once ruled.

One of the great masterpieces of Lombardic art is the *Christ in Majesty* altar frontal (the flat front of the altar that faces the congregation) of Ratchis, king of the Lombards (r. 744–749). Commissioned toward the mid eighth century by the pious Ratchis, who later abdicated his throne in order to become a monk,* this altar shows Christ flanked by two seraphim (six-winged angels) and four other angels. For the purposes of meaningful study, we will compare it with an earlier piece of sculpture from Constantinople. Together, the works should help us see the ways in which the "barbarian" art of the West borrowed from classical Mediterranean styles but differed from them radically in spirit and execution.

The earlier sculpture is an ivory panel that was created in Constantinople in the sixth century and portrays either Emperor Anastasius I (r. 491–518) or Emperor Justinian receiving the submission of various "barbarian" peoples. The triumphant emperor emerges on horseback out of the panel, while a female personification of earth supports his right foot. Beneath the horse's hooves, Asiatic Scythians and Indians offer tokens of submission. Behind the lance that the emperor holds, a soldier dressed in Scythian garments raises his hand in surrender. Farther to the emperor's right, a Roman general approaches, bearing a statuette of the spirit of Victory. A second winged Victory hovers over the mane of the emperor's horse. Crowning the whole composition is a bust of a youthful, beardless Christ in majesty, flanked by two angels. The Constantinopolitan artist has preserved Greco-Roman naturalism, particularly in regard to the bodies of humans and animals, and has also retained several traditional pagan symbols and motifs. At the same time, as we see in the figures of Christ and his flanking angels, the sculptor has transformed certain pre-Christian artistic types into figures representing Christian beliefs. This adaptation was certainly not new. Christians had been adapting pagan artistic conventions to their own needs since the first century A.D., and by the sixth century, such *Christ in Majesty* scenes were quite common.

The second *Christ in Majesty,* Ratchis's altar frontal, strikes us immediately as quite different from its Constantinopolitan counterpart. Whereas the sculpted ivory relief from Constantinople is boldly three dimensional, despite the constraints of the flat background into which the figures are set, the altar carving is two dimensional, even though the figures are sculpted in and not just painted on. Moreover, in contrast to Justinian's ivory panel, the Lombard artist appears to have been quite arbitrary in his depiction of human (and angelic) anatomy. The hands of the angels are grossly out of proportion to the rest of their bodies, and the length of an angel's arms is dictated only by the angel's distance from the *mandorla* (the almond-shaped halo of glory) that each helps to support. Classical Greco-Roman sculpted drapery defined human bodies and was often used to heighten the drama of a scene. The folds of a figure's clothes left no doubt that a flesh-and-blood person was underneath them. In Ratchis's altar, frontal drapery plays two quite different roles. It is simultaneously decorative and abstract. Like the decorative stars that are interspersed around the angels to symbolize Heaven, the drapery and exposed feet, hands, and faces combine to present only an *idea,* or abstract image, of real bodies; there is no effort to portray clothed bodies in a realistic manner.

This Lombardic *Christ in Majesty* violates virtually all of the canons of classical sculpture, but it works, and it works brilliantly. As a moving work of abstract art that touches the viewer on an emotional level, it is great art, but it certainly is not Greco-Roman.

QUESTIONS FOR ANALYSIS

1. How do we know that the figures on the bottom left of the panel (our right) of the Barberini ivory represent Indians? What message is implied by portraying peoples from such distant lands as Central Asia and India?
2. Compare these two reliefs with the *Christ Triumphant* mosaic from the archbishop's chapel at Ravenna (Chapter 1, source 5). Comment in depth about their respective similarities and dissimilarities. What inferences do you draw from this comparative analysis?
3. Which of these two works of art is closer to the attitudes and values expressed by Gregory of Tours? Why?
4. Consider this statement: "These two pieces serve as vivid images of the ways in which the barbarian West was moving away from the civilization of Greco-Roman antiquity, even as it found inspiration in that antique past. They furthermore demonstrate the growing cultural gap between the West and the civilization of Byzantium, which was emerging at Constantinople." Do you agree or disagree? Whichever is the case, do so in detail. (Before engaging in this exercise, you might want to study sources 11–13 in Chapter 3.)

The Barberini Ivory

Christ in Majesty, Altar Frontal of King Ratchis

Chapter 3

▼▼▼

Byzantium and Islam

The Mediterranean Sea gave shape and substance to the Roman Empire, and as the empire gave way to new realities, it was the Mediterranean that provided lands, peoples, and ancient ways of life and thought to new political and cultural amalgamations. The Mediterranean is an area of water, islands, and adjacent continental lands that covers more than one million square miles and encompasses southern Europe, North Africa, and much of Southwest Asia. The First Europe only inherited a portion of that vast region — essentially, the lands that stretched from the Iberian Peninsula to the northwestern Balkans. Most of the ancient Mediterranean was divided between two other successor civilizations, Byzantium and Islam, and it is to those two sibling cultures that we now turn.

Considerable cultural differences separated Byzantium from Islam, and both civilizations were quite different from the new society emerging in Western Europe. Yet despite their many dissimilarities, all three cultures drew heavily from two common, ancient roots: the monotheistic religious traditions of Southwest Asia and several thousand years of secular* ideas and institutions that we term *Hellenistic** culture. For this reason, we can justifiably think of the three as sibling heirs of the great Mediterranean community of related, civilized peoples that Rome had fashioned. Byzantium and Islam, however, were initially far richer beneficiaries of Hellenistic culture than was Europe, their poor relation. When the First Europe was still an essentially primitive culture, struggling to create an identity for itself, Byzantium and Islam had already created golden ages of political stability, economic vitality, and artistic and intellectual brilliance.

▼▼▼

Byzantium: From Justinian I to Basil II

While the former western portions of the Roman Empire were in the midst of a painful process of political breakdown and sweeping cultural transformation, the empire's eastern half was evolving more gently and with greater continuity into a new cultural synthesis called *Byzantine* civilization. Modern historians created the term to distinguish the Eastern Christian civilization centered at Constantinople, the site of the Ancient Greek city of *Byzantion* (*Byzantium* in Latin), from preceding Greco-Roman cultures. This new civilization resulted from the fusion of three key elements: the autocratic structure of the late Roman Empire (Chapter 1, sources 1 and 2); Eastern Orthodox* Christianity (Chapter 1, source 3); and the cultural heritage of the western Asiatic and Greek Hellenistic past.

In true Hellenistic fashion, the entire Byzantine world revolved around the orthodox emperor, who in theory was answerable to no one on earth. As a Christian, he could not play the part of a god-king, but he was the next best thing: the living image of God on earth, insofar as his imperial majesty was a pale reflection of the Glory of God. As such, the emperor was the link between the Christian Chosen People and their God (Chapter 2, source 10).

Under the leadership of these emperors, who styled themselves *isapostolos* (peer of the Apostles*) and *autokrator* (sole ruler of the world), the Eastern Christian Empire experienced close to a millennium of vitality. Some eighteenth-century European historians considered Byzantine civilization merely an unoriginal and degenerate fossilization of late antiquity, but nothing could be farther from the truth. Although the Byzantines saw their state as a living continuation of the Roman Empire and, therefore, called themselves *Romaioi* (Romans), in fact, by the middle of the sixth century, Constantinople had become the matrix of a new civilization that persisted and flourished to 1453, when the city of Constantinople finally fell to the forces of Islam. To be sure, over those nine hundred years, Byzantium experienced inevitable fluctuations in fortune and creativity, but by and large, Byzantine civilization was noted throughout its long history for economic prosperity and cultural brilliance. Moreover, long after 1453, Byzantine culture remained a living force in Russia and Eastern Europe's other Orthodox Christian societies, such as Bulgaria and Serbia, which had adopted Constantinople's religion and many of its other traditions.

Two of the following three documents shed light on two of Byzantium's early ages of special vitality, the eras of Justinian I and Basil II, during which the Eastern Roman Empire exerted powerful influence on its many neighbors. The third document reflects one of the most important characteristics of the Byzantine economy: intense regulation by the imperial government.

Justinian the Great: God's Deputy or a Devil?
▼▼▼

11 ▼ *Procopius, ON THE BUILDINGS and THE SECRET HISTORY*

The age of Justinian I (r. 527–565) was pivotal in the history of the Eastern Roman Empire. The last of the emperors of Constantinople to speak Latin as his native tongue, Justinian attempted to reconquer the West. The effort ultimately failed, but it did manage to transform Rome and much of Italy into a war-ravaged backwater and to strip the eastern empire of much needed resources. After Justinian's age, the Greek-speaking emperors and people of Constantinople were forced to look increasingly to their eastern, southern, and northern borders, thereby accelerating the impact of Asian influences on Byzantium's cultural development. A sincerely but narrowly pious man who took seriously his duties as God-anointed emperor, Justinian also promoted the cause of Christian *Orthodoxy* (correct thinking) in a cosmopolitan empire that contained large numbers of variant Christian beliefs and ways of interpreting the faith. The result was deep alienation, especially among Egyptian and Syrian subjects of the empire, and a consequent weakness that Islamic Arab forces would exploit in the next century.

For all of his large-scale miscalculations, Justinian ranks as one of Byzantium's greatest emperors; indeed, he often is referred to as *Justinian the Great,* the last Roman and first Byzantine emperor. Among his many accomplishments, he ordered and saw to completion the codification of imperial Roman law that had only been partially and inadequately completed by the jurists of Theodosius II (Chapter 1, source 2). He also commissioned the rebuilding of many of Constantinople's churches and public buildings following an especially destructive urban riot in 532. The greatest of all these edifices was the massive domed church of *Hagia Sophia* (Holy Wisdom), the first great example of a distinctly Byzantine style of architecture.

To celebrate Justinian's building projects, a Palestinian courtier named Procopius (d. after 562?) composed a work entitled *On the Buildings* around 553–554. Earlier, he had composed the first seven books of his *History in Eight Books,* also known as *The Wars,* a largely eyewitness account of Justinian's wars against the Persians, Vandals, and Goths, which were fought between 527 and 553. Both of these works were meant for widespread distribution and praised the emperor's actions and character in a most obsequious manner. Unknown to Justinian and the imperial censors, Procopius also wrote, probably in the year 550, a work he never intended to be seen in his own lifetime. Known today as *The Secret History,* this work purports to be a corrective to the laudatory *Wars,* the inside story of court life and policy making, and a true description of the characters of the emperor and his empress, Theodora.

The two excerpts that follow come from the *Buildings* and the slightly earlier *Secret History,* respectively. Together, they illustrate how and why Justinian the Great was and still is such a controversial ruler and individual.

QUESTIONS FOR ANALYSIS

1. According to *On the Buildings,* what were Justinian's greatest accomplishments?
2. According to *The Secret History,* what specific evils was Justinian guilty of?
3. Consider Justinian's supposed character flaws and vices. How would a partisan of Justinian interpret those qualities?
4. Why do you think Procopius composed *The Secret History,* and how trustworthy does it appear to be as a source? Does *On the Buildings* seem any more useful as a source? Do either or both of these histories have any value as sources? If so, what value? Please be specific in your answer. How do these two accounts illustrate the caution that historians must exercise when using any evidence?
5. According to Procopius in *On the Buildings,* what were the consequences of an emperor's enjoying a proper relationship with God? Now consider *The Secret History.* If the emperor did not have a proper relationship with God, what was, to Procopius's mind, the logical conclusion? What does this suggest about the ideological foundations of imperial power in Byzantium?
6. Assume that the ivory panel in Chapter 2, source 10, represents Justinian (as it probably does). Compose Procopius's dual commentary on it — first in the spirit of *On the Buildings* and then in the spirit of *The Secret History.*

In our time Justinian became emperor. He took over the state when it was tottering dangerously. He increased its size and made it far more glorious by driving from it the barbarians who had violated it from ancient times, as I have described in detail in my work on the wars. . . . Justinian did not refuse to acquire other states as well. At any rate, he won over many which in his time were already foreign to the Roman Empire, and he built innumerable new cities. And finding doctrine about God before his time wavering and being forced into many directions, he checked all the pathways leading to error and caused the faith to stand on one secure foundation. Besides this, he found that the laws were obscure because they had been multiplied unnecessarily and were in confusion because of their obvious contradiction. So he purified them of the mass of quibbles, and by greatly strengthening them, preserved them from contradiction.[1] By using his own initiative to remove possible causes of conspiracy and by satisfying those in need of a livelihood with gifts of money and by forcibly removing the fate which threatened them, he brought the state to blessedness. Further, he strengthened the Roman Empire, which was subject everywhere to barbarians, with large numbers of soldiers and fortified all its furthest points by building strongholds. As for the rest, most of it has been recorded in my other works: The good

---

[1]Justinian's *Corpus Iuris Civilis* (Body of Civil Law), which codified and clarified imperial Roman law.

that was done by his building shall be my present subject. . . .

As I have just said, he more than doubled the state in area and increased its power in other ways: And those who plotted against him, even to the extent of wanting his death, have not only lived to this day in the enjoyment of their property, even though they were openly caught, but actually still serve as Roman generals and enjoy the rank of consuls.[2] But now, as I said, I must go on to the buildings of this emperor, so that it may not come about that those who look upon them in the future may fail to believe because of their number and size that they are the work of one man. For many achievements of our ancestors are discredited because of their outstanding merits, if they have not been recorded in writing. The buildings in Byzantium will naturally be the foundation of the record. For the beginning of a task, according to the old saying, we must "put on a shining face."

At one period some of the common people and the dregs of the mob rose against the Emperor Justinian in Byzantium and caused the so-called Nika Revolt,[3] as I have described in detail without hiding anything in my work on the wars. Showing that they had taken up arms, not only against the emperor, but just as much against God in their wickedness, they dared to burn the Christian church (the Byzantines call this temple Wisdom,[4] thinking this name most appropriate to God), and God allowed them to accomplish this impiety in the foreknowledge of the beauty which this shrine was destined to attain when restored. So the whole church was burned down and lay in ruins. Not long after, the Emperor Justinian rounded it off so beautifully that if anyone had asked the Christians earlier whether they wanted the church to be destroyed and rebuilt like this, and had shown them the outlines

of what can now be seen, I think they would have immediately prayed to see the church in ruins so that it could be changed into its present form. In the event, the Emperor proceeded with all haste to the building, with no heed to expense, and collected all the craftsmen from all over the world. . . . This, too, was a sign of the honor in which God held the emperor, in that he procured in advance those who would be best to help him in his undertakings. One might reasonably admire the Emperor's own good sense also, in that he was able to select from all men those best adapted for the most serious tasks. . . .

And whenever anyone enters this church to pray, he perceives at once that this edifice has been so finely crafted not by any human power or skill but by the agency of God. Therefore his mind is lifted up toward God and exalted.

▾ ▾ ▾

DECEPTIVE AFFABILITY AND PIETY OF A TYRANT

Justinian, while otherwise of such character as I have shown, did make himself easy of access and affable to his visitors; nobody of all those who sought audience with him was ever denied: even those who confronted him improperly or noisily never made him angry. On the other hand, he never blushed at the murders he committed. Thus he never revealed a sign of wrath or irritation at any offender, but with a gentle countenance and unruffled brow gave the order to destroy myriads of innocent men, to sack cities, to confiscate any amount of properties.

One would think from this manner that the man had the mind of a lamb. If, however, anyone tried to propitiate him and in suppliance beg him to forgive his victims, he would grin like a

---

[2]See Chapter 2, source 9, note 25.

[3]January 532. The riot received its name from the fact that the rioters cried out "*Nika*" (Win!), the traditional chant of the crowds at the chariot races in the Hippodrome, where the riot began and ended. (See notes 29 and 31 for further information.)

[4]Hagia Sophia.

wild beast, and woe betide those who saw his teeth thus bared!

The priests* he permitted fearlessly to outrage their neighbors, and even took sympathetic pleasure in their robberies, fancying he was thus sharing their divine piety. When he judged such cases, he thought he was doing the holy thing when he gave the decision to the priest and let him go free with his ill-gotten booty: justice, in his mind, meant the priests' getting the better of their opponents. When he himself thus illegally got possession of estates of people alive or dead, he would straightway make them over to one of the churches, gilding his violence with the color of piety — and so that his victims could not possibly get their property back. Furthermore he committed an inconceivable number of murders for the same cause: for in his zeal to gather all men into one Christian doctrine, he recklessly killed all who dissented, and this too he did in the name of piety. For he did not call it homicide, when those who perished happened to be of a belief that was different from his own. . . .

He was untiring; and hardly slept at all, generally speaking; he had no appetite for food or drink, but picking up a morsel with the tips of his fingers, tasted it and left the table, as if eating were a duty imposed upon him by nature and of no more interest than a courier takes in delivering a letter. Indeed, he would often go without food for two days and nights, especially when the time before the festival called Easter enjoins such fasting. Then, as I have said, he often went without food for two days, living only on a little water and a few wild herbs, sleeping perhaps a single hour, and then spending the rest of the time walking up and down.

If, mark you, he had spent these periods in good works, matters might have been considerably alleviated. Instead, he devoted the full strength of his nature to the ruin of the Romans,

and succeeded in razing the state to its foundation. For his constant wakefulness, his privations and his labors were undergone for no other reason than to contrive each day ever more exaggerated calamities for his people. For he was, as I said, unusually keen at inventing and quick at accomplishing unholy acts, so that even the good in him transpired to be answerable for the downfall of his subjects. . . .

HOW JUSTINIAN KILLED A TRILLION PEOPLE

That Justinian was not a man, but a demon, as I have said, in human form,[5] one might prove by considering the enormity of the evils he brought upon mankind. For in the monstrousness of his actions the power of a fiend is manifest. Certainly an accurate reckoning of all those whom he destroyed would be impossible, I think, for anyone but God to make. Sooner could one number, I fancy, the sands of the sea than the men this emperor murdered. Examining the countries that he made desolate of inhabitants, I would say he slew a trillion people. For Libya,[6] vast as it is, he so devastated that you would have to go a long way to find a single man, and he would be remarkable. Yet eighty thousand Vandals capable of bearing arms had dwelt there, and as for their wives and children and servants, who could guess their number? Yet still more numerous than these were the Mauretanians,[7] who with their wives and children were all exterminated. And again, many Roman soldiers and those who followed them to Constantinople, the earth now covers; so that if one should venture to say that five million men perished in Libya alone, he would not, I imagine, be telling the half of it.

The reason for this was that after the Vandals were defeated,[8] Justinian planned, not how he might best strengthen his hold on the country,

---

[5]Procopius did not mean this in a metaphorical sense. Demons in human form were a major motif in Christian literature.

[6]A reference to Vandal North Africa.
[7]The people of western North Africa.
[8]This war lasted from 533 to 534.

nor how by safeguarding the interests of those who were loyal to him he might have the goodwill of his subjects: but instead he foolishly recalled Belisarius[9] at once, on the charge that the latter intended to make himself king (an idea of which Belisarius was utterly incapable),[10] and so that he might manage affairs there himself and be able to plunder the whole of Libya. Sending commissioners to value the province, he imposed grievous taxes where before there had been none. Whatever lands were most valuable, he seized, and prohibited the Arians from observing their religious ceremonies.[11] Negligent toward sending necessary supplies to the soldiers, he was overstrict with them in other ways; wherefore mutinies arose resulting in the deaths of many. For he was never able to abide by established customs, but naturally threw everything into confusion and disturbance.

Italy, which is not less than thrice as large as Libya, was everywhere desolated of men, even worse than the other country,[12] and from this the count of those who perished there may be imagined. The reason for what happened in Italy I have already made plain.[13] All of his crimes in Libya were repeated here; sending his auditors to Italy, he soon upset and ruined everything.

The rule of the Goths, before this war, had extended from the land of the Gauls to the boundaries of Dacia.[14] . . . The Germans held Cisalpine Gaul[15] and most of the land of the Venetians,[16] when the Roman army arrived in Italy. Sirmium and the neighboring country was in the hands of the Gepidae.[17] All of these he utterly depopulated. For those who did not die in battle perished of disease and famine, which as usual followed in the train of war. Illyria[18] and all of Thrace,[19] that is, from the Ionian Gulf[20] to the suburbs of Constantinople, including Greece and the Chersonese,[21] were overrun by the Huns,[22] Slavs[23] and Antes,[24] almost every year, from the time when Justinian took over the Roman Empire; and intolerable things they did to the inhabitants. For in each of these incursions, I should say, more than two hundred thousand Romans were slain or enslaved, so that all this country became a desert like that of Scythia.[25]

Such were the results of the wars in Libya and in Europe. Meanwhile the Saracens[26] were continuously making inroads on the Romans of the East, from the land of Egypt to the boundaries of Persia; and so completely did their work, that in all this country few were left, and it will never be possible, I fear, to find out how many thus perished. Also the Persians under Chosroes[27] three times invaded the rest of this Roman territory, sacked the cities, and either killing or carrying away the men they captured in the cities

---

[9]Constantinople's best general, Belisarius (ca. 505–565) had suppressed the Nika riot, conquered North Africa, and captured Rome in 536.

[10]Procopius had served as Belisarius's secretary and was quite loyal to the man. Apparently, he is correct here. Despite contrary rumors, Belisarius was totally loyal to Justinian.

[11]Like the Goths, the Vandals were Arian Christians.

[12]The Italian, or Gothic, War began in 536 and dragged on to 561.

[13]In his earlier history of the Gothic War.

[14]Modern Romania.

[15]Literally, "Gaul this side of the Alps." This refers to Italy north of the Po River, especially northwest Italy, which ancient Celtic tribes had inhabited.

[16]Northeast Italy.

[17]A Gothic people.

[18]The western, or Adriatic, shore of the Balkans.

[19]The eastern, or Black Sea, region of the Balkans.

[20]The Mediterranean region between southern Italy and Greece.

[21]A narrow peninsula in Thrace that extends along the European side of the Dardenelles, the strait that separates modern European Turkey from Asiatic Turkey.

[22]The so-called Cotrigur Huns and also the Avars, both of whom were Turkic horsepeople out of the steppes of Central Asia.

[23]Various Slavic-speaking pagan peoples who were moving into the northern Balkans.

[24]A conglomeration of people, possibly Indo-Iranians or Slavs, from north of the Black Sea. Justinian made them allies in 545; they disappear from history after 602.

[25]The desolate steppes of Central Asia.

[26]Arabs.

[27]Chosroes I (r. 531–578/579), king of kings of the Sassanian Empire of Persia, which encompassed Mesopotamia and Iran. He inherited a war with Justinian, which had been raging since 527. In 532 he and Justinian negotiated an Eternal Peace. Chosroes broke this peace in 540 when he invaded Byzantine Mesopotamia and Syria. In 561 both exhausted parties concluded a fifty-year truce.

and country, emptied the land of inhabitants every time they invaded it. . . .

For neither the Persians nor the Saracens, the Huns or the Slavs or the rest of the barbarians, were able to withdraw from Roman territory undamaged. In their inroads, and still more in their sieges of cities and in battles, where they prevailed over opposing forces, they shared in disastrous losses quite as much. Not only the Romans, but nearly all the barbarians thus felt Justinian's bloodthirstiness. For while Chosroes himself was bad enough, as I have duly shown elsewhere, Justinian was the one who each time gave him an occasion for the war. For he took no heed to fit his policies to an appropriate time, but did everything at the wrong moment: in time of peace or truce he ever craftily contrived to find pretext for war with his neighbors; while in time of war, he unreasonably lost interest, and hesitated too long in preparing for the campaign, grudging the necessary expenses; and instead of putting his mind on the war, gave his attention to stargazing and research as to the nature of God.[28] Yet he would not abandon hostilities, since he was so bloodthirsty and tyrannical, even when thus unable to conquer the enemy because of his negligence in meeting the situation.

So while he was emperor, the whole earth ran red with the blood of nearly all the Romans and the barbarians. Such were the results of the wars throughout the whole empire during this time. But the civil strife in Constantinople and in every other city, if the dead were reckoned, would total no smaller number of slain than those who perished in the wars, I believe. Since justice and

impartial punishment were seldom directed against offenders, and each of the two factions[29] tried to win the favor of the emperor over the other, neither party kept the peace. Each, according to his smile or his frown, was now terrified, now encouraged. Sometimes they attacked each other in full strength, sometimes in smaller groups, or even lay in ambush against the first single man of the opposite party who came along. For thirty-two years, without ever ceasing, they performed outrages against each other, many of them being punished with death by the municipal prefect.[30]

However, punishment for these offenses was mostly directed against the Greens.[31]

Furthermore the persecution of the Samaritans[32] and the so-called heretics* filled the Roman realm with blood. Let this present recapitulation suffice to recall what I have described more fully a little while since. Such were the things done to all mankind by the demon in flesh for which Justinian, as emperor, was responsible. But what evils he wrought against men by some hidden power and diabolic force I shall now relate.

During his rule over the Romans, many disasters of various kinds occurred: which some said were due to the presence and artifices of the Devil, and others considered were effected by the Divinity, Who, disgusted with the Roman Empire, had turned away from it and given the country up to the Old One.[33] The Scirtus River flooded Edessa,[34] creating countless sufferings among the inhabitants, as I have elsewhere written. The Nile, rising as usual, but not subsiding in the customary season, brought terrible calami-

---

[28]Justinian was avidly interested in subtle points of theology and believed himself to be a theologian.

[29]The two major circus factions — the Blues and the Greens. They were much more than just fans of chariot-racing teams. Their rivalries and, at times, mutual frustrations often resulted in mob violence.

[30]Constantinople's chief municipal official.

[31]See note 29. The Greens were especially troublesome for Justinian. They precipitated the Nika riot of 532 (note 3) when they staged a demonstration in the Hippodrome in which they complained of the arbitrary actions of imperial authorities, including the emperor.

[32]A nonorthodox Jewish sect with settlements in Palestine, Syria, Egypt, and Constantinople, they were centered in the hills of Samaria in central Israel. Rebelling against Byzantine authority in 529, they were ruthlessly crushed.

[33]The Devil.

[34]A city in what is today southeast Turkey.

ties to the people there, as I have also previously recounted. . . .

Earthquakes destroyed Antioch,[35] the leading city of the East; Seleucia, which is situated nearby; and Anazarbus, most renowned city in Cilicia. Who could number those that perished in these metropoles? Yet one must add also those who lived in Ibora; in Amasea, the chief city of Pontus; in Polybotus in Phrygia, called Polymede by the Pisidians; in Lychnidus in Epirus; and in Corinth: all thickly inhabited cities from of old. All of these were destroyed by earthquakes during this time, with a loss of almost all their inhabitants.[36] And then came the plague, which I have previously mentioned, killing half at least of those who had survived the earthquakes.[37] To so many men came their doom, when Justinian first came to direct the Roman state and later possessed the throne of autocracy.

---

[35]The chief city of Syria.
[36]These cities were located throughout the eastern empire. Nine major earthquakes were recorded in this entire region during 526–557. The death toll was staggering.

[37]A Mediterranean-wide pandemic of bubonic plague broke out in Egypt in 541 and reached Constantinople by May 542. Justinian contracted but survived the plague. By 600 the plague had essentially burnt itself out, but only after reducing the total population of the Mediterranean to about 60 percent or less of its previous level.

Economic Regulation
▼▼▼

12 ▼ *THE BOOK OF THE EPARCH*

The close governmental regulation of essential industries, trades, and services that we saw in the *Theodosian Code* (Chapter 1, source 2) continued to be a salient feature of imperial policy at Constantinople throughout Byzantium's long history. As far as the government was concerned, it was just as necessary to the well-being of the empire for the state to control the economy as it was for it to direct foreign relations. In the age of the Macedonian Dynasty (867–1056), when Byzantium was at the peak of its power and prosperity, the city of Constantinople had at least twenty-two different occupational guilds, all of which were directly supervised by the city's chief civil official, the *eparch*, or prefect. Unlike the laws governing late Roman guilds, Byzantine law did not require children to follow their parents into particular guilds. Indeed, guild membership was not automatically inherited; it was earned.

Sometime during the tenth century, an anonymous editor compiled in twenty-two chapters a collection of regulations regarding Constantinople's guilds. Known as *The Book of the Eparch*, this compendium illustrates clearly the ways in which the government attempted to direct the economy.

QUESTIONS FOR ANALYSIS

1. What obligations did these regulations lay upon bankers?
2. What obligations were laid upon grocers?

3. Grocers were prohibited from engaging in certain commercial practices, and their profit margin was strictly set by law. What philosophy lay behind such regulations?

4. What do you infer from the severity of the penalties imposed on bankers and grocers who engaged in illegal economic activities?

5. Considering the tone of these laws, what do you think was the likelihood that a significant number of people engaged in prohibited economic practices? Explain your answer.

6. Compare these guilds with the collegia that we saw in the *Theodosian Code*. How are they similar? How are they dissimilar? Which are more significant, the similarities or dissimilarities? What conclusions follow from your answers?

7. According to one historian, "Byzantium's economic regulations transformed its merchants and artisans into quasi civil officials and imposed police duties on them." Based on your reading of this source, do you agree or disagree? Why?

THE BANKERS.

1. Anyone who wishes to be nominated as a banker must be vouched for by respected and honest men who will guarantee that he will do nothing contrary to the ordinances; to wit, that he will not pare down, or cut, or put false inscriptions on *nomismata*[1] or *miliarisia*,[2] or set one of his own slaves in his place at his bank if he should happen to be occupied with some temporary duties, so that no trickery may thereby enter into the business of the profession. If anyone is caught in such practices, he shall be punished by the amputation of his hand.

2. The money-changers shall report to the prefect the forgers who station themselves in the squares and streets in order to prevent them from indulging in illegal practices. If they know of such and fail to report them, they shall suffer the aforementioned punishment.

3. The money-changers shall make no deduction from the value of an unadulterated *miliarision* which bears the genuine royal stamp, but shall accept it as equivilent to twenty-four *obols*.[3] However, if the condition of the coin is otherwise, it must be valued accordingly.[4] Those who disregard this injunction shall be scourged, shorn, and suffer confiscation.

4. Each banker shall keep two assistants to sort his coins. He must go surety for these, so that if one of them is detected acting contrary to the ordinances both he and the one who appointed him shall suffer the aforesaid penalties.

5. Any money-changer who receives a counterfeited *nomisma* or *miliarision,* and fails to report it to the prefect together with its possessor, shall be scourged, shorn, and banished.

6. The bankers must not give their subordinates account books or coins and station them in the squares and streets in order to receive the profit accruing from their activities. Even on occasions of distribution of largesses[5] or the performance of services for the emperor they shall not go away and abandon their banks. If anyone is caught doing so, he shall be beaten, shorn, and suffer confiscation. . . .

---

[1]Gold coins. *Nomismata* is the plural form of *nomisma*.
[2]Silver coins. *Miliarisia* is the plural form of *miliarision*. Twelve miliarisia equaled one nomisma.
[3]Bronze coins.

[4]The value of a coin derived from its true weight of silver or gold. Worn or defaced coins were worth less than full-weight coins.
[5]When money or goods were distributed to the city's populace in the emperor's name.

THE GROCERS.

1. The grocers shall open their shops in the square and streets throughout the whole city so that the necessities of life may easily be found. They shall sell meat, pickled fish, meal, cheese, honey, olive oil, green vegetables of all sorts, butter, solid and liquid pitch, cedar resin, hemp, flax, plaster, pottery vessels, bottles, nails, and all the other things sold by a bar-balance and not by twin scales. They are forbidden to engage in the trades of the perfumers, or soap-makers, or linen merchants, or tavern keepers, or butchers even in the slightest degree. If anyone is found acting contrary to these regulations, he shall be scourged, shorn, and banished.

2. If any grocer has in his possession weights or measures not marked with the seal of the prefect, or if he pares down gold coins, or if he withdraws from circulation *nomismata* of four or two quarters bearing the genuine imperial stamp, he shall be beaten, shorn, and banished.

3. If a grocer is caught cheating another in a purchase and raising the price agreed upon, he shall be fined ten *nomismata*.[6] Likewise one who exhibits his wares outside his shop on the Lord's Day or on another Holy Day[7] shall undergo the same penalty.

4. The grocers shall keep watch upon the imports that pertain to them, so that, if anyone not enrolled in their guild stores these up against a time of scarcity, he may be denounced to the prefect and called to account by him.

5. The grocers shall sell their goods in small quantities at a profit of two *miliarisia* on the *nomisma*.[8] If a calculation of their authorized gains shows that they are making a larger profit, they shall be scourged, shorn, and forced to give up this trade.

6. If any one of them secretly or openly raises the rental of another, he shall suffer the aforesaid penalty.

---

[6]The equivalent of the tax charged a fully laden ship leaving Constantinople; it could ruin an average small trader.

[7]Sunday is the Lord's Day; other holy days would be days of special religious commemoration, such as Epiphany (January 6) or Good Friday (the Friday before Easter).
[8]See notes 1 and 2.

Emperor Basil II and the Apogee of Byzantine Power
▼▼▼
13 ▼ *Michael Psellus, THE CHRONOGRAPHIA*

The history of Byzantium is one of peaks and valleys. The pattern of triumph, decline, and recovery repeated itself continuously until Byzantium's collapse in the mid fifteenth century. One key to understanding this cycle is the power invested in the God-ordained emperor (and empress). Rarely does an individual single-handedly alter in a radical way the historical course of an empire or any other large institution, but autocratic monarchs could and did play inordinately important roles in the unfolding of Byzantine fortunes. Like Justinian the Great (source 11), Basil II (r. 976–1025) dominated an age of Byzantine greatness. In fact, many historians see Basil II's reign as the political, military, and cultural apogee of Byzantine civilization.

Late in the eleventh century, Michael Psellus (1018–after 1081?), a monk,[*] scholar, and politician, composed the *Chronographia* (*Chronicle*), a series of imperial character sketches covering the period from the start of the reign of Basil II through that of Michael VII (r. 1071–1078). As far as Psellus was concerned, the empire's history was largely driven by the ways in which individual emperors and empresses responded to the challenges and temptations of office. In the following excerpt, Psellus describes the qualities that he believed allowed Basil II to rule so successfully.

QUESTIONS FOR ANALYSIS

1. What picture of Basil II emerges from this sketch?
2. According to Psellus, which of the emperor's personal qualities aided his success? How so?
3. How old was Psellus during Basil's reign? Might that fact be significant in evaluating his portrait of the emperor? Notwithstanding, does this sketch appear to ring true? Defend your answer.
4. Compare this character sketch with Procopius's two descriptions of Justinian. There are some striking differences between the portraits of Justinian I and Basil II. What are they? How do you explain them?
5. Can you discover any significant similarities? If so, what do you infer from them?
6. Based on your comparative analysis of Procopius and Psellus, what inferences have you drawn about the nature of the Byzantine imperial government? What qualities, for example, did successful emperors seem to share? What were some of the factors that precipitated imperial decline?
7. Consider the Barberini ivory (Chapter 2, source 10) in light of Procopius's *On the Buildings* and Psellus's *Chronographia.* Are any images of imperial power common to all three? If so, what are they, and what do they suggest about the Byzantine vision of the ideal emperor?

In his dealings with his subjects, Basil behaved with extraordinary circumspection. It is perfectly true that the great reputation he built up as a ruler was founded rather on terror than on loyalty. As he grew older and became more experienced he relied less on the judgment of men wiser than himself. He alone introduced new measures, he alone disposed his military forces. As for the civil administration, he governed, not in accordance with the written laws, but following the unwritten dictates of his own intuition, which was most excellently equipped by nature for the purpose. Consequently he paid no attention to men of learning: on the contrary, he affected utter scorn — towards the learned folk, I mean. It seems to me a wonderful thing, therefore, that while the emperor so despised literary culture, no small crop of philosophers and orators sprang up in those times. One solution of the paradox, I fancy, is that the men of those days did not devote themselves to the study of letters for any ulterior purpose: they cultivated literature for its own sake and as an end in itself, whereas the majority nowadays do not approach the subject of education in this spirit, but consider personal profit to be the first reason for study. Perhaps I should add, that though gain is the object of their zeal for literature, if they do not immediately achieve this goal, then they desist from their studies at once. Shame on them!

However, we must return to the emperor. Having purged the empire of the barbarians,[1] he dealt with his own subjects and completely subjugated them too — I think 'subjugate' is the right word to describe it. He decided to abandon his former policy, and after the great families had been humiliated and put on an equal footing with the rest, Basil found himself playing the game of power-politics with considerable success. He surrounded himself with favorites who were neither remarkable for brilliance of intellect, nor of noble lineage, nor too learned. To them were entrusted the imperial rescripts, and with them he was accustomed to share the secrets of state. However, since at that time the emperor's comments on memoranda or requests for favor were never varied, but only plain, straightforward statements (for Basil, whether writing or speaking, eschewed all elegance of composition) he used to dictate to his secretaries just as the words came to his tongue, stringing them all together, one after the other. There was no subtlety, nothing superfluous, in his speech.

By humbling the pride or jealousy of his people, Basil made his own road to power an easy one. He was careful, moreover, to close the exit-doors on the monies contributed to the treasury. So a huge sum of money was built up, partly by the exercise of strict economy, partly by fresh additions from abroad. Actually, the sum accumulated in the imperial treasury reached the grand total of 200,000 talents.[2] As for the rest of his gains, it would indeed be hard to find words adequately to describe them. All the treasures amassed in Iberia and Arabia, all the riches found among the Celts or contained in the land of the Scyths[3] — in brief, all the wealth of the barbarians who surround our borders — all were gathered together in one place and deposited in the emperor's coffers. In addition to this, he carried off to his treasure-chambers and sequestrated there, all the money of those who rebelled against him and were afterwards subdued. And since the vaults of the buildings made for this purpose were not big enough, he had spiral galleries dug underground, after the Egyptian style, and there he kept safe a considerable proportion of his treasures. He himself took no pleasure in any of it: quite the reverse indeed, for the majority of the precious stones, both the white ones (which we call pearls) and the colored brilliants, far from being inlaid in diadems or collars, were hidden away in his underground vaults. Meanwhile Basil took part in his processions and gave audience to his governors clothed merely in a robe of purple, not the very bright purple, but simply purple of a dark hue, with a handful of gems as a mark of distinction. As he spent the greater part of his reign serving as a soldier on guard at our frontiers and keeping the barbarians from raiding our territories, not only did he draw nothing from his reserves of wealth, but even multiplied his riches many times over.

On his expedition against the barbarians,[4] Basil did not follow the customary procedure of other emperors, setting out at the middle of spring and returning home at the end of summer. For him the time to return was when the task in hand was accomplished. He endured the rigors of winter and the heat of summer with equal indifference. He disciplined himself against thirst. In fact, all his natural desires were kept under stern control, and the man was as hard as steel. He had an accurate knowledge of the details of army life, and by that I do not mean the general acquaintance with the composition of his army, the relative functions of individual units in the whole

---

[1]Basil had put down several claimants to the imperial throne, along with their foreign allies. Also, between 990 and 995 he all but destroyed Bulgarian power in the north central regions of his empire, thereby earning the sobriquet "Bulgar-slayer."

[2]A *talent* was a weight of precious metal that varied according to time and place.

[3]In this context, *Iberia* means the land of Georgia near the Caucasus Mountains of Southwest Asia and not the Iberian Peninsula, where modern Portugal and Spain are located. The land of the Scyths is the steppe region of Eastern Europe and Central Asia.

[4]His campaign against the Bulgars; note 1.

body, or the various groupings and deployments suited to the different formations. His experience of army matters went further than that: the duties of the *protostate,* the duties of the *hemilochites,*[5] the tasks proper to the rank immediately junior to them — all these were no mysteries to Basil, and the knowledge stood him in good stead in his wars. Accordingly, jobs appropriate to these ranks were not devolved on others, and the emperor, being personally conversant with the character and combat duties of each individual, knowing to what each man was fitted either by temperament or by training, used him in this capacity and made him serve there.

Moreover, he knew the various formations suited to his men. Some he had read of in books, others he devised himself during the operations of war, the result of his own intuition. He professed to conduct his wars and draw up the troops in line of battle, himself planning each campaign, but he preferred not to engage in combat personally. A sudden retreat might otherwise prove embarrassing. Consequently, for the most part he kept his troops immobile. He would construct machines of war and skirmish at a distance, while the maneuvering was left to his light-armed soldiers. Once he had made contact with the enemy, a regular military liaison was established between the different formations of the Roman army. The whole force was formed up like a solid tower, headquarters being in touch with the cavalry squadrons, who were themselves kept in communication with the light infantry, and these again with the various units of heavy-armed foot. When all was ready, strict orders were given that no soldier should advance in front of the line or break rank under any circumstance. If these orders were disobeyed, and if some of the most valiant or daring soldiers did ride out well in front of the rest, even in cases where they engaged the enemy successfully, they could expect no medals or rewards for valor when they re-

sumed. On the contrary, Basil promptly discharged them from the army, and they were punished on the same level as common criminals. The decisive factor in the achievement of victory was, in his opinion, the massing of troops in one coherent body, and for this reason alone he believed the Roman armies to be invincible. The careful inspections he made before battle used to aggravate the soldiers and they abused him openly, but the emperor met their scorn with common sense. He would listen quietly, and then, with a gay smile, point out that if he neglected these precautions, their battles would go on for ever.

Basil's character was two-fold, for he readily adapted himself no less to the crises of war than to the calm of peace. Really, if the truth be told, he was more of a villain in wartime, more of an emperor in time of peace. Outbursts of wrath he controlled, and like the proverbial 'fire under the ashes,' kept anger hid in his heart, but if his orders were disobeyed in war, on his rerturn to the palace he would kindle his wrath and reveal it. Terrible then was the vengeance he took on the miscreant. Generally, he persisted in his opinions, but there were occasions when he did change his mind. In many cases, too, he traced crimes back to their original causes, and the final links in the chain were exonerated. So most defaulters obtained forgiveness, either through his sympathetic understanding or because he showed some other interest in their affairs. He was slow to adopt any course of action, but never would he willingly alter the decision, once it was taken. Consequently, his attitude to friends was unvaried, unless perchance he was compelled by necessity to revise his opinion of them. Similarly, where he had burst out in anger against someone, he did not quickly moderate his wrath. Whatever estimate he formed, indeed, was to him an irrevocable and divinely-inspired judgment.

---

[5]Both were junior officer ranks in the army.

Dar al-Islam:
From the Prophet to the Abbasids

Two great empires dominated western Eurasia in late antiquity: the Roman Empire and the Sassanian Empire, which controlled Iran and Iraq and threatened Rome's eastern provinces. Between and to the south of these imperial behemoths lay the Arabian Peninsula, whose harsh desert climate and hardy warrior people combined to keep both powers at bay, despite periodic attempts to incorporate this region into their respective empires.

Although desert sands covered most of the peninsula, Arabia was a key point of transit for goods passing between the Indian Ocean and the Mediterranean. *Hijaz,* a narrow, fertile strip of land along Arabia's western, or Red Sea, coast, contained several of the peninsula's major caravan towns, chief of which was Mecca. Mecca was also a religious center, drawing numerous pilgrims* to its most important sanctuary, the *Ka'bah,* where the images of numerous deities resided. Although Judaism and Christianity had made inroads into Arabia from Ethiopia, Syria-Palestine, and Egypt, the tribes of Arabia were largely polytheistic until the rise of a prophet in Mecca known as *Muhammad* (570–632), whose monotheistic teachings transformed Arabic culture and welded the Arabs into one of the most dynamic forces in the history of the world.

The faith that Muhammad preached was *Islam,* which means "submission" in Arabic. One who submits in a totally uncompromising manner to the will of the single, omnipotent God of the universe, known as *Allah* (The God), is a *Muslim.* The Prophet of Islam was a well-to-do merchant of Mecca, who around 610 began to receive visions in which he was called by God to preach God's Oneness, the imminence of the Resurrection of the dead, a divine Day of Judgment, an all-consuming hell fire for the unjust and unbelievers, and a paradise of bliss for the faithful. Muhammad believed that just as the Jews and the Christians had received their divine revelations from God, now the Arabs were receiving the full and final word of God through Muhammad himself, the last and greatest of the prophets but still only a man. Abraham, Moses, Jesus, and other prophets had been earlier messengers of God. Muhammad was the *seal* of these forerunners.

Most of Meccan society was initially unmoved by Muhammad's message, so in 622 Muhammad journeyed to the city of Yathrib, where he was able to establish a *theocratic* (ruled in the name of God) Muslim community. In his honor, the city was renamed *Medinat al-Nabi* (City of the Prophet), or, more simply, *Medina.* From Medina, Muhammad and his followers initiated a holy war against Mecca. In 630 Muhammad was able to re-enter Mecca in triumph and to transform the Ka'bah into Islam's chief shrine by cleansing it of all its pagan idols. The Prophet of Allah was now the most powerful chieftain in Arabia, and the various tribes of the peninsula soon were united under his leadership. When Muhammad died in

632, his closest friend (and father-in-law), Abu Bakr, assumed the title and office of *caliph* (deputy, or successor, of the Prophet), thereby accepting leadership over the family of Islam. Thanks to Abu Bakr's efforts at destroying secessionist elements, Islam remained a unified community under his stewardship (632–634), ready to explode out of its homeland, which it did under the second caliph, 'Umar (r. 634–644). Within a century, Muslim territory reached from the Pyrenees and Atlantic coast in Spain to the Indus Valley of India and China's far western borders.

Originally, the Arabs considered Islam their special revelation and had no intention of sharing the faith with their non-Arab subjects, but several factors combined to attract large numbers of non-Arab converts. These included Islam's uncompromising monotheism and the straightforwardness of its other central doctrines; the psychic and social security offered by membership in a totally integrated Muslim community, where one's entire life is subject to God's Word; and the desire to escape the second-class status of Islam's non-Muslim subjects. When the Abbasid caliphs (750–1258) established their court at Baghdad on the Tigris in 762, they claimed dominion over a multiethnic community bound together by one of the most attractive and fastest growing religions in the history of humanity. The culture of this world community, which Muslims call *Dar al-Islam* (the House of Submission), was a combination of many elements, of which the most important were Arabic, Persian, and Hellenistic.*

The documents that follow illustrate some of the striking ties between Islam and its Judaic and Christian sibling faiths as well as some of the ways in which early Islamic society interacted with these other monotheistic cultures.

The Children of the House of Imran

▼▼▼

14 ▼ *THE QUR'AN*

Muhammad was a teacher who spoke rather than wrote his message, and as long as the Prophet was alive, there was no compelling reason to set his words down in some definitive form. However, following Muhammad's sudden death in 632, Caliph Abu Bakr (r. 632–634) ordered one of the Prophet's companions, Zayd ibn Thabit, to collect from both oral and written sources all of Muhammad's inspired utterances. Subsequently, Caliph Uthman (r. 644–656) promulgated an official collection of these revelations and ordered all other versions destroyed. The sacred text that resulted from this work is known as the *Qur'an* (the Recitations), which Muslims believe contains, word for word, absolutely everything that God revealed to Muhammad and nothing else. As the full and final revelation of God, the Qur'an encompasses all that any human needs to know. Its verses, each a poetically perfect proclamation from Heaven, are both doctrine and law, governing essentially every aspect of a Muslim's life.

Islam without the Qur'an is unimaginable, insofar as it quickly became and remains the basis of every pious Muslim's education. As Islam spread beyond Arab ethnic boundaries, Muslims all over the world learned Arabic in order to study and recite (usually from memory) the sacred *surahs* (chapters) of this holy book. Because of the centrality of the Qur'an, Arabic literacy became the hallmark of Muslims from sub-Saharan West Africa to Southeast Asia. As far as Europe was concerned, Arabic language and culture had a profound impact on the evolution of Spanish and Portuguese cultures following the Muslim conquest of most of the Iberian Peninsula in the early eighth century.

The following excerpts come from the third of the Qur'an's one hundred fourteen surahs. Known as "The House of Imran," it deals with the connections between Islam and the faiths of Judaism and Christianity.

QUESTIONS FOR ANALYSIS

1. What evidence is there that Muhammad was experiencing difficulty converting Jewish and Christian Arabs?
2. How does the Qur'an portray Jews and Christians? What is Islam's relationship with these two faiths?
3. Do you see any parallels between this text and that of the Bible's Jewish and Christian Testaments? What do you infer from your answer?
4. What basic Muslim beliefs are reflected in this excerpt?
5. How does Islam differ from Judaism and Christianity?
6. How are Muslims to deal with nonbelievers? With those who attack them?

God
there is no god but He, the
Living, the Everlasting.

He has sent down upon thee the Book
with the truth, confirming what was before it,
and He sent down the Torah[1] and the Gospel[2]
aforetime, as guidance to the people,
and He sent down the Salvation.

As for those who disbelieve in God's signs, for
them awaits a terrible chastisement; God is
All-mighty, Vengeful.

From God nothing whatever is hidden
in heaven and earth. It is He who forms you
in the womb as He will. There is no god but
He,
the All-mighty, the All-wise.

It is He who sent down upon thee the Book,[3]
wherein are verses clear that are the Essence
of the Book. . . .

Our Lord, make not our hearts to swerve
after that Thou hast guided us; and give us
mercy from Thee;
Thou art the Giver.
Our Lord, it is Thou that shall gather
mankind for a day whereon is no doubt;
verily God will
not fail the tryst.[4] . . .

The true religion with God is Islam.

Those who were given the Book[5] were not at
variance
except after the knowledge came to them,
being insolent one to another.[6] And whoso

---

[1]"The Law," the first five books of the *Tanakh* (the Jewish Bible or, as Christians know it, the Old Testament), it is the basis of Judaic religion and life.
[2]The Christian New Testament.
[3]All three books of revelation: the Qur'an; the Gospels;[*] and the Torah.

[4]God's covenant, or pact, with humanity.
[5]Jews and Christians who respectively received from God the Torah and the Gospels.
[6]Through sheer insolence, especially toward one another, Jews and Christians strayed from the path of God's revelation.

disbelieves in God's signs, God is swift
    at the reckoning.
So if they dispute with thee, say: 'I have
surrendered my will to God, and whosoever
    follows me.'
And say to those who have been given the
    Book[7]
and to the common folk: 'Have you surren-
    dered?'
If they have surrendered, they are right
    guided;
but if they turn their backs, thine it is only
to deliver the Message; and God
        sees His servants.[8]
Those who disbelieve in the signs of God
and slay the Prophets without right,
and slay such men as bid to justice —
do thou give them the good tidings of
    a painful chastisement;
their works have failed in this world and the
    next;
        they have no helpers.
Hast thou not regarded those who were given
a portion of the Book, being called to the Book
of God, that it might decide between them,
and then a party of them turned away,
        swerving aside?
That, because they said, 'The Fire shall not
touch us, except for a number of days';
and the lies they forged have deluded them
    in their religion.
But how will it be, when We[9] gather them
for a day whereon is no doubt, and every soul
shall be paid in full what it has earned, and
    they
        shall not be wronged?

Say: 'O God, Master of the Kingdom,
Thou givest the Kingdom to whom Thou wilt,
and seizest the kingdom from whom Thou
    wilt,

Thou exaltest whom Thou wilt, and Thou
abasest whom Thou wilt; in Thy hand
is the good; Thou art powerful
        over everything.
Thou makest the night to enter into the day
and Thou makest the day to enter into the
    night,
Thou bringest forth the living from the dead
and Thou bringest forth the dead from the
    living,
and Thou providest whomsoever Thou wilt
    without reckoning.' . . .

Say: 'If you love God, follow me, and God
will love you, and forgive you your sins;
God is All-forgiving, All-compassionate.'
Say: 'Obey God, and the Messenger.'[10] But
if they turn their backs, God loves not
        the unbelievers.

    God chose Adam and Noah
    and the House of Abraham
    and the House of Imran[11]
    above all beings, the
    seed of one another;
    God hears, and knows.

    When the wife of Imran[12]
    said, 'Lord, I have vowed
    to Thee, in dedication,
    what is within my womb.
    Receive Thou this from me;
    Thou hearest, and knowest.'
    And when she gave birth to her
    she said, 'Lord, I have given
    birth to her, a female.'
    (And God knew very well
    what she had given birth to;
    the male is not as the female.)
    'And I have named her Mary,
    and commend her to Thee
    with her seed, to protect them

---

[7]Jews and Christians.
[8]God knows who are His submissive servants.
[9]God.
[10]Muhammad.

[11]Islam reveres the memory of two men named *Imran:* the
father of Moses and Aaron and the father of Mary, mother
of Jesus. The term *the House of Imran* seems to refer to the
family of the former.
[12]This clearly is the second Imran, the father of Mary.

from the accursed Satan.'
Her Lord received the child
with gracious favor. . . .

When the angels said,
'Mary, God gives thee good
tidings of a Word[13] from Him
whose name is Messiah,[14]
Jesus, son of Mary;
high honored shall he be
in this world and the next,
near stationed to God.
He shall speak to men
in the cradle, and of age,
and righteous he shall be.'
'Lord,' said Mary,
'how shall I have a son
seeing no mortal has
touched me?'[15] Even so,
God said, 'God
creates what He will.

When He decrees a thing
He does but say to it
"Be," and it is.
And He will teach him
the Book, the Wisdom,
the Torah, the Gospel,
to be a Messenger
to the Children of Israel
saying, "I have come to
you with a sign from
your Lord. I will create
for you out of clay as
the likeness of a bird;
then I will breathe into
it, and it will be a
bird,[16] by the leave of God.
I will also heal

the blind and the leper,
and bring to life the
dead, by the leave of God.
I will inform you too
of what things you eat,
and what you treasure up
in your houses. Surely
in that is a sign for you,
if you are believers.
Likewise confirming the
truth of the Torah that
is before me, and to make
lawful to you certain
things that before were
forbidden unto you.
I have come to you with
a sign from your Lord;
so fear you God, and
obey you me. Surely
God is my Lord and
your Lord; so serve Him.
This is a straight path".'

And when Jesus perceived
their unbelief, he said,
'Who will be my helpers
unto God?' The Apostles*
said, 'We will be helpers
of God; we believe in God;
witness thou our submission.
Lord, we believe in that
Thou hast sent down, and we
follow the Messenger.
Inscribe us therefore with
those who bear witness.'

And they devised, and God
devised, and God is
the best of devisers. . . .

---

[13]*Logos* in Greek; it is a term used by Christians to describe Jesus Christ, the Living Word of God. Christians believe that the Logos is co-eternal and co-divine with God the Father and God the Holy Spirit.*
[14]Hebrew for "the Anointed One"; *Christos* in Greek.
[15]She is a virgin. Compare this with the Gospel of Luke, 1:26–38.

[16]An echo of the so-called *Infancy Gospel,* 15:6, ascribed to the Apostle James the Less. This uncanonical, second-century collection of tales relating to Jesus' miracle-filled boyhood was well-known in the Christian communities of the eastern Mediterranean and Red Sea areas.

This We recite to thee
of signs and wise remembrance.
Truly, the likeness of
Jesus, in God's sight,
is as Adam's likeness;
He created him of dust,
then said He unto him,
'Be,' and he was.[17]
The truth is of God;
be not of the doubters.
And whoso disputes with thee
concerning him, after the
knowledge that has come to thee,
say: 'Come now, let us call
our sons and your sons,
our wives and your wives,
our selves and your selves,
then let us humbly pray
and so lay God's curse
upon the ones who lie.'
This is the true story.
There is no god but God,
and assuredly God is
the All-mighty, the All-wise.
And if they turn their backs,
assuredly God knows
the workers of corruption.

Say: 'People of the Book! Come now to a word
common between us and you, that we serve
none but God, and that we associate not
aught with Him,[18] and do not some of us take
others as Lords, apart from God.' And if
they turn their backs, say: 'Bear witness that
    we are Muslims.'

People of the Book! Why do you dispute
concerning Abraham? The Torah was not sent
down, neither the Gospel, but after him.[19]
    What,
        have you no reason?

Ha, you are the ones who dispute on what you
know; why then dispute you touching a matter
of which you know not anything? God knows,
        and you know not.
No; Abraham in truth was not a Jew,
neither a Christian; but he was a Muslim
and one pure of faith; certainly he was never
        of the idolaters.
Surely the people standing closest to Abraham
are those who followed him, and this
    Prophet,[20]
and those who believe; and God is the Protector
    of the believers.

There is a party of the People of the Book
yearn to make you go astray; yet none
they make to stray, except themselves, but
        they are not aware.
People of the Book! Why do you disbelieve
in God's signs, which you yourselves witness?
People of the Book! Why do you confound
the truth with vanity, and conceal the truth
        and that wittingly? . . .

Say: 'We believe in God, and that which has
    been sent
down on us, and sent down on Abraham and
    Ishmael,[21]
Isaac[22] and Jacob, and the Tribes,[23] and in that
    which was
given to Moses and Jesus, and the Prophets,
    of their
Lord; we make no division between any of
    them, and
        to Him we surrender.'
Whoso desires another religion than Islam,
    it shall
not be accepted of him; in the next world
    he shall
        be among the losers.

---

[17]Jesus was one of God's creatures; he is not divine.
[18]God has no divine associates; there is only one God.
[19]The Torah and the Gospels and, therefore, Jews and Christians postdate Abraham, the father of all Arabs and Jews.
[20]Muhammad.

[21]Abraham's elder son, from whom the Arabs (and, by spiritual extension, all Muslims) claim descent.
[22]Abraham's younger son, from whom the Hebrews are descended.
[23]The twelve tribes of Israel.

The *Dhimma*: A Contract with the People of the Book

▼▼▼

15 ▼ THE PACT OF 'UMAR

Islam exploded out of the Arabian Peninsula in the reign of Caliph 'Umar ibn 'Abd al-Khattab (r. 634–644). Earlier, when the armies of Islam's first caliph, Abu Bakr, began raiding the territories of their neighbors, they discovered lands ripe for conquest. Both the Sassanian and Byzantine empires had exhausted each other in a series of destructive wars that ran from 503 to 627, and they were further enervated by massive natural disasters and plague (source 11). In addition, the Byzantine Empire was rent by ethnic and religious dissension, especially in Syria-Palestine and Egypt. The Arabs, now united in a common cause, exploited these weaknesses in a series of lightninglike campaigns. By the time of 'Umar's death, the Byzantines had lost all of Syria-Palestine and Egypt to Islam, and the Arab conquest of the Sassanian Empire was virtually completed. Less than a century later, Muslim armies were battling Chinese armies deep in Central Asia and Frankish armies along the banks of the Loire River.

One vexing question facing the conquering Muslim armies was how to deal with their non-Muslim subjects, particularly Jewish and Christian "people of the book" (source 14). The following document, which purports to be the pact of peace offered by Caliph 'Umar I to the Christians of Syria around 637, was apparently written down in its present form in the ninth century, but it is supposedly based on the account of an early Muslim who died in 697. Even so, most Western scholars believe the pact is an anachronism and essentially reflects ninth-century realities, because it is too restrictive for the quite liberal age of Islam's first four "Rightly-Guided" caliphs (632–661) and the Umayyad Dynasty (661–750) that followed. Whatever its origins, the pact represented by this document is an excellent example of the *dhimma,* or contract of protection, offered to subject non-Muslims throughout most of premodern Islamic history. The non-Muslims who lived under this compact were known as *dhimmis.*

QUESTIONS FOR ANALYSIS

1. Why do you think non-Muslims were prohibited from teaching their children the Qur'an?
2. Why were dhimmis forbidden to use the very phrases and modes of dress employed by Muslims or even to adopt Muslim surnames?
3. How restrictive were these rules so far as the practice of Christianity was concerned?
4. What was the threatened consequence should a dhimmi break this pact or even be perceived as having broken it?

5. What was the purpose of this pact?
6. How would you characterize the dhimma and the status of the dhimmis?
7. Large numbers of Christians, Jews, Zoroastrians, and others in the regions conquered by Islam ultimately converted to Islam. Does this pact provide any evidence of one reason for some of the conversions? If so, what?

In the name of God, the Merciful, the Compassionate!

This is a writing to 'Umar from the Christians of such and such a city. When you[1] marched against us,[2] we asked of you protection for ourselves, our posterity, our possessions, and our co-religionists; and we made this stipulation with you, that we will not erect in our city or the suburbs any new monastery,* church, cell or hermitage;[3] that we will not repair any of such buildings that may fall into ruins, or renew those that may be situated in the Muslim quarters of the town; that we will not refuse the Muslims entry into our churches either by night or by day; that we will open the gates wide to passengers and travelers; that we will receive any Muslim traveler into our houses and give him food and lodging for three nights; that we will not harbor any spy in our churches or houses, or conceal any enemy of the Muslims.[4]

That we will not teach our children the Qur'an; that we will not make a show of the Christian religion nor invite any one to embrace it; that we will not prevent any of our kinsmen from embracing Islam, if they so desire. That we will honor the Muslims and rise up in our assemblies when they wish to take their seats; that we will not imitate them in our dress, either in the cap, turban, sandals, or parting of the hair; that we will not make use of their expressions of speech,[5] nor adopt their surnames; that we will not ride on saddles, or gird on swords, or take to ourselves arms or wear them, or engrave Arabic inscriptions on our rings; that we will not sell wine;[6] that we will shave the front of our heads; that we will keep to our own style of dress, wherever we may be; that we will wear belts round our waists.[7]

That we will not display the cross upon our churches or display our crosses or our sacred books in the streets of the Muslims, or in their market-places; that we will strike the clappers in our churches lightly;[8] that we will not recite our services in a loud voice when a Muslim is present; that we will not carry palm-branches[9] or our images[10] in procession in the streets; that at the burial of our dead we will not chant loudly or carry lighted candles in the streets of the Muslims or their market-places; that we will not take any slaves that have already been in the possession of Muslims, nor spy into their houses; and that we will not strike any Muslims.

All this we promise to observe, on behalf of ourselves and our co-religionists, and receive protection from you in exchange; and if we violate any of the conditions of this agreement, then we forfeit your protection and you are at liberty to treat us as enemies and rebels.

---

[1]Muslims.

[2]The Christians of Syria.

[3]The dwelling of a Christian hermit, or monk.* See sources 17 and 18 in Chapter 4.

[4]Several of these ordinances were taken directly from earlier imperial Roman laws regarding non-Christians.

[5]Muslims greet one another with certain qur'anic verses and similar affirmations of their faith.

[6]Muslims are forbidden to drink wine.

[7]Dhimmis wore leather or cord belts; Muslims wore silk and other types of cloth belts.

[8]Christian churches could not ring bells; the faithful were summoned to prayer by wooden clappers.

[9]On Palm Sunday, the Sunday that precedes Easter. This public procession commemorates Jesus' triumphal entry into Jerusalem.

[10]Islam has traditionally looked upon the use of sacred images as idolatry.

Relations with Constantinople in the Age of Harun al-Rashid

▼▼▼

16 ▼ *Abu'l-Faradj al-Isfahani,* KITAB AL-AGHANI

It is no exaggeration to state that the Abbasid Dynasty was at the height of its power in Caliph Harun al-Rashid's reign (786–809). The proud inhabitants of Iraq, the heartland of the Abbasid Empire, could boast with some justification that their region was, as one ninth-century Arab geographer described it, "the center of the world, the navel of the earth." Foreigners were almost as equally impressed by this empire and Caliph Harun, whose ambassadors traveled as far east as China and as far west as the Frankish lands of Charlemagne (Chapter 5, sources 24–27).

By 842, however, the Abbasid caliphs began a slide toward impotence that they never were able to reverse. They increasingly came under the influence and dominance of their political and military subordinates, to the point that by the tenth century, they were mere religious figureheads in an increasingly fractionalized Muslim world; they remained so until the effective end of their dynasty in 1258. As time went on, the presumed golden age of Caliph Harun al-Rashid became ever more brilliant in retrospect.

One tenth-century writer who contributed to the history and legend of Harun al-Rashid was the musicologist Abu'l-Faradj al-Isfahani (897–967). Al-Isfahani was close enough to Caliph Harun's reign to be well acquainted with the events and documents of that era but sufficiently removed in time to look back to it with longing. The medium for his recording this history was his *Kitab al-Aghani* (*Book of Songs*), a massive work in which he traced the history of Arabic music and poetry down to the end of the ninth century. Because of the centrality of poetry to Arabic culture, the *Kitab al-Aghani* became, in al-Isfahani's hands, a magisterial overview of Arabic civilization. The following excerpt, which recounts the history of Abbasid-Byzantine relations between 791 and 806, illustrates how al-Isfahani's interest in the history of Arabic poetry and song was the point of departure for a history of much wider scope.

QUESTIONS FOR ANALYSIS

1. How well acquainted was al-Isfahani with events that had taken place a century and a half earlier? Be specific in your analysis.
2. From the Abbasid perspective, what was the meaning of Nikephoros's paying the jizya?
3. Analyze Abu'l-Atahiya's poem. What does it tell us about the self-image of the Abbasid caliphate?
4. What does Abu Muhammad's poem tell us about the Muslim view of the dhimma?

5. **What does this entire account suggest about Abbasid-Byzantine relations around 800?**

A woman[1] came to rule over the Romans[2] because at the time she was the only one of their royal house who remained. She wrote to the caliphs al-Mahdi and al-Hadi and to al-Rashid[3] at the beginning of his caliphate with respect and deference and showered him with gifts. When her son grew up and came to the throne in her place, he brought trouble and disorder and provoked al-Rashid.[4] The empress, who knew al-Rashid and feared his power, was afraid lest the kingdom of the Romans pass away and their country be ruined. She therefore overcame her son by cunning and put out his eyes so that the kingdom was taken from him and returned to her.[5] But the people of their kingdom disapproved of this and hated her for it. Therefore Nikephoros, who was her secretary, rose against her, and they helped and supported him so that he seized power and became the ruler of the Romans.[6]

When he was in full control of his kingdom, he wrote to al-Rashid, "From Nikephoros, the king of Romans, to al-Rashid, the king of the Arabs, as follows: That woman put you and your father and your brother in the place of kings and put herself in the place of a commoner.[7] I put you in a different place and am preparing to invade your lands and attack your cities, unless you repay me what that woman paid you. Farewell!"

When his letter reached al-Rashid, he replied, "In the name of God, the Merciful and the Compassionate, from the servant of God, Harun, Commander of the Faithful, to Nikephoros, the dog of the Romans, as follows: I have understood your letter, and I have your answer. You will see it with your own eye, not hear it." Then he at once sent an army against the land of the Romans of a size the like of which was never heard before and with commanders unrivaled in courage and skill.[8] When news of this reached Nikephoros, the earth became narrow before him and he took counsel. Al-Rashid advanced relentlessly into the land of the Romans, killing, plundering, taking captives, destroying castles, and obliterating traces, until they came to the narrow roads before Constantinople, and when they reached there, they found that Nikephoros had already had trees cut down, thrown across these roads, and set on fire. The first who put on the garments of the naphtha-throwers[9] was Muhammad ibn Yazid ibn Mazyad. He plunged boldly through, and then the others followed him.

Nikephoros sent gifts to al-Rashid and submitted to him very humbly and paid him the poll tax for himself as well as for his companions.[10]

On this Abu'l-'Atahiya[11] said:

---

[1]Empress Irene ruled jointly with her son, Constantine VI, from 780 to 790 and again from 792 to 797 (see notes 4, 5, and 6).

[2]To the Arabs, the Christians of Constantinople were known as the *Rum* (the Romans).

[3]Al-Mahdi (r. 775–785); al-Hadi (r. 785–786); al-Rashid (r. 786–809).

[4]In October 790 Constantine VI (r. 780–797) managed to have himself declared sole ruler and shut his mother up in the palace; this only lasted until January 15, 792. Following Constantine's defeat by Arab and Bulgar forces in 791, he reinstated his mother as co-ruler.

[5]In 797 she staged a coup, had her son blinded, and ruled solely in her own name.

[6]Nikephoros, Irene's minister of finance, dethroned and banished her in 802 and ruled as Nikephoros I (802–811).

[7]Irene had preferred to pay tribute to Harun al-Rashid and earlier to his father al-Mahdi and brother al-Hadi, rather than fighting the Abbasids.

[8]In 803.

[9]The protective asbestos garments worn by soldiers who sprayed "Greek fire," a deadly combustible mixture of pitch and naphtha. The Byzantines had created this weapon and tried to keep its formula a secret, but the secret leaked out.

[10]This is the *jizya,* or poll tax, paid by all dhimmis (source 15) as a token of their submission to the authority of an Islamic ruler. Nikephoros was forced to pay the jizya for himself and his son out of his own purse.

[11]A famous Arabic poet who died in 825/826.

O Imam[12] of God's guidance, you have
become the guardian of religion, quenching the thirst of all who pray for rain.

You have two names drawn from righteousness [rashad] and guidance [huda], for you
are the one called Rashid and Mahdi,[13]

Whatever displeases you becomes loathsome; if anything pleases you, the people
are well pleased with it.

You have stretched out the hand of nobility
to us, east and west, and bestowed bounty
on both easterner and westerner.

You have adorned the face of the earth with
generosity and munificence, and the face
of the earth is adorned with generosity.

O, Commander of the Faithful, brave and
pious, you have opened that part of
benevolence which was closed!

God has destined that the kingdom should
remain to Harun, and God's destiny is
binding on mankind.

The world submits to Harun, the favored of
God, and Nikephoros has become the
dhimmi of Harun.

Then al-Rashid went back, because of what
Nikephoros had given him, and got as far as
Raqqa.[14] When the snow fell and Nikephoros
felt safe from attack, he took advantage of the
respite and broke the agreement between himself and al-Rashid and returned to his previous
posture. Yahya ibn Khalid,[15] let alone any other,
did not dare to inform al-Rashid of the treachery of Nikephoros. Instead, he and his sons offered money to the poets to recite poetry and
thereby inform al-Rashid of this. But they all
held back and refrained, except for one poet from
Jedda,[16] called Abu Muhammad, who was very
proficient, strong of heart and strong of poetry,
distinguished in the days of al-Ma'mun[17] and of
very high standing. He accepted the sum of
100,000 dirhams[18] from Yahya and his sons and
then went before al-Rashid and recited the following verses:

Nikephoros has broken the promise he gave
you, and now death hovers above him.

I bring good tidings to the Commander of
the Faithful, for Almighty God is
bringing you a great victory.

Your subjects hail the messenger who brings
the good news of his treachery.

Your right hand craves to hasten to that
battle which will assuage our souls and
bring a memorable punishment.

He paid you his poll tax and bent his cheek
in fear of sharp swords and in dread of
destruction.

[12]Religious leader. The Abbasids stressed their religious
functions in order to distance themselves from the
Umayyads, who had a reputation for being too secular* and
religiously lax.
[13]Harun's title, *al-Rashid,* means "the Rightly Guided." His
father and predecessor once removed (note 3) had borne
the title *al-Mahdi,* which also means "the Guided One."
These titles laid claim to the legitimacy of Islam's first four
Rightly Guided Caliphs and were a rejoinder against the
breakaway Isma'ili Shi'ites, who rejected the legitimacy of
the Umayyad and Abbasid caliphs and expectantly awaited
the coming of a messianic Mahdi who would disclose the
inner meaning of the Qur'an and rule the world with justice.
[14]A town on the middle Euphrates.

[15]The following story of the role played by Yahya ibn Khalid
and his sons in this affair is blatantly wrong. Yahya ibn
Khalid, a member of the Barmakid family, had served as
Harun al-Rashid's *vizier,* or chief official, from 786 to early
803. Because Yahya's sons al-Fadl and Dia'far were essentially co-viziers, this seventeen-year period is often known
as *the era of the Barmakids' reign.* Suddenly in January 803,
Harun al-Rashid stripped the family of all its offices and
possessions. Dia'far was executed, and his body was publicly exposed for a year. Yahya was arrested and died in
prison in 805. Al-Fadl died in prison in 808. With the
passage of time, the Barmakids passed into legend. Yahya
became a figure renowned for his wisdom and prescience.
Dia'far's legend preserved the memory of his literary eloquence, and al-Fadl was remembered for his generosity. We
can see all of these legendary qualities in this story.
[16]An Arabian port city on the Red Sea.
[17]Al-Rashid's son and successor, once removed (r. 813–833).
[18]Silver coins.

You protected him from the blow of swords
which we brandished like blazing torches.

You brought all your armies back from him
and he to whom you gave your protection
was secure and happy.

Nikephoros! If you played false because the
Imam was far from you, how ignorant and
deluded you were!

Did you think you could play false and
escape? May your mother mourn you!
What you thought is delusion.

Your destiny will throw you into its
brimming depths; seas will envelop you
from the Imam.

The Imam has power to overwhelm you,
whether your dwelling be near or far
away.

Though we may be neglectful the Imam
does not neglect that which he rules and
governs with his strong will.

A king who goes in person to the holy war!
His enemy is always conquered by him.

O you who seek God's approval by your
striving, nothing in your inmost heart is
hidden from God.

No counsel can avail him who deceives his
Imam, but counsel from loyal counsellers
deserves thanks.

Warning the Imam is a religious duty, an
expiation and a cleansing for those who
do it.

When he recited this, al-Rashid asked, "Has
he done that?" and he learned that the viziers
had used this device to inform him of it. He then
made war against Nikephoros while the snow
still remained and conquered Heraclea at that
time.[19]

---

[19]In 806 al-Rashid's forces captured the city of Heraclea
Pontica, which lay on the Black Sea, about one hundred
miles east of Constantinople.

Chapter 4

▼▼▼

Monks, Popes, Bishops, and Saints

The many different peoples who collectively comprised pagan society in the Roman Empire generally thought and worshipped in terms of holy places, such as temples and natural sites sacred to various deities. Christianity did not reject this phenomenon out of hand. Sites that had once been associated with such goddesses as Artemis, Diana, Isis, Minerva, and Athena, for example, were transformed into centers for the cult of the Virgin Mary. Similarly, other places that were associated with the lives and martyrdoms of Jesus and his saints, such as Jerusalem and Rome, became sacred Christian spaces. Nevertheless, Christianity brought about profound changes in the ways in which people related to the Sacred. During the fourth, fifth, and sixth centuries, Christian holy *people* — who, it was believed, possessed special religious powers — were fast replacing holy *spaces* as the main focal point of religious imagination and practice.

These holy people came in many guises and both sexes. As the following documents illustrate, they could be hermits who rejected the world or bishops* or laypeople who struggled within the world. What they had in common was that they were perceived as special friends of God who, by virtue of that relationship, offered protection and guidance to the people of God's community. One of the many consequences of this new emphasis on holy people, as opposed to holy places, was the formation of the early Roman papacy.*

▼▼▼

Monks

During the fourth and fifth centuries, many pious men and women sought escape from the new Christian-imperial order and what they perceived to be a corrupt and decaying society by going into the wastelands of Egypt, Syria-Palestine, and Anatolia.* These fugitives, who sought to live on the margins of society, are known as the *Desert Fathers,* or, more correctly, the *Desert Elders.* The Desert Elders included such colorful and unconventional characters as John the Dwarf, Moses the Black, and St. Mary the Harlot. Despite their many differences in background, they shared a number of characteristics. Chief among these was a desire to live the spirit of the Gospels* in a totally uncompromising manner, away from the evil influences of the world and alone with their God.

This flight to the desert became the foundation of Christian monasticism.* The first Desert Elders were usually hermits (also known as *anchorites*), who elected to live solitary lives in their desert refuges. The desert oases could support only a limited number of hermitages, however, and in time, many former hermits chose to join together into communities. Those who elected to live communally were known as *cenobites* (convent dwellers). By the end of the sixth century, cenobitic communities became the Christian monastic norm in the East and the West, but they never totally displaced hermits. Moreover, the lives and legends of the first desert hermits continued to inspire Christian monasticism through the ages. Whether anchorite or cenobite, Christian monks of every variety have universally claimed that their ways of life continue the tradition of the flight to the desert. Indeed, the very word *monk* comes from the Greek *monachos,* which means "one who lives alone." So, whether they live in communities or hermitages, monks are men and women dedicated to seeking and worshipping God apart from the distractions of the world.

The world, however, is not easily escaped, especially when it perceives monks as living Christian heroes who, by virtue of their successful struggles with the Devil, have gained a special spiritual strength that they can impart to the weaker members of society. On their part, monks, in obedience to the Christian call to save and transform the world and to reject its vain allures, have often been willing to offer themselves as agents of divine grace. Monks had always comprised an exceedingly small percentage of the population, but from the beginning of the flight to the desert, they became folk heroes of such magnitude that they, more than any other single group, were responsible for turning Christianity into a mass religion.

The following two sources illustrate the two major forms of monasticism that took shape in the West during the fifth and sixth centuries. Members of each played a profoundly important role in the eventual transformation of Western civilization. Indeed, it is nearly impossible to exaggerate the importance of their role in the evolution of the First Europe.

Establishing a Monastic Community
▼▼▼

17 ▾ *The Rule of Saint Benedict*

During the fourth and fifth centuries, Christian cenobitic monasticism spread into western Europe in various forms from its places of origin in the eastern Mediterranean. Like monasteries in the East, monastic organization varied widely among the first monasteries in the West. Most followed their own unique rules or adopted whatever regulations they admired from monastic houses near and faraway. Early in the sixth century, an Italian monk, whom history knows as *St. Benedict* (ca. 480–ca. 547), established a house for male religious recluses at Monte Cassino, which lies south of Rome, and there he presided as the monastery's father, or *abbot.*＊ Following the practices of his day, he composed a rule intended only for the monks of Monte Cassino and its few associated houses, and he liberally based his rule on earlier sets of monastic regulations. Despite this modest beginning, Benedict's rule became in time *the* Holy Rule of Western monasticism and the norm for all monastic life in the West.

Several reasons explain the success of Benedict's rule. As the following excerpts illustrate, St. Benedict was a proficient student of the human condition and crafted a rule that accorded with his insights. Beyond that, his rule was, and remains, highly adaptable. Benedict and his rule also enjoyed some influential patrons. Pope St. Gregory the Great (source 20), the first pope to have been a monk (but not one of Benedict's monks), celebrated the life and legend of Benedict in his widely disseminated *Dialogues,* a collection of stories about contemporary and near-contemporary saints in Italy. Gregory and his papal＊ successors also became special friends of the monks of Monte Cassino, who fled to Rome in the wake of the Lombards' destruction of their abbey＊ in 577. Just as important, eighth- and ninth-century Carolingian kings and emperors (Chapter 5) placed the weight of their authority behind the Rule of St. Benedict in a fairly successful attempt to reform and standardize monastic life within their lands.

Benedict's Holy Rule consists of a Prologue and seventy-three short chapters that offer practical instruction covering many different areas of monastic concern. Chief among these are how one enters and stays on the pathway to individual spiritual growth, the manner in which Benedict's ideal monastery is to be organized and governed, and the monks' day-to-day activities, especially their lives of prayer. The following selections provide a sample of Benedict's vision.

QUESTIONS FOR ANALYSIS

1. According to Benedict, what are the worst sins and abuses that monks can be guilty of? What does your answer suggest about his view of the ideal monastery and the purpose of the monastic life?

2. According to Benedict, what are the chief virtues of an ideal monk? What do you infer from your answer?

3. Why is the abbot so central to the Benedictine monastery? What sort of person should the ideal abbot be, and how should he govern the abbey?

4. Consider the various metaphors that Benedict employs when referring to his monastery and its monks. What do they suggest about his view of monastic life?

5. Monasticism has been defined as a system of organized *asceticism* (denial of one's bodily needs and pleasures for reasons of spiritual growth). Does this definition adequately encompass the monastic life, as set out in this rule? Do you think a sixth-century peasant would have found it unduly severe? Explain your answers.

6. One historian has written, "The rule of St. Benedict is characterized by good sense, a genuine concern for human frailties, and a balance of rigor and moderation." Do you agree or disagree? Please be specific in your answer.

7. Christian Europeans, especially during the period A.D. 700–1000, often considered the Benedictine community to be the model Christian family. Why would this be so?

PROLOGUE

Listen, son, to the master's precepts and incline the ear of your heart; freely accept and faithfully fulfill the admonitions of a loving father, so that through the labor of obedience you might return to Him from whom you have strayed by reason of the sloth of disobedience. My words are now addressed to you, whoever you might be, so that, by renouncing your own will, you might take up the strong and glorious weapons of obedience to fight for Christ, the True King. . . . We must, therefore, establish a school for service to the Lord. In establishing it we hope to ordain nothing that is harsh or heavy to bear. If, however, for adequate reason — the correction of faults or the preservation of charity — there is some disciplinary strictness herein, do not then and there be terrified and run away from the path of salvation, for its entrance is necessarily narrow. As we progress in the life of monas-

tic conversion[1] and faith, our hearts will be enlarged and, with the unspeakable sweetness of love, we shall run along the path of God's commandments so that, never forsaking His teachings but persevering in His doctrine right up to the moment of death in the monastery, we shall share in Christ's suffering through our patience and, thereby, deserve to be partakers also of His Kingdom.

CHAPTER 1

The Kinds of Monks

There are clearly four kinds of monks. The first kind consists of cenobites, namely, they who live in monasteries, doing spiritual battle under a rule and an abbot. The second kind consists of anchorites, namely, hermits. They are not in the first fervor of their monastic conversion, but after long testing in a monastery and with the as-

---

[1]Conversion of one's whole life and being. This is a long process that an individual undertakes *after* entering the monastery.

sistance of many brethren, they have learned how to fight against the devil. Well armed, they leave the fraternal ranks to engage in the solitary combat of the desert. Now alone and without another's help, but relying on their own strength and God's help, they are prepared to fight against the temptations of the flesh and the mind. The third kind of monks is that abominable one of sarabaites,[2] who, never having been hardened, like gold in a furnace, by any rule or experience, are as soft as lead. They keep faith with the ways of this world in their actions, and their tonsures[3] mark them out as liars before God. In twos, threes, and even singly, they live without a shepherd shut up in their own sheepfolds, not in those of the Lord. Their law is the satisfaction of their desires. Whatever they think of or choose to do, that they call holy; what they do not like, that they regard as illicit. The fourth kind of monks consists of those called gyrovagues.[4] They spend their entire lives wandering through various provinces, being entertained for three or four days at a time in the cells[5] of various monks, always wandering and never stable, slaves of their own wills and the allurements of gluttony. In all respects, they are worse than the sarabaites.

It is better to pass over in silence than to speak of the wretched way of life of all these [last two kinds of] monks. Therefore, let us proceed with God's help to provide for that strong kind of monks known as cenobites.

CHAPTER 2

What Sort of Man the Abbot Should Be

An abbot who is worthy of ruling a monastery must always remember what he is called and fulfill in his actions the name of one who is called a "superior." For he is believed to serve as the representative of Christ in the monastery and for that reason is called by His[6] title, according to the words of the apostle:* "You have received the spirit of the adoption of sons, whereby we cry Abba, Father."[7] . . . The abbot should always remember that at the dread Judgment of God two matters will be examined: his teaching and the obedience of his disciples. Let the abbot know that whatever lack of fruitfulness the Father[8] might discover in the sheep will be laid to the blame of the shepherd. On the other hand, if the shepherd has spent total diligence in the care of an unruly and disobedient flock and devoted his full attention to correcting their disorderly ways, then he will be found guiltless before God's tribunal. . . . Then, finally, let those sheep who were mindless of his care suffer the penalty of death itself.

Therefore, when anyone has received the name of abbot, he ought to lead his disciples by means of a twofold way of instruction. He should display all goodness and holiness by his deeds even more so than by his words. For disciples who are quick of mind, let him use words to expound the Lord's commandments; for those, however, who have hard hearts or are simpler of mind, let him demonstrate the divine precepts by his own actions. . . .

The abbot should not display preferential treatment for anyone in his monastery. He should not love one more than another, unless he has discovered him to be better in good works and obedience. A freeborn monk must not be given preference over one who enters the monastery from a state of servitude, unless there is some other rational ground for preference. . . . Whether slave or free, we are all one in Christ, and we owe equal military service under the same Lord.

---

[2]A Coptic word of derision that had its origins in the Egyptian desert.
[3]The shaven portion of a monk's head that signifies his rejection of the world's vanities.
[4]"Rolling wheels."

[5]The rooms or other residences of monks.
[6]Christ's.
[7]The Bible, St. Paul in the Epistle to the Romans, 8:15.
[8]God the Judge.

In his instruction, the abbot ought always observe the rule of the apostle, in which he states: "Reprove, persuade, rebuke."[9] This means he must behave differently at different times. Balancing threats with encouragement, he shows the rigor of a school master and the tender love of a father. This means he must sternly reprimand the undisciplined and restless, but he should earnestly implore the obedient, the meek, and the patient to advance in virtue. We advise him to rebuke and punish the negligent and rebellious. Let him not overlook the sins of offenders. Rather, as soon as they appear, he should cut them out by the roots, insofar as he is able to. . . .

The abbot ought always to remember what he is and what he is called and should know that more is expected from him to whom more has been entrusted. Let him also realize how difficult and arduous a task he has undertaken, of ruling souls and serving men of many different personalities. One he must encourage, another he must reprimand, another he must persuade — each according to his nature and intelligence. The abbot must adapt and conform himself to everyone in such a way, not only as not to suffer a loss in the flock entrusted to him but so that he might rejoice as his good flock increases. . . .

CHAPTER 23

Concerning Excommunication* for Faults

If any brother is contumacious, or disobedient, or proud, or a grumbler, or is found have set himself in opposition to any point of the Holy Rule or to have held in contempt the orders of his superiors, let such a monk be admonished secretly for a first and a second time by his superiors, as our Lord has commanded. If he does not amend his ways, let him be rebuked publicly in the presence of everyone. If even then he fails to correct himself, let him be excommunicated, provided that he understands the gravity of the penalty. If, however, he is stubborn, he must undergo corporal punishment.

CHAPTER 24

What the Measure of Excommunication Should Be

The measure of excommunication or punishment must be proportionate to the degree of the fault, and it is for the abbot to judge the level of all faults. If some brother is found guilty of lesser faults, he shall be excluded from sharing in the common meal. . . . Until he has made satisfaction, . . . he shall have his meal alone, after the community meal. If the brothers eat at the sixth hour,[10] let him eat at the ninth; if they eat at the ninth hour, he shall eat in the evening, until, after proper satisfaction, he obtains pardon.

CHAPTER 25

Graver Faults

The brother who is judged guilty of a graver fault shall be excluded both from the meal and the oratory.[11] Let none of the brothers consort with him or speak with him. He is to be left alone at the work assigned him, abiding in penitential grief and pondering that terrible sentence of the apostle: "This sort of man is handed over for the destruction of his flesh, so that his spirit might be saved on the day of the Lord."[12] Let him take his meals alone, in the measure and at the hour that the abbot considers suitable for him. Neither he nor the food given him may be blessed by anyone passing by. . . .

---

[9]St. Paul, Epistle to the Romans, 2:11.
[10]See note 15. Following Roman practice, monastic days and nights were each divided into twelve equal hours. The length of an hour, therefore, varied according to the season. The daytime sixth hour would be around noon in the early spring and early fall, the times of the equinox.

[11]The place devoted to daily community prayer.
[12]St. Paul, First Letter to the Corinthians, 5:5.

CHAPTER 27

How the Abbot Should Be Solicitous for the Excommunicated

The abbot should carry out with the deepest concern his responsibility for errant brothers, because it is not the healthy who need a physician but those who are ill. Like a wise physician, he should use every possible remedy. He should send *senpectae* (namely, prudent elder brothers),[13] who, in an almost secret manner, might comfort the troubled brother, induce him to make humble satisfaction, and console him, lest he be swallowed up by too much sorrow. And let it be as the apostle says, "that love for him be affirmed,"[14] and let everyone pray for him. For the abbot is obligated to use the greatest care and to exercise all prudence and diligence, lest he lose any of the sheep entrusted to him. For he should know that he has undertaken the care of unhealthy souls and not a despotic rule over healthy spirits. . . .

CHAPTER 28

Of Those Who, Though Often Corrected, Refuse to Change Their Ways

If any brother, though often corrected and even excommunicated for some offense, does not amend his ways, let him receive more severe correction. That is to say, he must be beaten. If even then he does not correct himself or, perhaps (may it not be so), he is so puffed up with pride that he wishes to defend his actions, then let the abbot act as any prudent physician would. If he has applied the poultices and ointments of his exhortations, if he has used the medicine of divine scripture, and if, finally, he has employed the cauterization of excommunication and blows

from a rod and now he sees that his work is fruitless, let him employ yet something stronger — his own prayers and those of all the brothers — so that God, who can do everything, might effect the cure of this sick brother. But if he is not made well even in this way, then let the abbot use the knife of amputation, . . . lest one diseased sheep infect the whole flock.

CHAPTER 29

Whether Brothers Who Leave the Monastery May Be Received Again

If a brother, who by his own fault left the monastery, wishes to return, he must first promise full amendment of the fault that occasioned his leaving. Then let him be received back in the lowest rank, as a test of his humility. Should he depart a second time, he may be received back again, and even for a third time, but he should understand that after that all prospect of return will be denied him. . . .

CHAPTER 33

Whether Monks May Possess Anything of Their Own

This vice should be totally rooted out of the monastery. No one should presume to give or accept anything without the abbot's permission or to possess anything of his own, anything whatever, be it a book, or writing tablets, or a pen, or whatever it might be. For monks should not have even their own bodies or wills at their own disposal. Rather, let them look to the monastery's father for all their necessities. It is unlawful to have anything that the abbot has not given or permitted. . . .

---

[13]The word means "playmate" in Greek and was used by Greek-speaking monks in the East to refer to monastic companions. In the West, it was mistakenly believed that the word derived from the Latin *senex* (old man). Therefore, it came to mean "wise old monastic teachers."

[14]St. Paul, Second Epistle to the Corinthians, 2:7.

CHAPTER 39

The Measure of Food

We believe that it suffices for the daily meal, whether at the sixth or ninth hour,[15] that every table have two cooked dishes, on account of individual infirmities. If, perhaps, a brother cannot eat one, he can eat the other. Therefore, let two cooked dishes suffice for all the brothers, but if any fruits or young vegetables are available, a third may be added. Let a full pound[16] of bread suffice for the day, whether there is one meal or both dinner and supper. If they are to have supper,[17] let the cellarer[18] hold back a third of a pound of that bread, to be served at supper. If their work happens to be heavier than normal, the abbot has the discretion and power to increase the allowance, should it be expedient. Above all else, however, gluttony must be avoided, and never must indigestion seize a monk, for there is nothing so unbecoming to every Christian as gluttony. . . . Young boys[19] shall not receive the same amount of food but less than their elders, and frugality will be the rule at all times. Except for the sick who are especially weak, everyone must abstain at all times from consuming the flesh of four-footed animals.

CHAPTER 40

The Measure of Drink

"Everyone has his own gift from God, one in this way, another in that."[20] Consequently, it is with some misgiving that we establish the amount of nourishment that others consume. Nevertheless, keeping in mind the frailty of weaker brothers, we believe that a *hemina*[21] of wine a day suffices for each. Those, however, to whom God gives the capacity for abstinence should understand that they will have their own special reward. If, however, local circumstances, or their work, or the heat of summer require more, the superior has the right to make that decision, but he must in all cases take care that neither excess nor inebriation creeps in. To be sure, we read that wine is in no way a fit drink for monks, yet because today's monks cannot be persuaded of that, let us at least agree upon this: to drink not to the point of satiety but more sparingly. For wine leads even the wise into infidelity. When the local circumstances are such that the above-mentioned quantity of wine cannot be had, but much less or even nothing at all, those who live there should bless God and not grumble. Above all else, we admonish them to abstain from grumbling! . . .

CHAPTER 73

The Full Observance of Righteous Behavior Is Not Established in This Rule

We have composed this rule so that, by practicing it in monasteries, we might show that we have attained, to some degree, honesty of character and the beginning of our monastic conversion. For him who would hasten to the perfection of monastic conversion, there are the teachings of the Holy Fathers,[22] whose observance leads one to the summit of perfection. What page or what utterance of the divinely inspired Old and New

---

[15]Benedict's monks normally ate their first and main meal only at the sixth hour of daylight (see note 10), even though they had risen for first prayers in the early morning hours, long before sunrise. They would then have a light supper in the evening. In times of ordinary fast, they ate only one meal and put it off until the ninth hour. In times of special fast, such as the penitential period of Lent, the forty days that precede Easter, the monks' sole meal for the day was a frugal supper that they ate just before the end of daylight.
[16]No one knows the weight of this sixth-century full pound.

[17]See note 15.
[18]The monastic official in charge of provisions.
[19]Who had been given by their parents to be educated in the monastery, with the understanding that they probably would take proper monastic vows upon reaching maturity.
[20]St. Paul, First Letter to the Corinthians, 7:7.
[21]No one really knows how much liquid constituted a sixth-century hemina.
[22]The great early teachers of Christian doctrine and morality.

Testaments is not an infallible norm for a human life? What book of the most holy Catholic Fathers does not proclaim the proper path by which we should make our way to the Creator? Then the *Collations of the Fathers,* and the *Institutes*[23] and the *Lives of the Fathers,*[24] and the Rule of our holy father Basil[25] — what else are they but instruments of virtue for good-living and

obedient monks? To us, however, who are slothful, who live badly, and who are negligent, they bring a blush of shame. Therefore, you, whoever you might be, who hurries toward the heavenly fatherland, fulfill, with Christ's help, this little rule written for beginners, and then you will attain at last, under God's protection, those heights of wisdom and virtue that we mentioned above.

---

[23]The *Collations* is better known as the *Conferences.* Both the *Conferences* and the *Institutes* were composed in Latin by John Cassian (ca. 360–432), based on his experiences among the monks of Syria-Palestine and Egypt, and both became standard instructional reading for monks in the West.

[24]The many different collections of biographies of the early desert saints.

[25]St. Basil the Great (330–379) — monk, theologian, Father of the Eastern Church, and bishop of Caesarea — is usually regarded as the father of Byzantine monasticism. He wrote no rule in the sense of Benedict's Holy Rule; his so-called Longer and Shorter Rules are really series of disconnected precepts. However, he, more than any other individual, infused Eastern cenobitic monasticism with vitality and made it an integral part of Eastern Christian culture.

A Celtic Monk Confronts Demons
▼▼▼
18 ▼ THE LIFE OF SAINT GALL

Two of the most important figures in the initial translation of monastic ways of life into Gaul were St. Martin of Tours (Chapter 2, source 9) and John Cassian of Marseilles (ca. 360–432), both of whom were deeply influenced by the way in which monastic communities functioned in Egypt. The Egyptian desert continued to breed monks who were very much spiritual athletes. Although they increasingly came to dwell in communities under the supervision of religious superiors, Egyptian monks largely continued to imitate the fervent asceticism and solitary lifestyles of the early anchorites of the desert.

In the fourth and fifth centuries, missionary monks such as St. Patrick (ca. 390–461), who were raised in Gaul under Egyptian-like monastic conditions, carried Christianity and monasticism into Ireland. This land of tribal societies embraced the Christianity that the monks transmitted from across the sea and adapted their uncompromisingly rigorous forms of monasticism to Celtic warrior culture.

One practice that was peculiar to Celtic monasticism was voluntarily making oneself a wandering exile for Christ, as a form of ultimate renunciation and as an expression of one's spiritual heroism. As a result, Irish monks spilled out of their homeland, carrying with them the Christian faith and Celtic monasticism. They set up monasteries from Iceland to Central Europe and northern Italy during the sixth and seventh centuries, and wherever possible, they preached the faith to pagans.

Thanks to Carolingian patronage of St. Benedict's Holy Rule, Celtic monasticism eventually gave way to Benedictinism, and monastic houses established in the wilderness by early Celtic missionaries were later converted into Benedictine monasteries. The Irish monastery that arose in the early seventh century on the spot where the present story took place, for example, was transformed into a model of Benedictine organization by the late eighth century. But before St. Benedict's rule and the order that it represented won the day, Celtic monks had several centuries in which to play their heroic role.

Two of the most notable Celtic hero-monks were Saint Columban (ca. 530–615) and his associate St. Gall (before 560–after 615), who both labored among the pagan countryfolk on the continent. The following story comes from the anonymous *Life of Saint Gall,* which possibly was written as late as 771 and describes the adventures of Columban and Gall around the year 612 in the region of Lake Constance, where modern southwest Germany and Switzerland meet.

QUESTIONS FOR ANALYSIS

1. What pre-Christian notions do Gall and his biographer accept? How have they placed these notions into a Christian framework?
2. How have these monks, and especially Gall, transformed this former site of pagan power into a Christian center?
3. How does this story illustrate the point made in the chapter introduction about the shift in cultic orientation from pagan sites to Christian holy people?
4. Why do you think missionaries such as Gall enjoyed such success among pagan rural populations?

There the brethren's hands made ready a dwelling, and the holy Columban fervently prayed to Christ in behalf of that place. The superstitious pagans worshiped three idols of gilded metal, and believed in returning thanks to them rather than to the creator of the world.

So Columban, the man of God, wished to destroy that superstition, and told Gall to talk to the people, since he himself excelled in Latin, but not in the language of that tribe. The people gathered at the temple for their wonted festival; but they were attracted by the sight of the strangers, not, however, by reverence for the divine religion. When they were assembled, Gall, the elect of God, fed their hearts with honeyed words, exhorting them to turn to their Creator, and to Jesus Christ the Son of God, who opened the gate of Heaven for the human race, sunk in indifference and uncleanness.

Then before them all he broke in pieces with stones the enthroned idols, and cast them into the depths of the lake. Then part of the people confessed* their sins and believed, but others were angry and enraged, and departed in wrath; and Columban, the man of God, blessed the water and sanctified the place, and remained there with his followers three years. . . .

Some time after, in the silence of the night, Gall, the elect of God, was laying nets in the water, and lo! he heard the demon of the mountain top calling to his fellow who dwelt in the depths of the lake. The demon of the lake answered, "I am here"; he of the mountain returned: "Arise, come to my aid! Behold the aliens come, and thrust me from my temple. Come, come! help me to drive them from our lands." The demon of the lake answered: "One of them is upon the lake, whom I could never harm. For I wished to break his nets, but see, I am vanquished and mourn. The sign of his prayer protects him always, and sleep never overcomes him."

Gall, the elect of God, heard this, and fortified himself on all sides with the sign of the cross, and said to them: "In the name of Jesus Christ, I command you, leave this place, and do not presume to harm any one here." And he hastened to return to the shore, and told his abbot[1] what he had heard.

When Columban, the man of God, heard this, he called the brethren together in the church, and made the accustomed sign.[2] Before the brethren could raise their voices, the voice of an unseen being was heard, and wailing and lamentation echoed from the mountain top. So the malicious demons departed with mourning, and the prayer of the brethren arose as they sent up their supplications to God.

----

[1]Columban.

[2]Of the Cross.

▼▼▼

Popes

Based upon some fragmentary, quite ambiguous evidence, it seems that first-century Christian communities were governed by boards of elders, or overseers. During the second century, however, such boards appear to have given way to rule by *bishops.* A bishop was a male cleric* who functioned as the sole chief priest* and administrative head of a regional church and who resided in the area's major city. By the time of Constantine the Great, bishops, especially those in the East, were the Church's chief clerical voices and leaders. The western half of the empire, of course, had its notable bishops, and in the age following Constantine, the bishop of one city — Rome — began slowly to emerge as claimant to the role of premier bishop in the West.

From the late third century on, the city of Rome rapidly lost its position of political primacy and was replaced in the West by such new imperial centers as Milan and Ravenna in Italy and Trier in Germany. When Constantinople was dedicated as the New Rome in 330, the whole center of imperial power shifted eastward. And when the last Roman emperor in the West was forced to abdicate in 476, the emperor residing at Constantinople became the sole legitimate ruler of an empire whose western regions were rapidly becoming fragmented, ungovernable by a single imperial authority, and quite un-Roman.

Even as Rome was losing its political power, its spiritual authority was ascending. Although every bishop theoretically received his powers directly from the apostles* and governed an essentially autonomous community, some bishops were recognized as deserving special respect and as having extraordinary authority, by virtue of the importance of their sees.* Included among these were the bishops of Alexandria in Egypt, Antioch in Syria, and Rome. Alexandria and Antioch were economically and politically important cities. In the fourth and fifth centuries, Rome was nowhere near as rich or politically significant, but it was still Rome — the sentimental heart of the empire — and that counted for quite a lot. Moreover, the Church of Rome alone could claim the bodies and, therefore, the inherited powers of Saints Peter and Paul, the Church's two greatest apostles. This was powerful spiritual ammunition in a culture that believed in the immediate intervention of heavenly patrons, especially patrons who allowed their relics* to reside in the churches of their devotees. Increasingly, and particularly from the pontificate* of Pope St. Leo I, known as *the Great* (r. 440–461), the bishops of Rome claimed to be the legal heirs of St. Peter, whom they believed had received special powers of governance over the Church directly from Jesus and who, according to tradition, had been Rome's first bishop. The main biblical underpinning for this claim was (and remains) the Gospel of St. Matthew (16:17–19), which Pope Gregory I quotes in source 20 of this chapter.

As a consequence of this Petrine claim, from the sixth century on, the bishops of Rome increasingly claimed exclusive right to the title *Pope,* or "Father" (*Papa* in Latin), a title that originally was applied to all bishops out of respect for their spiritual paternity. Although many other bishops were still accorded the title in the sixth century (Chapter 2, source 9), the Roman papacy's* case for sole claim on the title was gaining ground in the West. Moreover, as far as many popes of Rome were concerned, the title meant much more than just an acknowledgment of their spiritual fatherhood; it signified the bishop of Rome's legitimate claim to govern the Church with an authority analogous to the almost absolute power of a traditional Roman head of a household. During these early centuries, few persons outside of Rome were ready to accept or even acknowledge the implications of such claims, but the foundations had been laid for what would become the medieval papacy.

The following sources present some of the seminal writings of three of the most important popes of the Roman papacy's formative years: Gelasius I, Gregory I, and Gregory II. Each was instrumental in the Roman papacy's evolution into the most important church office in the West.

The Issue of Christian Authority
▼▼▼

19 ▾ *Pope Gelasius I,*
LETTER TO EMPEROR ANASTASIUS I and
ON THE BONDS OF ANATHEMA

In 494 Pope Gelasius I (r. 492–496) wrote to Emperor Anastasius I (Chapter 2, sources 9 and 10), complaining of the emperor's interference in church affairs. Separated from the emperor at Constantinople by an ever-widening gulf between the eastern and western portions of the empire and supported in Italy by Theodoric the Ostrogoth (Chapter 2, source 8), Gelasius felt confident enough to lecture Anastasius on the proper relationship between imperial and priestly powers. The first excerpt contains Gelasius's definition of the respective powers and areas of responsibility of priests and emperors, as set out in his letter to Anastasius. Two years later, Gelasius returned to the issue in a treatise entitled *On the Bonds of*

Anathema and more clearly spelled out the relationship between spiritual and worldly authority. In these two writings, Gelasius articulated one of the classic answers to a conundrum that would vex popes and emperors for many centuries to come.

QUESTIONS FOR ANALYSIS

1. According to Gelasius, who are Christendom's two authorities, and of them, whose responsibilities and authority are the greater? Why?
2. According to Gelasius, why are there two separate authorities in Christendom?
3. How does Gelasius view the Roman papacy? How does he view the emperor?
4. Strictly speaking, does Gelasius argue for a separation of church and state? If he does not go that far, what does he argue?
5. Compare Gelasius's views on the proper relationship of church and state with Augustine's vision of the City of God's use of the peace of this world (Chapter 1, source 4). Are their philosophies comparable? If not, how do they differ? What conclusions follow from your answers?
6. Review the Barberini ivory (Chapter 2, source 10). Would the emperor portrayed on that panel agree with Gelasius's interpretation of imperial power? Why or why not?

Two there are, august emperor, by which this world is chiefly ruled, the sacred authority of the priesthood and the royal power. Of these the responsibility of the priests is more weighty in so far as they will answer for the kings of men themselves at the divine judgment. You know, most clement son, that, although you take precedence over all mankind in dignity, nevertheless you piously bow the neck to those who have charge of divine affairs and seek from them the means of your salvation, and hence you realize that, in the order of religion, in matters concerning the reception and right administration of the heavenly sacraments,* you ought to submit yourself rather than rule, and that in these matters you should depend on their judgment rather than seek to bend them to your will. For if the bishops themselves, recognizing that the imperial office was conferred on you by divine disposition, obey your laws so far as the sphere of public order is concerned lest they seem to obstruct your decrees in mundane matters, with what zeal, I ask you, ought you to obey those who have been charged with administering the sacred mysteries? Moreover, just as no light risk attends pontiffs* who keep silent in matters concerning the service of God, so too no little danger threatens those who show scorn — which God forbid — when they ought to obey. And if the hearts of the faithful should be submitted to all priests in general who rightly administer divine things, how much more should assent be given to the bishop of that see which the Most High wished to be preeminent over all priests, and which the devotion of the whole church has honored ever since.[1] As Your Piety is certainly well aware, no

---

[1] The bishopric of Rome.

one can ever raise himself by purely human means to the privilege and place of him whom the voice of Christ has set before all, whom the church has always venerated and held in devotion as its primate.[2] The things which are established by divine judgment can be assailed by human presumption; they cannot be overthrown by anyone's power.

▼ ▼ ▼

It happened before the coming of Christ that certain men, though still engaged in carnal activities,[3] were symbolically both kings and priests, and sacred history tells us that Melchisedek[4] was such a one. The Devil also imitated this among his own people, for he always strives in a spirit of tyranny to claim for himself what pertains to divine worship, and so pagan emperors were called supreme pontiffs.[5] But when He[6] came who was true king and true priest, the emperor no longer assumed the title of priest,[7] nor did the priest claim the royal dignity — though the members of Him[8] who was true king and true priest, through participation in his na-

ture, may be said to have received both qualities in their sacred nobility so that they constitute a race at once royal and priestly. For Christ, mindful of human frailty, regulated with an excellent disposition what pertained to the salvation of his people. Thus he distinguished between the offices of both powers according to their own proper activities and separate dignities, wanting his people to be saved by healthful humility and not carried away again by human pride, so that Christian emperors would need priests for attaining eternal life and priests would avail themselves of imperial regulations in the conduct of temporal affairs. In this fashion spiritual activity would be set apart from worldly encroachments and the "soldier of God"[9] would not be involved in secular* affairs, while on the other hand he who was involved in secular affairs would not seem to preside over divine matters. Thus the humility of each order would be preserved, neither being exalted by the subservience of the other, and each profession would be especially fitted for its appropriate functions.

---

[2]The reference is to the pope, the entire Church's primate.*
[3]Activities of the flesh or worldly matters.
[4]King of Salem (an unidentified ancient city in Syria-Palestine, possibly pre-Israelite Jerusalem) and also its chief priest, Melchizedek blessed Abraham, father of the Hebrews (the Bible, Genesis, 14:17–20).
[5]Here Gelasius has the pre-Christian emperors of Rome in mind, each of whom claimed the title *Pontifex Maximus* (chief priest). The bishops of Rome took that title as their own in the late fourth century.

[6]Jesus.
[7]Gratian (r. 375–383), emperor in the West, was the first Christian Roman emperor to refuse the title *Pontifex Maximus,* just about the same time that the bishops of Rome were claiming the title.
[8]All Christians.
[9]A priest.

The Father of the Medieval Papacy

▼▼▼

20 ▼ *Pope Gregory I, LETTERS*

When Gregory I, known to history as *the Great,* assumed the papal* throne in 590, after his predecessor had died of bubonic plague, he noted sadly, "I, unworthy and weak as I am, have taken charge of an old and grievously shattered ship." That ship was Rome, Italy, and the western Roman Empire, and it was certainly shattered, but Gregory, who would guide the fortunes of the Western Church until his death on March 12, 604, proved worthy of his office and as equal as any human could have been to the great challenges facing him and Western society.

The challenges were stupendous. The plague that killed Gregory's predecessor had been ravaging the Mediterranean world since 541 and, in the process, had already killed off millions of people, from Constantinople to Spain (Chapter 3, source 11). Periodic famines and droughts also wreaked havoc with the West's rapidly declining population. In addition to natural disasters, invasions and wars added to the sum total of human misery. Imperial troops invaded Italy in 535 in an attempt to reconquer the peninsula from what Emperor Justinian (source 11) considered to be barbarian heretics˚ — the Ostrogothic successors of Theodoric (Chapter 2, source 8). The result was almost two decades of bitter warfare, which resulted in massive deurbanization and, in turn, ruined Italy economically. Rome became a malaria-ridden, derelict town of ruins and deserted fields. In 550 one contemporary wrote, "Nothing remains for the inhabitants of Italy to do but die." Shortly after the emperor's troops had driven the Ostrogoths out of Italy (and out of history), new Germanic invaders appeared in the peninsula. In 568 the Lombards arrived on the scene, thereby beginning a new cycle of destruction.

Faced with all of the crises that beset Rome and Italy, Pope Gregory could have spent his entire pontificate˚ simply responding to local disasters and needs. Indeed, this native-born Roman aristocrat, who earlier had served as one of Rome's civil leaders, devoted large amounts of energy as pope to caring for the spiritual and physical needs of the people of Italy. He even helped organize defenses against the Lombards.

Notwithstanding the local demands on his attention, Gregory did not neglect significant affairs far removed from Italy's borders. As several of the following letters show, Gregory believed himself responsible for matters that concerned all of Christendom, not just his besieged world of Italy. Consequently, he carried on lively correspondence with the emperor at Constantinople and with Eastern Christian bishops˚ and, perhaps most significant of all, dispatched in 596 a band of forty monks˚ to work as missionaries among the pagan Germanic settlers of faraway Britain. This act of religious charity, perhaps even optimism, in an age of general despair bore rich fruit in the centuries that followed. Through his actions, life, and writings, Gregory the Great played a crucial role in making the Roman papacy˚ the moral and spiritual leader of the West. In many respects, Gregory deserves the title *father of the medieval papacy.*

QUESTIONS FOR ANALYSIS

1. Consider the first letter. How did Gregory interpret the dramatic events of his day?
2. How might Gregory's interpretation have colored his missionary activities and policies in England (letters 4 and 5)?
3. Consider Gregory's letter to Emperor Maurice. How did Gregory view the emperor's role in Christendom? What did he expect from the emperor in

faraway Constantinople? What does this suggest about Gregory's view of the empire?

4. Review Augustine's *City of God* (Chapter 1, source 4). To what extent, if at all, were Gregory's ideas in accord with those of Augustine? What do you infer from your answer?

5. Would Gregory agree or disagree with Gelasius's views, as set forth in source 19? Why?

6. Why did Gregory take offense at John the Faster's use of the title *ecumenical patriarch?** What does this suggest about Gregory the man and the pope?

7. What do Gregory's letters to Constantinople and Alexandria suggest about his vision of the role of holy people in Christendom? Consider the letter to Abbot Mellitus. In Gregory's mind, how can holy people transform a previously pagan place into a site of Christian holiness?

8. The Roman papacy was constructed on the principle of Petrine primacy. What does your reading of letters 2 and 3 tell you about Gregory's view of papal primacy?

9. *Syncretism* is a term that refers to the adaptation of foreign cultural elements to a host culture. What do letters 4 and 5 suggest about the process of cultural syncretism, so far as Germanic society's adoption of Latin Christianity was concerned?

THE PRESENT AGE

1. To the clergy* of Milan

Take note that all the things of this world, which we used to hear[1] from sacred scripture were doomed to perish,[2] we see now in ruins. Cities are overthrown, fortresses uprooted, churches destroyed, and no tiller of the soil inhabits our land any more. The sword of man incessantly rages in our midst — we, the very few who are left. Along with this, calamities smite us from above.[3] Thus we see before our very eyes the evils that we long ago heard would descend upon the world, and the very regions of the earth have become like pages of books to us.[4] As all things pass away, we should reflect how all that we have loved was nothing. Look with anxious heart, therefore, upon the approaching day of the Eternal Judge

and, by repenting, anticipate its terrors. Wash away all the stains of your transgressions with your tears. Use lamentations that endure only for awhile to turn aside the wrath that hangs over you eternally. When our loving Creator comes to judge us, He will comfort us in direct proportion to what He now sees as the punishment that we inflict upon ourselves for our own transgressions.

THE EMPEROR AND THE CHURCH OF CONSTANTINOPLE

2. To Emperor Maurice[5]

Our most pious and God-appointed Lord, in addition to all the burdensome cares of empire, provides with true spiritual zeal for the preser-

---

[1]Note the verb is *hear,* not *read.* This is an essentially oral society, in which the Bible is read aloud to congregations.
[2]The portion of the Bible that Gregory refers to is the Book of Revelation, also known as the Apocalypse of St. John, the last book of the Christian New Testament, which deals with the last days of the world.
[3]A reference to the bubonic plague.

[4]Gregory's meaning is not totally clear here. He probably means that the horrors that Christians read about in the pages of the Book of Revelation (note 2) are now realities. He could also mean that the world's lands are now as fragile as papyrus.
[5]Ruled 582–602.

vation of Christian peace among the clergy. He righteously and correctly knows that no person can exercise proper rule on earth unless he knows how to deal with divine matters, and he also knows that the peace of the state depends on the peace of the universal Church. Indeed, Most Serene Lord, what human power, what strength of muscular arm, would dare raise a sacrilegious hand against the eminence of your most Christian empire, if all its priests* strove with one mind, as they ought, to win the Redeemer's favor for you by prayer and the merit of their lives? What sword of a most savage people[6] would advance with such cruelty to the slaughter of the faithful, were it not for the fact that the lives of us, who are called priests but who are not, are weighed down by perfidious deeds? . . . Our faults, which weigh down the forces of the state, sharpen the swords of the enemy. What shall we say for ourselves, who are unworthily set over God's people, when we oppress them with the burdens of our sins and destroy by example what we preach with our tongues? . . . Our bones are wasted by fasts, but we are bloated in our minds. Our body is covered with rags, but in the pride of our heart, we surpass the imperial purple. We lie in ashes but look down upon loftiness. Teachers of humility, we are masters of pride. . . . God has inspired my most pious Lord to deter war against the empire by first establishing peace within the Church and by deigning to bring back the hearts of its priests to harmony. This, indeed, is what I desire, and for myself, I give glad obedience to your most serene commands.

Since, however, it is not my cause, but God's, since the holy laws, since the venerable coun-

cils,* since the very commands of our Lord Jesus Christ are disturbed by the invention of a certain proud and haughty phrase, may you, My Most Pious Lord, cut out the sore and bind the resisting patient in the restraints of imperial authority. For in binding up these things tightly, you provide relief to the state, and when you cut off such things, you assure a longer reign for yourself.

To all who know the Gospel,* it is clear that the Lord verbally committed to the holy apostle,* Peter, the prince of all the apostles, care of the entire Church. . . . For to Peter it was said: "You are Peter, and upon this rock I will build My Church, and the gates of hell shall not prevail against it. And I will give you the keys of the Kingdom of Heaven; whatever you bind on earth will be bound also in heaven, and whatever you loose on earth will be loosed also in heaven."[7] Behold, Peter received the keys of the Kingdom of Heaven; the power to bind and loose is given him; the care of the entire Church is committed to him, and yet he is not called the *universal apostle.* Meanwhile, the most holy man, my fellow-priest John, attempts to be called universal bishop.[8] I am compelled to cry out: "O tempora, O mores!"[9]

Behold. All the regions of Europe are in the hands of barbarians, cities are overthrown, fortresses uprooted, provinces depopulated, no tiller of the soil inhabits the land,[10] idol worshippers rage and daily dominate — all to the slaughter of the faithful — and still priests, who ought to lie weeping on the ground and in ashes, seek for themselves names of vanity, and they take pride in new and profane titles.

---

[6]The Lombards.
[7]The Gospel of Matthew, 16:18.
[8]John IV, bishop of Constantinople, known as *John the Faster* (r. 582–595). See what Gregory wrote earlier in this letter about hypocritical fasters. Gregory was offended by John's use of the title *ecumenical patriarch.* The bishops of Rome, Constantinople, Alexandria, and Antioch all traditionally bore the title *patriarch,* in recognition of the special preeminence each enjoyed. However, the term *ecumenical* disturbed Gregory, because he assumed that it implied a claim to rule over the *universal* Church. In fact, the title simply meant that John was supreme with the region of his particular patriarchate.

[9]Oh, how lamentable this age and its customs!
[10]Compare these phrases with his letter to the clergy of Milan.

Do I, Most Pious Lord, defend my own cause? Am I resentful because of a wrong done me? No! It is the cause of Almighty God. It is the cause of the universal Church. . . . In honor of Peter, prince of the apostles, [the title *universal*] was offered by the venerable synod* of Chalcedon to the bishop of Rome.[11] But not one bishop of Rome has ever consented to use this unique title, lest, by giving something special to one priest, priests in general would be deprived of the honor due them. How is it, then, that we do not seek the glory of this title, even when it is offered, but another presumes to seize it for himself, even though it has not been offered? . . .

Behold. We all suffer offense in this matter. Let the author of the offense be brought back to a proper way of life, and all priestly quarrels will end. For my part, I am the servant of all priests,[12] as long as they live in a manner that befits priests. But whoever, through the swelling of vainglory, lifts up his neck against God Almighty and against the laws of the Church Fathers, I trust such a man will not bend my neck to himself, not even with a sword.

PETRINE PRIMACY

3. To Eulogius, bishop of Alexandria[13]

Your most sweet Holiness has spoken much in your letter to me about the chair[14] of Saint Pe-

ter, prince of the apostles, saying that he himself[15] now sits on it in the persons of his successors, . . . and, indeed, I gladly accepted all that was said, inasmuch as he[16] has spoken to me about Peter's chair who occupies Peter's chair. Although special honor to me in no way delights me, I greatly rejoice because you, Most Holy One, have given to yourself what you have bestowed on me. For who can be unaware that the holy Church has been made firm in the strength of the prince of the apostles, who derived his name from the firmness of his spirit, so that he was called *Petrus,* which comes from *petra.*[17] And to him it is said by the voice of Truth:[18] "I will give you the keys of the Kingdom of Heaven."[19] And again it is said to him: "When you are converted, strengthen your brothers."[20] And once more: "Simon, son of Jonah, do you love Me? Then feed My sheep."[21] It follows from this that although there are many apostles, so far as primacy is concerned, the see* of the prince of the apostles alone has grown strong in authority, which in three places is one see. For Peter himself exalted the see in which he deigned to reside and end his life on earth.[22] Peter himself honored the see to which he sent his disciple as evangelist.[23] Peter himself strengthened[24] the see in which, although he would leave it, he sat for seven years.[25] Because it is the see of one, and one see over which by Divine Authority three bishops now preside, whatever good I hear of you I impute to myself.

---

[11]Actually, canon* 28 of the Ecumenical Council of Chalcedon of 451 acknowledged that the five major patriarchs of the Church were the bishops of Rome, Constantinople, Alexandria, Antioch, and Jerusalem. It went on to state that the patriarchate of Constantinople enjoyed equal powers and privileges with that of Rome, because Constantinople was the New Rome. Pope Leo I (r. 440–461) found this canon so objectionable that he campaigned against its inclusion in the official records of the council, and he won the day by his persistence. Canon 28 was excised from the list of the council's decisions.

[12]Gregory's favorite title was *servant (or slave) of the servants (or slaves) of God,* which he is credited with coining.

[13]In Egypt.

[14]The *cathedra,* or "seat of power," the pope inherited from St. Peter.

[15]St. Peter.

[16]Eulogius.

[17]A Greek word that means *rock.*

[18]Jesus.

[19]Matthew, 16:19.

[20]Matthew, 22:32.

[21]The Gospel of John, 21:17.

[22]The see of Rome. According to tradition, Peter served as Rome's first bishop and died a martyr there in either 64 or 67.

[23]The see of Alexandria. According to tradition, Alexandria's first bishop was the evangelist,* or gospel author, St. Mark, who was sent there by St. Peter, his teacher.

[24]Note the verbs that Gregory employs: *exalted (sublimavit), honored (decoravit),* and *strengthened (firmavit).* Is this simply rhetorical variety, or does it imply something else?

[25]The see of Antioch in Syria. According to tradition, Peter served as Antioch's first bishop for seven years before leaving it for Rome.

If you believe anything good of me, impute this to your merits, because we are one in Him who says: "That they all may be one, as You, Father, are in Me and I in You, and that they may be one in Us."[26]

MISSIONARY POLICIES

4. To Augustine, bishop of the Angles[27]

Augustine's third question.

Inasmuch as there is one faith, why do the practices of churches differ? The Roman Church has one type of mass;* there is another in the churches of Gaul.

My brother, you are acquainted with the practices of the Roman Church, in which you have been nurtured. I wish, however, that if you have found any practices that might be more pleasing to God Almighty, be they the customs of the Church of Rome, or of Gaul, or of any Church whatsoever, you carefully select them out and diligently introduce to the Church of the Angles,[28] which is still new to the faith, whatever you have been able to collect from these many Churches. We ought not love things for their location; rather, we should love locations for the good things that are attached to them.

Therefore, choose from each particular Church those things that are holy, religious, and proper, and, collecting them as it were into a bundle, plant them in the minds of the Angles for their use.

5. To Mellitus, abbot traveling through Gaul[29]

Since the departure of our congregation that is with you, I have been most anxious because I have heard nothing about the success of your journey. When, however, Almighty God has brought you to our most reverend brother, Bishop Augustine, inform him that, after much deliberation, I have decided the following in regard to the issue of the Angles. The shrines of that people's idols should not be destroyed. Destroy only the idols that are in them. Take holy water and sprinkle it in these shrines. Build altars and deposit relics* in them. For if the shrines are well built,[30] it is necessary to transfer them from the worship of devils to the service of the True God. When the people see that their shrines are not destroyed, they will be able to banish error from their hearts and more comfortably come to places they are familiar with, now knowing and adoring the True God. Since they are also accustomed

---

[26]The Gospel of John, 17:21. The speaker is Jesus.

[27]Augustine, later known as *St. Augustine of Canterbury*, headed the group of forty Italian monks that Gregory dispatched in 596 to work as missionaries among the pagans of England. Augustine and his colleagues converted King Aethelbert and numerous Germans in the kingdom of Kent (see note 28). In 598 Augustine sent a letter to Pope Gregory, requesting answers to eleven issues that vexed him. The pope's illness prevented a speedy answer, but in 601 he sent back his answers, along with Augustine's commission as archbishop* of all of England. This excerpt presents Gregory's answer to one of those questions.

[28]According to the Venerable Bede, an early eighth-century historian (source 22), three different Germanic groups invaded England in the fifth century: Angles, Saxons, and Jutes. The kingdom of Kent, where Augustine began his work, was settled by Jutes, not Angles. The Angles largely settled in the north of England. As far as Gregory was concerned, however, all of the Germans of Britain were Angles. Indeed, the Angles were not that different from the Saxons and the Jutes, and what differences existed were soon submerged.

[29]Abbot Mellitus, who seems to have served as the abbot* of the Roman monastery* of St. Andrew (where Gregory had lived as a monk prior to being called out of monastic solitude by Pope Pelagius), headed the second wave of missionaries sent to England in 601. This letter, which reversed an earlier decision Pope Gregory had made concerning how pagan temples were to be dealt with, was intended to reach Mellitus as he journeyed through Gaul toward England. (See source 22 for additional information on Mellitus.)

[30]Inasmuch as ancient pagan Germans appear to have believed in worshiping out of doors, the Jutes, Angles, and Saxons probably had few, if any, structures of this sort. See Tacitus (Chapter 2, source 6) and also Charlemagne's Capitulary on Saxony (Chapter 5, source 26). Gregory seems to be viewing pagan religion with a distinctly Roman mindset.

to kill many oxen as sacrifices to demons, they should also have some solemn festivity of this sort but in a changed form. On that day of dedication[31] or on the feast days of the holy martyrs whose relics are deposited there, they may construct tents out of the branches of the trees that surround these shrines that have been transformed into churches, and they may celebrate that holy day with religious feasts. Do not let them sacrifice animals to the Devil any longer, but let them slay animals for their own eating in praise of God, and let them give thanks to the Giver of all for their full stomachs. In this way, while they retain some bodily pleasures they might more easily be able to incline their minds toward spiritual joys. Without a doubt, it is impossible to cut away everything all at once from hard hearts. One who strives to climb to the highest pinnacle must ascend by steps and paces, not by leaps.

---

[31]The day when the shrine has been consecrated to Christian use.

The Conflict over Icons

▼▼▼

21 ▼ *Pope Gregory II, LETTER TO EMPEROR LEO III*

Numerous factors, such as invasions by Lombards, Slavs, and Arabs, tended to pull Byzantium and the West apart, particularly after the age of Justinian I (Chapter 3, source 11). Despite these centrifugal forces, Italy and the Roman papacy* managed to maintain ties with Constantinople and the Eastern Church well into the eighth century. Indeed, in the century bracketed by the pontificates of Pope Theodore I (r. 642–649) and Pope Zacharias (r. 741–752), virtually every bishop* of Rome came from either Greek or Syrian stock. Contact, however, does not necessarily bring with it harmony or understanding, and during this era of the so-called Byzantine papacy, Rome and Constantinople had many disagreements on political and religious issues, the two being intimately connected.

These tensions reached a new level in 726, when Emperor Leo III (r. 717–742) inaugurated a program of *iconoclasm,* or "image breaking." Citing biblical injunctions against graven images, Leo and his advisors moved to stamp out what they considered to be an idolatrous practice: the use of sacred images, or *icons,* by the faithful in their worship. To be sure, educated churchpeople had often looked with bemusement and even suspicion on many popular practices and beliefs that had sprung up around some of the Church's more popular icons, especially those of Jesus and Mary. In their more extreme forms, some of the practices were nothing less than image worship. Yet Emperor Leo's attack on icons ran directly counter to an already centuries-old tradition of using, and even venerating, icons in order to raise the mind and heart of the worshiper to God.

Leo's program of iconoclasm, which became the official policy of the Byzantine Church down to 843 (except for a thirty-year hiatus from 786 to 816), infuriated large numbers of clerics,* monks,* and laity in the East and occasioned an equally severe reaction from the Roman papacy. In 726 or 727 Pope Gregory II (r. 715–731), a Syrian of Arabic heritage, sent the following letter to Emperor Leo in response to the imperial decree against sacred images. Unlike the angry masses in Constantinople and elsewhere in the East, who could be kept in line, at least momentarily, by imperial troops, Gregory II was sufficiently far removed from Byzantium to act with relative impunity. Even so, Emperor Leo's agent in Italy did plot, without success, the rebel pope's murder.

QUESTIONS FOR ANALYSIS

1. According to Gregory, how has Leo deviated from imperial tradition?
2. How does Gregory defend the use of icons?
3. On what grounds does Gregory base his refusal to bow to the emperor's edict?
4. Emperor Leo III once claimed, "I am the Deputy of Christ." Did Gregory II agree? Please explain your conclusion.
5. Consider the last paragraph, where Gregory refers to the support the papacy enjoys among the yet to be baptized* pagans of the West? What is his point? Does his argument have a basis in fact? Again, please explain.
6. What would Pope Gelasius I (source 19) have thought of this letter? What about Pope Gregory I (source 20)? Be specific in your answers.
7. Consider the assumptions that underlie this letter. Does Gregory II see the churches of Rome and Constantinople as essentially united or divided? On what reasoning do you base your inference?
8. Given the fact that neither Gregory nor Leo backed down, what do you suppose was the major impact of the Iconoclastic Controversy on East-West relations?

We have received the letter which you sent us by your ambassador Rufinus. We are deeply grieved that you should persist in your error, that you should refuse to recognize the things which are Christ's, and to accept the teaching and follow the example of the holy fathers,* the saintly miracle-workers and learned doctors.[1] . . . But you have followed the guidance of your own wayward spirit and have allowed the exigencies of the political situation at your own court to lead you astray. You say: "I am both emperor and bishop." But the emperors who were before you . . . proved themselves to be both emperors and bishops by following the true faith, by founding and fostering churches, and by displaying the same zeal for the faith as the popes. These emperors ruled righteously; they held synods[2] in harmony with the popes, they tried to establish true doctrines, they founded and adorned churches. Those who claim to be both emperors and priests* should demonstrate it by their works; you, since the beginning of your rule, have constantly failed to observe the decrees of the fathers. Wherever you found churches adorned and enriched with hangings you despoiled them. For what are our churches? Are they not made by hand of stones, timbers, straw, plaster, and lime? But they are also adorned with pictures and rep-

---

[1] The teachers, or doctors, of the Church. The word *doctor* originally meant "a teacher."

[2] Church councils,* especially the six ecumenical councils (note 8).

resentations of the miracles of the saints, of the sufferings of Christ, of the holy mother herself, and of the saints and apostles;* and men expend their wealth on such images. Moreover, men and women make use of these pictures to instruct in the faith their little children and young men and maidens in the bloom of youth and those from heathen nations; by means of these pictures the hearts and minds of men are directed to God. But you have ordered the people to abstain from the pictures, and have attempted to satisfy them with idle sermons, trivialities, music of pipe and zither, rattles and toys, turning them from the giving of thanks to the hearing of idle tales. You shall have your part with them, and with those who invent useless fables and babble of their ignorance. Hearken to us, emperor: abandon your present course and accept the holy Church as you found her, for matters of faith and practice concern not the emperor, but the pope, since we have the mind of Christ.[3] The making of laws for the Church is one thing and the governing of the empire another; the ordinary intelligence which is used in administering worldly affairs is not adequate to the settlement of spiritual matters. Behold, I will show you now the difference between the palace and the church, between the emperor and the pope; learn this and be saved; be no longer contentious. If anyone should take from you the adornments of royalty, your purple robes, diadem, sceptre, and your ranks of servants, you would be regarded by men as base, hateful, and abject; but to this condition you have reduced the churches, for you have deprived them of their ornaments and made them unsightly. Just as the pope has not the right to interfere in the palace or to infringe upon the royal prerogatives, so the emperor has not the right to interfere in the churches, or to conduct elections among the clergy,* or to consecrate, or to administer the sac-

raments,* or even to participate in the sacraments without the aid of a priest; let each one of us abide in the same calling wherein he is called of God.[4] Do you see, emperor, the difference between popes and emperors? If anyone has offended you, you confiscate his house and take everything from him but his life, or you hang him or cut off his head, or you banish him, sending him far from his children and from all his relatives and friends. But popes do not so; when anyone has sinned and has confessed,* in place of hanging him or cutting off his head, they put the gospel* and the cross about his neck, and imprison him, as it were, in the sacristy or the treasure chamber of the sacred vessels; they put him into the part of the church reserved for the deacons and the catechumens;[5] they prescribe for him fasting, vigils, and praise. And after they have chastened and punished him with fasting, then they give him of the precious body of the Lord and of the holy blood. And when they have restored him as a chosen vessel, free from sin, they hand him over to the Lord pure and unspotted. Do you see now, emperor, the difference between the Church and the empire? Those emperors who have lived piously in Christ have obeyed the popes, and not vexed them. But you, emperor, since you have transgressed and gone astray, and since you have written with your own hand and confessed that he who attacks the fathers is to be execrated, have thereby condemned yourself by your own sentence and have driven from you the Holy Spirit.* You persecute us and vex us tyrannically with violent and carnal hand. We, unarmed and defenseless, possessing no earthly armies, call now upon the prince of all the armies of creation, Christ seated in the heavens, commanding all the hosts of celestial beings, to send a demon upon you;[6] as the apostle says: "To deliver such a one unto Satan for the

---

[3]See St. Paul's First Letter to the Corinthians, 2:16.
[4]Ibid., 7:20.

[5]Catechumens, who were preparing to become baptized Christians, were not allowed to enter the main area of the church. In the room set aside for them, they were instructed in the faith by deacons.
[6]This is a formal curse, or sentence of excommunication.*

destruction of the flesh, that the spirit may be saved."[7] Do you see now, emperor, to what a pitch of impudence and inhumanity you have gone? You have driven your soul headlong into the abyss, because you would not humble yourself and bend your stubborn neck. When a pope is able by his teaching and admonition to bring the emperor of his time before God, guiltless and cleansed from all sin, he gains great glory from Him on the holy day of resurrection, when all our secrets and all our works are brought to light to our confusion in the presence of his angels. But we shall blush for shame, because you will have lost your soul by your disobedience, while the popes that preceded us have won over to God the emperors of their times. How ashamed we will be on that day, that the emperor of our time is false and ignominious, instead of great and glorious. Now, therefore, we exhort you to do penance; be converted and turn to the truth; obey the truth as you found and received it. Honor and glorify our holy and glorious fathers and doctors who dispelled the blindness from our eyes and restored us to sight. You ask: "How was it that nothing was said about images in six councils?"[8] What then? Nothing was said about bread or water, whether that should be eaten or not; whether this should be drunk or not; yet these things have been accepted from the beginning for the preservation of human life. So also images have been accepted; the popes themselves brought them to councils, and no Christian would set out on a journey without images, because they were possessed of virtue and approved of by God. We exhort you to be both emperor and bishop, as you have called yourself in your letter. But if you are ashamed to take this upon yourself as emperor, then write to all the regions to which you have given offence, that Gregory the pope and Germanos the patriarch* of Constantinople[9] are at fault in the matter of the images [that is, are responsible for the destruction of the images], and we will take upon ourselves the responsibility for the sin, as we have authority from God to loose and to bind all things, earthly and celestial; and we will free you from responsibility in this matter. But no, you will not do this! Knowing that we would have to render account to Christ the Lord for our office, we have done our best to convert you from your error, by admonition and warning, but you have drawn back, you have refused to obey us or Germanos or our fathers, the holy and glorious miracle-workers and doctors, and you have followed the teaching of perverse and wicked men who wander from the truth. You shall have your lot with them. As we have already informed you, we shall proceed on our way to the extreme western regions, where those who are earnestly seeking to be baptized are awaiting us. For although we have sent them bishops and clergymen from our church, their princes have not yet been induced to bow their heads and be baptized, because they hope to be received into the Church by us in person. Therefore we gird ourselves for the journey in the goodness of God, lest perchance we should have to render account for their condemnation and for our faithlessness. May God give you prudence and patience, that you may be turned to the truth from which you have departed; may he again restore the people to their one shepherd, Christ, and to the one fold of the orthodox* churches and prelates,* and may the Lord our God give peace to all the earth now and forever to all generations. Amen.

---

[7]St. Paul, First Letter to the Corinthians, 5:5.

[8]The (up-to-then) six ecumenical councils of the Church, whose decisions were considered infallible: Nicaea (held in 325); Constantinople (381); Ephesus (431); Chalcedon (451); II Constantinople (553); and III Constantinople (681). All had been held in the East under imperial patronage, and the bishops of Rome played negligible roles in most of them, except for Pope Leo I's impact on the Council of Chalcedon (source 20, note 11).

[9]Emperor Leo forced the resignation of Patriarch Germanos I (r. 715–730), because the patriarch opposed the edict against images.

▼▼▼

Bishops and Saints

Despite their intention to remain apart from the world, monks* could and did have an impact on the lives of common men and women, as sources 17 and 20 illustrate. Popes, by their policies, actions, and words, also influenced the lives of countless commoners. Yet so far as most people were concerned, the individuals who most represented the power of Christianity were the *secular clerics** and the saints, both living and dead, who resided among them.

*Secular** means "worldly," and in a clerical* context, it refers to the clergy* whose primary vocation is to live among the laity and to minister to its spiritual needs. As such, secular clerics stand in contrast to *regular clerics,** such as monks, whose primary vocation is to live apart from the world in communities governed by a special rule (*regula* in Latin). Whereas monks at this time usually lived in autonomous, self-governing monasteries,* secular clerics were part of a hierarchical network that tied small village churches to larger urban churches, where their bishops* and archbishops* resided. Most bishops had their *sees,** or seats of power, in small to moderate-sized towns and ruled over the secular clerics of the surrounding region, called a *diocese.** Bishops whose sees were located in larger or more politically important centers exercised more extensive authority by virtue of the size and importance of their sees. Known as an *archbishop,* each exercised supervisory rights over all other bishops whose dioceses were located in the *province** that centered on his seat of power. Many archbishops held regular provincial councils,* or *synods,** at which they and their subordinate bishops addressed provincewide issues. Yet so far as the vast majority of humanity in Christian Europe was concerned, the local diocesan bishop was as far up the ecclesiastical* ladder as an individual could or should go. He and his secular clergy constituted their Church, and certainly the Holy Father in faraway Rome was more remote and disassociated from their lives than even the great archbishop.

As Christianity expanded into pagan lands, often as a result of monastic missionaries, it became necessary to establish new archbishoprics and bishoprics in order to expand and solidify the gains made by the first wave of missionaries. Without the day-to-day ministrations of bishops, priests,* deacons,* and other secular clerics, it would not have been possible to transform Europe into a civilization that looked to Roman Catholic Christianity for moral and religious guidance.

Even more important to these Christian Europeans than the priests and bishops who guided them were the saints who protected them. We have already seen in Chapter 2, source 9, the power that the relics* of dead saints had on the imaginations and practices of Christians. In essence, they believed that saints never truly died. As tokens of their favor and power, saints left behind the mortal bodies they had shed, and whoever possessed and properly venerated these corporal relics had strong advocates in Heaven. Saints, however, were not just holy people from the past; they walked among God's people at all times. Each community had its local, still-breathing saints, who, according to wide opinion, lived heroically Christian lives and, by that heroism, brought blessings down on the entire community.

Sanctity, of course, is hard to define, and its blessings are often difficult to identify. What is holy zeal in one person's eyes might be erratic behavior in another's. Living saints were often controversial individualists, who lived on the margins of society and behaved in ways often considered eccentric and even unbalanced. For every person edified by the heroically holy actions of some putative living saint, there was probably another who found the zealot's enthusiasm disturbing.

The following two sources show saintly archbishops and a saintly commoner at work. The first document illustrates how the early seventh-century missionary archbishopric of Canterbury fared in the face of various crises. The second source illustrates how one late-ninth-century clerical author believed that a holy Saxon woman had spiritually protected and served her East German people. It also suggests that, in so doing, the woman had acted in ways that some might have perceived as decidedly eccentric and even unnatural.

The Trials and Triumphs
of England's Missionary Bishops
▼▼▼

22 ▼ *Bede the Venerable,*
HISTORY OF THE ENGLISH CHURCH
AND PEOPLE

St. Bede the Venerable (ca. 672–735) was a descendant of the pagan Angles who, in concert with their Germanic cousins, the Saxons and the Jutes, migrated into Britain during the fifth century and overwhelmed the Romanized Celtic inhabitants of the land they then transformed into England — the land of the Angles. These were the same people to whom Pope St. Gregory the Great had sent missionary monks at the end of the sixth century (source 20). The labors of these and other missionaries were successful, and by Bede's day, England was dotted with Catholic bishoprics* and monasteries.

Arguably the greatest historian in the West between A.D. 400 and 1100, Bede was a monk of the abbey* of Jarrow in the northern English kingdom of Northumbria. He entered that monastery at age seven and rarely left it (and then, only to visit other monastic houses for short visits). Although cloister walls enclosed his person, they failed to imprison his mind or fame. In later life, he became quite well known throughout Christian Europe for his spirituality and erudition. He was an outstanding classical scholar, a student of Greek and Hebrew as well as a master of Latin, who used his monastery's well-stocked library to great advantage. A prolific author, his writings ranged over a wide area of interests, but his greatest publication, and the work for which he is best remembered today, is his *History of the English Church and People*.

Bede's history traces the fortunes of Christianity in England down to the year 731. His precision, accuracy, and painstaking research techniques marked him as a first-rate historian in an age and culture that little appreciated or understood historical scholarship. He scrupulously investigated every available source in order to uncover all relevant facts. Moreover, his history bore the imprint of an orderly, as well as inquisitive, mind. Extraneous materials were culled, so that nothing detracted from his work's central theme: the triumphal progress of orthodox* Roman Catholic Christianity in England.

In the following selection, Bede recounts the adventures of three early seventh-century missionary bishops: Laurentius, Mellitus, and Justus. All three were Roman monks (but not Benedictines) whom Pope Gregory I had dispatched to England to assist Augustine in the conversion of the English, and each, in turn, served as archbishop of Canterbury. Although in theory, monks did not serve as secular clergy,* extraordinary times called for extraordinary measures.

QUESTIONS FOR ANALYSIS

1. Consider Aethelbert, Eadbald, Sathbert, and Sathbert's sons. What roles could and did kings and other great lords play in promoting or hampering the efforts of bishops?
2. How deeply had Christianity penetrated southern England during the first several decades of the seventh century?
3. If kings could offer protection to the Church and its clerics, what could the Church and its clerics offer kings in return?
4. Why was it St. Peter and not another saint who appeared to Laurentius and prevented his leaving England?
5. What sort of service and protection did these three bishops offer the Angles, Saxons, and other peoples of Britain? In addressing this question, it might be helpful to compare them with St. Gall (source 18).
6. Consider again the story of Mellitus and the fire. How did this prescientific society explain extraordinary natural phenomena?
7. These three bishops were monks, but in what ways did they differ from the ideal monk envisioned by St. Benedict (source 17)? Why do you think the Church used monks in this manner?
8. What evidence does this account provide that papal* Rome had, by the early seventh century, essentially replaced imperial Rome as the West's new center of focus and organization?

In the year of our Lord's incarnation 616,[1] which is the twenty-first year after Augustine and his companions were sent to preach to the English nation, Aethelbert, king of Kent, having most gloriously governed his temporal kingdom fifty-six years, entered into the eternal joys of the kingdom which is heavenly.[2] He was the third of the English kings that had the sovereignty of all the southern provinces that are divided from the northern by the river Humber, and the borders contiguous to the same,[3] but the first of the kings that ascended to the heavenly kingdom.[4] . . . King Aethelbert died on the 24th day of the month of February, twenty-one years after he had received the faith, and was buried in St. Martin's porch within the church of the blessed apostles* Peter and Paul,[5] where also lies his queen, Bertha.[6] Among other benefits which he conferred upon the nation, he also, by the advice of wise persons, introduced judicial decrees, after the Roman model; which, being written in English, are still kept and observed by them. Among which, he in the first place set down what satisfaction should be given by those who should steal anything belonging to the church, the bishop, or the other clergy, resolving to give protection to those whose doctrine he had embraced. . . .

But after the death of Aethelbert, the accession of his son Eadbald proved very prejudicial to the new Church; for he not only refused to embrace the faith of Christ, but was also defiled with such a sort of fornication, as the apostle testifies, was not heard of, even among the Gentiles; for he kept his father's wife.[7] By both which crimes he gave occasion to those to return to their former uncleanness, who, under his father, had, either for favor, or through fear of the king, submitted to the laws of faith and chastity. Nor did the perfidious king escape without divine punishment and correction; for he was troubled with frequent fits of madness, and possessed by an evil spirit. This confusion was increased by the death of Sabert, king of the East Saxons,[8] who departing to the heavenly kingdom, left three sons, still pagans, to inherit his temporal crown. They immediately began to profess idolatry, which, during their father's reign, they had seemed a little to abandon, and they granted free liberty to the people under their government to serve idols. And when they saw the bishop,[9] while celebrating mass* in the church, give the eucharist[10] to the people, they, puffed up with barbarous folly, were wont, as it is reported, to say to him, "Why do you not give us also that white bread, which you used to give to our father Saba, (for so they used to call him,) and which you still continue to give to the people in the church?" To whom he answered, "If you will be washed in that laver[11] of salvation, in which your father was washed, you may also partake of the holy bread of which he partook; but if you despise the laver of life, you may not receive the bread of life." They replied, "We will not enter into that laver, because we do not know that we stand in need of

---

[1] More than any other single work, Bede's history was instrumental in popularizing in the West the convention of dating all time in relation to the Year of Grace (Jesus' birth): hence, B.C. (before Christ) and A.D. (*Anno Domini,* "in the year of the Lord").

[2] Aethelbert (r. 560–616), king of Kent in southeastern England, who was converted to Christianity in 597.

[3] He was a *bretwalda,* or "king of kings," and his domain was all of southern England.

[4] The first English king to die a Christian.

[5] The monastic church that Augustine founded at Canterbury and that served as his cathedral,* or archiepiscopal seat. The dedication to Saints Peter and Paul stressed the new English Church's allegiance to the Roman papacy.*

[6] Aethelbert's first wife, a Christian who had been instrumental in her husband's patronage of these monastic missionaries and his conversion to Christianity. Compare her role with that of Clotilda in Chapter 2, source 9.

[7] A wife whom Aethelbert had apparently married after Bertha's death.

[8] The subkingdom of Essex. Sabert had been a subordinate king under Aethelbert.

[9] The bishop is Mellitus, whom we saw in source 20. Augustine had consecrated Mellitus as a bishop in 604 and sent him to London in Essex; there, he established his cathedral church, which he dedicated to St. Paul.

[10] The holy communion host, or consecrated bread, that Catholics and other Christians believe is the body of Christ.

[11] A large basin for ritual ablutions. Here, it means the baptismal* font.

it, and yet we will eat of that bread." And being often earnestly admonished by him, that the same could not be done, nor any one admitted to partake of the sacred oblation[12] without the holy cleansing, at last they said in anger, "If you will not comply with us in so small a matter as that which we require, you shall not stay in our province." And accordingly they obliged him and his followers to depart from their kingdom. Being forced from thence, he came into Kent, to advise with his fellow bishops, Laurentius and Justus,[13] what was to be done in that case; and it was unanimously agreed, that it was better for them all to return to their own country, where they might serve God in freedom, than to continue without any advantage among those barbarians, who had revolted from the faith. Mellitus and Justus accordingly went away first, and withdrew into Gaul, designing there to await the event of things. But the kings, who had driven from them the preacher of the truth, did not continue long unpunished in their heathenish worship. For marching out to battle against the nation of the West Saxons, they were all slain with their army. However, the people, having been once turned to wickedness, though the authors of it were destroyed, would not be corrected, nor return to the unity of faith and charity which is in Christ.

Laurentius, being about to follow Mellitus and Justus, and to quit Britain, ordered his bed to be laid the night before in the church of the blessed apostles, Peter and Paul, which has been often mentioned before; wherein having laid himself to take some rest, after he had poured out many prayers and tears to God for the state of the church, he fell asleep; in the dead of night,

the blessed prince of the apostles appeared to him, and scourging him a long time with apostolic severity, asked of him why he would forsake the flock which he had committed to him, or to what shepherds he would commit Christ's sheep that were in the midst of wolves? "Have you," said he, "forgotten my example, who, for the sake of those little ones, whom Christ recommended to me in token of his affection, underwent at the hands of infidels and enemies of Christ, bonds, stripes, imprisonment, afflictions, and lastly, the death of the cross,[14] that I might at last be crowned with Him?" Laurentius, the servant of Christ, being excited by these words and stripes, the very next morning repaired to the king, and taking off his garment, showed the scars of the stripes which he had received. The king, astonished, asked, "Who had presumed to give such stripes to so great a man?" And was much frightened when he heard that the bishop had suffered so much at the hands of the apostle of Christ for his salvation. Then abjuring the worship of idols, and renouncing his unlawful marriage, he embraced the faith of Christ, and being baptized,* promoted the affairs of the church to the utmost of his power.

He also sent over into Gaul, and recalled Mellitus and Justus, and commanded them freely to return to govern their churches, which they accordingly did, one year after their departure. Justus, indeed, returned to the city of Rochester, where he had before presided; but the Londoners would not receive Bishop Mellitus, choosing rather to be under their idolatrous high priests; for King Eadbald had not so much authority in the kingdom as his father, nor was he able to restore the bishop to his church against

---

[12]The eucharist,* which is offered as a sacrifice as well as an act of adoration and thanksgiving.

[13]Laurentius, whom Augustine had consecrated as his successor, succeeded Augustine as archbishop of Canterbury in 604 or 605 and served in that office until his death in 619, whereupon he was succeeded by Mellitus. When Mellitus died in 624, Justus, who had been bishop of Rochester since 604, became the fourth archbishop of Canterbury.

[14]According to tradition, Peter was fleeing Rome when he had a vision of Jesus, who was carrying a cross. Upon being asked by Peter where he was headed, Jesus replied, "To Rome to be crucified again." Peter then returned to Rome, was captured, and was crucified upside down.

the will and consent of the pagans. But he and his nation, after his conversion to our Lord, diligently followed the divine precepts. . . .

In this king's reign, the holy Archbishop Laurentius was taken up to the heavenly kingdom: he was buried in the church and monastery of the holy Apostle Peter, close by his predecessor Augustine, on the 2nd day of the month of February. Mellitus, who was bishop of London, was the third archbishop of Canterbury from Augustine; Justus, who was still living, governed the church of Rochester. These ruled the church of the English with much industry and labor, and received letters of exhortation from Boniface, bishop of the Roman apostolic see, who presided over the church after Deusdedit, in the year of our Lord 619.[15] Mellitus labored under an infirmity of body, that is, the gout; but his mind was sound, cheerfully passing over all earthly things, and always aspiring to love, seek, and attain to those which are celestial. He was noble by birth, but much nobler in mind.

In short, that I may give one testimony of his virtue, by which the rest may be guessed at, it happened once that the city of Canterbury, being by carelessness set on fire, was in danger of being consumed by the spreading conflagration; water was thrown over the fire in vain; a considerable part of the city was already destroyed, and the fierce flame advancing towards the bishop, when he, confiding in the divine assistance, where human failed, ordered himself to be carried towards the raging fire, that was spreading on every side. The Shrine of the Four Crowned Martyrs[16] was in the place where the fire raged most. The bishop being carried thither by his servants, the sick man averted the danger by prayer, which a number of strong men had not been able to perform by much labor. Immediately, the wind, which blowing from the south had spread the conflagration throughout the city, turning to the north, prevented the destruction of those places that had lain in its way, and then ceasing entirely, the flames were immediately extinguished. And thus the man of God, whose mind was inflamed with the fire of divine charity, and who was wont to drive away the powers of the air by his frequent prayers, from doing harm to himself, or his people, was deservedly allowed to prevail over the worldly winds and flames, and to obtain that they should not injure him or his.

---

[15]Pope Boniface V (r. 619–625), who followed Deusdedit (r. 615–618).

[16]According to one legend, they were four Christian sculptors who refused to carve idols of the gods and were consequently martyred during the reign of Diocletian. A major church known as *Quattuor Coronati* stood (and one still stands there) on Rome's Celian hill, not far from the monastery of St. Andrew, where Augustine and his companions had been monks. Augustine probably brought relics from this Roman church to Canterbury and there established a shrine dedicated to the Four Crowned Martyrs.

Sanctity in Ninth-Century Saxony
▼▼▼
23 ▼ *THE LIFE OF THE VIRGIN LIUTBIRG*

Laurentius, Mellitus, and Justus are *canonized* saints; that is, they are numbered among the holy persons listed in the official *canon,*[*] or authoritative list, of saints recognized by the Catholic Church. For every saint officially recognized by Rome, however, there were scores and even hundreds of holy people whose cults never extended beyond the communities in which they lived and died. This was especially so in the formative centuries of European Christianity, long before the Roman papacy* instituted a formal process of saintly canonization. Like their more famous counterparts, these local saints served as models of spiritual heroism, as it was understood by the society that venerated them, and they offered their neighbors, in both life and death, protection from evil in all its forms. Of course, not all of the saints' contemporaries saw them in this light. Some people, perhaps many, were disturbed by their local saints' often eccentric behavior.

One local saint whose behavior both edified and troubled those who knew her was the Saxon woman Liutbirg (ca. 800–ca. 876). Between 772 and 804 Charles the Great waged a war of conquest and conversion against the pagan Saxons to the northeast of his Frankish lands (Chapter 5, sources 24 and 26). Just about the time that Charles's soldiers and missionaries were completing the absorption of the Saxons into Charles's empire, Liutbirg was born, possibly to parents who were still pagans. Whatever the case, the young Liutbirg became a servant in the house of Countess Gisela, one of the most powerful Christian Saxon landholders of the early ninth century and daughter of Count Hessi, who had thrown his lot in with Charlemagne in 775. Liutbirg's personal qualities and skills soon endeared her to Gisela, who treated her like a daughter. Following Gisela's death sometime after 814, Liutbirg served Gisela's son and heir, Bernhard, as steward of his estates and all-around factotum. While functioning as a successful manager, Liutbirg also exhibited the qualities of a religious zealot; in time, she prevailed upon the reluctant Bernhard to allow her to put aside her managerial responsibilities in order to devote the rest of her life to prayer and self-mortification as an *inclusa,* or female religious shut-in — apparently, the first in all of Saxony. For reasons we can only guess at, the cult of St. Liutbirg never reached beyond her own home region, and even there it passed out of fashion after several centuries. Notwithstanding, Liutbirg's life and legend present an insightful picture of the strong role that one extraordinary holy woman could and did play in ninth-century Europe.

The following excerpts, which begin with Liutbirg's functioning as the manager of Count Bernhard's estates and end with her death in a hermitage, come from an anonymous biography dated about 876 and composed by a cleric* who obviously had known the then-dead holy woman. The genre to which this *vita,* or "life," belongs is known as *hagiography,* which literally means "something written about a saint." As we might expect, most hagiographical literature is one dimensional. The genre demands that the author focus on the subject's heroic virtues and spiritual life. Rarely do hagiographies provide any substantial detail about the holy person's life outside a religious context.

QUESTIONS FOR ANALYSIS

1. How did Liutbirg display her religious zeal while serving as Count Bernhard's steward? Why did she desire to do more?
2. Count Bernhard was troubled by some of Liutbirg's pious activities and her wish to do more. Why?

3. Consider the clerical author's treatment of these prehermitage years. What does he seem to think of Liutbirg's early enthusiasm and its consequences?

4. Why was Bishop Theotgrimus at first reluctant to grant Liutbirg permission to live in isolation?

5. Liutbirg eventually persuaded the count and the bishop* to grant her wish. How did she achieve this, and what do you infer from your answer?

6. Holy people who follow their own visions of godliness can be threatening to the established Church. Describe Liutbirg's relationship with the Church's hierarchy. Was she threatening to the Church? What inferences follow from your answers? Explain them in detail.

7. How did Liutbirg meet the temptations and dangers that beset her in her hermitage?

8. Compare Liutbirg's confrontation with demons with that of Saint Gall (source 18). Do you perceive any differences? If so, how do you explain them?

9. What sort of power and authority did Liutbirg have after her inclusion in her cell? What were the origins of that power?

10. What, if anything, is so significant about St. Martin of Tours's appearance to Liutbirg?

11. As far as you can infer, what does the author wish us to learn from this life of St. Liutbirg?

Bernhard was mindful that he had many possessions . . . , and to whichever of his properties he journeyed, he did not easily sustain the temporary absence of his venerable woman,[1] since she was the guardian and faithful steward of his properties.

Whenever she stayed anywhere for a period of time, she did not neglect to frequent the churches of God which she visited day and night. Assiduously attending divine worship, she spent the whole night without sleep, until the light of day. In her holy work, she bore not the slightest damage, so much that she was considered effective in every one of her undertakings, and her strenuous perseverance was held as a great miracle. It was clearly evident to all who knew her that the continuous labor was exacted not from the powers of her weak body, but by the aid of the Divine. The constancy of her mind was, without doubt, invigorated and breathed upon by a spirit from Heaven. Throughout this long, burdensome, serious duty she did not yield, she did not tire, she did not bend her neck. Always, with

unbroken powers, she was busy in her wrestling bout against the allures of the world and the filthiness of the flesh. She trampled, with the unharmed foot of chastity, lewdness of the body and flattering wantonness of the mind, which was advising licentiousness. With the hoe of sobriety she endeavored to pluck the prickly fruits from thorns with the roots of amusements.

As we anticipated, she was weakened by the fasts and vigils. Her body was enervated by her manual labor, just as it was consumed by abstinence. The color of her face changed, and her skin, sticking to her bones, attenuated her thinning appearance. The great part of this came about from her nocturnal vigils, which exposed her to the highest degree of danger. . . .

Then, that same count, seeing the appearance of her face, so thin and quite wasted in its meagerness, turned to her and asked those standing near him: "What illness does our beloved mother Liutbirg have?" The response given was that this could not be attributed to illness, but more to her perpetual abstinence and vigils, and that the

---

[1]Liutbirg.

ill treatment of her body was excessive. Continuously added to this was the dangerous nocturnal trip to the churches. This, it was common knowledge, was every night with the attendance of only one small little boy or little girl, and in her bare feet.

Astounded, the count called her to him and, in the customary manner, addressed her with honorific and flattering words, and said: "Why, dearest mother, you who have always offered yourself as a mirror of seriousness of morals and of honesty of life, excelling others, not only in your words but also in your deeds, why do you now endeavor to assure yourself, as if on a road of headlong descent, an early death, before the time predestined for you by God? It is indeed something feared even by armed men, when plundering, taking place day and night by pagans and falsely-named Christians, disturbs the hearts of strong men. Even if the danger of such great madness were absent, what else would you have offered yourself as, except willing prey for the teeth of wild beasts and for the bites of wolves? It could only be said, by those grieving or by our enemies, that your act was the utter folly of vain superstitions. The reputation of the excellence of your prior life would be counted as nothing."

Liutbirg immediately answered him, with lowered voice: "I beseech you, my lord, do not listen to the chattering of those most worthless men. They always, with rash mouth, heap insults upon those living piously and sensibly. They rage, with mad jaws, against good deeds, and with poisoned tongue tear them to pieces with all their might. . . . Where is the authority of those who were once great? Where are the riches of the wealthy? Where are the strongmen's powers which have been told about? Where are those wallowing in magnificent excess, and those servitors of insatiable gluttony or vile lust? Where indeed are those who have swallowed, in their perpetually thirsty mouth, whomever they could for the sake of gold and silver and property? Such are those,

the more they drink, the more they will thirst. These are the ones who store up these things, and don't know with whom they assemble; their money, acquired from robberies and thievings, follows its lovers to perdition. We do not fear them much, as the Lord says, 'Do not fear those who kill the body: they are not able to kill the soul; but rather fear him who is able to destroy both the body and the soul in Gehenna.'[2]

"What more than anything else can our wish be, than that the Lord make us earn his grace, and that our mortal body may merit becoming a partaker of his immortality in his kingdom?"

With these and other similar words, she guided the agitated mind of the count to pious tranquility, and the tumor of enraged frenzy, which had started to grow, vanished, sedated by the surgeon's blade. Turning to her, he said, 'With your feelings, which, in my opinion are more than divine, you have tied my heart so much to your just desires that I set utterly nothing against them; I beg, let Him, for whose name you have not been afraid to take hold of difficulties of such great gravity, carry out your prayers. And whatever your will may be, you will obtain."

She, exhilarated in her innermost heart by the words which revealed this sentiment, wished to throw herself at his feet, but he did not allow it. "I receive this with pleasure, my lord," she said, "with my heart thankful for the great favor of your piety, and with the gift divinely granted, I do not cease giving thanks with all my heart, if the petition is granted."

But he said, "Pray tell me, without concealment, what is in your heart. I confess myself, as I promised a little while age, determined by your reasonable petitions to offer, God willing, my life and powers." Then she, with a long, deep breath, and with tears breaking forth, said, "I am a very great sinner, lord, held back by many chains. Up to this point in my life, I have led a life spoiled with all desires and straying into all the pleasures of this world. . . . I ask your kindness of some place to live, so that I may be able

---

[2]The Gospel of Matthew, 10:28; *Gehenna* is hell.

to persist for the rest of my life in penitence for my offences, and to ask for blessings of those who, for the sake of God, visit upon me, a wretch, works of piety. This, so I believe, my lord, will be happily returned to you and to your mother of venerable memory, with a gift of uninterrupted duration. . . ."

Then he, with a peaceful face, responded, "And where will we be able to find a place of such great quietude, so that you might shelter secure, without the world's turbulent clatter and stormy disturbances?" Then she said, "I have already seen a place agreeable to me for the days of my unimportance. There, if your goodness ordered it made into a small cell, it will suffice as a habitation, and, delightful and pleasant, it will abound in place of the riches of the world for my lifetime.

He, admiring the self-possession of the small woman, and the confidence of her brave spirit, said, after a long silence: "The sentiment expressed by your words so far, that you attempt to undertake a life solitary, secluded, and sequestered from others who dwell together, is something not customary, as of yet, in these parts. The judgments of priests* and our bishop, more than those of the laity should be summoned especially for this."

She continued, "By no means, my lord, have I imagined such a thing should be begun, except that it be decided upon by holy and prudent examination by our rectors that the Lord's will, and not my own, should be carried out, and their counsel should be made known as to how these things should be undertaken."

They decided that the bishop and priests should agreeably air and wisely deliberate their position about these thoughts, within a suitable period of time. At the end of this conversation, having faith in the promises, she reverted to her cheerful spirit, completely submitting the hope of her affairs to divine goodness.

It happened, after some space of time, that the bishop of that province, Theotgrimus[3] of blessed memory, came to the house of the previously mentioned count. There had always been a firm friendship between them. He stayed all night, and on the next day, the venerable Liutbirg saw the timely opportunity to be present, and to disclose the secrets of her desirous mind to so great a counsellor. By God's arrangement, she found a suitable time and place, and humbly prostrating herself at the feet of the bishop, she declared, with submissive voice, her need of his clemency.

He was astounded in his mind, since she had previously been well known to him as one completely dedicated to virtuous behaviour. He knew that she was, to her lord, like a mother, so there was much sympathy in his heart, and he spoke to her with these kind words: "Ahh, beloved sister, explain freely whatever thoughts of your mind must be declared. God granting, you have spontaneously found in me a comforter of your anxiety."

She . . . mentioned that she was a sinner, and testified that she was guilty of innumerable offenses. In supplication, she implored his aid for the sins she had committed, and quickly laid out the thoughts her mind was concealing.

Alertly, he concentrated on the sentiment of her words, knowing that, as far as he was able, he should always be a supporter, rather than a rejector, of righteous desires and passions. After a short silence, he looked at her keenly and said: "Beloved daughter, bearing in mind that your soul's intention flows from a spring of piety, we feel that the way in which one might safely pursue this course must be deliberated beforehand with prudent counsel. Divine aid must be sought especially, so that with God, the author and ally of all good things, our deliberations in this matter come out well. With this helmsman at the beginning of such a voyage, it is possible to reach a safe harbor." And saying these things, he asked that Bernhard be summoned to him, and proposed to sit down with him. When they were sitting together, the bishop said to him: . . .

---

[3]Bishop of Halberstadt (r. 827–840).

"This is the path which our sister hastens to take up. But the army of adversaries that besets her in bands must be dealt with. They are in many, almost innumerable squadrons. Here is Pride, leading her multitude of soldiers. She raises up victory banners not only for evil deeds, but also for things well-done. There the phalanx of Covetousness, with its banners and many generals, at this moment presents arms soaked with brotherly blood.

"After that, on one side, the alluring camps of Lust hold a multitude of people by means of various pleasures. On the other side, Appetite and Gluttony, allies of Passion and Desire, sit barricaded. Here is Wrath, armed with torches; there the poisoned javelins of Jealousy and Hatred are bunched together. Here are the troops of Arrogance; there is Pretense, painted with many colors and protected by the allied veil of Falsehood. Here is the pit of Deceit, open in a wide abyss; there the thousand snares of Malice are hidden, with deeply dug traps all around. No one walks safely through them, unless he led by divine power. . . .

"It is known that demons are always deceptive, although, when they declare deceitful tricks as true, they sometimes are able to deceive those of simpler minds by placing before them a manifestation of truth, just as in the art of fishing, one holds in front of its mouth a hook enclosed with food pleasing to the fish. By this entrapment of the enticer, the fish is ensnared by the feasts in which it was accustomed to delight. Just so, our adversary, holding out in all directions the perverse pretense of his cleverness, is accustomed, as we have said, to seize the pious minds of simple folk with various spiders' webs. The point of the hidden sword vibrates especially in a show of truth while striking very negligent minds. . . .

"In spite of these and other countless dangers, the faithful person has been aroused in his soul and released from such illusions. Fortified by divine aid, the prudent mind, being aware far in advance of the frightful disturbances of the adversarial crowds, is freed from the traps of the enemy. . . . Commending itself in all things to divine protection, it easily will overcome such a massive attack, a legion of enemies with their villainous tricks, just as clouds will be scattered with the arriving wind, or fog by the shining sun, since the virtue of Christ, which destroyed their power, placed their leader[4] in eternal chains.

"And so their power, growing languid, will fail; just as when fire will have come over stalks of straw, they will return nothing other than the crackling of their delusion. Therefore, dearest daughter, caution is necessary, so that one may examine every direction with circumspection. If one stands firm, with unconquered mind, against the tricks, clever deceits, and spiritual villainy of the enemy, he might also be sufficient to bear impartially the slander and mockery of evil men, and the empty flatteries of some men and the praises of deceivers.

"Since one who will have preferred to start something extraordinary among those with whom he lived, strives to show, in the eyes of all, a miracle as if of some prodigy, and to open the mouths of many, it is then necessary to take the middle road. One must look ahead with the greatest care, falling neither to the right through vain glory, nor to the left into the pit of desperation. He must unfailingly supplicate divine aid that, Christ our Savior permitting, things which were begun arrive at a good end."

After the bishop had so advised her, she again humbled herself at his feet, repeating her thanks to him. "Thanks be to God. . . . I entrust my hope in Him who created me and arranged my life so far. I firmly believe in Him, by whose help, unworthy though I am, I will not be disappointed. Be mindful, therefore, holy priest, of your word, by which you have given me hope." . . . [Then] she said: I ask the benevolence of your piety toward me. Set the time and day, so that God's will concerning me, a wretch, might be fulfilled." Consequently, the bishop, along with

---

[4]The Devil.

the count, marveled greatly at her constancy of mind, and they both agreed to what she had asked be done and set a day to meet at the location she desired.

At the agreed upon time, the aforesaid bishop, with not a small number of priests and with a numerous collection of the second order[5] and those of the lower ranks,[6] blessed with his benediction the cell of the small house, now prepared for work. He blessed the cell with the water of aspersion.[7] When she had entered that house, which was as small as a hut, he forbade her to leave it, unless some extremely great necessity assailed. . . .

▷ While enclosed in her cell, Liutbirg is often visited by demons who torment and tempt her.

It is not possible to relate to anyone how she put up with the great number of snares of her enemies and the various trickeries of the devil she patiently endured, whether through the contrivances of hostile terrors or through the phantasms of his sly cleverness or through visions and hallucinations of celestial cities used by him. He always, in the manner of seduction, mixed true things with false, which made him more easily capable of dragging her unguarded mind from the recognition of truth to false ideas. . . .

Exhibiting another instrument to bodily eyes since he never ceases to extend more tightly the snares of his wickedness whether through perverse thoughts or wicked desires, he assailed her with terrors. One time, coming in the guise of a boy and sitting on the sill of the front window, he shouted to her. Prostrate in prayer, she did not give an answer to him. And he, with a louder shout, said: "Liutbirg, do you fear me?" Raising herself up, her prayer being finished, she said to him: "Why should I fear you, who have no power

except that which is allowed to you by God, in whose hand all powers exist? I fear him who has the power to destroy body and soul in Gehenna." But he responded: "If you do not fear me, I shall find you someone to fear." He left suddenly. He came again, bringing with him another spirit in the form of a little dog, and as they sat again in the window he asked if she was afraid of the two of them. Responding, she said: "I fear you two as much as I feared you alone before." Leaving again, they came back and brought with them a third who had the appearance of a goat with a bristly brow and a long beard and wide-set horns, threatening terribly with his visage, and presenting itself like an angry bull. And now the little dog wore a fierce expression and opened its jaws. And the little man asked if she was by now afraid of the three. To him she responded that as long as she was in the house of her lords, she feared [their] dogs more than these demons. And he said: "I will bring to you guests such that you will fear." And when those spirits left, she prostrated herself in prayer and cried to the Lord with her innermost heart that he might free her from the power of the enemy. And while she was intent in prayer, mice rushed into her cell, and such a multitude of them entered that neither the floor, nor the walls of the room, nor even the ceiling was visible. The entire surface of the little cell was so covered by the multitude of mice that the mice ran this way and that over her as she was prostrate in prayer. Because of the very multitude of such noisy vermin absolutely nothing, other than the filthy band of infestation, was [able to] move about in that entire room. Her prayer finally finished, she arose and took blessed water, which she had always at hand. Using this, along with litanies and prayers, she went around and sprinkled the cell and [thereby] put them into such flight that not one of the dirty horde there remained. . . .

---

[5]The reference is unclear. It could mean deacons* or high-ranking laypeople.
[6]A reference either to the five lowest orders of clergy,* below those of priest and deacon, or to lower social ranks of the laity.

[7]Holy water.

▷　While enclosed in her cell, Liutbirg's fame as a prophetess and living saint spreads throughout Saxony.

So it happened, as she had foretold, that she remained in the same cell for a thirty-year period, and whatever she had predicted, indubitably happened. It became manifestly apparent that the sure outcome always followed up the things she had predicted. Even Saint Martin[8] came to her in a true vision and advised her about the quality of food and clothing. He also preached with father-like words, telling about the force of prayer and about his whole way of life. After having fed on his consolatory conversations, as if on honeyed feasts, things which before seemed heavy were considered lighter.

She had conversation with men of special sanctity, indeed, most intimate discussion with those whom she knew were acquainted with and instructed in holy law. From them she plucked little flowers of their perfection, and it always happened that each left happy. Abbots[*] and bishops who had knowledge of her, either personally or through their messengers, commended themselves to her prayers and included her in theirs. Inspired with exchanged prayer, they rejoiced in the Lord.

Her bishop, Haymo,[9] of worthy memory, very often visited her with fatherly affection. He was a man of the greatest sanctity and erudition. She dwelt in his diocese,[*] and the means for her way of life belonged in his care and prudence. He left her instructed and edified by many words, and he kindly supported her with physical necessities.

A man surpassing all these things in our recollection and in the perfection of all virtues was Anskar,[10] a special athlete of Christ. He was archbishop of Bremen and cherished her with very great love of holy adoption. He came hurrying, as a devoted father, on the road of such great length; his visits cheered her with the greatest kindnesses and exceeding munificence. This venerable bishop voluntarily supported her, not only with the conversation of his presence, but also with physical subsidies of all necessities. He sent to her, for the satisfaction of the holy work to which she unceasingly stuck with the greatest zeal, beautiful looking girls. She educated them in psalmody[11] and artistic crafts, and, after teaching them, she permitted them to go, liberty having been granted, either to their relatives, or wherever they might want. . . .

We will now tell what we have heard about her death. A little while before she began to be ill, she made confession[*] to each of the priests who was summoned every day. At the same time she accepted their blessings with prayer, until the foreknown moment, the hour at which she had to return her spirit to God. She begged the priests gathered with the sisters, and the many others who were assembled, to offer prayers for her. She asked all to forgive her sins and, after taking the communion for the dead,[12] she fell prostate before the cross which she had attached above her window. With her arms stretched out in the likeness of the cross, and her head lowered to the ground, a voice was heard at the end of her prayer. This was: "You who deigned to ascend the gallows of the cross for us sinners, and You who had pity on the hanging robber, may You think me worthy to be pitied, since into Your hands I commend my spirit." And so, in the midst of psalm-singing and voices of the mourners, she returned her, as I believe, happy spirit to the Lord, to whom is honor and glory for ever.

---

[8]St. Martin of Tours (Chapter 2, source 9), one of the fathers of Gallican monasticism, the patron of the Frankish royal family, and the most popular saint in Frankish Gaul.
[9]Bishop of Halberstadt (r. 840–853).
[10]Called the *apostle of the North,* St. Anskar was archbishop[*] of Bremen (r. 831–865) and a leader in attempts to convert the Danes and Swedes.

[11]Singing psalms, or sacred songs.
[12]Known as *viaticum* (something to take on a journey), it is the holy communion, or eucharist,[*] taken by a person facing death.

Chapter 5

▼▼▼

The Carolingian Age

The *Merovingian* royal family, the dynasty begun by Clovis (Chapter 2, source 9), reigned in *Francia* (the land of the Franks) for two and a half centuries, but from at least the time of King Dagobert I (r. 622–638), the Merovingians' last reasonably effective monarch, Frankish nobles were increasingly able to rule their lives and lands largely undisturbed by the king. One partial corrective to this tendency toward political fragmentation and royal impotence was the growing power of a class of ministers known as the *mayors of the palace.* Originally aristocratic overseers of the king's household, the mayors became the principals behind the throne, and one mayor, Charles Martel (ca. 688–741), gave his name to a dynasty that, shortly after his death, became the new royal family of the Franks. That family, the *Carolingians,* not only replaced the Merovingians as kings, it produced Western emperors from 800 to 899.

In 751 Charles Martel's son and mayoral successor packed the last Merovingian king into a monastery* and, with papal* approval, began to reign as King Pepin I (r. 751–768). Pope Zacharias (r. 741–752) had countenanced this coup, in part because the papacy* was desperately searching for a defender against resurgent Lombard aggression in Italy. Given that the Iconoclastic Controversy (Chapter 4, source 21) effectively cut off the papacy from any hope of Byzantine help, the popes now looked across the Alps to the Franks for assistance, and King Pepin and his son Charles did not disappoint their papal friends. Despite the opposition of many of his Frankish followers, Pepin twice marched into Italy, where he momentarily blunted the Lombardic threat to the papacy. Renewed Lombard aggression brought King Charles (r. 768–814), Pepin's successor, into Italy, as well. Following a decisive military victory, Charles shut away the Lombard king in a monastery and in 774 assumed for himself the title *king of the Lombards.* He was well on his way to becoming *Charlemagne* — Charles the Great.

A quarter century later, on Christmas Day, 800, the people and clergy* of Rome acclaimed Charles emperor, and Pope Leo III placed an imperial crown on his head. The honor was deserved. Charles was clearly Western Europe's dominant monarch, and he held lands extensive enough to be termed an empire. More than that, many of his contemporaries saw him as the only logical heir of Roman imperial legitimacy. Unfortunately, Charlemagne's heirs were unable and unwilling to hold his empire together. By 843 Charles's three grandsons had divided it up into three smaller kingdoms, and the empire was effectively dead. Nonetheless, the largely honorific title of *emperor* remained alive, to be passed among various Carolingian monarchs throughout the rest of the century.

The feeble reign of Louis the Child, the last Carolingian king of the East Franks (or Germans), ended in 911, and the reign of Louis V, the last Carolingian monarch of the West Franks (we cannot call them *French* at such an early date), ended with his death in 987. With these events, the Carolingians passed out of history. Before this inglorious end, however, they had produced not only an empire and a modest renaissance in letters and the arts, they had, arguably, helped to usher in the First Europe. Many historians see Charles the Great as the first true European king and his reign as the beginning of Europe's misnamed *Middle Ages*.

The sources in this chapter shed light on some of the factors that contributed to the fairly rapid rise and almost equally as rapid demise of Carolingian greatness.

▼▼▼

Charlemagne

The imperial coronation of Charles the Great by Pope Leo III in St. Peter's basilica on Christmas Day, 800, certainly is a memorable symbol of the fusion of the First Europe's three constituent elements: the memory and legitimacy of the Roman Empire; Latin Christianity; and Germanic culture. As is true of all symbolically significant historical events, however, the myths and drama associated with this event tend to obscure the historical setting in which it took place.

The sources included in this section have been selected with an eye toward placing Charlemagne within that fuller historical context. Source 24 provides a Carolingian interpretation of Emperor Charles and his relationship with the Roman papacy. The three letters that comprise source 25 reflect Charles's mind and policies at the height of his powers, and source 26 provides a glimpse of the laws Charles issued as he wrestled with the realities of governing his lands before and after 800. Source 27 returns to themes already partially explored. Source 21 (Chapter 4) shed light on the mind of the Roman papacy regarding papal-imperial relations fully four decades before Charles succeeded to the Frankish royal throne in 768. Source 27 presents Pope Leo III's view of Charlemagne's relationship with the See* of St. Peter after Charles had been on the throne for fully three decades.

Charles the Great: A Carolingian Portrait
▼▼▼
24 ▼ *Einhard, THE LIFE OF CHARLES THE GREAT*

Charles the Great, or Charlemagne, king of the Franks and the Lombards and emperor in the West, ruled a major portion of continental Europe for close to half a century. During his lifetime, his herculean efforts to expand the boundaries of Christendom and impose an order based on his understanding of Christian principles won him a reputation that extended all the way to the court of Caliph Harun al-Rashid in Baghdad (Chapter 3, source 16). Within a few years of his death, as Carolingian unity and order began to crumble, Westerners fondly looked back on Charles's reign as a golden age.

One of Charles's many accomplishments was his patronage of scholarship on a modest but historically significant scale, a phenomenon often referred to as the *Carolingian Renaissance.* One of the scholars drawn to Charles's patronage was Einhard (ca. 770–840), a Frankish intellectual who arrived at Charles's court at Aachen, or Aix-la-Chappelle, in the 790s. Einhard was vastly talented in a wide variety of areas. As an architect, he supervised the construction of Charles's basilica at Aachen. Einhard also served Charles as an ambassador and was a poet of considerable skill. In all likelihood, he succeeded Alcuin as master of the court school when the Englishman retired in 796. Needless to say, Einhard came to know Charles quite well during the last two decades of the emperor's life. Following Charles's death, Einhard served as private secretary to Emperor Louis the Pious (r. 813–840), retiring in 830.

Early in his retirement years, probably between 830 and 833, Einhard undertook the task of writing a biography of Charles the Great. Basing this life of his late emperor, patron, and friend on the *Lives of the Twelve Caesars,* by the Roman historian Suetonius (ca. 69–140), Einhard implicitly argued that Charlemagne had been more than the equal of the early exemplars of Roman imperial greatness. Beyond that, Einhard set out to instruct Louis, Charles's son and successor, on the qualities that an effective Christian-Frankish emperor should have; this tutelage occurred at the very moment when family quarrels were pulling Louis's empire apart.

In the following excerpts, Einhard describes Charles's Saxon wars, his relations with his children, his love of learning, his character and piety, his relations with the Roman papacy (with special attention paid toward his imperial acclamation in 800), and Louis's imperial coronation in 813.

QUESTIONS FOR ANALYSIS

1. According to this excerpt, what were Charles's most sterling qualities? Which of them probably contributed to the success of his reign? Which of them contributed to the legend of Charlemagne as emperor-hero?

2. What light, if any, do these excerpts shed on Charles's patronage of learning?

3. Einhard tells us that Augustine's *City of God* was one of Charles's favorite mealtime readings. Review Chapter 1, source 4, and compose Charles's commentary on that excerpt in light of what you have learned about the man from this biography.

4. In what ways, if at all, did Charles act like a Christian emperor even before Christmas Day, 800? Understand the title *Christian emperor* in the sense of someone who inherited the responsibilities of Constantine, Justinian, and similar Christian Roman emperors. What do you conclude from your answer?

5. Einhard's statement that Charles initially had an aversion to the imperial title has puzzled some historians. From other sources, we know that on Christmas Day, 800, Pope Leo, perhaps to Charles's surprise, placed a crown on the Frankish king's head, and the people assembled in St. Peter's basilica acclaimed Charles emperor. Compare these facts with Einhard's treatment of that day, and also compare that Roman ceremony with the manner in which Louis the Pious was made emperor. Now can you think of any reason why Charles might have been displeased thirteen years earlier? (Note that Charles never returned to Rome after leaving in 801.)

No war ever undertaken by the Frankish nation was carried on with such persistence and bitterness, or cost so much labor, because the Saxons, like almost all the tribes of Germany, were a fierce people, given to the worship of devils and hostile to our religion, and did not consider it dishonorable to transgress and violate all law, human and divine. Then there were peculiar circumstances that tended to cause a breach of peace every day. Except in a few places, where large forests or mountain-ridges intervened and made the boundaries certain, the line between ourselves and the Saxons passed almost in its whole extent through an open country, so that there was no end to the murders, thefts, and arsons on both sides. In this way the Franks became so embittered that they at last resolved to make reprisals no longer, but to come to open war with the Saxons.

Accordingly, war was begun against them, and was waged for thirty-three successive years[1] with great fury; more, however, to the disadvantage of the Saxons than of the Franks. It could doubtless have been brought to an end sooner, had it not been for the faithlessness of the Saxons. It is hard to say how often they were conquered, and, humbly submitting to the king, promised to do what was enjoined upon them, gave without hesitation the required hostages, and received the officers sent them from the king. They were sometimes so much weakened and reduced that they promised to renounce the worship of devils and to adopt Christianity; but they were no less ready to violate these terms than prompt to ac-

---

[1]772 to 804, or thirty-two years.

cept them, so that it is impossible to tell which came easier to them to do; scarcely a year passed from the beginning of the war without such changes on their part. But the king did not suffer his high purpose and steadfastness — firm alike in good and evil fortune — to be wearied by any fickleness on their part, or to be turned from the task that he had undertaken; on the contrary, he never allowed their faithless behavior to go unpunished, but either took the field against them in person, or sent his counts with an army to wreak vengeance and exact righteous satisfaction.[2] At last, after conquering and subduing all who had offered resistance, he took ten thousand of those who lived on the banks of the Elbe, and settled them, with their wives and children, in many different bodies here and there in Gaul and Germany.[3] The war that had lasted so many years was at length ended by their acceding to the terms offered by the king; which were renunciation of their religious customs and the worship of devils, acceptance of the sacraments* of the Christian religion, and union with the Franks to form one people. . . .

The plan that he adopted for his children's education was, first of all, to have both boys and girls instructed in the liberal arts, to which he also turned his own attention. As soon as their years admitted, in accordance with the custom of the Franks, the boys had to learn horsemanship, and to practice war and the chase, and the girls to familiarize themselves with cloth-making, and to handle distaff and spindle, that they might not grow indolent through idleness, and he fostered in them every virtuous sentiment. . . . He was so careful of the training of his sons and daughters that he never took his meals without them when he was at home, and never made a journey without them; his sons would ride at

his side, and his daughters follow him, while a number of his bodyguard, detailed for their protection, brought up the rear. . . .

Charles was temperate in eating, and particularly so in drinking, for he abominated drunkenness in anybody, much more in himself and those of his household; but he could not easily abstain from food, and often complained that fasts injured his health. He very rarely gave entertainments, only on great feastdays, and then to large numbers of people. His meals ordinarily consisted of four courses, not counting the roast, which his huntsmen used to bring in on the spit; he was more fond of this than of any other dish. While at table, he listened to reading or music. The subjects of the readings were the stories and deeds of olden time: he was fond, too, of St. Augustine's books, and especially of the one entitled *The City of God.* He was so moderate in the use of wine and all sorts of drink that he rarely allowed himself more than three cups in the course of a meal.

Charles had the gift of ready and fluent speech, and could express whatever he had to say with the utmost clearness. He was not satisfied with ability to use his native language merely, but gave attention to the study of foreign ones, and in particular was such a master of Latin that he could speak it as well as his native tongue; but he could understand Greek better than he could speak it. He was so eloquent, indeed, that he might have been taken for a teacher of oratory. He most zealously cherished the liberal arts, held those who taught them in great esteem, and conferred great honors upon them. He took lessons in grammar from the deacon Peter of Pisa, at that time an aged man.[4] Another deacon, Albin of Britain, otherwise called Alcuin, a man of Saxon birth, who was the greatest scholar of the day, was his

---

[2]Charles's armies undertook at least eighteen separate campaigns in Saxony. Most did not result in any significant pitched battles; rather, the campaigns consisted of Frankish pacification efforts in the face of Saxon guerrilla warfare and stubborn private attempts to retain their culture (see source 26).

[3]In 804.

[4]When Charles captured Pavia, the Lombard capital, in 774, he found the grammarian Peter of Pisa teaching there and prevailed upon Peter to travel to Francia to serve as a teacher at the royal court.

teacher in other branches of learning.[5] The king spent much time and labor with him studying rhetoric,* dialectic,* and especially astronomy. He learned to make calculations, and used to investigate with much curiosity and intelligence the motions of the heavenly bodies. He also tried to write, and used to keep tablets and blanks in bed under his pillow, that at leisure hours he might accustom his hand to form the letters; however, as he began his efforts late in life, and not at the proper time, they met with little success.

He cherished with the greatest fervor and devotion the principles of the Christian religion, which had been instilled into him from infancy. Hence it was that he built the beautiful basilica at Aix-la-Chapelle, which he adorned with gold and silver and lamps, and with rails and doors of solid brass.[6] He had the columns and marbles for this structure brought from Rome and Ravenna, for he could not find such as were suitable elsewhere.[7] He was a constant worshiper at this church as long as his health permitted, going morning and evening, even after nightfall, besides attending mass.* He took care that all the services there conducted should be held in the best possible manner, very often warning the sextons[8] not to let any improper or unclean thing be brought into the building, or remain in it. He provided it with a number of sacred vessels of gold and silver, and with such a quantity of clerical* robes that not even the door-keepers, who filled the humblest office in the church, were obliged to wear their everyday clothes when in the performance of their duties. He took great

pains to improve the church reading and singing, for he was well skilled in both, although he neither read in public nor sang, except in a low tone and with others.

He was very active in aiding the poor, and in that open generosity which the Greeks call alms; so much so, indeed, that he not only made a point of giving in his own country and his own kingdom, but when he discovered that there were Christians living in poverty in Syria, Egypt, and Africa, at Jerusalem, Alexandria, and Carthage, he had compassion on their wants, and used to send money over the seas to them. The reason that he earnestly strove to make friends with the kings beyond seas was that he might get help and relief to the Christians living under their rule.[9] He cared for the church of St. Peter the Apostle at Rome above all other holy and sacred places, and heaped high its treasury with a vast wealth of gold, silver, and precious stones. He sent great and countless gifts to the popes; and throughout his whole reign the wish that he had nearest his heart was to re-establish the ancient authority of the city of Rome under his care and by his influence, and to defend and protect the church of St. Peter, and to beautify and enrich it out of his own store above all other churches. Nevertheless, although he held it in such veneration, only four times[10] did he repair to Rome to pay his vows and make his supplications during the whole forty-seven years that he reigned.

When he made his last journey thither, he had also other ends in view. The Romans had inflicted many injuries upon the Pontiff Leo,[11] tearing out

---

[5]Actually, he was an Angle. Called *Ealhwine* in his native Anglian and *Albinus* in Latin, Alcuin was a product of the intellectual milieu of Northumbria in England, one of early eighth-century Western Christendom's major centers of learning, thanks to churchmen such as Bede (Chapter 4, source 22). Alcuin served as the headmaster of Charles's palace school from 782 to 796 and then retired to the abbey* of Saint Martin of Tours, where he served as abbot* until his death in 804.

[6]All that remains of this great complex is Charles's octagonal private chapel, which now serves as a chapel in the cathedral* of Aachen.

[7]Many came from the former palace of the then defunct Byzantine exarch of Ravenna (Chapter 1, source 5).

[8]Persons charged with the church's maintenance.

[9]In 799 Charles sent an ambassador to Jerusalem to inquire about the conditions of the Christians living there. During the first decade of the ninth century, Charles exchanged several embassies with Caliph Harun al-Rashid, presumably because Charles was interested in the well-being of the many Christians living under the caliph's rule.

[10]774, 781, 787, and 800.

[11]Pope Leo III (r. 795–816) was attacked on April 25, 799, by factional opponents, including members of the family of the previous pope, Hadrian I. Although an attempt was made to blind Leo and cut out his tongue, thereby rendering him incapable of serving as a priest,* the attackers failed.

his eyes and cutting out his tongue, so that he had been compelled to call upon the king for help. Charles accordingly went to Rome,[12] to set in order the affairs of the Church, which were in great confusion, and passed the whole winter there. It was then that he received the titles of Emperor and Augustus, to which he at first had such an aversion that he declared that he would not have set foot in the church the day that they were conferred, although it was a great feast-day, if he could have foreseen the design of the pope. He bore very patiently with the jealousy which the Roman emperors[13] showed upon his assuming these titles, for they took this step very ill; and by dint of frequent embassies and letters, in which he addressed them as brothers, he made their haughtiness yield to his magnanimity,[14] a

quality in which he was unquestionably much their superior. . . .

Towards the close of his life,[15] when he was broken by ill-health and old age, he summoned Louis, king of Aquitania,[16] his only surviving son by Hildegard, and gathered together all the chief men of the whole kingdom of the Franks in a solemn assembly. He appointed Louis, with their unanimous consent,[17] to rule with himself over the whole kingdom, and constituted him heir to the imperial name; then, placing the diadem upon his son's head, he bade him be proclaimed Emperor and Augustus. This step was hailed by all present with great favor, for it really seemed as if God had prompted him to it for the kingdom's good; it increased the king's[18] dignity, and struck no little terror into foreign nations.

---

[12]Charles arrived on November 24, 800.
[13]In Constantinople.
[14]In 812 Emperor Michael I (r. 811–813) recognized Charles's imperial title in exchange for Venice and some territory in the Balkans.

[15]813.
[16]A region in modern southwest France.
[17]The consent of all leading Frankish nobles was needed to *ratify* a royal succession.
[18]Louis.

Carolingian Authority
▼▼▼

25 ▼ *Charles the Great, LETTERS*

The first two letters that follow were, in all likelihood, the literary creations of Alcuin of York (ca. 733–804). As was true of most of his royal and imperial contemporaries, Charles depended on his classically educated secretaries, such as Alcuin, to compose his letters. Although the words of the first two letters are Alcuin's, the ideas and policies contained in them undoubtedly had Charles's approval. Conceivably, Charles orally drafted the major points contained in his more important letters.

The first letter, which dates to around 787–789, was addressed to Baugulf, abbot* of Fulda (r. 780–802), and appears to be the sole surviving example of a number of similar letters that were dispatched to the most important bishops* and abbots in Charles's lands. Founded in 744, Fulda had been a Frankish royal abbey* since 764/765; that is, the Carolingians were its patrons and immediate lords. In Abbot Baugulf's day, Fulda was noted as a center of strict Benedictine observance and one of the premier centers of learning in the West.

The second letter was sent to Pope Leo III (r. 795–816) in 796, shortly after Charles's court received word of Leo's accession to the papal* throne. We must understand this letter in the context of Charles's checkered relations with Pope

Hadrian I (r. 772–795), Leo's predecessor. It was Hadrian who implored Charles to invade Lombardy in defense of the papacy,* thereby opening the way for Charles's conquest of the Lombards in 774. However, when Hadrian approved the decrees of the Second Council* of Nicaea of 787 that momentarily ended Byzantine iconoclasm, Charles's theologians discovered in the poor translation of the council's acts that Hadrian had sent the Frankish king reason to conclude that the pope had wandered too far in the direction of image worship. Consequently, Charles gave his approval to a four-volume work known as *The Carolingian Books,* which proceeded to set out for the pope and the entire Western Church the orthodox,* Carolingian position on the use of holy images.

The third letter is a formulaic epistle composed by some anonymous clerk long after Alcuin had left Charles's court. Addressed to Abbot Fulrad of Saint Quentin, a monastery* located about sixty miles outside Paris, the letter dates to around 806. Very much like the letter to Abbot Baugulf, this is the single extant example of a general letter — in this case, one sent to nobles and churchmen whom Charles expected to bring soldiers to his spring general assembly, or *May Field* (see source 26). All of Francia's secular* and religious lords were required to attend this annual convocation, and if Charles was planning a military campaign, those who owed military service were instructed to bring their armed retainers and specified supplies.

QUESTIONS FOR ANALYSIS

1. According to the letter to Abbot Baugulf, what was Charles's main reason for promoting education?
2. What allows us to infer that the letter to Baugulf was one of at least several similar letters?
3. Does the letter to Baugulf establish or outline a program of educational reform or organization? If not, what does the letter do? What do you conclude from your answer?
4. Consider Charles's letter to Pope Leo. What role(s) does Charles claim for himself? What role(s) does he assign the pope?
5. What do you infer from Charles's letter to Pope Leo about Charles's view of the Western Church and his relationship to that Church? Would Pope Gelasius (Chapter 4, source 19) have agreed? How about Pope Gregory II (source 21)?
6. The Carolingians were avid patrons of the Rule of Saint Benedict (Chapter 4, source 17) and attempted to impose it on all monastic houses within their lands. What evidence, however, does the letter to Abbot Fulrad present to suggest that Benedictine monasticism had changed since the days of Saint Benedict?
7. At the beginning of Charles's reign, every Frankish freeman was, theoretically, required to accompany the army whenever it was assembled. What evidence does this document provide to suggest that by the early ninth century, army service was increasingly the duty of professional warriors?

Why would this change have taken place? (Do not overlook the evidence provided by Einhard in source 24.)

8. What does this letter to Fulrad tell us about the mechanics of early ninth-century military operations?
9. What does it tell us about Charles's organizational abilities and the way in which his government functioned?

Charles, by the grace of God, king of the Franks and Lombards and patrician of the Romans,[1] to Abbot Baugulf and to all the congregation, also to the faithful committed to you, we have directed a loving greeting by our ambassadors in the name of omnipotent God.

Be it known, therefore, to your devotion pleasing to God, that we, together with our faithful, have considered it to be useful that the bishoprics and monasteries entrusted by the favor of Christ to our control, in addition, in the culture of letters also ought to be zealous in teaching those who by the gift of God are able to learn, according to the capacity of each individual, so that just as the observance of the rule[2] imparts order and grace to honesty of morals, so also zeal in teaching and learning may do the same for sentences, so that those who desire to please God by living rightly should not neglect to please him also by speaking correctly. For it is written: "Either from thy words thou shalt be justified or from thy words thou shalt be condemned."[3] For although correct conduct may be better than knowledge, nevertheless knowledge precedes conduct. Therefore, each one ought to study what he desires to accomplish, so that so much the more fully the mind may know what ought to be done, as the tongue hastens in the praises of omnipotent God without the hindrances of errors. For since errors should be shunned by all men, so much the more ought they to be avoided as far as possible by those who are chosen for this

very purpose alone,[4] so that they ought to be the special servants of truth. For when in the years just passed letters were often written to us from several monasteries in which it was stated that the brethren who dwelt there offered up in our behalf sacred and pious prayers, we have recognized in most of these letters both correct thoughts and uncouth expressions; because what pious devotion dictated faithfully to the mind, the tongue, uneducated on account of the neglect of study, was not able to express in the letter without error. Whence it happened that we began to fear lest perchance, as the skill in writing was less, so also the wisdom for understanding the Holy Scriptures might be much less than it rightly ought to be. And we all know well that, although errors of speech are dangerous, far more dangerous are errors of the understanding. Therefore, we exhort you not only not to neglect the study of letters, but also with most humble mind, pleasing to God, to study earnestly in order that you may be able more easily and more correctly to penetrate the mysteries of the divine Scriptures. Since, moreover, images,[5] tropes[6] and similar figures are found in the sacred pages, no one doubts that each one in reading these will understand the spiritual sense more quickly if previously he shall have been fully instructed in the mastery of letters. Such men truly are to be chosen for this work as have both the will and the ability to learn and a desire to instruct others. And may this be done with a zeal

---

[1]Pope Stephen II (r. 752–757) had bestowed this Roman title on King Pepin and his sons Charles and Carloman in 754.
[2]The Rule of St. Benedict for monks* and, more generally, all of the rules of the Church governing clerics* and laity.
[3]The Bible, the Gospel of St. Matthew, 12:37.

[4]Clerics and monks.
[5]Similes and metaphors.
[6]A *trope* is a word or phrase used in a nonliteral, or figurative, manner. It normally involves an alteration of the word's standard meaning.

as great as the earnestness with which we command it. For we desire you to be, as it is fitting that soldiers of the Church should be, devout in mind, learned in discourse, chaste in conduct and eloquent in speech, so that whosoever shall seek to see you out of reverence of God, or on account of your reputation for holy conduct, just as he is edified by your appearance, may also be instructed by your wisdom, which he has learned from your reading or singing, and may go away joyfully giving thanks to omnipotent God. Do not neglect, therefore, if you wish to have our favor, to send copies of this letter to all your suffragans[7] and fellow-bishops and to all the monasteries.

▼ ▼ ▼

Charles, by the grace of God king of the Franks and Lombards, and patrician of the Romans, to his holiness, Pope Leo, greeting. . . . Just as I entered into an agreement with the most holy father, your predecessor, so also I desire to make with you an inviolable treaty of mutual fidelity and love; that, on the one hand, you shall pray for me and give me the apostolic benediction,[8] and that, on the other, with the aid of God I will ever defend the most holy seat of the holy Roman Church. For it is our part to defend the holy Church of Christ from the attacks of pagans and infidels from without, and within to enforce the acceptance of the catholic faith. It is your part, most holy father, to aid us in the good fight by raising your hands to God as Moses did,[9] so that by your intercession the Christian people under the leadership of God may always and everywhere have the victory over the enemies of His holy name, and the name of our Lord Jesus Christ may be glorified throughout the world. Abide by the

canonical law* in all things and obey the precepts of the holy fathers always, that your life may be an example of sanctity to all, and your holy admonitions be observed by the whole world, and that your light may so shine before men that they may see your good works and glorify your father who is in Heaven.[10] May omnipotent God preserve your holiness unharmed through many years for the exalting of his holy Church.

▼ ▼ ▼

In the name of the Father, Son and Holy Ghost [Spirit*]. Charles, most serene, august, crowned by God, great pacific Emperor, and also, by God's mercy, king of the Franks and Lombards, to Abbot Fulrad.

Be it known to you that we have decided to hold our general assembly this year in the eastern part of Saxony, on the river Bode, at the place which is called Strassfurt.[11] Therefore, we have commanded you to come to the aforesaid place, with all your men well armed and prepared, on the fifteenth day before the Kalends of July, that is, seven days before the festival of St. John the Baptist.[12] Come, accordingly, so equipped with your men to the aforesaid place that thence you may be able to go well prepared in any direction whither our summons shall direct; that is, with arms and gear also, and other equipment for war in food and clothing. So that each horseman shall have a shield, lance, sword, dagger, bow and quivers with arrows; and in your carts utensils of various kinds, that is, axes, planes, augers, boards, spades, iron shovels, and other utensils which are necessary in an army. In the carts also supplies of food for three months, dating from the time of the assembly, arms and clothing for a

---

[7]Subordinate religious leaders; here, the heads of churches and monasteries subject to Fulda's supervision.
[8]The apostle's* blessing; here, the reference is to St. Peter. Since Pope Damasus I (r. 366–384), the bishops of Rome had claimed the title *Apostolic See** for the bishopric of Rome. In the West, the adjective *apostolic* soon came to be applied exclusively to the Roman papacy.

[9]Exodus, 17:11.
[10]The Gospel of Matthew, 5:16.
[11]Strassfurt was near Magdeburg, in the vicinity of Liutbirg's native land (Chapter 4, source 23) and about 483 miles from St. Quentin.
[12]June 17.

half-year. And we command this in general, that you cause it to be observed that you proceed peacefully to the aforesaid place, through whatever part of our realm your journey shall take you, that is, that you presume to take nothing except fodder, wood and water; and let the men of each one of your vassals[13] march along with the carts and horsemen, and let the leader always be with them until they reach the aforesaid place, so that the absence of a lord may not give an opportunity to his men of doing evil.

Send your gifts, which you ought to present to us at our assembly in the middle of the month of May, to the place where we then shall be; if perchance your journey shall so shape itself that on your march you are able in person to present these gifts of yours to us, we greatly desire it. See that you show no negligence in the future if you desire to have our favor.

---

[13]A soldier who had commended himself as the "man," or *vassal,** of a lord (see Chapter 6, source 31).

Charlemagne's Government
▼▼▼
26 ▼ *Charles the Great, CAPITULARIES*

The following two documents are known as *capitularies,* because each consists of a number of regulatory chapters (*capitula* in Latin), or articles. Capitularies generally were drafted at the annual general assemblies that Charles held prior to leading his army on campaign. At these meetings of "a people in arms," Charles convened his major secular* and ecclesiastical* lords and sought their advice on a variety of issues. The results of these deliberations were published as capitularies and had the force of law.

The first document is Charles's initial *Capitulary on Saxony,* which he issued in 785 at his Saxon outpost at Paderborn. As already noted, Charles's armies waged a series of campaigns in Saxony from 772 to 804 in a successful effort to conquer and Christianize this region. This capitulary sheds light on the means that Charles used to subjugate and convert the Saxons and some of the resistance that his efforts met.

The second document is known as the *Capitulary on the Missi,* which Charles issued in 802. Charles's *missi dominici* (the sovereign's envoys) were not permanent, full-time officials. Rather, they were lay and ecclesiastical lords who exercised special commissions to inquire into the activities of local counts, bishops,* and monasteries.* Working in pairs of one layman and one churchman, they traveled to a region comprising about six out of the empire's roughly three hundred counties, examined the state of affairs in their assigned areas, corrected minor irregularities, and reported major crimes and misdemeanors to the emperor. The Merovingians and King Pepin I had employed such agents, but it remained for Charles to make them a central part of his government. In theory, every part of Charles's empire received a visit from a pair of missi at least once a year.

QUESTIONS FOR ANALYSIS

1. Consider the Capitulary on Saxony. How does Charles employ "the carrot and the stick" to win over the Saxons to Christianity?
2. What does this document tell us about Saxon pagan practices? How credible is this testimony? In answering this, you might find it helpful to compare this document with Tacitus's *Germania* (Chapter 2, source 6).
3. How effective do you think these laws were in suppressing Saxon independence and paganism? Why do you conclude that?
4. In 797 Charles issued a second Capitulary on Saxony, which relaxed many of the severe features of the initial capitulary. Why do you think he did so?
5. Consider the oath expected of all freemen (chapters 2–9 of the Capitulary on the Missi). What does it suggest about the nature and extent of Charles's government?
6. Consider articles 10, 11, 14, 19, and 40 of the Capitulary on the Missi. What do these chapters allow us to infer about Charles's view of the imperial Church and its clerics*?
7. Carefully read the entire Capitulary on the Missi, and then review *The Salic Law* (Chapter 2, source 7). How had Frankish law, in both theory and practice, changed since the days of Clovis? How had it remained the same? What do you conclude from your answers?
8. Does either capitulary clearly distinguish between *crimes* and *sins?* What inferences do you draw from your answer?
9. After a careful reading of both capitularies, what do you infer was Charles's vision of his duties as king and emperor? For whom did he believe he had a special responsibility? How did he see his realm?

First, concerning the greater chapters[1] it has been enacted:

1. It is pleasing to all that the churches of Christ, which are now being built in Saxony and consecrated to God, should not have less, but greater and more illustrious honor than the shrines of the idols have had.

2. If any one shall have fled to a church for refuge, let no one presume to expel him from the church by violence, but he shall be left in peace until he shall be brought to the judicial assemblage; and on account of the honor due to God and the saints, and the reverence due to the church itself, let his life and all his members be granted to him. Moreover, let him plead his cause as best he can and he shall be judged; and so let him be led to the presence of the lord king, and the latter shall send him where it shall seem fitting to his clemency.

3. If any one shall have entered a church by violence and shall have carried off anything in it by force or theft, or shall have burned the church itself, let him be punished by death.

4. If any one, out of contempt for Christianity, shall have despised the holy Lenten fast[2] and shall have eaten flesh, let him be punished by death. But, nevertheless, let it be taken into consideration by a priest,* lest perchance any one from necessity has been led to eat flesh.

---

[1]The greater chapters concerned offenses that involved capital punishment; the lesser chapters dealt with noncapital offenses.

[2]The forty-day fast preceding Easter, during which meat and many other foods were prohibited.

5. If any one shall have killed a bishop or priest or deacon* let him likewise be punished capitally.

6. If any one, deceived by the devil, shall have believed, after the manner of the pagans, that any man or woman is a witch and eats men, and on this account shall have burned the person, or shall have given the person's flesh to others to eat, or shall have eaten it himself, let him be punished by a capital sentence.

7. If any one, in accordance with pagan rites, shall have caused the body of a dead man to be burned, and shall have reduced his bones to ashes, let him be punished capitally.

8. If any one of the race of the Saxons hereafter, concealed among them, shall have wished to hide himself unbaptized, and shall have scorned to come to baptism,* and shall have wished to remain a pagan, let him be punished by death.

9. If any one shall have sacrificed a man to the devil, and, after the manner of the pagans, shall have presented him as a victim to the demons, let him be punished by death.

10. If any one shall have formed a conspiracy with the pagans against the Christians, or shall have wished to join with them in opposition to the Christians, let him be punished by death; and whosoever shall have consented fraudulently to this same against the king and the Christian people, let him be punished by death.

11. If any one shall have shown himself unfaithful to the lord king, let him be punished with a capital sentence. . . . .

13. If any one shall have killed his lord or lady, let him be punished in a like manner.

14. If, indeed, for these mortal crimes secretly committed any one shall have fled of his own accord to a priest, and after confession* shall have wished to do penance, let him be freed by the testimony of the priest from death. . . .[3]

18. On the Lord's day no meetings or public judicial assemblages shall be held, unless perchance in a case of great necessity, or when war compels it, but all shall go to church to hear the word of God, and shall be free for prayers or good works. Likewise, also, on the special festivals they shall devote themselves to God and to the services of the Church, and shall refrain from secular assemblies.

19. Likewise, it has been pleasing to insert in these decrees that all infants shall be baptized within a year; we have decreed this, that if any one shall have refused to bring his infant to baptism within the course of a year, without the advice or permission of the priest, if he is a noble he shall pay 120 *solidi*[4] to the treasury; if a freeman, 60; if a *litus,*[5] 30.

20. If any one shall have contracted a prohibited or illegal marriage, if a noble, 60 *solidi;* if a freeman, 30; if a *litus,* 15.

21. If any one shall have made a vow at springs or trees or groves,[6] or shall have made an offering after the manner of the heathen and shall have partaken of a repast in honor of the demons, if he shall be a noble, 60 *solidi;* if a freeman, 30; if a *litus,* 15. If, indeed, they have not the means of paying at once, they shall be given into the service of the Church[7] until the *solidi* are paid.

22. We command that the bodies of Saxon Christians shall be carried to the church cemeteries, and not to the mounds of the pagans.

23. We have ordered that diviners and soothsayers shall be handed over to the churches and priests.

24. Concerning robbers and malefactors who shall have fled from one county to another, if

---

[3]From this point on, the capitulary deals with lesser chapters.

[4]For the value of a solidus (see Chapter 2, source 7, note 2).

[5]A *letus,* or *leet,* was someone whose class was midway between a free person and a slave (see ibid., note 5).

[6]Places sacred to Saxon deities. Pagan Germans believed that certain natural places possessed a special sanctity that made them locations in which they could contact their gods. Consequently, the pagan Germans conducted all of their religious rites in these open-air settings, having no enclosed temples. See Tacitus, Chapter 2, source 6, but also see Gregory I's letter to Abbot Mellitus (Chapter 4, source 20).

[7]As indentured servants.

any one shall receive them into his protection and shall keep them with him for seven nights, except for the purpose of bringing them to justice, let him pay our ban.[8] Likewise, if a count[9] shall have concealed them, and shall be unwilling to bring them forward so that justice may be done, and is not able to excuse himself for this, let him lose his office.

26. No one shall presume to impede any man coming to us to seek justice; and if any one shall have attempted to do this, he shall pay our ban. . . .

34. We have forbidden that Saxons shall hold public assemblies in general, unless perchance our *missus*[10] shall have caused them to come together in accordance with our command; but each count shall hold judicial assemblies and administer justice in his jurisdiction. And this shall be cared for by the priests, lest it be done otherwise.[11]

▼ ▼ ▼

1. Concerning the embassy sent out by the lord emperor.

Therefore, the most serene and most Christian lord emperor Charles has chosen from his nobles the wisest and most prudent men, both archbishops[12] and some of the other bishops also, and venerable abbots and pious laymen,[13] and has sent them throughout his whole kingdom, and through them he would have all the various classes of persons mentioned in the following chapters live in accordance with the correct law.

Moreover, where anything which is not right and just has been enacted in the law, he has ordered them to inquire into this most diligently and to inform him of it. He desires, God granting, to reform it. And let no one, through his cleverness or craft, dare to oppose or thwart the written law, as many are wont to do, or the judicial sentence passed upon him, or to do injury to the churches of God, or the poor, or the widows, or the wards, or any Christian. But all shall live entirely in accordance with God's precept, honestly and under a just rule, and each one shall be admonished to live in harmony with his fellows in his business or profession; the canonical clergy[14] ought to observe in every respect a canonical life without heeding base gain; nuns* ought to keep diligent watch over their lives; laymen and the secular clergy* ought rightly to observe their laws without malicious fraud; and all ought to live in mutual charity and perfect peace.

And let the *missi* themselves make a diligent investigation whenever any man claims that an injustice has been done him by any one, just as they desire to deserve the grace of omnipotent God and to keep their fidelity promised to Him, so that in all cases, in accordance with the will and fear of God, they shall administer the law fully and justly in the case of the holy churches of God and of the poor, of wards and widows, and of the whole people. And if there be anything of such a nature that they, together with the provincial counts, are not able of themselves

---

[8]The fine assessed by the king for breaking the peace or, in this case, harboring a fugitive criminal.

[9]Charles's local secular lords and representatives of his authority. Counties tended to be coterminous with episcopal dioceses,* which meant that the local count and the local bishop were the two leading individuals of the region. Chapter 34 of this capitulary describes several of their chief responsibilities. In addition, the counts raised troops, made public Charles's capitularies, collected revenues, and kept the peace. See Chapter 2, source 7, for evidence regarding Germanic counts in the age of Clovis.

[10]The singular of *missi* (see the next capitulary).

[11]Priests — and here, he probably means local bishops and abbots* — had the responsibility of supervising local government in order to assure that it was just and proper.

[12]When archbishops* were used as missi, they usually were commissioned to visit the subordinate, or suffragan, bishops within their own archiepiscopal provinces.*

[13]Initially, Charles had used low-ranking subordinates as missi, but by 802 he depended almost exclusively on important lords to fill these posts.

[14]Normally, this term refers to secular clerics* serving as functionaries within cathedral* churches. Such clerics are known individually as *canons*,* because they administer and live according to the canons, or rules, of the Church. As a group, these clerics are known as the cathedral's *chapter of canons.* In the context of this article, however, *canonical clergy* must mean monks* who live according to a special rule or set of canons.

to correct it and to do justice concerning it, they shall, without any reservation, refer it, together with their reports, to the judgment of the emperor; and the straight path of justice shall not be impeded by any one on account of flattery or gifts, or on account of any relationship, or from fear of the powerful.

2. Concerning the fidelity to be promised to the lord emperor.

He has commanded that every man in his whole kingdom, whether ecclesiastic or layman, and each one according to his vow and occupation, should now promise to him as emperor the fidelity which he had previously promised to him as king; and all of those who had not yet made that promise should do likewise, down to those who were twelve years old. And that it shall be announced to all in public, so that each one might know, how great and how many things are comprehended in that oath; not merely, as many have thought hitherto, fidelity to the lord emperor as regards his life, and not introducing any enemy into his kingdom out of enmity, and not consenting to or concealing another's faithlessness to him; but that all may know that this oath contains in itself the following meaning:

3. First, that each one voluntarily shall strive, in accordance with his knowledge and ability, to live completely in the holy service of God, in accordance with the precept of God and in accordance with his own promise, because the lord emperor is unable to give to all individually the necessary care and discipline.

4. Secondly, that no man, either through perjury or any other wile or fraud, or on account of the flattery or gift of any one, shall refuse to give back or dare to take possession of or conceal a serf* of the lord emperor, or a district, or land,

or anything that belongs to him; and that no one shall presume, through perjury or other wile, to conceal or entice away his fugitive fiscaline serfs[15] who unjustly and fraudulently say that they are free.

5. That no one shall presume to rob or do any injury fraudulently to the churches of God, or widows, or orphans, or pilgrims,* for the lord emperor himself, under God and His saints, has constituted himself their protector and defender.

6. That no one shall dare to lay waste a benefice[16] of the lord emperor, or to make it his own property.

7. That no one shall presume to neglect a summons to war from the lord emperor; and that no one of the counts shall be so presumptuous as to dare to excuse any one of those who owe military service, either on account of relationship, or flattery, or gifts from any one.

8. That no one shall presume to impede at all in any way a ban[17] or command of the lord emperor, or to tamper with his work, or to impede, or to lessen, or in any way to act contrary to his will or commands. And that no one shall dare to neglect to pay his dues or tax.

9. That no one, for any reason, shall make a practice in court of defending another unjustly, either from any desire of gain when the cause is weak, or by impeding a just judgment by his skill in reasoning, or by a desire of oppressing when the cause is weak. But each one shall answer for his own cause or tax or debt, unless someone is infirm or ignorant of pleading, for these the *missi,* or the chiefs who are in the court, or the judge who knows the case in question, shall plead before the court; or, if it is necessary, such a person may be allowed as is acceptable to all

---

[15]Serfs who worked on Charles's fiscal lands, or royal estates, from which he drew most of his income.

[16]In its narrowest sense, a *benefice* was a cleric's source of income (often land and its attached rents) and held only as long as the person functioned in that clerical office. Here, it means land and other sources of revenue that the emperor had given out to a relative, friend, or dependent. The person enjoyed the income from the benefice, but Charles retained legal ownership of it.

[17]A judicial fine or other sentence.

and knows the case well; but this shall be done wholly according to the convenience of the chiefs or *missi* who are present. But in every case it shall be done in accordance with justice and the law; and no one shall have the power to impede justice by a gift, reward, or any kind of evil flattery, or from any hindrance of relationship. And no one shall unjustly consent to another in anything, but with all zeal and good-will all shall be prepared to carry out justice.

For all the above mentioned ought to be observed by the imperial oath.

10. [We ordain] that bishops and priests shall live according to the canons and shall teach others to do the same.

11. That bishops, abbots, and abbesses* who are in charge of others, with the greatest veneration shall strive to surpass their subjects in this diligence and shall not oppress their subjects with a harsh rule or tyranny, but with a sincere love shall carefully guard the flock committed to them with mercy and charity, or by the examples of good works. . . .

14. That bishops, abbots and abbesses, and counts shall be mutually in accord, following the law in order to render a just judgment with all charity and unity of peace, and that they shall live faithfully in accordance with the will of God, so that always everywhere through them and among them a just judgment shall be rendered. The poor, widows, orphans, and pilgrims shall have consolation and defense from them; so that we, through the good-will of these, may deserve the reward of eternal life rather than punishment. . . .

19. That no bishops, abbots, priests, deacons, or other members of the clergy shall presume to have dogs for hunting, or hawks, falcons, and sparrow-hawks, but each shall observe fully the canons or rule of his order. If any one shall presume to do so, let him know that he shall lose

his office. And in addition he shall suffer such punishment for his misconduct that the others will be afraid to possess such things for themselves. . . .

27. And we command that no one in our whole kingdom shall dare to deny hospitality to rich, or poor, or pilgrims; that is, let no one deny shelter and fire and water to pilgrims traversing our country in God's name, or to any one traveling for the love of God, or for the safety of his own soul.

28. Concerning embassies coming from the lord emperor. That the counts and *centenarii*[18] shall provide most carefully, as they desire the good-will of the lord emperor, for the *missi* who are sent out, so that they may go through their territories without any delay; and the emperor commands all everywhere that they see to it that no delay is encountered anywhere, but they shall cause the *missi* to go on their way in all haste and shall provide for them in such a manner as they may direct. . . .

32. Murders, by which a multitude of the Christian people perish, we command in every way to be shunned and to be forbidden. . . . Nevertheless, lest sin should also increase, in order that the greatest enmities may not arise among Christians, when by the persuasions of the devil murders happen, the criminal shall immediately hasten to make amends and with all speed shall pay to the relatives of the murdered man the fitting composition for the evil done.[19] And we forbid firmly that the relatives of the murdered man shall dare in any way to continue their enmities on account of the evil done, or shall refuse to grant peace to him who asks it, but, having given their pledges, they shall receive the fitting composition and shall make a perpetual peace; moreover, the guilty one shall not delay to pay the composition. . . . But if any one shall have scorned to make the fitting composition,

---

[18]The *centenarii,* or "hundred leaders," were minor local officials, who were subject to the authority of the district count. Each county was divided into a number of hundreds. See *The Salic Law* (Chapter 2, source 7, note 1) for more information on the traditional Germanic hundred.

[19]See Chapter 2, source 7.

he shall be deprived of his property until we shall render our decision. . . .

40. Lastly, therefore, we desire all our decrees to be known in the whole kingdom through our *missi* now sent out, either among the men of the Church, bishops, abbots, priests, deacons, canons, all monks or nuns, so that each one in his ministry or profession may keep our ban or decree, or where it may be fitting to thank the people for their good-will, or to furnish aid, or where there may be need still of correcting anything. . . . Where we believe there is anything unpunished, we shall so strive to correct it with all our zeal and will that with God's aid we may bring it to correction, both for our own eternal glory and that of all our faithful.

Leo III and Charles the Great: A Papal Portrait
▼▼▼
27 ▼ *POPE LEO III'S LATERAN MOSAIC*

Pope Leo III was lavish in the money he spent beautifying papal* Rome, and one of his most ambitious building projects was adding two massive state reception halls to the papal residence known as the *Lateran Palace.* In the fashion of the times, the interiors of each hall were covered with mosaics.* One of the mosaics pictured a seated St. Peter flanked by two kneeling figures: Pope Leo III and King Charles. Inasmuch as the mosaic was completed sometime between 798 and April 799, Charles undoubtedly saw this artistic interpretation of papal-Frankish relations on his fateful last visit to Rome in 800/801. We can only wonder what he thought of it.

Time badly deteriorated the mosaic, and an attempt to remove and restore it in 1743 resulted in its destruction and replacement by a not totally trustworthy copy. What we see in this eighteenth-century copy is St. Peter, with the keys to the Kingdom of Heaven on his lap (Chapter 4, source 20), handing a *pallium* (a long white strip of cloth on which a cross is embroidered) to Pope Leo and a lance with attached battle standard to King Charles. The pallium that Leo receives is the sign of primatial* power worn by popes and archbishops.* Note that Peter, who is dressed in clerical* robes, wears one. Both the pope and the king have square *nimbuses,* or haloes, conventional signs that they are especially sanctified or powerful people who are still living; Peter has a round nimbus, a sign of canonized* sainthood. The four Latin inscriptions read (from top to bottom and left to right as we view the mosaic): "Saint Peter"; "Most Holy Lord Pope Leo"; "To Lord King Charles"; and "Blessed Peter, You Give Life to Pope Leo and You Give Victory to King Charles."

Several descriptions of the original mosaic differ from this copy in a few details. One sixteenth-century author tells us that all he could read in the bottom inscription was "Blessed Peter, Give . . . to Pope Leo and Victory . . . to King Charles." To the contrary, a seventeenth-century papal librarian saw in that same inscription the words "Blessed Peter, Give Charles the Crown, Life, and Victory." Probably the most trustworthy rendering of the mosaic's Latin inscriptions appears in an early eighteenth-century engraving by Bernard de Montfaucon, a student of Italian antiquities. Montfaucon read "Our Most Holy Lord

Pope Leo" over the pope's figure; "Our Lord King Charles" over Charles's figure; and "Blessed Peter, Give Life to Pope Leo and Give Victory to King Charles" in the inscription at the feet of all three figures. It is now impossible to say with certainty which reading is correct. Whatever the words might have been, the images in this public mosaic are eloquent enough.

QUESTIONS FOR ANALYSIS

1. **Is there anything significant about Leo being on St. Peter's right and Charles being on his left? Explain your answer.**
2. **What do you make of the fact that it is *Peter* who gives Charles the lance and not Jesus or God the Father?**
3. **Review the three preceding sources in this section. Now compose a Carolingian commentary on this mosaic.**

Pope Leo III's Lateran Mosaic

The Later Carolingians

Charlemagne's accomplishments were impressive, but they should not blind us to the fact that at the time, no single individual or generation could successfully counter the forces of localism that were dividing continental Europe into smaller, more governable units. In his Capitulary on the Missi of 802, Charles admitted that he was "unable to give all individually the necessary care and discipline." In fact, during the last years of his life, his empire had already begun to show signs of political fragmentation, as some local counts and high-ranking churchmen grabbed power, despite Charlemagne's best efforts to keep these lords in check.

Moreover, fragmentation was built into the very fabric of Frankish inheritance customs. Charles and his brother Carloman had shared equally in the division of Pepin's kingdom in 768, and it was only following Carloman's death in 771 that Charles was able to gain the whole kingdom. In accordance with time-honored Frankish custom, in 806 Charlemagne formally divided his lands among his three legitimate sons — Charles, Pepin, and Louis — with Charles, the eldest, receiving a substantially larger portion. Pepin, however, died in 810, and Charles died the following year, leaving Louis as the sole surviving heir. As a consequence, Louis was crowned co-emperor in 813 and succeeded to all of Charlemagne's lands the following year as *Louis I* (r. 813–840), also known as *Louis the Pious*. Just as promising for those who dreamed of a strong and unified empire was the fact that Louis, unlike his father, put aside the title *king of the Franks and of the Lombards* and referred to himself simply and forcefully as *August Emperor ruling by the divine ordination of Providence.* Louis certainly seems to have had a vision of a single, indivisible empire, but he also had several strong-willed, ambitious sons, each of whom wanted his part of the Carolingian patrimony. The result was civil war among Louis's sons, even during their father's lifetime. By 843 Louis's three surviving sons — Lothair, Charles the Bald, and Louis the German — had divided the empire into three kingdoms. With this, the Carolingian world had reached a new level of fragmentation from which there was no going back.

The general breakdown of Carolingian order and unity was hurried along by new invasions: notably, Vikings from Scandinavia; Muslim pirates from North Africa and Spain; and Magyars, or Hungarians, from the steppes of Central Asia. Once again, Western Christian society was under siege, and its destiny was simple: It must either fight off or absorb the new invaders or go under as an identifiable civilization. In the process of successfully meeting the challenge posed by the invaders, Western Europe emerged stronger and more resilient than ever before, but it also suffered heavy losses in the fight. One of its more notable losses was the passing away of the Carolingian Empire before the ninth century had ended.

Civil War among Charlemagne's Grandsons

▼▼▼

28 ▼ *Nithard, HISTORIES*

Nithard (ca. 795–845) — a grandson of Charlemagne by reason of the love affair between Charles's daughter Bertha and the court poet Angilbert — was a soldier, statesman, and chronicler of the troubles that beset the Carolingian Empire in the generation following Charles's death. As a partisan of Louis the Pious's youngest son, Charles the Bald, who was king of western Francia and later emperor (r. 843–877), Nithard participated as a warrior and negotiator in the fratricidal struggles that intermittently ravaged the empire from 830 to 842/843. The peace treaty of Verdun of 843, which settled the issue of how the empire was to be divided among Louis's three surviving sons, did not end the empire's woes, however, as Nithard's own life and death testify. This learned grandson of Charlemagne met his end in 845, fighting invading Vikings.

Nithard informs his readers that he undertook the task of recording the Carolingian family struggles of his day at the urging of his lord, Charles the Bald, and we should not be surprised, therefore, that this history consistently views events from the perspective of Charles's camp. Despite that interpretive prism, Nithard seems to present the events of the civil war as honestly as circumstances and loyalty allowed. Certainly, as the war dragged on, Nithard became more despondent over its destructive course, and in his later chapters, he showed an increasing lack of enthusiasm for his task as its chronicler.

In the following excerpts, Nithard outlines the origins of the civil war, chronicles its resolution in 842/843, and, as he ends his history, reflects on the differences between his own day and that of Charlemagne.

QUESTIONS FOR ANALYSIS

1. How did Louis use the Church to ensure that no one would challenge his hold on the throne? Did it work?
2. What evidence is there that even before the civil war, the empire was troubled by factional disputes and power-seeking lords? What does this suggest about the empire's structural weaknesses?
3. What fueled this civil war: ideology? something else? What do you conclude from your answer?
4. How specifically did the civil war accelerate the breakdown of imperial order, unity, and power? Please explain your answer.
5. How does this history help us understand why Charles I became Charlemagne in Western Europe's historical memory?

When Emperor Charles of blessed memory, rightfully called the Great by all nations, died at a ripe old age, about the third hour of the day, he left the whole of Europe flourishing. For in his time he was a man who so much excelled all others in wisdom and virtue that to everyone on earth he appeared both terrible and worthy of love and admiration. Thus, he made his whole reign in every way glorious and salutary, as was apparent to everyone. But above all I believe he will be admired for the tempered severity with which he subdued the fierce and iron hearts of Franks and barbarians. Not even Roman might had been able to tame these people, but they dared do nothing in Charles's empire except what was in harmony with the public welfare. He ruled happily as king for thirty-two years and held the helm of the empire with no less success for fourteen years.[1]

Louis was the heir of all this excellence. He was the youngest of Charles's legitimate sons and succeeded to the throne after the death of the others. As soon as he had certain news of his father's death, he came straightway from Aquitaine to Aachen. No one objected when he asserted his authority over the nobles arriving on the scene but reserved judgment on those whose loyalty seemed doubtful. At the beginning of his rule as emperor he ordered the immense treasures left by his father to be divided into three parts; one part he spent on the funeral; the other two parts he divided between himself and those of his sisters who were born in lawful wedlock. He also ordered his sisters to remove themselves instantly from the palace to their monasteries.[2] His brothers Drogo, Hugo, and Theodoric, who were still very young, he made

companions of his table and ordered to be brought up in his palace.[3] To his nephew Bernard, Pepin's son,[4] he granted the kingdom of Italy. Since Bernard defected from Louis a little later, he was taken prisoner and deprived of his sight as well as his life by Bertmund, governor of the province of Lyons.[5] From that time on Louis feared that his younger brothers[6] might later stir up the people and behave like Bernard. He therefore had them appear before his general assembly, tonsured them, and put them under free custody into monasteries.[7]

When this had been taken care of, he made his sons enter legal marriages and divided the whole empire among them so that Pepin was to have Aquitaine, Louis Bavaria, and Lothair, after his father's death, the whole empire.[8] He also permitted Lothair to hold the title of emperor with him. In the meantime Queen Irmengardis, their mother, died, and a short time later Emperor Louis married Judith, who gave birth to Charles.[9]

After Charles's birth, Louis did not know what to do for him since he had already divided the whole empire among his other sons. When the distressed father begged their help on Charles's behalf, Lothair finally gave his assent and swore that his father should give to Charles whatever part of the kingdom he wished. He assured Louis by oath that in the future he would be Charles's protector and defender against all enemies. But after being incited by Hugo, whose daughter Lothair had married, Mathfrid, and others, he later regretted what he had done and tried to undo it. This behavior did not in the least escape his father and Judith. So from then on Lothair secretly sought to destroy what his fa-

---

[1]In other words, he was king from 768 to 800 and emperor from 800 to 814.

[2]Gisela and Bertha, neither of whom ever married and who had led rather free love lives. Both retired to comfortable positions in female monasteries.*

[3]Three sons of Charlemagne, born as the results of extramarital affairs.

[4]Louis's late brother Pepin, also called *Carloman,* died in 811.

[5]The rebellion took place in 817, and Bernard was blinded and killed in 818.

[6]His illegitimate brothers Drogo, Hugo, and Theodoric.

[7]They were tonsured as monks* in 818; that is, their heads were shaved, which is a sign that the person has renounced the world.

[8]The division was worked out in 817 and ratified in 821.

[9]Louis and Judith married in 819, and Charles (the Bald) was born in 823.

ther had arranged. To help him counter Lothair's plot the father employed a man named Bernard, who was duke of Septimania.[10] He appointed Bernard his chamberlain, entrusted Charles to him, and made him the second man in the empire. Bernard recklessly abused the imperial power which he was supposed to strengthen and undermined it entirely.

At that time Alamannia[11] was handed over to Charles by decree.[12] Lothair, as if he had at last found a good reason to complain, called upon his brothers and the whole people to restore authority and order in the empire.[13] They all suddenly converged on Louis at Compiègne, made the queen take the veil, tonsured her brothers, Conrad and Rudolf, and sent them to Aquitaine to be held by Pepin. Bernard took to his heels and escaped to Septimania. His brother Herbert was captured, blinded, and imprisoned in Italy. When Lothair had taken over the government, he held his father and Charles in free custody.[14] He ordered monks to keep Charles company; they were to get him used to the monastic life and urge him to take it up himself.

But the state of the empire grew worse from day to day, since all were driven by greed and sought only their own advantage. On account of this the monks we have mentioned above, as well as other men who deplored what had happened, began to question Louis to see if he were willing to reconstruct the government and stand behind it if the kingdom were restored to him. Above all he was to promote religious worship, by which all order is protected and preserved. Since he readily accepted this, his restoration was quickly agreed upon. Louis chose Guntbald, a monk, and secretly sent him to his sons Pepin and Louis. Guntbald went ostensibly on religious business, but he promised that Louis would increase the kingdom of both Pepin and Louis if they would assist the men who wanted him back on the throne. The promise of more land made them only too eager to comply. An assembly was convoked,[15] the queen and her brothers were returned to Louis, and the whole people submitted again to his rule. Then those who had been on Lothair's side were taken before the general assembly[16] and either condemned to death or, if their lives were spared, sent into exile by Lothair himself. Lothair also had to be content with Italy alone and was permitted to go there only on the condition that in the future he would not attempt anything in the kingdom against his father's will.[17]

When matters rested at this and there seemed to be a moment's respite, the monk Guntbald, whom we mentioned above, immediately wanted to be second in the empire because he had done so much for Louis' restoration. But Bernard, who had formerly held this position, as I said before, tried eagerly to regain it. Also Pepin and Louis, although their kingdoms had been enlarged as promised, nevertheless both tried hard to be first in the empire after their father. But those who were in charge of the government at that time resisted their desires.

▷   This accord lasted only a short time. A second rebellion broke out in 833, resulting in Louis's momentary deposition. Although he was restored to the throne in 834, Louis's last years were troubled by the constant conflicts among his four sons and their followers. Pepin died in December 838, and Emperor Louis died in July 840, leaving Emperor Lothair and Kings Louis and Charles to continue their fight. We pick up the story in 841/842.

---

[10]The Mediterranean regions of Francia.
[11]Southwest Germany and western Switzerland.
[12]In late 829.
[13]Co-emperor Lothair, the villain of this history, did not initiate the rebellion; rather, a group of dissident magnates began the revolt. Lothair, who was in Italy at the time, joined the rebellion in May 830.

[14]This coup of 830 resulted in Louis's being kept at a monastery at Soissons and Lothair ruling as virtual sole emperor, even though Louis retained some influence on affairs.
[15]In October 830.
[16]In February 831.
[17]The division of 817 was now nullified. Lothair was no longer heir to the entire empire. Except for Lothair's Italy, the empire was divided up among Louis, Pepin, and Charles.

Since I consider the affairs of the Saxons to be very important, I believe that they should not be omitted. Emperor Charles, deservedly called the Great by all peoples, converted the Saxons by much effort, as is known to everyone in Europe. He won them over from the vain adoration of idols to the true Christian religion of God. From the beginning the Saxons have often proved themselves by many examples to be both noble and extremely warlike. This whole tribe is divided into three classes. There are those among them who are called *edhilingi* in their language; those who are called *frilingi,* and those who are called *lazzi;* this is in the Latin language nobles, freemen, and serfs.* In the conflict between Lothair and his brothers the nobility among the Saxons was divided into two factions, one following Lothair, the other Louis.

Since this was how matters stood, and Lothair saw that after his brother's victory the people who had been with him wished to defect, he was compelled by various needs to turn for help anywhere he could get it. So he distributed public property for private use; he gave freedom to some and promised it to others after victory; he also sent into Saxony to the immense number of *frilingi* and *lazzi,* promising them, if they should side with him, that he would let them have the same law in the future which their ancestors had observed when they were still worshipping idols. Since they desired this law above all, they adopted a new name, "Stellinga,"[18] rallied to a large host, almost drove their lords from the kingdom, and each lived as their ancestors had done according to the law of his choice. But Lothair had also called in the Norsemen to help him, had put some Christians under their lordship, and permitted them to plunder others.[19]

Louis thus feared that Norsemen and Slavs[20] might unite with the Saxons who called them-selves Stellinga, because they are neighbors, and that they might invade the kingdom to revenge themselves and root out the Christian religion in the area. . . .

At the same time the Norsemen laid waste Quentovic,[21] then crossed the sea from there and ravaged Hamwig[22] and Northunnwig,[23] too. But Lothair, when he had withdrawn as far as the bank of the Rhone, took up residence there and made use of the shipping on this river. By doing so he drew as many men as he could from all sides for his support. Still, he dispatched an envoy to his brothers, informing them that he was willing, if only he knew how, to send his magnates to them to negotiate about peace.

He received the answer that he should send anyone he wished and that he could easily find out where to come. They themselves, however, continued their march by Chalon to Troyes. When they had come as far as Mellecey, Joseph, Eberhard, Egbert, and others of Lothair's party came to them and declared that Lothair knew he had wronged God and his brothers and that he did not wish the conflict between them and the Christian people to last any longer. If they wished, they might add a little to the third part of the kingdom because of the imperial title which their father had granted to him and because of the dignity of the empire which their grandfather had added to the kingdom of the Franks. But if they did not wish to do that, they should only concede to him the third part of the whole kingdom with the exception of Lombardy, Bavaria, and Aquitaine. Each of them should rule his part of the kingdom with God's help as best he could. Each should enjoy the other's help and good will. To their subjects they should mutually grant peace and justice, and with God's will there should be eternal peace among them.

---

[18]The name's meaning is uncertain, but it might mean "associates" or "allies."

[19]In 841 Lothair ceded some territory in Frisia to Heriold, king of the Danes.

[20]Various Slavic peoples to the east of the empire, most of whom were still pagan.

[21]The Pas-de-Calais.

[22]Harwich, England.

[23]Norwich?

When Louis and Charles[24] heard this and when it pleased them and their entire people, they met in council* with their magnates and considered with grateful hearts what they should do about Lothair's proposals. They declared that this accord was what they had desired right from the very beginning of their quarrel and, although it could not be worked out because of the violations that were committed in the meantime, that they had often proposed it to Lothair. They thanked Almighty God, Whose help finally let them see their brother, through God's grace, ask for that peace and harmony which he had always rejected.

▷   A peaceful division of the empire finally was accepted by all three parties in late 842 (and later ratified at Verdun in August 843). Despite this apparent solution, Nithard ended his history with the following observation.

From this history, everyone may gather how mad it is to neglect the common good and to follow only private and selfish desires, since both sins

insult the Creator so much, in fact, that He turns even the elements against the madness of the sinner. I shall easily prove this by examples still known to almost everyone. In the times of Charles the Great of good memory, who died almost thirty years ago, peace and concord ruled everywhere because our people were treading the one proper way, the way of the common welfare, and thus the way of God. But now since each goes his separate way, dissension and struggle abound. Once there was abundance and happiness everywhere, now everywhere there is want and sadness. Once even the elements smiled on everything and now they threaten, as Scripture which was left to us as the gift of God, testifies: *And the world will wage war against the mad.*[25]

About this time, on March 20, there occurred an eclipse of the moon.[26] Besides, a great deal of snow fell in the same night and the just judgment of God, as I said before, filled every heart with sorrow. I mention this because rapine and wrongs of every sort were rampant on all sides, and now the unseasonable weather killed the last hope of any good to come.

---

[24]Louis and Charles had allied against Lothair in February 842.
[25]The Bible, the Book of Wisdom, 5:21.

[26]Actually, March 19, 843.

The End of an Empire
▼▼▼
29 ▼ *Regino of Prüm, CHRONICLE*

Chronicles were a popular form of historical record keeping in early Europe, especially among monastic writers. As the term suggests, chronicles followed a strict chronological, or year-by-year, format, and their authors normally displayed little or no attempt at meaningful interpretation of what they recorded. Given this restrictive format, chronicles were not full-fledged, narrative histories, but at their best, they were more than just a series of short, random notes on disconnected matters.

Regino (ca. 845–915), abbot* of the German Benedictine monastery* at Prüm from 892 to 899, composed a chronicle — the first of its kind in East Francia —

that traced the history of the West from A.D. 1 to 906. Regino was one of the most widely educated individuals of his age, and he borrowed extensively from ancient and more modern authors in his attempt to write a reasonably detailed account of the major religious and secular* events that preceded his own adulthood. Even when he finally reached the late ninth century and began recording contemporary events, Regino continued to use written sources, as well as oral testimony and his own experiences, to help fill out his accounts and to present his readers with a series of vivid stories and character sketches.

The following selections deal with some of the most important events and crises of Regino's day. We begin with the death of Emperor Charles III, known as *the Fat.* Following Charles's inability to stand up to the Vikings who besieged Paris in 885–886, an assembly of German nobles deposed him in 887 and then elected Arnulf of Carinthia, the son of Charles's brother Carloman, as king of East Francia (r. 887–899). Shortly thereafter, Charles the Fat died, earning his place in history as the last Carolingian emperor to claim rule over the entire empire, albeit briefly and ineffectually. Even though Carolingians continued to hold various regional kingships for awhile more and Arnulf bore the now largely empty title of *emperor* from 896 to 899, Charles III's deposition and death signaled, for all practical purposes, the end of the Carolingian Empire.

The second excerpt deals with the election of Odo, count of Paris, as king of West Francia, the first non-Carolingian king of that land since 751. The last several excerpts detail the impact of the Vikings and the Hungarians on late-ninth-century Carolingian society.

QUESTIONS FOR ANALYSIS

1. How convincing is Regino's portrait of Charles III? What about the reasons he offers to explain the empire's breakup? On what do you base these assessments?
2. What point of view underlies Regino's treatment of Charles III and the effects of his deposition and death?
3. Does Regino seem aware that the year 888 is a watershed in Carolingian history? Please explain your answer.
4. Why was Odo chosen as king of West Francia? What does this suggest about late-ninth-century political realities?
5. What does Regino's treatment of the Viking attacks of 888/889 suggest about these late-ninth-century invasions?
6. Why were the Vikings such a threat to continental Europe? For instance, did the subcontinent have any geographic features that made it especially vulnerable to Viking attacks? (You might want to consult a map as you ponder this issue.)
7. How did the Hungarian menace differ from the Viking threat? What do you conclude from your answer?

888.

In the 888th year of the Lord's Incarnation, on the day preceding the Ides of January,[1] Emperor Charles, the third of this name and dignity,[2] died and was buried at the monastery of Reichenau.[3] He was truly a most Christian prince who feared God, observed His mandates with his whole heart, scrupulously obeyed the Church's laws, was generous in his alms giving, was unceasing in his devotion to prayer and the chanting of psalms, was indefatigable in his single-minded praise of God, and entrusted his every hope and all his plans to divine disposition. Consequently, everything that happened to him happily turned out well. In fact, he easily took possession of all the Frankish kingdoms in a short space of time and without conflict or opposition — the same kingdoms that his predecessors had acquired with bloodshed and great labor. The fact, however, that, toward the end of his life, he was stripped of his offices and despoiled of all his possessions was a trial, we believe, designed not only for his purification but, more important, so that he could prove himself. Indeed, the common report is that he bore this with the utmost patience, keeping true to his vows to offer thanks [to God] in adversity as well as in prosperity. Therefore, he has already received, or will undoubtedly receive, the crown of life, which God promised those who love Him.

After his death, the kingdoms that had been obedient to his authority were unbound from their union and returned to their separate ways, as if destitute of a legitimate heir.[4] Now, not waiting for their natural lord,[5] each sets out to elect for itself a king from its own inner parts. This excited great impulses toward war, not because the Franks lacked princes who could rule these kingdoms with nobility, fortitude, and wisdom but because their equality of generosity, dignity, and power increased discord among them. No one so excelled the others that the rest would deign to submit themselves to his overlordship. Francia could have produced many princes well suited to guiding the course of the kingdom had not Fortune armed them for their mutual destruction, as they strove for excellence. . . .

Meanwhile, the people of Gaul gathered together and, with the consent of Arnulf and their own equal assent and consent, elected as their king Duke Odo,[6] . . . a vigorous man who exceeded all others in beauty of form, height, and magnitude of strength and wisdom. He ruled the commonwealth manfully, and in defense against the unremitting depredations by the Northmen, he proved indefatigable. . . .

In the same year, the Northmen, who were besieging the city of Paris, did something extraordinary and unheard of both in our own day and even in times past: When they realized that the city was beyond capture, they began to exert all their strength and every bit of their ingenuity on the following plan. Turning their backs to the city, they would leave it, thereby enabling their fleet and all their troops to sweep up the Seine.[7] In this way, they would enter the Yonne

---

[1]January 12.

[2]Charles III (r. 876–887), the youngest son of Louis II (the German) and therefore the great-grandson of Charlemagne, held a variety of titles and lands at various times. He was crowned emperor in 881, but only in 885 did he manage to unite all of Charlemagne's empire.

[3]It was located on an island in Lake Constance, the lake whose demonic spirit had been vexed by Saint Gall (see Chapter 4, source 18).

[4]Charles the Fat had no legitimate heir, his only son having been born to a lover. Arnulf had also been born out of wedlock. His illegitimacy, however, was not the reason for the empire's dissolution.

[5]Charles III had attempted, unsuccessfully, to adopt an imperial heir before his deposition.

[6]Odo, or Eudes, count of Paris, reigned until his death in 898. His family intermittently held the royal crown of West Francia until 987, when Hugh Capet, a direct descendant of Odo, ascended the throne following the short and inglorious reign of Louis V (r. 986–987), Europe's last Carolingian monarch. Thereafter, the family of Odo, now known as the *Capetians,* produced kings of France in an unbroken line of son following father until 1328.

[7]In other words, they would bypass Paris, which at this time was a small, fortified island in the Seine.

River and thus penetrate the borders of Burgundy without opposition. Because the Parisians, however, used every means to bar their passage upstream, the Northmen dragged their ships over dry land for more than two miles, and having by this stratagem avoided every risk, they once again floated them on the Seine's waters. Shortly thereafter, they left the Seine and, as they had planned, sailed with all possible speed up the Yonne, putting in at Sens.[8] There, they set up camp, blockaded that same city by siege for six straight months, and destroyed almost all of Burgundy with robbery, murder, and fire. But because the citizens of Sens vigorously fought back and because God protected them, the Northmen were not able to capture the aforementioned city in any way whatsoever, even though they tried to do so many times by the sweat of their efforts and by the cleverness of all their skills and war machines. . . .

889.

In the 889th year of the Lord's Incarnation, the Hungarians, an exceedingly ferocious people, who are crueler than any beast and so unheard of in earlier ages that they were unknown by name, moved out of the realms of Scythia[9] and out of the swamps that the Don creates in great volume by its flooding. . . . This people was expelled out of these lands and from their homes by a neighboring people called the *Pechenegs*,[10] because the Pechenegs surpassed them in numbers and valor and the land of their birth was not large enough to accommodate their growing population. Put to flight, therefore, by Pecheneg aggression, the Hungarians said farewell to their homeland and set out in search of inhabitable lands, where they could establish settlements. First, they roamed the wastelands of the Pannonians and the Avars,[11] seeking their daily food by hunting and fishing. Then, by repeated

aggressive attacks, they broke through the borders of the Carinthians, Moravians, and Bulgars[12] and killed a few by the sword and many thousands with arrows, which they shoot so skillfully from their bows made of horn that it is almost impossible to defend oneself against their strikes.

They do not know how to fight hand to hand in close battle formation or how to take cities by siege. Rather, they fight by charging forward on their horses or by retreating, often even pretending to flee. They also cannot fight for long periods of time. They would otherwise be unbearable if their energy and perseverance were as intense as their onslaught. Most of the time, they retire from combat when the battle is hottest, but shortly thereafter, they return from flight to fight, so that just when you believe you have won overwhelmingly, you are about to undergo the real challenge. Their type of fighting is all the more dangerous, insofar as other people are unacquainted with it. There is one difference between their way of fighting and that practiced by the Bretons;[13] the latter use javelins, and the former, arrows.

They live not in the manner of human beings but of wild animals. According to rumor, they feed on raw meat, drink blood, cut up into pieces the hearts of their captives, which they eat like medicine, are not influenced by compassion, and have no stomach for any type of proper behavior. They cut their hair right down to the skin with a knife. They ride horses all the time; they are accustomed to traveling, thinking, standing, and conversing on horseback. They expend great care in teaching their children and slaves to ride and shoot arrows. By temperament, they are boastful, quarrelsome, dishonest, and overly hasty. Inasmuch as they expect the same ferocity from women as they do from men, they constantly deprive themselves of rest for the sake of foreign and domestic disturbances. By nature, they are taciturn and are more likely to act than to speak.

---

[8]A town southeast of Paris.
[9]The steppes of Central Asia.
[10]Turkic nomads from Central Asia who moved into the region of the Volga in the ninth century.

[11]Essentially, the plains of what is today Hungary.
[12]Various peoples of Eastern Europe.
[13]See source 33, note 13.

Not only the aforementioned lands but even the greatest part of the kingdom of Italy suffered destruction from the cruelty of this most abominable people.

In the same year, the Northmen left Sens and returned to Paris with their whole army. Because the people of Paris totally barred them from proceeding down river, they set up camp again and attacked the city with all their might, but, thanks to God's help, the Northmen did not prevail. A few days later, they once again sailed up the Seine with their fleet, entered the Marne River, burned down the city of Troyes, and laid waste the land all about right up to the cities of Verdun and Toul.[14]

---

[14]All three lie alongside rivers: Troyes is on the Seine; Verdun is on the Meuse; and Toul is on the Moselle (Mosel).

Chapter 6

▼▼▼

Restructuring and Reordering Europe: A.D. 850–1050

Internal weaknesses, irresistible tendencies toward the creation of regional power blocs, and multiple invasions by non-Christian outsiders precipitated the collapse of Carolingian unity during the late ninth century. We would be very mistaken, however, to view the 800s and the century and a half that followed as an era of unmitigated disasters, unremitting invasions, universal political fragmentation, and total social dislocation.

To be sure, the western regions of the Carolingian Empire witnessed weak kings and, more so than elsewhere in Europe, the rise of local political units that historians generally refer to as *feudal** lordships. Early feudal warriors were all too often lawless elements in a chaotic world. Lords and their armed retainers fought seemingly incessant wars, as they jockeyed for power against other feudal warriors. Yet these same feudal soldiers often provided the only possible military defense against invaders and homebred bandits in the face of the breakdown of monarchic authority; this was especially true in West Francia. Feudal soldiers thereby provided a modicum of security at the local level, and by the mid eleventh century, some of them offered more than just minimal protection and order.

East Francia, the eastern Germanic area of the old Carolingian Empire, experienced far less disunity, and therefore less feudal particularism, than its western counterpart. Germany was divided among four great tribal entities — the Franks, Saxons, Swabians, and Bavarians — and each tribe retained its own identity, laws, and ducal leaders. Of these tribes, the Saxons, whom Charles the Great had violently introduced to Christianity, produced a series of especially vigorous dukes. In fact, one of them, Henry I, the Fowler (r. 918–936), managed to secure the kingship of Germany, thereby becoming the first non-Frank to reign as king of East Francia. His son and successor, Otto I (r. 936–973), known to history as *the Great,* went one step farther and re-established an empire that once again encompassed Italian and Germanic lands and peoples, although its boundaries were quite different than existed during Charlemagne's empire. Under Otto I, his son Otto II (r. 973–983), and grandson Otto III (r. 983–1002), the empire expanded its influence eastward into the lands of formerly pagan Slavic and Hungarian peoples. Thanks to the efforts of imperially sponsored missionaries and settlers, by A.D. 1000 the Roman Church could count Bohemia, Poland, and Hungary as members of its expanding community of Christian states.

A similar spread of Latin Christian civilization took place in Scandinavia, as Norse, Danish, and Swedish kings adopted Christianity as a means of increasing royal power. By the year 1000 Norway and Denmark, whose Viking raiders and colonists had proved to be such disturbing factors in Western Europe for well over a century, were on their way to becoming integral parts of Latin Europe's family of Christian states. The same was true of Sweden, whose wandering merchants, warriors, and settlers had originally concentrated more on the regions of Ukraine, Russia, and Byzantium than on Western Europe. Whereas Sweden opted for Latin Christianity, Kievan Russia, whose early Scandinavian settlers blended into a much larger Slavic population, adopted the faith and many of the cultural forms of Byzantium during the late tenth century and following.

In addition to this dramatic spread of Europe's eastern and northern frontiers and the relative pacification of two of its late Carolingian invaders — the Hungarians and the Vikings — Western Europe also witnessed the rise of England's first united monarchy and the consequent rise in that island of a well-governed state.

Intellectual, artistic, and educational renewal often accompanied political restructuring throughout Western Christendom. Despite the ravages of ninth- and tenth-century invasions and internecine wars, Western Europe was not plunged into a dark age. Indeed, as it would so many times in the centuries to follow, Western civilization displayed an amazing resilience and surprising regenerative powers.

All things considered, Western Europe circa 1050 was still beset by many problems and a good deal of internal disharmony. Yet it had turned the corner and was ready for its first great age of efflorescence.

▼▼▼

Early France: A World of Local Lordship

West Francia, which we can begin to call the *kingdom of France* as we approach the year 1000, suffered greatly from ninth-century Viking, Hungarian, and Saracen raids as well from all of the internal instabilities that hastened the collapse of Carolingian unity. As Regino of Prüm's chronicle implied, Count Odo of Paris was elected king in 888 largely because of his ability to defend the region around Paris, known as the *Île de France,* from Viking marauders. His effective power, however, did not spread far beyond Paris. When he died, the crown passed back to the Carolingian Dynasty in the person of Charles III, the Simple (r. 898–922), and he proved so ineffectual that in 911 he was forced to cede land at the mouth of the Seine to the Norse leader Rolf. Although Rolf became a Christian, married Charles's daughter, and swore nominal fealty[*] to Charles, this land served as the nucleus for the essentially autonomous duchy of Normandy. Royal inability to deal effectively with the crises that beset France continued throughout the tenth and eleventh centuries, even after the descendants of King Odo gained permanent possession of the French crown in 987.

In many ways, the tenth- and early eleventh-century history of France was the reverse of the histories of England and Germany. Namely, in France, great lords emerged at the regional level, usurping royal and ecclesiastical[*] lands and offices and turning what had been public duties in the age of Charlemagne into private rights. These lords built up armies of personal retainers and used their soldiers, increasingly known as *vassals,*[*] to govern and extend the lands subject to them.

The purpose of vassalage and its accompanying rite of *homage,* by which some-one became a lord's "man" and publicly acknowledged that fact in a symbolic act of submission, was to bind people in a relationship as sacred and permanent as that of blood kinship. As is ideally the case in any family relationship, each party incurred responsibilities toward the other. The vassal swore to serve his lord faithfully, usually as a soldier, and the lord swore to protect the life and honor of his vassal. Additionally, the lord often granted the vassal an office, stronghold, land, or some other source of revenue in return for that service. This grant, which eventually became known as a *feudum,* or *fief,*[*] serves as the root for that mystifying and not easily defined term *feudalism.*

Because feudal relations largely concerned illiterate soldiers, few sources exist for the early stages of feudalism — certainly, too few to allow us to trace its development in any meaningful detail. Moreover, few contemporaries thought it necessary to describe in detail what was fast becoming an accepted and quite common phenomenon. Notwithstanding these limitations, some documents are available that give us tantalizing glimpses of early feudal realities and ideals.

St. Odo of Cluny's *Life of Saint Gerald of Aurillac,* source 30, shows an early tenth-century count's attempts to govern his lands. In addition to what it says about Count Gerald, this source also provides valuable insight into the ideals that motivated Abbot Odo, one of the leading reformers of his age. In source 31, another notable churchman and advocate of reform, Bishop Fulbert of Chartres, provides a theoretical statement of the obligations of vassals and lords. Odo and Fulbert were not alone in their attempts to call feudal warriors to a higher standard of conduct. The documents that appear together as source 32 reflect two ways in which some southern French church leaders sought to lower the level of violence that resulted from the lords' often unrestricted use of their private armies.

The Ideal Tenth-Century Count?

▼▼▼

30 ▼ *Saint Odo of Cluny,* THE LIFE OF SAINT GERALD OF AURILLAC

The anonymous *Life of the Virgin Liutbirg* (Chapter 4, source 23) introduced the genre of hagiography. After reading a few saints' lives, it becomes clear that their authors were interested primarily in demonstrating the holiness of the women and men about whom they were writing and in providing edifying examples of heroic acts of sanctity. Consequently, hagiographies tend to be formulaic and hyperbolic. As historical sources, they often tell us more about popular religious values than they do about the actual people whose lives they purport to record. As long as we understand these characteristics, however, we can carefully mine hagiographies for meaningful information about the flesh-and-blood holy people whom they memorialize and the times in which they lived.

Around 930 St. Odo, the second abbot* of the Burgundian monastery* of Cluny (r. 927–942), under whom the abbey* became the foremost center of tenth-century monastic reform in the West, composed the life of St. Gerald of Aurillac (855–909), a count noted for his own patronage of Benedictine monasticism. Himself the son of a great lord and a person who had received an extensive secular* education prior to becoming a monk* at age nineteen, Odo felt a certain affinity for the saintly Gerald.

Odo informs us that Count Gerald longed to live the life of a hermit and secretly lived a quasi-monastic life to the day of his death. That included remaining celibate, thereby neglecting one of the primary concerns of his class — the perpetuation and extension of his family's power. However, Gerald did not totally abandon the world. He maintained to the end full involvement in the governance and defense of his lands. That continuing involvement, portrayed in the pages of this hagiography, allows us to see, however dimly, some of the secular realities of Gerald's society.

QUESTIONS FOR ANALYSIS

1. What constituted normal training for the sons of nobility? Why did Gerald's parents offer him an alternative education, and what do their motives suggest about what was expected of ninth- and tenth-century lords?

2. How had Gerald become count? What conclusion do you draw from your answer?
3. Gerald had vassals who had their own vassals. How do we know that? What sort of authority did Gerald exercise over these rear, or second-rank, vassals? What does your answer suggest about the nature of government in Gerald's day and region?
4. What does the gift that Gerald gave to the blind priest* tell you about the count's authority?
5. Consider the peasants who fled Gerald's lands. Why might they have considered him a less than ideal lord?
6. Review Chapter 5, source 26. What function had counts served under Charlemagne? What were Gerald's functions, and to whom did he answer for his actions as count? What do your answers suggest?
7. Based upon what Odo tells us about the background against which Gerald performed his holy works, how would you characterize this age?
8. What is Odo's vision of the ideal warrior-count? How realistic does that vision appear to be?

The man of God, Gerald, took his origin from that part of Gaul which was called by the ancients *Celtica,* in the territory which marches with that of Auvergne and Cahors and Albi, in the town or village of Aurillac.[1] His father was Gerald, his mother Adaltruda. He was so illustrious by the nobility of his birth, that among the families of Gaul his lineage is outstanding both for its possessions and the excellence of its life. For it is said that his parents held modesty and religion as a sort of hereditary dowry. Two witnesses among his ancestors are themselves sufficient to prove the point: namely St. Caesarius, the Bishop* of Arles, and the holy Abbot Aredius,[2] . . . And indeed the great quantity of estates endowed with serfs,* lying in various places, which came to Gerald by right of succession, testifies to the extent of their riches. . . .

When he had been born, . . . and weaned, and had come to that age in which the character of children may usually be discerned, a certain pleasing quality began to show itself in him, by which those who looked closely conjectured of what virtue the future man should be. For at an early age, as we often see, children through the incitements of their corrupt nature are accustomed to be angry and envious, and to wish to be revenged, or to attempt other things of this sort. But in the child Gerald a certain sweetness and modesty of mind, which especially graces youth, adorned his childish acts. By the grace of divine providence he applied himself to the study of letters, but by the will of his parents only to the extent of going through his psalter,[3] after that he was instructed in the worldly exercises customary for the sons of the nobility; to ride to

---

[1] Aurillac is located in south central France. Around 890 Count Gerald founded the monastery of St. Peter at Aurillac, which quickly became a center for Cluniac reform.

[2] St. Caesarius, archbishop* of Arles (r. 502–542), and St. Aredius (d. 591), a champion of Eastern forms of monasticism, were two of southern Gaul's most notable sixth-century churchmen.

[3] A book of psalms, or prayers for chanting, taken from the Bible.

hounds, become an archer, learn to fly falcons and hawks in the proper manner. But lest given to useless pursuits the time suitable for learning letters should pass without profit the divine will ordained that he should be a long time sick, though with such a sickness that he should be withdrawn from worldly pursuits but not hindered in his application to learning. And for a long time he was so covered with small pimples that it was not thought that he could be cured. For this reason his father and mother decided that he should be put more closely to the study of letters, so that if he should prove unsuited for worldly pursuits, he might be fitted for the ecclesiastical* state. So it came about that he not only learned the chant, but also learnt something of grammar.[4] And this was afterwards of much use to him, since, perfected by that exercise, his wits were sharpened for whatever he might wish to apply them to. He had a lively and discerning mind, and was not slow to learn anything to which he set himself.

While he was growing up his bodily strength consumed the harmful humors of his body. So agile was he that he could vault over the backs of horses with ease. And because, endowed with bodily strength as he was, he became very active, it was demanded of him that he accustom himself to military service. But the sweetness of the Scriptures, to the study of which he was greatly attracted, held his mind in pledge, so that, although he excelled in military exercises, nevertheless it was the charm of letters which attracted him. . . .

After the death of his parents, when he attained full power over his property, Gerald was not puffed up, as youths often are who boast of their grown-up mastery, nor did he change the modesty which was springing up in his heart. His power of ruling increased, but the humble mind did not grow haughty. He was compelled to be occupied in administering and watching over things which, as I have said, came to him by

hereditary right, and to leave that peace of heart, which he had to some extent tasted, to take up the weariness of earthly business. He could scarcely bear to leave the inner solitude of his heart, and he returned to it as soon as he could. . . .

He admitted these gnawing cares[5] unwillingly for the sake of the complaints of those who had recourse to him. For his dependents pleaded querulously saying: "Why should a great man suffer violence from persons of low degree who lay waste his property?", adding that, when these discovered that he did not wish to take vengeance they devoured the more greedily that which was rightfully his. It would be more holy and honest that he should recognize the right of armed force, that he should unsheathe the sword against his enemies, that he should restrain the boldness of the violent; it would be better that the bold should be suppressed by force of arms than that the undefended districts should be unjustly oppressed by them. When Gerald heard this he was moved, not by the attack made on him but by reason, to have mercy and to give help. Committing himself entirely to the will of God and the divine mercy, he sought only how he might visit the fatherless and widows and hold himself unspotted from this world. . . .

He therefore exerted himself to repress the insolence of the violent, taking care in the first place to promise peace and most easy reconciliation to his enemies. And he did this by taking care, that either he should overcome evil by good, or if his enemies would not come to terms, he should have in God's eyes the greater right on his side. And sometimes indeed he soothed them and reduced them to peace. When insatiable malice poured scorn on peaceful men, showing severity of heart, he broke the teeth of the wicked, that . . . he might snatch the prey from their jaws. He was not incited by the desire for revenge, as in the case with many, or led on by love of praise from the multitude, but by love of the poor, who

---

[4]Latin poetry and prose.

[5]The cares, or concerns, of this world.

were not able to protect themselves. He acted in this way lest, if he became sluggish through an indolent patience, he should seem to have neglected the precept to care for the poor. He ordered the poor man to be saved and the needy to be freed from the hand of the sinner. Rightly, therefore, he did not allow the sinner to prevail. But sometimes when the unavoidable necessity of fighting lay on him, he commanded his men in imperious tones, to fight with the backs of their swords and with their spears reversed. This would have been ridiculous to the enemy if Gerald, strengthened by divine power, had not been invincible to them. And it would have seemed useless to his own men, if they had not learned by experience that Gerald, who was carried away by his piety in the very moment of battle, had not always been invincible. When therefore they saw that he triumphed by a new kind of fighting which was mingled with piety, they changed their scorn to admiration, and sure of victory they readily fulfilled his commands. For it was a thing unheard of that he or the soldiers who fought under him were not victorious. But this also is certain, that he himself never wounded anybody, nor was wounded by anyone. . . . Let no one be worried because a just man sometimes made use of fighting, which seems incompatible with religion. No one who has judged his cause impartially will be able to show that the glory of Gerald is clouded by this. . . . Gerald did not fight invading the property of others, but defending his own, or rather his people's rights, knowing that the rhinoceros, that is, any powerful man, is to be bound with a thong that he may break the clods of the valley, that is, the oppressors of the lowly. . . .

It was lawful, therefore, for a layman to carry the sword in battle that he might protect defenseless people, as the harmless flock from evening wolves . . . and that he might restrain by arms or by the law those whom ecclesiastical censure was not able to subdue. It does not darken his glory, then, that he fought for the cause of God, for whom the whole world fights against the unwise. Rather is it to his praise that he always won openly without the help of deceit or ambushes, and nevertheless was so protected by God, that, as I said before, he never stained his sword with human blood. Hereafter, let him who by his example shall take up arms against his enemies, seek also by his example not his own but the common good. For you may see some who for love of praise or gain boldly put themselves in danger, gladly sustain the evils of the world for the sake of the world, and while they encounter its bitterness lose the joys, so to speak, which they were seeking. But of these it is another story. The work of Gerald shines forth, because it sprang from simplicity of heart. . . .

The poor and the wronged always had free access to him, nor did they need to bring the slightest gift to recommend their cause. For the more fully anyone brought his necessity to his notice, the more closely did he attend to his need. And now his goodness was heard of not only in neighboring, but also in distant regions. And because everyone knew his kindness to all, many found the solution of their difficulties in him. Nor did he disdain either personally or through his officials to interest himself in the affairs of the poor, and, as occasion offered, to give help. For often when he knew that there was fierce strife between litigants, on the day on which the cause was to be heard he had Mass* said for them, and implored the divine assistance for those whom, humanly speaking, he could not help. Nor did he allow any lord to take benefices[6] from a vassal

---

[6]Fiefs. The word *benefice* is ecclesiastical in origin and refers to any church office and its sources of revenue held by a cleric.* Because the early Carolingians distributed ecclesiastical benefices as fiefs to their more important retainers, the word became part of the feudal vocabulary, even while it retained its original ecclesiastical meaning.

because he was angry with him. But when the case was brought forward, partly by entreaty, partly by command, he allayed the exasperation. You might think the vigor of his justice severe in this one thing alone, that whenever a poor man was brought before a more powerful man, he was at hand to uphold the weaker, in such a way that the stronger was overcome without being hurt. For the rest, truly hungering after justice, he insisted on its being carried out not only among his own people but even among strangers. . . .

Robbers had taken possession of a certain wood, and plundered and murdered both passers-by and those who lived in the vicinity. Gerald, hearing of this, immediately gave orders for them to be captured. It happened, however, that a certain countryman was driven by fear to join them. But the soldiers who captured them, fearing that Gerald would either release them, or blame them for showing him the prisoners unpunished, forthwith put out the eyes of all of them. And so it came about that this countryman was blinded. Later he went into the district of Toulouse, and a long time afterwards, when Gerald heard that he had not been a companion of the robbers, he was very grieved, and asked if he was still alive, and where he had gone. Having learnt that he had gone to the province* of Toulouse, he sent him, so they say, a hundred solidi, ordering the messenger to ask pardon for him from the man.

How he mercifully consoled the afflicted, and often spared the guilty, may be seen from an example. His neighbors had afflicted a certain priest with increasing quarrels, to the point that they put out his eyes. The count consoled the man greatly by his words, urging him to be patient. But lest the consolation of words should seem meagre, he handed over to him a certain church in his jurisdiction by formal deed. After a little time one of those who had done violence to the priest was taken by the officers and shut up in prison, and this was forthwith announced to the

count as something over which he would rejoice. And he in haste, as though with the desire of punishing the man, went to the prison. But other cases arose which it was necessary to deal with on the next day, and so he ordered the accused to be kept till then. In the evening when the officers had gone home, he secretly ordered the jailer to refresh the man with food and drink. And because he had no shoes he allowed shoes to be given to him and permitted him to escape. On the next day when those who were attending the court came to the count, he ordered the accused to be brought forth, and some men whom the jailer had prepared to act on his behalf announced trembling that the accused had escaped. Gerald, wishing to conceal the truth, made as though to threaten the jailer, but soon he said, "It is well, for the priest has now forgiven the injury done to him."

So, two men in chains were presented to him accused of a great crime. The accusers insisted that he should order them forthwith to be hanged. He dissembled, because he did not wish to free them openly. For he so conducted himself in any good work, that the goodness did not appear too much. Looking therefore at the accusers, "If," he said, "they ought to die, as you say, let us first give them a meal in the customary manner." Then he ordered food and drink to be brought to them, and ordered them to be unbound so that they might eat. When they had eaten he gave them his knife saying, "Go yourselves and bring the osier[7] with which you must be hanged." Not far away was a wood which grew up thickly with saplings. Going into this as though looking for osiers and gradually penetrating further they suddenly disappeared, and so escaped the moment of death. Those who were present, understanding that it was with his consent, did not dare to search for them among the bushes. He punished either with fines or branding the accused who were, as far as could be judged from their appearance, confirmed in evil.

---

[7]Willow sapling.

But those who had done wrong not through seasoned malice but inadvertently, he set free uncondemned. It was unheard of, nevertheless, that anyone was punished by death or maiming in his presence. . . .

To his vassals he was so kind and peaceable that it was a matter of wonder to those who saw it. And they frequently complained that he was soft and timid, because he permitted himself to be injured by persons of low degree as though he had no authority. Nor was he easily or lightly annoyed, as lords generally are, by his critics. On one occasion he met a number of peasants who had left their holdings, and were moving into another province.[8] When he had recognized

them and inquired where they were going with their household goods, they replied that they had been wronged by him when he had given them their holdings. The soldiers who were accompanying him urged that he should order them to be beaten and made to go back to the holdings from which they had come. But he was unwilling, for he knew that both he and they had one Lord in heaven, who was accustomed rather, in the words of the Apostle,* to forbear threats,[9] and who was not used to raise the hand of His might against the fatherless.[10] He therefore permitted them to go where they thought they would be better off, and gave them permission to live there.

---

[8]This is extraordinary. They possibly were free peasants, but the author seems to imply that they were legally bound to the soil.

[9]The Bible, St. Paul, Epistle to the Ephesians, 6:9.
[10]The Book of Job, 31:21.

The Ideal Early Eleventh-Century Vassal?
▼▼▼

31 ▼ *Fulbert of Chartres,* LETTER TO DUKE WILLIAM V OF AQUITAINE

The following document, addressed to Duke William V of Aquitaine (r. 990–1029), comes from the pen of Fulbert, bishop* of Chartres (r. 1006–1028) and dates to around 1020. Apparently, William, who was embroiled in a dispute with his powerful vassal* Hugh of Lusignan over the issue of respective rights, requested that Fulbert, one of the age's most learned men, clearly enunciate the obligations owed to a lord by those who had sworn fidelity to him. Bishop Fulbert responded with a short treatise on the ideal relationship that should exist between lords and their vassals.

QUESTIONS FOR ANALYSIS

1. Why do you think Fulbert begins by listing the vassal's six *negative* duties? What might that imply about the times and feudal realities?
2. In addition to these negative duties, what must a vassal do *for* his lord? What do you think Fulbert means by a vassal's advising and aiding his lord?

3. Does the lord owe anything to his vassal? If so, what? What inferences do you draw from your answers?
4. What are the implied sanctions for any vassal or lord who fails to meet his obligations?
5. What picture emerges of early eleventh-century French feudalism* from this letter?

To William, most illustrious duke of the Aquitanians,[1] Bishop Fulbert, the favor of his prayers:

Requested to write something regarding the character of fealty,* I have set down briefly for you, on the authority of the books,[2] the following things. He who takes the oath of fealty to his lord ought always to keep in mind these six things: what is harmless, safe, honorable, useful, easy, and practicable. *Harmless,* which means that he ought not to injure his lord in his body; *safe,* that he should not injure him by betraying his confidence or the defenses upon which he depends for security; *honorable,* that he should not injure him in his justice,[3] or in other matters that relate to his honor;[4] *useful,* that he should not injure him in his property; *easy,* that he should not make difficult that which his lord can do easily; and *practicable,* that he should not make impossible for the lord that which is possible.

However, while it is proper that the faithful vassal avoid these injuries, it is not for doing this alone that he deserves his holding: for it is not enough to refrain from wrongdoing, unless that which is good is done also. It remains, therefore, that in the same six things referred to above he should faithfully advise and aid his lord, if he wishes to be regarded as worthy of his benefice* and to be safe concerning the fealty which he has sworn.

The lord also ought to act toward his faithful vassal in the same manner in all these things. And if he fails to do this, he will be rightfully regarded as guilty of bad faith, just as the former, if he should be found shirking, or willing to shirk, his obligations would be perfidious and perjured.

I should have written to you at greater length had I not been busy with many other matters, including the rebuilding of our city and church, which were recently completely destroyed by a terrible fire.[5] Though for a time we could not think of anything but this disaster, yet now, by the hope of God's comfort, and of yours also,[6] we breathe more freely again.

---

[1] Aquitaine was a duchy in southwest France.
[2] Here, Fulbert refers to several manuals from Roman antiquity that he had consulted. Fulbert also possibly studied various books of local feudal customs, which had the force of law in their relevant feudal territories.
[3] The right of justice, or hearing cases, was one of the clearest indicators of power and rank. More serious cases, especially capital cases, would be referred by a vassal to his lord's court.
[4] This word has a dual meaning: "honor," as we understand it, and "office." Fulbert seems to imply both meanings.

[5] On the night of September 7, 1020, the Carolingian-era cathedral* of St. Mary was destroyed by fire. Fulbert immediately began a fund-raising program to build a grander and larger church. This church would, in turn, be destroyed by fire in 1194, which led to the construction of the great Gothic cathedral that dominates Chartres today.
[6] Duke William became one of the new church's major patrons.

The Search for Peace

▼▼▼

32 ▼ THE PEACE OF GOD and THE TRUCE OF GOD

The early feudal* world was filled with violence, and as we might reasonably expect, nonmilitary persons and places were particularly at risk. Beginning in 989 regional church councils* in southern France demanded that warriors accord defenseless people and places a special *peace,* or immunity from violence. A bit later, other church councils in this same general area of France expanded the peace movement by legislating periods of truce, during which all normal fighting was prohibited.

Although it is doubtful that such efforts immediately influenced the behavior of most warriors, the peace movement had several long-term consequences. In 1095 a French pope, Urban II (r. 1088–1099), universalized the peace movement for all of Western Christendom by calling for an armed expedition to the Holy Land, in part as an effort to export violence from Christian Europe. The result was the First Crusade (Chapter 11, source 72). The peace movement also helped engender within Europe's professional warrior class a developing awareness that its members had special responsibilities to the Christian community. By the twelfth century, such consciousness, which was so extraordinary in Gerald of Aurillac's day (source 30), was expressed in the rapidly developing Code of Chivalry, or knightly behavior (Chapter 8, source 47, and Chapter 9, source 60).

The two documents that follow come from an age in which the peace movement was just getting underway as a localized phenomenon. The first source dates from 990 and is a proclamation of the Peace of God by Guy, bishop* of Puy. The second is the earliest known example of the Truce of God. Preserved as a communication from Reginbald, archbishop* of Arles, and several other high-ranking French clerics* to the clergy* of Italy, it dates from the period 1035–1041. In it, Archbishop Reginbald and his colleagues recommend that the Italian clergy adopt the Truce of God, which obviously has already been proclaimed in the Mediterranean province of Arles.

QUESTIONS FOR ANALYSIS

1. Consider Bishop Guy's statement: "Only the peace-loving shall see the Lord." Does this sentiment shed any light on the manner in which Abbot Odo wrote about Gerald of Aurillac's life (source 30)? How so?
2. Which persons and places are protected by Bishop Guy's Peace? Why are they so singled out?
3. Consider the allowed exceptions to these peace prohibitions. What do they suggest to you?
4. Article 7 seems out of place in Bishop Guy's Peace. Is it? If not, how does it fit in?

5. Consider Reginbald's statement: "This is the peace or truce of God that we have received from Heaven through the inspiration of God." What do you think: Was this empty rhetoric, or did he believe those words? What is the basis for your answer?

6. What sanctions are threatened against those who violate the Peace and the Truce? What impact do you think they would have on those so threatened?

7. Who will punish those who break the Truce of God? How does Reginbald justify this double penalty?

8. What is promised to those who observe the Truce of God? What impact do you think that promise would have on eleventh-century individuals?

9. Based on the tone and message of these two documents, what conclusions have you reached concerning life in southern France at the turn of the millennium?

In the name of the divine, supreme, and undivided Trinity. Guy of Anjou, by the grace of God bishop [of Puy], greeting and peace to all who desire the mercy of God. Be it known to all the faithful subjects of God, that because of the wickedness that daily increases among the people, we have called together certain bishops [names], and many other bishops, princes, and nobles. And since we know that only the peace-loving shall see the Lord, we urge all men, in the name of the Lord, to be sons of peace.

1. From this hour forth, no man in the bishoprics over which these bishops rule, and in these counties, shall break into a church, . . . except that the bishop may enter a church to recover the taxes that are due him from it.

2. No man in the counties or bishoprics shall seize a horse, colt, ox, cow, ass, or the burdens which it carries, or a sheep, goat, or pig, or kill any of them, unless he requires it for a lawful expedition.[1] On an expedition a man may take what he needs to eat, but shall carry nothing home with him; and no one shall take material for fortifying or besieging a castle except from his own lands or subjects.

3. Clergymen shall not bear arms; no one shall injure monks* or any unarmed persons who accompany them; except that the bishop or the archdeacon[2] may use such means as are necessary to compel them to pay the taxes which they owe them.

4. No one shall seize a peasant, man or woman, for the purpose of making him purchase his freedom, unless the peasant has forfeited his freedom. This is not meant to restrict the rights of a lord over the peasants living on his own lands or on lands which he claims.

5. From this hour forth no one shall seize ecclesiastical* lands, whether those of a bishop, chapter,* or monastery,* and no one shall levy any unjust tax or toll from them; unless he holds them as *precaria*[3] from the bishop or the brothers.

---

[1] A legitimate expedition undertaken by the king, the local lord, or some other duly constituted authority. This right goes back to Roman imperial law.

[2] Dioceses* were divided into four administrative districts known as *archdeaconries,* each under the supervision of an archdeacon.

[3] A *precarium* (the singular form) was a fief* held in precarious tenure; that is, it was not transferable by right of inheritance. Upon the death of the fief holder or following the end of the period of feudal contract, the precarium reverted to the rightful owner. Because churches could not, according to ecclesiastical law, permanently alienate land or other possessions, they tended to give out fiefs to their vassals* as precaria.

6. No one shall seize or rob merchants.

7. No layman shall exercise any authority in the matter of burials or ecclesiastical offerings; no priest* shall take money for baptism,* for it is the gift of the Holy Spirit.[4]

8. If anyone breaks the peace and refuses to keep it, he shall be excommunicated* and anathematized and cut off from the Holy Mother Church, until he makes satisfaction; if he refuses to make satisfaction, no priest shall say mass* or perform divine services for him, no priest shall bury him or permit him to be buried in consecrated ground; no priest shall knowingly give him communion; if any priest knowingly violates this decree he shall be deposed.

▼ ▼ ▼

In the name of God, the omnipotent Father, Son, and Holy Spirit.* Reginbald, archbishop of Arles, with Benedict, bishop of Avignon, Nithard, bishop of Nice, the venerable abbot* Odilo [of Cluny],[5] and all the bishops, abbots, and other clergy of Gaul, to all the archbishops, bishops, and clergy of Italy, grace and peace from God, the omnipotent Father, who is, was, and shall be.

1. For the salvation of your souls, we beseech all you who fear God and believe in him and have been redeemed by his blood, to follow the footsteps of God, and to keep peace one with another, that you may obtain eternal peace and quiet with Him.

2. This is the peace or truce of God that we have received from Heaven through the inspiration of God, and we beseech you to accept it and observe it even as we have done; namely, that all Christians, friends and enemies, neighbors and strangers, should keep true and lasting peace one with another from vespers[6] on Wednesday to sunrise on Monday, so that during these four days and five nights, all persons may have peace, and, trusting in this peace, may go about their business without fear of their enemies.

3. All who keep the peace and truce of God shall be absolved of their sins by God, the omnipotent Father, and His Son Jesus Christ, and the Holy Spirit, and by St. Mary with the choir of virgins, and St. Michael with the choir of angels, and St. Peter with all the saints and all the faithful, now and forever.

4. Those who have promised to observe the truce and have wilfully violated it, shall be excommunicated by God the omnipotent Father, and His Son Jesus Christ, and the Holy Spirit, from the communion of all the saints of God, shall be accursed and despised here and in the future world, shall be damned with Dathan and Abiram[7] and with Judas who betrayed his Lord,[8] and shall be overwhelmed in the depths of hell, as was Pharaoh in the midst of the sea,[9] unless they make such satisfaction as is described in the following:

5. If anyone has killed another on the days of the truce of God, he shall be exiled and driven from the land and shall make a pilgrimage* to Jerusalem, spending his exile there. If anyone has violated the truce of God in any other way, he shall suffer the penalty prescribed by the secular* laws and shall do double the penance prescribed by the canons.*

6. We believe it is just that we should suffer both secular and spiritual punishment if we break the promise which we have made to keep the

---

[4]God's grace is totally free and cannot be merited or purchased.

[5]The fifth abbot of Cluny (r. 999–1049), St. Odilo was the most important monk of his age. During his fifty-year reign, Cluny became the West's leading center of monastic life and reform.

[6]The early evening prayer; it is the next to last of the daily canonical hours,* or periods of prayer, required of monks and clerics.

[7]Two Israelites who plotted to overthrow Moses during the period of the desert wandering (The Bible, Numbers, 16:26, and Deuteronomy, 11:16).

[8]The apostle* who betrayed Jesus by handing him over to Jewish authorities.

[9]As Pharaoh's army pursued the departing Israelites, it was drowned in the Sea of Reeds (Exodus, 14:21–29).

peace. For we believe that this peace was given to us from Heaven by God; for before God gave it to his people, there was nothing good done among us. The Lord's Day was not kept, but all kinds of labor were performed on it.

7. We have vowed and dedicated these four days to God: Thursday, because it is the day of His ascension; Friday, because it is the day of His passion;[10] Saturday, because it is the day in which He was in the tomb; and Sunday, because it is the day of His resurrection; on that day no labor shall be done and no one shall be in fear of his enemy.

8. By the power given to us by God through the apostles, we bless and absolve all who keep the peace and truce of God; we excommunicate, curse, anathematize, and exclude from the Holy Mother Church all who violate it.

9. If anyone shall punish violators of this decree and of the truce of God, he shall not be held guilty of a crime, but shall go and come freely with the blessing of all Christians, as a defender of the cause of God. But if anything has been stolen on other days, and the owner finds it on one of the days of the truce, he shall not be restrained from recovering it, lest thereby an advantage should be given to the thief.

10. In addition, brothers, we request that you observe the day on which the peace and truce was established by us, keeping it in the name of the Holy Trinity. Drive all thieves out of your country, and curse and excommunicate them in the name of all the saints.

11. Offer your tithes* and the first fruits of your labors to God, and bring offerings from your goods to the churches for the souls of the living and the dead, that God may free you from all evils in this world, and after this life bring you to the kingdom of Heaven, through Him who lives and reigns with God the Father and the Holy Spirit, forever and ever. Amen.

---

[10]*Passion* means "suffering" here; Friday is the day on which Jesus died.

▼▼▼

England, the Ottonian Empire, and Eastern Europe: New Monarchic Order

The dictum "What does not destroy me makes me stronger" certainly holds true for England and Germany in the ninth and tenth centuries. In meeting the crisis of invasion, each emerged as a stronger, more centralized kingdom, and in the case of Germany, the result was an empire that rivaled Charlemagne's.

When Danish raiders first appeared on the southern coast of England in 787, four Anglo-Saxon kingdoms dominated the land and vied among themselves for hegemony: Northumbria in the north; Mercia in the Midlands; East Anglia in the southeast; and Wessex in the southwest. A century later, Danish invaders and colonists had effectively destroyed the power of three of those kingdoms, thereby clearing the field for the rise of the kingdom of Wessex as England's sole bulwark against pagan Danish rule. Led initially by Alfred the Great (r. 871–899), the kings of Wessex successfully rose to the challenge. Their successful defense of their kingdom and subsequent counterattack against Danish-held areas resulted in the eventual conversion of the Vikings in England to Christianity and the unification of all peoples and lands in England under the House of Wessex around 954. In the midst of these accomplishments, the kings of Wessex also labored, with some success, to reinvigorate the Anglo-Saxon Church and to raise the level of literacy and learning in their island kingdom. As the first document shows, it was none other than Alfred the Great who established the precedent of attacking the silent, internal enemies, illiteracy and ignorance, even while carrying on the battle against external menaces.

Germany, or East Francia, suffered from Viking raids out of neighboring Denmark and seasonal invasions by waves of Hungarian light cavalry out of the East. Beginning with King Henry I (r. 919–936), Saxony produced vigorous royal war leaders, who were able to contain the threat from Scandinavia and crush the Hungarians in two major battles. The scale of the threat posed by the Danes and the Hungarians, when combined with the Saxon kings' successes on the battlefield, resulted in the growth of royal power and the momentary diminution of ducal independence. The second monarch of the House of Saxony, Otto the Great (r. 936–973), built upon his father's successes to the point that in 962 he was master of Germany and much of Italy, lord over a number of vassal* states in the Slavic East, and recognized as emperor by the Roman papacy.* As the second document shows, Otto was able to use that power and prestige to dominate the Roman papacy and, when necessary, to depose a hostile pope.

Popes and German emperors, however, generally worked in concert in their successful attempts to expand the borders of Roman Catholic Christianity among the Scandinavians of the North and the Slavs and Hungarians of Eastern Europe. By A.D. 1050, Denmark, Norway, Sweden, Poland, Bohemia, Hungary, and Croatia had been added to the family of believers claimed by the Roman Church, and Norse adventurers had even carried the new faith to Iceland, Greenland, and North America. Meanwhile, Russians, Ukrainians, Bulgarians, and Serbs had accepted the faith and ecclesiastical* traditions of Constantinople. Old beliefs and religious practices still persisted in all the new Christian lands, but, except for Greenland and North America's Vinland, the momentum toward integration into the cultures of Western Europe and Byzantium was irresistible. As the third document suggests, one of the major reasons for this rapid expansion of Christianity's borderlands was that local lords sponsored the new religion as a means of strengthening their prestige and power at home.

King Alfred's Educational Program
▼▼▼

33 ▼ Alfred the Great, *LETTER TO BISHOP WERFRITH*

In the late eighth and early ninth centuries, Danish Vikings invaded a politically fragmented England and managed to conquer much of the eastern half of the island, an area that became known as the *Danelaw*. In this time of extreme crisis, the kingdom of Wessex produced a hero-king, Alfred (r. 871–899), who managed to turn the tide of war by defeating a great Danish army in 878, thereby saving his kingdom. He then began the slow process of extending his authority north and east, capturing London in 886. By the time of Alfred's death, much of non-Danish England was subject to his rule, and the process of nibbling away at Danish-held land was well underway. In the mid tenth century, Alfred's royal descendants completed the reconquest of the Danelaw and ruled as kings of all England.

Alfred was an able warrior, an efficient organizer, and an innovator in the area of military strategy. More than that, he was a scholar and a patron of education. Although he only began to study Latin at the age of thirty-eight, Alfred proved to be an excellent student of the language and its literature. Much like Charles the Great, Alfred gathered scholars at his court from far and wide and set them to the task of reforming learning throughout his kingdom. A major element of that educational program was their translation of selected Christian classics from Latin to Saxon, the vernacular language of Alfred's people. Not content with standing idly by while this work went on, King Alfred joined in the effort.

Sometime between 890–892, Alfred produced his initial translation, *The Book of Pastoral Care* by Pope Gregory the Great. By way of a preface to this work, Alfred addressed the following letter to his close friend Werfrith, bishop* of Worcester and the scholar who had begun the entire translation process with his own Saxon rendition of Gregory the Great's *Dialogues*. Because this was Alfred's first translation, the letter to Werfrith served the purpose of setting forth the king's educational program as well as the philosophy that underlay it.

QUESTIONS FOR ANALYSIS

1. How does Alfred characterize England prior to the Viking invasions? How does he characterize the Danish impact on England?
2. Based on this letter, what appears to have been the common language of ninth-century church services in England?
3. How did Alfred propose to improve England's level of learning?
4. Notwithstanding his program of Saxon education, Latin retained a place in Alfred's scheme. What was it, and what do you infer from that fact?
5. Compare this document with Charles the Great's letter to Abbot Baugulf (Chapter 5, source 25). For example, how does each monarch view the present level of learning in his realm? Why is each concerned over it, and what does each propose to do about it? What conclusions do you draw from your comparative analysis?

King Alfred greets Bishop Werfrith with loving words and with friendship.

I let it be known to you that it has very often come into my mind what wise men there formerly were throughout England, both within the Church and outside it; also what happy times there were then and how the kings who had power over the nation in those days obeyed God and His ministers; how they cherished peace, morality, and order at home, and at the same time enlarged their territory abroad; and how they prospered both in war and in wisdom. Often have

I thought, also, of the sacred orders,[1] how zealous they were both in teaching and learning, and in all the services they owed to God; and how foreigners came to this land in search of wisdom and instruction, which things we should now have to get from abroad if we were to have them at all.

So general became the decay of learning in England that there were very few on this side of the Humber[2] who could understand the rituals[3] in English, or translate a letter from Latin into English; and I believe that there were not many beyond the Humber who could do these things.[4] There were so few, in fact, that I cannot remember a single person south of the Thames[5] when I came to the throne. Thanks be to Almighty God that we now have some teachers among us. And therefore I enjoin you to free yourself, as I believe you are ready to do, from worldly matters, that you may apply the wisdom which God has given you wherever you can. Consider what punishments would come upon us if we neither loved wisdom ourselves nor allowed other men to obtain it. We should then care for the name only of Christian, and have regard for very few of the Christian virtues.

When I thought of all this I remembered also how I saw the country before it had been all ravaged and burned; how the churches throughout the whole of England stood filled with treasures and books. There was also a great multitude of God's servants, but they had very little knowledge of books, for they could not understand anything in them because they were not written in their own language.[6] When I remembered all this I wondered extremely that the good and wise men who were formerly all over England and had learned perfectly all the books, did not wish to translate them into their own language. But again I soon answered myself and said: "Their own desire for learning was so great that they did not suppose that men would ever become so indifferent and that learning would ever so decay; and they wished, moreover, that wisdom in this land might increase with our knowledge of languages." Then I remembered how the law was first known in Hebrew and when the Greeks had learned it how they translated the whole of it into their own tongue,[7] and all other books besides. And again the Romans, when they had learned it, translated the whole of it into their own language.[8] And also all other Christian nations translated a part of it into their languages.

Therefore it seems better to me, if you agree, for us also to translate some of the books which are most needful for all men to know into the language which we can all understand. It shall be your duty to see to it, as can easily be done if we have tranquility enough, that all the free-born youth now in England, who are rich enough to be able to devote themselves to it, be set to learn as long as they are not fit for any other occupation,[9] until they are well able to read English writing. And let those afterwards be taught more in the Latin language who are to continue learning[10] and be promoted to a higher rank.

When I remembered how the knowledge of Latin had decayed through England, and yet that many could read English writing, I began, among other various and manifold troubles of this king-

---

[1]The monastic* and clerical* orders.
[2]South of the Humber, a wide estuary and swampland on England's northeast coast, which separates Northumbria from central and southeast England.
[3]The Church's worship services.
[4]Quite a claim, inasmuch as the region of the northeast had been the home of the early eighth-century *Northumbrian Renaissance,* whose greatest exemplar was Bede the Venerable (Chapter 4, source 22).
[5]The River Thames was the kingdom of Wessex's northern boundary.
[6]They were in Latin and, in a few cases, Greek.

[7]The law he refers to is the sacred law contained in the Bible. During the Hellenistic* era, the Hebrew Bible was translated into various Greek editions for Hellenized Jews of the Diaspora who no longer spoke or read Hebrew.
[8]St. Jerome (345–420) produced the most successful Latin translation of the Bible, a work that became known as the *Vulgate* (common) Bible. Carolingian sponsorship played a major role in making Jerome's translation the standard Western Bible.
[9]Especially those not fit for military service.
[10]This follows Alfred's own educational odyssey. He learned to read and write Saxon after the age of twelve and turned to Latin twenty-five years later.

dom, to translate into English the book which is called in Latin *Pastoralis,* and in English *The Shepherd's Book,*[11] sometimes word for word, and sometimes according to the sense, as I had learned it from Plegmund, my archbishop,* and Asser, my bishop, and Grimbald, my mass*-priest,* and John, my mass-priest. And when I had learned it, as I could best understand it and most clearly interpret it, I translated it into English.

I will send a copy of this book to every bishopric in my kingdom, and on each copy there shall be a clasp worth fifty mancuses.[12] And I command in God's name that no man take the clasp from the book, or the book from the minster.[13] It is uncertain how long there may be such learned bishops as, thanks be to God, there now are almost everywhere; therefore, I wish these copies always to remain in their places, unless the bishop desires to take them with him, or they be loaned out anywhere, or any one wishes to make a copy of them.

---

[11]The bishop, according to Gregory the Great, is the shepherd, or pastor, of his people.

[12]A considerable weight of silver.

[13]Originally, the term meant a monastic church. Because England's first cathedral* churches were founded and served by monks* (Chapter 4, source 22), the term was sometimes applied to cathedral churches in general. Some English cathedrals, such as the Minster of York, retain the title to this day.

Otto I and the Papacy

▼▼▼

34 ▾ *Liudprand of Cremona, THE DEEDS OF OTTO*

Following the death of the king of Italy, Berengar I (r. 915–923), who enjoyed the title but not the authority of *emperor,* the imperial title died out in the West for lack of anyone strong enough to claim it. On February 2, 962, however, Pope John XII (r. 955–964) anointed the king of Germany, Otto I (r. 936–973), as emperor, thereby resurrecting the Western imperial office. Much like Charlemagne, upon whom he modeled himself, Otto was the most powerful monarch of his day in Western Europe and was remembered by posterity as worthy of the title *the Great.* Unlike Charles the Great, however, Otto carved out an empire in Germany and Italy that lived on for centuries after his death.

Liudprand (ca. 920–972), bishop* of Cremona, was an eyewitness to the birth of that empire, and his account, which covers the years 960–964, outlines in detail the events leading up to and following Otto's consecration as emperor. Liudprand, who came from an important Lombard family in northern Italy, initially served Berengar II, the marquis of Ivrea and king of Italy, but following a falling out with Berengar, Liudprand fled to Otto's court in Germany. Late in 961, as he marched toward Rome for his imperial anointment, King Otto installed Liudprand in the bishopric of Cremona in northern Italy as a reward for his services. In return, Liudprand proved to be a faithful instrument and publicist of Otto's Italian policies.

QUESTIONS FOR ANALYSIS

1. Why did John XII turn against Otto?
2. Why did the Roman synod* depose Pope John?
3. Review Pope Gregory I's letter to Emperor Maurice in source 20 of Chapter 4. How did Gregory's interpretation of Matthew, 16:18, differ from that proposed by the Roman synod of November 22, 963? What do you conclude from your comparative analysis?
4. What role did Otto play in judging and deposing Pope John? What role did Otto play in Pope Leo's election? What do you infer from your answers?
5. How does Liudprand deal with Pope John? Pope Leo VIII? What are your conclusions?
6. Note the ways in which Liudprand refers to Otto and what he says about the emperor's duties and actions. What do you infer from all of this?
7. In describing Otto's war against Berengar, Liudprand notes, "The holy apostles* Peter and Paul were fighting under his {Otto's} flag." Compare this with source 27 in Chapter 5. What conclusions do you draw from this comparison?
8. Consider both Alfred the Great and Otto the Great. In what ways did each man appear to be influenced by the life and legend of Charlemagne? What do your answers suggest about the impact of Charles the Great on European history?

Berengar and Adalbert were reigning,[1] or rather raging, in Italy, where, to speak the truth, they exercised the worst of tyrannies, when John, the supreme pontiff* and universal pope,[2] whose church had suffered from the savage cruelty of the aforesaid Berengar and Adalbert,[3] sent envoys from the holy church of Rome, in the persons of the cardinal* deacon* John and the secretary Azo, to Otto, at that time the most serene and pious king and now our august emperor, humbly begging him, both by letters and a recital of facts, for the love of God and the holy apostles Peter and Paul, who he hoped would remit his sins, to rescue him and the holy Roman Church entrusted to him from their jaws, and restore it to its former prosperity and freedom. While the Roman envoys were laying these complaints, Waldpert, the venerable archbishop* of the holy church of Milan, having escaped half-dead from the mad rage of the aforesaid Berengar and Adalbert, sought the powerful protection of the above mentioned Otto, at that time king and now our august emperor, declaring that he could no no longer bear or submit to the cruelty of

---

[1]The king of Lombardy, also known as the king of Italy, Berengar II and his son, Adalbert. Otto I's second wife, Adelaide, had a better claim to the crown of northern Italy, but Berengar had dispossessed her and had even imprisoned her for awhile before her marriage to Otto. In 952 Berengar had sworn fealty* to Otto, recognizing Otto as his overlord.

[2]John XII (r. 955–963). Originally named *Octavian,* John was the son of Alberic II (d. 954), the prince of Rome. Alberic had managed to secure Octavian's succession as prince of Rome and had also stage managed Octavian's future election as pope, once the then reigning Agapetus II (r. 946–955) died. Upon Agapetus's death a year after Alberic's own death, Octavian claimed the papal* throne and changed his name to *John.* He was not quite nineteen years of age when he acquired the office.

[3]Both men had designs on the extensive lands held by the papacy,* which were known as the *Patrimony of Saint Peter.*

Berengar and Adalbert and Willa,[4] who contrary to all human and divine law had appointed Manasses bishop of Arles to the see* of Milan.[5] He said that it was a calamity for his church thus to intercept a right that belonged to him and to his people.[6] After Waldpert came Waldo Bishop of Como,[7] crying out that he also had suffered a like insult at the hands of Berengar, Adalbert and Willa. . . .

The most pious king was moved by their tearful complaints, and considered not himself but the cause of Jesus Christ. Therefore, although it was contrary to custom, he appointed his young son Otto as king,[8] and leaving him in Saxony collected his forces and marched in haste to Italy. There he drove Berengar and Adalbert from the realm at once, the more quickly inasmuch as it is certain that the holy apostles Peter and Paul were fighting under his flag. The good king brought together what had been scattered and mended what had been broken, restoring to each man his due possessions. Then he advanced on Rome to do the same again.

There he was welcomed with marvelous ceremony and unexampled pomp, and was anointed as emperor by John the supreme bishop and universal pope. To the church he not only gave back her possessions but bestowed lavish gifts of jewels, gold and silver. Furthermore Pope John and all the princes of the city swore solemnly on the most precious body of Saint Peter that they would never give help to Berengar and Adalbert. Thereupon Otto returned to Pavia[9] with all speed.

Meanwhile, Pope John, forgetful of his oath and the promise he had made to the sacred emperor, sent to Adalbert asking him to return and swearing that he would assist him against the power of the most sacred emperor. For the sacred emperor had so terrified this Adalbert, per-secutor of God's churches and of Pope John, that he had left Italy altogether and had gone to Fraxinetum[10] and put himself under the protection of the Saracens. The righteous emperor for his part could not understand at all why Pope John was now showing such affection to the very man whom previously he had attacked in bitter hatred. Accordingly he called together some of his intimates and sent off to Rome to inquire if this report was true. On his messengers' arrival they got this answer, not from a few chance informants, but from all the citizens of Rome: — "Pope John hates the most sacred emperor, who freed him from Adalbert's clutches, for exactly the same reason that the devil hates his creator. The emperor, as we have learned by experience, knows, works and loves the things of God: he guards the affairs of church and state with his sword, adorns them by his virtues, and purifies them by his laws. Pope John is the enemy of all these things. What we say is a tale well known to all. As witness to its truth take the widow of Rainer his own vassal,* a woman with whom John has been so blindly in love that he has made her governor of many cities and given to her the golden crosses and cups that are the sacred possessions of St Peter himself. Witness also the case of Stephana, his father's mistress, who recently conceived a child by him and died of an effusion of blood. If all else were silent, the palace of the Lateran,[11] that once sheltered saints and is now a harlot's brothel, will never forget his union with his father's wench, the sister of the other concubine Stephania. Witness again the absence of all women here save Romans: they fear to come and pray at the thresholds of the holy apostles, for they have heard how John a little time ago took women pilgrims* by force to his bed, wives, widows and virgins alike. Witness the churches of

---

[4]Berengar's wife.

[5]The city of Milan was the key to control of the Lombard Plain. Berengar desired to install his own archbishop, Manasses, in this strategically important see.

[6]By tradition, bishops were *canonically* *elected* by the clergy* and laity of their cities (see Chapter 10, source 65).

[7]Another northern Italian diocese.*

[8]The future Emperor Otto II (r. 973–983). Otto was fifteen in 961, when this was happening.

[9]The capital of the kingdom of Lombardy (also known as the kingdom of Italy, even though most of the peninsula lay outside of royal control).

[10]A stronghold on the Riviera held by Muslim pirates.

[11]The papal palace in Rome.

the holy apostles, whose roof lets the rain in upon the sacrosanct altar, and that not in drops but in sheets. The woodwork fills us with alarm, when we go there to ask God's help. Death reigns within the building, and, though we have much to pray for, we are prevented from going there and soon shall be forced to abandon God's house altogether. Witness the women he keeps, some of them fine ladies who, as the poet says, are as thin as reeds by dieting, others everyday buxom wenches. It is all the same to him whether they walk the pavement or ride in a carriage and pair. That is the reason why there is the same disagreement between him and the holy emperor as there is of necessity between wolves and lambs. That he may go his way unchecked, he is trying to get Adalbert, as patron, guardian and protector."

When the envoys on their return gave this report to the emperor, he said: — "He is only a boy, and will soon alter if good men set him an example. I hope that honorable reproof and generous persuasion will quickly cure him of these vices." . . .

▷   After fruitless negotiations between the pope and Otto's envoys, Pope John receives Adalbert back in Rome. In September 963 Otto marches on Rome, and Pope John and Adalbert flee the city.

The citizens welcomed the holy emperor and all his men into their town, promising again to be loyal and adding under a strong oath that they would never elect or ordain a pope except with the consent and approval of the august Caesar Otto the lord emperor and his son King Otto.

Three days later at the request of the bishops and people of Rome a synod was held in the church of St Peter, attended by the emperor and the Italian archbishops. . . .

When all had taken their seats and complete silence was established, the holy emperor began thus: "How fitting it would have been for the lord pope John to be present at this glorious holy

synod. I ask you, holy fathers,* to give your opinion why he has refused to attend this great gathering, for you live as he does and share in all his interests." Thereupon the Roman bishops and the cardinal priests* and deacons together with the whole populace said: — "We are surprised that your most holy wisdom deigns to ask us this question: even the inhabitants of Iberia and Babylonia and India know the answer to it. John is not now even one of those who come in sheep's clothing and within are ravening wolves: his savageness is manifest, he is openly engaged in the devil's business, and he makes no attempt at disguise." The emperor replied: — "It seems to us right that the charges against the pope should be brought forward seriatim, and that the whole synod should then consider what course we should adopt." . . .

▷   A number of charges of sacrilege, sin, unbelief, and improper behavior are leveled against John, including the claim that he murdered a Roman cleric* by castrating him. Otto is hesitant to accept these charges as true, without John's having a chance to clear himself, presumably by taking an oath of innocence, as Leo III had done to clear his name in December 800. Consequently, the synod sends John an invitation to return to Rome to answer the charges.

After reading this letter, the pope sent the following reply: "Bishop John, servant of God's servants, to all the bishops. We hear say that you wish to make another pope. If you do, I excommunicate* you by Almighty God, and you have no power, to ordain no one or celebrate mass.*"

When this answer was read in the holy synod, the . . . synod returned the following reply to the lord pope: — "To the supreme pontiff and universal pope lord John, Otto, august emperor by the grace of God, and the holy synod assembled at Rome in God's service, send greeting in the Lord's name. At our last meeting of the sixth of November[12] we sent you a letter containing the charges made against you by your

---

[12]963.

accusers and their reasons for bringing them. In the same letter we asked your highness to come to Rome, as is only just, and to clear yourself from these allegations. We have now received your answer, which is not at all of a kind suited to the character of this occasion but is more in accordance with the folly of rank indifference. There could be no reasonable excuse for not coming to the synod. But messengers from your highness ought certainly to have put in an appearance here, and assured us that you could not attend the holy synod owing to illness or some such insuperable difficulty. There is furthermore a sentence in your letter more fitting for a stupid boy than a bishop. You excommunicated us all if we appointed another bishop to the see of Rome, and yet gave us power to celebrate the mass and ordain clerical functionaries. You said: — 'You have no power to ordain no one.' We always thought, or rather believed, that two negatives make an affirmative, if your authority did not weaken the verdict of the authors of old. However, let us reply, not to your words, but to your meaning. If you do not refuse to come to the synod and to clear yourself of these charges, we certainly are prepared to bow to your authority. But if — which Heaven forbid! — under any pretence you refrain from coming and defending yourself against a capital charge, especially when there is nothing to stop you, neither a sea voyage, nor bodily sickness, nor a long journey, then we shall disregard your excommunication, and rather turn it upon yourself, as we have justly the power to do. Judas, who betrayed, or rather who sold, Our Lord Jesus Christ, with the other disciples received the power of binding and loosing from their Master in these words: — 'Verily I say unto you, Whatsoever ye shall bind on earth shall be bound in heaven: and whatsoever ye shall loose on earth shall be loosed in heaven.' As long as Judas was a good man with his fellow disciples, he had the power to bind and loose. But when he became a murderer for greed and wished to destroy all men's lives, whom

then could he loose that was bound or bind that was loosed save himself, whom he hanged in the accursed noose?" This letter was written on the twenty-second day of November and sent by the hand of the cardinal priest Adrian and the cardinal deacon Benedict.

When these latter arrived at Tivoli,[13] they could not find the pope: he had gone off into the country with bow and arrows, and no one could tell them where he was. Not being able to find him they returned with the letter to Rome and the holy synod met for the third time. On this occasion the emperor said: "We have waited for the pope's appearance, that we might complain of his conduct towards us in his presence: but since we are now assured that he will not attend, we beg you earnestly to listen to an account of his treacherous behavior. We hereby inform you, archbishops, bishops, priests, deacons, clerics, counts, judges and people, that Pope John being hard pressed by Berengar and Adalbert, our revolted subjects, sent messengers to us in Saxony, asking us for the love of God to come to Italy and free him and the church of St Peter from their jaws. We need not tell you how much we did for him with God's assistance: you see it to-day for yourselves. But when by my help he was rescued from their hands and restored to his proper place, forgetful of the oath of loyalty which he swore to me on the body of St Peter, he got Adalbert to come to Rome, defended him against me, stirred up tumults, and before my soldiers' eyes appeared as leader in the campaign equipped with helmet and cuirass. Let the holy synod now declare its decision." Thereupon the Roman pontiffs[14] and the other clergy and all the people replied: "A mischief for which there is no precedent must be cauterized by methods equally novel. If the pope's moral corruption only hurt himself and not others, we should have to bear with him as best we could. But how many chaste youths by his example have become unchaste? How many worthy men by association with him have become reprobates? We therefore

---

[13]A town in central Italy.

[14]Here, the term means the clergy of Rome at the synod.

ask your imperial majesty that this monster, whom no virtue redeems from vice, shall be driven from the Holy Roman Church, and another be appointed in his place, who by the example of his goodly conversation may prove himself both ruler and benefactor, living rightly himself and setting us an example of like conduct." Then the emperor said: "I agree with what you say; nothing will please me more than for you to find such a man and to give him control of this holy universal see."

At that all cried with one voice: — "We elect as our shepherd Leo, the venerable chief notary of the holy Roman church, a man of proved worth deserving of the highest sacerdotal rank. He shall be the supreme and universal pope of the Holy Roman Church, and we hereby reprobate the apostate[15] John because of his vicious life." The whole assembly repeated these words three times, and then with the emperor's consent escorted the aforesaid Leo to the Lateran Palace amid acclamations, and later at the due season in the church of St Peter elevated him to the supreme priesthood by holy consecration and took the oath of loyalty towards him.[16]

---

[15]Someone who has abandoned the faith.

[16]Pope Leo VIII (r. 963–965).

The Apostolic King of Hungary
▼▼▼

35 ▼ *Pope Sylvester II,*
LETTER TO SAINT STEPHEN OF HUNGARY

When we last saw the Hungarians, whom Regino of Prüm characterized as an "exceedingly ferocious people, . . . crueler than any beast" (Chapter 5, source 29), they were devastating late-ninth-century Europe. A Finno-Ugric people out of the Great Steppes of Eurasia, the Hungarians (or *Magyars,* as they called themselves) were quite terrifying for late-ninth- and early tenth-century Europe. "Lord, preserve us from the arrows of the Hungarians" was a constant prayer in Central Europe and northern Italy.

The Magyars continued to be a menace until Otto I inflicted a crushing defeat upon them in 995 at the Lechfeld in southern Germany. Soon thereafter, they settled down in a region defined by the Middle Danube and the Pannonian Plain, a land they transformed into Hungary, and began receiving Christian missionaries, especially from Germany.

All three Ottonian emperors were enthusiastic patrons of this missionary work, especially the young and idealistic Otto III (r. 983–1002). Otto III — who variously styled himself as *servant of the Apostles** and *servant of Jesus Christ* — envisioned a Christian empire in which pope and emperor worked harmoniously to create a society permeated by Christian principles. To that end, he appointed to the papacy* Gerbert of Aurillac, the foremost scholar of his day, a former monk* of the monastery* founded by St. Gerald of Aurillac (source 30) and teacher of several of Europe's leading intellectuals, including Fulbert of Chartres (source 31). Gerbert, the first person from the kingdom of France to advance to the papal* throne, assumed the name *Sylvester II* (r. 999–1003).

The name change was highly significant. The first Sylvester had been bishop*
of Rome in the time of Constantine the Great. According to tradition, it was
Sylvester I (r. 314–335) who had converted and baptized* the Roman emperor.
Just as significant, according to tradition and a forged eighth-century document
known as *The Donation of Constantine,* Emperor Constantine I had conferred on
Pope Sylvester I authority over Rome, Italy, and "the lands of the West," just
before he transferred his capital to Constantinople. There was no truth to these
legends, although they were almost universally believed in the West. On his part,
Otto III dismissed *The Donation of Constantine* as a fraud but probably believed
that Sylvester I and Constantine had worked together closely. Therefore, Gerbert's
assumption of the name *Sylvester* betokened his determination to work alongside
this latter-day Constantine to create a Christian commonwealth on earth, and
that included supporting the empire's missionary activities among the Slavs, Scandinavians, and Magyars.

On their part, the Hungarian leaders, beginning with Duke Géza (r. 972–997),
were more than willing to accept Christianity, but they wanted no part of German overlordship. As part of his program of welcoming missionaries while keeping Otto's empire at arm's length, Géza's son Vajk (r. 997–1038), who changed his
name to *Stephen* (which means "crown" in Greek), submitted his land and people
directly to papal overlordship. In return, he was invested as king on Christmas
Day, 1000, with a crown sent him by Pope Sylvester II. For his successful efforts
in converting his people to Catholic Christianity, King Stephen was declared a
saint in 1083.

The document that follows is Pope Sylvester's letter of 1000, in which he officially conferred the title of *king* on Stephen. Never before had any pope bestowed
a royal title on anyone, although Pope Zacharias had indirectly given his approval
to Pepin's palace coup in 751.

QUESTIONS FOR ANALYSIS

1. What relationship did this letter establish between Hungary and the
   papacy?
2. What relationship did it establish between the king of Hungary and the
   pope?
3. What powers and honors did the grant confer on the king?
4. Based on your answers to the preceding questions, what do you conclude
   were, to Stephen's mind, the benefits to be gained from accepting the
   crown from the pope?
5. Why you think Pope Sylvester made this grant?
6. Otto III approved the pope's action. What do you think Otto might have
   had in mind?
7. In the late eleventh century and following, the papacy interpreted
   Sylvester's granting of a crown as an important precedent. How do you
   think these later popes viewed the act?

Sylvester, bishop, servant of the servants of God, to Stephen, king of the Hungarians, greeting and apostolic benediction. Your ambassadors, especially our dear brother, Astricus, bishop of Colocza,[1] were received by us with the greater joy and accomplished their mission with the greater ease, because we had been divinely forewarned to expect an embassy from a nation still unknown to us. ... Surely, according to the apostle: "It is not of him who wills nor of him who runs, but of God who shows mercy";[2] and according to the testimony of Daniel: "He changes the times and the seasons; he removes kings and sets up kings; he reveals the deep and secret things; he knows what is in the darkness";[3] for in him is that light which, as John teaches, "lights every man who comes into the world."[4] Therefore we first give thanks to God the Father, and to our Lord Jesus Christ, because he has found in our time another David,[5] and has again raised up a man after his own heart to feed his people Israel, that is, the chosen race of the Hungarians. Secondly, we praise you for your piety toward God and for your reverence for this Apostolic See,* over which, not by our own merits, but by the mercy of God, we now preside. Finally, we commend the liberality you have shown in offering to St. Peter yourself and your people and your kingdom and possessions by the same ambassadors and letters. For by this deed you have clearly demonstrated that you already are what you have asked us to declare you.[6] But enough of this; it is not necessary to commend him whom God himself has commended and whose deeds openly proclaim to be worthy of all commendation. Now therefore, glorious son, by

the authority of omnipotent God and of St. Peter, the prince of apostles, we freely grant, concede, and bestow with our apostolic benediction all that you have sought from us and from the Apostolic See; namely, the royal crown and name, the creation of the metropolitanate* of Gran,[7] and of the other bishoprics.[8] Moreover, we receive under the protection of the holy Church the kingdom which you have surrendered to St. Peter, together with yourself and your people, the Hungarian nation; and we now give it back to you and to your heirs and successors to be held, possessed, ruled, and governed. And your heirs and successors, who shall have been legally elected by the nobles, shall duly offer obedience and reverence to us and to our successors in their own persons or by ambassadors, and shall confess themselves the subjects of the Roman Church, who does not hold her subjects as slaves, but receives them all as children. They shall persevere in the catholic faith and the religion of our Lord and Savior Jesus Christ, and strive always to promote it. And because you have fulfilled the office of the apostles in preaching Christ and propagating his faith, and have tried to do in your realm the work of us and of our clergy,* and because you have honored the same prince of apostles above all others, therefore by this privilege we grant you and your successors, who shall have been legally elected and approved by the Apostolic See, the right to have the cross borne before you as a sign of apostleship,[9] after you have been crowned with the crown which we send and according to the ceremony which we have committed to your ambassadors. And we likewise give you full power by our apostolic authority to

---

[1]The see* of Kalocsa in central Hungary. Stephen transformed it from a bishopric to an archbishopric.*
[2]The Bible, Epistle to the Romans, 9:16.
[3]Daniel, 2:21–22.
[4]The Gospel of John, 1:9.
[5]The king who ruled ancient Israel as its model king from around 1000 to 961 B.C.
[6]A king.

[7]Esztergom, called *Gran* in German. Esztergom was Stephen's capital. Its bishop was now, by Sylvester's act, an archbishop and primate* of the Hungarian Church. By transforming Esztergom into a metropolitan archdiocese,* Pope Sylvester made Hungary ecclesiastically* independent of Germany.
[8]Eleventh-century Hungary had two archbishoprics and eight suffragan bishoprics.
[9]The kings of Hungary claimed the title *Apostolic King* into the twentieth century.

control and manage all the churches of your realm, both present and future, as divine grace may guide you, as representing us and our successors. All these things are contained more fully and explicitly in that general letter which we have sent by our messenger to you and to your nobles and faithful subjects. And we pray that omnipotent God, who called you even from your mother's womb to the kingdom and crown, and who has commanded us to give you the crown which we had prepared for the duke of Poland,[10] may increase continually the fruits of your good works, and sprinkle with the dew of his benediction this young plant of your kingdom, and preserve you and your realm and protect you from all enemies, visible and invisible, and, after the trials of the earthly kingship are past, crown you with an eternal crown in the Kingdom of Heaven.

---

[10]Duke Boleslaw the Mighty of Poland (r. 992–1025), an active patron of Christian missionary work, desired a royal crown and had reason to believe he would receive it around the year 1000. He remained a ducal vassal* of the emperor, however, until 1024, when he finally received his royal crown from the papacy.

▼▼▼

Visions of the World

So far, this chapter has dealt only with high and mighty men — a rather small percentage of any society's total population. This emphasis on Europe's secular* and ecclesiastical* male leaders is a consequence of the extant sources from this era, which were largely produced by such leaders or their male clerical* secretaries. Needless to say, if we were to depend exclusively on these documents, we would have a very skewed and incomplete view of early European civilization.

Happily, a few (unhappily, too few) sources exist that show the world from the perspectives of the First Europe's all too silent majorities, but even in these cases, the authors were members of educated, privileged classes. Source 36 — an excerpt from a play by Roswitha of Gandersheim, a high-born, well-educated, tenth-century German churchwoman — provides the strong voice of a woman who trumpeted the moral strength of her sex. Source 37 is far less artful, the product of the rather gullible French monk* Ralph Glaber, but in its lack of sophistication, Ralph's work sheds bright light on eleventh-century popular religious beliefs and movements. Far more than any other source in this chapter, it reflects history from the bottom up.

Four Women of Courage
▼▼▼

36 ▼ *Roswitha of Gandersheim, SAPIENTIA*

Roswitha, whose name has many spelling variations (including *Hrotswitha* and *Hrotsvit*), was born in Saxony around 935 and lived past 973. As a young woman, she entered the monastery* of Gandersheim, a religious house reserved exclusively for high-born women and patronized by the Saxon emperors of Germany. Gerberga II, one of the two abbesses* during Roswitha's years at Gandersheim, was the niece of Emperor Otto I. As befit their class and their monastery's extensive lands, the abbesses of Gandersheim were powerful women who exercised the rights of lordship over their lands, held law courts, and dispatched soldiers to the king's army. The nuns* and canonesses* of Gandersheim were also well educated in the Latin classics, and Roswitha was one of the most learned of them all. In addition, she was a playwright and poet of considerable skill. Indeed, she was Saxony's first Latin poet, Germany's first dramatist, and Europe's first female historian. If there was an Ottonian Renaissance, as many medievalists argue, then Roswitha was one of its leading lights.

Roswitha's most famous literary creation is a cycle of six didactic plays that she produced for her sisters at Gandersheim. The six plays, which are thematically and structurally interconnected, deal with the lives, virtues, and holy deaths of various early Christian women and men. One of the more striking aspects of her six-part morality drama is that Roswitha always balances examples of male and female *virtus,* which means, simultaneously, "virtue," "courage," and "power." One play has three male martyrs; another has three female martyrs. In one play, a man delivers a learned discourse on the mathematical basis of music; in another, a woman lectures Emperor Hadrian on mathematical theory.

The selection that follows comes from the sixth and last play, *Sapientia,* which deals with the martyrdoms of three young sisters — Faith, Hope, and Charity — and the enduring devotion to God of their mother, Sapientia, whose name means "wisdom" in Latin. As their names suggest, each woman is an *allegorical* representation of a prime Christian virtue. The term *allegory,* which is Greek in origin, means "to speak in other terms." The play, therefore, is an extended metaphor, and each woman is a metaphorical character.

The excerpt begins at the court of the second-century Roman emperor Hadrian, where he is discussing affairs of state with his counselor Antiochus.

QUESTIONS FOR ANALYSIS

1. How does Hadrian initially perceive the women brought before him? What is Antiochus's initial attitude toward the same women? From the context of the play, what seems to have been Roswitha's purpose in depicting these attitudes?

2. Some commentators have concluded that Sapientia, or Wisdom, is an allegorical representation of Holy Mother the Church. Do you agree or disagree? If you agree, what inferences do you draw from this interpretation? If you disagree, explain why.

3. In what ways does Roswitha seem to help her audience identify with the women? Why do you think she would want to do that?

4. Review the Rule of St. Benedict (Chapter 4, source 17). Gandersheim was noted for its strict adherence to St. Benedict's Rule. What elements of this play would particularly appeal to a Benedictine nun?

5. What seem to be the main points the playwright wishes her audience to take away from this play? How convincingly has she made those points?

6. Modern students tend to view medieval people (and especially medieval church people) as humorless and exceedingly serious at all times. Does Roswitha fit that model? Defend your answer.

SCENE I

ANTIOCHUS. My Lord Emperor, what desire has your servant but to see you powerful and prosperous? What ambition apart from the welfare and peace and greatness of the state you rule? So when I discover anything that threatens the commonwealth or your peace of mind I try to crush it before it has taken root.

HADRIAN. In this you show discretion, Antiochus. Our prosperity means your advantage. Witness the honors that we never tire of heaping on you.

ANTIOCHUS. Your Grace's welfare is so dear to me that I do not seek to disguise what is hostile to your interests, but immediately bring it to your notice and denounce it!

HADRIAN. Do you praise yourself for this? If you withheld such information you would be guilty of treason to our Imperial Majesty.

ANTIOCHUS. I have never been disloyal.

HADRIAN. I do not question it. Come, if you have discovered some new danger, make it known to us.

ANTIOCHUS. A certain alien woman has recently come to this city with her three children.

HADRIAN. Of what sex are the children?

ANTIOCHUS. They are all girls.

HADRIAN. And you think that a handful of women threaten danger to the state?

ANTIOCHUS. I do, and very grave danger.

HADRIAN. Of what kind?

ANTIOCHUS. A disturbance of the peace.

HADRIAN. How?

ANTIOCHUS. What disturbs the peace and harmony of states more than religious differences?

HADRIAN. I grant you that. The whole Roman Empire witnesses to the serious troubles they can cause. The body politic is infected by the corpses of slaughtered Christians.

ANTIOCHUS. This woman of whom I speak is urging the people of this country to abandon the religion of their fathers and embrace the Christian faith.

HADRIAN. But have her words any effect?

ANTIOCHUS. Indeed they have. Our wives hate and scorn us to such an extent that they will not deign to eat with us, still less share our beds.

HADRIAN. This is a real danger, I admit.

ANTIOCHUS. You must protect yourself.

HADRIAN. That stands to reason. Let the woman be brought before me, and I will examine her and see what can be done.

ANTIOCHUS. You wish me to summon her?

HADRIAN. I have said it. . . .

▷ Antiochus takes the women into custody and brings them to the emperor's court.

SCENE III

ANTIOCHUS. That is the emperor you see there, seated on his throne. Be careful what you say to him.

SAPIENTIA. The word of Christ forbids us to take thought as to what we ought to say. His wisdom is sufficient for us.

HADRIAN. Are you there, Antiochus?

ANTIOCHUS. At your service, my lord.

HADRIAN. Are these the women whom you have arrested on account of their Christian opinions?

ANTIOCHUS. Yes, lord.

HADRIAN. I am amazed at their beauty; I cannot help admiring their noble and dignified manner.

ANTIOCHUS. Waste no time in admiring them, my lord. Make them worship the gods.

HADRIAN. It would be wiser to ask it as a favor to me at first. Then they may yield.

ANTIOCHUS. That may be best. This frail sex is easily moved by flattery.

HADRIAN. Noble matron, if you desire to enjoy my friendship, I ask you in all gentleness to join me in an act of worship of the gods.

SAPIENTIA. We have no desire for your friendship. And we refuse to worship your gods.

HADRIAN. You will try in vain to rouse my anger. I feel no indignation against you. I appeal to you and your daughters as lovingly as if I were their own father.

SAPIENTIA. My children are not to be cozened by such diabolical flattery. They scorn it as I do.

FAITH. Yes, and laugh at it in our hearts.

ANTIOCHUS. What are you muttering there?

SAPIENTIA. I was speaking to my daughters.

HADRIAN. I judge from appearances that you are of noble race, but I would know more — to what country and family you belong, and your name.

SAPIENTIA. Although we take no pride in it, I come of noble stock.

HADRIAN. That is easy to believe.

SAPIENTIA. My parents were princes of Greece, and I am called Sapientia.

HADRIAN. The splendor of your ancestry is blazoned in your face, and the wisdom of your name sparkles on your lips.

SAPIENTIA. You need not waste your breath in flattering us. We are not to be conquered by fair speeches.

HADRIAN. Why have you left your own people and come to live here?

SAPIENTIA. For no other reason than that we wished to know the truth. I came to learn more of the faith which you persecute, and to consecrate my daughters to Christ.

HADRIAN. Tell me their names.

SAPIENTIA. The eldest is called Faith, the second Hope, the youngest Charity.

HADRIAN. And how old are they?

SAPIENTIA. What do you say, children? Shall I puzzle his dull brain with some problems in arithmetic?

FAITH. Do, mother. It will give us joy to hear you. . . .

▷ Sapientia proceeds to dazzle and confuse Hadrian with a learned discourse on mathematical theory.

HADRIAN. Little did I think that a simple question as to the age of these children could give rise to such an intricate and unprofitable dissertation.

SAPIENTIA. It would be unprofitable if it did not lead us to appreciate the wisdom of our Creator, and the wondrous knowledge of the Author of the world, Who in the beginning created the world out of nothing, and set everything in number, measure, and weight, and then, in time and the age of man, formulated a science which reveals fresh wonders the more we study it.

HADRIAN. I had my reasons for enduring your lecture with patience. I hope to persuade you to submit.

SAPIENTIA. To what?

HADRIAN. To worshipping the gods.

SAPIENTIA. That we can never do.

HADRIAN. Take warning. If you are obstinate, you will be put to the torture.

SAPIENTIA. It is in your power to kill the body, but you will not succeed in harming the soul.

ANTIOCHUS. The day has passed, and the night is falling. This is no time to argue. Supper is ready.

HADRIAN. Let these women be taken to the prison near our palace, and give them three days to reflect.

ANTIOCHUS. Soldiers, see that these women are well guarded and given no chance of escape.

SCENE IV

SAPIENTIA. Oh, my dearest ones! My beloved children! Do not let this narrow prison sadden you. Do not be frightened by the threat of sufferings to come.

FAITH. Our weak bodies may dread the torture, but our souls look forward with joy to the reward.

SAPIENTIA. You are only children, but your understanding is ripe and strong. It will triumph over your tender years.

HOPE. You must help us with your prayers. Then we shall conquer.

SAPIENTIA. This I pray without ceasing, this I implore — that you may stand firm in the faith which I instilled into you while you were infants at my breast.

CHARITY. Can we forget what we learned there? Never.

SAPIENTIA. I gave you milk. I nourished and cherished you, that I might wed you to a heavenly bridegroom,[1] not to an earthly one. I trusted that for your dear sakes I might be deemed worthy of being received into the family of the Eternal King.

FAITH. For His love we are all ready to die.

SAPIENTIA. Oh, children, your words are sweeter to me than nectar!

HOPE. When we come before the tribunal you will see what courage our love will give us.

SAPIENTIA. Your mother will be crowned by your virginity and glorified by your martyrdom.

CHARITY. Let us go hand in hand to the tyrant and make him feel ashamed.

SAPIENTIA. We must wait till the hour comes when we are summoned.

FAITH. We chafe at the delay, but we must be patient.

SCENE V

HADRIAN. Antiochus, bring the Greek prisoners before us.

ANTIOCHUS. Step forward, Sapientia. The emperor has asked for you and your daughters.

SAPIENTIA. Walk with me bravely, children, and persevere with one mind in the faith. Think only of the happiness before you — of the martyr's palm.[2]

HOPE. We are ready. And He is with us for Whose love we are to be led to death.

HADRIAN. The three days' respite which of our clemency we granted you is over. If you have profited by it, obey our commands.

SAPIENTIA. We have profited by it. It has strengthened our determination not to yield.

ANTIOCHUS. It is beneath your dignity to bandy words with this obstinate woman. Have you not had enough of her insolence and presumption?

HADRIAN. Am I to send her away unpunished?

ANTIOCHUS. By no means.

HADRIAN. What then?

ANTIOCHUS. Address yourself to the little girls. If they defy you, do not spare them because of their tender years, but have them put to death. That will teach their obstinate mother a lesson.

HADRIAN. I will do as you advise.

ANTIOCHUS. This way you will succeed.

HADRIAN. Faith, there is the venerated statue of the great Diana.[3] Carry a libation[4] to the holy goddess, and you will win her favor.

FAITH. What a foolish man the emperor must be to give such an order!

HADRIAN. What are you muttering there? Behave yourself and do not laugh.

FAITH. How can I help laughing? Such a lack of wisdom is ludicrous.

HADRIAN. Whose lack of wisdom?

FAITH. Why, yours!

ANTIOCHUS. You dare to speak to the emperor so!

FAITH. I speak the truth.

ANTIOCHUS. This is not to be endured!

FAITH. What is it but folly to tell us to insult the Creator of the world and worship a bit of metal!

ANTIOCHUS. This girl is crazy — a raving lunatic! She calls the ruler of the world a fool!

FAITH. I have said it, and I am ready to repeat it. I shall not take back my words as long as I live.

---

[1]Jesus Christ.
[2]A metaphor for victory that refers to the palm, or laurel branch, accorded Olympic winners.

[3]The virgin goddess of the hunt.
[4]An offering of wine.

ANTIOCHUS. That will not be long. You deserve to die at once for such impudence.

FAITH. I wish for nothing better than death in Christ.

HADRIAN. Enough of this! Let ten centurions[5] take turns in flaying her with scourges.

ANTIOCHUS. She deserves it.

HADRIAN. Most valiant centurions, approach, and wipe out the insult which has been offered us.

ANTIOCHUS. That is the way.

HADRIAN. Ask her now, Antiochus, if she will yield.

ANTIOCHUS. Faith, will you now withdraw your insults to the Imperial Majesty, and promise not to repeat them?

FAITH. Why now?

ANTIOCHUS. The scourging should have brought you to your senses.

FAITH. These whips cannot silence me, as they do not hurt at all.

ANTIOCHUS. Cursed obstinacy! Was there ever such insolence?

HADRIAN. Although her body weakens under the chastisement, her spirit is still swollen with pride.

FAITH. Hadrian, you are wrong. It is not I who am weakening, but your executioners. They sweat and faint with fatigue.

HADRIAN. Antiochus, tell them to cut the nipples off her breasts. The shame will cow her.

ANTIOCHUS. I care not about the means, so long as she is forced to yield.

FAITH. You have wounded my pure breast, but you have not hurt me. And look! Instead of blood a stream of milk gushes from my wounds.

HADRIAN. Put her on a gridiron, and let fire be placed beneath so that she may be roasted to death.

ANTIOCHUS. She deserves a terrible death for her boldness in defying you.

FAITH. All you do to cause me suffering is a source of bliss to me. I am as happy on this gridiron as if it were a little boat at sea!

HADRIAN. Bring a brazier full of pitch and wax, and place it on the fire. Then fling this rebellious girl into the boiling liquid.

FAITH. I will leap into it joyfully of my own accord.

HADRIAN. So be it.

FAITH. I laugh at your threats. Look! Am I hurt? I am swimming merrily in the boiling pitch. Its fierce heat seems as cool to me as the morning dew.

HADRIAN. Antiochus, what can we do with her?

ANTIOCHUS. She must not escape.

HADRIAN. She shall be beheaded.

ANTIOCHUS. That seems the only way of conquering her.

FAITH. Now let my soul rejoice and exult in the Lord.

SAPIENTIA. O Christ, invincible Conqueror of Satan, give my child, Faith, endurance to the end!

FAITH. Holy and dear mother, say a last farewell to your daughter. Kiss your firstborn, but do not mourn for me, for my hands are outstretched to the reward of eternity.

SAPIENTIA. Oh, my daughter, my darling dear, I am not dismayed — I am not distressed! I bid you farewell rejoicing. I kiss your mouth and eyes, weeping for joy. My only prayer is that beneath the executioner's sword you may keep the mystery of your name inviolate.

FAITH. Oh, my sisters, born of the same womb, give me the kiss of peace, and prepare yourselves for the struggle!

HOPE. Help us with your prayers. Pray with all your might that we may be found worthy to follow in your footsteps.

FAITH. Listen to the words of our holy mother. She has always taught us to despise the things of earth that we may gain those which are eternal.

---

[5]Roman military officers who commanded one hundred troops each.

CHARITY. We shall obey her in everything. We want to be worthy of eternal joy.

FAITH. Come, executioner, do your duty, and put an end to my life.

SAPIENTIA. I embrace the severed head of my dead child, and as I cover it with kisses I praise You, O Christ, Who have given the victory to a little maid.

▷ The other two sisters undergo similar heroic and miracle-laden deaths. Unbroken, Sapientia carries the bodies of her daughters to a spot three miles outside of Rome. There, with the help of holy matrons, she buries them and prays over the grave of these new martyrs, asking God to allow her also to die. Her wish is granted as she commends her soul to God.

Popular Religious Attitudes in Early Eleventh-Century France

37 ▼ *Ralph Glaber, FIVE BOOKS OF HISTORY*

Ralph Glaber (ca. 985–ca. 1050) entered a monastery* around the age of twelve. It was a fairly common practice to commend boys and girls as young as seven to monasteries in the hope that they would receive decent educations, find reasonably secure and meaningful lives within the cloister, and take life-long monastic vows, once they reached the age of maturity. Many of these children, such as Bede the Venerable (Chapter 4, source 22), undoubtedly developed into adult monks* and nuns* who were at peace with their way of life. Yet many others were less than comfortable with the monastic profession that had been imposed upon them. Ralph Glaber appears to have fit into the latter category, at least for most of his monastic years.

Ralph led a restless monastic existence, wandering among seven or eight monasteries in his native Burgundy, including the great abbey* of Cluny, where he spent five years. There, he came under the influence of Abbot* Odilo (source 32, note 5), who seems to have helped settle Ralph's turbulent spirit, at least for awhile. Whatever the case, Ralph dedicated his work of history, a project he had begun prior to arriving at Cluny in 1030, to Odilo. By reason of his travels and his association with Cluny, which served as the matrix of a massive religious network, Ralph was able to gather tales from a wide variety of people. The result was *Five Books of History,* which cover the period from 900 to 1047.

Ralph's history is filled with factual errors and abounds with every sort of fantastic story. Once dismissed as a worthless historical source, Ralph's work is now prized by social historians who seek to understand the beliefs, attitudes, and actions of Europe's nonelites, including the peasants.

QUESTIONS FOR ANALYSIS

1. What does the story of Leutard suggest about religious belief and life at the level of the peasantry?

2. Consider the actions of Bishop Jebuin. What do they tell you about the role and responsibilities of diocesan* bishops?*

3. What did some Christians in the West believe about the Jews' supposed role in the destruction of the church of the Holy Sepulcher? What was the consequence of that mistaken belief? What do those events and Ralph's manner of treating them suggest about Western Christian attitudes toward Judaism and Jews?

4. What does this source imply about the place of Jerusalem in the religious imagery of Western Christians?

5. Compare what Ralph tells us about the Peace of God with source 32. What do you conclude from your comparative analysis?

6. What is the overall tone of this source, and what do you infer from your answer?

7. What does this source suggest about Europe's recuperative powers?

CONCERNING LEUTARD, THE INSANE HERETIC*

Toward the end of the year 1000 a peasant named Leutard was living in Gaul at a village called Vertus in the district of Châlons. As the outcome of the affair proved, it was possible to believe him to be the envoy of Satan, for his perverse insanity had this beginning. He was spending some time in a field to finish his farmwork when, worn out by his labor, he fell asleep. It seemed to him that a great swarm of bees entered his body, through nature's secrets and, noisily issuing from his mouth, stung him mercilessly. When he was much agitated by their goads they seemed to speak to him and to teach him to do many things impossible to men. Exhausted at last, he got up and returned home and dismissed his wife as if he were divorcing her by evangelical* precept. Going out as though to pray he entered a church, seized the cross and ground to bits the image of Our Savior.

Those who saw this were frightened out of their wits, believing him to be insane, as indeed he was. But since they were impressionable rustics, he persuaded them that he accomplished these things by a wonderful revelation of God. Moreover, he spoke in discourses of no value and devoid of truth and, wishing to appear as a teacher, he tried to undo the teachings of the masters.

For he kept saying that the giving of tithes* was in every way superfluous and senseless. And as with other heresies* which, in order to deceive cleverly, cloak themselves in Holy Writ, to which in fact they are opposed, so also this fellow maintained that the prophets had in part told useful things, but in part things not to be believed.

In a short time, by his reputation, as though by the intellect of a sane and devout person, he drew to himself a considerable part of the crowd. When Jebuin, the elderly and most learned bishop of Châlons in whose diocese, it seems, he was, ascertained this, he ordered the man to be brought to him. When he had questioned him about all he discovered that he had said and done, he [Leutard] decided to conceal the poison of his evil, and tried to obtain for himself evidence that he had not given instruction about the Holy Scriptures. When the most wise bishop heard these things which were not in agreement, indeed more disgraceful than reprehensible, he showed that the man had become an insane heretic and he recalled the partly deceived people from their madness and duly restored them to the Catholic faith. But he [Leutard], seeing himself defeated and no longer flattered by the crowd, drowned himself in a well.

▼ ▼ ▼

CONCERNING THE OVERTHROWING OF THE TEMPLE OF JERUSALEM AND THE SLAUGHTER OF THE JEWS

At that same time, that is in the ninth year after the millennium just mentioned, the church at Jerusalem which contained the sepulcher of Our Lord and Savior[1] was completely demolished by order of the King of Babylon.[2] The reason for this destruction is known to have had the origin we are about to describe. Since a great multitude of people from all over the world was constantly going to Jerusalem on account of this great memorial of the Lord, the envious devil again began to pass on to the worshippers of the true faith the poison of his iniquity through the race of the Jews who were accustomed to him. There was at the royal city of Orléans in Gaul a considerable number of these people who were found to be more puffed up and envious and audacious than others of their race. And these, after they formed a plan, seduced by bribery a certain good-for-nothing man, obviously a tramp in pilgrim's* garb, named Rotbert, a runaway serf* from the monastery of St. Mary Melerensis. After carefully taking him in, they directed him to the king of Babylon with letters written in Hebrew characters on little leaves of parchment attached to an iron staff in such a way that they could not by any chance be separated from it.

He set out and brought to the aforementioned prince the letters full of deceit and wickedness [which said] that unless he destroyed the venerable home of the Christians very quickly he would discover that he was wholly without authority in the neighboring kingdom with the Christians occupying it. When the prince heard these things he was immediately seized with anger and sent his own men to Jerusalem to demolish completely the temple mentioned above. They went there and did as they were commanded; but they did not succeed in their attempt to shatter the vaulted tomb of the sepulcher with iron hammers.[3] Then in like manner they did destroy the church of the holy martyr, St. George, in Ramla,[4] whose spiritual strength had greatly terrified the Saracen people. Indeed, it was reported that those desiring to enter were often stricken with blindness.

When, therefore, as we said, the temple was destroyed, it became clear after a short time that this most impious deed had been perpetuated by the wickedness of the Jews. And so it was spread abroad throughout the entire world and decreed by the common consent of all Christians that all the Jews should be entirely expelled from their lands and cities. Thus, everywhere regarded with hatred, expelled from cities, some put to the sword, others drowned in rivers or destroyed by various kinds of death, many even took their own lives in various ways. Therefore, when an evidently deserved punishment had been inflicted upon them, only a few of them could be found in the Roman world.[5] Then also it was decreed by the bishops and forbidden to any Christian to do any business with them.[6] If, however, any of them desired to be converted to the grace of baptism* and to reject all Jewish customs and practices, they ordained that such persons should so receive baptism. And many did this, more out of love of the present life and fear

---

[1] Jesus' empty tomb, which was enshrined in a fourth-century church erected by Constantine the Great and renovated in the seventh century.

[2] The Fatimid Caliph of Egypt al-Hakim (r. 996–1020), who declared himself a manifestation of God and ordered the destruction of the church of the Holy Sepulcher in 1009. He mysteriously disappeared in 1020. *Babylon* was a term commonly used in the West to refer to Muslim Egypt.

[3] Wrong. The tomb was destroyed. A masonry replica replaced it when the church was rebuilt (see note 8).

[4] St. George was a legendary warrior saint. Ramla is in Palestine.

[5] France and the empire, which constituted the focus of Ralph's history. Ralph greatly exaggerates this persecution's impact on the overall Jewish population of Western Europe. Plenty of evidence indicates that there were quite large Jewish communities in Western Europe during the last decade of the eleventh century (see Chapter 11, source 74).

[6] This is simply not true.

of death than for the sake of the joys of eternal life. For some of them who had dishonestly requested that they be made [Christian], shamelessly returned a little later to their former ways.

. . . About five years after the destruction of the temple, a few of the fugitive and wandering Jews, who had survived the slaughter mentioned above by hiding in out-of-the-way places, began to appear in cities. And inasmuch as it is fitting, although to their confusion, that some of them remain for the future either to confirm their own wickedness or as testimony to the shedding of Christ's blood, we verily believe that the animosity of the Christians toward them through the intervention of Divine Providence had for some time abated. Moreover, in that same year, with the aid of divine mercy, the mother of the same prince, that is the Emir of Babylon, a very devout Christian woman named Mary, began to rebuild with polished and squared stones the temple of Christ which her son had ordered destroyed. And her husband, in fact the father of him of whom we are speaking, as though another Nicodemus,[7] is said to have been clothed secretly as a Christian.[8] Then from all over the world an incredible number of persons exultantly journeying toward Jerusalem brought gifts to the restored house of God.

▼ ▼ ▼

CONCERNING PEACE AND ABUNDANCE IN THE ONE THOUSANDTH YEAR OF THE PASSION OF OUR LORD

In the one thousandth year from the passion of Our Lord,[9] following the famine recounted above,[10] and when the storm clouds obeying the divine mercy and goodness quieted, the smiling face of the skies began to clear and to blow with agreeable breezes, and by calm fair weather to show forth the magnaminity of the Creator. All the lands of the earth, flourishing in a friendly manner, began to portend an abundance of fruit by driving away famine. Then for the first time, in the region of Aquitaine, councils* of bishops, abbots, and other men devoted to holy religion from the entire people began to be assembled. Many bodies of saints and countless gifts of holy relics* were brought before them. Thereafter, throughout the Arelate, Lyonnais, all of Burgundy as far as the remote areas of France, it was proclaimed throughout all dioceses that in certain places councils* should be assembled by prelates* and magnates of the entire country for the purpose of re-establishing peace and the teaching of holy faith. On hearing this, a great multitude of all the people, the great, the middle class, and the humble, eagerly came forth ready to obey whatever might be commanded by the pastors of the church. Indeed, it seemed almost as though a voice from heaven were speaking to men on earth. For the disasters of times past still worried everyone and they all feared lest they could not enjoy the good things to come.

A list was drawn up, both of those things which were prohibited and those actions to be offered freely pledged to Almighty God. And most important among the latter was the preservation of an inviolable peace so that men of every condition, whatever their previous perils, might now travel unarmed without fear. The brigand or robber of another's property was to be fined by giving up his possessions or be subject to severe bodily punishment to the extent of the law. Nevertheless, in holy places the honor and reverence due the churches was to be shown,

---

[7]Nicodemus was a secret follower of Jesus who gave his grave to his executed master.
[8]There is no truth to this story of Mary, the supposed mother of al-Hakim, and her husband. Following al-Hakim's disappearance, Emperor Constantine IX of Constantinople (r. 1042–1055) financed the rebuilding of the church between 1042 and 1048.

[9]By Ralph's calculation, 1033.
[10]A terrible famine took place between 1030 and 1033. In the previous chapter, Ralph reports massive loss of life and examples of cannibalism.

so that if anyone guilty of sin in any form whatsoever sought refuge there he should go without injury, except someone who had violated the pact of peace just mentioned. When such a one was taken from the altar he was to suffer the prescribed punishment. Similarly, all clerics,* monks and nuns [were to be respected] so that a person passing through the region with them should suffer no violence from anyone.

Many things were decided in these councils which we are disposed to refer to at length. It should be especially noted that it was unanimously agreed by a perpetual decree that there was to be abstinence from wine on the sixth day of each week and from flesh on the seventh, unless by chance serious illness prevented it or the observance of an important feast intervened. And if something caused this regime to be relaxed a little, three poor persons were then to be supplied with sustenance. Many were the healings of the sick brought about in these gatherings of holy men. But that it might not seem a trifling thing to anyone, there was in many broken skin and torn flesh, and much blood was shed as limbs, lately bent, were restored to their original state. All this, as in other cases where there had been doubt, restored faith. Everyone was ardently inspired by these things to raise a staff to heaven through the hands of the bishops, and with their palms extended cried to God with one voice, "Peace, peace, peace!" so that this might be a symbol of the perpetual pact on this between themselves and God to which they had agreed; and for the reason that, thanks to the confirmation of peace when five years had elapsed, this very wonder might be accomplished by all. For at length in the same year there was a greater abundance of grain and wine and other fruits than could have been hoped for in the ensuing five years. Except for meat or special breadstuffs, some food was inexpensive. In fact, there was the semblance of that great rejoicing of the Israelites. Nor did things prosper less in the third and fourth years following.

Part Two

▾▾▾

The High Middle Ages:
European Efflorescence and
Expansion: A.D. *1050–1300*

The First Europe had weathered the crises of the ninth and tenth centuries. Changed and even battered by those challenges, it had not been broken. As we saw in the last chapter, Europeans displayed an amazing resilience. They beat off Muslim attackers from the Mediterranean. They even managed to absorb their two other formidable foes, the Vikings and the Magyars, thereby substantially expanding the borders of European civilization. By the mid eleventh century, Europe was preparing for one of its most creative eras, a period that many historians refer to as the *High Middle Ages* — essentially, the period from around 1050 to 1300.

As the following chapters illustrate, a number of breakthroughs and developments characterized the High Middle Ages. This era witnessed significant changes in the ways in which Europeans related to their Christian God and the Catholic Church, which claimed to speak for that God. During these centuries, significant social and economic developments took place that affected all levels of society and resulted in the creation of a new dynamic class — the *bourgeoisie.* In the realms of the intellect and the creative arts, European thinkers and artists produced timeless masterpieces and, much to their credit, continued innovating and exploring new avenues of inquiry and expression throughout the High Middle Ages, rather than smugly continuing to proceed along comfortable, known avenues. In the political arena, proto-nation states emerged in England and France during the thirteenth century, and, what is more, the seeds of later French absolutism and English constitutional monarchy were firmly planted by 1300. Everywhere throughout Europe the rule of political pluralism prevailed, providing this young civilization with one of its most distinctive characteristics and most dynamic driving forces — the competition of political forces. No single emperor, king, or even pope was ever able to bend all, or even most, of Europe to his will, although many tried. In the eventually futile drive to create a monolithic society governed by a single supreme power on earth, popes, emperors, and kings quarreled incessantly throughout these two and a half centuries and beyond. The result was a rich variety of sophisticated political theory regarding church-state relations and clearer definitions of what it meant to be Western European Christians.

In the process of defining who they *were,* Western European Christians equally defined who they were *not.* This creation of a more clearly delineated *us* and *them* resulted in a number of movements against Christian Europe's perceived enemies, including homebred non-Christians and heretics,* as well as *infidels* (nonbelievers) in Iberia, northeast Europe, and across the Mediterranean waters. Western Europe waged its brand of Christianity against the unbelievers, particularly Muslims, and in the process stamped Western civilization, perhaps forever, with a crusader mentality. Long after the crusades to the lands of the eastern Mediterranean had ended, Western Europeans and their trans-oceanic progeny in the Americas and elsewhere retained the notion that the world could be made better through the use of idealistically driven violence.

In addition to this idea, the crusades also helped open up the West to a wider world beyond the geographic boundaries of the European subcontinent. Western crusaders established overseas colonies in the eastern Mediterranean, thereby creating better conduits than Europe had had for centuries for the influx of ideas and goods from the East. What is more, the crusader spirit ultimately drove late-thirteenth-century Europeans to the far reaches of China and, two centuries after that, to the shores of the Americas. Europe and the world would never be the same as a result of Europe's crusader drive and the many other developments that took shape in the West between 1050 and 1300.

Chapter 7

▼▼▼

New Religious Trends

Europe of the High Middle Ages produced a wide assortment of religious expressions that, regardless of their differences, shared a focus on the personal relationship that exists between God-redeemed humanity and a loving God who deigned to become a human in order to perfect human nature through grace. This new religious mood tended to emphasize Jesus the Suffering Man and Mary the loving Mother of God and of all humanity, rather than Jesus the Judge or God the angry Father.

The first manifestations of this new religious vision appeared in Europe's monasteries* during the eleventh and twelfth centuries. Here, we discover, among both traditional and new monastic groups, an emphasis on discovering God within the human soul and on living a life modeled upon that of Jesus. The new spirituality of the monasteries particularly stressed pure love of God, the saints, and fellow humans, especially one's monastic colleagues. With the growing importance of urban centers in the twelfth and thirteenth centuries, we find new forms of spirituality also springing up in towns and cities. Some of those movements were exceedingly orthodox* and functioned well within the boundaries of traditional Catholicism, even as they expanded its modes of pious expression. Other urban religious movements ultimately proved to be quite heterodox* and challenged, thereby, the authority and teachings of the established Church.

Challenges to ecclesiastical* authority, as well as impulses to offer humans a more perfect Church, resulted in attempts to reform the Church and its members, both lay and clerical.* Such challenges also resulted in more rigid definitions of what constituted proper Christian behavior and belief and what constituted error. The established Church not only sought the moral reformation of its clergy* and laity, thereby calling them to higher standards of behavior, it also sought to excise from its midst those who were perceived as insulting this loving God and His Church. Efforts to cleanse the Church of dissident members often produced terror and bloodshed in the name of serving a loving God.

▼▼▼

The Different Faces of Piety

The dynamism of the High Middle Ages is reflected in the era's multiple religious innovations, many of which reflected a new spirit of religious optimism that saw the average human being as someone worthy and capable of cooperating with God in achieving salvation. Beginning toward the late eleventh century, new monastic movements sprang up, especially in northern Italy and eastern France, that paradoxically emphasized retreat from the increasingly attractive snares of the world but also service to that world. Of all the new orders of monks,* the most important during the twelfth century was the Order of Cîteaux, which was founded in Burgundy in 1098. The order's most dynamic member, St. Bernard of Clairvaux, composed the sermon that appears as source 38.

Source 38 and source 39 reflect the cult of the Virgin Mary, as seen from two perspectives: that of a monk and that of the masses. The veneration of Mary, the Mother of Jesus, was as old as Christianity itself and was especially important among Eastern Christians. In the course of the twelfth and thirteenth centuries, partly as a result of influences from Constantinople, the cult of Mary, the loving Mother of humanity, made a quantum leap in the West. Churches, particularly cathedrals,* were dedicated in dramatically increasing numbers throughout Western Europe to *Notre Dame* — Our Lady. In Mary, the West had a model of human perfectibility and a patroness before the throne of Heaven.

The twelfth and thirteenth centuries also witnessed widespread questioning of and outright rejection of mainstream Catholic beliefs and practices, including the cult of saints. Source 40 introduces the Waldensians, one of several significant heretical* religious movements that rocked the Church of the High Middle Ages.

In countering heretical trends, most of which had sprung up in Europe's newly important urban centers, the Church employed many expedients. Of all of them, the mendicant friars,* particularly the Franciscans, proved to be the Roman Church's most popular means of defending itself against the assaults of Waldensians and other heterodox critics who assailed it for its perceived venality, corruption, and spiritual irrelevance. Source 41 introduces St. Francis, "the little poor man of Assisi," who is, without a doubt, the most charismatic individual in early thirteenth-century Europe.

The Monastic Cult of Mary

▼▼▼

38 ▼ Saint Bernard of Clairvaux, *HOMILY ON THE VIRGIN MARY*

It is difficult to exaggerate the impact that St. Bernard of Clairvaux (1090–1153) had upon his society. Born of noble stock and educated in the rhetorical* arts, Bernard entered the new monastery of Cîteaux in 1112, taking with him all five of his brothers and several other male relatives. The young Bernard's leadership qualities and fervor were evident from the outset of his monastic life. Three years later, in 1115, he was sent out from the mother house of Cîteaux to establish the monastery of Clairvaux, over which he served as abbot* to the day of his death.

Although Bernard was dedicated to the Cistercian ideals of self-abnegation and retreat from the world, his zeal and obvious talents for eloquent expression brought him into contact with virtually all of the major characters and controversies of the first half of the twelfth century. Bernard took it upon himself to attack what he believed to be Cluny's relaxation of the rigor of the Rule of St. Benedict and to lecture Pope Eugenius III (r. 1145–1153), a good friend and former subordinate at Clairvaux, on the shortcomings of the contemporary papacy.* Additionally, Bernard almost single-handedly launched the Second Crusade (1147–1148), and he led the assault on the rational theology of Peter Abelard (Chapter 9, source 53).

In spite of his involvement in the affairs of Greater Christendom, Bernard was devoted to his monks at Clairvaux and remained their constant teacher. The following selection consists of excerpts from the second of four *homilies,* or sermons, that Bernard delivered to his monks in celebration of the vigil of the feast of the Virgin's Nativity. Collectively, they are sometimes referred to as *On the Praises of the Virgin Mother.* Here, Bernard comments on the text from the Gospel* of Saint Luke, in which the Angel Gabriel announces to the Virgin Mary that God has chosen her to bear the Messiah.

QUESTIONS FOR ANALYSIS

1. What particular virtues of Mary does Bernard emphasize in this homily? Why would he emphasize them to his monastic audience?
2. One of Mary's titles was *the New Eve.* What did it mean?
3. According to Bernard, what role did Mary play in human redemption? What inferences do you draw from your answer?
4. Consider the last passage in this homily. According to Bernard, what functions does Mary now perform? What inferences do you draw from your answer?

5. Historians often speak of twelfth-century monasticism's new emphasis on *affective,* or emotional, spirituality. How, if at all, does this document provide an example of that phenomenon?
6. What might be the implications for a culture that created two feminine models: Eve and Mary?

The Angel Gabriel was sent from God unto a city of Galilee, named Nazareth, to a virgin espoused to a man whose name was Joseph, of the house of David; and the Virgin's name was Mary.[1]

1. No one doubts that the new song which shall be given to be sung in the Kingdom of God by virgins alone, shall be sung by her, the Queen of Virgins, with the rest or rather first among the rest. I imagine to myself that besides the song, which though for virgins alone, yet shall be common to all virgins, she will give joy to the City of God by some more sweet and beautiful canticle, whose heart-searching modulations, no other among virgins shall be found worthy to catch and to repeat because it shall belong to none but her to sing it, who alone was honored with the glory of Maternity and of the Divine Son. But if she glories in her maternity, it is not in herself, but in Him who was born of her. He who was born of her is God; and He shall bestow upon His Mother special glory in Heaven, as she was presented with special grace on earth, so that she conceived and bore miraculously and as a virgin. For the only kind of birth which befitted God was to be born of a virgin, and it befitted the Virgin that Him whom she should bring forth should be God. And the Creator of men, when He desired to become Man and to be born into the world, had of necessity to choose His Mother from among the human race; or rather to form her for Himself such as should be worthy of Him, and as He should approve. He willed therefore that she should be a pure virgin, from

whom a pure offspring should proceed, to purge the sin of all. And He willed that she who should give to the world Him who is meek and humble in heart, should herself be humble, since He would show in Himself an example, as salutary as necessary to all men, of those virtues. He therefore who had before inspired in her the determination of virginity, and the merit of humility, He bestowed upon her, being a virgin, the honor of maternity. This is shown by the fact that the Angel proclaimed her to be full of grace,[2] which he would not have been able to do if she had had only a small degree of excellence that was not the full fruit of grace.

2. So then, that she, who should conceive and bring forth the Most Holy One, might be holy in body, she received the gift of virginity; and that she might be holy in mind, she received that of humility. Adorned therefore with the jewels of these two virtues, conspicuous by double beauty, both of body and mind, like the dwellers in Heaven in sweetness and grace, the royal Virgin obtained for herself the approval of the King, who sent to her from on high a heavenly messenger. We learn this from the Evangelist,* when he tells us that an Angel was sent of God to a virgin. "From God" he says "to a virgin": that is from the lofty to the lowly, from the Lord to the servant, from the Creator to the creature. What condescension by God! and what excellence in the Virgin! Come, maidens and mothers; all who since Eve and because of Eve have brought forth and are still bringing forth, in sorrow.[3] Come to that virginal couch; enter if you

---

[1] The Bible, the Gospel of St. Luke, 1:26–27.
[2] The Vulgate Latin translation of Gabriel's greeting to Mary is "Hail, you who are full of grace, the Lord is with you."

[3] Following her sin in the Garden of Paradise, God curses Eve, the Mother of all humanity, by telling her that she (and, therefore, all women) shall bear children in pain: Genesis, 3:16.

can, that modest chamber of your sister. For behold, God sends to the Virgin, and an Angel addresses Mary. Lend your ear and listen to what he announces; and what you hear might perhaps console you.

3. Rejoice, O father Adam; and do you, O Eve our mother, exult even more. As you are the parents of all, so you have been their destroyers;[4] and, unhappy as you are, their destroyers before they had even come into the world. Be consoled now, because of this your daughter, and that she is of such excellence. Be consoled the first, you from whom the evil first began and from whom it has fallen back upon all women. For the time draws near when that ancient reproach shall be done away, and man shall have no longer anything to reproach to woman: man, I say, who did not hesitate to excuse himself as rashly as cruelly in accusing her: *The woman whom Thou gavest to be with me, she gave me of the tree, and I did eat.*[5] Wherefore hasten, O Eve, to Mary; hasten, O mother to daughter. Let the daughter answer for the mother, take away her reproach and give to her father for her a just satisfaction. For if it was by woman that man fell, it is by woman also that he is raised up. What hadst thou, O Adam, to say of thy sin? *The woman whom Thou gavest to be with me, she gave me of the tree, and I did eat.* But these are words of malice, and by them your fault is increased, not removed. But Wisdom has overcome malice; when it found in the treasury of unfailing bounty, the occasion for pardon which God in questioning you sought to elicit, but sought in vain. A woman is rendered for a woman, but a wise in place of a foolish, a humble for a proud. This one, instead of offering the fruit of a tree which brings death, brings you to taste of the Fruit of the Tree of Life; and in place of the bitterness of that poisonous food, prepares for you the sweetness of the fruit of eternal happiness. Change therefore the words of unjust accusation into those of returning thanks, and say:

"Lord, the woman Thou gavest me, has given to me of the Tree of Life, and I have eaten; and because in that fruit Thou has bestowed upon me life, it is sweeter than honey to my mouth."

For behold, with this purpose was the Angel sent unto the Virgin. O Virgin, truly admirable and most worthy of all honor; woman singularly to be venerated, admirable above others, who repairs the ill which your ancestors have caused, and are the means of restoring life to their descendants.

4. *An Angel,* says the Evangelist, *was sent unto a Virgin;* a virgin in body, in mind, in intention; in a word such as the Apostle* describes, *holy both in body and in spirit,*[6] not found newly nor by chance, but chosen from the beginning, foreknown by the Most High and prepared for His work, kept safe by Angels, indicated by Patriarchs* and foretold by Prophets. Search the Scriptures, and you will approve what I say. Do you desire that I should adduce some testimonies drawn from thence? To mention a few out of very many, what other does God seem to have predicted, when He said to the serpent: *I will put enmity between thee and the woman?* And if you hesitate to believe that He spoke of Mary, hear what follows: *She shall bruise thy head.*[7] To whom was that victory reserved, if not to Mary? Without doubt she bruised the envenomed head, who trampled under foot every suggestion of evil, whether from the pride of mind, or the allurements of the flesh. . . .

17. The verse of the Evangelist ends thus: *And the Virgin's name was Mary.* Let us say a few words upon this name also. The word Mary means *Star of the Sea,* which seems to have a wonderful fitness to the Virgin Mother. For she is fitly compared to a star; for just as a star sends forth its ray without injury to itself, so the Virgin, remaining a virgin, brought forth her Son. The ray does not diminish the clearness of the star, nor the Son of the Virgin her Virginity. She is

---

[4]By virtue of their Original Sin in the Garden of Paradise.
[5]Genesis, 3:12. Adam claimed that Eve had led him astray.
[6]The First Epistle to the Corinthians, 7:34.

[7]Genesis, 3:15. The serpent in the Garden of Paradise symbolizes the Devil.

even that noble star risen out of Jacob,[8] whose ray enlightens the whole world, whose splendor both shines in the Heavens and penetrates into Hell: and as it traverses the lands, it causes minds to glow with virtues more than bodies with heat, while vices it burns up and consumes. She, I say, is that beautiful and admirable star, raised of necessity above this great and spacious sea of life, shining with virtues and affording an illustrious example. Whosoever you are who know yourself to be tossed about among the storms and tempests of this troubled world rather than to be walking peacefully upon the shore, turn not your eyes away from the shining of this star, if you would not be overwhelmed with the tempest. If the winds of temptation arise, if you are driving upon the rocks of tribulation, look to the star, invoke Mary. If you are tossed upon the waves of pride, of ambition, of envy, of rivalry, look to the star, invoke Mary. If wrath, avarice, temptations of the flesh assail the frail skiff of your mind, look to Mary. If you are troubled by the greatness of your crimes, confused by the foulness of your conscience, and desperate with the horror of judgment, you feel yourself drawn into the depth of sorrow and into the abyss of despair; in dangers, in difficulties, in perplexities: invoke and think of Mary. Let not the name depart from heart and from lips; and that you may obtain a part in the petitions of her prayer, do not desert the example of her life. If you think of and follow her you will not go wrong, not despair if you beg of her. With her help you will not fall or be fatigued; if she is favorable you will be sure to arrive; and thus you will learn by your own experience how rightly it is said: *The Virgin's name was Mary.* But now let us stop for a little, that we may not have merely a passing glance at the luster of the great light. For to use the words of the Apostles *It is good for us to be here;*[9] it is a happiness to be able to contemplate in silence what a labored discourse could not sufficiently explain. But in the meantime the pious contemplation of that brilliant star will give us new ardor for what remains to be said.

---

[8]Jacob was the son of Isaac and grandson of Abraham. God changed Jacob's name to *Israel* and blessed him, thereby making him the father of all Israelites: Genesis, 32:23–30.

[9]The words of the Apostle Peter at Jesus' transfiguration: Matthew, 17:4; Mark, 9:5; and Luke, 9:33.

The Popular Cult of Mary

▼▼▼

39 ▼ *Jacques de Vitry, EVERYDAY SERMONS*

Bernard of Clairvaux addressed his homilies on the Virgin to fairly sophisticated, well-read monks.* But what about the laity, particularly unlettered laypeople? What were they told of the Virgin, and how did they view her? The thirteenth century abounded in preachers' handbooks and other collections of edifying materials for use by clerics* teaching religious values to mass audiences, and from them we can garner many insights into the popular religious mind.

Jacques de Vitry (ca. 1170–1240), a patron of evangelical* religious reform at all levels of society, was one of his age's leading advocates of the use of entertaining morality stories, or *exempla* (the singular is *exemplum*), to bring sermons alive. A scholar at the university of Paris, a historian, bishop* of Acre in the crusader kingdom of Jerusalem, and finally a cardinal* of the Roman Church, Bishop Jacques was also one of Europe's foremost preachers and, moreover, a leading theoretician of the art of homiletics. Among his many writings, Vitry prepared several collections of sermons for the edification of preachers less gifted than he. The following stories come from his *Sermones vulgares,* or *Everyday Sermons,* which organizes its sample sermons according to the class and condition of each intended audience. The first story appears in a sermon aimed at married people, and the latter, in a sermon for virgins and young girls.

QUESTIONS FOR ANALYSIS

1. Consider the first story. Why did the Virgin intervene on behalf of these two sinners?
2. What is the moral of the story?
3. What does the story assume about the Virgin's powers?
4. Jacques de Vitry spent a good deal of effort preaching against heretics[*] (sources 40, 42, and 43). What does this story suggest about some of this Catholic preacher's concerns?
5. What is the moral of the second story?
6. In both stories, the Virgin, of all people, seems to wink at adultery. Is this so? How do you explain the Virgin's behavior, and what does it suggest about popular thirteenth-century notions of the Virgin?
7. What do these stories seem to suggest about popular notions of sexuality?
8. How would you describe the particular religious vision or spirit expressed in these two Virgin stories?
9. In what ways are the two stories consonant with Bernard of Clairvaux's portrait of the Virgin? How, if at all, do they differ? What conclusions follow from your answers?

A certain very religious man told me that this happened in a place where he had been staying. A virtuous and pious matron came frequently to the church and served God most devoutly day and night. There also came a certain monk, the guardian and treasurer of the monastery,[*] who had a great reputation for piety, and truly devout he was. When, however, the two frequently conversed together in the church concerning religious matters, the devil, envying their virtue and reputation, tempted them very sorely, so that the spiritual love was changed to carnal. Accordingly they fixed upon a night when the monk was to leave his monastery, taking the treasures of the church, and the matron her home, with a sum of money which she should steal from her husband.

After they had fled, the monks, on rising in the morning, saw that the chests had been bro-

ken open and the treasures of the church stolen; and not finding the monk, they quickly pursued him; likewise the husband his wife. Overtaking the monk and the woman with the treasure and money, they brought them back and threw them into prison. So great was the scandal throughout the whole country, and so much were all religious persons reviled, that the harm from the infamy and scandal was far greater than from the sin itself.

Then the monk, restored to his senses, began with many tears to pray to the blessed Virgin, whom from infancy he had always served, and never before had any such misfortune happened to him. Likewise the said matron began urgently to implore the aid of the blessed Virgin, whom regularly, day and night, she had been accustomed to salute and kneel in prayer before her image. At length the blessed Virgin, very angry, appeared, and after she had sorely upbraided them, she said: "I can obtain the remission of your sins from my Son, but what can I do about such a dreadful scandal? For you have so befouled the name of religious persons before all the people, that in the future no one will trust them. The harm you have done is almost irremediable."

Nevertheless the merciful Virgin, overcome by their prayers, summoned the demons who had caused the deed and enjoined upon them that, as they had caused the scandal to religion, they must bring it to an end. As they were not able to resist her commands, after much anxiety and various conferences, they found a way to remove the infamy. In the night they placed the monk in his church, and, repairing the broken receptacle as it was before, they placed the treasure in it. Also after replacing the money in it they closed and locked the chest which the matron had opened. And they set the woman in her room and in the place where she was accustomed to pray by night.

When the monks found the treasure of their monastery, and their brother praying to God just as he had been accustomed to do, and the husband saw his wife, and the money was found just as it had been before, they became stupefied and wondered. Rushing to the prison, they saw the monk and the woman in fetters just as they had left them; for one of the demons was seen by them transformed into the likeness of a monk and another into the likeness of a woman. When everybody in the whole city had come together to see the miracle, the demons said in the hearing of all, "Let us go, for sufficiently have we deluded these people by causing them to think evil of religious persons." And, saying this, they suddenly disappeared. Then all threw themselves at the feet of the monk and of the woman and demanded pardon.

Behold how great infamy and scandal and what inestimable damage the devil would have wrought against religious persons, if the blessed Virgin had not aided them.

▼ ▼ ▼

I heard tell of a certain woman from the diocese* of Artois[1] whose husband fell in love with another woman and consequently treated his wife badly and his adulterous mistress generously. The wife, finding herself unable to do anything else about it, frequently cried aloud for grief directly before an image of Holy Mary and complained to the Holy Virgin about this whore who had stolen her husband from her. Then, on a certain night, as the wife began to sleep a little bit, following a long, tearful vigil before the Virgin's image, the image seemed to answer her with these words: "I cannot avenge you so far as that woman is concerned, because, although she is a sinner, every day she genuflects before me one hundred times while saying, 'Ave Maria.'"[2] Upon waking, the wife went away filled with deep sorrow, and when, on a certain day, she happened upon the other woman, the wife said to her: "You are a wretched whore for having seduced and stolen away my man. I complained about you in person to the Blessed Virgin, but you have so enchanted her by saluting her one hundred times each day with your filthy mouth that she does not wish to do justice for me in your case. Rather, she told me that she could not avenge me because you daily genuflect before her one hundred times, but I will complain about you to her Son, who will not fail me so far as justice is concerned. He will take vengeance on you." The woman, realizing that the Blessed Virgin, whom she had dishonored, had abstained from punishing her (even though she was a sinner) because of the service she rendered her, was deeply moved and fell at the wife's feet, swearing before God and the wife that no longer would she commit sin with her husband. And so the Blessed Virgin made peace between them and made amends to the wife with the very best sort of vindication.

---

[1]In France.

[2]"Hail Mary."

Twelfth-Century Popular Heresy:
The Waldensians

▼▼▼

40 ▼ *Stephen of Bourbon,*
A TREATISE ON VARIOUS
SUBJECTS FOR SERMONS

The new piety and religious emotionalism of the High Middle Ages produced dissenters, as well as Roman Catholic saints, and out of dissent came *heresy,* or teachings contrary to the doctrines of the established Church. Religious disaffection and heresy were certainly known in Europe before 1100, but in the twelfth and thirteenth centuries, heretical* sects proliferated to a point where they seemed to threaten the very existence of the Roman Church. One of the most threatening of these movements, as far as the Church of Rome was concerned, was a group of individuals known collectively as the *Waldensians* (or *Waldenses*), also known as the *Poor of Lyons.*

Around 1170 a wealthy merchant of Lyons in southeastern France named *Waldes* underwent a religious conversion, renounced his earthly riches, began preaching repentance and a life of poverty, and soon attracted numerous followers. There was nothing intrinsically revolutionary or threatening about Waldes's initial religious fervor. This era witnessed many mainstream religious enthusiasts, including the early Cistercians, who claimed to be pursuing the *vita apostolica* (apostolic life) — a life of total poverty modeled upon the presumed poverty of Jesus and his apostles.* In 1179 Waldes sought and received papal* permission to lead a life of evangelical* poverty but was forbidden to preach publicly because of his lay status. Waldes and his disciples refused to accept this limitation and continued preaching. In 1184 Pope Lucius III excommunicated* Waldes and his sect, and within a decade, the Waldensians, who by then had spread well beyond France, were challenging the Roman Church's doctrine that Jesus had created a special priesthood* to serve as *the* intermediary between God and the laity. Rejecting the notion that ordained clerics* were necessary for preaching the Gospel,* performing religious rites, and dispensing the sacraments,* the Waldensians preached the universal priesthood of all true Christians, regardless of learning, class, or gender.

The following description of Waldensian origins comes from the writings of Stephen of Bourbon (d. 1261), a Catholic priest, preacher, and active member of the Inquisition (source 43). Although Stephen wrote after 1249 about events that took place several decades before his own birth, he seems fairly well informed about Waldes and the early Waldensian movement, even though he does confuse the sequences of some events.

QUESTIONS FOR ANALYSIS

1. According to Stephen, where and how had Waldes and his followers gone wrong?
2. What does the tone and message of Stephen's account of Waldes's so-called error suggest about the Roman Church of the late twelfth and thirteenth centuries?
3. According to Stephen, why were the Waldensians particularly dangerous?
4. The established Church particularly feared heretical movements that excited the fervor of the laity. What was it about the Waldensians that could have excited such fervor?
5. How did Waldes and his followers deviate from the established Church?
6. The word *heresy* means "choice" in Greek. What light does this shed upon Waldes's heresy?
7. How did Waldes and his followers exhibit the religious ideals and new piety of their age?

Now, the Waldenses are so named from the founder of this heresy, who was named Waldes.[1] They are also called the Poor of Lyons because it was in that city that they entered upon their life of poverty. They also refer to themselves as the Poor in Spirit because of what the Lord said, "Blessed are the poor in spirit."[2] Verily, they are poor in spirit — in spiritual blessings and in the Holy Spirit.*

The sect began in this way, according to what I have heard from several persons who observed its earliest members and from a certain priest, named Bernard Ydros, in the city of Lyons, who was himself quite respected and well-to-do and a friend of our brethren.[3] When he was a young man and a scribe, he was employed by Waldes to write in the vernacular the first books pos-

sessed by those people, while a certain grammarian, Stephen of Anse by name — whom I often encountered — translated and dictated them to him. Stephen, a prebendary[4] of the cathedral* of Lyons, subsequently came to a sudden death by falling from the upper story of a house which he was building.

There was in that city a rich man named Waldes, who was not well educated, but on hearing the Gospels was anxious to learn more precisely what was in them. He made a contract with these priests, the one to translate them into the vernacular and the other to write them down at his dictation. This they did, not only for many books of the Bible but also for many passages from the Fathers,[5] grouped by topics, which are called Sentences.[6] When this citizen had pored

---

[1]Modern textbooks commonly refer to him as *Peter Waldo,* but twelfth- and thirteenth-century sources do not support the later tradition that named him *Peter.* That name first appeared in documents dating from the second half of the fourteenth century (see note 8).

[2]From the Bible, the Sermon on the Mount in the Gospel of Matthew, 5:3.

[3]The Order of Preachers, or Dominicans, a religious congregation of Catholic mendicant friars* (sources 41 and 43) that arose in the early thirteenth century to combat heresy. Stephen of Bourbon entered the Dominican Order around 1220.

[4]A *prebend* was the source of income that a cleric or monk received to enable him to perform the duties of his office. By transference, the term was also applied to the office itself. Hence, a *prebendary* held a prebend.

[5]The early teachers of Christian doctrine, whose writings were especially authoritative. In the West, the four major Fathers were Ambrose, Jerome, Augustine (Chapter 1, source 4), and Pope Gregory the Great (Chapter 4, source 20). Many others, such as Benedict (Chapter 4, source 17), also were accorded the honor of being referred to as *Fathers of the Church.*

[6]Citations and excerpts from theological authorities that are arranged topically.

over these texts and learned them by heart, he resolved to devote himself to evangelical perfection, just as the apostles had pursued it. Selling all his possessions, in contempt of the world he broadcast his money to the poor and presumptuously arrogated to himself the office of the apostles. Preaching in the streets and the broad ways the Gospels and those things that he had learned by heart, he drew to himself many men and women that they might do the same, and he strengthened them in the Gospel. He also sent out persons even of the basest occupations to preach in the nearby villages. Men and women alike, stupid and uneducated, they wandered through the villages, entered homes, preached in the squares and even in the churches, and induced others to do likewise.

Now, when they had spread error and scandal everywhere as a result of their rashness and ignorance, they were summoned before the archbishop* of Lyons, whose name was John, and were forbidden by him to concern themselves with expounding the Scriptures or with preaching.[7] They, in turn, fell back on the reply made by the apostles. Their leader, assuming the role of Peter, replied with his words to the chief priests: "We ought to obey God, rather than men"[8] — the God who had commanded the apostles to "Preach the gospel to every creature."[9] He asserted this as though the Lord had said to them what He said to the apostles; the latter, however, did not presume to preach until they had been clothed with power from on high, until

they had been illuminated by the best and fullest knowledge, and had received the gift of tongues.[10] But these persons, that is to say, Waldes and his fellows, fell first into disobedience by their presumption and their usurpation of the apostolic office, then into contumacy, and finally under the sentence of excommunication. After they were driven out of these parts and were summoned to the council* which was held in Rome before the Lateran Council, they remained obdurate and were finally judged to be schismatics.[11] Thereafter, since they mingled in Provence and Lombardy[12] with other heretics whose errors they imbibed and propagated, they have been adjudged by the Church most hostile, infectious, and dangerous heretics, who wander everywhere, assuming the appearance but not the reality of holiness and sincerity. The more dangerous the more they lie hidden from sight, they conceal themselves under various disguises and occupations. Once there was captured a leader of their sect who carried with him the trappings of various crafts by which he could transform himself like Proteus.[13] If he were sought in one disguise and realized the fact, he would change to another. Sometimes he wore the garb and marks of a pilgrim,* at others he bore the staff and irons of a penitent, at still other times he pretended to be a cobbler or a barber or a harvester, and so on. Others do the same. This sect began about the year of our Lord 1170, in the episcopacy* of John, called "of the Fair Hands," archbishop of Lyons.[14]

---

[7]Stephen is slightly confused here. Archbishop Guichard (r. 1165–1181) forbade them to preach, probably before 1179. His successor, John of the Fair Hands (r. 1181–1193), expelled Waldes and his followers from Lyons sometime after becoming archbishop in 1181.

[8]The Bible, Acts of the Apostles, 5:29. Such attempts to draw parallels between St. Peter, the Prince of the Apostles, and Waldes might be a major factor behind the tradition that gave Waldes the name *Peter* (see note 1).

[9]The Gospel of Mark, 16:15.

[10]The infusion of the Holy Spirit on Pentecost: Acts of the Apostles, 2:1–4.

[11]Stephen is again confused about some basic facts. The Waldensians were driven out of Lyons in or after 1181; they were condemned in 1184 at the Council of Verona in northern Italy, not in Rome. The Lateran Council he refers to must be the Fourth Lateran Council of 1215 (source 42), which condemned all current heresy, not the Third Lateran Council of 1179, in which Pope Alexander III had approved Waldes's apostolic lifestyle.

A *schismatic* is someone who has broken away from the Church and is, therefore, in schism.

[12]Provence is in southeast France; Lombardy is in north central Italy.

[13]A minor Greek sea god.

[14]See note 7.

The Franciscan Spirit

▼▼▼

41 ▼ *Saint Francis of Assisi, TESTAMENT*

The parallels between Waldes and Francis of Assisi (1181–1226) are striking and the differences, revealing. Born the son of a well-to-do textile merchant of Assisi in Italy and a French woman, the future founder of the Franciscans was baptized* *Giovanni,* or *John.* The nickname by which he later became known, *Franciscus,* or "the little Frenchman," was one that stuck. Very much like Waldes, Francis underwent a profound religious conversion that led him to renounce all worldly possessions and to preach repentance, peace, and love. Also like Waldes, he attracted like-minded followers from his hometown and sought papal* approval for his way of life. In 1209 or 1210 Francis and his few companions traveled to Rome, where they received the verbal approval of Pope Innocent III (sources 42 and 66). Thus was born what Francis called the *Order of Friars Minor,* or *Lesser Brethren.* More popularly, his followers are known as *Franciscans.*

The Franciscans, like their great thirteenth-century counterparts, the *Dominicans,* were a new type of clergy,* being neither monks* nor secular clerics.* They were *mendicant friars,* which means "begging brothers." Traditional cenobitic* monks, such as those who followed the Rule of St. Benedict (Chapter 4, source 17), had always eschewed personal property, even though their monasteries* might be and often were exceedingly rich and powerful institutions. Francis, however, had no intention of becoming a monk or of founding a monastic order. He also had no intention of allowing himself or his followers to possess any worldly wealth, either as individuals or as a corporation. Practicing what they believed was total apostolic* poverty, Francis and his early disciples owned nothing, not even the clothes on their bodies, and worked or begged for their daily food and no more. In return, they preached and attempted to live the Gospel* to its fullest. Originally possessing no buildings of any sort, the Friars Minor conducted their ministry in the open air, in marketplaces, and in whatever churches local clerics* might invite them temporarily.

The poetic simplicity by which Francis embraced the *vita apostolica* and the way in which he seemed to personify the highest religious ideals of his age earned for him the devotion of popes and peasants alike. Thousands flocked to follow Francis, and before his death, Friars Minor were preaching to Christians all over Europe and among Muslims in Spain, North Africa, and the Holy Land.

As the Franciscan movement grew, its burgeoning numbers and unexpected success necessitated a certain amount of organization. In 1223 the Franciscans adopted, with papal approval, a formal rule that trained church lawyers had helped draft. What had begun as an attempt by a single, charismatic individual to follow the Gospels literally was now changing into a major religious order with its own administrative framework. The very size and growing complexity of the Order of Friars Minor threatened the heroic standards of poverty set by Francis and his earliest disciples. As these events unfolded, Francis's health seriously declined, he became more immersed in mystical prayer and solitude, and he handed over leadership of his order to more practical people.

Shortly before his death in 1226, Francis composed a final testament for the instruction of his brethren, in which he summed up the essence of his life and vision in order to remind them of the order's foundations and spirit.

QUESTIONS FOR ANALYSIS

1. How, according to Francis, did he arrive at his religious conversion?
2. What does this testament tell you about Francis's vision of the Friars Minor?
3. From what Francis tells about himself, what parallels can you find between his life and religious vision and that of Waldes?
4. Francis clearly identifies the basic differences that set him apart from Waldes. What were they?
5. A Waldensian Church still exists today, but it is quite small. From the evidence, what factors seem to have contributed to Francis's success and Waldes's failure?
6. Why did Francis not want glosses on the Rule or on his testament? What conclusion follows from your answer?
7. What light does Francis's testament shed on the ideals and piety of his age?

The Lord gave to me, Brother Francis, thus to begin to do penance; for when I was in sin it seemed to me very bitter to see lepers, and the Lord Himself led me among them and I showed mercy to them. And when I left them, that which had seemed to me bitter was changed for me into sweetness of body and soul. And afterwards I remained a little and I left the world. And the Lord gave me so much faith in churches and that I would simply pray and say thus: "We adore Thee Lord Jesus Christ here and in all Thy churches which are in the whole world, and we bless Thee because by Thy holy cross Thou hast redeemed the world."

After that the Lord gave me, and gives me, so much faith in priests* who live according to the form of the holy Roman Church, on account of their order, that if they should persecute me, I would have recourse to them. And if I had as much wisdom as Solomon[1] had, and if I should find poor priests of this world, I would not preach against their will in the parishes* in which they

live. And I desire to fear, love, and honor them and all others as my masters; and I do not wish to consider sin in them, for in them I see the Son of God and they are my masters. And I do this because in this world, I see nothing corporally of the most high Son of God himself except His most holy Body and Blood, which they receive and they alone administer to others.[2] And I will that these most holy mysteries be honored and revered above all things and that they be placed in precious places. Wheresoever I find His most holy Names and written words in unseemly places, I wish to collect them, and I ask that they may be collected and put in a becoming place. And we ought to honor and venerate all theologians and those who minister to us the most holy Divine Words as those who minister to us spirit and life.

And when the Lord gave me some brothers, no one showed me what I ought to do, but the Most High Himself revealed to me that I should live according to the form of the holy Gospel.

---

[1] An ancient king of Israel who had requested and received the gift of wisdom from God.

[2] The only physical presence of Jesus available to Francis is the consecrated Eucharist* — the bread and wine that priests alone can transform into Jesus' body and blood.

And I caused it to be written in few words and simply, and the Lord Pope confirmed it for me.[3] And those who came to take this life upon themselves gave to the poor all that they might have and they were content with one tunic, patched within and without, by those who wished, with a cord and breeches, and we wished for no more.

We clerics said the [Divine] Office* like other clerics;[4] the laybrothers[5] said the *Paternoster,*[6] and we remained in the churches willingly enough. And we were simple and subject to all. And I worked with my hands and I wish to work and I wish firmly that all the other brothers should work at some labor which is compatible with honesty. Let those who know not [how to work] learn, not through desire to receive the price of labor but for the sake of example and to repel idleness. And when the price of labor is not given to us, let us have recourse to the table of the Lord, begging alms from door to door.

The Lord revealed to me this saluation, that we should say: "The Lord give thee peace."[7] Let the brothers take care not to receive on any account churches, poor dwelling-places, and all other things that are constructed for them, unless they are as is becoming the holy poverty which we have promised in the Rule, always dwelling there as strangers and pilgrims.*

I strictly enjoin by obedience on all the brothers that, wherever they may be, they should not dare, either themselves or by means of some interposed person, to ask any letter in the Roman curia either for a church or for any other place, nor under pretext of preaching, nor on account of their bodily persecution,[8] but, wherever they are not received let them flee to another land to do penance, with the blessing of God. And I wish to obey the minister general of this brotherhood[9] strictly and the guardian whom it may please him to give me.[10] And I wish to be so captive in his hands that I cannot go or act beyond his obedience and his will because he is my master. And although I am simple and infirm, I desire withal always to have a cleric who will perform the office with me as it is contained in the Rule.[11]

And let all the other brothers be found to obey their guardian and to perform the office according to the Rule. And those who may be found not performing the office according to the Rule and wishing to change it in some way, or who are not Catholics, let all the brothers wherever they may be, if they find one of these, be bound by obedience to present him to the custos who is nearest to the place where they have found him.[12] And the custos shall be strictly bound, by obedience, to guard him strongly day and night as a prisoner so that he cannot be snatched from his hands until he shall personally place him in the hands of his minister.[13] And the minister shall be firmly bound by obedience to send him by such brothers as shall watch him day and night like a prisoner until they shall present him to the Lord of Ostia, who is master protector, and corrector of this brotherhood.[14]

---

[3]Apparently, he refers here to Pope Innocent III's oral confirmation of 1209/1210 and not to the more formal Rules of 1221 and 1223.

[4]Francis successfully resisted becoming a monk or a priest, but Pope Innocent would not allow him to remain a layman. In 1209 or 1210 Francis was ordained a deacon.*

[5]Most early Franciscans were not ordained clerics. This changed in the generations following Francis's death.

[6]The "Our Father," or Lord's Prayer.

[7]Francis had a reputation throughout northern and central Italy as a peacemaker.

[8]They were not to appeal to the papal court (*curia*) for churches or other possessions, for preaching privileges, or even for protection.

[9]Francis had surrendered leadership of the Order of Friars Minor to a minister general. Legally, he was now just another brother.

[10]This guardian would be the superior, or head, of the small community to which Francis was attached.

[11]The Rules of 1221 and 1223 enjoined Franciscan clerics to say the daily Office according to the rite of the papal court.

[12]The *custos* was a regional superior.

[13]Apparently, he means the provincial minister and not the minister general. The Franciscans divided their preaching world into large provinces,* each of which was headed by a provincial minister. Beneath the provincial ministers were regional custodians, and beneath them were the heads of small communities.

[14]Ugolino, cardinal*-bishop* of Ostia, kinsman of Pope Innocent III, and the future Pope Gregory IX (r. 1227–1241), served as cardinal-protector of the order. Francis had requested Cardinal Ugolino for this office.

And let not the brothers say: This is another Rule; for this is a remembrance, a warning, and an exhortation and my Testament which I, little Brother Francis, make for you, my blessed brothers, in order that we may observe in a more Catholic way the Rule which we have promised to the Lord.[15] And let the minister general and all the other ministers and custodes be bound by obedience not to add to these words or to take from them. And let them always have this writing with them beside the Rule. And in all the chapters[16] they hold, when they read the Rule let them read these words also. And I strictly enjoin on all my brothers, clerics and laics, by obedience, not to put glosses[17] on the Rule or on these words

saying: Thus they ought to be understood; but as the Lord has given me to speak and to write the Rule and these words simply and purely, so shall you understand them simply and purely and with holy operation observe them until the end.

And whoever shall observe these things may he be filled in Heaven with the blessing of the Most High Father and may he be filled on earth with blessing of His Beloved Son together with the Holy Spirit,* the Paraclete,[18] and all the Powers of Heaven and all the saints. And I, Brother Francis, your little one and servant, in so far as I am able, I confirm to you within and without this most holy blessing. Amen.

---

[15]Francis probably saw all three Rules — 1209/1210, 1221, and 1223 — as variations on the same basic Rule.
[16]Meetings of the brothers; here, major convocations. The term *chapter* has its origins in Benedictine tradition. Benedictine monks meet daily in the morning to discuss important affairs. Each meeting begins with the reading of a chapter or portion of a chapter of the Rule, so that over the course of a year, each monk hears the entire Rule read aloud several times from start to finish. Because of this, the assembly became known as a *chapter meeting,* or simply a *chapter.* Later, the term was applied to bodies of cathedral* canons* (hence, chapters of canons) and assemblies of mendicant friars.*

[17]Written interpretations, or commentaries.
[18]The Comforter or Helper — one of the Holy Spirit's titles and attributes.

▼▼▼

The Drive to Create an Ordered Christian Society

Having defined themselves as members of God's family, Western European Christians implicitly set for themselves the task of being worthy of that family. No matter what else they disagreed on, preachers such as Bernard of Clairvaux, Waldes, and Jacques de Vitry agreed that all too often clerics* and laity fell far short of the high standards of behavior demanded of them by a God who had redeemed them but still required their full cooperation in achieving salvation. Continuing attempts to order, reform, and cleanse Christian society were therefore woven into the fabric of Europe's High Middle Ages.

The first reading illustrates how the thirteenth-century Church attempted to regulate its clergy* and laity. The second reading is an example of that same Church's policies toward those individuals who deviated from its doctrines.

Reforming Western Christendom
▼▼▼
42 ▼ *DECREES OF THE FOURTH LATERAN COUNCIL*

At least as early as the third century A.D., Christian bishops* occasionally met in regional *synods,** or councils,* where they collectively dealt with common matters affecting their communities. In 325 the practice went a significant step farther when a council of over three hundred bishops, representing dioceses* spread all over the Roman Empire and from as far away as Persia, met at Nicaea in Asia Minor in order to settle the Arian Controversy (Chapter 2, source 9, note 19). Although the vast majority of the bishops who gathered in 325 came from eastern Mediterranean cities, the Council of Nicaea is recognized as the first *ecumenical,** or general, council of the Church.

The theory behind ecumenical councils is that the Church is the repository of God's truth. Therefore, when its leaders assemble in a plenary session that represents the entire Church, their decisions on doctrine are assumed to be God inspired and infallible. In the years between 325 and 870, eight ecumenical councils convened. Each was held in the East under the authority of the emperor at Constantinople and was called at a moment when the universal Church seemed to be at a critical juncture, especially in regard to the faith. As far as the Eastern, or Byzantine, Church was (and is) concerned, the last ecumenical council met at Constantinople between 869 and 870.

Beginning, however, in 1123, the popes of Rome initiated the practice of convening, solely on their own authority, ecumenical councils in Rome. These councils (which, in fact, represented only the Western Church) met at the Lateran Basilica of St. John, next to the papal* palace, and were occasions for public displays of papal authority, as well as meetings designed to address the problems facing Western Christendom. The Lateran Councils of 1123, 1139, and 1179 were spectacular, but they were dwarfed in size and historic significance by Innocent III's Fourth Lateran Council of 1215.

From the beginning of his reign in 1198, Pope Innocent declared that his dual primary objectives were recovery of Jerusalem (which Islam had reconquered in 1187) and reform of the Church. To achieve those ends, Pope Innocent planned to hold an ecumenical council. Toward the end of his eventful pontificate* and after much preparation, his general council finally assembled in November 1215 and met throughout the month. In attendance were some 412 bishops and archbishops;* about 800 abbots* and other monastic* representatives; the ambassadors of the Western emperor and of the Latin emperor of Constantinople (Chapter 11, source 76); ambassadors from the kings of France, England, Aragon, Portugal, Hungary, Cyprus, Jerusalem, and a number of Italian city-states; and even a representative from the patriarch* of Alexandria (Chapter 4, source 20). In three public sessions, the council passed seventy *canons,** or decrees, aimed at regulating and reforming the Church. Additionally, it published a detailed policy statement on measures to be taken for the recovery of the Holy Land.

The following canons suggest the scope of the council's attempts to impose order on Western society.

QUESTIONS FOR ANALYSIS

1. How did the Fourth Lateran Council attempt to deal with the problem of heresy?* What do these measures suggest about the level of the problem, as far as the Church was concerned?
2. How did the council attempt to set the clergy apart from the rest of society? In what ways were its decrees concerning the clergy a response to the problem of heresy? What other motives, if any, might be behind this policy?
3. What do the various canons concerning the clergy suggest about some of the current practices that the council sought to change?
4. What is so significant about canon 21?
5. Consider canon 62. What abuses and criticisms does it address? After having studied the canon, what do you infer was the Church's official policy regarding relics?*
6. What was the Church's policy toward non-Christians?
7. How could someone such as Innocent III possibly see canons 68 and 69 as proceeding from the same philosophy that underlay canons 15, 16, and 18? What conclusions follow from your answer?
8. How, if at all, are these canons illustrative of the new spirituality alluded to in the chapter introduction?

3. On heretics*

We excommunicate* and anathematize[1] every heresy raising itself up against this holy, orthodox* and catholic faith which we have expounded above.[2] We condemn all heretics, whatever names they may go under. They have different faces indeed but their tails are tied together inasmuch as they are alike in their pride. Let those condemned be handed over to the secular* authorities present, or to their baliffs, for due punishment. Clerics are first to be degraded from their orders. The goods of the condemned are to be confiscated, if they are lay persons, and if clerics they are to be applied to the churches from which they received their stipends. Those who are only found suspect of heresy are to be struck with the sword of anathema, unless they prove

their innocence by an appropriate purgation, having regard to the reasons for suspicion and the character of the person. Let such persons be avoided by all until they have made adequate satisfaction. If they persist in the excommunication for a year, they are to be condemned as heretics. Let secular authorities, whatever offices they may be discharging, be advised and urged and if necessary be compelled by ecclesiastical* censure, if they wish to be reputed and held to be faithful, to take publicly an oath for the defence of the faith to the effect that they will seek, in so far as they can, to expel from the lands subject to their jurisdiction all heretics designated by the church in good faith. Thus whenever anyone is promoted to spiritual or temporal author-

---

[1]Declare cursed.

[2]Canon 1, entitled "On the Catholic Faith," is a declaration of official religious belief.

ity, he shall be obliged to confirm this article with an oath. If however a temporal lord, required and instructed by the church, neglects to cleanse his territory of this heretical filth, he shall be bound with the bond of excommunication by the metropolitan* and other bishops of the province.* If he refuses to give satisfaction within a year, this shall be reported to the supreme pontiff[3] so that he may then declare his vassals* absolved from their fealty* to him and make the land available for occupation by Catholics so that these may, after they have expelled the heretics, possess it unopposed and preserve it in the purity of the faith — saving the right of the suzerain[4] provided that he makes no difficulty in the matter and puts no impediment in the way. The same law is to be observed no less as regards those who do not have a suzerain.

Catholics who take the cross and gird themselves up for the expulsion of heretics shall enjoy the same indulgence, and be strengthened by the same holy privilege, as is granted to those who go to the aid of the holy Land.[5] Moreover, we determine to subject to excommunication believers who receive, defend or support heretics. We strictly ordain that if any such person, after he has been designated as excommunicated, refuses to render satisfaction within a year, then by the law itself he shall be branded as infamous and not be admitted to public offices or councils or to elect others to the same or to give testimony. He shall be intestable, that is he shall not have the freedom to make a will nor shall succeed to an inheritance. Moreover nobody shall be compelled to answer to him on any business whatever, but he may be compelled to answer to them. If he is a judge, sentences pronounced by him shall have no force and cases may not be brought before him; if an advocate, he may not be allowed to defend anyone; if a notary, documents drawn up by him shall be worthless and condemned along with their condemned author; and in similar matters we order the same to be observed. If however he is a cleric, let him be deposed from every office and benefice,* so that the greater the fault the greater be the punishment. If any refuse to avoid such persons after they have been pointed out by the church, let them be punished with the sentence of excommunication until they make suitable satisfaction. Clerics should not, of course, give the sacraments* of the church to such pestilent people nor give them a Christian burial nor accept alms or offerings from them; if they do, let them be deprived of their office and not restored to it without a special indult of the Apostolic See.* Similarly with regulars,[6] let them be punished with losing their privileges in the diocese in which they presume to commit such excesses.

There are some who holding to the form of religion but denying its power (as the Apostle* says),[7] claim for themselves the authority to preach, whereas the same Apostle says, How shall they preach unless they are sent?[8] Let therefore all those who have been forbidden or not sent to preach, and yet dare publicly or privately to usurp the office of preaching without having received the authority of the apostolic see or the catholic bishop of the place, be bound with the bond of excommunication and, unless they repent very

---

[3]The pope.
[4]His secular overlord; normally, a king.
[5]This is a reference to the crusade then being waged in Languedoc (southern France) against Cathars and other heretics by crusaders from northern France. The papacy* granted all crusaders a *plenary indulgence,* or forgiveness of all penalties owed, on earth or in purgatory* after death, for sins committed against God. Privileges included papal protection of the crusader's person, family, and property and suspension of all debts while serving under the crusade vow. In fact, crusaders enjoyed quasi-clerical legal status, as far as canon law* was concerned.

[6]Regular clerics.*
[7]The Bible, St. Paul, Second Epistle to Timothy, 3:5.
[8]St. Paul, Epistle to the Romans, 10:15.

quickly, be punished by another suitable penalty. We add further that each archbishop or bishop, either in person or through his archdeacon[9] or through suitable honest persons, should visit twice or at least once in the year any parish* of his in which heretics are said to live. There he should compel three or more men of good repute, or even if it seems expedient the whole neighborhood, to swear that if anyone knows of heretics there or of any persons who hold secret conventicles or who differ in their life and habits from the normal way of living of the faithful, then he will take care to point them out to the bishop. The bishop himself should summon the accused to his presence, and they should be punished canonically if they are unable to clear themselves of the charge or if after compurgation[10] they relapse into their former errors of faith. If however any of them with damnable obstinacy refuse to honor an oath and so will not take it, let them by this very fact be regarded as heretics.[11] We therefore will and command and, in virtue of obedience, strictly command that bishops see carefully to the effective execution of these things throughout their dioceses, if they wish to avoid canonical penalties. If any bishop is negligent or remiss in cleansing his diocese of the ferment of heresy, then when this shows itself by unmistakeable signs he shall be deposed from his office as bishop and there shall be put in his place a suitable person who both wishes and is able to overthrow the evil of heresy. . . .

11. On schoolmasters

Zeal for learning and the opportunity to make progress is denied to some through lack of means. The Lateran council[12] therefore dutifully decreed that "in each cathedral* church there should be provided a suitable benefice for a master who shall instruct without charge the clerics of the cathedral church and other poor scholars, thus at once satisfying the teacher's needs and opening up the way of knowledge to learners." This decree, however, is very little observed in many churches. We therefore confirm it and add that not only in every cathedral church but also in other churches with sufficient resources, a suitable master, elected by the chapter[13] or by the greater and sounder part of it, shall be appointed by the prelate* to teach grammar and other branches of study, as far as is possible, to the clerics of those and other churches. The metropolitan church[14] shall have a theologian to teach scripture to priests* and others and especially to instruct them in matters which are recognized as pertaining to the cure of souls. The income of one prebend* shall be assigned by the chapter to each master, and as much shall be assigned by the metropolitan* to the theologian. The incumbent does not by this become a canon but he receives the income of one as long as he continues to teach. If the metropolitan church finds providing for two masters a burden, let it provide for the theologian in the aforesaid way but get adequate provision made for the grammarian in another church of the city or diocese. . . .

14. On punishing clerical incontinence

In order that the morals and conduct of clerics may be reformed for the better, let all of them strive to live in a continent and chaste way, especially those in holy orders. Let them beware of every vice involving lust, especially that on account of which the wrath of God came down from heaven upon the sons of disobedience, so that

---

[9]The chief administrative officer of the diocese.

[10]To clear themselves by taking a sacred oath, and, if necessary, to present others who would swear as to their orthodoxy (see Chapter 2, source 7, note 8).

[11]Waldensians, Cathars, and other heretics refused to take oaths, claiming that to do so violated biblical injunctions. Thus, refusing to take an oath was *prima facie* evidence of heresy.

[12]The Third Lateran Council.

[13]The chapter* of canons (see source 41, note 16).

[14]The provincial, or archiepiscopal, church.

they may be worthy to minister in the sight of Almighty God with a pure heart and an unsullied body. Lest the ease of receiving pardon prove an incentive to sin, we decree that those who are caught giving way to the vice of incontinence are to be punished according to canonical sanctions, in proportion to the seriousness of their sins. We order such sanctions to be effectively and strictly observed, in order that those whom the fear of God does not hold back from evil may at least be restrained from sin by temporal punishment. Therefore anyone who has been suspended for this reason and presumes to celebrate divine services, shall not only be deprived of his ecclesiastical benefices but shall also, on account of his twofold fault, be deposed in perpetuity. Prelates* who dare to support such persons in their wickedness, especially if they do it for money or for some other temporal advantage, are to be subject to like punishment. Those clerics who have not renounced the marriage bond, following the custom of their region, shall be punished even more severely if they fall into sin, since for them it is possible to make lawful use of matrimony.[15]

15. On preventing drunkenness among the clergy

All clerics should carefully abstain from gluttony and drunkenness. They should temper the wine to themselves and themselves to the wine. Let no one be urged to drink, since drunkenness obscures the intellect and stirs up lust. Accordingly we decree that that abuse is to be entirely abolished whereby in some places drinkers bind themselves to drink equal amounts, and that man is most praised who makes the most people drunk

and himself drains the deepest cups. If anyone shows himself worthy of blame in these matters, let him be suspended from his benefice or office, unless after being warned by his superior he makes suitable satisfaction. We forbid all clerics to hunt or to fowl, so let them not presume to have dogs or birds for fowling.

16. On the dress of clerics

Clerics should not practice callings or business of a secular nature, especially those that are dishonorable. They should not watch mimes, entertainers and actors. Let them avoid taverns altogether, unless by chance they are obliged by necessity on a journey. They should not play at games of chance or of dice, nor be present at such games. They should have a suitable crown and tonsure,[16] and let them diligently apply themselves to the divine services and other good pursuits. Their outer garments should be closed and neither too short nor too long. Let them not indulge in red or green cloths, long sleeves or shoes with embroidery or pointed toes, or in bridles, saddles, breast-plates[17] and spurs that are gilded or have other superfluous ornamentation. Let them not wear cloaks with sleeves at divine services in a church, nor even elsewhere, if they are priests or parsons, unless a justifiable fear requires a change of dress. They are not to wear buckles or belts ornamented with gold or silver, or even rings except for those whose dignity it befits to have them. All bishops should wear outer garments of linen in public and in church, unless they have been monks,* in which case they should wear the monastic habit; and let them not wear their cloaks loose in public but rather fastened together behind the neck or across the chest. . . .

---

[15]Certain areas under the rule of the Church of Rome — such as Sicily, southern Italy, and the recently conquered Latin Empire of Constantinople (Chapter 11, source 76) — had priests who followed the Byzantine rite. The Byzantine Church allowed men studying for the priesthood to marry and then to advance to the priesthood while remaining married. Such married priests could never remarry and could not become bishops.

[16]The shaved crown of a man's head that indicated his clerical status.
[17]For their horses.

18. On sentences involving either the shedding of blood or a duel being forbidden to clerics

No cleric may decree or pronounce a sentence involving the shedding of blood, or carry out a punishment involving the same, or be present when such punishment is carried out. If anyone, however, under cover of this statute, dares to inflict injury on churches or ecclesiastical persons, let him be restrained by ecclesiastical censure. A cleric may not write or dictate letters which require punishments involving the shedding of blood; in the courts of princes this responsibility should be entrusted to laymen and not to clerics. Moreover no cleric may be put in command of mercenaries or crossbowmen or suchlike men of blood; nor may a subdeacon,* deacon* or priest practise the art of surgery, which involves cauterizing and making incisions; nor may anyone confer a rite of blessing or consecration on a purgation by ordeal of boiling or cold water or of the red-hot iron,[18] saving nevertheless the previously promulgated prohibitions regarding single combats and duels.[19] . . .

21. On confession* being made, and not revealed by the priest, and on communicating at least at Easter

All the faithful of either sex, after they have reached the age of discernment, should individually confess all their sins in a faithful manner to their own priest at least once a year, and let them take care to do what they can to perform the penance imposed on them. Let them reverently receive the sacrament* of the eucharist* at least at Easter unless they think, for a good reason and on the advice of their own priest, that they should abstain from receiving it for a time. Otherwise they shall be barred from entering a church during their lifetime and they shall be denied a Christian burial at death. Let this salutary decree be frequently published in churches, so that nobody may find the presence of an excuse in the blindness of ignorance. If any persons wish, for good reasons, to confess their sins to another priest let them first ask and obtain the permission of their own priest; for otherwise the other priest will not have the power to absolve or to bind them. The priest shall be discerning and prudent, so that like a skilled doctor he may pour wine and oil over the wounds of the injured one. Let him carefully inquire about the circumstances of both the sinner and the sin, so that he may prudently discern what sort of advice he ought to give and what remedy to apply, using various means to heal the sick person. Let him take the utmost care, however, not to betray the sinner at all by word or sign or in any other way. If the priest needs wise advice, let him seek it cautiously without any mention of the person concerned. For if anyone presumes to reveal a sin disclosed to him in confession, we decree that he is not only to be deposed from his priestly office but also to be confined to a strict monastery* to do perpetual penance. . . .

27. On the instruction of ordinands

To guide souls is a supreme art. We therefore strictly order bishops carefully to prepare those who are to be promoted to the priesthood and to instruct them, either by themselves or through other suitable persons, in the divine services and the sacraments of the church, so that they may be able to celebrate them correctly. But if they presume henceforth to ordain the ignorant and unformed, which can indeed easily be detected, we decree that both the ordainers and those ordained are to be subject to severe punishment. For it is preferable, especially in the ordination of priests, to have a few good ministers than many bad ones, for if a blind man leads another blind man, both will fall into the pit. . . .

---

[18]Note 9 of source 7, Chapter 2, describes the ordeal of boiling water and note 37 of source 44, Chapter 8, describes the ordeal of hot iron.

[19]The Third Lateran Council had forbidden tournaments and other forms of recreational combat. The prohibition went essentially unheeded by Europe's warrior classes (see Chapter 9, source 60).

62. That saints' relics may not be exhibited outside reliquaries, nor may newly discovered relics be venerated without authorization from the Roman church

The Christian religion is frequently disparaged because certain people put saints' relics up for sale and display them indiscriminately. In order that it may not be disparaged in the future, we ordain by this present decree that henceforth ancient relics shall not be displayed outside a reliquary[20] or be put up for sale. As for newly discovered relics, let no one presume to venerate them publicly unless they have previously been approved by the authority of the Roman Pontiff.* Prelates, moreover, should not in future allow those who come to their churches, in order to venerate, to be deceived by lying stories or false documents, as has commonly happened in many places on account of the desire for profit. We also forbid the recognition of alms-collectors,[21] some of whom deceive other people by proposing various errors in their preaching, unless they show authentic letters from the Apostolic See or from the diocesan bishop. Even then they shall not be permitted to put before the people anything beyond what is contained in the letters. . . .

Let those who are sent to seek alms be modest and discreet, and let them not stay in taverns or other unsuitable places or incur useless or excessive expenses, being careful above all not to wear the garb of false religion. Moreover, because the keys of the church are brought into contempt and satisfaction through penance loses its force through indiscriminate and excessive indulgences, which certain prelates of churches do not fear to grant, we therefore decree that when a basilica[22] is dedicated, the indulgence shall not be for more than one year,[23] whether it is dedicated by one bishop or by more than one, and for the anniversary of the dedication the remission of penances imposed is not to exceed forty days. We order that the letters of indulgence, which are granted for various reasons at different times, are to fix this number of days, since the Roman Pontiff himself, who possesses the plenitude of power,[24] is accustomed to observe this moderation in such things.

63. On simony*

As we have certainly learnt, shameful and wicked exactions and extortions are levied in many places and by many persons, who are like the sellers of doves in the temple,[25] for the consecration of bishops, the blessing of abbots and the ordination of clerics. There is fixed how much is to be paid for this or that and for yet another thing. Some even strive to defend this disgrace and wickedness on the grounds of long-established custom, thereby heaping up for themselves still further damnation. Wishing therefore to abolish so great an abuse, we altogether reject such a custom which should rather be termed a corruption. We firmly decree that nobody shall dare to demand or extort anything under any pretext for the conferring of such things or for their having

---

[20]A vessel, often made of gold or silver, used for holding and displaying relics.

[21]Official collectors of charitable contributions who offered indulgences in return for so-called freely given alms for some specific cause, such as a crusade or the building of a hospital.

[22]A church to which the pope has granted special privileges and therefore a site to which penitents travel on pilgrimage.*

[23]According to thirteenth-century Catholic theology, one could decrease the amount of afterlife spent in purgatory either through penance and other acts of piety and self-deprivation in this world or by earning special indulgences. The year mentioned here does not mean a year less in purgatory; rather, it means the equivalent of the unknown amount of merit earned by a year's worth of normal penance.

[24]The fullness of ecclesiastical power. See Chapter 10, source 66, for a letter by Innocent III regarding the papacy's plenitude of power.

[25]The Gospels* of Matthew, 21:12; Mark, 11:15; and John, 2:14.

been conferred. Otherwise both he who receives and he who gives such an absolutely condemned payment shall be condemned with Gehazi and Simon.[26] . . .

66. *On the same with regard to the avarice of clerics*

It has frequently been reported to the Apostolic See that certain clerics demand and extort payments for funeral rites for the dead, the blessing of those marrying, and the like; and if it happens that their greed is not satisfied, they deceitfully set up false impediments.[27] On the other hand some lay people, stirred by a ferment of heretical wickedness, strive to infringe a praiseworthy custom of Holy Church, introduced by the pious devotion of the faithful, under the pretext of canonical scruples.[28] We therefore both forbid wicked exactions to be made in these matters and order pious customs to be observed, ordaining that the church's sacraments are to be given freely but also that those who maliciously try to change a praiseworthy custom are to be restrained when the truth is known, by the bishop of the place. . . .

68. *That Jews should be distinguished from Christians in their dress*

A difference of dress distinguishes Jews or Saracens[29] from Christians in some provinces, but in others a certain confusion has developed so that they are indistinguishable. Whence it sometimes happens that by mistake Christians join with Jewish or Saracen women, and Jews or Saracens with Christian women. In order that the offence of such a damnable mixing may not spread further, under the excuse of a mistake of this kind, we decree that such persons of either sex, in every Christian province and at all times, are to be distinguished in public from other people by the character of their dress — seeing moreover that this was enjoined upon them by Moses himself, as we read.[30] They shall not appear in public at all on the days of lamentation and on passion Sunday; because some of them on such days, as we have heard, do not blush to parade in very ornate dress and are not afraid to mock Christians who are presenting a memorial of the most sacred passion[31] and are displaying signs of grief. What we most strictly forbid, however, is that they dare in any way to break out in derision of the Redeemer. We order secular princes to restrain with condign punishment those who do so presume, lest they dare to blaspheme in any way Him who was crucified for us, since we ought not to ignore insults against Him who blotted out our wrongdoings.

69. *That Jews are not to hold public offices*

It would be too absurd for a blasphemer of Christ to exercise power over Christians. We therefore renew in this canon, on account of the boldness of the offenders, what the council of Toledo[32] providently decreed in this matter: we forbid Jews to be appointed to public offices, since under cover of them they are very hostile to Christians. If, however, anyone does commit such an office to them let him, after an admonition, be curbed by the provincial council, which we order to be held annually,[33] by means of an appropriate sanction. Any official so appointed shall be denied commerce with Christians in business

---

[26]Two biblical villains who tried to sell and buy spiritual favor and power: IV Kings 5:20, and Acts of the Apostles, 8:9–24.

[27]For example, claiming false impediments to a legitimate marriage, thereby refusing to conduct the marriage ceremony.

[28]The pious custom is offering a donation to the presiding cleric, in order to help support him and his office (compare this with note 21). Certain heretics, such as the Waldensians (source 40), claimed such gifts were illegal (uncanonical) and contrary to Holy Scripture.

[29]Muslims.

[30]Leviticus 19:19 and elsewhere in the Bible.

[31]Jesus' suffering and death.

[32]In the year 589.

[33]Canon 6 of IV Lateran ordered each archbishop, along with his subordinate bishops, to hold an annual provincial* council in order to implement the reforms of the General Council, especially in regard to the reformation of the clergy.

and in other matters until he has converted to the use of poor Christians, in accordance with the directions of the diocesan bishop, whatever he has obtained from Christians by reason of his office so acquired, and he shall surrender with shame the office which he irreverently assumed. We extend the same thing to pagans.

The Inquisitorial Process

▼▼▼

43 ▼ *David of Augsburg,*
ON THE INQUISITION OF HERETICS

Canon 3 of the Fourth Lateran Council (source 42) required archbishops* and bishops* to inquire into the possible existence of heresy* in their provinces* and dioceses* and further required local lords to lend them full assistance in defending the faith. The efficacy of such local efforts varied widely and generally proved less than satisfactory, as far as the papacy* was concerned. The next logical step was to set up a body of inquisitors, who were responsible directly to the Roman papacy and charged with seeking and rooting out heresy. The seminal act in the evolution of what became known in popular lore as the *Inquisition* took place in 1231, when Pope Gregory IX (r. 1227–1241) commissioned the Dominican prior* of Regensburg in Germany as a papal* judge and ordered him to travel about as he deemed necessary, seeking out heretics* wherever he could find them. Gregory also invested this judge with the authority to commission other Dominicans to assist him.

Use of the mendicant friars* (initially the Dominicans and a bit later the Franciscans) in the work of itinerant inquisition was a masterstroke. They were unattached to local parishes* and dioceses and owed their loyalty only to the papacy and their respective orders. Moreover, they had reputations as superior preachers and, at least initially, were widely respected for their piety. The Dominicans and later the Franciscans were also noted for their theological learning.

During the late thirteenth century, the Inquisition took shape as the Church's most effective weapon against heterodox* belief. Modern myth to the contrary, however, the medieval Inquisition was not an organized department of papal government that reached into every corner of Europe, and it was not directed from a central office in Rome. Throughout the thirteenth and fourteenth centuries, it was no more than a set of disconnected inquisitions commissioned by various popes and bishops who increasingly used the willing services of Dominican and Franciscan inquisitors. Notwithstanding the Inquisition's lack of centralized organization, inquisitorial practices were remarkably consistent across Europe by 1300.

Toward the last quarter of the thirteenth century, an inquisitor's handbook, entitled *On the Inquisition of Heretics,* appeared, probably the work of the German Franciscan inquisitor David of Augsburg (d. 1271) and based on his experiences with Waldensian Christians. In that book, he described some of difficulties that inquisitors faced when interrogating suspected heretics. Apparently, the problems and procedures that David described remained constant into the fourteenth century. In 1323 or 1324 the Dominican friar Bernard Gui (ca. 1261–ca. 1331), an inquisitor who worked in the region of southern France known as *Toulouse,* produced the *Inquisitor's Manual,* which described in great detail the methods of inquisition that had evolved over the past century. In his book, Gui reproduced from David of Augsburg's earlier handbook the dialogue that follows. This dialogue, which apparently was consistent with Gui's own wide experiences, illustrates an encounter between a trained inquisitor and someone accused of Waldensian beliefs.

QUESTIONS FOR ANALYSIS

1. What evidence is there that the accused has been coached or has prepared for this confrontation?
2. What gives him away as a Waldensian?
3. The person before the inquisitor clearly wants to preserve both his conscience and his life. What do you think his chances are of escaping with both? On what do you base that conclusion?
4. Consider this statement from a historian: "Most conscientious inquisitors saw themselves as having two immediate objectives in any examination of a suspected heretic: to extract a humble confession from the sinner and to lead that person to seek mercy and forgiveness. To achieve such ends, the subtlest and the crudest methods of interrogation were equally used." Please evaluate the worth of this statement in light of the evidence presented in the source. Do you agree or disagree with this historian? Why?

When a heretic is first brought up for examination, he assumes a confident air, as though secure in his innocence. I ask him why he has been brought before me. He replies, smiling and courteous, "Sir, I would be glad to learn the cause from you."

I. You are accused as a heretic, and that you believe and teach otherwise than Holy Church believes.

A. (Raising his eyes to heaven, with an air of the greatest faith) Lord, thou knowest that I am innocent of this, and that I never held any faith other than that of true Christianity.

I. You call your faith Christian, for you consider ours as false and heretical. But I ask whether you have ever believed as true another faith than that which the Roman Church holds to be true?

A. I believe the true faith which the Roman Church believes, and which you openly preach to us.

I. Perhaps you have some of your sect at Rome whom you call the Roman Church. I, when I preach, say many things, some of which are common to us both, as that God lives, and you believe some of what I preach. Nevertheless you may be a heretic in not believing other matters which are to be believed.

A. I believe all things that a Christian should believe.

I. I know your tricks. What the members of your sect believe you hold to be that which a

Christian should believe. But we waste time in this fencing. Say simply, Do you believe in one God the Father, and the Son, and the Holy Spirit?*

A. I believe.

I. Do you believe in Christ born of the Virgin, suffered, risen, and ascended to heaven?

A. (Briskly) I believe.

I. Do you believe the bread and wine in the mass* performed by the priests* to be changed into the body and blood of Christ by divine virtue?

A. Ought I not to believe this?

I. I don't ask if you ought to believe, but if you do believe.

A. I believe whatever you and other good doctors[1] order me to believe.

I. Those good doctors are the masters of your sect; if I accord with them you believe with me; if not, not.

A. I willingly believe with you if you teach what is good to me.

I. You consider it good to you if I teach what your other masters teach. Say, then, do you believe the body of our Lord Jesus Christ to be in the altar?

A. (Promptly) I believe.

I. You know that a body is there, and that all bodies are of our Lord. I ask whether the body there is of the Lord who was born of the Virgin, hung on the cross, arose from the dead, ascended, etc.?

A. And you, sir, do you not believe it?

I. I believe it wholly.

A. I believe likewise.

I. You believe that I believe it, which is not what I ask, but whether you believe it.

A. If you wish to interpret all that I say otherwise than simply and plainly, then I don't know what to say. I am a simple and ignorant man. Pray don't catch me in my words.

I. If you are simple, answer simply, without evasions.

A. Willingly.

I. Will you then swear that you have never learned anything contrary to the faith which we hold to be true?

A. (Growing pale) If I ought to swear, I will willingly swear.

I. I don't ask whether you ought, but whether you will swear.

A. If you order me to swear, I will swear.

I. I don't force you to swear, because as you believe oaths to be unlawful, you will transfer the sin to me who forced you; but if you will swear, I will hear it.

A. Why should I swear if you do not order me to?

I. So that you may remove the suspicion of being a heretic.

A. Sir, I do not know how unless you teach me.

I. If I had to swear, I would raise my hand and spread my fingers and say, "So help me God, I have never learned heresy or believed what is contrary to the true faith."

Then trembling as if he cannot repeat the form, he will stumble along as though speaking for himself or for another, so that there is not an absolute form of oath and yet he may be thought to have sworn. If the words are there, they are so turned around that he does not swear and yet appears to have sworn. Or he converts the oath into a form of prayer, as "God help me that I am not a heretic or the like"; and when asked whether he had sworn, he will say: "Did you not hear me swear?" And when further hard pressed he will appeal, saying: "Sir, if I have done amiss in aught, I will willingly bear the penance, only help me to avoid the infamy of which I am accused through malice and without fault of mine." But a vigorous inquisitor must not allow himself to be worked upon in this way, but proceed firmly till he makes these people confess their error, or

---

[1]Teachers; in this instance, teachers of sacred theology.

at least publicly abjure heresy, so that if they are subsequently found to have sworn falsely, he can, without further hearing, abandon them to the secular* arm. If one consents to swear that he is not a heretic, I say to him, "If you wish to swear so as to escape the stake,[2] one oath will not suffice for me, nor ten, nor a hundred, nor a thousand, because you dispense each other for a certain number of oaths taken under necessity, but I will require a countless number. Moreover, if I have, as I presume, adverse witnesses against you, your oaths will not save you from being burned. You will only stain your conscience without escaping death. But if you will simply confess your error, you may find mercy." Under this anxiety, I have seen some confess.

---

[2]Those who remained adamant in their heresy, as well as backsliders (those who relapsed into heresy, after having initially confessed and having successfully begged for mercy), were handed over to secular authorities for public execution by burning.

Chapter 8

▼▼▼

The Secular Orders of Society

Around the year 1000, Bishop Adalbero of Laon (r. 977–1030) composed a poem addressed to King Robert II of France (r. 996–1031), in which he identified society's three orders, or classes: those who pray (the ecclesiastical* order); those who fight (the knightly order); and those who work (the unfree peasantry). According to Adalbero, each order supported the other two. The bishop,* however, then plaintively noted: "The world has been at peace as long as this system has prevailed. Now laws are growing weaker, and already peace has vanished. The morals of people change and so does the division of society."

Adalbero's lament over the apparent breakdown of morality and social order was certainly one way of interpreting what was taking place in early eleventh-century Western Europe, as towns and cities were beginning to become important driving forces for economic and social change. In the process, a new class emerged — the *bourgeoisie,* or urban dwellers. We might wonder how many of the former peasants and younger sons of the military class who took up residence in towns to pursue lives as artisans and merchants would have agreed with Adalbero's assessment.

In the previous chapter, we looked at those who prayed — Europe's clergy.* In this chapter, we will consider the secular* orders. First, we will examine the backbone of medieval European civilization — the peasantry. Then, we will look at those who fought — Europe's warrior class. Finally, we will consider those who lived in urban environments, Europe's new and often disturbing class or, more correctly, classes — the bourgeoisie.

▼▼▼

Those Who Work the Land

According to Adalbero of Laon, the peasantry was "an unfortunate class that possesses nothing without suffering." This observation probably was correct, so far as the vast majority of peasants, particularly the unfree, were concerned in his day. As the three sources in this section suggest, however, such a sweeping generalization fails to take into account the wide variety of status, possessions, privileges, and opportunities that separated various peasants from one another.

Eleventh-Century Law in the Rhineland
▼▼▼

44 ▼ *Burchard of Worms,*
THE LAWS AND STATUTES OF THE
FAMILY OF SAINT PETER OF WORMS

In 1023 Burchard, bishop of Worms (r. 1000–1025), issued a code of laws for all his lay dependents — free and unfree, urban and rural. Worms, a city situated on the banks of Germany's Rhine River, was one of the empire's important administrative centers, and its bishop wielded considerable secular, as well as ecclesiastical, power. As bishop, Burchard was the greatest landholder in the region, possessing a considerable number of estates in the countryside and a fair percentage of the real estate within the city walls of Worms. He let out some of his rural lands as fiefs* to military vassals,* who owed him regular knight service and dues but who governed the peasants on their fief-estates free of Burchard's supervision. The rest of his country property was cultivated by peasants who were dependent directly upon Burchard and were supervised by the bishop's various agents.

To Burchard's mind, all of the people directly dependent upon him were members of the *family of St. Peter,* the patron saint of Worms, and in his code, the bishop attempted to establish a system of norms and sanctions for this extended family. Although his code contains some provisions that clearly relate only to members of the family of St. Peter who resided in the city of Worms, most of the laws, at least in part, deal with peasants who tilled the countryside estates of St. Peter. To be sure, this code predates by a quarter century the period from 1050 to 1300, and most of its statutes were not new laws but rather well-established customs that Bishop Burchard now saw fit to set in writing. Nevertheless, the code reflects many of the conditions and trends of rural life that continued in northern Europe throughout the High Middle Ages.

QUESTIONS FOR ANALYSIS

1. Consider the prologue, which offers interesting glimpses of some of the realities of Bishop Burchard's day. What inferences do you draw from this single paragraph?
2. Consider sections 2, 11, and 21. What do they allow you to infer about the value of land and serfs* in the eleventh century?
3. Section 10 apparently refers to serfs inheriting land. Why do you think that the son inherits all land that carries a servile bond? Consider section 14 in light of your answer.
4. This code points out a number of differences in status and fortune among the servile members of the family of St. Peter. What were those differences, and what inferences do you draw from your answer?
5. What forces were at work that tended to reduce serfs to the lowest class? What counterforces were at work that allowed for upward mobility?
6. A number of these laws provide interesting insights into the status of female peasants in the family of St. Peter. What picture emerges of the roles of women?
7. What do these statutes tell us about eleventh-century legal principles and procedures?
8. What overall picture of peasant life on the estates of St. Peter emerges from this document?

Because of the frequent lamentations of my unfortunate subjects and the great injustice done them by many who have habitually wronged the family of St. Peter, imposing different laws upon them and oppressing all the weaker ones by their unjust judgments and decisions, I, Burchard, bishop of Worms, with the advice of my clergy, knights, and of all my family, have ordered these laws to be written, in order that hereafter no advocate,[1] nor vidame,[2] nor official,[3] nor any other malicious person may be able to add any new law to the detriment of the aforementioned family, but that the whole family, rich and poor alike, may have the same law.

1. If anyone of the family of St. Peter legally marries a woman who is also a member of the family, and gives her a dower[4] and she has peaceable possession of it for a year and a day, then if the man dies, the wife shall hold the whole of the dower until she dies. When the woman dies, if they had no children, the dower goes to the nearest heirs of the man. If the woman dies first, the same disposition shall be made of it. If after marriage they acquire property, when one of them dies, the other shall have it and do what he will with it. If the wife brought any property to her husband at the time of marriage, at the death of both, their children, if they have any, shall in-

---

[1] A layman who represented the bishop and his church in all secular matters, especially those that involved military service or coercion. In theory, he protected the church and was its secular arm. His duties included holding three regular court sessions in the course of the year and collecting fines in the bishop's name. Many advocates took advantage of their positions to extort money from the church's dependents and from the church itself.

[2] The advocate's assistant.
[3] See sections 2 and 12. This was probably a local village leader who presided over the village's court in the name of the bishop.
[4] The *bride price* that the groom brings to the marriage and bestows on his wife.

herit it. If they have no children, it shall return to her relatives unless she gives it away before her death. If the children die after inheriting it, it shall return to the nearest relatives of their mother.

2. If anyone has inherited a piece of land with serfs, and becomes poor and is forced to sell it, he must first, in the presence of witnesses, offer to sell it to his nearest heirs. If they will not buy it, he may sell it to any member of the family of St. Peter. If a piece of land has, by judicial process, been declared forfeited to the bishop,[5] and any one of the heirs of the one who held it wishes to pay the back dues, he may do so and receive the land. But if no heir wishes to pay the back dues, the local official may let the land to any member of the family he may wish, and the one thus receiving it shall hold it. If after a few years someone comes and says: "I am the heir. I was poor, I was an orphan, I had no means of support, so I left home and have been supporting myself in another place by work," and if he tries by his own testimony alone to dispossess him who, with the consent of the bishop, received the land, and who has cultivated it well[6] and improved it, he shall not be able to do so. For since there was no heir at the time who was willing to pay the back dues, let him to whom the local official gave it keep it. For [it may be said to the new claimant]: "If you were the heir, why did you go away? Why did you not stay at home and look after your inheritance?" No hearing shall be granted him unless he has a good and reasonable excuse. If anyone who has a piece of land by hereditary right dies leaving a child as heir, and this child is not able to render the service due, and there is a near relative who is will-

ing to render the due service for this land until the heir becomes of age, he may do so. But let the heir not be disinherited because of his youth. We beg that he may be treated mercifully in this matter [that is, that he may receive his inheritance when he comes of age].

3. If anyone on our domain land[7] dies leaving an inheritance, his heir shall receive it without being bound to give us a present,[8] and thereafter he shall render the due service for it.

4. If any member of the family dies leaving free property,[9] unless he has given it away, his nearest heirs shall inherit it.

5. If anyone in the presence of witnesses and with the consent of his wife parts with any piece of property, no matter what it is, the bargain shall stand unless there is some other good reason for breaking it.

6. If anyone sells his land or his inheritance to another member of the family in the presence of one of his heirs, and that heir does not object at the time, he shall never afterwards have the right to object. If an heir were not present, but, after learning of the sale, did not object within that year, he shall afterwards not have the right to object to it.

7. If anyone is, by the judgment of his fellows, put "into the bishop's hand,"[10] he and all his possessions are in the bishop's power.

8. If anyone takes some of his fellows and does some injustice to a member of the family, he shall pay a fine for himself and for his accomplices and each one of them shall pay his own fine.

9. Five pounds of the *wergeld*[11] of a *fisgilinus*[12] go to the bishop's treasury and two and one-half pounds go to his friends [kin].

10. If a man and his wife die leaving a son

---

[5]Because the holder has not rendered due services or paid required dues.

[6]Who has managed it well. The serfs provide the actual labor.

[7]Lands held directly by the bishop and cultivated by his peasants.

[8]As a form of inheritance tax, the lord would often, by custom, demand the holding's best animal or some other such so-called gift.

[9]Land held without dues, service, or bondage. Such land was known as an *allod* (see Chapter 2, source 7). Serfs could purchase allodial land out of their surplus (see section 10).

[10]Someone who has been convicted of a serious felony in a village or other court.

[11]"Person money," or the fine paid for a homicide (see Chapter 2, source 7, note 13).

[12]A rank, or class, of serf (see sections 13, 16, and 22).

and a daughter, the son shall receive the inheritance of the servile land,[13] and the daughter shall receive the clothing of her mother and all the cash on hand. Whatever other property there is shall be divided equally between them.

11. If anyone has received a piece of land and serfs by inheritance, and takes to his bed because of illness so that he cannot ride on horseback or walk alone, he shall not alienate the land and serfs to the disadvantage of his heirs, unless he wishes to give something for the salvation of his soul.[14] All his other property he may give to whomever he wishes.

12. In order that there may not be so many perjuries, if any member of the family has done some wrong to a fellow-member in the matter of land, or vineyards, or any other less important thing, and the case has been brought before the local official, we desire that the local official shall, with the aid of his fellows, decide the case without having anyone take an oath.

13. If any *fisgilinus* does an injustice, either great or small, he shall, like the *dagewardus*,[15] pledge five solidi[16] to the treasury of the bishop and pay five solidi as settlement to him to whom he did the wrong, if he is of the same society.[17] If he is outside his society he shall pledge one ounce [of silver] and no oath shall be taken.

14. If anyone from the bishop's domain lands marries someone who belongs to a fief which is held from the bishop,[18] he shall continue to be under the bishop's jurisdiction. If anyone[19] from such a fief marries someone from the bishop's domain land, he shall continue under the jurisdiction of the lord of the fief on which he lives.

15. If anyone marries a foreign woman,[20] when he dies two-thirds of their possessions shall go to the bishop.

16. If a *fisgilinus* marries a *dagewarda*,[21] their children shall be of the lower rank; and likewise if a *dagewardus* marries a *fisgilina*. . . .

21. If anyone of the family of St. Peter buys a piece of land and serfs from a free man, or has acquired it in any other way, he shall not dispose of it to anyone outside of the family, unless he exchanges it.[22]

22. If anyone attempts to reduce a *fisgilinus* to the rank of a *dagewardus* and subject him to an unjust poll tax,[23] the *fisgilinus* shall prove his rank by the testimony of seven of his nearest relatives, but he shall not hire them for this purpose. If the charge is made that his father was not a *fisgilinus,* two female witnesses shall be taken from his father's family and one from his mother's. If it is said that his mother was not of that rank, two shall be taken from her family and one from his father's family, unless he can prove his rank by the testimony of the *Schoeffen*[24] or of his relatives.

23. If any member of the family enters the house of another with an armed force and violates his daughter, he shall pay to her father, or to her guardian, three times the value of every piece of clothing which she had on when she was seized, and to the bishop his ban[25] for each piece of clothing. And he shall also pay to her father a triple fine and the bishop's ban. And because the law of the church does not permit him to marry her, he shall appease her family by giving to twelve members of it twelve shields and as many lances and one pound of money. . . .

29. If the bishop wishes to take a *fisgilinus* into

---

[13]Land held under bondage, for which one owed the duties of a serf.

[14]Bequeath a piece of property to a church or abbey* in return for prayers for his soul.

[15]A rank, or class, of serf (see sections 16 and 22).

[16]See Chapter 2, source 7, note 2.

[17]Possibly, this means the same village.

[18]Land held by one of the bishop's vassals.

[19]In both cases, the *anyone* is a male.

[20]A woman from outside the family of St. Peter.

[21]Two different classes of serfs. The feminine form of the noun ends in *a* (e.g., *dagewarda*); the male form ends in *us* (e.g., *dagewardus*).

[22]For other land and serfs.

[23]A head tax that was the sign of bondage.

[24]Local judges; the singular is *Schoeffe.*

[25]A fixed sum (in this case, 60 solidi) that served as the base for all fines.

his service, he may put him to work under the chamberlain, or the cup-bearer, or the steward, or the master of the horse,[26] or under the official who has charge of the bishop's lands and collects the dues from them.[27] But if he does not wish to serve the bishop in any of these departments of the bishop's household, he may pay four denars[28] every time the bishop is summoned by the king to call out his men for the purpose of fighting, and six when the bishop is summoned to accompany the emperor to Rome, and he must attend the three regular sessions of court which are held every year, and then he may serve whomsoever he wishes.[29]

30. Homicides take place almost daily among the family of St. Peter, as if they were wild beasts. The members of the family rage against each other as if they were insane and kill each other for nothing. Sometimes drunkenness, sometimes wanton malice is the cause of a murder. In the course of one year thirty-five serfs of St. Peter belonging to the church of Worms have been murdered without provocation. And the murderers, instead of showing penitence, rather boast and are proud of it. Because of the great loss thus inflicted on our church, with the advice of our faithful subjects, we have made the following laws in order to put an end to such murders. If any member of the family of St. Peter kills a fellow member except in self-defence, that is, while defending either himself or his property, we decree that he shall be beaten and his head shaved,

and he shall be branded on both jaws with a red-hot iron, made for this purpose, and he shall pay the *wergeld* and make peace in the customary way with the relatives of the man whom he killed. And those relatives shall be compelled to accept this. If the relatives of the slain man refuse to accept it and make war on the relatives of the murderer, anyone of the latter may secure himself against their violence by taking an oath that he knew nothing of the murder and had nothing to do with it. If the relatives of the slain man disregard such an oath and try to injure the one who took it, even though they do not succeed in doing so, they shall be beaten and have their heads shaved, but they shall not be branded on the jaws. But if they kill him or wound him, they shall be beaten and their heads shaved, and they shall be branded on the jaws. If a murderer escapes, all his property shall be confiscated, but his relatives, if they are innocent, shall not be punished for him. If the murderer does not flee, but, in order to prove his innocence,[30] wishes to fight a duel with some relative of the slain man, and if he wins, he shall pay the *wergeld* and satisfy the relatives of the slain man.[31] If no relative of the slain man wishes to fight a duel with the murderer, the murderer shall clear himself before the bishop with the ordeal of boiling water,[32] and pay the *wergeld,* and make peace with the relatives of the slain man, and they shall be compelled to accept it. If through fear of this law the relatives of the slain man go to another

---

[26]The chamberlain was master of the bishop's chamber; over time, his office evolved into that of chief of staff. The steward was the person in charge of the kitchen and all food except for drink, which was the cupbearer's sole responsibility. The master of horse was responsible for the horses and all transportation.

[27]The advocate (see note 1).

[28]See Chapter 2, source 7, note 2.

[29]These privileged serfs were known as *ministeriales* (singular: *ministerialis*). Because of their presumed loyalty, they were increasingly used by the kings and great lords of Germany throughout the century and well beyond. Not only did they serve as trusted agents of administration, some even gained the right to serve as mounted warriors, while remaining in bondage to a lord. As their responsibilities and honors increased, the ministeriales evolved into a hereditary class, and their descendants became free knights and lower nobles.

[30]He wishes to prove that he killed in self-defense.

[31]But he will not be beaten, branded, or shaven.

[32]See Chapter 2, source 7, note 9, and Chapter 7, source 42, canon 18.

family,[33] and incite them to violence against the relatives of the murderer, if they will not clear themselves by a duel,[34] they shall clear themselves before the bishop by the ordeal of boiling water, and whoever is proven guilty by the ordeal shall be beaten, his head shaved, and he shall be branded on the jaws. If any member of the family who lives in the city kills a fellow member except in self-defence, he shall be punished in the same way, and besides he shall pay the bishop's ban, and the *wergeld,* and make peace with the relatives of the slain man, and they shall be compelled to accept it. If any foreigner who cultivates a piece of St. Peter's land, kills a member of the family of St. Peter except in self-defence, he shall either be punished in the same way, or he shall lose his fief and he shall be at the mercy of the advocate and the family of St. Peter.[35] If anyone who is serving us or one of our officials commits such a crime, it shall be left to us to punish him as we, with the advice of our subjects, may see fit.

31. If one member of the family has a dispute with another about anything, such as fields, vineyards, serfs, or money, if possible, let it be decided by witnesses without oaths. If it cannot be decided in that way, let both parties to the case produce their witnesses in court. After the witnesses have testified, each for his side, two men shall be chosen, one from each side, to decide the suit by a duel. He whose champion is defeated in the duel shall lose his suit, and his witnesses shall be punished for bearing false witness, just as if they had taken an oath to it.

32. If any member of the family commits a theft not because of hunger, but from avarice and covetousness, or habit, and the stolen object is worth five solidi or more, and it can be proved that the thief, either in a public market or in a meeting of his fellow members, has restored the stolen object, or given a pledge to do so, we decree for the prevention of such crimes that as a punishment of his theft the thief shall lose his legal status — that is, if anyone accuses him of a crime, he cannot clear himself by an oath,[36] but must prove his innocence by a duel or by the ordeal of boiling water or red-hot iron.[37] The same punishment shall be inflicted on one who is guilty of perjury, or of bearing false witness, and also on one who is convicted by duel of theft, and of those who plot with the bishop's enemies against the honor and safety of his lord, the bishop.

---

[33]People outside the family of St. Peter.
[34]To prove they did not incite these outsiders.
[35]They may legitimately carry on a feud with him and even slay him.

[36]Normally, free persons could, in some cases, clear themselves simply on their own oaths or with the help of oathhelpers, or *compurgators* (Chapter 2, source 7, note 8).
[37]An ordeal in which a blessed, red-hot piece of iron was carried to a stipulated location. Otherwise, the test was like the ordeal of boiling water.

Twelfth-Century Peasant Colonists beyond the Elbe
▼▼▼

45 ▼ Frederick of Hamburg, *CHARTER OF PRIVILEGES*

Odo of Cluny wrote of disgruntled peasants who left the lands of Count Gerald of Aurillac and struck out for greener pastures, without the count's hindering them (Chapter 6, source 30). Such lordly benevolence was rare in any century, but from the age of Charlemagne onward, German lords intermittently encouraged peasant colonists to immigrate to the lands east of the Elbe River. In Charles the Great's day, the Elbe was the boundary separating Christian Germans from pagan Slavs, and Charlemagne and his successors sought to change that by making war and creating settlements in the east. The process was slow and suffered many setbacks. In 1066 and again in 1072, for example, Slavs attacked and virtually destroyed the port city of Hamburg on the lower, or northern, reaches of the Elbe. Despite such disasters, the work of colonizing, converting, and Germanizing the region between the Elbe and Oder Rivers and beyond continued on well into the High Middle Ages.

In 1106 Frederick, archbishop* of Hamburg and Bremen (r. 1104–1123), authorized establishment of a colony of peasant settlers in lands that lay directly east of his archdiocese,* and in the charter that appears here, he prescribed the terms under which the colonists would be bound. The document is typical of the increasingly frequent charters of privileges that were aimed at attracting farmers into former wastelands in Western Europe and the frontier lands of Central and Eastern Europe.

QUESTIONS FOR ANALYSIS

1. What privileges did Archbishop Frederick grant these settlers?
2. How has he bound the settlers to him? Conversely, what freedoms has he granted them?
3. How were these peasants governed compared with those from the family of St. Peter (source 44)? What significant differences do you find?
4. Based on your answers to the first three questions, what do you infer was the legal status of these farmers? Were they serfs,* or were they free?
5. Why was Bishop Frederick willing to grant such privileges to the colonists? What, in other words, did he get out of this?
6. Why would farmers be willing to settle in the "Wild East"?
7. Compare these colonists with the peasants described in Burchard of Worms's code of laws (source 44). What picture emerges of possible avenues of upward mobility open to European farmers during the High Middle Ages?

1. In the name of the holy and undivided Trinity.* Frederick, by the grace of God bishop* of Hamburg, to all the faithful in Christ, gives a perpetual benediction. We wish to make known to all the agreement which certain people living this side of the Rhine, who are called Hollanders,[1] have made with us.

2. These men came to us and earnestly begged us to grant them certain lands in our bishopric, which are uncultivated, swampy, and useless to our people. We have consulted our subjects about this and, considering that this would be profitable to us and to our successors, have granted their request.

---

[1] The eastern side of the Rhine. These Hollanders came from the same general area known today as *Holland.*

3. The agreement was made that they should pay us every year one denarius[2] for every hide of land.[3] We have thought it necessary to determine the dimensions of the hide, in order that no quarrel may hereafter arise about it. The hide shall be 720 royal rods long and thirty royal rods wide.[4] We also grant them the streams which flow through this land.

4. They agreed to give the tithe* according to our decree, that is, every eleventh sheaf of grain, every tenth lamb, every tenth pig, every tenth goat, every tenth goose, and a tenth of the honey and of the flax. For every colt they shall pay a denarius on St. Martin's day,[5] and for every calf an obol.[6]

5. They promised to obey me in all ecclesiastical* matters according to the decrees of the holy fathers,* the canonical law,* and the practice in the diocese* of Utrecht.[7]

6. They agreed to pay every year two marks[8] for every 100 hides for the privilege of holding their own courts for the settlement of all their differences about secular* matters. They did this because they feared they would suffer from the injustice of foreign judges. If they cannot settle the more important cases they shall refer them to the bishop. And if they take the bishop with them[9] for the purpose of deciding one of their trials, they shall provide for his support as long as he remains there by granting him one-third of all the fees arising from the trial; and they shall keep the other two-thirds.

7. We have given them permission to found churches wherever they may wish on these lands. For the support of the priests* who shall serve God in these churches we grant a tithe of our tithes from these parish* churches.[10] They promised that the congregation of each of these churches should endow their church with a hide for the support of their priest. The names of the men who made this agreement with us are: Henry, the priest, to whom we have granted the aforesaid churches for life; and the others are laymen, Helikin, Arnold, Hiko, Fordolt, and Referic. To them and to their heirs after them we have granted the aforesaid land according to the secular laws and to the terms of this agreement.

---

[2]See Chapter 2, source 7, note 2.
[3]According to ancient Germanic tradition, a *hide* was the amount of land needed to support one peasant family for a full year.
[4]The royal *rod* was close to the modern rod, which equals sixteen and a half feet (5.03 meters), making this hide about thirteen and a half acres.
[5]November 11.
[6]A penny.

[7]The settlers' home diocese in the Netherlands, about 175 miles southwest from Bremen, and subject to the archdiocese of Cologne on the Rhine.
[8]The word means "half pound," and normally it referred to a measure of silver. The weight of a mark of silver ranged between 237 and 260 grams, depending on local standards.
[9]That is, if they summon the bishop of Hamburg-Bremen to their colony.
[10]*Tithe* means "a tenth," so the bishop will keep nine-tenths of the tithes for his own church.

Thirteenth-Century Land Leases in Italy
▼▼▼
46 ▼ *TWO PADUAN LAND CONTRACTS*

Increasingly from the twelfth century onward, central and northern Italian urban residents leased out land they owned in the nearby countryside to peasants who contracted to work the land in return for a set rent. When that rent was primarily a portion of the annual produce, the lease arrangement was known as a *mezzadria* and the sharecropper was known as a *mezzadrio* (plural: *mezzadri*). In many respects, the mezzadria was the rural corollary to Italy's emerging urban centers (source 50), and the mezzadri were peasant counterparts to Italy's bourgeois entrepreneurs.

The first document illustrates a typical thirteenth-century mezzadria, and the second illustrates another type of lease, a long-term one in which sharecropping was not part of the contract. Both contracts come from the city of Padua, near Venice, and date to 1223.

QUESTIONS FOR ANALYSIS

1. Is the *Albertino* mentioned in the first document a serf* or a free peasant? On what evidence do you base your answer?
2. What about the *Albertino* mentioned in the second document? Is this the same person who appears in the first contract? What does the evidence allow you to say about the *Albertino* of the second contract?
3. How does the status of each *Albertino* compare with that of the peasants of the family of St. Peter? With that of the Hollander colonists? What conclusions follow from your comparative analysis?
4. How would you characterize the differences between the two leases, and how do you explain those differences?

Symeon, notary,[1] invests Albertino of Abate di Camponogara according to the law of rent for ten years with a piece of land lying in that place. . . . The aforesaid Albertino pledges to guarantee and defend the same land up to the aforesaid period to ten years that the aforesaid Albertino and his heirs have and hold the aforesaid land according to the law of rent up to the period of the ten years. Hence the aforesaid Albertino promises and agrees with the abovementioned Symeon, notary, in good faith and without fraud to work and plant, to drain and ditch the land and to plant willows, and to give to him [Symeon] a third part of the crop delivered to his house in Padua at Albertino's expense. Every year for ten years also [he will give] a shoulder and cake at the feast of St. Stephen [December

26]; and at Shrove Tuesday,[2] two capons; at Easter twelve eggs; and at the feast of All Saints [November 1] a duck or a goose; and at the feast of St. Justina [October 7], twenty *soldi*.[3] He is held to make these payments with the obligation of all of the goods present and future which he might own to pay all his dues and if there are damages to his part of the crop, he must still meet the aforementioned requirements and make good the damage with oath and other means of approval.

▾ ▾ ▾

John, by the grace of God prior* of the monastery* of S. Ciprian, with the consent and will of his brothers here present, namely Valentino and Peter and others, for 100 Venetian *lire de piccoli*[4]

---

[1]A professional who specialized in drawing up private and public documents (see Chapter 12, source 84).
[2]The Tuesday before Ash Wednesday, the day when the penitential season of Lent begins. Shrove Tuesday is also known as *Mardi Gras* (Fat Tuesday) and *Carnival,* because it is the last chance for feasting before forty days of fasting.

[3]Not a coin at this time but a unit of *money of account.* One *solido* equaled twenty pennies or one twelfth of a *lira,* or pound (see note 4). A Venetian document of 1224 stipulates that the wages for an archer or a first-class sailor are 2 to 3 solidi a day.
[4]Literally, "a pound of small pennies." A lira, like a solido, was a unit of value and not a coin. It was worth 240 pennies, each made from a copper-silver alloy.

which he has confessed to have accepted numbered and accounted by himself in the name of the monastery and for the monastery from Albertino of Luciano, he [John] renounced all exceptions and agrees himself paid for the time of the contract, and together with his aforementioned brothers accepted this money for the use of the monastery. Now he [John] invests the same Albertino according to the law of the perpetual lease with a piece of land of building property with a house built upon it and with a court and garden belonging to it, lying in the city of Padua in the district of S. Lucia. It is bound on one side by a public road, on the other by [the land of] Egidiolo Filora, on one end by Symeon, notary, and on the other by Peter. Thus that the lease or the investiture of a lease ought to be renewed every 29 years. At each renewal, Albertino and his heirs will have to give John or his successors, ten Venetian *soldi di piccoli* and, in turn, Albertino and his heirs ought to have, hold and possess the aforementioned piece of land with court and gar-

den and with the house built on it with all his will and according to the law of perpetual lease renewable every 29 years. As is said, without contradiction from or petition to John and his successors, [Albertino and his heirs ought to have] right of accession, entrance, entering and leaving, with the road and ditches and aqueducts, with above and below the ground and with all things that belong to these property, and with all rights, actions, and law, real and personal of the same land and buildings which belong to the aforementioned John in the name of the same monastery. Except according to the law and condition asserting and saying that the same land with building cannot be given, alienated or in any way obligated to any other except to the aforesaid Albertino, and it is free of all service. And if more than the said price will be demanded, it will be given and conceded to him purely and irrevocably, as is contained above in the contract of the lease.

▼▼▼

Those Who Fight

Early medieval warriors were largely unruly individuals, little concerned with moral standards, and as a group, they were generally low born and enjoyed low social status. During the High Middle Ages, much of this changed, as Europe's feudal* warriors evolved into a landed class. In the course of this transformation, many of these warriors developed a new self-image, whereby they saw themselves as belonging to a special, hereditary order of society, which possessed certain unique values, virtues, and modes of behavior that ennobled them and justified their power, privileges, and ways of life.

Toward the end of the eleventh century and the beginning of the twelfth, feudal warriors began to articulate a code of knightly conduct that later generations would term *chivalry*. Ideally, chivalric principles and customs governed the life and conduct of the *chevalier,* or mounted knight, but reality and ideal diverged, more often than not. The first selection illustrates an important early stage in the development of a code of chivalry as an ideal, if not a total reality.

Feudal warriors were becoming a defined class, with their own social niche and manners; they were also developing their own codes of law, which defined the reciprocal duties and privileges of vassals* and their lords. The second document presents an example of late-twelfth-century feudal law.

The Ideal Feudal Warrior?
▼▼▼
47 ▼ *THE SONG OF ROLAND*

In the tenth-century world of St. Gerald of Aurillac (Chapter 6, source 30), feudalism was, at best, a rather ill-defined mass of arrangements and customs, all of which somehow revolved around relationships that bound warrior-landholders to their military retainers and the people whom they governed. By the early eleventh century, feudal relationships had sufficiently become a part of regular life (at least in the kingdom of France) that Fulbert of Chartres could attempt to define the feudal contract (source 31). By 1100 feudal ways had become so deeply ingrained in the life and psyche of France's warrior class that they provided the ethos for France's earliest and greatest epic poem, *The Song of Roland.*

This anonymous *chanson de geste,* or "song of heroic deeds," which was composed in Old French around 1100, relates the legendary last battle of Count Roland and his companions. The story is loosely based on a minor disaster suffered by Charlemagne in 778. While his army was returning from an expedition in northern Spain, Christian Basques ambushed and wiped out his baggage train and rear guard in the mountain pass of Roncesvalles. Among the fallen was Roland, lord of the Breton frontier. We know little else about this skirmish or the historical Roland. When Roland re-emerges several centuries later, however, he has been transformed into Charlemagne's nephew and the greatest champion in the emperor's holy war against Islam, and the Basque bandits have become an enormous Muslim army. Charlemagne, who was only thirty-six at the time of the ambush and twenty-two years shy of his eventual coronation as emperor, has metamorphosed into a Moses-like patriarch* more than 200 years old, who rules as God's sole agent on earth over a united Christian world. He, his nephew, and his nephew's companions are now Frenchmen, even though there had been no France or French culture in Charlemagne's day. Likewise, even though feudalism was in its infancy when Charles the Great's Frankish kingdom served as Western Christendom's focal point, *The Song of Roland* assumes a society permeated by feudal relationships and values.

The story revolves around the themes of feudal loyalty and honor. Roland has unwittingly offended his stepfather, Ganelon, who, in revenge, enters into a conspiracy with the Saracen (Muslim) king, Marsilion, to deliver up Roland and the rest of the flower of French knighthood. Ganelon then arranges for Roland to command the emperor's rear guard, knowing that the Saracens plan to ambush it and that Roland will be too proud to sound his horn for reinforcements. Such is the case. Despite the entreaties of Oliver, his closest friend, Roland does not sound the horn until the battle is lost and 20,000 Christian soldiers lie dead. The emperor returns too late to prevent his nephew's death but manages to exact revenge by destroying all Muslim forces in Spain and consigning Ganelon to death by torture.

The selection that follows describes the opening and final stages of Roland's last fight and reflects the warrior values of feudal society in the era of the First Crusade (1095–1102).

QUESTIONS FOR ANALYSIS

1. Why does Roland not wish to sound his horn? Why does Oliver initially urge Roland to blow the horn but later tells him that it would be shameful to do so? What conclusions follow from your answers?
2. How does Roland define a vassal's duty? Would Oliver remove or add anything to that list? With which of these two warriors, Roland or Oliver, would Fulbert of Chartres agree more? Why?
3. Why do these warriors give names to their weapons, and why does Roland attempt to destroy Durendal before he dies? What inferences do you draw from your answers?
4. Consider the words and actions of Roland, Oliver, and Turpin, and from them, draw up a list of the components comprising the late-eleventh-century Code of Chivalry. Do you see any potentially contradictory values or practices? If so, how do you explain them?
5. How does the author express the salvation of Roland's soul in feudal terms? What inferences do you draw from this scene?
6. What role does religion play in this epic? Would Abbot Odo of Cluny (Chapter 6, source 30) agree with Archbishop Turpin's sermon and the poem's overall religious vision? What conclusions follow from your answers to these questions?
7. To what degree is this poem saturated with feudal values?

The pagans[1] arm themselves with Saracen[2] coats of triple-layered chain mail.[3] They buckle on helmets made in Saragossa[4] and strap on swords of Viennese steel. Their shields are handsome, and their lances, crafted in Valencia,[5] are tipped with white, blue, and scarlet streamers. They leave behind their pack mules and riding horses and, mounting their war-horses, ride forth in right formation. The day is fair and the sun bright, and all their gear glistens in the light.

To add to the splendor, they sound a thousand trumpets. So great is the clamor, the sound carries to the Franks.[6]

Upon hearing it, Oliver says to Count Roland: "Sir comrade, I think we are now going to battle the Saracens." Roland answers: "May God so grant it. If we make a stand here for our monarch, we are only doing what is expected of good men. A man ought to be willing to suffer pain and loss for his lord. He should endure extremes of heat and cold and should be ever ready to lose hide and hair in his lord's service. Let each of us now be sure to strike hard blows, so that no bard may sing ill of us in his songs. Pagans are wrong, and Christians are right. On my part, I will not set a bad example."

---

[1] At this time, the age of the First Crusade (Chapter 11), European Christians were generally ignorant of the fact that Muslims are monotheists and, therefore, not pagans.

[2] Originally, *Saracen* was a term the Romans used to designate an inhabitant of Arabia; later, it became a general Western synonym for *Muslim*.

[3] Knee-length garments of interconnected iron rings (chain mail) that protected the torso and thighs.

[4] A city in northeast Spain that Christian forces captured from Islam in 1118. This reference suggests the poem predates that date.

[5] A region in eastern Spain.

[6] The Christian army. By 1100, *Frank* was a generic term for Western European Christian, used particularly by Byzantines and Muslims. Whereas Europeans saw it as an honorable name, to eastern Mediterranean peoples, it was often a synonym for *barbarian*.

Oliver says: "The heathen army is massive, and our numbers are few. Roland, my good friend, sound your horn. Charles will hear it and return with his whole army." Roland replies: "That would be a foolish act, for by so doing I would lose all fame in sweet France. I prefer to strike hard blows with Durendal,[7] so that its blade is bloodied right up to the hilt. These foul pagans made a mistake in coming to this mountain pass. I pledge that they have not long to live."

"Roland, my comrade, blow your horn. Charles will hear it, return with his army, and the king and his barons will aid us." Roland answers: "God forbid that my family be shamed by my actions or any dishonor fall on fair France. No, I will fight with Durendal, the good sword girded here at my side, and you will see its blade fully reddened. The pagans asked for trouble when they gathered their army. I pledge that all of them will die." . . .

Oliver says: "I see no shame here. I have seen the Saracens of Spain, they cover the hills and valleys, the scrubland and the plains. Numerous are the ranks of this hostile people, and we are but a small band of comrades." Roland answers: "This only inflames my desire. May God and His angels forbid that France should suffer any loss because of me. I would rather die than dishonor myself. The more we act like warriors, the more the emperor loves us."

Roland is valiant, Oliver is wise, and both are courageous. Once armed and on their horses, they would rather die than flee the battlefield. . . .

Close at hand is Archbishop Turpin.[8] He now spurs his horse to the crest of a knoll and delivers a sermon to the Franks: "Lord barons, Charles placed us here, and it is a man's duty to die for his monarch. Now help defend Christianity. It is certain you will have to fight, for here are the Saracens. Confess* your sins and beg God's mercy. For the salvation of your souls, I will absolve your sins. Should you die, you will die as holy martyrs, and you will have exalted seats in Paradise." The Franks dismount and kneel, and the archbishop blesses them. As their penance,[9] he commands them to use their swords.

▷ Despite a courageous stand, the rear guard is overwhelmed.

Count Roland, aware of the great slaughter of his men, turns to Oliver, saying: "Noble comrade, for God's sake, what do you think? See how many good men lie on the ground. We ought to weep for sweet France, the fair, that has lost such barons. Ah, my king and friend, would that you were here now! Oliver, my brother,[10] what should we do? How shall we send the king news of this?" "I do not know," says Oliver, "but I would prefer to die than dishonor myself." Then Roland says: "I will blow my horn, and Charles, as he crosses the mountains, will hear it. I swear that the Franks will return." Oliver then replies: "That would be shameful for you to do and would dishonor your family. It would be a disgrace they would carry to their graves. You would not blow the horn when I told you to do so, now I advise you not to sound it. To do so now would be useless." . . .

Roland asks: "Why are you angry with me?" Oliver answers: "Comrade, you have no one to blame but yourself. Valor tempered by wisdom is not foolishness, and prudence is better than pride. Because of your folly these Franks have died. Never again will King Charles enjoy our service. Had you taken my advice, my lord Charles would have been here, and this battle

---

[7]The name of Roland's sword.

[8]Archbishop* of the church of Reims and, along with Roland and Oliver, one of the Twelve Peers of France. *Peer* means "equal"; these twelve champions are socially the emperor's equals by virtue of their birth, prowess, and worth to him. Although a priest,* Turpin is also a fighter.

[9]After receiving absolution of his or her sins from God through the agency of a priest, the penitent is required by the priest to perform some penitential act as a token of contrition. Depending on the severity of the sins forgiven, the act could range from saying simple prayers to making a pilgrimage* to the Holy Land.

[10]His brother-in-arms and intended brother-in-law.

would have ended differently. King Marsilion would have been captured or killed. Your valor, Roland, has been our undoing. We shall never again fight for the great Emperor Charles, who will have no equal till the end of time. Now you must die, and France will be shamed by its loss. Today our loyal friendship will be ended; before night falls we will be sorrowfully parted."

The archbishop, hearing them quarrel, goads his horse with spurs of pure gold, rides to them, and rebukes them both, saying: "Sir Roland, and you, Sir Oliver, in God's name, I pray you, stop this strife. Your horn will give us little help now, yet it is better if you blow it. Should the king come, he will avenge us, and the pagans will not depart from here rejoicing. Our Frankish comrades will dismount and find us dead and mutilated. They will lay us on stretchers placed on the backs of pack mules and will mourn us in sorrow and pity. They will bury us in churches, so that our corpses are not eaten by wolves, swine, and dogs."

"Sir, you speak well and correctly," says Roland. Whereupon he sets his horn to his lips and blows it with all his might. . . . A good thirty leagues away they hear it resound. Charles and his whole army hear it, and the king remarks: "Our men

are engaged in battle." . . . With anguish and deep torment, Count Roland blows his horn with all his might, to the point that bright blood spurts out of his mouth, and the vessels of his brain are ruptured. . . .

Roland knows his time is over. . . . He has laid himself down beneath a pine tree, his face turned toward Spain. He begins to remember many things: all the lands he has conquered, sweet France, the noble lineage from which he is descended, and Charlemagne, his lord, who raised him in his own household. He cannot keep back his tears and sighs. But not forgetting himself, he confesses his sins and begs God's mercy: "Father, You who are truth itself, who raised Lazarus from the dead[11] and saved Daniel from the lions,[12] preserve my soul from all the dangers that beset it because of the sins I have committed throughout my life." He holds out his right glove to God, and Saint Gabriel[13] takes it from his hand. His head sinks down to rest on his arm. With clasped hands he meets his end. God sends down His cherubim[14] and Saint Michael, who saves us from the perils of the sea,[15] and with them comes Saint Gabriel, and they carry the soul of the count to paradise.

---

[11]A friend whom Jesus raised from the dead.
[12]A Jewish prophet protected by God while in a lion's den.
[13]An archangel and messenger of God.
[14]An order of angels.

[15]St. Michael the Archangel, a warrior saint. The island monastery* of Mont-Saint-Michel off the Breton coast is dedicated to St. Michael, the protector of sailors.

Feudal Law
▼▼▼

48 ▼ *"Glanville,"*
CONCERNING THE LAWS AND CUSTOMS OF THE KINGDOM OF ENGLAND

As noted in Chapter 6, vassals* served lords in return for fiefs.* Originally, a fief, or *fee,* was anything of value, but increasingly, it became a grant of land over which the vassal ruled in the lord's name. During the eleventh century, fiefs tended to become hereditary, passing to the vassal's oldest surviving male heir. Feudal soldiers, therefore, who several generations earlier had generally been hired thugs in the employ of warlords, were becoming landed nobles and gentry. As this rising class gained power and status, it developed complex bodies of law to regulate relationships between lords and vassals, especially regarding the tenure of fiefs.

Around 1190 someone who was intimately versed in the laws and legal procedures that had taken shape in England in the reign of Henry II (Chapter 10, source 63) composed a treatise on English royal law and custom. Tradition has assigned its authorship to Ranulf de Glanville, England's *justiciar,* or vice-regent in charge of administration and justice, from 1180 to 1189. Modern scholars, however, question that ascription. The author, whoever he might have been, sheds a great deal of light upon all aspects of King Henry's legal reforms and shows how feudal law functioned in England toward the close of the twelfth century.

QUESTIONS FOR ANALYSIS

1. Why could women not perform *homage?* That being the case, how did they inherit their fathers' fiefs in the absence of brothers or nephews?
2. Could women be lords under twelfth-century Anglo-Norman feudal law? Why or why not?
3. On the basis of your answers to questions 1 and 2, what do you infer about the status of women under late-twelfth-century English feudal law?
4. What was a *liege,* or chief, lord, and what do the rules governing vassal–liege lord relations suggest about the complexities of feudal relationships?
5. When and why could a vassal legitimately fight or oppose his lord? What does this suggest about the feudal contract?
6. How and why might a vassal lose his fief? What conclusions follow from your answer?
7. Chapter IV deals with reciprocal vassal-lord obligations. In brief, what were they?
8. Consider Chapters VIII through X. How do late-twelfth-century English customs and laws regarding *aids* indicate that feudal arrangements and feudal society in general had changed significantly since the tenth and early eleventh centuries?
9. Are the principles enunciated by "Glanville" consonant with what we discovered in Fulbert of Chartres's letter and *The Song of Roland?* If so, how? If not, how do they differ?

BOOK IX. *Chap. I.*   It remains to continue upon the subject of performing homage[1] and receiving reliefs.[2] Upon the death of the father or any other ancestor, the lord of the fee is bound from the first to receive the homage of the true heir, whether the heir has attained full age or not, provided always that he be male. For females cannot by law perform any homage, although, generally speaking, they are wont to do fealty to their lords.[3] But if they are married their husbands ought to do homage to their lords for their fee; if, I mean, homage be due in respect of such fees. If, however, the heir be male and a minor, the lord of the fee is not entitled by law to the wardship[4] of the heir or of his holding until he has received the homage of the heir; because it is a general principle that no one can exact from an heir, whether he is of age or not, any service, whether a relief or otherwise, until he has received the homage of the heir in respect of that holding for which the service is claimed. But a person may perform homage to several lords on account of different fees, but of these homages one should be the chief and should be liege homage,[5] and this must be performed to the lord from whom the person performing homage holds his chief tenement. Homage ought to be done in this manner, namely, that he who performs it shall so become the man of his lord that he shall bear faith to him for the tenement in respect of which he performs homage, and shall preserve the earthly honor of his lord in all things save the faith due to the king and to his heirs. From

this it is evident that a vassal cannot injure his lord without breaking the faith involved in homage, unless perhaps in his own defence, or unless on the order of the king he joins the king's army when it goes against his lord. Generally speaking, the law holds that no one can, without breaking the faith implied in homage, do anything which tends to deprive his lord of his inheritance, or do anything to the dishonor of his body. If then a tenant has, in respect of several fees, done homage to different lords who afterwards make war upon each other, and the chief lord should command the tenant to go in person with him against another of his lords, he ought to obey this command saving, however, the service due to the other lord in respect of the fee held from him. From what has been said it therefore follows that if a tenant should do anything contributing to the disinheritance of his lord, and should be convicted of it, he and his heirs shall according to the law lose forever the fee held of this lord. The same consequence will follow if the tenant lays violent hands on his lord to hurt him, or puts him to shame, and this be lawfully proved in court[6] against the tenant. But it may be asked whether anyone can be compelled to defend himself against the lord in the lord's court against such charges; and whether his lord can, by the judgment of his own court, distrain[7] the tenant so to do, without the precept of the king or of his justices or without the king's writ or that of his chief justice. The law indeed permits a lord by the judgment of his court to summon

---

[1]Literally, "to become one's man." It was the ceremonial act whereby one became *the man,* or vassal, of a lord. In a society that was still largely illiterate, ceremonial acts had a special force. In this act, the new vassal usually knelt before his lord, signifying his dependence, and often received from his lord a weapon as a sign of his military service. The act of homage was often accompanied by a sacred oath of *fealty,** or loyalty.

[2]The money or goods paid to a lord by a vassal upon inheriting a fief. This inheritance tax usually equaled the value of one year's income from the fief. See source 44, note 8, for a reference to the type of inheritance tax that was often extorted from serfs.*

[3]The oath of fealty (see note 1).

[4]A vassal who owed military service had to be twenty-two or older; if he was younger, he became the lord's ward. During the period of wardship, the lord took possession of the fief and used its revenues as he saw fit, being bound only to maintain the ward in "an honorable manner" and to allow the ward to inherit the fief upon reaching his majority.

[5]Liege homage was the recognition that service to one lord superseded all obligations to any other lord.

[6]Normally, the lord's feudal court, where the vassal will be judged by his peers, or fellow vassals, but it could also be the king's court.

[7]Seize and compel.

and distrain one who has paid him homage to appear in court, and unless such a one can purge himself against the charge of his lord by three persons, or as many as the court shall decide, he shall be amerced[8] to the lord to the extent of the whole fee that he holds from this lord. It may also be inquired whether a lord can distrain one who has paid him homage to appear in his court to answer for a service which the lord claims has not been rendered, or of which some part has been withheld. The answer is that the lord may by law well do so, and this even without the precept of the king or his justices. And in such a controversy the lord and the man who has paid him homage may submit their dispute to the duel,[9] or to the Grand Assize[10] by means of one of the tenant's peers who duly witnesses to the fact that he has seen the tenant himself or his ancestors perform such service for the fee to the lord or his ancestors, and is prepared to prove the fact. And if the tenant be convicted of this charge, he shall by law be disinherited of the whole fee which he holds of his lord. If, however, anyone is unable to constrain his tenants, it then becomes necessary to have recourse to the [king's] court. Every free male person may perform homage, whether of full age or otherwise, whether clerk or layman. But consecrated bishops[*] are not accustomed to perform homage to the king even for their baronies; but merely fealty accompanied by an oath. But bishops-elect[11] are wont to do homage previous to their consecration. . . .

Chap. III.   Homage may, however, be done to any free person whether male or female, whether of full age or otherwise, and whether clerk or lay. But it should be understood that if a person has done homage for a tenement to a woman who afterwards marries, then he shall be compelled to repeat it to her husband for the same tenement. If, however, anyone has by agreement made in court recovered a tenement against another who had previously paid a relief for it to the chief lord, it may be questioned whether the person so recovering the tenement ought to pay any further relief for it.

Chap. IV.   There ought to be a reciprocal obligation of fidelity between lordship and homage. Nor does the tenant owe more to his lord in respect of homage than the lord owes to the tenant on account of lordship, reverence alone excepted. Hence if one person gives to another any land in return for service and homage, which land is afterwards recovered against the tenant by a third party, the lord shall be bound to warrant such land to him or to return him an adequate equivalent. It is otherwise, however, in the case of a man who holds a fee from another as his inheritance and in this character has done homage, because in this instance although he lose his land the lord shall not be bound to give him an equivalent. . . .

Chap. VIII.   After it has been settled between the lord and the heir of the tenant concerning the giving and receiving of a reasonable relief, the heir may exact reasonable aids[12] in respect of this from his own men. This, however, must be done with moderation in accordance with the number and resources of their fees lest they should be too much oppressed or should lose their contenement.[13] But nothing certain is fixed concerning the giving and exacting of aids of this kind except that the conditions we have noted must be always observed. There are also other cases in which a lord can exact from his men simi-

---

[8]Handed over for punishment. An Old French legal term, it means "to be at the mercy of."
[9]Actual combat fought between the defendant (or his or her champion) and the lord's champion. The winner was obviously the one in the right.
[10]The king's court.

[11]Someone who has been elected but not yet consecrated as bishop.
[12]Money payments made to the lord to aid him in time of need.
[13]The property necessary to enable a vassal to maintain his position.

lar aids, always observing the prescribed form: as when his son and heir is made a knight, and when he gives his eldest daughter in marriage. But whether lords can exact aids to maintain private war is doubtful. The opinion which prevails is that they cannot lawfully distrain their tenants[14] for such a purpose except in so far as the tenants agree. But with respect to the payment of reasonable aids, lords may of their own right, without the king's precept or that of his justices, but by the judgment of their own court, distrain their tenants by such of their chattels as may be found within their fees or if necessary by their fees themselves; provided always that the tenants are dealt with according to the judgment of the lord's court and consistently with its reasonable custom. If therefore a lord may thus distrain his tenants to pay such reasonable aids, much stronger is the argument that he may lawfully distrain in the same manner for a relief, or for any other service necessarily due to him in respect of the fee. If, however, a lord is unable by judgment to compel his tenant to render his due and customary services, then recourse must be had to the king or to his chief justice, and he shall obtain the following writ:

Chap. IX.

The king to the sheriff[15] greeting. I order you to compel N. justly and without delay to render to R. the due and customary services which he ought to render in respect of the tenement he holds of him in such-and-such a village, as can be reasonably shown to be due to the lord, lest complaint be made again in respect of default of justice. Witness, etc.

Chap. X.   When the plea proceeds by virtue of this writ, the plaintiff shall in the shire court and before the sheriff demand his dues, whether they consist of reliefs or other things, according to the custom of the shire court. And if the plaintiff shall prove his case, then the tenant shall render the reasonable relief to his lord, and shall in addition be amerced to the sheriff, it being a recognized principle that the amercement which results from any suit dealt with and decided in the shire court belongs to the sheriff. The amount of such amercement has, it is true, been determined by no general assize, but is regulated by the custom of the different shires, in one shire more, in another less.

---

[14]Their feudal vassals and anyone else who held land from the lord under any sort of contract.

[15]The shire reeve, or official representative of the king in a shire, an administrative division of the kingdom.

▼▼▼

Urban Dwellers

People who lived in towns and cities did not constitute a single, monolithic class. To refer to them simply as a *middle class* is to overlook the significant economic, social, and political differences that divided them into many different classes. Despite this fact, urban dwellers did share some important characteristics that set them apart from most other Europeans.

Perhaps the most important of these common characteristics was that urban dwellers were, by and large, free. Europe's cities and towns, which were rapidly proliferating in number and expanding in size from the eleventh to the fourteenth century, were centers of industrial creativity and commercial exchange. Effective production and commerce were best carried on by people unhampered by the servile bonds of serfdom.*

Not only were most urban dwellers personally free, they also enjoyed a large measure of self-defense and self-government. The Germanic word *burg* — from which we derive such terms for townspeople as *burgesses, burghers,* and *bourgeoisie* — originally meant a fortified site. Cities and towns were encircled by walls, and those walls guaranteed their inhabitants at least a modicum of physical security. Free people who are capable of defending themselves tend to be self-governing. At the very least, a town would secure from a local lord or the king a charter of liberties that limited the extent to which any external authority could intervene in the town's fiscal, political, and judicial affairs. A few towns and cities in Italy went farther and became independent of all but the most nominal forms of outside control. This often occurred when a sworn association of townspeople, known as a *commune,* formed to gain independence from the local bishop* or from imperial authority. If necessary (and it often was necessary), commune members were prepared to fight to win and maintain their independence. Although communes could be found in many areas of Europe, most notably Flanders and France, it was only in Italy, Europe's epicenter of urbanization, that a handful of communes successfully transformed their hometowns into city-states.

The first two sources illustrate different types of urban settlements and the people who dwelt therein: a chartered royal borough in England and a self-governing city in Italy. The third source provides insights into the status and legal rights of the Jews of Speyer, in Germany's Rhineland, and the last source gives tantalizing glimpses of townspeople along Christian Europe's Iberian frontier.

The Merchants of Southampton
▼▼▼
49 ▼ *ORDINANCES OF THE GILD MERCHANT OF SOUTHAMPTON*

Southampton, a port town on England's southeast shore, was already an ancient center of handicraft and trade when Duke William of Normandy invaded England in 1066 and burned down the town in his successful campaign to gain the English crown. For almost a full century thereafter, the town languished under the realm's early Anglo-Norman monarchs. Under William I's great-grandson, Henry II (r. 1154–1189), however, who was also count of Anjou and duke of Aquitaine, Southampton was drawn into a trading network with south-central and southwestern France, which became the basis for the town's new prosperity. Carrying prime English wool to St. Malo, Nantes, La Rochelle, and Bordeaux, Southampton's merchants returned with agricultural products, especially wines from western France. Sailing northeast to the textile centers of the Low Countries, such as Bruges and Antwerp, Southampton's merchants exchanged wool for manufactured cloth and a wide variety of luxury goods. The town's reversal of fortune during the latter half of the twelfth century and following became the impetus for its development into a favored royal borough and the rise in power of its guild of merchants.

In the days of King Henry I (r. 1100–1135), Southampton was part of the royal *demesne,* or crown lands, and was governed directly by the king's *reeve,* or deputy. During the first year of the reign of King John (1199–1216), the situation changed dramatically when the king granted the burgesses of Southampton the perpetual right to assess, regulate, and collect all of their tolls and taxes in return for an annual payment of 200 pounds sterling to the royal treasury. Southampton now had limited self-government under royal authority.

The group that took the lead in securing the privileges of self-government was Southampton's *guild* (or gild) of merchants. No surviving records mention the borough's guild, or association, of merchants before the reign of Henry I, but its origins probably date back well into the pre-Conquest era. The following document, which lists the rules of Southampton's merchant guild, was transcribed in the fourteenth century, but most of its ordinances date from before 1300. The first eighteen regulations seem to be the oldest, but many others also reflect twelfth- and thirteenth-century realities. Regardless of when they became custom and law, these ordinances clearly show the inner workings and power of a fairly typical late-thirteenth-century guild of merchants.

QUESTIONS FOR ANALYSIS

1. Guilds often originated as religious confraternities. What evidence is there that the guild of merchants continued to have religious purposes?
2. What social functions did the guild have?
3. How did the guild protect its members?
4. How and why did the guild regulate entry into its membership?
5. How and why did the guild regulate trade?
6. Consider items 24, 25, and 63. What is their intent? What does this suggest about the economic and social principles that underlay the guild?
7. Consider items 13, 14, 16, and 22. What police and judicial powers does the guild claim over nonmembers?
8. Consider items 27 and 32. By what right does the guild mandate the type of officers who will govern Southampton, their duties, and the manner in which municipal elections will be held?
9. Study items 1, 8, 27, 32, and 35 as a block. Who do you think serves as the borough's chief alderman? Why have you reached that conclusion?
10. What do your answers to questions 7, 8, and 9 suggest about the guild's power and place in the community?
11. Upon whose authority does the guild ultimately depend for its powers and position?

1. In the first place, there shall be elected from the gild merchant, and established, an alderman,[1] a steward,[2] a chaplain,[3] four skevins,[4] and an usher.[5] And it is to be known that whosoever shall be alderman shall receive from each one entering into the gild fourpence,[6] the steward, twopence; the chaplain, twopence; and the usher, one penny. And the gild shall meet twice a year: that is to say, on the Sunday next after St. John the Baptist's day,[7] and on the Sunday next after St. Mary's day.[8]

2. And when the gild shall be sitting, no one of the gild is to bring in any stranger, except when required by the alderman or steward. And the alderman shall have a sergeant[9] to serve before him, the steward another sergeant, and the two skevins a sergeant, and the other two skevins a sergeant, and the chaplain shall have his clerk.

3. And when the gild shall sit, the alderman is to have, each night, so long as the gild sits, two gallons of wine and two candles, and the steward the same; and the four skevins and the chaplain, each of them one gallon of wine and one candle, and the usher one gallon of wine.

4. And when the gild shall sit, the lepers of La Madeleine[10] shall have of the alms of the gild, two sesters[11] of ale, and the sick of God's House and of St. Julian[12] shall have two sesters of ale. And the Friars Minor[13] shall have two sesters of ale and one sester of wine. And four sesters of ale shall be given to the poor wherever the gild shall meet.

5. And when the gild is sitting, no one who is of the gild shall go outside of the town for any business, without the permission of the steward. And if any one does so, let him be fined two shillings,[14] and pay them.

6. And when the gild sits, and any gildsman is outside of the city so that he does not know when it will happen, he shall have a gallon of wine, if his servants come to get it. And if a gildsman is ill and is in the city, wine shall be sent to him, two loaves of bread and a gallon of wine and a dish from the kitchen; and two approved men of the gild shall go to visit him and look after his condition.

7. And when a gildsman dies, all those who are of the gild and are in the city shall attend the service of the dead, and gildsmen shall bear the body and bring it to the place of burial. And whoever will not do this shall pay according to his oath, two pence, to be given to the poor. And those of the ward[15] where the dead man shall be ought to find a man to watch over the body the night that the dead shall lie in his house. And so long as the service of the dead shall last, that is to say the vigil and the mass,[*] there ought to burn four candles of the gild, each candle of two pounds weight or more, until the body is buried. And these four candles shall remain in the keeping of the steward of the gild.

8. The steward ought to keep the rolls[16] and the treasure of the gild under the seal of the alderman of the gild.

9. And when a gildsman dies, his eldest son or his next heir shall have the seat of his father, or of his uncle, if his father was not a gildsman, and of no other one; and he shall give nothing

---

[1]Literally, "the senior man."
[2]The official in charge of the guild's property.
[3]A priest.[*]
[4]Attendants. Originally, they seem to have had minor functions in the guild, but they evolved into a body of four elders.
[5]Originally, the doorkeeper and sergeant-at-arms.
[6]Two hundred forty pence make one pound sterling.
[7]June 24.
[8]Presumably, the feast of Mary's Conception, December 8. Another document states that this second meeting date was the Sunday following the feast day of St. Hilary (January 14).

[9]To be understood in the sense of a servant and secretary.
[10]A leper hospital that was established just north of the town around 1173.
[11]A *sester* was approximately four gallons.
[12]The hospital of St. Julian, also known as *God's House* (*Hôtel Dieu*), which was founded in 1196/1197.
[13]Franciscan friars[*] settled in the borough in 1233/1234.
[14]Twelve pence (note 6) made a shilling, and twenty shillings constituted a pound sterling.
[15]Neighborhood.
[16]The records, which were on parchment rolls.

for his seat. No husband can have a seat in the gild by right of his wife, nor demand a seat by right of his wife's ancestors.

10. And no one has the right or power to sell or give his seat in the gild to any man; and the son of a gildsman, other than his eldest son, shall enter into the gild on payment of ten shillings, and he shall take the oath of the gild.

11. And if a gildsman shall be imprisoned in England in time of peace, the alderman with the steward and with one of the skevins shall go, at the cost of the gild, to procure the deliverance of the one who is in prison.

12. And if any gildsman strikes another with his fist and is convicted thereof, he shall lose the gild until he shall have bought it back for ten shillings, and taken the oath of the gild again like a new member. And if a gildsman strikes another with a stick, or a knife, or any other weapon, whatever it may be, he shall lose the gild and the franchise,[17] and shall be held as a stranger until he shall have been reconciled to the good men of the gild and has made recompense to the one whom he has injured, and has paid a fine to the gild of twenty shillings; and this shall not be remitted.

13. If any one does an injury, who is not of the gild, and is of the franchise[18] or strikes a gildsman and is reasonably convicted, he shall lose his franchise and go to prison for a day and a night.

14. And if any stranger or any other who is not of the gild nor of the franchise strikes a gildsman, and is reasonably convicted thereof, let him be in prison two days and two nights, unless the injury is such that he should be more severely punished.

15. And if a gildsman reviles or slanders another gildsman, and a complaint of it comes to the alderman, and if he is reasonably convicted thereof, he shall pay two shillings fine to the gild, and if he is not able to pay he shall lose the gild.

16. And if anyone who is of the franchise speaks evil of a gildsman, and is convicted of this before the alderman, he shall pay five shillings for a fine or lose the franchise.

17. And no one shall come to the council of the gild if he is not a gildsman.

18. And if anyone of the gild forfeits the gild by any act or injury, and is excluded by the alderman and the steward and the skevins and the twelve sworn men of the city;[19] and he wishes to have the gild again, he shall do all things anew just as one who has never been of the gild, and shall make amends for his injury according to the discretion of the alderman and the aforesaid approved men. And if anyone of the gild or of the franchise brings a suit against another outside of the city, by a writ or without a writ, he shall lose the gild and the franchise if he is convicted of it.

19. And no one of the city of Southampton shall buy anything to sell again in the same city, unless he is of the gild merchant or of the franchise. And if anyone shall do so and is convicted of it, all which he has so bought shall be forfeited to the king; and no one shall be quit of custom unless he proves that he is in the gild or in the franchise, and this from year to year.

20. And no one shall buy honey, fat, salt herrings, or any kind of oil, or millstones, or fresh hides, or any kind of fresh skins, unless he is a gildsman: nor keep a tavern for wine, nor sell cloth at retail, except in market or fair days;[20] nor keep grain in his granary beyond five quarters, to sell at retail, if he is not a gildsman; and whoever shall do this and be convicted shall forfeit all to the king.

21. No one of the gild ought to be partner or joint dealer in any of the kinds of merchandise before mentioned with anyone who is not of the gild, by any manner of coverture, or art, or contrivance, or collusion, or in any other manner. And whosoever shall do this and be convicted,

---

[17]Membership in the borough; from the Old French, meaning "endowed with freedom."
[18]A burgess of Southampton (see note 17).
[19]See item 32.

[20]Weekly or twice-weekly market days were when farmers and fishermen brought food into the town for sale. Fairs were seasonal and substantially larger markets, at which foreign merchants were welcome.

the goods in such manner bought shall be forfeited to the king, and the gildsman shall lose the gild.

22. If any gildsman falls into poverty and has not the wherewithal to live, and is not able to work or to provide for himself, he shall have one mark[21] from the gild to relieve his condition when the gild shall sit. No one of the gild nor of the franchise shall avow[22] another's goods for his by which the custom of the city shall be injured. And if any one does so and is convicted, he shall lose the gild and the franchise; and the merchandise so avowed shall be forfeited to the king.

23. And no private man nor stranger shall bargain for or buy any kind of merchandise coming into the city before a burgess of the gild merchant, so long as the gildsman is present and wishes to bargain for and buy this merchandise; and if anyone does so and is convicted, that which he buys shall be forfeited to the king.

24. And anyone who is of the gild merchant shall share in all merchandise which another gildsman shall buy or any other person, whosoever he is, if he comes and demands part and is there where the merchandise is bought, and also if he gives satisfaction to the seller and gives security for his part. But no one who is not a gildsman is able or ought to share with a gildsman, without the will of the gildsman.

25. And if any gildsman or other of the city refuse a part to the gildsman in the manner above said, he[23] shall not buy or sell in that year in the town, except his victuals.

26. And if any merchant of the town buys wine or grain so that all the risk shall be on the buyer, he shall not pay custom for this merchandise. And if any risk is upon the seller, he[24] shall pay.

27. It is provided that the chief alderman of the town, or the bailiffs[25] and the twelve sworn men, shall give attention to the merchants as well strangers as private men, as often as it shall be required, to see that they have sufficient security for their debts, and recognisance from their debtors; and the day of this shall be enrolled before them, so that if the day is not kept, on proof by the creditor, the debtor should be then distrained[26] according to the recognisance which he has made, in lands and chattels, to give satisfaction according to the usage of the town, without any manner of pleading, so that the men of the town should not have damage by the default of payment of the debtors aforesaid.

28. And if any gildsman for any debt which he may owe will not suffer himself to be distrained, or when he has been distrained, shall break through, or make removal or break the king's lock,[27] and be convicted thereof, he shall lose his gildship until he has bought it again for twenty shillings, and this each time that he offends in such manner. And he shall be none the less distrained until he has made satisfaction for the debt he owes; and if he will not submit to justice as aforesaid and be thereof convicted, he shall go to prison for a day and a night like one who is against the peace; and if he will not submit to justice let the matter be laid before the king and his council in manner aforesaid. . . .

32. Every year, on the morrow of St. Michael,[28] shall be elected by the whole community of the town, assembled in a place provided, to consider the estate and treat of the common business of the town — then shall be elected by the whole community, twelve discreet men to execute the king's commands, together with the bailiffs, and to keep the peace and protect the franchise, and to do and keep justice to all persons, as well poor

---

[21]A half pound of silver; it could support an early thirteenth-century family modestly for about half a year.
[22]Claim.
[23]The person who refused to share.
[24]The buyer.

[25]Officers of the town who maintained law and order; supervised markets, weights, and measures; registered debts; and kept customs and tax records (see item 32).
[26]Compelled.
[27]The royal seal on his goods that have been taken as security.
[28]September 30, the day after the feast of St. Michael.

as rich, natives or strangers, all that year; and to this they shall be sworn in the form provided. And these twelve discreet men shall choose the same day two discreet men from among themselves and the other profitable and wise men to be bailiffs for the ensuing year, who shall take care that the customs shall be well paid; and they shall receive their jurisdiction the day after Michaelmas, as has been customary. And this shall be done from year to year, so that the bailiffs shall be renewed every year, and the twelve aforesaid, if there is occasion. The same shall be done as to clerk and sergeants of the city, in making and removing. . . .

35. The common chest[29] shall be in the house of the chief alderman or of the steward, and the three keys of it shall be lodged with three discreet men of the aforesaid twelve sworn men, or with three of the skevins, who shall loyally take care of the common seal, and the charters and the treasure of the town, and the standards, and other muniments of the town; and no letter shall be sealed with the common seal, nor any charter taken out of the common-chest but in the presence of six or twelve sworn men, and of the alderman or steward; and nobody shall sell by any kind of measure or weight that it is not sealed, under forfeiture of two shillings. . . .

63. No one shall go out to meet a ship bringing wine or other merchandise coming to the town, in order to buy anything, before the ship be arrived and come to anchor for unlading; and if any one does so and is convicted, the merchandise which he shall have bought shall be forfeited to the king.

---

[29]Of the borough.

Italian Communal Government
▼▼▼

50 ▼ *John of Viterbo,*
BOOK ON THE GOVERNMENT OF CITIES

The thirteenth-century burgesses of Southampton enjoyed limited self-rule under royal charter. In northern Italy, to the contrary, a number of communes in the twelfth and thirteenth centuries managed to wrest control of their urban governments away from all imperial, feudal,* and ecclesiastical* authorities and to set up independent entities.

If such townsfolk were to govern themselves, they needed to understand the nature of government and how it functioned. Consequently, beginning with the University of Bologna, schools of law proliferated in Italy and elsewhere from the late eleventh century onward, and jurists composed a number of treatises on the theory and practice of good government. One of the most famous of such works is the thirteenth-century *Book on the Government of Cities,* by the Italian lawyer John of Viterbo. We know little about the author, and even the date of the work's composition is uncertain; some scholars have dated it as early as 1228, and others as late as sometime after 1261.

In the following excerpts, John, quoting from Roman law, explains why cities exist and defines the role of the *podesta,* the chief municipal official in many northern Italian city-states of the thirteenth century. Podestas were often professional, salaried magistrates brought in from outside and given one-year contracts, generally renewable upon review, to govern the city. Because many Italian cities suffered from family and class conflicts, they often recruited foreign chief executives on the theory that only an outsider could treat all persons and groups in an evenhanded manner.

QUESTIONS FOR ANALYSIS

1. Consider what John tells us about the primary function of a city. What does this suggest about medieval towns?
2. Are the podesta's powers absolute or limited? How so?
3. Is there any evidence to support the statement that thirteenth-century Italian cities tended to employ foreign-born podestas because they alone seemed to promise evenhanded governance? If so, what?
4. John refers to the inhabitants of a city as "citizens." Why is that significant?
5. According to John, "Matters that touch all must be approved by all." What does this mean? Does he envision the ideal city as a democracy? If not, what is his understanding of a city's constitution and reason for existence?
6. Compare Southampton with the city described here. What do they have in common? How do they differ? Which are more significant, the similarities or the differences? What conclusions follow from your answers to these questions?

THE MEANING OF "CITY"

A city, indeed, is said to be the liberty of its citizens or the defense of its inhabitants, as is said of a fortified town, for its walls are constructed to serve as a bulwark for those dwelling within. This word *civitas* [city] is syncopated, and so its aforementioned meaning comes from the three syllables that *civitas* contains within itself: namely, *ci, vi,* and *tas. Ci* stands for *citra* [apart from]; *vi* stands for *vim* [oppression]; *tas* stands for *habitas* [you dwell]. It follows that *civitas* means "you dwell apart from oppression." One resides there without oppression, because the governor of the city will protect men of more humble station so that they do not suffer injury at the hands of more powerful men (for, "We cannot be the equals of the more powerful").[1] Likewise, "it is not right for anyone to be oppressed by his adversary's might; if this is the case, it certainly reflects the ill-will of the person governing the province." Likewise, because everyone's house is his most secure refuge and place of shelter, no one ought to drag him from there against his will, nor is it natural that anyone in a city be constrained by violent fear, etc. Likewise, one

---

[1]This and the following quotation come from the *Digest,* one of four collections of late-Roman imperial law compiled under the authority of Emperor Justinian I (Chapter 3, source 11), which cumulatively comprise the *Corpus Iuris Civilis,* or *Body of Civil Law.* Medieval European lawyers assumed Roman law was still valid, particularly in Italian and German imperial areas, because they believed their society was a natural and legal continuation of the Roman Empire.

speaks correctly of immunity, because inhabitants are made immune by the walls and towers of their city and are protected within it from hostile foreigners and personal enemies.

THE CREATION OF CITIES

Cities, indeed, were created or founded for a particular purpose. I do not speak of the holy, celestial city of Jerusalem, called "the Great City," the city of our God, whose explanation I leave to theologians and prophets, because it is not my intention to consider Heaven. Rather, I speak of cities in this world, which have been founded so that anyone may hold on to his possessions and his guardianship of his belongings will not be disturbed. . . .

THE PODESTA'S OATH

The podesta's oath is, in fact, normally administered by a judge: "You, Lord B., shall swear on the Holy Gospels,* which you hold in your hands, to administer the affairs and business of this city pertaining to your office and to rule, unite, govern, maintain, and hold safe this city, its surrounding countryside and district, and all people and every person, the small as well as the great, foot soldiers as well as knights,[2] and to maintain and protect their rights and to preserve and assure the observance of the established law regarding minors and adults, especially little children, orphans, widows, and other people worthy of pity, and everyone else who will come to petition or answer charges under your jurisdiction and that of your judges. Likewise, to defend,

preserve, and maintain churches, shrines, hospitals, and other revered places, roads, pilgrims,* and merchants; to keep inviolate the constitution of this city, on which you are swearing with a sound and pure conscience, saving exceptions, if any exceptions have been made, putting aside hatred, love, fraud, favor, and every sort of deceit, according to our sound and pure common understanding, from the next first day of January for one year and the whole day of the first of January." Having said these words, let him who has administered the oath say, "Just as I have administered, so you, Lord B., will swear; and you promise to respect the commune of Florence,[3] and you will honor it in good faith and without fraud, guile, and any sort of deceit. So may God and these holy Gospels of God aid you." Following this, the judges, notaries, chamberlains, the podesta's knight or knights, and even his squires[4] swear oaths. . . .

THE PODESTA'S CONSULTATION WITH THE COUNCIL ON COMPLEX ISSUES

To be sure, in those situations that are complex or serious or pertain to the essential interests of the city, he ought to confer with the council,[5] once it has been assembled, and should do so again and again if the nature of the matter demands it. . . . For then the podesta can act decisively with the knowledge and advice of the city council. . . . If the gravity of the situation requires greater counsel, others from among the wiser element of the citizenry should be summoned to render advice, after they have been

---

[2]Only well-to-do citizens could afford a knight's armor, weapons, and horses; poorer citizens served as infantry.

[3]Florence, an industrial and commercial city in the northern Italian region of Tuscany, had a commune since at least 1200.

[4]A podesta generally brought with him a large retinue of his own trained assistants, who would be given positions of responsibility within the commune during the podesta's term of office. Such assistants included notaries (legal secretaries), chamberlains (financial officers), knights (the podesta's bodyguards), and squires* (personal attendants).

[5]Councils, composed of aristocrats and rich merchants who often joined forces to create a town's first commune, were initially the normal governing bodies of Italy's independent urban centers. During the thirteenth century, many councils found it necessary to surrender executive power to podestas.

elected by the city at large. To wit: representatives of the judges and those experienced in the law, representatives from the consuls of merchants and bankers[6] and from the priors of the trades,[7] and other appropriate persons. . . . For matters that touch all should be approved by all, and let unanimous agreement determine what benefits everyone.

---

[6]The elected heads of the merchant-banker associations, or guilds.

[7]The elected heads of the other trade and artisan guilds.

The Jews of Speyer
▼▼▼

51 ▼ *Rudegar Huozman,*
CHARTER TO THE JEWS OF SPEYER

We would be blind to the realities of history if we overlooked medieval Europe's non-Christian minorities. Jews, in particular, played a role in the cultural, social, and economic history of Europe that was disproportionate to their relatively small numbers. Despite Christian antipathy and often blatant hostility toward Judaism, as reflected in the Ralph Glaber's *Five Books of History* (Chapter 6, source 37) and canons 68 and 69 of the Fourth Lateran Council (Chapter 7, source 42), vibrant Jewish communities proliferated and grew throughout Europe, especially following the eleventh-century revival of commerce.

It would be a mistake to think of medieval Jews as people totally barred from landholding; some were farmers, and some were even estate owners. Even so, it is true that most Jews dwelt in towns and cities during the High Middle Ages. It would also be a mistake to think that urban Jews only supported themselves by money lending and smalltime commerce. Their occupations were as varied as those of their Christian neighbors, with the exception that Jews generally did not serve as professional warriors. However, the eleventh and twelfth centuries witnessed the growth of the feudal* and guild systems, whose participants had to be Christian. Thus, Jews found themselves increasingly excluded from landholding and the lucrative trades and crafts that guilds monopolized in Europe's larger towns and cities. Consequently, Jewish entrepreneurs turned increasingly to banking in order to support themselves, and this included lending money at interest, as well as exchanging money. Such bankers, however, were always a minority within their Jewish communities.

Whether bankers, merchants, artisans, or manual laborers, Europe's Jews contributed greatly to the economic upswing of cities and towns from England to Poland, from Scandinavia to the Mediterranean. A number of lords even welcomed Jews into the towns that they ruled, in the hope that they would prove to be an economic leaven.

As the following document illustrates, Jews were viewed as members of a distinctive, even marginal social order, which meant they were not subject to the same laws as Christians. Therefore, Jews were given special charters that defined their privileges, obligations, and status within the communities in which they settled. The charter that appears here dates from 1080 and was granted by Bishop Rudegar, lord of the town of Speyer in Germany's Rhineland. We will see in Chapter 11, source 74, what happened to the Jews of the Rhineland a few years later.

When reading this document, do not be misled by Bishop Rudegar's characterization of Speyer. As a significant port for waterborne commerce along the Rhine River, the town had been an episcopal see* since the fourth century and was enclosed by a wall as early as the tenth century. Speyer's huge Romanesque cathedral* (Chapter 9), the largest of its style in all of Germany, had been completed in 1061 and already held the bodies of two emperors, Conrad II and Henry III. The present emperor, Henry IV (r. 1056–1106), was an avid patron of the town and its cathedral, where his father was buried. Speyer was anything but a village.

QUESTIONS FOR ANALYSIS

1. Why has the bishop* settled Jews in Speyer? What does his expressed reason suggest about the Jews' economic reputation?
2. What does the bishop's action suggest about methods of urban development in his age?
3. Is there any evidence of anti-Semitism in this document? Please explain your answer.
4. How does the bishop attempt to protect the Jews of Speyer?
5. What economic activities do these Jews engage in?
6. What religious privileges does this charter guarantee?
7. What political-social privileges does the charter grant?
8. In what ways are the Jews of Speyer treated as an entity separate from their Christian neighbors?
9. What overall picture of Jewish-Christian relations in Speyer emerges from your answers to questions 1–8?

1. In the name of the holy and undivided Trinity.* I, Rudeger, by cognomen Huozman, humble bishop of Speyer, when I wished to make a city of my village of Speyer, thought that it would greatly add to its honor if I should establish some Jews in it. I have therefore collected some Jews and located them in a place apart from the dwellings and association of the other inhabitants of the city; and that they may be protected from the attacks and violence of the mob, I have surrounded their quarter with a wall. The land for their dwellings I had acquired in a legal way; for the hill I secured partly by purchase and partly by trade, and the valley I received as a gift from the heirs who possessed it. I have given them this hill and valley on condition that they pay every year three and one-half pounds of money coined in the mint of Speyer, for the use of the brothers.[1]

2. I have given them the free right of changing gold and silver coins and of buying and selling everything they wish within their own walls and outside the gate clear up to the boat-landing [on the Rhine] and also on the wharf itself.

---

[1] Monks* of an unnamed monastery,* possibly the abbey* of St. Germanus.

And they have the same right throughout the whole city.

3. Besides, I have given them a piece of the land of the church as a burial-ground. This land they shall hold forever.

4. I have also granted that, if a Jew comes to them from some other place and is their guest for a time, he shall pay no tolls [to the city].

5. The chief priest* of their synagogue shall have the same position and authority among them as the mayor of the city has among the citizens. He shall judge all the cases which arise among them or against them. If he is not able to decide any case it shall be taken before the bishop or his chamberlain.

6. They are bound to watch, guard, and defend only their own walls, in which work their servants may assist them.

7. They may hire Christian nurses and Christian servants.[2]

8. The meats which their law forbids them to eat they may sell to Christians, and the Christians may buy them.

9. To add to my kindness to them I grant them the most favorable laws and conditions that the Jews have in any city of the German kingdom.

---

[2]Many laws forbade Jews from hiring Christian servants, based on the assumption that no Christian should be subjected to Jewish authority.

A Frontier Town in Spain
▼▼▼
52 ▼ THE FUERO *OF CUENCA*

As part of the centuries-long process of Christian reconquest of the Iberian Peninsula, a land that Arabic-speaking Muslims called *al-Andalus,* the forces of King Alfonso VIII of Castile (r. 1158–1214) captured the town of Cuenca in central Spain in 1177. Soon thereafter, a bishopric* was established in the town, and new settlers were encouraged to take up residence in the former Muslim stronghold. Part of the attraction of settling there was undoubtedly the detailed *fuero,* or charter, that King Alfonso granted to the inhabitants of this prosperous town. Granted probably in the period 1189–1190, the *Fuero of Cuenca* became the model for similar municipal charters granted to many other urban communities in the region.

Cuenca's *fuero* formalized a considerable number of regional traditions. Moreover, it established a body of rules and regulations born out of a need to establish permanent Castilian control over a vital frontier town that faced challenges from Muslim lords to the south and the Christian king of Aragon, whose own frontiers lay but a few miles to the east.

The selections that appear here provide a glimpse of the complex social interaction that existed in the culturally diverse settlements along the Christian-Muslim frontier in the age of the *Reconquista* and the impact of the pressing military needs that this life engendered.

QUESTIONS FOR ANALYSIS

1. Why do you think the town council had the right to deny settlement privileges to anyone of whom it did not approve?
2. Why do you think that certain mounted knights were exempt from fortification taxes?
3. In what specific ways do these excerpts illustrate "the impact of . . . pressing military needs"?
4. What does statute II.32 allow you to infer about the social, economic, and legal status of the women of Cuenca?
5. What function did the bathhouse apparently have in Cuenca?
6. What do these statutes suggest about the status of the town's Jews?
7. What do these statutes seem to suggest about Jewish-Christian relations?
8. What inferences do you draw from the legal penalties prescribed by these statutes?
9. What overall picture emerges from this document of life in late-twelfth-century Cuenca?

I. CONCESSION OF THE CHARTER AND THE OUTLINE OF ITS PRIVILEGES

5. *Concerning the Settlers within the Boundaries*

The town council reserves the right to deny settlement privileges to anyone of whom they do not approve, without risk of subsequent fine.

6. *That No Citizen Pay Tribute*

Anyone owning a house in the town who has family members residing in it is free of all taxes in perpetuity. This exemption does not include the levies for the upkeep of the walls of the town and for fortifications and towers in lands under the town's control. However, a mounted knight owning a horse worth fifty *mencales*[1] or more is exempt from fortification taxes, and he passes that right to his heirs.

▾ ▾ ▾

II. STATUTES REGARDING PROPERTY HOLDINGS

32. *Concerning the Bathhouse and the Testimony of Women*

Men may use the common bathhouses on Tuesdays, Thursdays, and Saturdays. Women may enter on Mondays and Wednesdays. Jews enter on Fridays and Sundays. No one, neither woman nor man, pays more than a half-penny entry fee. Servants and children of residents enter free of charge. If a man enters any part of the bathhouse premises on the women's day for bathing, he is liable to a fine of ten gold coins.[2] He pays the same fine for spying on women in the bath on those days. However, if a woman should enter a bathhouse on a day reserved for men or be found there at night, and because of this the woman is publicly dishonored or harmed in some way, she has no right to bring charges of a kind sufficient to exile the offending man. On the other hand,

---

[1]Probably gold coins and possibly Muslim gold dinars, coins that circulated freely in Castile.

[2]See note 1.

if a man commits these acts against a woman on the women's bathing day or steals her clothing, he will be thrown from the cliffs of the town.[3] Officials can gather testimony from women at the bathhouse, the bakehouse, at the fountain and river,[4] and also at the spinners' and weavers' workplaces. Female witnesses should be wives or daughters of residents of the town.

If a Christian intrudes in a bathhouse on the Jewish bathing day or if a Jew intrudes on the Christian bathing days, resulting in either person attacking or killing the other, no formal accusations will be accepted from either of the persons or their relatives.

The bathhouse manager provides bathers with all bathing necessities, such as water and the like. Failing to provide these necessities will make the manager liable for a fine of ten solidi,[5] five to be paid to the Master of the Marketplace and five to the complainant. Anyone stealing bathhouse equipment will have his ears cut off; if bathers'

belongings are worth a total of ten mencales or more, then the thief shall be thrown off the town cliffs.

▼ ▼ ▼

XXIX. LAWSUITS BETWEEN CHRISTIANS AND JEWS

29. No One May Take Weapons out of Town for Sale

For the sake of town security, the charter establishes that no one, Christian, Muslim, or Jew, is permitted to take wooden or iron weapons from the town. Anyone caught doing so will pay a fine of twenty solidi. Those who take such weapons for the normal military purpose of fighting the enemy will not be liable for such a fine. Likewise, weapons and golden or silver vessels cannot be removed from Cuenca.

---

[3]The town is located between two high cliffs.
[4]Where women gather to wash laundry.

[5]Silver coins, as opposed to the gold mencal (see note 1).

Chapter 9

▼▼▼

New Intellectual and Artistic Expressions

The period 1050 to 1300 was one of the West's most fecund eras of cultural creativity. Intellectually and artistically, Europe proved capable of dazzling breakthroughs and, equally as dazzling, of constant renewal, revision, and restructuring of yesterday's novelties.

In the intellectual arena, European scholars applied in new ways classical Greek modes of rational analysis to their studies of theology, moral philosophy, law, and a variety of other critical subjects. Toward the end of the eleventh century, scholars were already using early sixth-century Latin translations of the elementary logical treatises of the Greek philosopher and scientist Aristotle (384–322 B.C.) as the basis for testing the limits of human reason to cast light on basic religious and ethical issues. From the middle of the twelfth century onward, schoolmasters and students avidly searched for, collected, and studied Latin translations of the more advanced logical and scientific works of Aristotle, as well as commentaries on his works by Muslim and Jewish scholars. By 1160, the whole body of Aristotle's logic was known in the West, and by the end of the century, the same was true for his extant scientific treatises, which Europe initially acquired from Spain and Sicily through Arabic translations of the original Greek texts. This swift influx of Greek rationalism, particularly the more advanced levels of Aristotelian logic, revolutionized education and had a profound effect on Latin Christianity's approach to theology. Europe's schoolmasters inaugurated an exciting period of intellectual flowering, which many historians term the *Renaissance of the Twelfth Century*.

The work of thirteenth-century intellectuals was no less impressive. They carried forward the breakthroughs of the twelfth century and expanded them on a number of fronts. By the middle of the century, European scholars had access to better, more literal translations of Aristotle's works directly from the Greek texts. Perhaps the most characteristic and daring achievement of this second century of Christian Aristotelianism was that a significant number of Europe's best teachers constructed encyclopedic syntheses, or *summae,* in a variety of fields, especially theology and law. Early twelfth-century scholars had been largely wandering students and teachers, but thirteenth-century lovers of learning gravitated toward Europe's newest intellectual arenas — the universities. Although universities attracted thinkers representing a wide variety of schools of thought and approaches to learning, their means of investigation and instruction were refined variations on the methods of rational analysis championed by so many twelfth-century predecessors.

In the area of the visual arts and architecture, twelfth- and thirteenth-century Europe witnessed the maturation of Romanesque forms and the creation and perfection of the Gothic vision. Solid, earthbound Romanesque structures fittingly served a prosperous society that was sure it had a future, whereas soaring Gothic churches symbolized the energy that drove that society. The essence of Gothic construction is the opposition of contrary forces to create an edifice that seems to defy gravity. Thrust and counterthrust, particularly through use of a serendipitous architectural device known as the *flying buttress,* result in a complex structure whose sheer beauty and size reflect the faith and pride of the society that created it. Such an achievement was fitting for a civilization that contained so many creative tensions and gloried in the conflict of ideas.

High-medieval literature also reflects in its variety, complexity, and maturity a society that had achieved a high level of creative sophistication. Latin and vernacular poems that sang of heavenly aspirations and carnal pleasures, knightly epics and Arthurian romances, satires and parodies, popular tales both pious and bawdy, witty animal fables, plays that interwove comic and solemn scenes, biographies and autobiographies, and histories of every sort — all were part of the rich fabric of European letters.

A large body of evidence supports the conclusion that the High Middle Ages was an era of tremendous intellectual and artistic flowering, and much of that efflorescence drew its initial inspiration from classical Greek and Roman models, as the following sources illustrate. As they also illustrate, rather than slavishly imitating the ancients, medieval Europeans adapted Greco-Roman patterns of thought and artistic creativity to express the ideals and aspirations of a civilization that differed radically from classical antiquity.

▼▼▼

Reason and Revelation
in the Schools of Paris

As a religious culture based on what its adherents believe to be divine revelation, Christianity has continually wrestled with the issue of the proper relationship of faith to reason. What legitimate role, if any, does human reason have in shedding light upon God's revealed truths and the mysteries of the faith? Is it licit for a believer to pursue secular° scholarship and science? If rational studies and religious doctrine seem to contradict one another, which is to be preferred?

In the West, this quandary was intensified by the fact that Christian Europe was an heir not only of Jewish monotheism but also of Greek philosophy and science. The Christian West embraced Greek rationalism as an intellectual tool because a significant number of early Western Christian authorities, especially St. Augustine of Hippo (354–430) and Boethius (480–524), used elements borrowed from Greco-Roman philosophy and rhetoric° to elucidate the Christian faith.

Thanks in large part to monastic° scholars, who preserved and studied the surviving texts of Roman antiquity, as well as the works of the early Christian writers, a fair amount of Europe's Greco-Roman heritage survived the vagaries and disasters of the Early Middle Ages. Yet for all of the continued vitality of monasticism throughout the eleventh and twelfth centuries, cathedral° schools, located in the West's rapidly developing urban centers, were replacing monasteries° as Europe's premier intellectual centers by the year 1100. Learned monks° emphasized traditional, conservative subjects, such as classical literature and history, and approached theology as a form of prayer (Chapter 7, source 38). The secular clerics° who attended and taught at the cathedral schools were no less pious, but they emphasized the more dynamic subjects of dialectic° (logic) and law and approached theology as a form of speculative philosophy. Whereas monastic schools tended to focus on the writings of Greco-Roman moralists and Christian spiritual authors, twelfth-century urban schoolmasters and their students turned increasingly to the fourth-century B.C. works of Aristotle. For these urban intellectuals, Aristotle's books on dialectic became tools that they hoped would enable them to understand more fully both Heaven and earth and thereby to function more effectively as dual citizens of the City of God and the City of Man.

By the late twelfth century, some urban cathedral schools had evolved into Europe's (and the world's) first universities: chartered corporations, or guilds, of masters and students that offered standardized curricula leading to recognized teaching licenses, or degrees, in certain core disciplines, namely, the liberal arts, theology, canon° and civil law, and medicine. Although we cannot date their precise beginnings, by 1200 Europe already had three universities — Bologna, Paris, and Oxford — and many more would be established within the next several centuries. Of all the branches of learning taught at Europe's universities, none was more prestigious or demanding than theology, and of all the schools of theology, Paris was preeminent. After about 1150, whenever medieval Christian Europe was confronted with a weighty religious issue, it usually turned to the masters of theology at Paris for guidance.

The first two documents in this section illustrate two of the most significant periods and personalities in the evolution of Paris as Christian Europe's center for theological studies. In the first source, we see Peter Abelard, peripatetic scholar and champion of faith illuminated by reason, who flourished in the period before Paris had an established university. In many respects, Master Peter and his contemporaries were the teachers who turned Paris into Europe's leading center of theological study and creativity. The second source comes from the pen of the University of Paris's greatest thirteenth-century theologian, St. Thomas Aquinas, arguably the most brilliant mind of his generation and culture. Together, Abelard and Aquinas point out the ways in which reason and revelation coexisted in the urban schools of the High Middle Ages. The third source, which was composed in the year that Aquinas retired from his professorial chair at Paris, illustrates a residual problem that vexed some masters at Paris who wished to apply the principles of philosophy to the study of divine revelation.

Understanding through Questioning
▼▼▼
53 ▼ *Peter Abelard, SIC ET NON*

If the last decades of the twentieth century constitute the age of the computer, then we might say that the twelfth century was the age of dialectic. *Dialectic,* also known as *logic,* is the opposition of contrary principles in order to reach hidden and deeper truths. In twelfth-century Europe, dialectic represented order and harmony to a society that was all too aware of the chaos of life. Like the modern computer revolution, twelfth-century dialectic provided European scholars with both a medium of analysis and a system for categorizing information and insight. Moreover, like contemporary prophets of the computer, many medieval scholastics exaggerated the potential benefits of dialectic. Even so, it is no exaggeration to state that the great theological, philosophical, and legal systems of Western Europe's High Middle Ages were based on dialectic.

The most influential early champion of dialectic was Peter Abelard (1079–1142), a teacher of logic and theology at Paris and elsewhere, whose life and loves were themselves filled with contradictions. Abelard was one of a handful of early twelfth-century thinkers who turned logic to the service of theology, thereby offering Western Europe a new and revolutionary approach to religious truth.

The following selection comes from the preface to a textbook that Abelard compiled sometime after 1120. Entitled *Sic et Non* (*Yes and No*), this work presented Abelard's students with 158 theological issues, such as "Should human faith be based on reason, or no?" and "Is God the author of evil, or no?" Each of these deliberately provocative titles was followed by groups of apparently conflicting texts culled from the Bible and other authoritative sources, which seemed either to support (*sic*) or deny (*non*) the proposition under consideration. Abelard's students were then expected to apply the rules of logic and reason to resolve the apparent quandaries. As any good teacher would, Abelard provided his students with sufficient hints on how to wrestle successfully with the problems by laying down in his preface a series of general rules of textual analysis.

QUESTIONS FOR ANALYSIS

1. How does Abelard regard the Bible? Does he believe that its authors could have erred? How does he explain the apparent contradictions and errors that appear in portions of the Bible?
2. According to Abelard, what factors can contribute to one's misunderstanding a text from scripture or the Church Fathers?*
3. Does Abelard accept all texts as equally authoritative? If not, what order of priority has he established?
4. Is Abelard a religious skeptic, or does he believe that there is an absolute standard of religious truth that humans can know?
5. "Abelard's prologue to *Sic et Non* gently points out to his students that simply citing authorities is not sufficient in their discussion and analysis of theological issues." What does this anonymous comment mean? If the citation of authorities was not sufficient, what did Abelard expect of his students?
6. What is Abelard's philosophy of education?
7. Did Abelard place any limits on human reason? What conclusions follow from your answer?

Among the multitudinous words of the holy Fathers[1] some sayings seem not only to differ from one another but even to contradict one another. Hence it is not presumptuous to judge concerning those by whom the world itself will be judged, as it is written, "The saints shall judge nations,"[2] and, again, "You shall sit and judge."[3] We do not presume to rebuke as untruthful or to denounce as erroneous those to whom the Lord said, "He who hears you hears me; he who despises you despises me."[4] Bearing in mind our foolishness we believe that our understanding is defective rather than the writing of those to whom the Truth Himself said, "It is not you who speak but the spirit of your Father who speaks in you."[5] Why should it seem surprising if we, lacking the guidance of the Holy Spirit* through whom those things were written and spoken, the Spirit impressing them on the writers, fail to understand them? Our achievement of full understanding is impeded especially by unusual modes of expression and by the different significances that can be attached to one and the same word, as a word is used now in one sense, now in another. Just as there are many meanings so there are many words. Tully says that sameness

---

Source: Excerpted from Brian Tierney, Donald Kagan, and L. Pearce Williams, *Great Issues in Western Civilization,* Second Edition. Copyright © 1972 by Random House. Reprinted with permission of The McGraw-Hill Companies.

[1] The Fathers of the Church.

[2] The Bible, the Book of Wisdom, 3:8. Inasmuch as Abelard was quoting this and other scriptural passages from memory, it only loosely conforms to the established text, as preserved in Jerome's Vulgate Bible.
[3] The Gospel of Matthew, 19:28, and the Gospel of Luke, 22:30.
[4] The Gospel of Luke, 10:16.
[5] The Gospel of Matthew, 10:20.

is the mother of satiety in all things, that is to say it gives rise to fastidious distaste,[6] and so it is appropriate to use a variety of words in discussing the same thing and not to express everything in common and vulgar words. . . .

We must also take special care that we are not deceived by corruptions of the text or by false attributions when sayings of the Fathers are quoted that seem to differ from the truth or to be contrary to it; for many apocryphal writings[7] are set down under names of saints to enhance their authority; and even the texts of divine Scripture are corrupted by the errors of scribes. That most faithful writer and true interpreter, Jerome,[8] accordingly warned us, "Beware of apocryphal writings. . . ." Again, on the title of Psalm 77 which is "An Instruction of Asaph," he commented, "It is written according to Matthew that when the Lord had spoken in parables and they did not understand, he said, 'These things are done that it might be fulfilled which was written by the prophet Isaias,[9] *I will open my mouth in parables.'*[10] The Gospels* still have it so. Yet it is not Isaias who says this but Asaph." Again, let us explain simply why in Matthew and John it is written that the Lord was crucified at the sixth hour but in Mark at the third hour.[11] There was a scribal error, and in Mark too the sixth hour was mentioned, but many read the Greek *epismo* as *gamma.*[12] So too there was a scribal error where "Isaias" was set down for "Asaph." We know that many churches were gathered together from among ignorant gentiles. When they read in the Gospel, "That it might be fulfilled which was written by the prophet Asaph," the one who first wrote down the Gospel began to say, "Who is

this prophet Asaph?" for he was not known among the people. And what did he do? In seeking to amend an error he made an error. We would say the same of another text in Matthew. "He took," it says, "the thirty pieces of silver, the price of him that was prized, as was written by the prophet Jeremias."[13] But we do not find this in Jeremias at all. Rather it is in Zacharias.[14] You see then that here, as before, there was an error. If in the Gospels themselves some things are corrupted by the ignorance of scribes, we should not be surprised that the same thing has sometimes happened in the writings of later Fathers who are of much less authority. . . .

It is no less important in my opinion to ascertain whether texts quoted from the Fathers may be ones that they themselves have retracted and corrected after they came to a better understanding of the truth as the blessed Augustine[15] did on many occasions; or whether they are giving the opinion of another rather than their own opinion . . . or whether, in inquiring into certain matters, they left them open to question rather than settled them with a definitive solution. . . .

In order that the way be not blocked and posterity deprived of the healthy labor of treating and debating difficult questions of language and style, a distinction must be drawn between the work of later authors and the supreme canonical* authority of the Old and New Testaments. If, in Scripture, anything seems absurd you are not permitted to say, "The author of this book did not hold to the truth" — but rather that the codex is defective or that the interpreter erred or that you do not understand. But if anything

---

[6]Marcus Tullius Cicero (106–43 B.C.), a Roman rhetorician* and politician. Taken from his *On Rhetorical Invention,* 1, 41, 76.

[7]Counterfeit texts or works wrongly ascribed to a certain author.

[8]Saint Jerome (345–420), one of the four major Fathers of the Western Church.

[9]Several different Hebrew prophets of the sixth century B.C., whose cumulative sayings comprise the Book of Isaiah.

[10]The Gospel of Matthew, 13:35.

[11]Either Abelard refers to a faulty text or his memory fails him. Matthew, Mark, and Luke all state that Jesus' crucifixion began at the sixth hour, or noon (the daylight hours being divided into twelve equal units, or *hours*). John does not mention the hour.

[12]He argues that the symbol for *6,* the Greek letter *zeta* (not *epismo*), was mistakenly read as *gamma,* the third letter in the Greek alphabet and the symbol for *3.*

[13]The Gospel of Matthew, 27:9. Jeremiah, or Jeremias, was a Hebrew prophet of the seventh and sixth centuries B.C.

[14]A prophet of the late sixth century B.C.

[15]Chapter 1, source 4.

seems contrary to truth in the works of later authors, which are contained in innumerable books, the reader or auditor is free to judge, so that he may approve what is pleasing and reject what gives offense, unless the matter is established by certain reason or by canonical authority (of the Scriptures). . . .

In view of these considerations we have undertaken to collect various sayings of the Fathers that give rise to questioning because of their apparent contradictions as they occur to our memory. This questioning excites young readers to the maximum of effort in inquiring into the truth, and such inquiry sharpens their minds. Assiduous and frequent questioning is indeed the first key to wisdom. Aristotle, that most perspicacious of all philosophers, exhorted the studious to practice it eagerly, saying, "Perhaps it is difficult to express oneself with confidence on such matters if they have not been much discussed. To entertain doubts on particular points will not be unprofitable." For by doubting we come to inquiry; through inquiring we perceive the truth, according to the Truth Himself. "Seek and you shall find," He says, "Knock and it shall be opened to you."[16] In order to teach us by His example He chose to be found when He was about twelve years old sitting in the midst of the doctors and questioning them, presenting the appearance of a disciple by questioning rather than of a master by teaching, although there was in Him the complete and perfect wisdom of God.[17] Where we have quoted texts of Scripture, the greater the authority attributed to Scripture, the more they should stimulate the reader and attract him to the search for truth. Hence I have prefixed to this my book, compiled in one volume from the saying of the saints, the decree of Pope Gelasius[18] concerning authentic books, from which it may be known that I have cited nothing from apocryphal books. I have also added excerpts from the Retractations of St. Augustine, from which it will be clear that nothing is included which he later retracted and corrected.

---

[16]The Gospel of Matthew, 7:7.
[17]A reference to Jesus' questioning of the Temple elders when his family journeyed to Jerusalem for Passover: Luke, 2:41–50.

[18]Pope Gelasius I (r. 492–496).

Thirteenth-Century Rational Theology
▼▼▼

54 ▼ *Saint Thomas Aquinas,*
SUMMA CONTRA GENTILES

Abelard's use of dialectic* to probe theological questions disturbed some conservative church leaders, including St. Bernard of Clairvaux (Chapter 7, source 38), who complained, "He corrupts the faith of simple people and sullies the purity of the Church." Despite this sharp opposition and two official condemnations by French church councils* of some of Abelard's teachings, the rationalism that Abelard championed won the day in the schools of the West. Significantly, however, no subsequent master who constructed a book of questions dared to leave the issues unresolved, as Abelard had done in his *Sic et Non.* It seems that what most alienated the majority of Abelard's detractors was not so much his rationalism as his style and personality.

Notwithstanding his arrogance and enemies, Abelard, more than any other individual, helped transform Paris into Europe's premier academic center. Sometime after Abelard's death but well before 1200, the masters of Paris formed a teaching guild, or *universitas,* which enjoyed a monopoly on higher education in the city.

The University of Paris attracted students and teachers from all over Europe, and of all its thirteenth-century alumni and teachers, the greatest was undoubtedly St. Thomas Aquinas (1225–1274), a Dominican friar* and professor of theology at Paris. Born into a minor Italian noble family, Thomas entered the monastery* of Monte Cassino at age five and remained there until 1239. He left the abbey* to continue his studies in Naples, where he entered the Order of Preachers, or Dominicans, in 1245. Thomas then went to Paris to study and from there went to Cologne, where he was a pupil of St. Albert the Great, early thirteenth-century Christian Europe's greatest Aristotelian scholar. In 1252 Thomas returned to Paris, to teach as well as to study. In 1256 he became a master of theology and was appointed to one of the two theological chairs the university reserved for mendicant friar* professors. In 1258 Aquinas began the first of his two great *summae* of theology, a labor that he completed in 1264.

Known as the *Summa contra gentiles,* or *A Comprehensive Treatise in Opposition to the Unbelievers,* Thomas's initial summa was a handbook for Dominican missionaries in Spain, who needed rational defenses of Catholic belief in their debates with learned Muslims who did not accept the authority of the Bible. Agreeing that "it is necessary to have recourse to natural reason to which all people give assent," Aquinas constructed a natural theology based on the principles of Aristotelian philosophy. In essence, he attempted to demonstrate that certain limited elements of the Catholic faith could be arrived at without the benefit of divine revelation. In contrast, his later, more mature and comprehensive *Summa theologiae* (*A Synthesis of Theology*), which he composed (but never completed) between 1265 and 1273, was a vast tome of revelation and philosophy aimed at Catholic students of theology. This latter masterwork was predicated on the assumption that humanity needs revelation and faith because "only a few people come to rationally acquired truth about God, and only after a long time and with the admixture of error."

In the following excerpt from Book I of the *Summa contra gentiles,* Aquinas addresses the relationship of reason and revelation.

QUESTIONS FOR ANALYSIS

1. According to Thomas, what are the two truths?
2. According to Aristotle and Aquinas, what is the essence of human knowledge? Put another way, what, in general terms, can humans know?
3. How do human minds proceed to knowledge and understanding?
4. According to Aquinas, what are the limits of the human mind? Why, for example, cannot human minds penetrate into the essence of God?
5. Granted that humans cannot know God's essence, what can they know about God, and how do they attain this understanding?

6. According to Aquinas, why is it foolish to reject divine revelation just because "it does not make sense"?

7. According to Aquinas, can reason and revelation, science and faith, truly conflict? Why or why not? What if they appear to conflict?

CHAPTER III

In What Way It Is Possible to Make Known the Divine Truth

Since, however, not every truth is to be made known in the same way, *and it is the part of an educated man to seek for conviction in each subject, only so far as the nature of the subject allows,*[1] as the Philosopher[2] most rightly observes as quoted by Boethius,[3] it is necessary to show first of all in what way it is possible to make known the aforesaid truth.

Now in those things which we hold about God there is truth in two ways. For certain things that are true about God wholly surpass the capability of human reason, for instance that God is three and one:[4] while there are certain things to which even natural reason can attain, for instance that God is, that God is one, and others like these, which even the philosophers proved demonstratively of God, being guided by the light of natural reason.

That certain divine truths wholly surpass the capability of human reason, is most clearly evident. For since the principle of all the knowledge which the reason acquires about a thing, is the understanding of that thing's essence, because according to the Philosopher's teaching the principle of a demonstration is *what a thing is,* it follows that our knowledge about a thing will be in proportion to our understanding of its essence. Wherefore, if the human intellect comprehends the essence of a particular thing, for instance a stone or a triangle, no truth about that thing will surpass the capability of human reason. But

this does not happen to us in relation to God, because the human intellect is incapable by its natural power of attaining to the comprehension of His essence: since our intellect's knowledge, according to the mode of the present life, originates from the senses: so that things which are not objects of sense cannot be comprehended by the human intellect, except in so far as knowledge of them is gathered from sensibles. Now sensibles cannot lead our intellect to see in them what God is, because they are effects unequal to the power of their cause. And yet our intellect is led by sensibles to the divine knowledge so as to know about God that He is, and other such truths, which need to be ascribed to the first principle. Accordingly some divine truths are attainable by human reason while others altogether surpass the power of human reason.

Again. The same is easy to see from the degrees of intellects. For if one of two men perceives a thing with his intellect with greater subtlety, the one whose intellect is of a higher degree understands many things which the other is altogether unable to grasp; as instanced in a yokel who is utterly incapable of grasping the subtleties of philosophy. Now the angelic intellect surpasses the human intellect more than the intellect of the cleverest philosopher surpasses that of the most uncultured. For an angel knows God through a more excellent effect than does man, for as much as the angel's essence, through which he is led to know God by natural knowledge, is more excellent than sensible things, even than the soul itself, by which the human intellect mounts to the knowledge of God. And the

---

[1] A quotation from Aristotle's *Nichomachean Ethics.*
[2] Aristotle, whom Thomas always referred to respectfully as "the Philosopher."

[3] An early sixth-century scholar. See the introduction to this section.
[4] The doctrine and mystery of the Trinity.*

divine intellect surpasses the angelic intellect much more than the angelic surpasses the human. For the divine intellect by its capacity equals the divine essence, wherefore God perfectly understands of Himself what He is, and He knows all things that can be understood about Him: whereas the angel knows not what God is by his natural knowledge, because the angel's essence, by which he is led to the knowledge of God, is an effect unequal to the power of its cause. Consequently an angel is unable by his natural knowledge to grasp all that God understands about Himself: nor again is human reason capable of grasping all that an angel understands by his natural power. Accordingly just as a man would show himself to be a most insane fool if he declared the assertions of a philosopher to be false because he was unable to understand them, so, and much more, a man would be exceedingly foolish, were he to suspect of falsehood the things revealed by God through the ministry of His angels, because they cannot be the object of reason's investigations.

Furthermore. The same is made abundantly clear by the deficiency which every day we experience in our knowledge of things. For we are ignorant of many of the properties of sensible things, and in many cases we are unable to discover the nature of those properties which we perceive by our senses. Much less therefore is human reason capable of investigating all the truths about that most sublime essence.

With this the saying of the Philosopher is in accord where he says that *our intellect in relation to those primary things which are most evident in nature is like the eye of a bat in relation to the sun.*

To this truth Holy Writ also bears witness. For it is written: *Will you comprehend the steps of God and will you find out the Almighty perfectly?* and: *Behold God is great, exceeding our knowledge,*[5] and: *We know in part.*[6]

Therefore all that is said about God, though it cannot be investigated by reason, must not be forthwith rejected as false. . . .

CHAPTER VII

That the Truth of Reason Is Not in Opposition to the Truth of the Christian Faith

Now though the aforesaid truth of the Christian faith surpasses the ability of human reason, nevertheless those things which are naturally instilled in human reason cannot be opposed to this truth. For it is clear that those things which are implanted in reason by nature are most true, so much so that it is impossible to think them to be false. Nor is it lawful to deem false that which is held by faith, since it is so evidently confirmed by God. Seeing then that the false alone is opposed to the true, as evidently appears if we examine their definitions, it is impossible for the aforesaid truth of faith to be contrary to those principles which reason knows naturally.

Again. The same thing which the disciple's mind receives from its teacher is contained in the knowledge of the teacher, unless he teach insincerely, which it were wicked to say of God. Now the knowledge of naturally known principles is instilled into us by God, since God Himself is the author of our nature. Therefore the divine Wisdom also contains these principles. Consequently whatever is contrary to these principles, is contrary to the divine Wisdom; wherefore it cannot be from God. Therefore those things which are received by faith from divine revelation cannot be contrary to our natural knowledge.

Moreover. Our intellect is stayed by contrary arguments, so that it cannot advance to the knowledge of truth. Wherefore if conflicting knowledges were instilled into us by God, our intellect would thereby be hindered from knowing the truth. And this cannot be ascribed to God.

---

[5]See the Bible, the Book of Job, especially 11:7 and 36:26.

[6]St. Paul, First Epistle to the Corinthians, 13:9.

Furthermore. Things that are natural are unchangeable, so long as nature remains. Now contrary opinions cannot be together in the same subject. Therefore God does not instill into man any opinion or belief contrary to natural knowledge.

Hence the Apostle* says: *The word is nigh thee even in thy heart and in thy mouth. This is the word of faith which we preach.*[7] Yet because it surpasses reason some look upon it as though it were contrary thereto; which is impossible.

This is confirmed also by the authority of Au-

gustine who says: *That which truth shall make known can nowise be in opposition to the holy books whether of the Old or of the New Testament.*[8]

From this we may evidently conclude that whatever arguments are alleged against the teachings of faith, they do not rightly proceed from the first self-evident principles instilled by nature. Wherefore they lack the force of demonstration, and are either probable or sophistical arguments, and consequently it is possible to solve them.

---

[7]St. Paul, Epistle to the Romans, 10:8.

[8]St. Augustine of Hippo's *Commentary on the Book of Genesis.*

Ensuring Theological Correctness
▼▼▼

55 ▼ *A STATUTE OF 1272 FOR THE ARTS FACULTY OF PARIS*

Not every thirteenth-century church leader and intellectual shared Thomas Aquinas's serene confidence that true philosophy cannot conflict with the true faith. After all, Aristotle "the Philosopher" had maintained that the world is eternal, a proposition that no orthodox* Christian (or Jew or Muslim) could accept. As early as 1215, the papal* legate Robert de Courçon forbade lectures on the scientific and metaphysical books of Aristotle in a body of statutes that he drew up for the masters and students of Paris. In his papal bull of 1231, which granted the University of Paris wide-ranging privileges, Gregory IX (r. 1227–1241) continued the official prohibition on previously banned books of science "until they have been examined and purged of all suspicion of heresy."* An official list of courses offered by the liberal arts faculty in 1255, however, included Aristotle's *Ethics, Physics, Metaphysics,* and *On Animals* among the core books required of all students. Apparently, they had been examined and found acceptable in the quarter century since Pope Gregory's bull. Despite this triumph of the Aristotelian canon, many church leaders remained skeptical of the legitimacy of philosophical pursuits and the orthodoxy of certain Parisian masters. In 1270 Bishop Stephen of Paris publicly condemned and excommunicated* all who taught thirteen notorious heresies, including the notion that the world is eternal. It is in this context that we must study the statute of April 1272, which follows.

QUESTIONS FOR ANALYSIS

1. What exactly does this statute prohibit?

2. By implication, what does it permit?
3. Is it a direct attack on Aristotelian philosophy?
4. If not, what is it, and what does it represent?

Statute of the Faculty of Arts[1] against Artists[2] Treating Theological Questions and That No One Shall Dare to Determine against the Faith Questions Which Touch the Faith as Well as Philosophy

To each and all the sons of Holy Mother Church who now and in the future shall see the present page, the masters of logical science[3] or professors of natural science[4] at Paris, each and all, who hold and observe the statute and ordinance of the venerable father Symon by divine permission cardinal* priest* of the title of St. Cecilia, legate[5] of the Apostolic See,* made after separate deliberation of the nations,[6] and who adhere expressly and entirely to the opinion of the seven judges appointed by the same legate in the same statute, greeting in the Saviour of all. All should know that we masters, each and all, from the preceding abundant and considered advice and deliberation of good men concerning this, wishing with all our power to avoid present and future dangers which by occasion of this sort might in the future befall our faculty, by common consent, no one of us contradicting, on the Friday preceding the Sunday on which is sung *Rejoice Jerusalem,*[7] the masters one and all being convoked for this purpose in the church of Ste. Geneviève at Paris, decree and ordain that no master or bachelor[8] of our faculty should presume to determine or even to dispute any purely theological question, as concerning the Trinity* and Incarnation[9] and similar matters, since this would be transgressing the limits assigned him, for the Philosopher[10] says that it is utterly improper for a non-geometer to dispute with a geometer.

But if anyone shall have so presumed, unless within three days after he has been warned or

---

[1]The University of Paris consisted of four faculties. The faculty of arts provided a basic program that centered on the Seven Liberal Arts:* grammar, rhetoric,* dialectic,* arithmetic, geometry, music, and astronomy. Of these, dialectic was the premier discipline. After seven or eight years of study, a student took an examination that, if passed, earned him the title *Master of Arts* and a license to teach the arts. If he chose, he could then advance to study in one of the higher, professional faculties. At Paris, the three graduate faculties were medicine, canon law,* and theology. Other universities had a fourth advanced faculty — civil, or Roman, law.*
[2]Masters of Arts.
[3]Those who teach dialectic.
[4]Those who specialize in the arts and use the Aristotelian books of science.
[5]A *papal legate* exercised papal power in respect to his mission. This particular legate held the title of *cardinal-priest* of the church of St. Cecilia in Rome, which means he was a high-ranking official of the papal court.

[6]The masters of Paris's faculty of arts divided themselves into four *nations,* or ethnic divisions: the French Nation (which, by virtue of linguistic and cultural ties, included masters from Languedoc, Spain, Portugal, Italy, and crusader-held areas in the eastern Mediterranean, as well as from the lands around the Île de France); the Nation of the Picards, whose members came from northeast France and the Low Countries; the apparently homogenous Norman Nation; and the English-German Nation, which included English, Scots, Irish, Welsh, Germans, Poles, Scandinavians, Hungarians, and other Northern Europeans who did not fit anywhere else. Each nation had its own officers, seal, customs, patron saints, and feast days and met in secret.
[7]The fourth Sunday of Lent, which in 1272 fell on April 3; the preceding Friday was April 1.
[8]A Bachelor of Arts was an apprentice teacher on the path to becoming a Master of Arts, who had reached a level of expertise, after two or more years of study, whereby his master allowed him to hold a public disputation as a means of demonstrating his ability. Afterward, he would help by instructing first-year students. Some students accepted bachelor status as a terminal rank; thus was born the B.A. degree.
[9]The birth of God the Son in the person of Jesus.
[10]Aristotle.

required by us he shall have been willing to re- voke publicly his presumption in the classes or public disputation where he first disputed the said question, henceforth he shall be forever de- prived of our society. We decree further and or- dain that, if anyone shall have disputed at Paris any question which seems to touch both faith and philosophy, if he shall have determined it contrary to the faith, henceforth he shall forever be deprived of our society as a heretic,* unless he shall have been at pains humbly and devoutly to revoke his error and his heresy, within three days after our warning, in full congregation or else- where where it shall seem to us expedient. Add- ing further that, if any master or bachelor of our faculty reads or disputes any difficult passages or any questions which seem to undermine the faith, he shall refute the arguments or text so far as they are against the faith or concede that they are absolutely false and entirely erroneous, and

he shall not presume to dispute or lecture fur- ther upon this sort of difficulties, either in the text or in authorities, but shall pass over them entirely as erroneous. But if anyone shall be re- bellious in this, he shall be punished by a pen- alty which in the judgment of our faculty suits his fault and is due. Moreover, in order that all these may be inviolably observed, we masters, one and all, have sworn on our personal security in the hand of the rector[11] of our faculty and we all have spontaneously agreed to be so bound. In memory of which we have caused this same stat- ute to be inscribed and so ordered in the register of our faculty in the same words. Moreover, ev- ery rector henceforth to be created in the faculty shall swear that he will cause all the bachelors about to incept in our faculty to bind themselves to this same thing, swearing on their personal security in his hand. Given at Paris the year of the Lord 1271, the first day of April.[12]

---

[11]The head of the arts faculty; he was elected by the four nations (note 6), with each nation casting a single vote. His tenure at this time was brief, lasting from four to six weeks. At first, the rector represented only the arts faculty, but eventually, he became the chief officer of the entire university because the arts faculty easily outnumbered all three advanced faculties combined.

[12]By modern reckoning, April 1, 1272. The calendar of Paris began the new year on Easter Sunday, which in 1272 fell on April 24.

▼▼▼

Romanesque and Gothic Art

Romanesque is a style of eleventh- and twelfth-century architecture, sculpture, and painting remotely based on the inspiration of late-Roman models. The most characteristic and easily identifiable Romanesque creations are the solid stone churches with rounded-arch construction that can be found, with significant regional variations, throughout much of Western Europe. Spread over an area that stretched from the Mediterranean to the North Sea and from England to Germany, Romanesque churches were the products of Europe's first major effort at building large, permanent structures of stone on a widespread basis. In their overall shape and massive size, Romanesque churches were distant echoes of Roman basilicas, but, as was true of everything else that the medieval Europeans borrowed from antiquity, classical elements were radically altered to reflect the realities, tastes, and spirit of a distinctly new civilization. One major area in which Romanesque architects broke away from the tradition of the Roman basilica was in their use of ornate sculpture on both the exterior portals and the interior columns of their churches, thereby providing the impetus for the West's rediscovery of the possibilities of sculpture as an artistic medium — a medium that would be raised to a high art in the age of the *Gothic* church.

Just as Romanesque forms varied widely by region, so, too, the Romanesque did not uniformly give way to the Gothic style throughout Western Europe. Most of Germany and the Mediterranean remained wedded to the Romanesque style long after the Gothic had swept through northern France and into England. It was only during the Late Middle Ages (1300–1500) that Gothic art spread throughout the greater part of Western Europe. Primarily northern French in origin, with probable Islamic influences from eastern Mediterranean lands recently opened up to the West by the crusades, the Gothic style is expressed in such great late-twelfth- and thirteenth-century cathedrals* as Chartres, Amiens, Rheims, Strasbourg, Canterbury, and Lincoln. Distinguished by their pointed arches and ribbed vaults, Gothic churches were noted for their walls of stained glass, in contrast to the thick walls of masonry that characterized Romanesque's "heavenly fortresses." On the exterior of their great churches, however, Gothic architects continued to perfect the art of sculpture begun so well by their Romanesque predecessors.

The following pieces of art illustrate several important aspects of the Romanesque and Gothic styles. The first set of two artifacts shows an extraordinary Romanesque nude and the Roman prototype that probably served as the model for that sculpture. The second set of artifacts presents three statues in the round: the Romanesque *Notre Dame la Brune* of Tournus Abbey* and two Gothic allegorical figures from the cathedral of Strasbourg, which allow us to see how the Gothic vision differed from the Romanesque. The third set allows us to compare examples of thirteenth-century Byzantine and Gothic art styles, which, in turn, suggests some of the cultural differences that separated the Christian civilizations of Byzantium and Western Europe.

A Romanesque Temptress
▼▼▼

56 ▼ *Giselbertus, EVE, and Anonymous, A GALLO-ROMAN RELIEF*

Most Romanesque sculptors are nameless to us. Giselbertus is one of a handful of exceptions. This master sculptor, who designed and carved the entire program of sculptures for the church of St. Lazare in the Burgundian city of Autun between about 1120 and 1135, proudly placed his signature directly beneath the figure of Christ, who dominates the center of the west portal's *Last Judgment tympanum* — the carved space over the church entrance between the arch and the *lintel* (the horizontal stone that runs directly over the double door). "Giselbertus hoc fecit," which translates as "Giselbertus made this," proclaims to the world the artist's achievement and prominence. One cannot imagine the church's patron, Bishop Etienne de Bage (r. 1112–1139), allowing any run-of-the-mill artisan to place his name in such a prominent place on a church that Pope Innocent II consecrated in 1132.

Just as interesting and original as his *Last Judgment,* which art historians unanimously judge to be one of the great masterpieces of Romanesque art, is Giselbertus's sculpture of Eve's temptation. Eve was originally part of the now largely lost *Fall of Adam and Eve* relief that ran the length of the lintel of the north portal, the church's primary entrance. Unfortunately, most of the north portal sculptures were removed, scattered, and destroyed in the eighteenth century, and the Eve fragment survived only by being built into a nearby house in 1769, where it remained until discovered in 1856.

This reclining nude, which has no known counterpart in Romanesque art, is alive with motion. Eve is portrayed lying on the ground, resting on her elbow and knees and about to pick a fruit from a heavily laden branch that is being bent toward her by a satanic serpent. The extant remains of the serpent can be seen lying across Eve's lower leg. She seems to be whispering to a now-lost Adam, who probably was also recumbent. By placing Eve and presumably Adam in such a position, Giselbertus cleverly overcame the spatial limitations of a long but narrow block of stone. In meeting this challenge, however, the master sculptor probably drew inspiration from late-Gallo-Roman sculptures that were abundantly available in this region of eastern France.

The second artifact is a Gallo-Roman relief of a young reclining woman that today resides at the museum at Beaune, a city that lies only a few miles to the northeast of Autun. If not this particular sculpture, which dates from the last centuries of the Roman Empire, could not a similar monument from Burgundy's rich Gallo-Roman heritage have sparked Giselbertus's daring breakthrough?

QUESTIONS FOR ANALYSIS

1. How has Giselbertus dealt with the human body?
2. Giselbertus's relief has been characterized as "sensuous." Do you agree? If so, how could Giselbertus and Bishop Etienne justify placing such a sculpture over the church's main entrance?
3. What emotions did Giselbertus seem to want to stir in the viewer?
4. Review Bernard of Clairvaux's *Homily on the Virgin Mary* (Chapter 7, source 38). How does Bernard's vision of Mary, whom medieval churchmen apotheosized as *the New Eve,* differ from Giselbertus's portrait of Eve? Based on that analysis, what do you infer is the message of Giselbertus's *Eve?*
5. What parallels can you discover between *Eve* and the Gallo-Roman reclining nude? What differences do you find? Do you think it likely that Giselbertus used the late-Roman relief as a model? Explain your answer.
6. Assuming that Giselbertus was inspired by that late-Roman nude, how did he reinterpret the piece?
7. Granted the uniqueness of Giselbertus's genius and of his sculpture of Eve, can we still draw some conclusions about the Romanesque world's treatment of the human being? If so, what are they?

Eve

A Gallo-Roman Relief

Romanesque and Gothic Sculpture

▼▼▼

57 ▼ *NOTRE DAME LA BRUNE, ECCLESIA, and SYNAGOGA*

Part of Giselbertus's genius is revealed in his decision to carve the figures in deep relief, producing sharp contrasts of light and shade and rounded images that seem to leap out at the viewer. His technique appears to have borrowed almost as much from the tradition of late-Roman freestanding sculpture as it did from the medium of Roman relief carving.

Although Romanesque sculptors worked largely in relief, they did produce some small votive statues in the round, largely of the Virgin and Child. These statues, which display a profound Byzantine influence, were honored items at certain pilgrimage* sites that dotted the West. The first statue that appears here is a Virgin and Child known as *Notre Dame la Brune* (The Dark Madonna) from the abbey* church of St. Philbert at Tournus, a small Burgundian settlement to the southeast of Autun. The monastery* of St. Philbert was a popular pilgrimage site, due to the fact that it possessed the relics* of the early Christian martyr St. Valerien, as well as the bones of St. Philbert, a ninth-century monastic reformer. Pilgrims visiting the church undoubtedly prayed before *Notre Dame la Brune*, seeking the protection of both the Mother and the Christ Child. The statue, which is made of gilded cedar, depicts the Virgin seated on a columned throne, with Jesus on her lap. In his left hand, he holds the Gospels,* and with his right hand, he blesses his worshippers. Stylistic elements strongly suggest that the statue was crafted in the second half of the twelfth century.

The second and third statues come from the cathedral* of Strasbourg in what was then the southwest German region of Alsace. (Today, it is part of France.) Strasbourg cathedral is the Rhineland's finest example of the early thirteenth-century High Gothic style, and it ranks among the grandest of Europe's great churches. Its statuary is similarly renowned for its delicacy and naturalism. Dating from the period 1225 to 1230, these two statues are allegorical representations of *Ecclesia* (The Church) and *Synagoga* (The Synagogue) and originally graced the left and right sides of the cathedral's south entrance. The word *allegory* is Greek in origin and means "to speak in other terms." Thus, each of these allegorical sculptures is a metaphor in stone.

Between about 1140 and 1200, the period of Early Gothic, Western sculpture underwent a revolution in its representation of the human body. This change was comparable to what Ancient Greece experienced between 500 and 450 B.C., as both civilizations advanced rapidly from archaic carvings to highly naturalistic effigies. Just as Athens served as the locus for Hellas's sculptural revolution, the medieval European renaissance in sculpture had its focal point — the lands of the Île de France and immediately adjacent territories. Strangely, it was not Italy, which still retained vivid memories of its classical past, where this medieval revival of classical forms and sculptural esthetics first took shape. Byzantine and Romanesque styles continued to dominate Italy, southern France, the rest of the Mediterranean lands of the West, and most of Germany well into the thirteenth century. Rather, northern France, particularly the regions of **Paris** and **Champagne**, served as the first home of Gothic naturalism. By the 1220s, its influence had spread as far east as Strasbourg on the Rhine.

QUESTIONS FOR ANALYSIS

1. Consider *Notre Dame la Brune*. How does the sculptor approach the problem of depicting the human body? How would you characterize his overall technique? In addressing these questions, pay particular attention to such items as the Virgin's drapery and hands, the Christ Child's face and head, and both figures' expressions and postures. You might want to compare the Virgin's hands with those of the angels in *The Altar of King Ratchis* (Chapter 2, source 10).

2. Describe the emotions that the artist of *Notre Dame la Brune* meant to engender in those who venerated the statue.

3. How closely, if at all, does this Virgin conform to the mental image of the Virgin created by another twelfth-century Burgundian, Bernard of Clairvaux (Chapter 7, source 38)? Explain your answer.

4. Describe and interpret each of the symbols associated with *Ecclesia* and *Synagoga*. What, for example, is the book that *Synagoga* holds? What is the sculptor's message? Compare that message with canons 68 and 69 of the Fourth Lateran Council (Chapter 7, source 42). What conclusion follows from your analysis?

5. Compare the clothing and bodies of *Ecclesia* and *Synagoga* with those of the Virgin and Christ Child. What conclusion follows from this comparison?

6. Compare the drapery and bodies of *Ecclesia* and *Synagoga* with the figures on the Barberini Ivory (Chapter 2, source 10). What conclusion follows from this comparison?

7. Compare Giselbertus's *Eve* with these two Gothic statues. What inferences do you draw?

Notre Dame la Brune

Ecclesia

Synagoga

Two Thirteenth-Century
Representations of the Virgin

▼▼▼

58 ▼ *THE DORMITION OF THE CATHEDRAL OF STRASBOURG and THE DORMITION OF THE CHURCH OF SAINT MARY PERIBLEPTOS*

By the thirteenth century, Eastern and Western Christians disagreed over many issues (Chapter 11, source 76), but they equally regarded Mary, the Mother of Jesus, as the most lovable and loving of all God's saints. Both Byzantine and Latin Christians revered Mary as the fully human yet sinless Mother of God, who served as advocate for all humanity before her Son's throne (Chapter 7, sources 38 and 39).

The cult of Mary resulted in the creation of a massive volume of paintings and statues of the Virgin Mother in both the East and West. One of the more popular themes, especially in Byzantium, was the *Dormition,* or "Falling Asleep," of Mary. According to a tradition equally accepted in the East and West, when Mary died, her incorruptible body was assumed into Heaven. With body and soul reunited, she was crowned Queen of Heaven.

The two illustrations represent typical thirteenth-century High Gothic and Late Byzantine renderings of the Dormition. The first is a relief carving on a tympanum at the same south portal of Strasbourg cathedral* where *Ecclesia* and *Synagoga* originally stood (source 57). Like those two statues, the carving dates from around 1230. The other is a wall painting from the Serbian Church of St. Mary Peribleptos and dates to around 1295. During the thirteenth century, Serbia, which is located in the central Balkans, was culturally part of Byzantine civilization, whereas its immediate Balkan neighbor to the north, Croatia, had accepted Roman Catholicism.

Both pieces of art employ many of the same features. A "sleeping" Virgin is surrounded by mourning apostles.* St. Peter is at the far left, at the head of the bed, and St. Paul is at the far right, at the foot of the bed. Jesus dominates the central background, where he tenderly holds his mother's winged soul in his arms. In the Strasbourg sculpture, a kneeling St. Mary Magdalene, one of Jesus' most important female disciples, grieves at the bedside, but she is absent in the Serbian painting. In her place is an incense brazier. These iconographic similarities suggest a westward spread of Byzantine artistic motifs, as well as an essential theological agreement between the two separated branches of Christendom. Similarly, the differences in style and artistic execution help us better understand the ways in which the two Christian civilizations parted.

QUESTIONS FOR ANALYSIS

1. Which scene seems more naturalistic? Which scene seems to emphasize more the mystery or other worldliness of the faith? How so?

2. Judging from these scenes, which Christian tradition do you think emphasized the cult of the Risen, Glorified Christ? Which emphasized the suffering Jesus? Which tradition probably placed greater emphasis on the Nativity (Christmas)? Why have you drawn these inferences?

3. If each scene represents a different devotional emphasis and a different way of perceiving humanity's relationship with the Divine, what can you say about the two Christian cultures that produced them?

4. Based on your answer to question 1, reconsider *Notre Dame la Brune.* Does that statue also represent the mystery and other worldliness of the faith?

5. Gothic was largely an urban artform, and it has been said that High Gothic was a perfect medium for the expression of bourgeois religious values and aspirations. What does this mean? Does the Strasbourg scene strike you as particularly bourgeois? If so, in what ways?

6. Compare the Strasbourg Mary with Giselbertus's *Eve* in source 56. How has the artist made this New Eve appear as the sinless counterpart to humanity's original sinner?

Dormition, Cathedral of Strasbourg

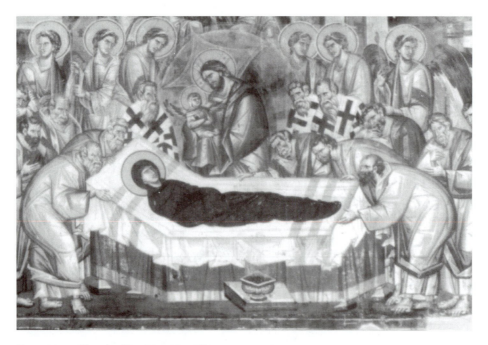

Dormition, Church of St. Mary Peribleptos

Literature

Europe's literary production during the High Middle Ages was as varied, sophisticated, and original as its other intellectual and artistic achievements. European writers composed both secular* and religious works, as well as works that bridged the two spheres; they expressed themselves in poetry and prose and wrote in Latin and a variety of vernacular tongues. Jacques de Vitry's popular tales, for example, were Latin prose pieces that revolved around religious issues (Chapter 7, source 39), whereas *The Song of Roland* was an Old French poem that blended religious sentiments with secular issues (Chapter 8, source 47).

If this section contained sources representative of the entire spectrum of twelfth- and thirteenth-century literature, it would exceed all reasonable limits of length. Therefore, it centers on only three of the most characteristic and original genres of literature in this era: poetry, romance, and parody. Although the selected sources do not represent the full range of this civilization's literary creativity, they suggest some of its variety.

Secular and Religious Poetry
▼▼▼

59 ▼ The Archpoet, "THE CONFESSION OF GOLIAS," Francis of Assisi, "THE CANTICLE OF THE CREATURES," and Thomas of Celano? "DIES IRAE"

Clerics* composed all three of the following poems, but their works represent several different visions of Heaven and earth.

The first poet represented here was one of the twelfth century's most original secular Latin poets and possibly its most gifted. Known only as *the Archpoet,* he was attached to the household of Rainald of Dassel, archbishop* of Cologne and archchancellor of Emperor Frederick I. Although the Archpoet probably composed a large body of work, only ten of his poems, all crafted between 1159 and 1165, are known today. Of these, the most famous is "The Confession of Golias." *Golias* is the Latin variation of the name *Goliath,* the Philistine giant whom David slew and whom Christian biblical commentators interpreted as a symbol of monstrous depravity and sensuality run wild. Golias commanded the literary allegiance of an unorganized band of fun-loving clerical poets, who styled themselves "the tribe of Golias," or *Goliards,* and lightheartedly celebrated their and Golias's larger-than-life appetites and habits. The Archpoet takes this literary conceit and creates a piece of poetic magic. Is he boasting of his life as a pleasure-seeking *bon vivant,* or has he repented?

With Francis of Assisi, there was no doubt. He repented and spent the remainder of his days doing penance for his youthful excesses (Chapter 7, source 41). Francis lived a life of poetic simplicity, in which he devoted himself, heart and soul, to uncompromising devotion to "My Lady Poverty," a metaphorical personification of the life of mendicancy* that he had embraced. Francis also expressed his religious vision in several hymns that he composed in his native Umbrian dialect, thereby becoming Italy's first significant vernacular poet. His most famous and beloved hymn is "The Canticle of the Creatures," which he began in 1225, when he was almost totally blind and suffering excruciating pain. According to one thirteenth-century biographer, Francis was moved to create his hymn in order help rectify the way in which humans misused and misperceived this divinely created world. He added the final verses about Sister Death shortly before his own death in 1226, and as he lay dying, he requested that his two closest companions sing the canticle for him.

Some commentators also claim to find the Franciscan spirit in the third poem, "Dies Irae" (Day of Wrath), a hymn that describes the Last Judgment, when Jesus will return to earth to judge all humanity. Tradition ascribes its authorship to Thomas of Celano (ca. 1190–ca. 1260), Francis of Assisi's first major biographer, but most modern scholars prefer to regard it as the work of an anonymous genius. The poem borrows heavily from some twelfth-century hymns, but the earliest manuscripts of the entire hymn date from the thirteenth century. It is possible that Thomas of Celano or some other, now unknown Franciscan friar* put the hymn into its final form. All great poetry defies translation, but our translator has managed to capture much of the percussionlike rhythm that hammers home the message of "Dies Irae."

QUESTIONS FOR ANALYSIS

1. What are the Archpoet's admitted sins?
2. From whom does he beg forgiveness, and what sort of absolution does he seek?
3. In light of your answers to 1 and 2, how would you characterize the spirit and message of the Archpoet's poem?
4. In "The Canticle of the Creatures," does Francis direct his praise at creation? Does he praise God because of creation? If neither of these, what role does creation play in this hymn?
5. What misconceptions and misuses of nature does Francis appear to want to rectify?
6. Do any of the Romanesque or Gothic art pieces in section 1 share any of the spirit of "The Confession of Golias"? Is there a connection between any of these sculptures and "The Canticle of the Creatures"? Explain your answers.
7. Do you perceive a shift in mood in stanza 8 of "Dies Irae"? What is that shift, and how do you explain it?
8. Many modern commentators believe they see a Franciscan tone in "Dies Irae." Where might that be? Compare this poem with Francis's *Testament*

(Chapter 7, source 41) and "The Canticle of the Creatures." Do you see any connections? If so, describe them.

9. What does your study of these three poems tell you about the High Middle Ages?

THE CONFESSION OF GOLIAS

Indignation's fiery flood
  Scalds my inmost being;
I must chew a bitter cud,
  One conclusion seeing:
Light of substance is my blood,
  Restlessness decreeing,
So that down the wind I scud
  Like a dead leaf fleeing.

Let the wise man place his seat
  On the rock firm founded.
Hither, thither, I must beat
  By my follies hounded.
With the flowing stream I fleet,
  So my doom is sounded;
'Neath the arch of heaven my feet
  Nowhere yet have grounded.

Like a hapless ship I fare
  Left without a sailor,
Like a bird on ways of air,
  Some poor lost cloud-scaler;
Not a jot for chains I care,
  Nor for key nor jailer.
Sinful flesh is frail, I swear.
  Mine's the same — but frailer!

Dull and dour sobriety
  Never takes my money,
Give me loose society
  Where the jokes are funny;
Love will bring variety,
  Toil that's sweet as honey.
Pillars of propriety,
  Have you hearts as sunny?

Down the primrose path I post
  Straight to Satan's grotto,
Shunning virtue, doing most
  Things that I ought not to;
Little hope of heaven I boast,
  Charmed by pleasure's otto:
Since the soul is bound to roast
  Save the skin's my motto.

Hear me, prelate[1] most discreet,
  For indulgence crying:
Deadly sin I find so sweet
  I'm in love with dying;
Every pretty girl I meet
  Sets my heart a-sighing:
Hands off! ah, but in conceit
  In her arms I'm lying.

Much too hard it is, I find,
  So to change my essence
As to keep a virgin mind
  In a virgin's presence.
Rigid laws can never bind
  Youth to acquiescence;
Light o' loves must seek their kind,
  Bodies take their pleasance.

Who that in a bonfire falls
  Is not scorched by flame there?
Who can leave Pavia's walls[2]
  Pure as when he came there?
Venus'[3] beckoning finger calls
  Youths with sportive aim there,
Eyes make captive willing thralls,
  Faces hunt for game there.

---

[1] Here, he refers directly to Rainald of Dassel, the prelate* of Cologne.

[2] A city in northern Italy, where the Archpoet resided with his patron. Archbishop Rainald and his entourage accompanied Emperor Frederick Barbarossa's campaign in northern Italy, which stretched from 1161 to 1165.

[3] The Roman goddess of love.

Give the chaste Hippolytus[4]
  One day in Pavia,
He'll not long be virtuous;
  Next day you will see a
Lover most solicitous.
  Love's their one idea:
'Mid these towers so numerous
  Dwells no Alethea.[5]

Next, I'm called in terms precise
  Monstrous fond of gaming;
Losing all my clothes at dice
  Gains me this worth naming:
While outside I'm cool as ice,
  Inwardly I'm flaming,
Then with daintiest device
  Poems and songs I'm framing.

Third, the tavern — here I dread
  Lies detraction's kernel:
Long on tavern joys I've fed,
  Never shall I spurn all
Till these eyes shall see instead
  Choirs from realms supernal
Changing for the newly dead
  Requiem[6] eternal.

My intention is to die
  In the tavern drinking;
Wine must be at hand, for I
  Want it when I'm sinking.
Angels when they come shall cry,
  At my frailties winking:
"Spare this drunkard, God, he's high,
  Absolutely stinking!"

Cups of wine illuminate
  Beacons of the spirit,
Draughts of nectar elevate
  Hearts to heaven, or near it.
Give me tavern liquor straight,
  Gouty lords may fear it —
Pah! their watered stuff I hate.
  Drawer, do you hear it?

Public life, there's no mistake,
  Certain poets find irking;
Courts they willingly forsake,
  In seclusion lurking;
There they study, drudge, and wake,
  No endeavor shirking,
Hoping one great poem to make
  Ere they cease from working.

Starveling rhymesters, when they thirst
  Water is their potion!
City din they count accurst
  And the crowd's commotion.
Foundlings by the Muses[7] nursed,
  Fame's their only notion:
Fame they sometimes win, but first
  Die of their devotion.

Nature grants us each a price,
  Fitly used, it waxes;
Mine in verse — not fasting — lies.
  Fasting so relaxes,
Any stripling half my size
  Bumps me off my axis.
Thirst and fasting I despise
  Worse than death and taxes.

One free gift from nature's stock
  Each man draws, and rightly;
Mine's for verse and getting chock
  Full of liquor nightly.
Broach the landlord's oldest crock
  Till I've mellowed slightly:
Good wine makes the fancies flock
  Copiously and brightly.

Let the verse be as the wine.
  Grasp this true technique well,
And like me, until you dine,
  Neither write nor speak well.
Fasting, while I peak and pine,
  Nothing comes in sequel;
Feast me, and these songs of mine
  Ovid[8] could not equal.

---

[4]A mythic Greek horseman who was noted for his chastity.
[5]The Greek goddess of truth.
[6]The mass for the dead.

[7]The nine Greek goddesses of the arts.
[8]A Roman poet and satirist who lived between 43 B.C. and
A.D. 17.

Inspiration's wooed in vain,
　Fancy stays retired,
Till my craving guts obtain
　All they have desired;
Then let mighty Bacchus[9] reign
　Till I'm duly fired,
Phoebus[10] rushes to my brain —
　Lord, but I'm inspired!

Thus I stand condemned, but by
　My own accusation;
See, the courtiers prophesy
　My deserved damnation;
Yet not one can testify,
　For his own salvation,
He is better armed than I
　'Gainst the world's temptation.

Even here before thy throne,
　Prince and true confessor,[*]
Following the rule made known
　By our Intercessor,
Let him cast at me the stone,
　Be the bard's oppressor,
Who can swear that he alone
　Never was transgressor.[11]

See, I've labored to record
　All my heart confesses;
Fulsome brews from pleasure's board —
　I spit out the messes!
Changed at last, I hasten toward
　This new life that blesses.
Man sees but the face; thou, Lord,
　Knowest the heart's recesses.

Now to virtue reconciled,
　Base desires I quiet,
Sweep and scour my sin-defiled
　Soul to purify it.
See me now a new-born child,
　New milk is my diet;

In my heart no more shall wild
　Vanities run riot.

Gracious prince, Cologne's elect[12]
　Archbishop and warden,
Grant me mercy, nor reject
　One who sues for pardon.
Deign my penance to direct,
　Lest my heart should harden,
No commands will I neglect:
　Plant me in thy garden.

Pity me, thy suppliant,
　Let no thunder rumble.
Lion, king of beasts, doth grant
　Mercy to the humble.
O ye kings, were mercy scant
　Heaven itself would crumble.
Tasting bitters when they want
　Sweets will make men grumble.

▼ ▼ ▼

THE CANTICLE OF THE CREATURES

Most high, all-powerful, all good, Lord!
　All praise is yours, all glory, all honor
　And all blessing.
To you, alone, Most High, do they belong.
　No mortal lips are worthy
　To pronounce your name.
All praise be yours, my Lord, through all that
　　you have made,
　And first my lord Brother Sun,
　Who brings the day; and light you give to
　　us through him.
How beautiful is he, how radiant in all his
　　splendor!
　Of you, Most High, he bears the likeness.

---

[9]The Greco-Roman god of wine and revelry.
[10]Phoebus Apollo was a Greco-Roman god, second in power only to his father, Zeus, king of the gods. Among his many attributes, he was the patron of poetic inspiration.

[11]A reference to Jesus' injunction "Let whoever is without sin cast the first stone [at a sinner]." The Bible, the Gospel of John, 8:7.
[12]Rainald, who was elected (chosen by Emperor Frederick) archbishop of Cologne in 1159.

All praise be yours, my Lord, through Sister
   Moon and Stars;
  In the heavens you have made them, bright
  And precious and fair.
All praise be yours, my Lord, through Brothers
   Wind and Air,
   And fair and stormy, all the weather's
    moods,
   By which you cherish all that you have
    made.
All praise be yours, my Lord, through Sister
   Water,
  So useful, lowly, precious and pure.
All praise be yours, my Lord, through Brother
   Fire,
   Through whom you brighten up the night.
   How beautiful is he, how gay! Full of power
    and strength.
All praise be yours, my Lord, through Sister
   Earth, our mother,
   Who feeds us in her sovereignty and
    produces
   Various fruits with colored flowers and
    herbs.
All praise be yours, my Lord, through those
   who grant pardon
   For love of you; through those who endure
   Sickness and trial.
Happy those who endure in peace,
  By you, Most High, they will be crowned.
All praise be yours, my Lord, through Sister
   Death,
   From whose embrace no mortal can escape.
Woe to those who die in mortal sin!
  Happy those She finds doing your will!
  The second death can do no harm to them.
Praise and bless my Lord, and give him thanks,
  And serve him with great humility.

▼ ▼ ▼

DIES IRAE

Day of wrath, that day of burning!
Earth shall end, to ashes turning:
Thus sing saint and seer, discerning.

Ah, the dread beyond expression
When the Judge in awful session
Searcheth out the world's transgression.

Then is heard a sound of wonder:
Mighty blasts of trumpet-thunder
Rend the sepulchers asunder.

What can e'er that woe resemble,
Where even death and nature tremble
As the rising throngs assemble!

Vain, my soul, is all concealing;
For the book is brought, revealing
Every deed and thought and feeling.

On his throne the Judge is seated,
And our sins are loud repeated,
And to each is vengeance meted.

Wretched me! How gain a hearing,
When the righteous falter, fearing,
At the pomp of his appearing?

King of majesty and splendor,
Fount of pity, true and tender,
Be, thyself, my strong defender.

From thy woes my hope I borrow:
I did cause thy way of sorrow:[13]
Do not lose me on that morrow.

Seeking me, thou weary sankest,
Nor from scourge and cross thou shrankest;
Make not vain the cup thou drankest.

Thou wert righteous even in slaying:
Yet forgive my guilty straying,
Now, before that day dismaying.

---

[13]Christians believe that Jesus died to atone for humanity's
sins.

Though my sins with shame suffuse me,
Though my very moans accuse me,
Canst thou, Loving One, refuse me!

Blessed hope! I have aggrieved thee:
Yet, by grace the thief believed thee,[14]
And the Magdalen received thee.[15]

Though unworthy my petition,
Grant me full and free remission,
And redeem me from perdition.

Be my lot in love decreed me:
From the goats[16] in safety lead me;
With thy sheep[17] forever feed me.

When thy foes are all confounded,
And with bitter flames surrounded,
Call me to thy bliss unbounded.

From the dust I pray thee, hear me:
When my end shall come, be near me;
Let thy grace sustain and cheer me.

Ah, that day, that day of weeping,
When, no more in ashes sleeping,
Man shall rise and stand before thee!
Spare him, spare him, I implore thee!

---

[14]The "good thief" who was crucified alongside Jesus and to whom Jesus promised salvation: The Gospel of Luke, 23:39–43.

[15]St. Mary Magdalene; according to tradition, a former prostitute (see source 58).
[16]The damned.
[17]The saved.

Courtly Romance
▼▼▼

60 ▾ *Chrétien de Troyes, EREC AND ENIDE*

The Song of Roland (Chapter 8, source 47) introduced us to a tough, masculine camp world, where women played minimal roles. Roland's fiancée, Aude, only appears at the end of the epic in order to drop dead upon hearing of Roland's death; the tougher, strong-minded Bramimonde, Muslim queen of Spain, plays a larger part and survives her husband's death. She, however, winds up as war booty and is sent off to France to be converted "through love" to Christianity.

During the twelfth century, however, a new, countervailing vision emerged of women and their role within chivalric society. As early as the last years of the eleventh century, *troubadour* lyric poets in Languedoc, the southeastern region of the kingdom of France, were singing the praises of court women (women who often exercised extensive powers over their domains) and extolling the virtues of a refined love that ennobled the lover. Turning on its head the feudal* virtue of loyalty to a lord, the troubadours pledged undying devotion to their *ladies,* who were the arbiters of and reasons for proper courtly conduct, or *courtoisie.* Troubadour conventions traveled north into the heartland of France, east into Germany, southeast into Italy, and across the channel into England.

Toward the middle of the twelfth century, literary artists in the Île de France created a new form of vernacular literature, the *courtly romance,* in order to provide a new voice to troubadour visions of love's redemptive qualities. The romance (*romanz* in Old French) was an extended story, in either verse or prose, that dealt with extraordinary feats of love and knightly prowess in the setting of a mythical, idealized past. The origin of the term probably derives from the fact that the earliest romances dealt with "Roman" themes — the fabled feats of certain ancient warriors, such as Alexander the Great, whom Europeans knew through extant Latin (Roman) sources.

The fully evolved romance was generally set against one of four thematic backgrounds: the siege of Troy, the age of Alexander the Great, the era of Charlemagne, and, most popular of all, the company of King Arthur and his knights. This last cycle of stories derived largely from Celtic legends regarding a shadowy but apparently historical sixth-century British warrior leader, whom twelfth-century romancers metamorphosed into the ideal chivalric knight.

The greatest and earliest writer of Arthurian romances was Chrétien de Troyes, a learned cleric* who served at the court of Countess Marie of Champagne and about whom little else is known. Apparently, he was born around 1140 and seems to have died sometime before 1200. His extant body of work includes five romances. The first is *Erec and Enide,* which dates to around 1170, making it the earliest surviving Arthurian romance.

In *Erec and Enide,* Chrétien examines and resolves the chivalric conflict that affects a happily married couple, Erec, prince of Outer Wales, and his new bride, Enide. The question is: Is marital bliss an impediment to martial duty? The excerpt opens with Erec at a tournament that he visits while residing at the court of King Arthur.

QUESTIONS FOR ANALYSIS

1. Compare Erec's reasons for fighting with those of Count Roland. What conclusions do you draw from this comparison?
2. Consider Erec's knightly attributes. How do they conform to those of Roland and Oliver? How do they differ? What conclusions follow from your answers?
3. Compare the mood that pervades Chrétien's description of knightly society with the mood of *The Song of Roland.* Is the world of the romance substantially different from that of the epic? What conclusions follow from your answer?
4. Why does Erec temporarily abandon knightly pursuits, and what price does he pay? How is be brought back to his sense of duty?
5. According to Chrétien's standards, who has the purer or better love and sense of marital responsibility, Erec or Enide? Why do you conclude that? Without even reading the rest of the romance, whose love do you think will prove to be the means by which the other partner is redeemed?
6. Consider the women in this selection. How are they portrayed, and what roles do they play? What sort of power, if any, do they have? What conclusions follow from your answers?
7. The chivalric world portrayed here was a literary creation. Notwithstanding, do you think this imaginative world had any impact on the way in which real people behaved? On what do you base your answer?

— A month after Pentecost[1] the tournament assembled, and the jousting began in the plain below Tenebroc. Many an ensign of red, blue, and white, many a veil and many a sleeve were bestowed as tokens of love. Many a lance was carried there, flying the colors argent and green, or gold and azure blue. There were many, too, with different devices, some with stripes and some with dots. That day one saw laced on many a helmet of gold or steel, some green, some yellow, and others red, all aglowing in the sun; so many scutcheons[2] and white hauberks;[3] so many swords girt on the left side; so many good shields, fresh and new, some resplendent in silver and green, others of azure with buckles of gold; so many good steeds marked with white, or sorrel, tawny, white, black, and bay: all gather hastily. And now the field is quite covered with arms. On either side the ranks tremble, and a roar rises from the fight. The shock of the lances is very great. Lances break and shields are riddled, the hauberks receive bumps and are torn asunder, saddles go empty and horsemen tumble, while the horses sweat and foam. Swords are quickly drawn on those who tumble noisily, and some run to receive the promise of a ransom,[4] others to stave off this disgrace. Erec rode a white horse, and came forth alone at the head of the line to joust, if he may find an opponent. From the opposite side there rides out to meet him Orguelleus de la Lande, mounted on an Irish steed which bears him along with marvellous speed. On the shield before his breast Erec strikes him with such force that he knocks him from his horse; he leaves him prone and passes on. Then Raindurant opposed him, son of the old dame of Tergalo, covered with blue cloth of silk; he was a knight of great prowess. Against one another now they

charge and deal fierce blows on the shields about their necks. Erec from a lance's length lays him over on the hard ground. While riding back he met the King of the Red City, who was very valiant and bold. They grasp their reins by the knots and their shields by the inner straps. They both had fine arms, and strong swift horses, and good shields, fresh and new. With such fury they strike each other that both their lances fly in splinters. Never was there seen such a blow. They rush together with shields, arms, and horses. But neither girth nor rein nor breast-strap could prevent the king from coming to earth. So he flew from his steed, carrying with him saddle and stirrup, and even the reins of his bridle in his hand. All those who witnessed the jousting were filled with amazement, and said it cost him dear to joust with such a goodly knight. Erec did not wish to stop to capture either horse or rider, but rather to joust and distinguish himself in order that his prowess might appear. He thrills the ranks in front of him. Gawain[5] animates those who were on his side by his prowess, and by winning horses and knights to the discomfiture of his opponents. I speak of my lord Gawain, who did right well and valiantly. In the fight he unhorsed Guincel, and took Gaudin of the Mountain; he captured knights and horses alike: my lord Gawain did well. Girflet the son of Do, and Yvain, and Sagremor the Impetuous, so evilly entreated their adversaries that they drove them back to the gates, capturing and unhorsing many of them. In front of the gate of the town the strife began again between those within and those without. There Sagremor was thrown down, who was a very gallant knight. He was on the point of being detained and captured, when Erec spurs to rescue him, breaking his lance into splinters upon one

---

[1]The feast of Pentecost is held on the seventh Sunday after Easter. This tournament, therefore, was held in late spring or early summer.
[2]Shields.
[3]A long tunic of chain mail. See Chapter 8, source 47, note 3.

[4]This type of early tournament was known as a *melée.* Two groups of knights charged one another like two hostile armies, and each knight sought to defeat as many opponents as possible because he could hold for ransom the person, arms, and horse of anyone whom he forced to surrender.
[5]King Arthur's nephew and the principal hero of the Arthurian cycle. Chrétien places Gawain first and Erec second among all the knights of the Round Table.

of the opponents. So hard he strikes him on the breast that he made him quit the saddle. Then he draws his sword and advances upon them, crushing and splitting their helmets. Some flee, and others make way before him, for even the boldest fears him. Finally, he distributed so many blows and thrusts that he rescued Sagremor from them, and drove them all in confusion into the town. Meanwhile, the vesper[6] hour drew to a close. Erec bore himself so well that day that he was the best of the combatants. But on the morrow he did much better yet; for he took so many knights and left so many saddles empty that none could believe it except those who had seen it. Every one on both sides said that with his lance and shield he had won the honors of the tournament. Now was Erec's renown so high that no one spoke save of him, nor was any one of such goodly favor. In countenance he resembled Absalom,[7] in language he seemed a Solomon,[8] in boldness he equalled Samson,[9] and in generous giving and spending he was the equal of Alexander.[10] On his return from the tourney Erec went to speak with the king.[11] He went to ask him for leave to go and visit his own land; but first he thanked him like a frank, wise, and courteous man for the honor which he had done him; for very deep was his gratitude. Then he asked his permission to leave, for he wished to visit his own country, and he wished to take his wife with him. This request the king could not deny, and yet he would have had him stay. He gives him leave and begs him to return as soon as possible; for in the whole court there was no better or more gallant knight, save only his dear nephew Gawain; with him no one could be compared. But next after him, he prized Erec most, and held him more dear than any other knight.

Erec wished to delay no longer. As soon as he had the King's leave, he bid his wife make her preparations and he retained as his escort sixty knights of merit with horses and with dappled and grey furs. As soon as he was ready for his journey, he tarried little further at court, but took leave of the queen[12] and commended the knights to God. The queen grants him leave to depart. At the hour of prime he set out from the royal palace. In the presence of them all he mounted his steed, and his wife mounted the dappled horse which she had brought from her own country; then all his escort mounted. Counting knights and squires, there were full seven score[13] in the train. After four long days' journey over hills and slopes, through forests, plains, and streams, they came on the fifth day to Carnant, where King Lac[14] was residing in a very charming town. No one ever saw one better situated; for the town was provided with forests and meadow-land, with vineyards and farms, with streams and orchards, with ladies and knights, and fine, lively youths, and polite, well-mannered clerks who spent their incomes freely, with fair and charming maidens, and with prosperous burghers. Before Erec reached the town, he sent two knights ahead to announce his arrival to the king. When he heard the news, the king had clerks, knights, and damsels quickly mount, and ordered the bells to be rung, and the streets to be hung with tapestries and silken stuffs, that his son might be received with joy; then he himself got on his horse. Of clerks there were present fourscore, gentle and honorable men, clad in grey cloaks bordered with sable. Of knights there were full five hundred, mounted on bay, sorrel, or white-spotted steeds. There were so many burghers and dames that no one could tell the number of them. The king

---

[6]The early evening prayer that signals the end of the workday.
[7]The third son of King David of Israel; Absalom was noted for his perfect beauty.
[8]King David's last son and successor; Solomon was noted for his wisdom.

[9]A biblical figure noted for his superhuman strength and ability to kill Philistines.
[10]Alexander the Great.
[11]Arthur.
[12]Queen Guinevere, Arthur's wife.
[13]One hundred forty.
[14]Erec's father.

and his son galloped and rode on till they saw and recognized each other. They both jump down from their horses and embrace and greet each other for a long time, without stirring from the place where they first met. Each party wished the other joy: the king makes much of Erec, but all at once breaks off to turn to Enide. On all sides he is in clover: he embraces and kisses them both, and knows not which of the two pleases him the more. As they gaily enter the castle, the bells all ring their peals to honor Erec's arrival. The streets are all strewn with reeds, mint, and iris, and are hung overhead with curtains and tapestries of fancy silk and satin stuffs. There was great rejoicing; for all the people came together to see their new lord, and no one ever saw greater happiness than was shown alike by young and old. First they came to the church, where very devoutly they were received in a procession. Erec kneeled before the altar of the Crucifix, and two knights led his wife to the image of Our Lady. When she had finished her prayer, she stepped back a little and crossed herself with her right hand, as a well-bred dame should do. Then they came out from the church and entered the royal palace, when the festivity began. That day Erec received many presents from the knights and burghers: from one a palfrey[15] of northern stock, and from another a golden cup. One presents him with a golden pigeon-hawk, another with a setter-dog, this one a greyhound, this other a sparrowhawk, and another a swift Arab steed, this one a shield, this one an ensign, this one a sword, and this a helmet. Never was a king more gladly seen in his kingdom, nor received with greater joy, as all strove to serve him well. Yet greater joy they made of Enide than of him, for the great beauty which they saw in her, and still more for her open charm. She was seated in a chamber upon a cushion of brocade which had been brought from Thessaly.[16] Round about her was many a fair lady; yet as the lustrous gem outshines the brown flint, and as the rose excels the poppy, so was Enide fairer than any other lady or damsel to be found in the world, wherever one might search. She was so gentle and honorable, of wise speech and affable, of pleasing character and kindly mien. No one could ever be so watchful as to detect in her any folly, or sign of evil or villainy. She had been so schooled in good manners that she had learned all virtues which any lady can possess, as well as generosity and knowledge. All loved her for her open heart, and whoever could do her any service was glad and esteemed himself the more. No one spoke any ill of her, for no one could do so. In the realm or empire there was no lady of such good manners. But Erec loved her with such a tender love that he cared no more for arms, nor did he go to tournaments, nor have any desire to joust; but he spent his time in cherishing his wife. He made of her his mistress and his sweetheart. He devoted all his heart and mind to fondling and kissing her, and sought no delight in other pastime. His friends grieved over this, and often regretted among themselves that he was so deep in love. Often it was past noon before he left her side; for there he was happy, say what they might. He rarely left her society, and yet he was as open-handed as ever to his knights with arms, dress, and money. There was not a tournament anywhere to which he did not send them well apparelled and equipped. Whatever the cost might be, he gave them fresh steeds for the tourney and joust. All the knights said it was a great pity and misfortune that such a valiant man as he was wont to be should no longer wish to bear arms. He was blamed so much on all sides by the knights and squires that murmurs reached Enide's ears how that her lord had turned craven about arms and deeds of chivalry, and that his manner of life was greatly changed. She grieved sorely over this, but she did not dare to show her grief; for her lord at once would take affront, if

---

[15]A riding horse, as opposed to a charger, or war horse.

[16]Northeast Greece.

she should speak to him. So the matter remained a secret, until one morning they lay in bed where they had had sport together. There they lay in close embrace, like the true lovers they were. He was asleep, but she was awake, thinking of what many a man in the country was saying of her lord. And when she began to think it all over, she could not keep back the tears. Such was her grief and her chagrin that by mischance she let fall a word for which she later felt remorse, though in her heart there was no guile. She began to survey her lord from head to foot, his well-shaped body and his clear countenance, until her tears fell fast upon the bosom of her lord, and she said: "Alas, woe is me that I ever left my country! What did I come here to seek? The earth ought by right to swallow me up when the best knight, the most hardy, brave, fair, and courteous that ever was a count or king, has completely abjured all his deeds of chivalry because of me. And thus, in truth, it is I who have brought shame upon his head, though I would fain not have done so at any price." Then she said to him: "Unhappy thou!" And then kept silence and spoke no more. Erec was not sound asleep and, though dozing, heard plainly what she said. He aroused at her words, and much surprised to see her weeping, he asked her: "Tell me, my precious beauty, why do you weep thus? What has caused you woe or sorrow? Surely it is my wish to know. Tell me now, my gentle sweetheart, and take care to keep nothing back, why you said that woe was me? For you said it of me and of no one else. I heard your words plainly enough." Then was Enide in a great plight, afraid and dismayed. "Sire," says she, "I know nothing of what you say." "Lady, why do you conceal it? Concealment is of no avail. You have been crying; I can see that, and you do not cry for nothing. And in my sleep I heard what you said." "Ah! fair sire, you never heard it, and I dare say it was a dream." "Now you are coming to me with lies. I hear you

calmly lying to me. But if you do not tell me the truth now, you will come to repent of it later." "Sire, since you torment me thus, I will tell you the whole truth, and keep nothing back. But I am afraid that you will not like it. In this land they all say — the dark, the fair, and the ruddy — that it is a great pity that you should renounce your arms; your reputation has suffered from it. Every one used to say not long ago that in all the world there was known no better or more gallant knight. Now they all go about making game of you — old and young, little and great — calling you a recreant. Do you suppose it does not give me pain to hear you thus spoken of with scorn? It grieves me when I hear it said, and yet it grieves me more that they put the blame for it on me. Yes, I am blamed for it, I regret to say, and they all assert it is because I have so ensnared and caught you that you are losing all your merit, and do not care for aught but me. You must choose another course, so that you may silence this reproach and regain your former fame; for I have heard too much of this reproach, and yet I did not dare to disclose it to you. Many a time, when I think of it, I have to weep for very grief. Such chagrin I felt just now that I could not keep myself from saying that you were ill-starred." "Lady," said he, "you were in the right, and those who blame me do so with reason. And now at once prepare yourself to take the road. Rise up from here, and dress yourself in your richest robe, and order your saddle to be put on your best palfrey."

▷   Erec and Enide now set out on a series of adventures that will enable them to reaffirm their love in a manner that allows Erec to become a worthy king of Outer Wales and Enide to become his equally worthy queen. By striking a balance between love and adventure, marriage and knightly duty, Erec and Enide emerge as the equals of Arthur and Guinevere.

The Voice of Parody

▼▼▼

61 ▼ THE GOSPEL ACCORDING TO THE MARKS OF SILVER

The Archpoet's "The Confession of Golias" (source 59) parodies the sacramental* rite of auricular confession, in which a penitent formally confesses his sins before a priest* and humbly requests absolution. *Parody* is the mimicking of a well-known text or ceremony in order to achieve a humorous effect that reaches the level of absurdity. Because medieval students were trained to write in imitation of the Latin masters of antiquity, they developed a feeling for genre, style, and cadence that enabled them, when the mood struck, to burlesque everything from the sonorous poetry of Virgil to the most sacred texts of the Church. Thus, the Archpoet took the traditional prayer "God have mercy on this sinner" and changed it to "Spare this drunkard, God, he's high" simply by substituting a single word, *potatori* (drunkard), for *peccatori* (sinner).

One of the most successful parodies of the High Middle Ages was *The Gospel According to the Marks of Silver,* which dates from around 1200 and today exists in three different versions. Whoever composed it (and it was clearly written and revised by several authors) assumed that the reader would immediately recognize the biblical texts that were being parodied. The parody opens with the words "Here begins the holy Gospel* according to the marks of silver," an almost exact echo of the words that precede the gospel reading in each celebration of the mass,* the Church's central religious ceremony. However, instead of hearing the Gospel according to the Evangelist* Mark, the audience hears or reads the gospel according to the marks of silver (a *mark* being a half pound of precious metal). The tone of absurdity has now been set, and what follows is a delicious perversion of one of the core messages of the Gospels: "Do not store up riches on earth . . . for your heart will always be where your riches are" (Matthew, 6:19–21, and Luke 12:33–34).

This selection is the shortest and oldest of the three extant gospel parodies. The notes that accompany the text refer to the biblical passages that are being twisted for comic effect. You will find it helpful to read those passages from the Bible in order to understand more fully the authors' art and message.

QUESTIONS FOR ANALYSIS

1. Who or what is being ridiculed in this parody, and what is the work's message?
2. What sort of persons composed and read this work with pleasure?
3. Is this parody an assault on Christianity? On Roman Catholicism? On the Church? On something else? Or is it even an assault on anything?

4. Review sources 40, 41, and 42 of Chapter 7. Then compose commentaries on this parody by Waldes, Francis of Assisi, and Pope Innocent III, all of whom were alive around the time it was composed. What would each man think of the message and its manner of presentation?

Here begins the Gospel according to the marks of silver. In that time, the pope said unto the Romans: "When the Son of Man comes to the seat of Our majesty,[1] first say unto him, 'Friend, wherefore art thou come?'[2] But if he should persevere in his knocking and give thee nothing,[3] cast him forth into the outer darkness."[4] And it came to pass that a certain poor cleric* came to the lord pope's court and cried out, saying: "Have mercy even unto me, ye doorkeepers of the pope, because the hand of poverty has touched me.[5] For I am needy and poor, and I beg thee to relieve my calamitous misery."[6] They, however, upon hearing this were right indignant and said: "Friend, thy poverty go with thee to damnation.[7] Get thee behind me, Satan, because ye taste not of the things that savor of money.[8] Amen, Amen, I say unto thee, thou shalt not enter into the joy of thy Lord, until thou hast given the very last penny."[9] And the pauper went away and sold his cloak and tunic and everything that he owned, and he gave to the cardinals,* and the doorkeep-

ers, and the chamberlains.[10] But they said: "And this, what is it among so much?" And they cast him out before the gates,[11] and he going forth wept bitterly[12] and could not be consoled.

Thereafter there came to the court a certain rich, fat, well-fed,[13] and bloated cleric, who had committed murder while engaging in a riot.[14] He first gave to the doorkeeper, in the second place to the chamberlain, and in the third place to the cardinals.[15] And they took counsel among themselves as to who of them should have received the most.[16] But the lord pope, hearing that his cardinals and ministers had received so many gifts from the cleric, took ill well unto death.[17] Then the rich cleric sent unto him a sweet elixir of gold and silver, and straightway he was recovered.[18] Then the lord pope called unto himself his cardinals and ministers and said unto them: "Brothers, be watchful lest anyone seduce thee with empty words.[19] For I give unto you an example that even as much as I take, ye also should take."[20]

---

[1]The Gospel of Matthew, 25:31.
[2]The Gospel of Matthew, 26:50.
[3]The Gospel of Luke, 11:5–13, and the Gospel of Matthew, 7:7–11.
[4]The Gospel of Matthew, 25:30.
[5]The Gospel of Matthew, 15:22.
[6]The Book of Job, 19:21, and Psalm 69.
[7]Acts of the Apostles, 8:20.
[8]The Gospel of Mark, 8:33.
[9]The Gospel of Matthew, 5:26.
[10]The Gospel of Matthew, 13:44–46.
[11]The Gospel of Matthew, 22:13.
[12]The Gospel of Matthew, 26:75.
[13]The Book of Deuteronomy, 32:15.
[14]The Gospel of Mark, 15:7.
[15]The Gospel of Matthew, 25:14–15.
[16]The Gospel of Matthew, 20:10.
[17]St Paul, Letter to the Philippians, 2:27.
[18]The Gospel of John, 5:9.
[19]St. Paul, Letter to the Ephesians, 5:6.
[20]The Gospel of John, 13:15.

Chapter 10

▼▼▼

Political Theory and Reality

Chapters 6 and 8 illustrate the importance of feudal* arrangements in the political ordering of France, Germany, and England, and the same was true, to a lesser degree, for some regions of Italy, Spain, and Eastern Europe. Yet the story of European politics and political theory during the High Middle Ages cannot be reduced simply to feudal relationships.

The following sources reveal something of the variety and vitality of political theory and reality from the eleventh through the thirteenth centuries. The theories represented here include the notions of priestly* imperial power, papal* theocratic supremacy, separation of secular* and ecclesiastical* authority, and constitutional limitation of royal power. The realities were equally diverse: the growth of royal juridical power in England, as well as a movement to make the English monarch subject to his own laws; the development of the cult of the king as father of his people in France; struggles between the papacy* and the empire; the decentralization of power in Germany; and the development of parliamentary, representative assemblies in Spain and England. All things considered, the High Middle Ages was an especially productive era for the development of new political institutions and theory.

The Power of Monarchs

The powers of Europe's monarchs varied considerably according to time, place, and circumstance. Up until the thirteenth century, the kings of Germany, who also ruled over northern Italy by virtue of their imperial title, largely managed to maintain the power they had inherited from Otto I and his immediate tenth-century successors (Chapter 6, source 34), and in some respects they expanded on that power. The Anglo-Saxon and Danish kings of England ruled effectively over a fairly compact, reasonably well-governed island-kingdom from the middle of the tenth century onward, but following William of Normandy's conquest of England in 1066, the power of English kings reached a new level of effectiveness, as Norman feudal traditions were joined to native Anglo-Saxon institutions to create one of the most centralized kingdoms in Europe. French monarchs lagged behind their colleagues in England and Germany in creating an effective royal establishment; however, between 1090 and 1123, the last thirty-three years of Philip II's reign, French royal power increased dramatically due to an increase in the royal demesne and the development of new governmental machinery.

The three sources that appear here reflect both theory and reality. The first illustrates the ideology that buttressed royal authority during the eleventh century, especially in Germany. The second shows the new twelfth-century legal functions and authority of the English crown. The third provides an insight into the importance of King Louis IX in the growth of French royal authority in the thirteenth century.

Emperor Henry II as Judge

▼▼▼

62 ▼ *THE GOSPEL BOOK OF MONTE CASSINO*

Charles the Great and his immediate successors had claimed that the monarch, be he king or emperor, was *the* God-appointed defender of righteousness, the punisher of the wicked, and the champion of orthodox* Christianity. According to Carolingian ideology, a proper monarch served as society's chief moral agent and provided an atmosphere that was as conducive to the salvation of souls as it was to the preservation of bodies (Chapter 5, sources 25 and 26). What is more, as the "Lord's anointed servant," the monarch assumed a priestly aura.

The Saxon monarchs of Germany accepted this definition of monarchic authority and attempted to rule accordingly, as the following piece of evidence suggests. It is a full-page manuscript illustration from *The Gospel Book of Monte Cassino.* The painting, which appears in a copy of the Gospels* that Emperor Henry II (r. 1002–1024) presented to the abbey* of Monte Cassino in 1022 or 1023, represents the emperor sitting in judgment. The last emperor of the Saxon Dynasty established by Otto I (Chapter 6, source 34), Henry II was noted for his piety and incessant attempts to establish peace during a reign filled with wars and rebellions. Pope Eugenius III acknowledged Henry's efforts by officially declaring him a saint in 1146.

Henry II fills the center of the picture, enthroned within a large circle. In his right hand, he holds an *orb,* a symbol of sovereign authority. The Latin inscription surrounding him declares, "Henry shines forth on his ancestral throne of empire, Caesar and Augustus, worthy of the dignity of the imperial robe of state." In addition to the white and purple robe of state, a long cloth, known as a *stole,* is draped over the emperor's left shoulder and crosses at his right hip. Originally a badge of Roman consular and imperial rank, the Church adopted the stole in the fourth century as a sacramental* garment for priests and deacons.* The emperors at Constantinople, however, continued to wear the stole as part of their *imperialia,* and apparently, so did the Saxon emperors of Germany. Perhaps significantly, Emperor Henry wears his stole in the manner of a deacon. Compare Henry's stole with the pallium worn by Saint Peter in Chapter 5, source 27.

Four smaller circles surround Henry's circle. Above him, God the Holy Spirit,* the divine source of illumination and wisdom, descends from Heaven in the form of a dove. The words that encircle this image are "Merciful Spirit, God, bounteously bless the king." Beneath Henry's feet, a person is about to be executed by sword, and the accompanying words read, "At the emperor's behest, Law and Right condemn the tyrant." Flanking the emperor are two allegorical court attendants: Wisdom (*Sapientia*) on his right and Prudence (*Prudentia*) on his left. Their inscriptions assure us that the emperor is fit for his office by virtue of his wisdom and prudence. The four corners of the picture present additional allegorical figures. Clockwise, they are Justice (*Iustitia*), Piety (*Pietas*), Right (*Ius*), and Law (*Lex*).

QUESTIONS FOR ANALYSIS

1. What geometric pattern do these the five circles combine to create? What seems to be the message of that pattern?
2. Compare Henry's posture and body language with those of Christ in Chapter 2, source 10, and Chapter 9, sources 57 and 58. What similarities do you find? Which are more significant, the similarities or the differences? What conclusions follow from your answers?
3. This picture establishes three vertical relationships. The most important one is the relationship involving Emperor Henry and the circles above and below him. What is the artist's message?
4. What are the other two vertical relationships, and what are their messages?
5. There are also three horizontal relationships. What are they, and what do they symbolize?
6. Compare this painting with the Lateran mosaic of Pope Leo III (Chapter 5, source 27). Are their overall messages similar or different? To what degree? What do you conclude from your answers?

Emperor Henry II as Judge

The King's Justice
▼▼▼
63 ▼ *THE ASSIZE OF CLARENDON*

The theory of *sacral,* or priestly,* kingship, in which the monarch acted as the deputy of the Divine Judge, reached its apogee in the eleventh century and then gave way to the more secular* notion of the monarch as the supreme legislator who imposed rational order on his realm. The transition from a liturgical to a law-based kingship is quite apparent in England after 1066.

The conquest of England by William, duke of Normandy, was a watershed in English history, in large part because William imposed on an already centralized, well-governed country an Anglo-Norman feudal* regime that allowed him to govern his new realm more closely than had any of his European counterparts. William I's two immediate successors, William II (r. 1087–1100) and Henry I (r. 1100–1135), shared their father's strengths. King Henry I, known as *the Lion of Justice,* was especially successful in creating a peaceful kingdom ruled by a strong monarchy. His death, however, occasioned nineteen years of civil war and local brigandage, due to a disputed royal succession. In 1154 the twenty-one-year-old duke of Normandy and count of Anjou and Maine, a great-grandson of William the Conqueror, assumed the crown of England, pacified his new kingdom, and reigned as Henry II until his death in 1189. Although King Henry II was very much a French prince, with far-flung interests well beyond his English kingdom, he proved to be one of England's greatest medieval monarchs and possibly its most innovative legislator. History has accorded him the title *Father of English Common Law,* with *common law* being understood as royal laws and legal procedures common to all English free persons. Even though free people were a minority in twelfth-century England, this was a significant step in the direction of greater royal authority because the alternative to the king's common law was an inherited patchwork quilt of local customs and jurisdictions.

Henry filled his thirty-five-year reign with a constant series of decrees aimed at directing all important civil and criminal cases to his increasingly professional royal courts. One of the earliest and most important of King Henry's innovative edicts was the Assize of Clarendon of 1166, which widened the scope of royal justice to include the indictment and prosecution of major felons throughout the realm. The term *assize,* which means "a sitting" in Old French, primarily meant a court session. It could, however, as is the case here, also refer to the law enacted at a session of the king's court.

The sworn *inquest jury,* mentioned in article 1 of the assize, deserves special notice, inasmuch as it is the direct ancestor of the modern Anglo-American *grand jury,* which indicts rather than establishes the guilt or innocence of an accused person. Henry II's Anglo-Norman predecessors had occasionally commanded their sheriffs to gather small groups of neighbors who were *juried,* or placed under oath (*jurati*), and required to provide a *verdict,* or true answer (*verum dictum*), to some specific question. The most dramatic use of inquest juries was when William the Conqueror's agents gathered information for his Domesday survey of

1086. It was Henry II, however, who transformed the institution into a regular and permanent arm of royal justice.

The text that appears here was preserved as an appendix to the chronicle* of Roger of Hoveden, which was completed in 1201. This probably explains why its language is so unlegalistic and imprecise in places.

QUESTIONS FOR ANALYSIS

1. Exactly what process do articles 1–13 set in motion?
2. What evidence shows that this assize did not end all private jurisdictions and nonroyal courts? On the other hand, how did it severely curtail their activities?
3. What does the crown gain from this assize?
4. Consider articles 12–14. What do they suggest about King Henry's attitude toward trial by ordeal?
5. What role did the accused's reputation and past record play in the process established by this assize? How might King Henry have justified the courts' use of this type of evidence?
6. How did the Assize of Clarendon deal with the issue of homeless and rootless people? Why do you think it took such measures?
7. How did Henry attempt to set up a countrywide system for identifying and apprehending criminal fugitives?
8. What does the assize tell us about the workings of Henry's police and judicial system in 1166?

Here begins the Assize of Clarendon, made by king Henry II, with the approval of the archbishops,* bishops,* abbots,* counts and barons of all England.

1. In the first place the aforesaid king Henry, by the counsel of all his barons, for the preservation of peace and the maintenance of justice, has decreed that an inquest shall be made for each county,[1] and for each hundred[2] by twelve of the more lawful men of the hundred, and by four of the more lawful men of each vill,[3] upon oath that they will speak the truth: whether in their hundred or in their vill there is any man who, since the lord king has been king, has been charged or

publicly exposed as being a robber or murderer or thief; or any one who is a concealer of robbers or murderers or thieves. And let the justices[4] inquire into this before them, and the sheriffs before them.

2. And he who is found through the oath of the aforesaid to have been charged or publicly exposed as being a robber or murderer or thief, or a concealer of them, since the lord king has been king, shall be seized and go to the ordeal of water,[5] and shall swear that, to the value of five shillings,[6] so far as he knows, he was not a robber or murderer or thief or concealer of them since the lord king has been king.

---

[1] The traditional Anglo-Saxon *shire,* which the Normans retained but renamed *county.* It was an administrative-judicial division of the realm under the supervision of a sheriff, or *shire reeve.*

[2] A division of a county, or shire. See Chapter 2, source 7, note 1, and Chapter 5, source 26, note 18, for its ancient Germanic origins.

[3] An agricultural community.

[4] Royal itinerant judges.

[5] See Chapter 2, source 7, note 9, and Chapter 7, source 42, note 18.

[6] A weight of silver. Twenty shillings constituted a pound sterling. See Chapter 8, source 49, note 14.

3. And if the lord of the man who was seized, or his steward or his men, seek him by pledge[7] within three days after he has been seized, he and his chattels shall be held back under pledge until he has made his law.[8]

4. And when a robber or murderer or thief, or concealers of them, has been seized through the aforesaid oath, if the justices have not come sufficiently quickly into that county where they have been taken, the sheriffs shall send word to the nearest justice through some knowledgeable man, that they have seized such men; and the justices shall send back word to the sheriffs where they wish those men to be conducted before them: and the sheriffs shall bring them before the justices. And with them they shall bring, from the hundred and vill where they were seized, two lawful men to bring the record for the county and hundred as to why they were seized; and there they will make their law before the justice.

5. And in the case of those who were seized through the aforesaid oath of this assize, no one shall have court or justice or chattels save the lord king in his court before his justices;[9] and the lord king shall have all their chattels.[10] But in the case of those who shall be seized in another way than by this oath, it shall be as is customary and ought to be.

6. And the sheriffs who seized them shall lead them before the justice without any other summons than they have then. And when the robbers or murderers or thieves, or concealers of them, who shall be seized through the oath or otherwise, are delivered to the sheriffs, they shall receive them immediately without delay.

7. And in those counties where there are no jails, let them be made in a borough or in some castle of the king with the king's money and from his woods if they are near, or from some nearby woods, in view of the king's servants; to the end that in them the sheriffs may have guarded those who have been seized, by the ministers and their servants who are used to doing this.

8. The lord king wills also that all shall come to the county courts to take this oath; so that no one shall stay away on account of any liberty[11] that he has, or court or soke[12] that he may have, but that they shall come to take this oath.

9. And let there be no one inside or outside his castle, nor even in the honor of Wallingford,[13] who shall forbid the sheriffs to enter into his court or his land to take the view of frankpledge;[14] and let all be under sureties: and let them be sent before the sheriffs under frankpledge.

10. And in the cities or boroughs no one may have men, or receive in his home or on his land or in his soke, those whom he will not take in hand to present before the justice if they be wanted, or are in frankpledge.

11. And no one may be in a city or borough or castle, or outside it, nor also in the honor of Wallingford, who shall forbid the sheriffs to enter into his land or soke to seize those who have been charged or publicly exposed as being robbers or murderers or thieves, or concealers of the same, or outlaws or charged with regard to the forest;[15] the king commands that they shall help the sheriffs seize them.

12. And if anyone shall be seized possessed of robbed or stolen goods, if he has been defamed

---

[7]Posted bond for him.

[8]He will be free under bond until he has undergone trial by ordeal (made his law).

[9]The king's judges alone shall try them and confiscate their goods.

[10]If they are found guilty or are exiled (see article 14).

[11]Special exemption or privilege.

[12]A holdover from Anglo-Saxon times, it was the right of local jurisdiction often granted by royal charter. Within the Anglo-Norman feudal system, it was normally one of a feudal lord's rights.

[13]An important fief,* or honor, that recently had been forfeited to the crown. Here, it serves as an example of the fact that even royal lands are not exempt from the assize.

[14]A police and bail system established by the Normans, whereby men of the lower classes were organized into groups of ten persons and took oaths to be mutually responsible for one another. If one of the ten was accused of a crime, the other nine were obligated to produce him or make good on the damage. Sheriffs were required to visit each village and borough twice a year to make sure that everyone who owed this obligation was duly sworn. Clerics,* nobles, knights, free landholders, merchants, and other such people were exempt from frankpledge.

[15]Persons who violated the king's forest rights. No one could hunt in the king's forests without special permission.

and has a bad reputation from the public, and has no warranty,[16] he will not have law.[17] And if he is not notorious, on account of the stolen things he has, he shall go to the ordeal by water.

13. And if anyone shall confess before lawful men, or in the hundred court, to robbery or murder or theft, or the concealing of those committing them, a ! afterwards wants to deny it, he shall not have law.

14. Moreover, the lord king wills also that those who shall be tried and absolved by the law, if they are of very bad repute and are publicly and disgracefully defamed by the testimony of many and lawful men, shall abjure the lands of the king, so that within eight days they shall cross the sea unless the wind detains them; and, with the first wind that they have afterwards, they shall cross the sea; and they shall not return any more to England unless by the mercy of the lord king: both there and if they return, they shall be outlawed; and if they return they shall be seized as outlaws.

15. And the lord king forbids that any waif, that is, a vagrant or unknown person, shall be sheltered any where except in a borough, and there he shall not be sheltered more than a night, unless he become ill there, or his horse, so that he can show an obvious excuse.

16. And if he is there more than one night, he shall be seized and held until his lord shall come to give surety for him, or until he himself shall procure good sureties; and likewise he shall be seized who sheltered him.

17. And if any sheriff shall send word to another sheriff that men have fled his county into another county on account of robbery or murder or theft, or the concealing of them, or for outlawry, or for an accusation with regard to the king's forest, he shall seize them: and also if he knows it of himself or through others that such men have fled into his county, let him seize them

and hold them in custody until he has good sureties from them.

18. And all sheriffs shall cause a record to be kept of all fugitives who fled their counties; and they shall do this in the presence of the county courts; and they shall carry the names written to the justices when first they come to them, so that they may be sought for throughout England, and their chattels may be taken for the use of the king.

19. And the lord king wills that when the sheriffs receive the summons of the itinerant justices to appear before them with the men of their counties, they shall assemble them and inquire for all who have newly come into their counties since this assize; and they shall release them under surety that they come before the justices, or they shall hold them in custody until the justices come to them, and then they shall bring them before the justices.

20. Moreover, the lord king forbids monks* or canons* or any religious house to receive anyone of the lower class as monk or canon or brother, until they know of what reputation he is, unless he is sick unto death.

21. The lord king forbids, moreover, anyone in all England to receive in his land or his soke or home under him anyone of that sect of renegades who were excommunicated* and branded at Oxford.[18] And if anyone receives them, he himself shall be at the mercy of the lord king; and the house in which they have been shall be carried outside the vill and burned. And each sheriff shall swear that he will observe this, and shall make all his ministers swear this, and the stewards of the barons, and all the knights and freeholders of the counties.

22. And the lord king wills that this assize shall be kept in his kingdom as long as it shall please him.

---

[16]A bond, or surety, as in frankpledge.

[17]See note 8 for the meaning of *law*. The person is to be punished immediately, without any trial.

[18]Cathar *heretics,* who believed in two divine forces: one, a god of goodness and spirit; the other, a god of darkness and physical matter.

The Ideal King?

▼▼▼

64 ▼ Jean de Joinville,
THE BOOK OF THE HOLY WORDS AND
GOOD DEEDS OF OUR KING, SAINT LOUIS

Henry II ruled over a realm that was far more centralized and better governed than the France of King Louis VII (r. 1137–1180). Moreover, Henry, as feudal[*] lord of the western half of the kingdom of France, controlled a vast collection of duchies and counties that collectively dwarfed the modest amount of territory around Paris that King Louis directly held. A century later, however, the king of France was master of most of his realm and one of the most powerful monarchs in Western Europe. By 1300 the roots of later French royal absolutism had been set.

Much of this dramatic turnabout came as a result of the policies of two monarchs: Philip II (r. 1180–1223), who pursued an opportunistic agenda that enabled him to enlarge the royal domain enormously, largely at the expense of King John of England (r. 1199–1216); and Philip's grandson, Louis IX (r. 1226–1270), who managed to combine a pious determination to rule justly and well with a firmness of character that made it possible for him to achieve many of his domestic objectives. Although he promoted and led two costly and disastrous crusades against Muslim powers in North Africa, Louis IX managed to retain a high level of popularity throughout his kingdom. Indeed, he was very likely the most beloved of all medieval French monarchs, and the affection he earned bore rich dividends for his royal successors. A measure of the love and respect accorded Louis IX is evident in the fact that the Roman Church declared him a saint in 1297.

Jean de Joinville (ca. 1224–1317) was one of the king's greatest admirers and, in turn, one of the kingdom's most respected feudal lords. Jean, who served as the *seneschal,* or senior administrator, of the count of Champagne, accompanied Louis on the king's first crusade, a six-year campaign that resulted in the capture and imprisonment of the king and his army in Egypt in 1250. In the course of their shared crusade, the two men became close friends, and Joinville was accorded the honor of being invested as a royal vassal.[*] They remained friends for the rest of Louis's life, even though Joinville refused to accompany the king on his second crusade in 1270, arguing that his duty lay in protecting the people of Champagne, not in campaigning overseas. Louis died on that crusade, and Joinville lived on to serve several other monarchs.

Joinville's was one of the strongest voices in promoting Louis's canonization as a saint, and following that successful campaign, he turned to recording his memories of St. Louis at the request of Queen Jeanne of Navarre, wife of King Philip IV (r. 1285–1314). Between 1305 and 1309 Joinville dictated his remembrances and dedicated the resulting work to the future King Louis X (r. 1314–1316), Louis IX's great-grandson.

Joinville began his biography of St. Louis by recounting examples of the king's chief virtues. The initial excerpt comes from that material. The second excerpt deals with the Great Ordinance of December 1254, which Louis published less than six months after his return from crusading in the East.

QUESTIONS FOR ANALYSIS

1. How did Joinville think he should depict St. Louis's piety, and what does his picture suggest about the religious values of his society?
2. Modern students of politics often equate *piety* in a secular* leader with *weakness*. Was Louis a weak king? On what do you base your judgment?
3. Against what specific abuses did Louis aim the Great Ordinance of 1254?
4. Compare the manner in which Louis dispensed justice in the first excerpt with the Great Ordinance of 1254. What do these two views of the king's justice tell us about the man and his age?
5. Based on what Joinville tells us about Louis, what do you think thirteenth-century society expected of its monarchs?
6. Louis IX has been characterized as the monarch who took the first steps toward what would become, centuries later, the formidable edifice of French royal absolutism. Does this source contain any evidence to support that judgment? Explain your answer.
7. How did King Louis see his duty toward God, Christianity, the Church, and his people?
8. This biography is the reminiscences of an old man, who is looking back on events that took place more than a half century earlier. Does this fact appear to compromise at all the value of this source? If so, to what degree? On what evidence do you base your judgment?

The Devotions of St. Louis — How He Did Justice in His Land

The rule of his land was so arranged that every day he heard the hours sung,[1] and a *Requiem* mass[2] without song; and then, if it was convenient, the mass of the day, or of the saint,[3] with song. Every day he rested in his bed after having eaten, and when he had slept and rested, he said, privately in his chamber — he and one of his chaplains together — the office for the dead;[4] and after he heard vespers.[5] At night he heard compline.[6]

A gray-friar[7] came to him at the castle of Hyères, there where we disembarked;[8] and said in his sermon, for the king's instruction, that he had read the Bible, and the books pertaining to heathen princes, and that he had never found, either among believers or misbelievers, that a kingdom had been lost, or had changed lords,

---

[1] The seven canonical hours.*
[2] The mass* for the dead.
[3] Each daily mass has a special theme or is dedicated to the memory of a particular saint or holy event.
[4] Special prayers for the dead.
[5] The sixth canonical hour; it marks the end of the workday.

[6] The seventh and last canonical hour; it marks the end of the day.
[7] A Franciscan. The friar* was Hugh of Barjols, a renowned preacher.
[8] On July 3, 1254, the day he reached French territory following his six-year crusade.

save there had first been failure of justice. "Therefore let the king, who is going into France, take good heed," said he, "that he do justice well and speedily among his people, so that our Lord allow his kingdom to remain in peace all the days of his life." . . .

The king forgot not the teaching of the friar, but ruled his land very loyally and piously, as you shall hear. . . .

Ofttimes it happened that he would go, after his mass, and seat himself in the wood of Vincennes,[9] and lean against an oak, and make us sit round him. And all those who had any case in hand came and spoke to him, without hindrance of usher, or of any other person. Then would he ask, out of his own mouth, "Is there any one who has a case in hand?" And those who had a case in hand stood up. Then would he say, "Keep silence all, and you shall be heard in turn, one after the other." Then he would call my Lord Peter of Fontaines and my Lord Geoffry of Villette, and say to one of them, "Settle me this case."

And when he saw that there was anything to amend in the words of those who spoke on his behalf, or in the words of those who spoke on behalf of any other person, he would himself, out of his own mouth, amend what they had said. Sometimes have I seen him, in summer, go to do justice among his people in the garden of Paris. . . . And he would cause a carpet to be laid down, so that we might sit round him, and all the people who had any case to bring before him stood around. And then would he have their cases settled, as I have told you afore he was wont to do in the wood of Vincennes.

St. Louis Refuses an Unjust Demand Made by the Bishops

I saw him, yet another time, in Paris, when all the prelates* of France had asked to speak with him, and the king went to the palace to give them audience. And there was present Guy of Auxerre, the son of my Lord William of Mello, and he spoke to the king on behalf of all the prelates, after this manner: "Sire, the lords who are here present, archbishops* and bishops,* have directed me to tell you that Christendom, which ought to be guarded and preserved by you, is perishing in your hands." The king crossed himself when he heard that word, and he said, "Tell me how that may be."

"Sire," said Guy of Auxerre, "it is because excommunications* are at the present day so lightly thought of that people suffer themselves to die before seeking absolution, and will not give satisfaction to the Church. These lords require you therefore, for the sake of God, and because it is your duty, to command your provosts and bailiffs[10] to seek out all such as suffer themselves to remain excommunicated for a year and day, and constrain them, by seizure of their goods, to have themselves absolved."

And the king replied that he would issue such commands willingly whensoever it could be shown to him that the excommunicated persons were in the wrong. The bishops said they would accept this condition at no price whatever, as they contested his jurisdiction in their cases. Then the king told them he would do no other; for it would be against God and reason if he constrained people to seek absolution when the clergy* were doing them wrong. "And of this," said the king, "I will give you an example, namely that of the count of Brittany, who, for seven years long, being excommunicated, pleaded against the prelates of Brittany, and carried his case so far that the Apostle condemned them all.[11] Wherefore, if I had constrained the count of Brittany, at the end of the first year, to get himself absolved, I should have sinned against God and against him." Then the prelates resigned themselves; nor did I ever hear tell that any further steps were taken in the aforesaid matters.

---

[9]A community just east of Paris.

[10]*Prévôts* and *baillis,* who served as royal financial, administrative, and judicial agents.

[11]The Apostle* is the pope. The count appealed to the papal* court and there won his case against the prelates of Brittany.

The Uprightness of St. Louis

The peace that he made with the king of England[12] was made against the advice of his council, for the council said to him: "Sire, it seems to us that you are giving away the land that you make over to the king of England; for he has no right thereto, seeing that his father lost it justly." To this the king replied that he knew well that the king of England had no right to the land, but that there was a reason why he should give it him, "for," said he, "we have two sisters to wife, and our children are cousins;[13] wherefore it is fitting that there should be peace between us. Moreover a very great honor accrues to me through the peace that I have made with the king of England, seeing that he is now my vassal, which he was not before."[14]

▼ ▼ ▼

How the King Reformed His Bailiffs, Provosts, and Mayors — and How He Instituted New Ordinances

After King Louis had returned to France from overseas, he bore himself very devoutly towards our Savior, and very justly towards his subjects; wherefore he considered and thought it would be a fair thing, and a good, to reform the realm of France. First he established a general ordinance for all his subjects throughout the realm of France, in the manner following: —

"We, Louis, by the grace of God, king of France, ordain that Our bailiffs, viscounts, provosts, mayors,[15] and all others, in whatever mat-

ter it may be, and whatever office they may hold, shall make oath that, so long as they hold the said office, or perform the functions of bailiffs, they shall do justice to all, without exception of persons, as well to the poor as to the rich, and to strangers as to those who are native-born; and that they shall observe such uses and customs as are good and have been approved.

"And if it happens that the bailiffs or viscounts, or others, as the sergeants or foresters,[16] do anything contrary to their oaths, and are convicted thereof, we order that they be punished in their goods, or in their persons, if the misfeasance so require; and the bailiffs shall be punished by Ourselves, and others by the bailiffs.

"Henceforward the other provosts, the bailiffs and the sergeants shall make oath to loyally keep and uphold Our rents and Our rights, and not to suffer Our rights to lapse or to be suppressed or diminished; and with this they shall swear not to take or receive, by themselves or through others, gold, nor silver, nor any indirect benefit, nor any other thing, save fruit or bread, or wine, or other present, to the value of ten sous,[17] the said sum not being exceeded.

"And besides this, they shall make oath not to take, or cause to be taken, any gift, of whatever kind, through their wives, or their children, or their brothers, or their sisters, or any other persons connected with them; and so soon as they have knowledge that any such gifts have been received, they will cause them to be returned as soon as may be possible. And, besides this, they shall make oath not to receive any gift, of what-

---

[12]In 1258–1259, Louis and Henry III of England negotiated the Treaty of Paris, whereby Henry renounced all claims to Normandy, Anjou, Maine, Touraine, and Poitou — French fiefs* that King Philip II had wrested from King John of England, Henry's father, in return for a large sum of money and clear possession of the duchy of Gascony as a feudal fief held directly from the king of France.

[13]Margaret, Louis's wife, and Eleanor, the wife of Henry III, were sisters.

[14]Louis IX now had some control over Henry III's actions in France, insofar as Henry was the enfeoffed duke of Gascony. Consequently, the king of France could once again hear appeals from the ducal court of Gascony.

[15]See note 10 for provosts and bailiffs. Viscounts were minor royal agents in northern France, and mayors were the elected heads of urban communities that had been granted by royal charter a measure of self-government.

[16]Lesser officials. Foresters were charged with maintaining the northern royal forests. Sergeants were armed agents, mounted and dismounted, and functioned throughout the realm.

[17]Twenty sous equaled one livre, or pound; the royal livre of France was 367.1 grams of silver.

ever kind, from any man belonging to their bailiwicks,[18] nor from any others who have a suit or may plead before them.

"Henceforth they shall make oath not to bestow any gift upon any men who are of Our council, nor upon their wives or children, or any person belonging to them; nor upon those who shall receive the said officers' accounts on Our behalf, nor to any persons whom we may send to their bailiwicks, or to their provostships, to inquire into their doings. And with this they shall swear to take no profit out of any sale that may be made of Our rents, Our bailiwicks, Our coinage, or anything else to Us belonging.

"And they shall swear and promise, that if they have knowledge of any official, sergeant, or provost, serving under them, who is unfaithful, given to robbery and usury,[19] or addicted to other vices whereby he ought to vacate Our service, then they will not uphold him for any gift, or promise, or private affection, or any other cause, but punish and judge him in all good faith.

"Henceforward Our provosts, Our viscounts, Our mayors, Our foresters, and Our other sergeants, mounted and dismounted, shall make oath not to bestow any gift upon their superiors, nor upon their superiors' wives, nor children, nor upon any one belonging to them.

"And because We desire that these oaths be fairly established, We order that they be taken in full assize,[20] before all men, by clerks and laymen, knights and sergeants, notwithstanding that any such may have already made oath before Us; and this We ordain so that those who take the oaths may avoid the guilt and the sin of perjury, not only from the fear of God and of Ourselves, but also for shame before the world.

"We will and ordain that all Our provosts and bailiffs abstain from saying any word that would bring into contempt God, or our Lady, or the saints; and also that they abstain from the game of dice and keep away from taverns. We ordain that the making of dice be forbidden throughout Our realm, and that lewd women be turned out of every house; and whosoever shall rent a house to a lewd woman shall forfeit to the provost, or the bailiff, the rent of the said house for a year.

"Moreover, We forbid Our bailiffs to purchase wrongfully, or to cause to be purchased, either directly, or through others, any possession or lands that may be in their bailiwick, or in any other, so long as they remain in Our service, and without Our express permission; and if any such purchases are made, We ordain that the lands in question be, and remain, in Our hands.

"We forbid Our bailiffs, so long as they shall be in Our service, to marry any sons or daughters that they may have, or any other person belonging to them, to any other person in their bailiwick, without Our special sanction; and moreover We forbid that they put any such into a religious house in their bailiwick, or supply them with any benefice* of holy Church, or any other possession; and moreover We forbid that they obtain provisions or lodgings from any religious house, or near by, at the expense of the religous persons. This prohibition as concerns marriages and the acquisition of goods, as stated above, does not apply to provosts, or mayors, nor to others holding minor offices.

"We order that no bailiff, provost, or any other, shall keep too many sergeants or beadles,[21] to the burdening of our people; and We ordain that the beadles be appointed in full assize, or else be not regarded as beadles. When sergeants are sent to a distant place, or to a strange county, We ordain that they be not received without letters from their superiors.

"We order that no bailiff or provost in Our service shall burden the good people in his jurisdiction beyond what is lawful and right; and that

---

[18]The region administered by a bailiff.
[19]Lending out money at interest.
[20]Full council. Here, *assize* refers to the meeting, or court, at which these oaths are taken.

[21]The word means "subordinates." Like the sergeants, they were minor officials.

none of Our subjects be put in prison for any debt save in so far as such debt may be due to Ourselves only.

"We ordain that no bailiff levy a fine for a debt due by any of Our subjects, or for any offence, save in full and open court, where the amount of such fine may be adjudged and estimated, with the advice of worthy and competent persons, even when the fine has already been considered by them (informally? passage obscure). And if it happens that the accused will not wait for the judgment of Our court, which is offered him, but offers for the fine a certain sum of money, such as has been commonly received aforetime, we ordain that the court accept such sum of money if it be reasonable and convenient; and, if not, we ordain that the fine be adjudicated upon, as aforesaid, even though the delinquent place himself in the hands of the court. We forbid that the bailiffs, or the mayors, or the provosts, should compel Our subjects, either by threats or intimidation, or any chicanery, to pay a fine in secret or in public, or accuse any save for reasonable cause.

"And We ordain that those who hold the office of provost, viscount, or any other office, do not sell such office to others without Our consent; and if several persons buy jointly any of the said offices, We order that one of the purchasers shall perform the duties of the office for all the rest, and alone enjoy such of its privileges in respect of journeyings,[22] taxes,[23] and common charges, as have been customary aforetime.

"And We forbid that they sell the said offices to their brothers, nephews, or cousins, after they have bought them from Us; and that they claim any debts that may be due to themselves, save such debts as appertain to their office. As regards their own personal debts, they will recover them by authority of the bailiff, just as if they were not in Our service.

"We forbid Our bailiffs and provosts to weary our subjects, in the causes brought before them, by moving the venue from place to place. They shall hear the matters brought before them in the place where they have been wont to hear them, so that Our subjects may not be induced to forego their just rights for fear of trouble and expense.

"From henceforth we command that Our provosts and bailiffs dispossess no man from the property which he holds, without full inquiry, or Our own special order; and that they impose upon Our people no new exactions, taxes and imposts; and that they compel no one to come forth to do service in arms, for the purpose of exacting money from him; for We order that none who owes Us service in arms shall be summoned to join the host without sufficient cause, and that those who would desire to come to the host in person should not be compelled to purchase exemption by money payment.

"Moreover, we forbid Our bailiffs and provosts to prevent grain, wine, and other merchandise from being taken out of Our kingdom, save for sufficient cause; and when it is convenient that these goods should not be taken out of the kingdom, the ordinance shall be made publicly, in the council of worthy and competent elders, and without suspicion of fraud or misdoing.

"Similarly We ordain that all bailiffs, viscounts, provosts, and mayors do remain, after they have left office, for the space of forty days in the land where such office has been exercised — remaining there in person, or by deputy — so that they may answer to the new bailiffs in respect of any wrong done to such as may wish to bring a complaint against them."

By these ordinances the king did much to improve the condition of the kingdom.

---

[22]The privilege of being housed, fed, and entertained at the expense of his hosts while traveling on official business.

[23]The right to collect royal revenues in a particular region was often farmed out for a substantial fee to a provost. The provost's profit (or loss) was the difference between what he collected and what he had paid the royal treasury for this right.

▼▼▼

Monarchs and Popes in Conflict

Between 1050 and 1300 monarchs and popes engaged in a series of power struggles that had profound repercussions on the course of Western civilization.

As early as the late fifth century, Pope Gelasius I had defined the two separate spheres of authority enjoyed by priests* and kings (Chapter 4, source 19), but his carefully crafted distinction had no immediately perceptible impact on political thought in either the East or the West. The emperors at Constantinople continued to govern their empire as an indivisible whole, perceiving no meaningful distinction between their power over secular* officials and their authority over priests (Chapter 2, source 10, and Chapter 3, source 11). Charlemagne and his imperial and royal successors in the West saw themselves in much the same light and acted accordingly (Chapter 5, sources 25 and 26; Chapter 6, source 34). On their part, a number of influential popes and other church leaders (but certainly not all) roundly declared the spiritual independence and even primacy of the priestly sphere (Chapter 4, sources 20 and 21; Chapter 5, source 27).

The claims of Western churchpeople to independence and at least a moral superiority over secular rulers were vitiated by the fact that the Church of the West was intimately involved with every aspect of secular government. Church leaders, such as Bishop Burchard of Worms (Chapter 8, source 44), were powerful lords, whose ecclesiastical* offices brought with them wide-ranging military and political responsibilities and great wealth.

In the last quarter of the eleventh century, these inherent tensions and contradictions sparked a half-century-long struggle between the empire and the papacy* known as the *Investiture Controversy.* The combatants eventually resolved some of their differences in 1122, but the core tensions remained unresolved.

During the twelfth and thirteenth centuries, the papacy reached the height of its moral authority and simultaneously constructed mechanisms of government that transformed the Roman Church into one of the most organized and powerful entities in Europe. Approximately at the same time, a number of monarchic states in the West were building up their own governmental systems that enabled monarchs such as Henry II of England, Louis IX of France, and the early Hohenstaufen emperors to govern their lands more completely than ever before. The result was a continuing cycle of church-state controversies.

The fact that neither popes nor monarchs were ever able to overwhelm the other proved ultimately fruitful, so far as Western political culture was concerned. Slowly, ever so slowly, some observers began to articulate the political theory that there are two powers, church and state, each with its separate sphere of activity. Just as monarchs were not priests, so priests could not legitimately interfere in the governance of secular states.

A Half Century That Shook the West

▼▼▼

65 ▼ *FOUR DOCUMENTS FROM THE INVESTITURE CONTROVERSY*

The Investiture Controversy was a struggle between the papacy and the Western empire that raged from 1075 to 1122 and ostensibly centered on the issue of lay lords investing high-ranking churchpeople with their offices and the symbols of their spiritual powers. In fact, however, the issues were far more complex than that.

The immediate background to the Investiture Controversy lay in successful attempts to free the Roman papacy from the control of local Roman factions and to reform the moral life of the Roman clergy,* especially of the man who held the keys of St. Peter. Emperor Henry III (r. 1039–1056) played a major role in this reformation from 1046 until his death in 1056. During that decade, he appointed four successive reform-minded popes from the ranks of the German clergy. His death at a youthful age and the succession of a child as king of Germany created a power vacuum that allowed more radical clerical* reformers to take increasing control of the papacy. The radicals, led by Cardinal Humbert of Silva Candida and Hildebrand, archdeacon of the Roman Church, blamed lay control of the Church and its priests for what they perceived to be the moral degeneracy of Christendom. Their argument was simple: The laity, by virtue of its immersion in the corruption of this world, corrupted clerics whenever and wherever it controlled them, even when the laypeople were pious emperors. The situation was ripe for confrontation when the young Henry IV (r. 1056–1106) came of age and endeavored to assert traditional imperial rights over the Church, and the situation reached a point of crisis when Archdeacon Hildebrand assumed the papal* throne as Gregory VII (r. 1073–1085).

The first document, known as the *Dictatus Papae* (The Pope's Proclamation), appeared in the official collection of Pope Gregory's correspondence for March 1075 under the title "What Is the Power of the Roman Pontiffs?*" It is clearly not a letter. The best-informed opinion is that, in the normal course of events, each of the twenty-seven assertions in this list would have been supported by citations from the Bible and other authoritative sources. It was, in other words, the outline of a church lawyer's uncompleted brief or, more correctly, a proposed collection of canons* that was never published. As sketchy as it is, the document provides good insight into the program and mindset of the papal party as the situation was beginning to heat up but before the controversy became full blown.

The second document is a letter of January 24, 1076, that Henry IV sent to Pope Gregory, in response to the pope's letter of December 1075, in which Gregory had warned Henry to fall in line and obey papal mandates regarding papal attempts to reform the Church, or else be ready to suffer the consequences. Henry's reply, which was drafted at a synod* of imperial church leaders that Henry had convened at Worms, was the opening salvo in what became a half-century war of words and swords.

The third document is Gregory's first excommunication* and deposition of King Henry in February 1076. In January 1077 Henry performed penance before the pope at Canossa in northern Italy and was readmitted into the Church, but soon thereafter, he fell to quarrelling with the pope again. In March 1080 Gregory declared Henry once again deposed.

Gregory's proclamations of deposition could not prevent Henry from capturing Rome in 1084 and installing his own antipope. Gregory escaped capture and went into exile, where he died, reportedly proclaiming, "I have loved Righteousness and hated iniquity, and, therefore, I die in exile." Surely, this is the confident cry of triumph of a self-professed martyr.

Despite Henry's apparent victory, the controversy dragged on between the papal reform party, which elected its own successor to Gregory VII, and the imperial party and its antipope. Finally, with both sides exhausted, Henry IV's son and successor, Henry V (r. 1106–1125), entered into a peace treaty with Pope Calixtus II (r. 1119–1124), which history knows as the *Concordat of Worms of 1122*. The concordat, which is the fourth and last document, settled the issue over which the two parties had struggled so bitterly for so long. Or did it?

QUESTIONS FOR ANALYSIS

1. What powers does Gregory claim over other clerics in the *Dictatus Papae?* What powers does he claim over princes?

2. Based on your answers to question 1, what do you conclude was Gregory's vision of the pope's place in Christendom?

3. Compose a commentary on the *Dictatus Papae* by any one of the following: Pope Gelasius I; Pope Gregory I; Charlemagne; Pope Leo III.

4. What charges does Henry IV bring against Pope Gregory VII, and what does Henry do about them?

5. The *Dictatus Papae* and King Henry's letter of January 1076 reveal two views of how the earthly Church functions. What are those views, and how, if at all, do they differ?

6. Consider the tone and arguments of Henry's letter to Gregory. Why is it reasonable to infer that churchmen loyal to Henry composed it? Why would many high-ranking prelates* agree with the message of this letter?

7. Consider the tone of Gregory's letter that excommunicates and deposes Henry and its implied world view. What insight does that letter give you into the mind and personality of Pope Gregory?

8. Consider Gregory's letter in the light of the Peace and Truce of God (Chapter 6, source 32). Do these documents share any common elements or spirit? If so, what do you conclude?

9. What issues did the Concordat of Worms settle? Were there any important issues that it did not address? If so, what? All things considered, how successfully did the concordat resolve the basic issues of the Investiture Controversy?

DICTATUS PAPAE

1. That the Roman church was established by God alone.
2. That the Roman pontiff* alone is rightly called universal.[1]
3. That he alone has the power to depose and reinstate bishops.*
4. That his legate,[2] even if he be of lower ecclesiastical* rank, presides over bishops in council,* and has the power to give sentence of deposition against them.
5. That the pope has the power to depose those who are absent.[3]
6. That, among other things, we ought not to remain in the same house with those whom he has excommunicated.
7. That he alone has the right, according to the necessity of the occasion, to make new laws, to create new bishoprics. . . .
8. That he alone may use the imperial insignia.[4]
9. That all princes shall kiss the foot of the pope alone.
10. That his name alone is to be recited in the churches.
11. That the name applied to him belongs to him alone.[5]
12. That he has the power to depose emperors.
13. That he has the right to transfer bishops from one see* to another when it becomes necessary.
14. That he has the right to ordain as a cleric anyone from any part of the church whatsoever.
15. That anyone ordained by him may rule [as bishop] over another church. . . .

16. That no general synod may be called without his order.[6]
17. That no action of a synod and no book shall be regarded as canonical[7] without his authority.
18. That his decree can be annulled by no one, and that he can annul the decrees of anyone.
19. That he can be judged by no one.
20. That no one shall dare to condemn a person who has appealed to the Apostolic See.*
21. That the important cases of any church whatsoever shall be referred to the Roman Church.
22. That the Roman Church has never erred and will never err to all eternity, according to the testimony of the holy scriptures.
23. That the Roman pontiff who has been canonically ordained[8] is made holy by the merits of St. Peter. . . .
24. That by his command or permission subjects may accuse their rulers.
25. That he can depose and reinstate bishops without the calling of a synod.
26. That no one can be regarded as catholic who does not agree with the Roman Church.
27. That he has the power to absolve subjects from their oath of fidelity to wicked rulers.

▼ ▼ ▼

THE LETTER OF HENRY IV TO GREGORY VII, JANUARY 24, 1076

Henry, king not by usurpation, but by the holy ordination of God, to Hildebrand, not pope, but false monk.*

---

[1] The pope alone has universal authority over all churches.
[2] A papal representative who possesses delegated papal power.
[3] From a council. And the pope can do so without giving them a hearing.
[4] A claim based on the eighth-century forgery known as *The Donation of Constantine.* See the introduction to source 35, Chapter 6. According to the forged donation, Constantine ceded to Pope Sylvester I the prerogative of wearing all imperial insignia, as well as giving him dominion over Rome, Italy, and all the western regions.

[5] He alone may bear the title *pope.*
[6] In a moment of strength following the Concordat of Worms, the papacy would call its own *ecumenical council,** the First Lateran Council in 1123. See the introduction to source 42 of Chapter 7.
[7] Legal.
[8] Legally elected and consecrated.

This is the salutation which you deserve, for you have never held any office in the Church without making it a source of confusion and a curse to Christian men instead of an honor and a blessing. To mention only the most obvious cases out of many, you have not only dared to touch the Lord's anointed, the archbishops,* bishops, and priests; but you have scorned them and abused them, as if they were ignorant servants not fit to know what their master was doing. This you have done to gain favor with the vulgar crowd. You have declared that the bishops know nothing and that you know everything; but if you have such great wisdom you have used it not to build but to destroy. Therefore we believe that St. Gregory, whose name you have presumed to take, had you in mind when he said: "The heart of the prelate is puffed up by the abundance of subjects, and he thinks himself more powerful than all others."[9] All this we have endured because of our respect for the papal office, but you have mistaken our humility for fear, and have dared to make an attack upon the royal and imperial authority[10] which we received from God. You have even threatened to take it away, as if we had received it from you, and as if the empire and kingdom were in your disposal and not in the disposal of God. Our Lord Jesus Christ has called us to the government of the empire, but he never called you to the rule of the Church. This is the way you have gained advancement in the Church: through craft you have obtained wealth; through wealth you have obtained favor; through favor, the power of the sword; and through the power of the sword, the papal seat, which is the seat of peace;[11] and then from the seat of peace you have expelled peace. For you have incited subjects to rebel against their prelates by teaching them to despise the bishops, their rightful rulers. You have given to laymen the authority over priests, whereby they condemn and depose those whom the bishops have put over them to teach them.[12] You have attacked me, who, unworthy as I am, have yet been anointed to rule among the anointed of God, and who, according to the teaching of the fathers,* can be judged by no one save God alone, and can be deposed for no crime except infidelity. For the holy fathers in the time of the apostate Julian did not presume to pronounce sentence of deposition against him, but left him to be judged and condemned by God.[13] St. Peter himself said: "Fear God, honor the king" [1 Pet. 2:17]. But you, who fear not God, have dishonored me, whom He has established. St. Paul, who said that even an angel from heaven should be accursed who taught any other than the true doctrine, did not make an exception in your favor, to permit you to teach false doctrines. For he says: "But though we, or an angel from heaven, preach any other gospel* unto you than that which we have preached unto you, let him be accursed" [Gal. 1:8]. Come down, then, from that apostolic* seat which you have obtained by violence; for you have been declared accursed by St. Paul for your false doctrines and have been condemned by us and our bishops for your evil rule. Let another ascend the throne of St. Peter, one who will not use religion as a cloak of violence, but will teach the life-giving doctrine of that prince of the apostles. I, Henry, king by the grace of God, with all my bishops, say unto you: "Come down, come down, and be accursed through all the ages."

▼ ▼ ▼

---

[9]Pope St. Gregory the Great, *The Pastoral Rule.* See Chapter 4, source 20.

[10]Actually, Henry had not yet been crowned emperor by the pope. He was only king of Germany and emperor-elect.

[11]Henry claims that Gregory had usurped the papal throne. There had been an irregularity when Gregory was elected pope, insofar as the people of Rome enthusiastically acclaimed the popular Hildebrand as pope, even before the cardinals* had voted. The cardinals then elected him pope.

[12]A reference to the fact that Gregory and other radical reformers within the papal party had called upon Europe's laity to reject sinful bishops and priests, especially those guilty of simony* and lay investiture.

[13]A reference to Emperor Julian the Apostate (r. 361–363), who rejected Christianity and attempted to reinstate state worship of the ancient Greco-Roman deities.

GREGORY VII'S FIRST EXCOMMUNICATION AND DEPOSITION OF HENRY IV

St. Peter, prince of the apostles, incline your ear to me, I beseech you, and hear me, your servant, whom you have nourished from my infancy and have delivered from my enemies who hate me for my fidelity to you. You are my witness, as are also my mistress, the mother of God, and St. Paul your brother, and all the other saints, that your holy Roman church called me to its government against my own will, and that I did not gain your throne by violence; that I would rather have ended my days in exile than have obtained your place by fraud or for worldly ambition. It is not by my efforts, but by your grace, that I am set to rule over the Christian world which was specially entrusted to you by Christ. It is by your grace and as your representative that God has given to me the power to bind and to loose in heaven and in earth. Confident of my integrity and authority, I now declare in the name of omnipotent God, the Father, Son, and Holy Spirit,* that Henry, son of the emperor Henry, is deprived of his kingdom of Germany and Italy; I do this by your authority and in defense of the honor of your church, because he has rebelled against it. He who attempts to destroy the honor of the Church should be deprived of such honor as he may have held. He has refused to obey as a Christian should, he has not returned to God from whom he had wandered, he has had dealings with excommunicated persons, he has done many iniquities, he has despised the warnings which, as you are witness, I sent to him for his salvation, he has cut himself off from your Church, and has attempted to rend it asunder; therefore, by your authority, I place him under the curse. It is in your name that I curse him, that all people may know that you are Peter, and upon your rock the Son of the living God has built his Church, and the gates of hell shall not prevail against it.

---

[14]Pope Paschal II had crowned Henry V as emperor in 1111, during a time of momentary accord.
[15]Delegated royal powers.

▼ ▼ ▼

THE CONCORDAT OF WORMS

The Oath of Calixtus II

Calixtus, bishop, servant of the servants of God, to his beloved son, Henry, by the grace of God emperor of the Romans,[14] Augustus.

We hereby grant that in Germany the elections of the bishops and abbots* who hold directly from the crown shall be held in your presence, such elections to be conducted canonically* and without simony or other illegality. In the case of disputed elections you shall have the right to decide between the parties, after consulting with the archbishop of the province* and his fellow-bishops. You shall confer the regalia[15] of the office upon the bishop or abbot elect by the scepter,[16] and this shall be done freely without exacting any payment from him; the bishop or abbot elect on his part shall perform all the duties that go with the holding of the regalia.

In other parts of the empire the bishops shall receive the regalia from you in the same manner within six months of their consecration, and shall in like manner perform all the duties that go with them. The undoubted rights of the Roman Church, however, are not to be regarded as prejudiced by this concession. If at any time you shall have occasion to complain of the carrying out of these provisions, I will undertake to satisfy your grievances as far as shall be consistent with my office. Finally, I hereby make a true and lasting peace with you and with all of your followers, including those who supported you in the recent controversy.

The Oath of Henry V

In the name of the holy and undivided Trinity.*

For the love of God and his holy church and of Pope Calixtus, and for the salvation of my soul,

---

[16]The emperor (or king of Germany) could invest the new prelate with secular powers by touching him (or her, in the case of an imperial abbess*) with the imperial scepter.

I, Henry, by the grace of God, emperor of the Romans, Augustus, hereby surrender to God and his apostles, Sts. Peter and Paul, and to the holy Catholic Church, all investiture by ring and staff.[17] I agree that elections and consecrations shall be conducted canonically and shall be free from all interference. I surrender also the possessions and regalia of St. Peter which have been seized by me during this quarrel, or by my father in his lifetime, and which are now in my possession, and I promise to aid the Church to recover such as are held by any other persons. I restore also the possessions of all other churches and princes, clerical or secular, which have been taken away during the course of this quarrel, which I have, and promise to aid them to recover such as are held by any other persons.

Finally, I make true and lasting peace with Pope Calixtus and with the holy Roman Church and with all who are or have ever been of his party. I will aid the Roman Church whenever my help is asked, and will do justice in all matters in regard to which the Church may have occasion to make complaint.

---

[17]The symbols of a prelate's office.

A Papal Rejoinder to the Byzantine Emperor
▼▼▼
66 ▾ *Innocent III, SOLITAE*

Innocent III (r. 1198–1216) was arguably the most dynamic and powerful pope of the High Middle Ages. Only thirty-seven years of age when he ascended the papal* throne, Innocent brought to his office vigor, a sense of high purpose, and an exalted vision of the pope's place within Christendom. We have already seen Innocent the church reformer (Chapter 7, source 42); we now turn to Innocent the articulator of papal power.

During his more than eighteen years as pope, Innocent was embroiled in numerous struggles with secular* and ecclesiastical* lords and dispatched large numbers of letters that articulated his position on a variety of issues. Innocent and his secretaries composed many of those letters not only for the moment but with an eye toward the future, inasmuch as the pope endeavored to provide church lawyers and subsequent popes with a body of authoritative texts that, more fully than ever before, defined the place of the pope within Christendom. Papal letters that address important legal and constitutional points are known as *decretals,* and Innocent's decretals proved to be a treasure trove for canon* lawyers in his own day and well beyond. In 1209 or 1210 the pope sent a collection of his important decretals to the masters and students at the University of Bologna, Europe's premier center for legal studies, for use in the law courts and lecture halls. One of the decretals contained in the collection was *Solitae,* a letter he wrote in late 1200 to Emperor Alexius III of Constantinople. As is true of all papal letters, the decretal's title derives from its opening word, which means "usual."

In 1198 Alexius had initiated relations with the new pope in the hope of reaching a political alliance against a common enemy, Philip of Hohenstaufen, a claimant to the kingship of Germany and the Western imperial title. Innocent responded to this overture by insisting that the emperor first must submit the Byzantine Church to the authority of the Roman papacy* and promise to aid the upcoming crusade (Chapter 11, source 76) before any political alliance was possible. In early 1199 Alexius dispatched a second letter to Rome, in which he attempted to dismiss politely the pope's arguments and preconditions, while leaving the door open for an alliance. Innocent's second letter to the emperor, composed in late 1199, left no doubt that he was serious and would accept nothing less than the Byzantine Church's submission to his papal primacy and Alexius's crusade cooperation. In 1200 Alexius replied with a now lost third letter that apparently was franker in tone and message than his two earlier dispatches to Rome. *Solitae* was the pope's reply.

QUESTIONS FOR ANALYSIS

1. What arguments had Alexius made in his letter of 1200? What do those arguments suggest about relations between emperors and priests* in Byzantium?
2. According to Innocent III, what is the proper relationship between the papacy and temporal authority? On what assumptions does the pope base that view?
3. How does Innocent view the papacy in relation to the Byzantine Empire?
4. How does Innocent view the papacy in relation to the universal Church? What is the basis for that vision?
5. Based on this letter, how would you characterize papal-Byzantine relations at the opening of the thirteenth century?
6. Assume that you are a canon lawyer,* writing a commentary on this decretal. What are the decretal's salient points, and what conclusions would you reach from this text?

TO ALEXIUS, EMPEROR OF CONSTANTINOPLE

With Our usual affection for you, We have received the letter Your Imperial Excellency dispatched to Us through the person of Our beloved son, the archdeacon of Durazzo,[1] a prudent and faithful man. Through your letter we learned that the letter we had sent to you through the office of Our beloved son and chaplain, John, who was then serving as a legate of the Apostolic See,* had arrived in your empire and was read.

As you intimated to Us in your letter, however, Your Imperial Sublimity is astonished that We seem to have reproached you in some small way, although We remember that We wrote what We wrote not in a spirit of reproach but rather in the gentle spirit of bringing something to your attention. We have gathered from your letter that your reading of what Saint Peter, the prince of

[1]Modern Durrës, an Adriatic port city in what is today Albania. It was then in Venetian hands and served as an economic and cultural point of exchange between the eastern and western regions of the Mediterranean.

the apostles,* wrote, "For the sake of God, be subject to every human creature, as much as to the king, who is the preeminent authority, as to the lords, for they are sent by God to punish evildoers and to praise the doers of good,"[2] served not as the cause of your wonder but as a convenient opportunity. What caused Us even more reasonably to wonder is that His Imperial Highness wished, through these words and others that he introduced, to place the empire above the priestly dignity and power, and from the authoritative text quoted above he desired to draw out a triple argument. The first argument is based on the text "be subject." The second is based on what follows that: "to the king, who is the preeminent authority." The third is based on the words that are appended directly to that: "to punish evildoers and to praise the doers of good." Imagining through the first argument that the priesthood is a subordinate state, through the second that the empire has precedence, through the third that emperors have received jurisdiction over priests, as well as laypeople, and, indeed, the power of the sword over priests![3] Inasmuch as some priests are good men and some are evildoers, he who, according to the Apostle, bears the sword for the punishment of evildoers and for the praise of the doers of good, is able to punish with the sword of vengeance priests who dare to deviate into evildoing, because the Apostle does not distinguish between priests and everyone else.

Doubtless, had you paid more careful attention to the person speaking these words and the people to whom he was speaking and the meaning of the words, you would not have drawn such an interpretation from the text. For the Apostle is writing to his subordinates, and he has been urging on them the virtue of humility. It was in this context that he said "be subject," because he wanted to place on the priesthood the yoke of subservience and to confer the authority of guidance on those persons to whom he urged priests to be subject. It follows from this also that any slave whatsoever has received power over priests when he says, "to every human creature." Regarding what follows, however, "to the king, who is the preeminent authority," we do not deny that the emperor, to be sure, is preeminent in temporal matters. But the pontiff* has precedence in spiritual affairs, which are as superior to temporal concerns as the body is to the soul. Let it also be noted that the statement was not simply "be subject," but "for the sake of God" was added, nor is the text pure and simply "to the king, who is the preeminent authority," but rather the phrase "as much as" is introduced, perhaps not without reason. What follows, however, "to punish evildoers and to praise the doers of good," should not be understood as meaning that the king or emperor has received the power of the sword over all, the good and the evil, but only over those who, by using the sword, are given over to the jurisdiction of the sword, according to what the Truth[4] said: "All who take up the sword shall perish by the sword."[5] For no one can or should judge another person's servant, because, as the Apostle notes, a servant stands or falls with his lord.[6] On that point you also introduced the argument that although Moses and Aaron were brothers in the flesh, Moses was the prince of the people and Aaron had more priestly power,[7] and Joshua,[8] his[9] successor, received ruling authority over priests.[10] Also King David was superior to Abiathar, the chief priest.[11] Moreover, although Moses was prince of the people, he was

---

[2]The Bible, the First Epistle of Peter, 2:13.

[3]The power to try and punish clerics.* The Church claimed total jurisdiction over all clerics and other members of the Church, who, according to canon law,* were subject to ecclesiastical tribunals, not secular* courts.

[4]Jesus.

[5]The Gospel of Matthew, 26:52.

[6]St. Paul, Epistle to the Romans, 14:4.

[7]See the Book of Exodus, chapters 4 and 7, and the Book of Numbers, 16:40.

[8]Moses's assistant; he became the leader of the Israelites following Moses's death: Deuteronomy, 34:9.

[9]Presumably the reference is to Moses, but grammatically it would seem to refer to Aaron.

[10]See the Book of Joshua.

[11]The First Book of Samuel, 22:20–23.

also a priest, who anointed Aaron as priest,[12] and the Prophet recognized Moses's priesthood when he said: "Moses and Aaron were His priests."[13]

The higher authority entrusted to Joshua that you wrote about should be interpreted more in accordance with the spirit of the text rather than the letter, because, as the Apostle writes: "The letter kills, but the spirit gives life."[14] Joshua, who led his people into the Promised Land,[15] symbolized the person of the True Jesus.[16] Also, although David possessed the royal diadem, he governed the priest Abiathar not as a consequence of his royal dignity but on account of his authority as a prophet. Whatever was long ago true in the Old Testament now is otherwise in the New Testament, because Christ was made a Priest unto eternity according to the order of Melchizedek[17] and offered Himself as a sacrifice to God the Father not as a king but as a priest on the altar of the cross, through which He redeemed the human family.

In regard particularly to him who is the successor of Saint Peter and the vicar of Christ, you should have been able to perceive the nature of the special privilege of priesthood from what was said not by just anyone but by God, not to a king but to a priest who was not of royal lineage but from a family of priestly succession, namely, from the priests who lived in Anathoth: "Behold, I have placed you over peoples and kingdoms, so that you might uproot and scatter, build and plant."[18] It is also said in divine law: "Do not slander the god-like, and do not speak evil of the prince of your people."[19] These words place priests before kings, calling the former gods and the latter princes.

Moreover, you ought to know that God made two great lights in the firmament of heaven, a greater light and a lesser light — the greater light to preside over the day, the lesser light to preside over the night. Each is great, but one is greater, because the Church is signified by the word "heaven," according to what the Truth said: "The Kingdom of Heaven is like the human head of a household who gathered workers at the break of day in his vineyard."[20] The word "day" we understand to mean "spiritual," and "night" means "carnal," according to the testimony of the Prophet: "Day utters the word to day, and night proclaims knowledge to night."[21] God gave, therefore, to the firmament of heaven, that is the Universal Church, two great lights. That is, He instituted two dignities, which are pontifical authority and royal power. The one, however, that rules over days, that is over spiritual matters, is greater; the one that rules over nights, that is over carnal matters, is lesser. Thus it is recognized that the difference between the sun and the moon is as great as that between pontiffs and kings.

If His Imperial Highness carefully considers these matters, he would neither make nor permit Our venerable brother, the patriarch* of Constantinople, a truly great and honorable member of the Church, to sit on the left next to his footstool,[22] when other kings and princes rev-

---

[12]The Book of Exodus, 29:1–46.

[13]Psalms, 99:6.

[14]The Second Letter of St. Paul to the Corinthians, 3:6.

[15]The Book of Joshua, 3:1–17.

[16]*Jesus* (*Iesous*) is the Greek form of the Hebrew name *Joshua* (*Jehoshua* or *Jeshua*), which means "God is salvation." Because of his name and pivotal role in Hebrew salvation history, Joshua, the ancient leader of the Israelites (note 8), served as a foreshadowing of Jesus Christ, as far as medieval Christian biblical commentators were concerned. Throughout this letter, Innocent uses the Latin *Iesus* to refer to both Joshua and Jesus Christ.

[17]The Epistle to the Hebrews, 5:6, putatively composed by St. Paul but probably not his work. Melchizedek was the priest-king of ancient Salem (Jerusalem?), who presented Abraham, father of the Hebrews, with an offering of bread and wine and blessed him: The Book of Genesis: 14:18–20. Christian biblical commentators saw him as a foreshadowing of Jesus Christ.

[18]These are the words with which God commissioned Jeremiah, a late-seventh-century B.C. priest of Anathoth, as a prophet: the Book of Jeremiah, 1:10.

[19]The Book of Exodus, 22:28.

[20]The Gospel of Matthew, 20:1.

[21]The Book of Psalms, 19:2.

[22]John X Camaterus (r. 1198–1206), the patriarch of Constantinople, was the highest-ranking bishop* in the Byzantine Church. Although the patriarchs were imperial appointees and were subject to a high degree of scrutiny by the emperor, they generally were accorded great honor and authority and were not treated anywhere near as shoddily as Pope Innocent believed.

erently rise in the presence of archbishops* and bishops, as they should, and assign them an honorable seat next to themselves. For, as We believe, Your Prudence is not ignorant of the fact that the exceedingly pious Constantine[23] showed such honor to priests.

For, even though We have not written in rebuke, We may, nevertheless, very reasonably rebuke, as Saint Paul the apostle is recorded to have written, by way of instruction, to Bishop Timothy: "Preach, persist both when it is convenient and when it is inconvenient, importune, censure, implore, rebuke with all patience and learning."[24] For Our mouth ought not to be bound, but it ought to be open to all, lest We be, as the Prophet says, "mute dogs who do not want to bark."[25] For this reason Our correction should not annoy you but rather should be accepted, because a father chides the son whom he loves, and God censures and castigates those whom He loves. We, therefore, carry out the duty of the pastoral office when we entreat, accuse, rebuke, and take pains to win over to those things that are pleasing to the Divine Will, when it is convenient and when it is inconvenient, not just everyone else but even emperors and kings. For all of Christ's sheep were committed to us, in the person of Saint Peter, when the Lord said, "Feed My sheep,"[26] not making any distinction between these sheep and those, in order to show that anyone who does not recognize Peter and his successors as teachers and pastors is outside His flock. Because it is so well known, we need hardly mention what the Lord said to Peter and, in the person of Peter, to his successors: "Whatsoever you bind on earth will be bound in Heaven, and whatsoever you permit on earth will be permitted in Heaven,"[27] excepting nothing when He said "whatsoever." In truth, We do not wish to

pursue this any longer, lest We seem contentious or attracted to something of this sort, because, should it be advantageous to boast, one should prefer to boast not of some mark of honor but of his onerous burden, not of his magnitude but of his disquietude. For this reason, the Apostle boasts of his infirmities.[28] We have learned that it is written: "Everyone who exalts himself shall be humbled, and everyone who humbles himself shall be exalted;"[29] and further, "The greater you are, the more you should humble yourself in all things;"[30] and elsewhere, "God resists the proud but gives glory to the humble."[31] Because of that we describe Our exaltation in humility, and We regard Our greatest exaltation to be Our humility. For this reason also We write and confess that We are the servants, not only of God, but of the servants of God and, in the Apostle's words, We are debtors equally to the wise and the foolish.[32]

Your Highness knows whether or not We have been able to lead Your Imperial Excellency to welcoming the good and the useful through Our letter and whether We have advised you of proper and honorable courses of actions, because We remember that We invited you to nothing other than the unity of the Church and aid for the land of Jerusalem. May He, Who breathes where He wills and Who holds the hearts of princes in His hand, so inspire your mind that you acquiesce to Our advice and counsel and do that which should deservedly produce honor for the Divine Name, profit for the Christian religion, and the salvation of your soul. We, however, will do what We know is expedient, no matter what you might do.

Would that you made it a point to imitate better in word and deed the devotion to the Apostolic See of your illustrious predecessor, the

[23]Constantine I (Chapter 1, source 3).
[24]The Second Letter of Paul to Timothy: 4:2.
[25]The Book of Isaiah, 56:10.
[26]The Gospel of John, 21:15–17.
[27]The Gospel of Matthew, 16:19.
[28]St. Paul, Second Epistle to the Corinthians, 11:30.

[29]The Gospel of Luke, 14:11 and 18:14.
[30]Ecclesiasticus or the Wisdom of Joshua Ben Sirach, 3:18.
[31]Proverbs, 3:34; the Epistle of James, 4:6; the First Epistle of Peter, 5:15.
[32]St. Paul, Epistle to the Romans, 1:14.

Emperor Manuel of glorious memory,[33] so that, through its aid and counsel, things might go better for you and your empire, as they did for him. Would that you, at least from this time onward, make up for what up you have neglected up to this point. The aforementioned archdeacon, however, can faithfully tell Your Excellency what he has heard from Us.

---

[33]Emperor Manuel I Comnenus (r. 1143–1180) had courted the goodwill of the papacy as he struggled with a variety of eastern and western enemies, including the Western emperor, Frederick I, and the Venetians.

A Middle Ground
▼▼▼

67 ▼ John of Paris, A TREATISE ON ROYAL AND PAPAL POWER

As we have seen, initially popes and emperors and later popes and the kings of Europe's new royal states struggled with one another to assert ultimate sole authority over the lives of their Christian subjects. The fact that neither popes nor secular* rulers were ever able to overwhelm the other resulted in a growing feeling among some observers that perhaps there are two powers, church and state, which have legitimate but different claims upon a subject's loyalty.

The clearest medieval articulator of this position was John of Paris, a French Dominican priest* and student of the theology and political philosophy of Thomas Aquinas (Chapter 9, source 54). Both Aquinas and John were deeply influenced by thirteenth-century Europe's rediscovery of Aristotle's *Politics*, a fourth-century B.C. treatise that eloquently presented the position that the sovereign state originates from natural human needs and is necessary for full human development. Around 1302 Friar* John composed *A Treatise on Royal and Papal Power,* in which he argued that civil government and the priesthood have separate roles to play in guiding human conduct. Although his was a minority voice in the ongoing struggle between secular and sacred authority, John of Paris represents an important school of thought and a foreshadowing of what would become, so many centuries later, the Western notion of separation of church and state.

QUESTIONS FOR ANALYSIS

1. According to John of Paris, what are humanity's two ends, or goals, and how is each attained?
2. Why is civil government natural and necessary?
3. Why is the priesthood higher in dignity than secular authority?
4. In what ways is secular authority greater than priestly authority?
5. How has John denied the claims of the *Dictatus Papae?*

6. How has John refuted the core assumption of Innocent III's "two lights" argument?

7. John of Paris cites *Solitae* in defense of a conclusion that differs radically from that of Pope Innocent. What does this suggest about medieval canon law?*

8. Compose rejoinders to John of Paris's views by either Henry IV or Alexius III *and* one of the two popes whom we have seen in this chapter, Gregory VII or Innocent III.

9. Compare John of Paris's political theory with that of Pope Gelasius I (Chapter 4, source 19). Where do they agree and/or disagree? Which are more significant, the similarities or the differences? Explain your answer.

First it should be known that kingship, properly understood, can be defined as the rule of one man over a perfect multitude so ordered as to promote the public good. . . . Such a government is based on natural law and the law of nations.[1] For, since man is naturally a civil or political creature . . . it is essential for a man to live in a multitude and in such a multitude as is self-sufficient for life. The community of a household or village is not of this sort, but the community of a city or kingdom is, for in a household or village there is not found everything necessary for food, clothing and defense through a whole life as there is in a city or kingdom. But every multitude scatters and disintegrates as each man pursues his own ends unless it is ordered to the common good by some one man who has charge of this common good. . . .

Next it must be borne in mind that man is not ordered only to such a good as can be acquired by nature, which is to live virtuously, but is further ordered to a supernatural end which is eternal life, and the whole multitude of men living virtuously is ordered to this. Therefore it is necessary that there be some one man to direct the multitude to this end. If indeed this end could be attained by the power of human nature, it would necessarily pertain to the office of the human king to direct men to this end, for

we call a human king him to whom is committed the highest duty of government in human affairs. But since man does not come to eternal life by human power but by divine . . . this kind of rule pertains to a king who is not only man but also God, namely Jesus Christ . . . and because Christ was to withdraw his corporal presence from the Church it was necessary for him to institute others as ministers who would administer the sacraments* to men, and these are called priests. . . . Hence priesthood may be defined in this fashion. Priesthood is a spiritual power of administering sacraments to the faithful conferred by Christ on ministers of the Church. . . .

From the foregoing material it is easy to see which is first in dignity, the kingship or the priesthood. . . . A kingdom is ordered to this end, that an assembled multitude may live virtuously, as has been said, and it is further ordered to a higher end which is the enjoyment of God; and responsibility for this end belongs to Christ, whose ministers and vicars are the priests. Therefore the priestly power is of greater dignity than the secular and this is commonly conceded. See *Dist.* 96 C.10, "As gold is more precious than lead so the priestly order is higher than the royal power."[2] And in the *Decretales* 1.33.6 it is said that as the sun excels the moon so spiritualities

---

[1] Laws common to civilized peoples that govern their international dealings.

[2] A quotation from Gratian's *Concordance of Discordant Canons,* known popularly as *The Decretum.* Compiled circa 1140, it became the standard primary textbook of canon law.

excel temporalities.[3] And likewise Bernard to Pope Eugenius, Book I,[4] "Which seems to you the greater dignity, the power of forgiving sins or of dividing estates? But there is no comparison." It is as if he would say, "The spiritual power is greater; therefore it excels in dignity."

But if the priest is greater in himself than the prince and is greater in dignity, it does not follow that he is greater in all respects. For the lesser secular power is not related to the greater spiritual power as having its origin from it or being derived from it as the power of a proconsul is related to that of the emperor, which is greater in all respects since the power of the former is derived from the latter. The relationship is rather like that of a head of a household to a general of armies, since one is not derived from the other but both from a superior power. And so the secular power is greater than the spiritual in some things, namely in temporal affairs, and in such affairs it is not subject to the spiritual power in any way because it does not have its origin from it but rather both have their origin immediately from the one supreme power, namely the divine. Accordingly the inferior power is not subject to the superior in all things but only in those where the supreme power has subordinated it to the greater. A teacher of literature or an instructor in morals directs the members of a household to a nobler end, namely the knowledge of truth, than a doctor who is concerned with a lower end, namely the health of bodies, but who would say therefore the doctor should be subjected to the teacher in preparing his medicines? For this is not fitting, since the head of the household who established both in his house did not subordinate the lesser to the greater in this respect. Therefore the priest is greater than the prince in spiritual affairs and, on the other hand, the prince is greater in temporal affairs. . . .

Concerning the ecclesiastical* power of censure or correction it should be known that, directly, it is only spiritual, for it can impose no penalty in the external court but a spiritual one, except conditionally and incidentally. For though the ecclesiastical judge has to lead men back to God and draw them away from sin and correct them, he has to do this only in the way laid down for him by God, which is to say by cutting them off from the sacraments and from the company of the faithful and by similar measures which are proper to ecclesiastical censure. I said "conditionally" in reference to one who is willing to repent and accept a pecuniary penalty, for the ecclesiastical judge cannot impose any corporal or pecuniary penalty for a crime as a secular judge can, except only on one who is willing to accept it. . . . I said "incidentally" because if a prince was a heretic* and incorrigible and contemptuous of ecclesiastical censures, the pope might so move the people that he would be deprived of his secular dignity and deposed by the people. The pope might do this in the case of an ecclesiastical crime, of which cognizance belonged to him, by excommunicating* all who obeyed such a man as a lord, and thus the people would depose him, and the pope "incidentally." So too, if the pope on the other hand behaved criminally and brought scandal on the Church and was incorrigible, the prince might indirectly excommunicate him and "incidentally" bring about his deposition by warning him personally or through the cardinals.* And if the pope were unwilling to yield the emperor might so move the people as to compel him to resign or be deposed by the people, for the emperor could, by taking securities or imposing corporal penalties, prevent each and everyone from obeying him or serving him as pope. So each can act toward the other, for both pope and emperor have jurisdiction universally and everywhere, but the one has spiritual jurisdiction, the other temporal.

As for the argument that corporeal beings are ruled by spiritual beings and depend on them as on a cause, I answer that an argument so constructed fails on many grounds. Firstly because

---

[3]*Solitae* (source 66). The citation is to the official collection of decretals authorized by Pope Gregory IX in 1234.

[4]Bernard of Clairvaux's treatise *On Consideration,* which he addressed to his friend and former monastic* subordinate, Pope Eugenius III.

it assumes that royal power is corporeal and not spiritual and that it has charge of bodies and not of souls which is false, as is said above, since it is ordained, not for any common good of the citizens whatsoever, but for that which consists in living according to virtue. Accordingly the Philosopher[5] says in the *Ethics*[6] that the intention of a legislator is to make men good and to lead them to virtue, and in the *Politics*[7] that a legislator is more estimable than a doctor since the legislator has charge of souls, the doctor of bodies.

[5]For John, as for Aquinas, Aristotle was the *Philosopher.*
[6]Aristotle's *Nichomachaean Ethics.*

[7]Aristotle's *Politics,* whose rediscovery by thirteenth-century Europe occasioned a revolution in political thought.

▼▼▼

Limited Government in Spain, England, and Germany

The High Middle Ages witnessed the development of increasingly efficient, centralized monarchies in the Spanish kingdoms of Castile-León and Aragon, as well as in England, France, and elsewhere. It also saw the rediscovery of Aristotle's political philosophy, which provided a rational justification for the secular,* sovereign state. In both fact and theory, quite a few European monarchic states were far stronger in 1300 than they had been in 1100, although that was not the case for either the kingdom of Germany or the empire.

Paradoxically, the growth of royal power in thirteenth-century Spain and England was accompanied by the development of institutions that emphasized the right and *duty* of the king's subjects to advise the king, to give consent to royal actions, and even to oppose those royal actions that seemed to violate tradition, good order, and the king's law.

The thirteenth-century empire, meanwhile, was undergoing crises that ultimately undermined the power of the emperor, while simultaneously building up the independent authority of German princes and northern Italian lords and communes.

Representative Government in Spain
▼▼▼

68 ▼ *Alfonso IX, DECREES OF 1188, Alfonso X, ORDINANCES OF THE CORTES OF SEVILLE IN 1252, and Pedro III, ORDINANCE OF 1283*

During the High Middle Ages, and especially in the thirteenth and fourteenth centuries, representative, parliamentary assemblies of one sort or another appeared all over Europe. England, Scandinavia, the empire, the kingdom of Sicily, Poland, Hungary, France, Christian Spain, the Roman Church, the Dominican

Order — all of these and more witnessed the rise and institutionalization of assemblies of representatives who individually wielded full authority to speak and act for those who had sent them and, as a body, possessed full power to bind by their decisions all elements of the greater body that they, as a whole, represented. We have already seen one such representative assembly, the Fourth Lateran Council (Chapter 7, source 42). As in the case of the general councils* of the twelfth and thirteenth centuries that were assembled at the command of powerful popes, most representative assemblies began as convenient instruments of monarchic policy that enabled rulers to govern efficiently and with a fair measure of popular support. However, as fifteenth-century English Parliament and the early fifteenth-century General Councils of the Church (Chapter 13, source 88) would later show, these representative assemblies were potentially curbs on monarchic authority. Although they received their legitimacy from the rulers who assembled them and were largely subject to monarchic control, once in session, they often displayed a certain independence of mind.

Spain holds a special place in the history of medieval representative assemblies because it is there, in the northern kingdom of León, that we find the first instance of representatives from towns being summoned to a royal council, or *cortes*. The origins of León's parliamentary development can be found in the first year of the reign of King Alfonso IX (r. 1188–1230). The young, inexperienced Alfonso IX, facing the enmity of his neighbor and cousin, King Alfonso VIII of Castile (Chapter 8, source 52), sought to secure the broad support of his subjects by holding an extraordinary meeting of his cortes in April 1188. The decrees enacted at that council are significant because they provide the first evidence of the convocation of representatives of the towns to the royal court, where previously only high-ranking churchmen and nobles had served as the king's counselors. The phrase *citizens chosen from each city* implies a process whereby each city council elected or designated representatives to act on its behalf at the king's court. In later times, those representatives would be called *procurators* and would receive full powers to act for and to bind their constituents.

After a separation of more than seventy years, the kingdoms of Castile and León were reunited in 1230, thereby allowing their single monarch to muster vast resources in a renewed campaign of expansion at the expense of Muslim states to the south. This resulted in the capture of Seville in 1248 and the conquest of the greater part of Andalusia, or southern Spain, by 1252. During the reign of Alfonso X (r. 1252–1284), the cortes of Castile-León developed the composition and functions that would characterize it for the remainder of the Middle Ages. In the first cortes of his reign, held in Seville in October 1252, a royal ordinance was passed that set the pattern for the future.

The greater part of the ordinance is concerned with setting prices for clothing and other goods, prohibiting the export of certain types of goods deemed necessary for the welfare of the realm (such as horses), regulating the dress of Jews and Muslims, and limiting the formation of guild associations, except for purely religious purposes. The three articles that follow provide an example of the types of regulations that this cortes passed. More important for our purposes is the preamble, which sets forth the king's official reasons for convening the assembly and informs us of the parliament's composition.

East of Castile-León, in the Mediterranean kingdom of Aragón, the *corts,* as it was known in the Catalan tongue, began to take shape during the thirteenth century and achieved its fullest development in the fourteenth and fifteenth centuries. The third document is pivotal in the parliamentary history of Catalonia. In it, Pedro (or Pere) III (r. 1276–1285), king of Aragón and count of Barcelona, defined and established in 1283 the fundamental rights of the Catalan corts.

QUESTIONS FOR ANALYSIS

1. What principle does article 2 of Alfonso IX's decree establish?
2. What principle does article 3 of that same decree establish?
3. According to Alfonso X, why had he convened the *cortes* of Seville?
4. What does this text allow you to infer about the assembly's purpose and powers and the relative influence of the townspeople who attended?
5. What principle does article 9 of the ordinances of 1283 establish?
6. What principle does article 11 establish?
7. Consider the Catalan document as a whole. What powers and rights does it give the corts, and in what ways are they different from those enjoyed by the earlier cortes of Castile-León? What conclusions follow from your answer?

DECREES ENACTED BY ALFONSO IX OF LEÓN IN THE CURIA OF LEÓN, 1188

1. In the name of God. When I, Lord Alfonso, King of León and Galicia, celebrated a *curia*[1] at León with the archbishop* [of Santiago de Compostela] and the bishops* and magnates of my kingdom and with the elected citizens of each city, I determined and I affirmed by oath that I would preserve for all the people of my kingdom, both clergy* and laity, the good customs which they had established by my predecessors.

2. I also established and I swore that if anyone should make or say to me any denunciation about someone, I would make that denunciation known to the one accused without delay. And if he [the accuser] cannot prove in my *curia* the denunciation which he has made, he shall suffer the penalty which the accused would have suffered if the accusation had been proved. I also swore that because of an accusation made to me about someone or an evil thing that was said about him, I would never do harm or injury either to his person or to his goods until I summoned him by my letters to come to my *curia* to

---

[1]A medieval Latin term meaning "court." The king's *curia* was a plenary assembly over which the monarch presided and to which he called all of his chief counselors who rendered him "advice and consent." As a plenary assembly, the king's court could and did consider any and all matters that the king and his counselors deemed appropriate. In modern terms, it was an executive, legislative, and judicial body.

make his law according as my *curia* should command. And if [the accusation] is not proved, the one who made the charge shall suffer the aforesaid penalty and shall also pay the expenses incurred by the accused in coming and going [to my court].

3. I also promised that I would not make war or peace or treaty without the counsel of the bishops, nobles, and good men[2] by whose counsel I ought to be guided.

▾ ▾ ▾

ALFONSO X, KING OF CASTILE-LEÓN, ENACTS AN ORDINANCE IN THE CORTES OF SEVILLE IN 1252

Don Alfonso, by the grace of God, king of Castile, Toledo, León, Galicia, Sevilla, Córdoba, Murcia, and Jaén, to the [municipal] council of Burgos[3] and its district and of the whole province, health and grace. Know that I saw the agreements that my great-grandfather King Alfonso [VIII] and my father King Fernando [III] made for their benefit and that of their people and of their entire realm. [Those agreements] were not observed at that time because of the wars and great pressures that occurred. Now when God wished that my father the king — may God pardon him — should conquer the land with God's favor and with the help and service that you gave him, you showed me the injuries that you received because the agreements were not observed as they should have been. And because you also showed me the injuries that you received many times because of the objectionable things that were done and the

great scarcity of goods to be sold, I thought it right and proper that those agreements that they made and which we now agree on for the benefit of myself and of all of you ought to be observed. I made these agreements with the counsel and consent of my uncle, Don Alfonso de Molina, and my brothers, Fadrique, Felipe, and Manuel, and of the bishops, magnates, knights, and [military] orders[4] and the good men of the towns, and of other good men who were with me. And I do this out of the great desire that I have to protect you from harm and from wrongful acts that result in injury to you, and to improve you in everything so that you may be richer and better off and may have more and be worth more and may be able to better serve me. The agreements are these: . . .

11. I also command that craftsmen of whatever craft they may be shall not join together against the people, but each one shall sell his work as best he can. . . .

14. I also command that confraternities and wrongful sworn associations or evil assemblies that are injurious to the realm and to the diminution of my lordship are not to be created, except to give food to the poor . . . or to bury the dead. . . . Nor are there to be magistrates to judge the confraternities except those appointed by me in the towns according to law. . . .

41. I also command that no Christian woman shall nurse the child of a Jew or of a Moor, nor shall a Jewish woman nurse any Christian. The one who does so will be fined 10 *maravedís*[5] for each day that she does so.

▾ ▾ ▾

---

[2]Upstanding people of sound judgment. Here, it probably meant persons, other than nobles and prelates,* who resided at the royal court and served the king in some capacity or other.

[3]The text of this copy of the ordinance appears in a *cuaderno,* or small bound notebook, addressed to the municipal council of Burgos; other copies were sent to other towns of the kingdom.

[4]Spain had a number of military orders on its soil participating in the Reconquest. A creation of the twelfth century and following, the military orders combined a life of religious commitment with one of fighting the enemies of Western Christendom, especially Muslims.

[5]Not a coin but a money of account. One *maravedí* was equivalent to ninety Castlian *burgaleses* or ninety-six Leónese *leoneses,* coins made of billon, an alloy of silver and copper. This same cortes of 1252 set the price of a shield and saddle of the highest quality at twenty maravedís.

CONSTITUTIONS OF PEDRO III, KING OF ARAGÓN AND COUNT OF BARCELONA, AT THE CORTS OF BARCELONA, 1283

In the name of God. When we, Pedro, king of Aragón and Sicily[6] by the grace of God, following the paths of our predecessors and willingly seeking the tranquility of our subjects, ordered a General Court of the Catalans to be celebrated in Barcelona, there assembled in the Court bishops, prelates, religious, barons, knights, citizens, and townsmen of Catalonia. . . . And each and everyone of the aforesaid asked . . . us to give assent to certain petitions and chapters as our constitutions and ordinances. . . .

9. We wish, we establish, and we also ordain that if we or our successors wish to make any general constitution or statute in Catalonia, we shall make it with the approbation and consent of the prelates, barons, knights, and citizens [of the towns] of Catalonia or of the greater and wiser part of those summoned. . . .

18. That once a year, at that time that seems most convenient to us, we and our successors will celebrate in Catalonia a General Court for the Catalans, in which, with our prelates, religious, barons, knights, citizens, and townsmen, we will treat of the good estate and reformation of the land. We shall not be bound to celebrate the said Court if we are prevented by any any just reason.

---

[6]King Pedro had conquered the island of Sicily in 1282.

Limitations on Royal Power in England
▼▼▼

69 ▼ *MAGNA CARTA*

The late-twelfth-century treatise on English law and custom that tradition ascribes to Ranulf de Glanville defined many of the reciprocal obligations and rights that bound feudal* lords and vassals* in the age of Henry II (Chapter 8, source 48). Just as the vassal was expected to serve the lord faithfully, the lord incurred an obligation to protect the vassal's honor, status, and well-being. A lord's failure to live up to such commitments could justify a vassal's rebellion and defiance of his lord. This built-in tension within feudalism often resulted in a fair amount of violence between parties who, rightly or wrongly, believed themselves aggrieved. This tension also gave rise to some interesting constitutional developments in England.

Early in the thirteenth century, many of the great lords of England believed that Henry II's son, King John (r. 1199–1216), was abusing his royal feudal privileges and generally treating all of his subjects, but especially the nobles, in a shoddy manner. The result was a baronial revolt in which the rebels sought not to depose or injure John, their liege lord, but to force him to acknowledge that he was equally subject to all the customs and laws of England, even though, as sovereign monarch, he was the source of justice and law. With the aid of the burghers of London and the archbishop* of Canterbury, who were equally disenchanted with the king's heavy-handed attempts to raise money in order to defend his continental possessions, the rebel barons forced John, on June 15, 1215, to agree to a list of reforms. Known originally as the *Articles of the Barons,* the document eventually became known as *Magna Carta de Libertatibus,* or *The Great Charter of Liberties.*

Despite the efforts of the English king's nominal feudal overlord, Pope Innocent III, to quash the barons' articles, the charter would not go away. In order to rally support to his cause, John's son, King Henry III (r. 1216–1272), issued revised versions of the charter of liberties in 1216, 1217, and 1225. It was the fourth version, which Henry granted upon reaching adulthood in 1225, that subsequent English kings constantly reconfirmed in return for support and financial assistance. As a result, *Magna Carta* became a living reminder of the limits of royal power in England.

The following extracts are taken from the original articles of 1215. Articles 12, 15, 52, and 61 were dropped from Henry III's revisions of the charter, but they are included here as evidence of the historical context in which the *Great Charter* first took shape.

QUESTIONS FOR ANALYSIS

1. Judging from the guarantees that John was forced to give, in what ways had he abused his royal and feudal rights? In addressing this question, refer back to what "Glanville" tells us of feudal rights.
2. How did the barons propose to prevent John from extorting uncustomary or unreasonable sums of money from them in the future?
3. What did the archbishop of Canterbury, the burghers of London, and the barons' own vassals get for their support of the rebellion?
4. How does the *Great Charter* deal with women, and what inferences do you draw from your answer?
5. Consider articles 12 and 14 in light of what you have studied in source 68. What was this common council? What do you think it will become?
6. Consider article 61. What were the barons trying to accomplish in that article? On what feudal principle was it based? What do you infer from the fact that it was dropped as early as 1216?
7. Which of the charter's clauses seem the most familiar to you? Why? What do you infer from your answer?
8. Some historians have characterized the *Great Charter* as a document that protects the narrow class interests of the baronage. What do you think of this judgment?

John, by the grace of God, king of England, lord of Ireland, duke of Normandy and Aquitaine, count of Anjou,[1] to the archbishops, bishops,* abbots,* earls, barons, justiciars, foresters, sheriffs, reeves, servants, and all bailiffs and his faithful people greeting. . . .

1. In the first place, we have granted to God, and by this our present charter confirmed, for us and for our heirs forever, that the English Church shall be free, and shall hold its rights entire and its liberties uninjured; and we will that it be thus observed; which is shown by this, that the freedom of elections, which is considered to be most important and especially necessary to the English Church, we, of our pure and spontaneous will, granted, and by our charter confirmed, before the contest between us and our barons had arisen; and obtained a confirmation of it by the lord Pope Innocent III.;[2] which we shall observe and which we will shall be observed in good faith by our heirs forever.

We have granted moreover to all free men[3] of our kingdom for us and our heirs forever all the liberties written below, to be had and holden by themselves and their heirs from us and our heirs.

2. If any of our earls or barons, or others holding from us in chief[4] by military service shall have died, and when he has died his heir shall be of full age and owe relief,[5] he shall have his inheritance by the ancient relief; that is to say, the heir or heirs of an earl for the whole barony of an earl a hundred pounds; the heir or heirs of a baron for a whole barony a hundred pounds; the heir or heirs of a knight for a whole knight's fee a hundred shillings[6] at most; and who owes less

let him give less according to the ancient custom of fiefs.

3. If moreover the heir of any one of such shall be under age, and shall be in wardship,[7] when he comes of age he shall have his inheritance without relief and without a fine.

4. The custodian of the land of such a minor heir shall not take from the land of the heir any except reasonable products, reasonable customary payments, and reasonable services, and this without destruction or waste of men or of property; and if we shall have committed the custody of the land of any such a one to the sheriff or to any other who is to be responsible to us for its proceeds, and that man shall have caused destruction or waste from his custody we will recover damages from him, and the land shall be committed to two legal and discreet men of that fief, who shall be responsible for its proceeds to us or to him to whom we have assigned them; and if we shall have given or sold to any one the custody of any such land, and he has caused destruction or waste there, he shall lose that custody, and it shall be handed over to two legal and discreet men of that fief who shall be in like manner responsible to us as is said above. . . .

7. A widow, after the death of her husband, shall have her marriage portion and her inheritance immediately and without obstruction, nor shall she give anything for her dowry or for her marriage portion, or for her inheritance, which inheritance her husband and she held on the day of the death of her husband; and she may remain in the house of her husband for forty days after his death, within which time her dowry shall be assigned to her.

---

[1]John had lost Normandy and Anjou to Philip Augustus, but he still claimed them as feudal principalities.
[2]Between 1207 and 1213, John quarrelled with Pope Innocent over the appointment of Stephen Langton as archbishop of Canterbury. Faced with a French invasion in 1213, John gave in, granting the English Church the right of free elections, and then went one dramatic step farther by surrendering England to the pope and receiving it back as a feudal fief.* By this act, John secured Innocent's support in his struggles against the baronage.

[3]Maybe fifty percent of the adult male population; quite possibly less than that.
[4]Any vassal, secular* or ecclesiastical,* who held a major fief directly from the king, as opposed to a rear vassal, who was a vassal of a vassal.
[5]See Chapter 8, source 48, note 2.
[6]Five pounds.
[7]See Chapter 8, source 48, note 4.

8. No widow shall be compelled to marry so long as she prefers to live without a husband, provided she gives security that she will not marry without our consent, if she holds from us, or without the consent of her lord from whom she holds, if she holds from another.[8] . . .

12. No scutage[9] or aid[10] shall be imposed in our kingdom except by the common council of our kingdom,[11] except for the ransoming of our body, for the making of our oldest son a knight, and for once marrying our oldest daughter, and for these purposes it shall be only a reasonable aid; in the same way it shall be done concerning the aids of the city of London.

13. And the city of London shall have all its ancient liberties and free customs,[12] as well by land as by water. Moreover, we will and grant that all other cities and boroughs and villages and ports shall have all their liberties and free customs.

14. And for holding a common council of the kingdom concerning the assessment of an aid otherwise than in the three cases mentioned above, or concerning the assessment of a scutage, we shall cause to be summoned the archbishops, bishops, abbots, earls, and greater barons by our letters under seal; and besides we shall cause to be summoned generally, by our sheriffs and bailiffs all those who hold from us in chief, for a certain day, that is at the end of forty days at least, and for a certain place; and in all the letters of that summons, we will express the cause of the summons, and when the summons has thus been given the business shall proceed on the appointed day, on the advice of those who shall be present, even if not all of those who were summoned have come.

15. We will not grant to any one, moreover, that he shall take an aid from his free men, except for ransoming his body, for making his oldest son a knight, and for once marrying his oldest daughter; and for these purposes only a reasonable aid shall be taken.

16. No one shall be compelled to perform any greater service for a knight's fee, or for any other free tenement than is owed from it. . . .

20. A free man shall not be fined for a small offence, except in proportion to the measure of the offence; and for a great offence he shall be fined in proportion to the magnitude of the offence, saving his freehold;[13] and a merchant in the same way, saving his merchandise; and the villain shall be fined in the same way, saving his wainage,[14] if he shall be at our mercy; and none of the above fines shall be imposed except by the oaths of honest men of the neighborhood.[15]

21. Earls and barons shall be fined only by their peers,[16] and only in proportion to their offence.

22. A clergyman shall be fined, like those before mentioned, only in proportion to his lay holding, and not according to the extent of his ecclesiastical benefice.* . . .

28. No constable or other bailiff of ours shall take anyone's grain or other chattels, without immediately paying for them in money, unless he is able to obtain a postponement at the good will of the seller. . . .

35. There shall be one measure of wine throughout our whole kingdom, and one mea-

---

[8]A lord had the right to deny a vassal's widow permission to marry a specific person, if he believed such a marriage would place an enemy or other undesirable person in charge of the deceased vassal's fief. As the widow's guardian, the lord faced the temptation to marry off her and her late husband's fief to the highest bidder or some lackey.

[9]From the Latin *scutum* (shield), this was money paid in place of required military service. Generally, John preferred to collect scutage so that he could hire mercenaries, while his vassals preferred to meet their obligations by going into the field.

[10]See Chapter 8, source 48, note 12.

[11]The feudal council of all his tenants-in-chief.

[12]Customs and privileges secured by royal charter.

[13]Land held freely without feudal or manorial obligation.

[14]Here, *villain* means an unfree peasant, or serf.* *Wainage* was that portion of the harvest that the serf was allowed to keep for food and seed.

[15]See source 63.

[16]Their equals; that is, other vassals. Every vassal had the right to trial by the lord's council of vassals. See Chapter 8, source 48, note 6.

sure of ale, and one measure of grain, that is the London quarter, and one width of dyed cloth. . . .

39. No free man shall be taken or imprisoned or dispossessed, or outlawed, or banished, or in any way destroyed, nor will we go upon him, nor send upon him, except by the legal judgment of his peers or by the law of the land.[17]

40. To no one will we sell, to no one will we deny, or delay right or justice.

41. All merchants shall be safe and secure in going out from England and coming into England and in remaining and going through England, as well by land as by water, for buying and selling, free from all evil tolls, by the ancient and rightful customs, except in time of war, and if they are of a land at war with us; and if such are found in our land at the beginning of war, they shall be attached without injury to their bodies or goods, until it shall be known from us or from our principal justiciar in what way the merchants of our land are treated who shall then be found in the country which is at war with us; and if ours are safe there, the others shall be safe in our land. . . .

52. If any one shall have been dispossessed or removed by us without legal judgment of his peers, from his lands, castles, franchises, or his right, we will restore them to him immediately; and if contention arises about this, then it shall be done according to the judgment of the twenty-five barons, of whom mention is made below concerning the security of the peace. . . .

54. No one shall be seized nor imprisoned on the appeal of a woman concerning the death of any one except her husband. . . .

60. Moreover, all those customs and franchises mentioned above which we have conceded in our kingdom, and which are to be fulfilled, as far as pertains to us, in respect to our men; all men of our kingdom as well clergy* as laymen, shall ob-

serve as far as pertains to them, in respect to their men.

61. Since, moreover, for the sake of God, and for the improvement of our kingdom, and for the better quieting of the hostility sprung up lately between us and our barons, we have made all these concessions; wishing them to enjoy these in a complete and firm stability forever, we make and concede to them the security described below; that is to say, that they shall elect twenty-five barons of the kingdom, whom they will, who ought with all their power to observe, hold, and cause to be observed, the peace and liberties which we have conceded to them, and by this our present charter confirmed to them; in this manner, that if we or our justiciar,[18] or our bailiffs, or any of our servants shall have done wrong in any way toward any one, or shall have transgressed any of the articles of peace or security; and the wrong shall have been shown to four barons of the aforesaid twenty-five barons, let those four barons come to us or to our justiciar, if we are out of the kingdom, laying before us the transgression, and let them ask that we cause that transgression to be corrected without delay. And if we shall not have corrected the transgression or, if we shall be out of the kingdom, if our justiciar shall not have corrected it within a period of forty days, counting from the time in which it has been shown to us or to our justiciar, if we are out of the kingdom; the aforesaid four barons shall refer the matter to the remainder of the twenty-five barons, and let these twenty-five barons with the whole community of the country distress and injure us in every way they can; that is to say by the seizure of our castles, lands, possessions, and in such other ways as they can until it shall have been corrected according to their judgment, saving our person and that of our queen, and those of our children; and when

---

[17]Feudal vassals have the right to trial by their peers; everyone else will be tried according to the customs and laws governing his or her group and the alleged offense. In 1215 that meant trial by ordeal, in most criminal cases.

[18]The vice-regent in charge of administration and justice. See Chapter 8, source 48.

the correction has been made, let them devote themselves to us as they did before. And let whoever in the country wishes take an oath that in all the above-mentioned measures he will obey the orders of the aforesaid twenty-five barons, and that he will injure us as far as he is able with them, and we give permission to swear publicly and freely to each one who wishes to swear, and no one will we ever forbid to swear. All those, moreover, in the country who of themselves and their own will are unwilling to take an oath to the twenty-five barons as to distressing and injuring us along with them, we will compel to take the oath by our mandate, as before said. And if any one of the twenty-five barons shall have died or departed from the land or shall in any other way be prevented from taking the above mentioned action, let the remainder of the aforesaid twenty-five barons choose another in his place, according to their judgment, who shall take an oath in the same way as the others. In all those things, moreover, which are committed to those five and twenty barons to carry out, if perhaps the twenty-five are present, and some disagreement arises among them about something, or if any of them when they have been summoned are not willing or are not able to be present, let that be considered valid and firm which the greater part of those who are present arrange or command, just as if the whole twenty-five had agreed in this; and let the aforesaid twenty-five swear that they will observe faithfully all the things which are said above, and with all their ability cause them to be observed. And we will obtain nothing from any one, either by ourselves or by another by which any of these concessions and liberties shall be revoked or diminished; and if any such thing shall have been obtained, let it be invalid and void, and we will never use it by ourselves or by another.

Limitations on Imperial Power in Germany
▼▼▼

70 ▼ *Frederick II,*
STATUTE IN FAVOR OF THE PRINCES

The Western empire reached its apogee of power during the reigns of the early Hohenstaufen emperors, Frederick I (r. 1152–1190) and his son, Henry VI (r. 1190–1197). Despite the often successful efforts of Frederick and Henry to extend the emperor's authority and prestige, they were never able to transform the kingship of Germany and the imperial crown that came with it into a hereditary possession. Both remained elective offices, with election in the hands of the great princes of Germany. This proved to be a fatal flaw that ultimately cost the empire dearly, when Henry died at a young age, leaving behind an infant son. Henry's unexpected death in Sicily, as he was mustering a great crusade army, precipitated more than a decade of civil war, as the Hohenstaufens fought with the Welf family for the crowns of Germany, Italy, and the empire. In the course of the civil war, the princes of Germany gained greatly at the expense of monarchic authority.

Fortune finally favored Henry VI's son, Frederick II (r. 1212–1250), who was crowned king of Germany in 1212 and in 1220 received the imperial crown. Although Frederick II had an exalted vision of his imperial power and attempted with substantial success to create an absolute monarchy based upon a highly organized bureaucracy in his native kingdom of Sicily, imperial administration in his German and northern Italian lands had almost totally broken down since 1197. Due to his conflicts with the papacy,* which began in 1227 and continued to the day of his death in 1250, Frederick never had the opportunity to reassert strong imperial control over Germany.

To make matters worse, Emperor Frederick handed over the crown of Germany to his young son Henry (VII), who proved too weak to stand up to the great ecclesiastical* and secular* princes. Henry tried to ally the crown with the rich cities of Germany, whose leagues threatened the territorial powers of the princes. This ploy so alienated the great lords that in 1231, they extorted from him a charter known as *The Statute in Favor of the Princes,* which largely recapitulated a charter of privileges that Emperor Frederick had granted to Germany's ecclesiastical princes in 1220, ironically in order to gain their support for young Henry's election as king. Now these wide-sweeping rights of self-government were extended to Germany's secular princes, and Emperor Frederick had no choice but to ratify the charter in May 1232.

QUESTIONS FOR ANALYSIS

1. What rights does this charter grant the princes?
2. What constraints does it lay upon the king?
3. What does this charter give to or take away from other classes?
4. This statute has been characterized as hostile to urban interests. Was it? Please be specific in your analysis.
5. If this statute was antiurban, what reasons explain it?
6. "The *Statute in Favor of the Princes* represented a complete retreat from the principle of royal sovereignty." Please comment on this anonymous quotation.
7. Compare this document with *Magna Carta*. How does each restrict the exercise of royal power? Are those restrictions similar or different? Are the constitutional consequences of the restrictions similar or different? In short, where does each document leave the king/emperor relative to his great lords and other subjects?

In the name of the holy and undivided Trinity.* Frederick II, by divine mercy emperor of the Romans, Augustus, king of Jerusalem,[1] king of Sicily.

1. No new castles or cities shall be erected by us or by anyone else to the prejudice of the princes.

2. New markets shall not be allowed to interfere with the interests of former ones.

3. No one shall be compelled to attend any market against his will.

4. Travelers shall not be compelled to leave the old highways, unless they desire to do so.

5. We will not exercise jurisdiction within the ban-mile[2] of our cities.

---

[1]By virtue of his marriage to the heiress of Jerusalem.

[2]The area outside a city's walls that was subject to its jurisdiction.

6. Each prince shall possess and exercise in peace according to the customs of the land the liberties, jurisdiction, and authority over counties and hundreds which are in his own possession or are held as fiefs* from him.

7. Centgrafs[3] shall receive their office from the prince or from the person who holds the land as a fief.

8. The location of the hundred court[4] shall not be changed without the consent of the lord.

9. No nobleman shall be amenable to the hundred court.

10. The citizens who are known as *phalburgii*[5] shall be expelled from the cities.

11. Payments of wine, money, grain, and other rents, which free peasants have formerly agreed to pay [to the emperor], are hereby remitted, and shall not be collected henceforth.

12. The serfs* of princes, nobles, ministerials,[6] and churches shall not be admitted to our cities.[7]

13. Lands and fiefs of princes, nobles, ministerials, and churches, which have been seized by our cities, shall be restored and shall never again be taken.

14. The right of the princes to furnish safe-conduct within the lands which they hold as fiefs from us shall not be infringed by us or by anyone else.

15. Inhabitants of our cities shall not be compelled by our judges to restore any possessions which they may have received from others before they moved there.

16. Notorious, condemned, and proscribed persons shall not be admitted to our cities; if they have been, they shall be driven out.

17. We will never cause any money to be coined in the land of any of the princes which shall be injurious to his coinage.

18. The jurisdiction of our cities shall not extend beyond their boundaries, unless we possess special jurisdiction in the region.

19. In our cities the plaintiff shall bring suit in the court of the accused.

20. Lands or property which are held as fiefs shall not be pawned without the consent of the lord from whom they are held.

21. No one shall be compelled to aid in the fortifying of cities unless he is legally bound to render that service.

22. Inhabitants of our cities who hold lands outside shall pay to their lords or advocates[8] the regular dues and services, and they shall not be burdened with unjust exactions.

23. If serfs, freemen subject to advocates, or vassals* of any lord, shall dwell within any of our cities, they shall not be prevented by our officials from going to their lords.

---

[3]Each was a count (*graf* in German) who ruled over a hundred, an administrative-judicial division of a county.
[4]See note 3.
[5]Literally, "boundary-marker citizens." These were nonresidents who lived outside a city's rural boundary, or *ban-mile,* but possessed the rights of citizenship in the city.
[6]Formerly serfs who served as warriors and ministers, they

were now a class of petty nobility. See Chapter 8, source 44, note 29.
[7]Cities that enjoyed imperial charters of liberty and were directly subject to the emperor, at least in theory. Most were quite independent of any external control.
[8]A layperson who served as the defender and judge of a church's secular property. See Chapter 8, source 44, note 1.

"What Affects All Should Be Approved by All"

▼▼▼

71 ▼ Edward I, SUMMONS TO PARLIAMENT, 1295

John of Viterbo noted in his treatise on city government: "Matters that touch all should be approved by all." This dictum, which comes from Justinian's sixth-century *Code of Civil Law,* became a common cliché among thirteenth-century jurists because it conformed to the widespread notion that a representative assembly, presided over by a monarch, was the most effective and legitimate expression of sovereign power, as we saw in source 68.

The most enduring representative body to emerge in the thirteenth century was the English Parliament, which began to take shape as a representative assembly in the reign of Edward I (r. 1272–1307). *Parliamentum* derives from the Old French *parler* (to talk), and originally it meant any body that met to discuss any issue. The most important deliberative body in thirteenth-century England was the king's *Great Council* of major feudal* lords, whose composition varied, depending on the matters the king wished to place before it. When the matter revolved around war plans, lay earls and barons would predominate; when the matter touched on ecclesiastical* issues, prelates* predominated. In good feudal fashion, the king consulted with his lay and clerical* vassals* periodically in order to benefit from their expertise and, just as importantly, to rally their support for his policies. On its part, the baronage valued its prerogative to advise and consent to royal actions directly affecting it. Thus, articles 12 and 14 of *Magna Carta* (source 69) specifically stipulated that the king could not impose scutage or new levies of money on his vassals without the approval of the council of royal tenants-in-chief.

The Great Council was first called a *parliament* in 1236, and thereafter, the term became increasingly attached to it. Despite its new name, parliament remained, as it had been since the days of William the Conqueror, a feudal assembly of royal vassals. In 1265, however, Simon de Montfort, leader of a baronial revolt against Henry III, summoned to a small parliament of rebel lords two knights from each county and two burgesses from each borough. By including representatives from the commons, he hoped to rally support to his fading cause. He was wrong. Although the illegality of Montfort's parliament meant that this was not a binding precedent, King Henry's son and successor, Edward I, experimented with the expediency of occasionally summoning representatives from the commons to his parliaments, beginning with his initial one in 1273.

In 1295 Edward summoned to parliament representatives from thirty-seven counties, one hundred ten cities and boroughs, and the lower clergy,* as well as all of the usual great lords and prelates of the realm and his royal "small council" of professional jurists and administrators. Historians often refer to this meeting as the *Model Parliament,* but of the twenty subsequent parliaments that Edward called, only three followed the model of 1295 and only twelve included representatives from the counties and boroughs. Even so, the parliament of 1295 was a landmark because of the precedent it set, and increasingly in the early fourteenth century, representatives from the commons were summoned to parliament. From the middle of the fourteenth century onward, they were present whenever the king called a parliament.

In 1295 King Edward was facing crises on several fronts. Wales and Scotland, two lands he had recently invaded and occupied, were in rebellion, and King Philip IV of France had recently invaded Gascony, the continental duchy that Louis IX had bestowed as a fief* on Edward's father, Henry III (source 64). In light of these problems, which would necessitate his raising a massive amount of financial support from his subjects, the king decided to summon a larger than usual parliament to his residence at Westminster, even though he had met with his Great Council a few months earlier.

The three documents that follow represent the different types of writs of summons that Edward's secretariat despatched to prelates, great lords, and sheriffs throughout the realm.

QUESTIONS FOR ANALYSIS

1. To what feelings and loyalties does the writ to Archbishop* Robert appeal? What does your answer suggest about attitudes in late-thirteenth-century England?
2. Note that the writs to Archbishop Robert and Earl Edmund stipulate that when they assemble at Westminster, they are to consider, ordain, and do whatever might be necessary in the present crisis. How does the writ to the sheriff of Northamptonshire differ in this regard? Is this significant? If so, what might it suggest about the reason behind King Edward's summoning of representatives from the counties, cities, and boroughs?
3. Consider the dates of these three documents. Do they seem to have any significance? If so, what?
4. In light of your answers to questions 2 and 3, what do you conclude was Edward's view of the relationship between the representatives from the commons and the Great Council?
5. What does it seem that Edward thought he was he doing by summoning parliament? Did he see doing so as sharing his sovereign power? If not this, then what?
6. Compare Edward's parliament with the Spanish representative assemblies in source 68. What strike you as being the most significant similarities? The most significant differences? What do you conclude from your answers?

The King to the venerable father in Christ, Robert, by the same grace Archbishop of Canterbury, Primate of all England, greeting:*

As a most just law, established by the careful providence of sacred princes, exhorts and decrees that what affects all by all should be approved, so also, very evidently, should common danger be met by means provided in common. You know sufficiently well, and it is now, as we believe, divulged through all regions of the world, how the king of France fraudulently and craftily deprives us of our land of Gascony by withholding it unjustly from us.

Now, however, not satisfied with the before-mentioned fraud and injustice, having gathered together for the conquest of our kingdom a very great fleet and an abounding multitude of warriors, with which he has made a hostile attack on our kingdom and the inhabitants of the same kingdom, he now proposes to destroy the English language altogether from the earth, if his power should correspond to the detestable proposition of the contemplated injustice, which God forbid.

Because, therefore, darts seen beforehand do less injury, and your interest especially, as that of the rest of the citizens of the same realm, is concerned in this affair, we command you, strictly enjoining you in the fidelity and love in which you are bound to us, that on the Lord's day next after the feast of St. Martin,[1] in the approaching winter, you be present in person at Westminster,[2] citing beforehand the dean and chapter* of your church,[3] the archdeacons[4] and all the clergy of your diocese,* causing the same dean and archdeacons in their own persons, and the said chapter by one suitable proctor,[5] and the said clergy by two, to be present along with you, having full and sufficient power[6] from the same chapter and clergy, to consider, ordain, and provide, along with us and with the rest of the prelates and principal men and other inhabitants of our kingdom, how the dangers and threatened evils of this kind are to be met.

Witness the king, at Wangham, the 30th of September.[7]

▾ ▾ ▾

The King to his beloved and faithful relative, Edmund, Earl of Cornwall, greeting:
Because we wish to have a consultation and meeting with you and with the rest of the principal men of our kingdom, as to provision for remedies against the dangers which in these days are threatening our whole kingdom, we command you, strictly enjoining you in the fidelity and love in which you are bound to us, that on the Lord's day next after the feast of St. Martin, in the approaching winter, you be present in person at Westminster, for considering, ordaining, and doing, along with us and with the prelates and the rest of the principal men and other inhabitants of our kingdom, as may be necessary for meeting dangers of this kind.

Witness the king, at Canterbury, the 1st of October.[8]

▾ ▾ ▾

The King to the Sheriff of Northamptonshire:
Since we intend to have a consultation and meeting with the earls, barons, and other principal men of our kingdom with regard to providing remedies against the dangers which are in these days threatening the same kingdom, and on that account have commanded them to be with us on the Lord's day next after the feast of St. Martin, in the approaching winter, at Westminster, to consider, ordain, and do as may be necessary for the avoidance of those dangers, we strictly require you to cause two knights from the aforesaid county, two citizens from each city in the same county, and two burgesses from each borough, of those who are especially discreet and capable of laboring, to be elected without delay, and to cause them to come to us at the aforesaid time and place.

Moreover, the said knights are to have full and sufficient power for themselves and for the community of the aforesaid county, and the said citizens and burgesses for themselves, and the communities of the aforesaid cities and boroughs separately, then and there, for doing what shall then be ordained according to the common council in the premises; so that the aforesaid business shall not remain unfinished in any way for defect of this power. And you shall have there the names of the knights, citizens, and burgesses, together with this writ.

Witness the king, at Canterbury, on the 3d of October.[9]

---

[1]The first Sunday after November 11, the feast of St. Martin.
[2]The royal residence that lay just west of the city of London. Today, it is the site of the houses of Parliament.
[3]The chapter of canons* of Canterbury Cathedral* was headed by a *dean.*
[4]The archbishop's chief archdiocesan* administrators.
[5]A delegate, or representative.
[6]Full power to represent in all matters those who sent them and to bind them by the actions taken at Westminster.

[7]Similar writs were sent to the archbishop of York, eighteen bishops,* sixty-seven abbots,* and the heads of three religious orders.
[8]Similar writs were sent to six other earls and forty-one barons.
[9]Every other sheriff throughout the realm received a similar letter.

Chapter 11

▾▾▾

The Crusades: Expanding Europe's Horizons

Following the collapse of Roman political unity, the West, to a great extent, lost direct and easy contact with North Africa and the lands of the eastern Mediterranean. To be sure, the early eighth-century Muslim conquest of most of the Iberian peninsula and continued Byzantine presence in Italy and Sicily assured emerging Europe of some contact with the ancient cultures of North Africa and the Levant. Moreover, Western merchants, particularly Italians, continued to carry on some limited commerce across the wine-dark waters of the Mediterranean. Notwithstanding this trickle of Western activity, Muslim and Byzantine ships dominated the Mediterranean up to the late eleventh century, and the West was definitely a minor player in trans-Mediterranean affairs.

North of the Alps and Pyrenees, the story was different. Although Western Europeans faced the barriers of wilderness and often hostile pagan societies, they doggedly pushed out the boundaries of their civilization into the hinterlands well before the eleventh century. Christian monks* brought the faith and Western civilization to tribal Ireland in the fifth century, and Irish missionaries, in turn, carried Christianity and its culture to the pagans of the other British Isles and the continent (Chapter 4, source 18). Charles the Great waged what was tantamount to a holy war of conquest and conversion against the pagan Saxons to his northeast (Chapter 5, source 26), and the converted Saxons, in turn, played a pivotal role in the introduction of Western Christian civilization into the lands of Eastern Europe (Chapter 6, source 35) and Scandinavia. By the year 1000, Christian Scandinavians had established colonies in Iceland, along the eastern shore of

Greenland, and, for a few years, in Newfoundland and perhaps elsewhere in North America.

Scandinavian expansion across the waters of the North Atlantic had little overall effect on Europe and its world view. However, new Western activity in the Iberian peninsula and central Mediterranean during the early eleventh century proved to be the opening round of a series of holy wars and overseas adventures that took European colonists into the biblical land of Syria-Palestine by 1100 and even brought a handful of Western missionaries and merchants all the way to China by the late thirteenth century.

From the late eighth century onward, various Christian leaders had warred against the Muslims of Iberia. Charles the Great had even conquered Barcelona in 810 and pushed as far south as the Ebro River in northeast Spain. It was only with the collapse of the caliphate of Cordoba in 1031, however, that Spanish and French Christian warriors began to pick up the tempo of their raids along the fluid frontier that separated Muslim and Christian states and shift from largely defensive counterthrusts to offensive operations. By midcentury, the *Reconquista* — the Christian reconquest of the Iberian peninsula — was underway (Chapter 8, source 52). This centuries-long series of wars, truces, and shifting alliances would not be completed until 1492, when Grenada, the last Muslim stronghold in Spain, fell to the armies of Aragon and Castile. One of the immediate effects of the Reconquista, however, was its contribution to a growing feeling in the eleventh-century Christian West that holy war against Islam was a legitimate expression of piety.

Similarly, Italian cities and princes were fighting Muslims long before the First Crusade (1096–1101) was launched. Between 827 and 902, Muslim invaders conquered Sicily, and around that same period, Saracen pirates established numerous fortifications along the coasts of Italy and Provence. Thanks, in large measure, to the vigorous leadership of Pope John X, a Christian coalition defeated the Muslim pirates of Italy in 915 and ended the days of their occupation of Italian mainland bases. Muslim seafaring raiders from island strongholds and North Africa still harassed European merchants off the coast of Italy until the maritime cities of Pisa and Genoa made the waters around Italy safe for waterborne commerce around the year 1000. By midcentury, the same Pisans and Genoese were on the offensive, raiding Muslim ports in Sicily and North Africa. The tide had turned, and Europe was now ready to expand into the larger Mediterranean, at the expense of Islam.

All of this served as context for Pope Gregory VII's call in 1074 for an armed expedition against the Seljuk Turks. The pope proposed to lead the army himself — an army whose goal was the liberation of the Christians of the East. He even suggested that after relieving Turkish pressure on Constantinople, the army might push on to free Jerusalem from Muslim control. The momentous events of the Investiture Controversy precluded Gregory's ever realizing this dream, but the reform papacy* did not forget the idea. Another reform pope, Urban II, took up the call for a papally sponsored holy war against Islam in 1095, thereby launching a series of expeditions that would have a profound impact on Europe, its Muslim and Byzantine neighbors, and, ultimately, the world.

▼▼▼

The Crusade Ideal

In 1071 the Seljuk Turks, recent converts to Islam, destroyed a Byzantine army at Manzikert in eastern Anatolia.* By sweeping through Anatolia, the Seljuks deprived the Eastern Roman Empire of its heartland and threatened the very city of Constantinople. When Emperor Alexius I (r. 1081–1118) appealed to Pope Urban II (r. 1088–1099) for help in attracting European mercenaries for the imperial army, the pope responded by issuing an impassioned call for military action at the Council* of Clermont in southeast France on November 27, 1095.

The response to Urban's idealistic appeal was astounding. Between 1096 and 1101, three major waves of crusaders left Europe for the Holy Land; altogether, maybe as many as 130,000 men, women, and children participated, of whom probably only about ten percent were professional warriors. Urban had unleashed a phenomenon that was to engage much of Europe's energy for the next several centuries and would touch all levels of society. Just as importantly, the crusade, as an ideal, remained part of the Western mindset long after the Holy Land ceased to be a focal point of serious crusading endeavors. Columbus and the *conquistadores* who followed him to the Americas saw themselves as latter-day crusaders, and right down to our own day, political and spiritual leaders continually employ the metaphor of crusade when they wish to rally the public to right wrongs and battle evil.

Crusade means "to carry a cross," the reference being to Jesus' injunction that all His followers must bear their crosses if they are to be worthy of being His apostles.* More specifically, a medieval crusade was an armed expedition against an enemy of the Church that was blessed and authorized by a legitimate ecclesiastical* authority, normally, the pope. In the course of the twelfth and thirteenth centuries, the Church launched crusades against Muslims in the Iberian Peninsula, pagans in the Baltic, and heretics* and political opponents of the papacy in Europe, but the primary focus of the crusade movement was the liberation of the Holy Land from Islam. Crusaders took sacred public vows to undertake their holy work, and they received a special legal status and privileges as a consequence of their vows. More than that, they believed they received God's favor and the promise of forgiveness of the divinely mandated penalties that they owed for their sins. The following sources provide insights into why so many Western Europeans believed that the crusade was a legitimate expression of Christian piety.

Two Versions of Urban II's Summons to a Crusade

▼▼▼

72 ▼ *Fulcher of Chartres, A JERUSALEM HISTORY, and Robert the Monk, A JERUSALEM HISTORY*

Four major accounts of Pope Urban II's speech at Clermont exist. All, however, were written down five or more years after the event, and none was a verbatim transcription. Several of the reporters might have been working from notes taken at Clermont or shortly thereafter, but that is not a certainty. Compounding the problem is the likelihood that the events and outcome of the crusade influenced how some or all of the reporters remembered and reconstructed Urban's speech. One other point to keep in mind is that medieval historians, like their Greco-Roman predecessors, approached the speeches that they purported to report as opportunities for demonstrating their own rhetorical skills. Therefore, the words and phrases they set down were usually their own and not those of their historical characters.

Two of the most important and interesting attempts to replicate Pope Urban's sermon came from the pens of two clerics,* Fulcher of Chartres and Robert the Monk. A comparative analysis of their sermon versions could conceivably allow a historian to compile a reasonably valid list of the major points, arguments, and passions that the pope raised at Clermont, but we will never know exactly what Pope Urban said at Clermont.

Fulcher (1059–ca. 1127), a priest* of Chartres in the Île de France, seems to have been present at Clermont in 1095, although nowhere does he claim that distinction. What is certain is that he participated in the second wave of the First Crusade, the so-called Crusade of the Nobles. In 1096 he set out for the East in the company of Stephen, count of Blois and Chartres, and subsequently became the chaplain of Baldwin of Boulogne, who seized the principality of Edessa in 1098. Fulcher accompanied Baldwin from Edessa to Jerusalem in 1100, when his lord became King Baldwin I of the new crusader kingdom of Jerusalem. Probably a year later, in 1101, Fulcher began to write down his history of the crusade and the subsequent fortunes of the Latin kingdom of Jerusalem. He carried his history down to 1127, apparently, the year of his death. Because his account of Urban's speech appears at the beginning of his history, we can be reasonably sure that he set it down in or around 1101. Some historians have concluded that Fulcher consulted a now-lost copy of the decrees of the council as he turned to composing his history.

Robert, former abbot* of the monastery* of Saint-Rémi in Champagne, was at the Council of Clermont in his capacity as an abbot. Following his forced retirement around 1097, Robert had the leisure to compose a history of the First Crusade sometime between about 1106 and his death in 1122. Robert did not participate in the crusade's military campaigns, but he probably visited recently conquered Jerusalem around 1100. His history reflects his lack of personal experience of the crusade's pivotal battles, inasmuch as it is largely an embellished recasting of an anonymous eyewitness account known as the *Gesta Francorum* (*The Deeds of the Franks*). At several places in his history, however, Robert deviates from the *Gesta;* the most notable of these deviations is his detailed attempt to replicate the sense of Urban's words in 1095.

As you compare the two accounts, note the different ways in which Fulcher and Robert introduce the pope's sermon. Fulcher begins with the pope's addressing the assembled clerics on the issue of church reform and then moves on to the crusade sermon. Robert tells us that after the council had disposed of ecclesiastical matters, the pope delivered his crusade sermon in a public square.

QUESTIONS FOR ANALYSIS

1. How does Fulcher tie the crusade into the papal* reform movement? How does he connect it with the Peace and Truce of God movements?
2. According to Fulcher, how does Urban redefine knighthood?
3. Consider questions 1 and 2 in regard to Robert's account. Does he touch on these same issues?
4. According to Robert, how did the pope attempt to keep this movement from getting out of hand?
5. Make two lists, side by side. In one, list all of the similarities between the two sermons. In the other, list all of the significant dissimilarities. For example, to whom does the pope make his appeal? To whom does the pope promise "remission of sins"? Are Jerusalem and the Holy Sepulcher mentioned as crusade objectives in both sermons?
6. On the basis of these lists, what do you conclude were the points that, without a doubt, were in the pope's actual sermon? What points do you think *probably* or very likely were in the sermon? Do any points seem spurious or unlikely to you? Be ready to defend your answers.
7. On the basis of your analysis, who appears to be the better reporter, Fulcher or Robert, or can we even answer that question?

"Most beloved brethren[1]: Urged by necessity, I, Urban, by the permission of God chief bishop* and prelate over the whole world, have come into these parts as an ambassador with a divine admonition to you, the servants of God. I hoped to find you as faithful and as zealous in the service of God as I had supposed you to be. But if there is in you any deformity or crookedness contrary to God's law, with divine help I will do my best to remove it. For God has put you as stewards over His family to minister to it. Happy indeed will you be if He finds you faithful in your stewardship. You are called shepherds; see that you do not act as hirelings. But be true shepherds, with your crooks[2] always in your hands. Do not go to sleep, but guard on all sides the flock committed to you. For if through your carelessness or negligence a wolf carries away one of your sheep, you will surely lose the reward laid up for you with God. And after you have been bitterly scourged with remorse for your faults, you will be fiercely overwhelmed in hell, the abode of death. For according to the Gospel* you are the salt of the earth.[3] But if you fall short in your duty, how, it may be asked, can it be salted? O how great the need of salting! It is indeed necessary for you to correct with the salt of wisdom this foolish people which is so devoted to the pleasures of this world, lest the Lord, when He may wish to speak to them, find them putrefied by their sins, unsalted and stinking. For if He shall find worms, that is, sins, in them, because you have been negligent in your duty, He will command them as worthless to be thrown into the abyss of unclean things. And because you cannot restore to Him His great loss, He will surely condemn you and drive you from His loving presence. But the man who applies this salt should be prudent, provident, modest, learned, peaceable, watchful, pious, just, equitable, and

pure. For how can the ignorant teach others? How can the licentious make others modest? And how can the impure make others pure? If anyone hates peace, how can he make others peaceable? Or if anyone has soiled his hands with baseness, how can he cleanse the impurities of another? We read also that if the blind lead the blind, both will fall into the ditch.[4] But first correct yourselves, in order that, free from blame, you may be able to correct those who are subject to you. If you wish to be the friends of God, gladly do the things which you know will please Him. You must especially let all matters that pertain to the church be controlled by the law of the church. And be careful that simony* does not take root among you, lest both those who buy and those who sell [church offices] be beaten with the scourges of the Lord through narrow streets and driven into the place of destruction and confusion.[5] Keep the church and the clergy* in all its grades entirely free from the secular* power. See that the tithes* that belong to God are faithfully paid from all the produce of the land; let them not be sold or withheld. If anyone seizes a bishop let him be treated as an outlaw. If anyone seizes or robs monks,* or clergymen, or nuns,* or their servants, or pilgrims,* or merchants, let him be anathema.[6] Let robbers and incendiaries and all their accomplices be expelled from the church and anathematized. If a man who does not give a part of his goods as alms is punished with the damnation of hell, how should he be punished who robs another of his goods? For thus it happened to the rich man in the Gospel; for he was not punished because he had stolen the goods of another, but because he had not used well the things which were his.[7]

"You have seen for a long time the great disorder in the world caused by these crimes. It is so bad in some of your provinces, I am told, and

---

[1]Here, the pope addresses fellow prelates.*
[2]The shepherd's crook, or curved staff. Bishops and abbots carried a ceremonial staff as a symbol of their pastoral duties.
[3]The Bible, the Gospel of Matthew, 5:13.
[4]The Gospel of Matthew, 15:14.

[5]In his description of the crusaders' taking Jerusalem on July 15, 1099, Fulcher noted that the terrified "heathens" ran in terror through the narrow streets. Many of them fled to the Temple Mount, where they were slaughtered. The parallel was probably deliberate.
[6]Cursed and excommunicated.*
[7]The Gospel of Luke, 16:19.

you are so weak in the administration of justice, that one can hardly go along the road by day or night without being attacked by robbers; and whether at home or abroad, one is in danger of being despoiled either by force or fraud. Therefore it is necessary to reenact the truce, as it is commonly called, which was proclaimed a long time ago by our holy fathers.* I exhort and demand that you, each, try hard to have the truce kept in your diocese.* And if anyone shall be led by his cupidity or arrogance to break this truce, by the authority of God and with the sanction of this council he shall be anathematized."[8]

After these and various other matters had been attended to, all who were present, clergy and people, gave thanks to God and agreed to the pope's proposition. They all faithfully promised to keep the decrees. Then the pope said that in another part of the world Christianity was suffering from a state of affairs that was worse than the one just mentioned. He continued:

"Although, O sons of God, you have promised more firmly than ever to keep the peace among yourselves and to preserve the rights of the Church, there remains still an important work for you to do. Freshly quickened by the divine correction, you must apply the strength of your righteousness to another matter which concerns you as well as God. For your brethren who live in the East are in urgent need of your help, and you must hasten to give them the aid which has often been promised them. For, as the most of you have heard, the Turks and Arabs have attacked them and have conquered the territory of Romania[9] as far west as the shore of the Mediterranean and the Hellespont, which is called the Arm of St. George.[10] They have occupied more and more of the lands of those Christians, and have overcome them in seven battles. They have killed and captured many, and have destroyed the churches and devastated the empire. If you

permit them to continue thus for awhile with impunity, the faithful of God will be much more widely attacked by them. On this account I, or rather the Lord, beseech you as Christ's heralds to publish this everywhere and to persuade all people of whatever rank, foot-soldiers and knights, poor and rich, to carry aid promptly to those Christians and to destroy that vile race from the lands of our friends. I say this to those who are present; it is meant also for those who are absent. Moreover, Christ commands it.

"All who die by the way, whether by land or by sea, or in battle against the pagans, shall have immediate remission of sins. This I grant them through the power of God with which I am invested. O what a disgrace if such a despised and base race, which worships demons, should conquer a people which has the faith of omnipotent God and is made glorious with the name of Christ! With what reproaches will the Lord overwhelm us if you do not aid those who, with us, profess the Christian religion! Let those who have been accustomed unjustly to wage private warfare against the faithful now go against the infidels and end with victory this war which should have been begun long ago. Let those who, for a long time, have been robbers, now become knights. Let those who have been fighting against their brothers and relatives now fight in a proper way against the barbarians. Let those who have been serving as mercenaries for small pay now obtain the eternal reward. Let those who have been wearing themselves out in both body and soul now work for a double honor. Behold! on this side will be the sorrowful and poor, on that, the rich; on this side, the enemies of the Lord, on that, his friends. Let those who go not put off the journey, but rent their lands and collect money for their expenses; and as soon as winter is over and spring comes, let them eagerly set out on the way with God as their guide."

---

[8]The Council of Clermont renewed the Truce of God of 1041, which prohibited fighting from Wednesday evening to Monday morning and during the period of all church festivals and times of penance, such as Lent. On the truce (as well as the Peace of God), see Chapter 6, source 32.

[9]A Western term for the East Roman, or Byzantine, Empire.
[10]The narrow strait that separates Asia from Europe.

▼ ▼ ▼

In 1095 a great council was held in Auvergne, in the city of Clermont. Pope Urban II, accompanied by cardinals* and bishops, presided over it. It was made famous by the presence of many bishops and princes from France and Germany. After the council had attended to ecclesiastical matters, the pope went out into a public square, because no house was able to hold the people, and addressed them in a very persuasive speech, as follows: "O race of the Franks, O people who live beyond the mountains,[11] O people loved and chosen of God, as is clear from your many deeds, distinguished over all other nations by the situation of your land, your Catholic faith, and your regard for the holy Church, we have a special message and exhortation for you. For we wish you to know what a grave matter has brought us to your country. The sad news has come from Jerusalem and Constantinople that the people of Persia,[12] an accursed and foreign race, enemies of God, 'a generation that set not their heart aright, and whose spirit was not steadfast with God,'[13] have invaded the lands of those Christians and devastated them with the sword, rapine, and fire. Some of the Christians they have carried away as slaves, others they have put to death. The churches they have either destroyed or turned into mosques.[14] They desecrate and overthrow the altars. They circumcise the Christians[15] and pour the blood from the circumcision on the altars or in the baptismal* fonts. Some they kill in a horrible way by cutting open the abdomen, taking out a part of the entrails and tying them to a stake; they then beat them and compel them to walk until all their entrails are drawn out and they fall to the ground. Some they use as targets for their arrows. They compel some to stretch out their necks and then they try to see whether they can cut off their heads with one stroke of the sword. It is better to say nothing of their horrible treatment of the women. They have taken from the Greek empire a tract of land so large that it takes more than two months to walk through it. Whose duty is it to avenge this and recover that land, if not yours? For to you more than to other nations the Lord has given the military spirit, courage, agile bodies, and the bravery to strike down those who resist you. Let your minds be stirred to bravery by the deeds of your forefathers, and by the efficiency and greatness of Charles the Great, and of Louis his son, and of the other kings who have destroyed Turkish kingdoms,[16] and established Christianity in their lands. You should be moved especially by the holy grave of our Lord and Savior[17] which is now held by unclean peoples, and by the holy places which are treated with dishonor and irreverently befouled with their uncleanness.

"O bravest of knights, descendants of unconquered ancestors, do not be weaker than they, but remember their courage. If you are kept back by your love for your children, relatives, and wives, remember what the Lord says in the Gospel: 'He that loveth father or mother more than me is not worthy of me';[18] 'and everyone that hath forsaken houses, or brothers, or sisters, or father, or mother, or wife, or children, or lands for my name's sake, shall receive a hundredfold and shall inherit everlasting life.'[19] Let no possessions keep you back, no solicitude for your property. Your land is shut in on all sides by the sea and mountains, and is too thickly populated. There is not much wealth here, and the soil

---

[11]As viewed from Italy.

[12]The Seljuk Turks, who had conquered Iran and Iraq, occupied the lands of ancient Persia, but they were not Persians.

[13]The Book of Psalms, 78:8.

[14]Places of Islamic worship.

[15]Muslim males are circumcised. Therefore, Urban claims the Turks forcibly convert Eastern Christians to Islam.

[16]A reference to the West's earlier defeat of such Turkic peoples out of Inner Asia, such as the Avars and Magyars. Charlemagne's armies defeated the Avars, who had been around since the sixth century; the Magyars (Chapter 5, source 29; Chapter 6, source 35) attacked Western Europe during the ninth century.

[17]The Holy Sepulcher — Jesus' empty tomb. See Chapter 6, source 37, notes 1–3.

[18]The Gospel of Matthew, 10:37.

[19]The Gospel of Matthew, 19:29.

scarcely yields enough to support you. On this account you kill and devour each other, and carry on war and mutually destroy each other. Let your hatred and quarrels cease, your civil wars come to an end, and all your dissensions stop. Set out on the road to the holy sepulcher, take the land from that wicked people, and make it your own. That land which, as the Scripture says, is flowing with milk and honey, God gave to the children of Israel. Jerusalem is the best of all lands; more fruitful than all others, as it were a second Paradise of delights. This land our Savior made illustrious by his birth, beautiful with his life, and sacred with his suffering; He redeemed it with his death and glorified it with his tomb. This royal city is now held captive by her enemies, and made pagan by those who know not God. She asks and longs to be liberated and does not cease to beg you to come to her aid. She asks aid especially from you because, as I have said, God has given more of the military spirit to you than to other nations. Set out on this journey and you will obtain the remission of your sins and be sure of the incorruptible glory of the Kingdom of Heaven."

When Pope Urban had said this and much more of the same sort, all who were present were moved to cry out with one accord, "It is the will of God, it is the will of God." When the pope heard this he raised his eyes to heaven and gave thanks to God, and, commanding silence with a gesture of his hand, he said: "My dear brethren, today there is fulfilled in you that which the Lord says in the Gospel, 'Where two or three are gathered together in my name, there am I in the midst.'[20] For unless the Lord God had been in

your minds you would not all have said the same thing. For although you spoke with many voices, nevertheless it was one and the same thing that made you speak. So I say unto you, God, who put those words into your hearts, has caused you to utter them. Therefore let these words be your battle cry, because God caused you to speak them. Whenever you meet the enemy in battle, you shall all cry out, 'It is the will of God, it is the will of God.' And we do not command the old or weak to go, or those who cannot bear arms. No women shall go without their husbands, or brothers, or proper companions, for such would be a hindrance rather than a help, a burden rather than an advantage. Let the rich aid the poor and equip them for fighting and take them with them. Clergymen shall not go without the consent of their bishop, for otherwise the journey would be of no value to them. Nor will this pilgrimage be of any benefit to a layman if he goes without the blessing of his priest. Whoever therefore shall determine to make this journey and shall make a vow to God and shall offer himself as a living sacrifice, holy, acceptable to God,[21] shall wear a cross on his brow or on his breast. And when he returns after having fulfilled his vow he shall wear the cross on his back. In this way he will obey the command of the Lord, 'Whosoever doth not bear his cross and come after me is not worthy of me.'"[22] When these things had been done, while all prostrated themselves on the earth and beat their breasts, one of the cardinals, named Gregory, made confession* for them, and they were given absolution for all their sins. After the absolution, they received the benediction and the permission to go home.

---

[20]The Gospel of Matthew, 18:20.
[21]St. Paul's Epistle to the Romans, 12:1.

[22]The Gospel of Luke, 14:27.

Illuminating the Crusade
▼▼▼

73 ▼ *FOUR THIRTEENTH-CENTURY MANUSCRIPT MINIATURES*

The crusades excited an outpouring of artistic expression in Europe, particularly from about 1100 to around 1250, the most intensive period of crusading activity. In addition to crusade histories, authors composed poems, songs, and popular tales that focused on the ideals and all-too-often grim realities of crusading. Visual artists displayed an equal fascination with holy war. It was the rare thirteenth-century Gothic church that did not have sculptures and stained glass windows portraying crusade themes. The other end of the spectrum of the visual arts was manuscript illumination — the illustration of hand-produced books through the use of decorated letters, marginal drawings, and small paintings known as *miniatures*. Manuscript production reached a high point of sophistication in this era, and crusade histories provided illuminators with a rich variety of possibilities.

The four miniatures printed here appear on the initial page of a thirteenth-century French translation and continuation of William of Tyre's late-twelfth-century history of the crusader states in Palestine. Here we see, in four connected scenes, a graphic portrayal of the meaning of Urban II's crusade message. The miniature in the upper-left corner portrays Christ's crucifixion. Immediately flanking the cross are two Roman centurions. The Virgin stands in the far left of the picture, and St. John the Apostle is in the far right. The picture in the upper right depicts Urban II preaching the crusade to a crowd of five men and one woman; three of the listeners, two men and a woman, kneel in the foreground, while three men stand in the background. The lower-left square shows a kneeling crowned pilgrim,* possibly King Baldwin I of the Latin kingdom of Jerusalem, praying before the Holy Sepulcher. The lower-right miniature portrays three kneeling men worshipping an idol in Jerusalem, while two onlookers, a man and a woman, stand behind them.

QUESTIONS FOR ANALYSIS

1. Each miniature is connected to the other three. What is the relationship of each picture to its three neighbors? In addressing this question, pay attention to the characters who appear in each scene, as well as the overall scene itself.
2. On the basis of your answers to question 1, what do you conclude is the overall message of this group of miniatures?
3. How well has the artist captured the spirit and message of Urban's crusade sermon? Has the artist left out any important elements?

Four Miniatures

Crusade Reality

Urban II characterized the crusade as an act of heroic self-sacrifice and love in which a main objective was to rescue the Christians of the East. As happens all too often, though, reality deviated greatly from the ideal.

The crusaders who marched eastward in 1096 and in the nearly two hundred years that followed were a mixed lot, drawn from all levels of society. They shared several common characteristics, however. Most went on crusade out of a desire to gain salvation, as they believed they would merit God's grace through their sacrifices and sufferings. Notwithstanding the allure of adventure and possible riches in the land of milk and honey, the majority of crusaders looked upon the expedition as one of great physical deprivation and hazard but also as the central sacramental* moment of their lives. Pain was certain, but spiritual gain was even more certain. A second common characteristic is that the crusaders believed that violence could be an effective tool in combating evil. More than that, they believed that God commanded holy warfare in both the Bible and in their own day.

Religious fervor and a proclivity to use armed might to achieve desirable ends are a volatile combination, as many people who encountered the crusaders discovered. The first two of the following documents show crusaders as viewed by European Jews and a Muslim Arab. The third illustrates how the crusades also managed to drive a wedge of mutual hostility between Byzantium and the West.

Crusaders and Jews
▼▼▼
74 ▼ *Solomon Bar Simson, CHRONICLE*

The First Crusade spilled out of Europe in three major waves. The first wave, which left Europe in early 1096, consisted of a number of disorganized and often poorly armed contingents of enthusiastic individuals drawn largely but not exclusively from the lower orders of society. Due to poor leadership and poorer discipline, these groups left swaths of destruction in their paths, as they marched to their own destruction in Anatolia.* By late August 1096, the so-called People's Crusade was over, its members largely dead or enslaved. The second wave was more successful. Consisting largely of independent armies of warriors and associated followers and led by some of France's greatest lords, the different elements of the Nobles' Crusade left Europe serially in late 1096 and rendezvoused in Constantinople in early 1097. Despite discord, defections, and hardships, the grand crusader army managed to capture several major cities and their surrounding territories in the Holy Land. The crowning achievement of this crusade was the bloody capture of Jerusalem on July 15, 1099, and the creation of the Latin kingdom of Jerusalem the following year. The third wave of the crusade was a series of ill-fated expeditions to shore up the newly created crusader states. Launched between 1100 and 1101, these expeditions proved ineffective and mainly met disaster.

One of the contingents that participated in the crusade's first wave was led by Emicho, count of Leiningen in the Rhineland. Emicho, who held lands between the Rhenish cities of Mainz and Worms, was a notorious robber baron, whom even Christian chroniclers of the crusade excoriated as a self-serving fraud. Jewish chroniclers had even worse things to write about Emicho and his followers.

In May of 1096 Emicho's crusaders marched northward (not exactly a direct route to the Holy Land) along the Rhine and, in the words of the Christian chronicler Ekkehard of Aura, "persecuted the hated race of Jews wherever they found them and strove either to destroy them completely or to compel them to become Christians." On May 3 Emicho's band unsuccessfully stormed the synagogue of Speyer, killing eleven Jews in the process. John, the bishop* of Speyer, then intervened with troops and took all surviving Jews into his castle, where he protected them from further harm. He even cut off the hands of some citizens of Speyer who had aided the crusaders. Frustrated at Speyer, Emicho's followers marched to Worms, where more than eight hundred Jews perished as a result of the attacks upon them. Hearing of the massacre, the Jews of nearby Mainz petitioned the city's bishop, Ruthard, for protection, paying him a large amount of silver to this end. On May 27 the crusaders arrived at Mainz's gates, where they were greeted by Christian townspeople who threw open the gates to them. In 1140 Solomon Bar Simson composed the following account of the horrors visited upon the Jews of Mainz.

QUESTIONS FOR ANALYSIS

1. Bar Simson places in the crusaders' mouths a rationale for their attacks on the Jews. Leaving aside the issue of how Bar Simson has the crusaders refer to their faith, does it seem to be a likely motive? Why or why not?
2. Is there any evidence here that religious zeal might not have been the only motive for attacking the Jews? Explain your answer.
3. According to Bar Simson, why did God allow this persecution to happen?
4. How did the Jews of Mainz respond psychologically and physically to the attacks on them?
5. Refer to article 6 of Bishop Rudegar's charter to the Jews of Speyer (Chapter 8, source 51). Why is it logical to conclude that the Jews of Mainz had similar rights and responsibilities?
6. Consider the acts of self-martyrdom, which had their parallels in earlier Jewish history and in other Jewish communities attacked by the crusaders. How did the Jewish martyrs justify the acts? What do they suggest about the values and mindset of the Jews of Mainz? Perhaps your answer to question 3 might offer some clues.
7. What does this account suggest about the level of knowledge that Christians and Jews had of one another at the time of the First Crusade? What does it suggest about their attitudes toward one another?
8. Compare the values, attitudes, and world view exhibited in Bar Simson's account with those exhibited in sources 72 and 73. What conclusions do you reach?

At this time arrogant people, a people of strange speech, a nation bitter and impetuous, Frenchmen and Germans, set out for the Holy City, which had been desecrated by barbaric nations, there to seek their house of idolatry[1] and banish the Ishmaelites[2] and other denizens of the land and conquer the land for themselves. They decorated themselves prominently with their signs, placing a profane symbol — a horizontal line over a vertical one — on the vestments of every man and woman whose heart yearned to go on the stray path to the grave of their Messiah. Their

---

[1]The church that housed the sites of both Mount Calvary, where Jesus was crucified, and the Holy Sepulcher. See Chapter 6, source 37, notes 1, 2, 3, and 8.

[2]Muslims, who claim religious descent from Abraham through his elder son, Ishmael.

ranks swelled until the number of men, women, and children exceeded a locust horde covering the earth. . . . Now it came to pass that as they passed through the towns where Jews dwelled, they said to one another: "Look now, we are going a long way to seek out the profane shrine and to avenge ourselves on the Ishmaelites, when here, in our very midst, are the Jews — they whose forefathers murdered and crucified him for no reason. Let us first avenge ourselves on them and exterminate them from among the nations so that the name of Israel will no longer be remembered, or let them adopt our faith and acknowledge the offspring of promiscuity."[3]

When the Jewish communities became aware of their intentions, they resorted to the custom of our ancestors, repentance, prayer, and charity. The hands of the Holy Nation turned faint at this time, their hearts melted, and their strength flagged. They hid in their innermost rooms to escape the swirling sword. They subjected themselves to great endurance, abstaining from food and drink for three consecutive days and nights, and then fasting many days from sunrise to sunset, until their skin was shriveled and dry as wood upon their bones. And they cried out loudly and bitterly to God. . . .

However, God, the maker of peace, turned aside and averted His eyes from His people, and consigned them to the sword. No prophet, seer, or man of wise heart was able to comprehend how the sin of the people infinite in number was deemed so great as to cause the destruction of so many lives in the various Jewish communities. The martyrs endured the extreme penalty normally inflicted only upon one guilty of murder. Yet, it must be stated with certainty that God is a righteous judge, and we are to blame.

Then the evil waters prevailed. The enemy unjustly accused them of evil acts they did not do, declaring: "You are the children of those who killed our object of veneration, hanging him on a tree;[4] and he himself had said: 'There will yet come a day when my children will come and avenge my blood.'[5] We are his children and it is therefore obligatory for us to avenge him since you are the ones who rebel and disbelieve in him. Your God has never been at peace with you. Although He intended to deal kindly with you, you have conducted yourselves improperly before Him. God has forgotten you and is no longer desirous of you since you are a stubborn nation. Instead, He has departed from you and has taken us for His portion, casting His radiance upon us."

When we heard these words, our hearts trembled and moved out of their places. We were dumb with silence, abiding in darkness, like those long dead, waiting for the Lord to look forth and behold from heaven. . . .

At midday the evil Emicho, oppressor of the Jews, came to the gate with his entire horde. The townspeople opened the gate to him, and the enemies of the Lord said to one another: "See, they have opened the gate for us; now let us avenge the blood of the crucified one."

When the people of the Holy Covenant, the saints, the fearers of the Most High, saw the great multitude, a vast horde of them, as the sand upon the seashore, they clung to their Creator. They donned their armor and their weapons of war, adults and children alike, with Rabbi Kalonymos, the son of Rabbi Meshullam, . . . at their head. But, as a result of their sufferings and fasts, they did not have the strength to withstand the onslaught of the foe. The troops and legions surged in like a streaming river until finally Mainz was completely overrun from end to end. . . .

The Jews armed themselves in the inner court of the bishop, and they all advanced toward the gate to fight against the errant ones and the burghers. The two sides fought against each other around the gate, but as a result of their trans-

---

[3]In Christian-Jewish polemic, Jews argued that Mary, Jesus' mother, conceived without being married. Christians argued that Jesus was born to a married couple, but his mother was a virgin and the conception was God's work.

[4]The cross.

[5]Compare this with the Bible, the Gospel of Matthew, 27:25.

gressions the enemy overpowered them and captured the gate. The hand of the Lord rested heavily on His people, and all the Gentiles assembled against the Jews in the courtyard to exterminate them. Our people's strength flagged when they saw that the hand of evil Edom[6] was prevailing against them. The bishop's people, who had promised to help them, being as broken reedstaffs, were the first to flee, so as to cause them to fall into the hands of the enemy. The bishop himself fled from his church, for they wanted to kill him, too, because he had spoken in favor of the Jews. The enemy entered the courtyard on the third day of Sivan,[7] the third day of the week — a day of darkness and gloom, a day of clouds and thick darkness; let darkness and the shadow of death claim it for their own. Let God not inquire after it from above, nor let the light shine upon it. Alas for the day on which we saw the torment of our soul! O stars — why did you not withhold your light? Has not Israel been compared to the stars and the twelve constellations, according to the number of Jacob's sons? Why, then, did you not withhold your light from shining for the enemy who sought to eradicate the name of Israel?

When the people of the Sacred Covenant saw that the Heavenly decree had been issued and that the enemy had defeated them and were entering the courtyard, they all cried out together — old and young, maidens and children, menservants and maids — to their Father in Heaven. They wept for themselves and for their lives and proclaimed the justness of the Heavenly judgment, and they said to one another: "Let us be of good courage and bear the yoke of the Holy Creed, for now the enemy can only slay us by the sword, and death by the sword is the lightest of the four deaths.[8] We shall then merit eternal life, and our souls will abide in the Garden of Eden

in the presence of the great luminous mirror forever."

All of them declared willingly and wholeheartedly, "After all things, there is no questioning the ways of the Holy One, blessed be He and blessed be His Name, Who has given us His Torah[9] and has commanded us to allow ourselves to be killed and slain in witness to the Oneness of His Holy Name. Happy are we if we fulfill His will, and happy is he who is slain or slaughtered and who dies attesting the Oneness of His Name. Such a one is destined for the World-to-Come, where he will sit in the realm of the saints — Rabbi Akiba and his companions, pillars of the universe, who were killed in witness to His Name.[10] Moreover — for such a one a world of darkness is exchanged for a world of light, a world of sorrow for one of joy, a transitory world for an eternal world."

Then in a great voice they all cried out as one: "We need tarry no longer, for the enemy is already upon us. Let us hasten and offer ourselves as a sacrifice before God. Anyone possessing a knife should examine it to see that it is not defective, and let him then proceed to slaughter us in sanctification of the Unique and Eternal One, then slaying himself — either cutting his throat or thrusting the knife into his stomach."

Upon entering the courtyard, the enemy encountered some of perfect piety, including Rabbi Isaac, son of Rabbi Moses, uprooter of mountains. He extended his neck and was the first to be decapitated. The others wrapped themselves in their fringed prayer shawls and sat in the courtyard waiting to expedite the will of their Creator, not wishing to flee within the chambers just to be saved for temporal life, for lovingly they accepted Heaven's judgment. The foe hurled stones and arrows at them, but they did not scurry to flee; the enemy smote all whom they

---

[6]Another name for Esau, Jacob's half-brother. Esau was the father of the Edomites, the sworn enemy of the Children of Israel: The Book of Genesis, 36:1–43.
[7]May 27, 1096.
[8]The four talmudic methods of execution were by stoning, burning, strangulation, and beheading.

[9]The Law, which consists of the first five books of the Tanakh, or Jewish Bible.
[10]Martyrs of the second century A.D.

found there with their swords, causing slaughter and destruction.

Those Jews in the chambers, seeing what the enemy had inflicted upon the saints, cried out: "There is none like our God unto whom it would be better to offer our lives." The women girded their loins with strength and slew their own sons and daughters, and then themselves. Many men also mustered their strength and slaughtered their wives and children and infants. The most gentle and tender of women slaughtered the child of her delight. They all arose, man and woman alike, and slew one another. The young maidens, the brides, and the bridegrooms looked out through the windows and cried out in a great voice: "Look and behold, O Lord, what we are doing to sanctify Thy Great Name, in order not to exchange You for a crucified scion who was despised, abominated, and held in contempt in his own generation, a bastard son conceived by a menstruating and wanton mother."

Thus the precious children of Zion, the people of Mainz, were tested with ten trials as was our Father Abraham. . . . They, too, bound their children in sacrifice, as Abraham did his son Isaac,[11] and willingly accepted upon themselves the yoke of fear of Heaven, of the King of Kings, the Blessed Holy One. Refusing to gainsay their faith and replace the fear of our King with an abominable stock, bastard son of a menstruating and wanton mother, they extended their necks for slaughter and offered up their pure souls to their Father in Heaven. The saintly and pious women acted in a similar manner, extending their necks to each other in willing sacrifice in witness to the Oneness of God's name — and each man likewise to his son and brother, brother to sister, mother to son and daughter, neighbor to neighbor and friend, bridegroom to bride, fiancé to his betrothed; each first sacrificed the other and then in turn yielded to be sacrificed, until the streams of blood touched and mingled, and the blood of husbands joined with that of their wives,

the blood of fathers with that of their sons, the blood of brothers with that of their sisters, the blood of teachers with that of their pupils, the blood of bridegrooms with that of their brides, the blood of community deacons with that of their scribes, the blood of babes and sucklings with that of their mothers — all killed and slaughtered in witness to the Oneness of the Venerated and Awesome Name. . . .

The enemy came into the chambers, they smashed the doors, and found the Jews still writhing and rolling in blood; and the enemy took their money, stripped them naked, and slew those still alive, leaving neither a vestige nor a remnant. Thus they did in all the chambers where children of the Sacred Covenent were to be found. But one room remained which was somewhat difficult to break into; there the enemy fought till nightfall.

When the saints saw that the enemy was prevailing over them and that they would be unable to withstand them any longer, they acted speedily; they rose up, men and women alike, slaughtered the children. Then the righteous women hurled stones from the windows on the enemy, and the enemy threw rocks back at them. The women were struck by the stones, and their bodies and faces were completely bruised and cut. They taunted and reviled the errant ones with the name of the crucified, despicable, and abominable son of harlotry, saying: "In whom do you place your trust? In a putrid corpse!" The misled ones then approached to smash the door.

Who has seen or heard of an act like the deed of the righteous and pious young Mistress Rachel, daughter of Isaac, son of Asher, and wife of Judah? She said to her friends: "Four children have I. Have no mercy on them either, lest those uncircumcised ones come and seize them alive and raise them in their ways of error. In my children, too, shall you sanctify the Holy Name of God."[12] One of her friends came and took the knife to slaughter her son. When the "mother of the sons"

---

[11]The Book of Exodus, 22:1–14.

[12]The act of self-martyrdom is often called *kiddush ha-Shem* (sanctification of the [Divine] Name).

saw the knife, she cried loudly and bitterly and smote her face and breast, and said: "Where is Your grace, O Lord?" With an embittered heart she [the mother] said to her companions: "Do not slaughter Isaac before his brother Aaron, so that he [Aaron] will not see the death of his brother and flee." A friend took the boy and slew him. A delightful little child he was. The mother spread her sleeves to receive the blood, according to the practice in the ancient Temple sacrificial rite.[13] The lad Aaron, upon seeing that his brother had been slaughtered, cried: "Mother, do not slaughter me," and fled, hiding under a box.

She also had left two daughters, Bella and Madrona, modest and beautiful maidens. The maidens took the knife and sharpened it, so that it would have no notch.[14] They extended their throats, and the mother sacrificed them to the Lord, God of Hosts, Who commanded us not to depart from His pure doctrine, and to remain wholehearted with Him, as it is written: "Thou shalt be wholehearted with the Lord thy God."[15]

When this pious woman had completed sacrificing her three children to their Creator, she raised her voice and called to her son: "Aaron, Aaron, where are you? I will not spare you either, or have mercy on you." She drew him out by his feet from under the box where he had hid-

den and slaughtered him before the Exalted and Lofty God. Then she placed them all on her arms, two children on one side and two on the other, beside her stomach, and they quivered beside her, until finally the enemy captured the chamber and found her there sitting and lamenting over them. They said to her: "Show us the money you have in your sleeves"; but when they saw the slaughtered children, they smote and killed her upon them, and her pure soul expired. . . .

When the father saw the death of his four children, beautiful in form and appearance, he cried bitterly and threw himself on the sword in his hand, and was thus disemboweled. He writhed in his blood on the road together with the others quivering and writhing in their blood. The enemy slew all who remained inside and stripped them naked. "See, O Lord, and behold, how abject I am become."[16]

The errant ones then began to rage tumultuously in the name of the crucified one, having their way with all those found in the chamber of the bishop; and there was not a single survivor. They raised their banners, and in an uproar proceeded to the remainder of the community in front of the count's courtyard. They besieged them, too, until they had taken the gatehouse of the courtyard, and slew those who were there.[17]

---

[13]The Book of Exodus, 29:18–21.
[14]The knife used for ancient Temple sacrifices had to be perfectly sharp.
[15]Deuteronomy, 18:13.

[16]The Book of Lamentations, 1:11.
[17]One early twelfth-century Jewish source estimates that thirteen hundred Jews died at Mainz that day.

Crusaders and Muslims

▼▼▼

75 ▼ Usamah ibn Munqidh, *THE BOOK OF REFLECTIONS*

According to both Fulcher of Chartres and Robert the Monk, Pope Urban II characterized the Muslim Turks as barbarians who were guilty of inhumane outrages against the Christians of the East. Moreover, those who took up the challenge to fight these "pagans" were following the Divine Will and thereby earned God's friendship. We have already seen how Jews in Western Europe had a different opinion regarding the crusaders. Imagine what Muslims in the East thought.

One of the most telling commentaries on crusader behavior in Syria-Palestine comes from the memoirs of Usamah ibn Munqidh (1095–1188), an Arab-Muslim warrior and gentleman of Syria. Born in the year in which the First Crusade was called, Usamah lived long enough to see Jerusalem reconquered in 1187 by his friend and patron Saladin, sultan of Egypt and Syria. Late in life, sometime past his ninetieth birthday, Usamah undertook the narration of his memoirs. Although his descriptions of the Western "Franks" constitute only a small segment of this amiably rambling work, they are among the autobiography's most fascinating and insightful sections.

QUESTIONS FOR ANALYSIS

1. According to Usamah, what are the Franks' chief deficiencies?
2. Does he acknowledge any virtues or positive qualities on their part?
3. *Acculturation* is the process whereby one ethnic group adopts the cultural traits of another. Can you find any evidence of this phenomenon in Usamah's account? Explain your answer.
4. What evidence do you see of friendly, or at least peaceful, relations between the crusaders and the Muslims of Syria-Palestine? To what do you ascribe such relations?
5. Despite such relations, what the elements separated the crusaders and Muslims?
6. What is the general tone and overall message of Usamah's commentary on the Franks?

AN APPRECIATION OF THE FRANKISH CHARACTER

Their Lack of Sense

Mysterious are the works of the Creator, the author of all things! When one comes to recount cases regarding the Franks,[1] he cannot but glorify Allah (exalted is he!) and sanctify him, for he sees them as animals possessing the virtues of courage and fighting, but nothing else; just as animals have only the virtues of strength and carrying loads. I shall now give some instances of their doings and their curious mentality.

In the army of King Fulk,[2] son of Fulk, was a Frankish reverend knight who had just arrived from their land in order to make the holy pilgrimage* and then return home. He was of my intimate fellowship and kept such constant company with me that he began to call me "my brother." Between us were mutual bonds of amity and friendship. When he resolved to return by sea to his homeland, he said to me:

My brother, I am leaving for my country and I want you to send with me your son (my son, who was then fourteen years old, was at that time in my company) to our country, where he can see the knights and learn wisdom and chivalry. When he returns, he will be like a wise man.

Thus there fell upon my ears words which would never come out of the head of a sensible

---

[1]To the peoples of the eastern Mediterranean, all Western Europeans were *Franks,* or *Franj.*

[2]Fulk, count of Anjou and king of Jerusalem (r. 1131–1143).

man; for even if my son were to be taken captive, his captivity could not bring him a worse misfortune than carrying him into the lands of the Franks. However, I said to the man:

By your life, this has exactly been my idea. But the only thing that prevented me from carrying it out was the fact that his grandmother, my mother, is so fond of him and did not this time let him come out with me until she exacted an oath from me to the effect that I would return him to her.

Thereupon he asked, "Is your mother still alive?" "Yes," I replied. "Well," said he, "disobey her not." . . .

Newly Arrived Franks Are Especially Rough: One Insists That Usamah Should Pray Eastward

Everyone who is a fresh emigrant from the Frankish lands is ruder in character than those who have become acclimatized and have held long association with the Muslims. Here is an illustration of their rude character.

Whenever I visited Jerusalem I always entered the Aqsa Mosque,[3] beside which stood a small mosque which the Franks had converted into a church. When I used to enter the Aqsa Mosque, which was occupied by the Templars,[4] who were my friends, the Templars would evacuate the little adjoining mosque so that I might pray in

it. One day[5] I entered this mosque, repeated the first formula, "Allah is great," and stood up in the act of praying, upon which one of the Franks rushed on me, got hold of me and turned my face eastward saying, "This is the way you should pray!" A group of Templars hastened to him, seized him, and repelled him from me. I resumed my prayer. The same man, while the others were otherwise busy, rushed once more on me and turned my face eastward, saying, "This is the way you should pray!" The Templars again came in to him and expelled him. They apologized to me, saying, "This is a stranger who has only recently arrived from the land of the Franks and he has never before seen anyone praying except eastward." Thereupon I said to myself, "I have had enough prayer." So I went out and have ever been surprised at the conduct of this devil of a man, at the change in the color of his face, his trembling and his sentiment at the sight of one praying towards the *qiblah.*[6]

Another Wants to Show to a Muslim God As a Child

I saw one of the Franks come to al-Amir[7] Mu'in-al-Din (may Allah's mercy rest upon his soul!) when he was in the Dome of the Rock[8] and say to him, "Do you want to see God as a child?" Mu'in-al-Din said, "Yes." The Frank walked ahead of us until he showed us the picture of Mary with Christ (may peace be upon him!) as an infant in her lap. He then said, "This is God

---

[3]Al-Aqsa mosque on Jerusalem's Temple Mount, the site of Judaism's first and second Temples of the Lord.

[4]The earliest, largest, and most famous of the military orders (Chapter 10, source 68, note 4). Knights joining the orders took religious vows of poverty, chastity, and obedience, pledging to live the remainder of their days under quasi-monastic* rules, but they remained warriors, fighting against unbelievers in Syria-Palestine and elsewhere. The Templars received their name from the fact that King Baldwin II of Jerusalem (r. 1118–1131) granted them lodging in his palace, the former Muslim mosque of al-Aqsa (note 3), which the crusaders mistakenly called *Solomon's Temple.*

[5]Around 1140.

[6]The niche in every mosque that indicates the direction of Mecca, toward which all Muslims pray. Depending on where a mosque is in relation to Mecca, the *qiblah* can point in any direction of the compass. To the contrary, it was the custom of Roman, or Latin, Christians to build all altars so that the priests* and worshippers standing before them faced east, the general direction of Jerusalem from West Europe. Ironically, the church of the Holy Sepulcher, the site in Jerusalem in whose direction Latin Christians in Europe prayed, lies about four hundred yards northwest of al-Aqsa.

[7]*Amir* (commander) was a title bestowed on military leaders and local lords.

[8]Located on the Temple Mount near al-Aqsa mosque, this late-seventh-century Muslim shrine sits above the rock tip of Mount Moriah, the site that tradition identifies as the holy of holies of the temple of Solomon.

as a child." But Allah is exalted far above what the infidels say about him! . . .

Their Judicial Trials: A Duel

I attended one day a duel in Nablus between two Franks. The reason for this was that certain Muslim thieves took by surprise one of the villages of Nablus. One of the peasants of that village was charged with having acted as guide for the thieves when they fell upon the village. So he fled away. The king sent and arrested his children. The peasant thereupon came back to the king and said, "Let justice be done in my case. I challenge to a duel the man who claimed that I guided the thieves to the village." The king then said to the tenant who held the village in fief,* "Bring forth someone to fight the duel with him." The tenant went to his village, where a blacksmith lived, took hold of him and ordered him to fight the duel. The tenant became thus sure of the safety of his own peasants, none of whom would be killed and his estate ruined.

I saw this blacksmith. He was a physically strong young man, but his heart failed him. He would walk a few steps and then sit down and ask for a drink. The one who had made the challenge was an old man, but he was strong in spirit and he would rub the nail of his thumb against that of the forefinger in defiance, as if he was not worrying over the duel. Then came the viscount, i.e., the lord of the town, and gave each one of the two contestants a cudgel and a shield and arranged the people in a circle around them.

The two met. The old man would press the blacksmith backward until he would get him as far as the circle, then he would come back to the middle of the arena. They went on exchanging blows until they looked like pillars smeared with blood. The contest was prolonged and the viscount began to urge them to hurry, saying, "Hurry on." The fact that the smith was given to the use of the hammer proved now of great advantage to him. The old man was worn out

and the smith gave him a blow which made him fall. His cudgel fell under his back. The smith knelt down over him and tried to stick his fingers into the eyes of his adversary, but could not do it because of the great quantity of blood flowing out. Then he rose up and hit his head with the cudgel until he killed him. They then fastened a rope around the neck of the dead person, dragged him away and hanged him. The lord who brought the smith now came, gave the smith his own mantle, made him mount the horse behind him and rode off with him. This case illustrates the kind of jurisprudence and legal decisions the Franks have — may Allah's curse be upon them!

Ordeal by Water

I once went in the company of al-Amir Mu'in-al-Din (may Allah's mercy rest upon his soul!) to Jerusalem. We stopped at Nablus. There a blind man, a Muslim, who was still young and was well dressed, presented himself before al-amir carrying fruits for him and asked permission to be admitted into his service in Damascus.[9] The amir consented. I inquired about this man and was informed that his mother had been married to a Frank whom she had killed. Her son used to practice ruses against the Frankish pilgrims and cooperate with his mother in assassinating them. They finally brought charges against him and tried his case according to the Frankish way of procedure.

They installed a huge cask and filled it with water. Across it they set a board of wood. They then bound the arms of the man charged with the act, tied a rope around his shoulders and dropped him into the cask, their idea being that in case he was innocent, he would sink in the water and they would then lift him up with the rope so that he might not die in the water; and in case he was guilty, he would not sink in the water. This man did his best to sink when they dropped him into the water, but he could not do

---

[9] One of the two major Muslim-held cities in Syria.

it. So he had to submit to their sentence against him — may Allah's curse be upon them! They pierced his eyeballs with red-hot awls.

Later the same man arrived in Damascus. Al-Amir Mu'in-al-Din (may Allah's mercy rest upon his soul!) assigned him a stipend large enough to meet all his needs and said to a slave of his, "Conduct him to Burhan-al-Din al-Balkhi (may Allah's mercy rest upon his soul!) and ask him on my behalf to order somebody to teach this man the Qur'an and something of Muslim jurisprudence. . . .

A Frank Domesticated in Syria Abstains from Eating Pork

Among the Franks are those who have become acclimatized and have associated long with the Muslims. These are much better than the recent comers from the Frankish lands. But they constitute the exception and cannot be treated as a rule.

Here is an illustration. I dispatched one of my men to Antioch[10] on business. There was in Antioch at that time al-Ra'is Theodoros Sophianos,[11] to whom I was bound by mutual ties of amity. His influence in Antioch was supreme. One day he said to my man, "I am invited by a friend of mine who is a Frank. You should come with me so that you may see their fashions." My man related the story in the following words:

I went along with him and we came to the home of a knight who belonged to the old category of knights who came with the early expeditions of the Franks. He had been by that time stricken off the register and exempted from service, and possessed in Antioch an estate on the income of which he lived. The knight presented an excellent table, with food extraordinarily clean and delicious. Seeing me abstaining from food, he said, "Eat, be of good cheer! I never eat Frankish dishes, but I have Egyptian women cooks and never eat except their cooking. Besides, pork never enters my home."[12]

I ate, but guardedly, and after that we departed.

As I was passing in the market place, a Frankish woman all of a sudden hung to my clothes and began to mutter words in their language, and I could not understand what she was saying. This made me immediately the center of a big crowd of Franks. I was convinced that death was at hand. But all of a sudden that same knight approached. On seeing me, he came and said to that woman, "What is the matter between you and this Muslim?" She replied, "This is he who has killed my brother Hurso." This Hurso was a knight in Afamiyah who was killed by someone of the army of Hamah. The Christian knight shouted at her saying, "This is a bourgeois [i.e., a merchant] who neither fights nor attends a fight." He also yelled at the people who had assembled, and they all dispersed. Then he took me by the hand and went away. Thus the effect of that meal was my deliverance from certain death.

---

[10]The chief Christian city of Syria; it fell to the crusaders in 1098.

[11]The name indicates he was a Greek.

[12]Islamic law prohibits the eating of pork, because it is an unclean food.

Crusaders and Greeks

▼▼▼

76 ▼ *Gunther of Pairis,* *HYSTORIA CONSTANTINOPOLITANA*

Because of their location, the Greeks of Byzantium found themselves, usually unwillingly, caught up in the conflict of the crusades. Although Emperor Alexius I had applied to the West for help against the Turks, he never imagined that his empire would be invaded by waves of often poorly disciplined Western Christians trekking eastward to do battle for the Holy Land. To be sure, Urban II had called upon Western Europeans to rush to the rescue of their Eastern Christian siblings, but as far as many Byzantines were concerned, the pope's summons to action resulted in nothing less than a barbarian invasion from the West. In her history of her father's reign, Anna Comnena (1083–after 1148), daughter of Emperor Alexius I, characterized the Western crusaders as unstable, greedy for money, and always ready to break their word.

Before the First Crusade was over, Latin and Greek Christians had already clashed on the field of battle, although these initial skirmishes were not terribly serious, except to the people who died in them. During the twelfth century, as Latin fortunes suffered a number of reverses in the Holy Land, two additional major crusades were sent eastward, the Second Crusade (1147–1149) and the Third Crusade (1189–1192). Each further exacerbated Latin-Byzantine relations by engendering increasingly sharp conflicts and misunderstandings.

Following the Muslim recapture of Jerusalem in 1187 and the failure of the Third Crusade to retake the holy city, the West was especially eager to strike back at Islam. In the early thirteenth century, a force made up largely of French warriors and Venetian sailors planned to strike at Islam by capturing Alexandria in Egypt, thereby relieving pressure on the embattled Latin settlements in the Holy Land. That particular assault never took place. Rather, circumstances led the army and fleet of the Fourth Crusade (1202–1204) to Constantinople, where the crusaders became embroiled in a dynastic power struggle between rival imperial claimants. Eventually, the crusaders attacked Constantinople on April 12, 1204, and captured it the following day. After three days of brutal looting, the crusaders settled down and established the Latin Empire of Constantinople (1204–1261).

The Byzantines regained their capital city in 1261, but their empire was, by then, largely a shadow of its former self. Just as significant, the events of 1204 caused the final and, until today, irreconcilable rupture between the Roman Catholic and Eastern Orthodox* branches of Christianity.

One of the participants in the April 1204 looting of Constantinople was Martin, abbot* of the Cistercian monastery* of Pairis, which was located in the Vosges mountains of German-speaking Alsace. Upon his return to Pairis in 1205, Martin commissioned one of the monastery's brothers, Gunther, to compose an account of the abbot's adventures on the crusade. Gunther (ca. 1150?–after 1210?), already an accomplished scholar and poet, took this opportunity to construct the

Hystoria Constantinopolitana (*A Constantinopolitan History*), a masterpiece of art-fully intermingled prose and poetry, whose purpose was to reveal the ways of God to humanity.

In the following two selections, Gunther uses prose and poetry to pass judgment on Constantinople; to explain the reasons, both human and divine, behind the crusaders' decision to travel to that city in 1203; and to justify the assault of April 1204. The first selection appears in Chapter 11 of Gunther's twenty-five-chapter history. Here, at the pivotal point in his story, the author stops to reflect on the meaning of what is about to unfold. The second selection serves as a poetic explanation of why and how the crusaders attacked the Christian city of Constantinople.

QUESTIONS FOR ANALYSIS

1. According to Gunther, do either the crusaders or God hate the Byzantines or wish to destroy them? Explain your answer.
2. According to Gunther, why did God will the crusader capture of Constantinople?
3. What is Gunther's attitude toward Greek Christians?
4. According to Gunther, in what ways were the crusaders' motives to go to Constantinople a mixture of piety and greed? What does this suggest about crusader motives in general? Does Gunther judge them severely for this? Again, explain your answer.
5. The *Hystoria Constantinopolitana* has numerous echoes of Robert the Monk's *Historia Iherosolymitana*. How do the two selections echo Robert's version of Urban's speech (source 72)? How do they alter Urban's message? What purpose and message lie behind Gunther's artistry here?
6. What do these two selections suggest about relations between the two churches in the early thirteenth century?

Now the series of events which had led our people to this constraining crisis can be condensed as follows. When the royal youth Alexius (as was mentioned above)[1] came to the encampment accompanied by messengers and a letter from King Philip[2] and after he had deeply moved the princes of our army through his personal entreaties and extravagant promises, everyone gradually began, as we said, to lean in his favor and toward support of his case. This tendency was encouraged by various factors: first, out of consideration for the influence of King Philip, who was imploring our people so urgently on his behalf; next, because it seemed to them right (if they could

---

[1] Prince Alexius Angelos sought help in the West to restore his deposed father, Isaac II (r. 1185–1195 and 1203), whom Alexius III (Chapter 10, source 66) had deposed. When the crusade army restored Isaac to the throne in 1203, the crusaders insisted that Prince Alexius be made co-emperor. Alexius IV (r. 1203–1204) was killed in an anticrusader palace coup, and his death precipitated the eventual April attack on the city.

[2] Philip of Swabia, king of Germany (r. 1197–1208), was Prince Alexius's brother-in-law and supported the young man's overtures to the crusade army for help.

effect it) to restore the kingdom's legitimate heir to his throne, from which he had been cruelly deposed; then also because of the youth's entreaties and his promises that, if he were restored, he would be able, both then and afterward, to offer significant assistance to all pilgrims.[3] Moreover, it helped that they knew that this very city was rebellious and offensive to the Holy Roman Church, and they did not think its conquest by our people would displease very much either the supreme pontiff[4] or even God. Also, the Venetians, whose fleet they were using, were particularly urging it, partly in hope of the promised money (for which that race is extremely greedy) and partly because their city, supported by a large navy, was, in fact, arrogating to itself sovereign mastery over that entire sea. Through the union of all of these factors and, perhaps, of others, it happened that all unanimously found in favor of the young man and promised him their aid.

Yet there was also, we believe, another far older and more powerful reason than all of these, namely, the decision of Divine Goodness, which so arranged, through this pattern of events, that this people, proud because of its wealth, should be humbled by their very pride and recalled to the peace and concord of the Holy Catholic Church. It certainly seemed proper that this people, which otherwise could not be corrected, should be punished by the death of a few[5] and the loss of those temporal goods with which it had puffed itself up; that a pilgrim people should grow rich on spoils from the rich and the entire land pass into our power; and that the Western Church, illuminated by the inviolable relics* of which these people had shown themselves unworthy, should rejoice forever.[6] It is, in any case, significant that the oft-mentioned city, which had always been faithless to pilgrims,[7] following (by God's will) a change of citizenry, will remain faithful and supportive and render us aid in fighting the barbarians and in capturing and holding the Holy Land — an aid that is more significant because of its closer proximity. Anyway, all of these matters would be unsettled had that people been conquered by persons of another faith, heathen or heretic,* or (what would have been most disastrous) had it been forced to convert to their error. Therefore, I believe these considerations, surely hidden from us, yet manifest to Him who foresees all, were of utmost importance to God. It was because of them that those monumental and miraculous events, of which we shall speak, were conducted to their outcome along a fixed but secret path.

▾ ▾ ▾

Break in! Now, honored soldier of Christ,
   Break in!
Break into the city which Christ has given to
   the conqueror.
Imagine for yourself Christ, seated on a gentle
   ass,[8]
The King of Peace, radiant in countenance,
   leading the way.
You fight Christ's battles. You execute Christ's
   vengeance,

---

[3]Crusaders were considered to be pilgrims* of a special sort, *armed* pilgrims, and they enjoyed all of the special privileges the Church accorded pilgrims.

[4]Pope Innocent III. See Innocent's letter to Alexius III (Chapter 10, source 66). From the Western perspective, the Greek Church had broken away from obedience to papal* authority. From the Byzantine perspective, the pope claimed powers that rightly belonged to the entire Church, which was guided by the Orthodox emperor and the community of all right-believing bishops.*

[5]Gunther maintains, wrongly, that only a handful of Greeks died in the April battles.

[6]Among the objects seized in the sack of the city, the holy relics of the saints and especially of Jesus (such as his Shroud, or burial cloth) were highly prized. Abbot Martin piously looted a church and brought home a treasure trove of relics, which Gunther ironically referred to as "the spoils of sacred sacrilege."

[7]From the Western perspective, Constantinople had worked actively to ruin the Second and Third Crusades. In fact, the Byzantines had little sympathy for the crusades or the crusaders.

[8]According to the gospels* of Matthew, Mark, and Luke, Jesus entered Jerusalem in triumph, seated on a donkey. Christians commemorate this event on Palm Sunday, the Sunday preceding Easter.

By Christ's judgment. His will precedes your
 onslaught.
Break in! Rout menaces; crush cowards; press
 on more bravely;
Shout in thundering voice; brandish iron, but
 spare the blood.
Instill terror, yet remember they are brothers
Whom you overwhelm, who by their guilt
 have merited it for sometime.
Christ wished to enrich you with the wrongdo-
 ers' spoils,
Lest some other conquering people despoil
 them.
Behold, homes lie open, filled with enemy
 riches,

And an ancient hoard will have new masters.
Yet you, meanwhile, curbing heart and hand,
Postpone and disdain the pillage of goods until
 the right moment!
Throw yourself on the timorous; press firmly
 upon the conquered;
Do not allow the fatigued to recover and
 regain strength.
Immediately upon the enemy's expulsion from
 the entire city,
There will be time for looting; it will be
 proper to despoil the conquered.

▼▼▼

The Mongol Challenge

In 1211 Mongol horsemen began an assault on China under the leadership of a chieftain named *Temuchin* (1167?–1227), who had recently conquered and united most of the tribes of the steppe grasslands of Mongolia. In recognition of that unification, Temuchin had assumed the title *Chinggis* (or *Ghengis*) *Khan* (univer- sal lord) in 1206. Well before the conquest of northern China was completed, Mongol armies wheeled westward in 1219, to invade the Muslim empire of Khwarazm, which stretched from Central Asia to the Persian Gulf. This inva- sion, in turn, led to a Mongol reconnaissance in force into Christian Georgia in the Caucasus and the Russian states that lay north of Georgia. Beginning early in 1221, the Mongols spent more than two years devastating and scouting the lands of the Russian steppes. When they withdrew in 1223, they left with an intimate knowledge of Russia and adjacent lands, as well as with large amounts of booty.

Following a fourteen-year interlude, Batu Khan, a grandson of the now de- ceased Chinggis Khan, and his brilliant general Subedai led a new assault on Russia in late 1237. This time, the Mongols came to conquer. Kiev, the premier city of thirteenth-century Russia, fell in December 1240, and in early 1241 Mongol detachments swept into Poland and Hungary. In Poland, they burned Cracow to the ground on March 24 and destroyed an army of combined crusader military orders at Liegnitz on April 9. The following day, Mongol invaders in Hungary eliminated a massive Hungarian army at the River Sajó. All of Poland and Hun- gary lay helpless before the invaders, and in July 1241 Mongol raiding parties reached the outskirts of Vienna in Austria. No power in the West seemed capable of stopping the Mongols' drive to the Atlantic.

Fortuitously for Western Europe, Ogedai, Chinggis Khan's successor as khan of khans, died in Mongolia in December 1241. Probably in reaction to news of this event, Batu Khan abandoned his plans for further westward campaigning in 1242 and retreated to the lower Volga steppes, where he set up the khanate of the Golden Horde. The Mongols never returned in force to Hungary and Poland and, therefore, never pushed into Western Europe.

The West, however, had no way of knowing in 1242 that the Mongol drive into Europe had reached its farthest extent. The Mongols remained a major concern for Europe for the rest of the century. As the sources contained in this section illustrate, the West exhibited an ambivalent attitude toward these horsemen from Mongolia. The Mongols were fiercesome invaders whose cruelty was legendary among thirteenth-century European writers and preachers. They had already wiped out two Latin Christian armies in orgies of bloodshed. What was next? At the same time, the Mongols were doing even greater damage to Muslim armies and states in Central and West Asia. What if the Roman Church could convert the Mongols to its brand of Christianity and join with these new friends of Christ in a final, glorious crusade against Islam? This dream ultimately led European Christian missionaries to China before the century had ended.

Saint Louis, Prester John, and the Tartars

▼▼▼

77 ▼ *Jean de Joinville,* *THE BOOK OF THE HOLY WORDS AND GOOD DEEDS OF OUR KING, SAINT LOUIS*

In 1227 Emperor Frederick II successfully negotiated the return of Jerusalem to Christian authority, and for a little more than a decade and a half, a Latin king of Jerusalem again reigned in the holy city. This ended in 1244, when Jerusalem fell to the sultan of Egypt's army. The recapture of Jerusalem by Muslim forces spurred King Louis IX to embark on a crusade, which he did in 1248 (Chapter 10, source 64). On his way to the Holy Land, Louis spent some time on the island of Cyprus, where he received two Christian ambassadors from Eljigidei, commander of Mongol forces in Southwest Asia, with an offer of an alliance against Islam. At that moment, the Mongols were pressing against Baghdad, which they would capture in 1258, and they welcomed crusader action against Egypt or Jerusalem, hoping it would draw off Muslim energies. King Louis responded by dispatching several Dominican friars[*] as emissaries to the khan of khans, not realizing that the Great Khan had recently died and his widow was serving as regent. The regent received the emissaries at her camp deep in Central Asia and sent back the message that Joinville records in St. Louis's biography.

We have already analyzed an excerpt from Joinville's memorial to King Louis in Chapter 10, so this author needs no introduction; two points merit mention, however. First, the papacy[*] had already sent two embassies to the Mongols, in 1245 and 1247, to protest their attacks on Christians, to ascertain Mongol intentions regarding Europe, and to discover if they could be converted to Roman

Christianity. Both legations were curtly informed that the pope should submit to the Great Khan's authority. Then, in a sudden change of tone and policy, the Mongols sent their own envoys to the papal* court in 1248 with a secret proposal for an alliance against a common enemy, probably Islam. Although none of these early contacts had any concrete results, King Louis's exchange of emissaries with the Mongols should be understood within this wider context. Second, Joinville mentions *Prester John* (John the priest), whom the Mongols had supposedly conquered. Prester John was a mythic emperor and priest* of some lost Christian people in the far regions of Asia. The Prester John myth, which took shape in twelfth-century Europe, was born partly out of the West's vague knowledge of distant Christian cultures in Asia and Africa and partly out of its crusading zeal to discover new Christian allies in the war against Islam.

Although Prester John was only a myth, there were, in fact, Christian societies flourishing well beyond the boundaries of Western Europe and Byzantium. They included the Ethiopians of northeast Africa, the so-called St. Thomas Christians of the western coast of India, and the *Nestorian* Church, which stretched from Iraq to China. The Nestorians, who constituted the largest Christian group in the grasslands of Central and East Asia, originated as a sect in fifth-century Syria. After Nestorian beliefs were declared heretical* in 431 and again in 451, many believers migrated eastward. By the seventh century, Nestorianism had taken root among some Turkic tribes in the steppes on both sides of China's northwestern border. It was probably the Nestorians, more than any other group of distant Christians, who provided the West with continuing reason to believe that a powerful Christian emperor was out there, somewhere, waiting to link up with his Western co-religionists.

QUESTIONS FOR ANALYSIS

1. What overall picture of the Mongols does Joinville give us?
2. How does his account mix fact and fancy?
3. Overall, how well informed about the Mongols does Joinville appear to be? Explain your answer.
4. Consider the story given here of the Mongols' victory over Prester John. If there was no Prester John, from where do you think the story originated? What was its purpose?
5. Consider the story of the Mongol prince, which has no basis in fact. What was its message, and what do you think were its origin and purpose?
6. How did the Mongol regent greet King Louis's overtures, and how did the king respond to the Mongols' answer to his emissaries?
7. What general conclusions do you draw from your answers to questions 1, 4, 5, and 6? In other words, how did the Europeans view the Mongols, and how did the Mongols regard the Europeans in the mid thirteenth century?

*How the Tartars Chose a Chief
to Shake Off the Yoke of Prester John,
and of the Emperor of Persia*

While the king was sojourning in Cyprus, envoys came from the Tartars[1] and gave him to understand that they would help him to conquer the kingdom of Jerusalem from the Saracens. The king sent back these envoys, and sent with them, by his own envoys, a chapel[2] which he had caused to be fashioned all in scarlet; and in order to draw the Tartars to our faith, he had caused all our faith to be imaged in the chapel: the Annunciation of the angel, the Nativity, the baptism[*] that God was baptised withal, and all of the Passion, and the Ascension, and the coming of the Holy Ghost;[3] and with the chapel he sent also cups, books, and all things needful for the chanting of the mass,[*] and two Preaching Brothers[4] to sing the mass before the Tartars.

The king's envoys arrived at the port of Antioch;[5] and from Antioch it took them full a year's journeying, riding ten leagues[6] a day, to reach the great king of the Tartars. They found all the land subject to the Tartars, and many cities that they had destroyed, and great heaps of dead men's bones.

They inquired how the Tartars had arrived at such authority, and killed and utterly confounded so many people; and this was how, as the envoys reported it to the king: The Tartars came, being there created, from a great plain of sand where no good thing would grow. This plain began from certain rocks, very great and marvelous, which are at the world's end, towards the East; and the said rocks have never been passed by man, as the Tartars testify. And they said that within these rocks are enclosed the people of Gog and Magog, who are to come at the end of the world, when Antichrist shall come to destroy all things.[7]

In this plain dwelt the people of the Tartars; and they were subject to Prester John, and to the emperor of Persia,[8] whose land came next to his, and to several other misbelieving kings, to whom they rendered tribute and service every year, for the pasturage of their beasts, seeing they had no other means of livelihood. This Prester John, and the king of Persia, and the other kings, held the Tartars in such contempt that when they brought their rents they would not receive them face-wise, but turned their backs upon them.

Among the Tartars was a wise man, who journeyed over all the plains, and spoke with the wise men of the plains, and of the different places, and showed them in what bondage they stood, and prayed them all to consider how best they might find a way of escape from the bondage in which they were held. He wrought so effectu-

---

[1]Western Europeans mistakenly referred to the Mongols as *Tartars,* a corruption of *Tatars,* the name of a tribe of Turko-Mongol steppe people who had been the hereditary enemy of the Mongols but who intermarried with them. Chinggis Khan had exterminated the Tatars as an identifiable people, but the name lived on and became associated with the Mongols. In the West, the name *Tatar* was corrupted to *Tartar* and became the object of a pun that the thirteenth-century English historian Matthew Paris recorded in his *Greater Chronicle.*[*] The classical Latin name for *hell* was *Tartarus;* hence, the Mongols were the "the horsemen from hell."

[2]A portable altar.

[3]The central events of Jesus Christ's redemptive mission: the annunciation to Mary that she was chosen to bear the Messiah and her acceptance of that choice; the birth of Jesus; Jesus' baptism in the River Jordan by John the Baptist; Jesus' suffering and death; his ascension into Heaven forty days after his resurrection; and the descent of the Holy Spirit[*] on the first members of the Church ten days after Jesus' ascension.

[4]The Dominicans are officially known as the *Order of Preachers.* Actually, the embassy contained three Dominicans. The head of the legation was Andrew of Longjumeau, who spoke Farsi (Persian) and had already visited the Mongol encampment in Southwest Asia, probably on the papal mission of 1247.

[5]In Syria.

[6]Thirty miles.

[7]Two mythic evil giants and their followers. The New Testament's Book of Revelation, 20: 7–10, notes that following the thousand-year reign of Christ on earth and just before the Final Judgment of all humanity, Satan will escape captivity and muster the people of Gog and Magog to attack God's people, but God will defeat them.

[8]The shah of Khwarazm. Chinggis Khan invaded and conquered his empire, which stretched from Persia eastward to Samarqand, roughly from modern Iran to Uzbekistan and Kazakstan. The shah's power never extended to Mongolia.

ally that he gathered them all together at the end of the plain, over against the land of Prester John, and explained matters to them. And they answered that whatever he desired, that they would do. And he said that they would achieve nothing unless they had a king and lord over them. And he taught them after what manner they might obtain a king; and they agreed.

And this was the manner: out of the fifty-two tribes that there were, each tribe was to bring an arrow marked with its name; and by consent of all the people it was agreed that the fifty-two arrows so brought should be placed before a child aged five years; and the arrow that the child took first would mark the tribe from which the king would be chosen. When the child had so lifted up one of the arrows, the wise men caused all the other tribes to draw back; and it was settled that the tribe from which the king was to be chosen should select among themselves fifty-two of the wisest and best men that they had. When these were elected, each one brought an arrow marked with his name. Then was it agreed that the man whose arrow the child lifted up should be made king. And the child lifted up one of the arrows, and it was that of the wise man by whom the people had been instructed. Then were the people glad, and each rejoiced greatly. And the wise man bade them all be silent, and said: "Lords, if you would have me to be your king, swear to me by Him who made the heavens and the earth, that you will keep my commandments." And they swore it.[9]

The ordinances that he established had for purpose the maintenance of peace among the people; and they were to this effect: that none should steal another man's goods, nor any man strike another, on penalty of losing his fist; that no man should have company with another's wife or daughter, on penalty of losing his fist, or his

life. Many other good ordinances did he establish among them for the maintenance of peace.[10]

Victory of the Tartars over Prester John — Vision of One of Their Princes — His Conversion

After he had established order and arrayed them, the king spoke in this wise: "Lords, the most powerful enemy that we have is Prester John. And I command you to be all ready, on the morrow, to fall upon him; and if it so happens that he defeats us — which God forbid! — let each do as best he can. And if we defeat him, I order that the slaying last three days and three nights, and that none, during that space, be so rash as to lay hand on the booty, but all be bent on slaying the people; for after we have obtained the victory, I will distribute the booty, duly and loyally, so that each shall hold himself well paid." To this they all agreed.

On the morrow they fell upon their enemies, and, as God so willed, discomfited them. All those whom they found in arms, and capable of defence, they put to the sword; and those whom they found in religious garb, the priests and other religious people, they slew not. The other people belonging to Prester John's land, who were not in that battle, made themselves subjects of the Tartars.

One of the princes of the tribes spoken of above,[11] was lost for three months, so that no one had news of him; and when he came back he was neither thirsty nor hungry, for he thought he had remained away no more than one night at the most. The news that he brought back was this: that he had gone to the top of a tall hillock and had found thereon a great many folk, the fairest folk that he had ever seen, the best clothed and the best adorned; and at the end of the hillock he saw sitting, a king, fairer than the rest,

---

[9]The wise man is Chinggis Khan. He actually united the Mongols through conquest.
[10]Tradition ascribed a Great *Yasa,* or code of law, to Chinggis Khan. Laws similar to the prohibitions listed here are contained in various versions of the Yasa.

[11]The Mongol tribes.

and better clothed, and better adorned; and this king sat upon a throne of gold. At his right sat six kings, crowned, richly adorned with precious stones, and at his left six kings. Near him, at his right hand, was a queen kneeling, and she prayed and besought him to think upon her people; at his left hand knelt a man of exceeding beauty, and he had two wings resplendent as the sun. And round the king was a great abundance of fair folk with wings. Then the king called the prince to him, and said: "Thou art come from the host of the Tartars." And he replied: "Sire, that is so, truly." And the king said: "Thou shalt go to thy king and tell him that thou hast seen me, who am lord of heaven and earth; and thou shalt tell him to render thanks to me for the victory I have given him over Prester John, and over his people. And thou shalt tell him also, as from me, that I give him power to bring the whole earth under his subjection." "Sire," said the prince, "how will he then believe me?" "Thou shalt tell him to believe thee by these signs: that thou shalt go and fight against the emperor of Persia, with three hundred of thy people, and no more;[12] and in order that your great king may believe that I have power to do all things, I shall give thee the victory over the emperor of Persia, who will do battle against thee with three hundred thousand armed men, and more; and before thou goest to do battle against him, thou shalt ask of thy king to give thee the priests and men of religion whom he has taken in the [late] battle; and what these teach, that thou shalt firmly believe, thou and all thy people." "Sire," said the prince, "I cannot go hence, if thou dost not cause me to be shown the way."

Then the king turned towards a great multitude of knights, so well armed that it was a marvel to see them; and he called one of them, and said: "George, come hither."[13] And the knight came and knelt before him. Then the king said to him: "Rise, and lead me this man safe and sound to his tent." And this the knight did at the dawning of a certain day.

As soon as all his people saw the prince, they made such joy of him, as did all the host likewise, that it was past the telling. He asked the great king to give him the priests, and he gave them to him; and then the prince and all his people received the priests' teaching so favorably that they were all baptised. After these things the prince took three hundred men-at-arms, and caused them to be confessed* and to make ready for battle, and then went and fought against the emperor of Persia, and defeated him, and drove him from his kingdom, so that the said emperor came flying to the kingdom of Jerusalem; and this was the same emperor who discomfited our people, and took Count Walter of Brienne prisoner.[14] . . .

Manners of the Tartars —
Pride of Their King —
St. Lewis Repents of Having
Sent an Envoy to Him

The people of this Christian prince were so numerous that the king's envoys told us that he had in his camp eight hundred chapels on wagons. Their manner of living is such that they eat no bread, and live on meat and milk. The best meat they have is horseflesh; and they put it to lie in brine and dry it afterwards, so that they can cut it as they would black bread. The best beverage they have, and the strongest, is mare's milk, flavored with herbs.[15] There was presented

[12]Chinggis Khan's army of invasion of 1219 contained tens of thousands of soldiers.
[13]St. George, a legendary holy warrior, was a patron saint of the crusades.

[14]Walter of Brienne, count of Jaffa, was one of the ill-fated defenders of Jerusalem. When the last shah of the Khwarazm Empire (note 8) died in 1231, large numbers of his now leaderless troops allied with the sultan of Egypt against the crusaders in Syria-Palestine. The Khwarazmians captured Jerusalem in August 1244.
[15]*Qumiz,* a drink of fermented mare's milk that Mongols still favor today.

to the great king of the Tartars a horse laden with flour, who had come a three-months journey's distance; and he gave it to the envoys of the king.

There are among them a great many Christian folk who hold the creed of the Greeks, and there are, besides, the Christians of whom we have already spoken, and others. These Christians the Tartars send against the Saracens when they wish to make war on the Saracens; and contrariwise they use the Saracens in any war against the Christians. All manner of childless women go with them to war, and they give pay to such women as they would do to men, according to their strength and vigor.[16] And the king's envoys told us that the men and women soldiers ate together in the quarters of the chiefs under whom they served; and that the men dared not touch the women in any sort, because of the law that their first king had given them.

The flesh of all manner of beasts dying in the camp is eaten. The women who have children see after them, and take care of them; and also prepare the food of the people who go to battle. They put the raw meat between their saddles and the lappets of their clothing, and when the blood is well pressed out, they eat it quite raw.[17] What they cannot eat, there and then, they throw into a leather bag; and when they are hungry they open the bag and always eat the oldest bits first. Thus I saw a Khorasmin, one of the emperor of Persia's people, who guarded us in our imprisonment,[18] and when he opened his bag we held our noses, for we could not bear it, because of the stink that came out of his bag.

But now let us go back to the matter in hand, and tell how the great king of the Tartars,[19] after he had received the king's envoys and presents, sent to gather together, under safe conduct, several kings who had not as yet submitted to him; and when they were come he caused the king's chapel to be pitched, and spoke to them after this manner: "Lords, the king of France has sued for mercy, and submitted himself to us, and behold here is the tribute he has sent us; and if you do not submit yourselves to us we will send and fetch him for your destruction." Many there were who, through fear of the French king, placed themselves in subjection to that Tartar king.

With the king's envoys returned[20] other envoys from the great king of the Tartars, and these brought letters to the king of France, saying: "A good thing is peace; for in the land where peace reigns those that go about on four feet eat the grass of peace; and those that go about on two feet till the earth — from which good things do proceed — in peace also. And this thing we tell you for your information; for you cannot have peace except if you have it with us. For Prester John rose up against us, and such and such kings" — and he named a great many — "and we have put them all to the sword. So we admonish you to send us, year by year, of your gold and of your silver, and thus keep us as your friend; and if you will not do this, we will destroy you and your people, as we have done to the kings already named." And you must know that it grieved the king sorely that he had ever sent envoys to the great king of the Tartars.

---

[16]Women had a fairly high status in Mongol society, and some seem to have played significant roles in war.

[17]Beef tartar, a delicacy that combines lean raw meat, raw egg, and various condiments, is supposedly a modern version of this food. Although a number of ancient and medieval Western authors claimed that the Huns, Mongols, and other steppe horse nomads dried their meat in this manner, many modern scholars dismiss this evidence as unfounded myth.

[18]When Joinville was held prisoner in Egypt. See Chapter 10, source 64.

[19]Actually, his widow.

[20]Around April 1251. They met the king in the crusader kingdom of Jerusalem.

A Franciscan Missionary in China
▼▼▼
78 ▼ *John of Monte Corvino,* LETTER TO THE WEST

Despite disappointment at the Mongols' reception of their early embassies to the Great Khan and his lieutenants, popes and kings in the West did not abandon hope of converting the Mongols to Roman Christianity and allying with them against Islam. On their part, various Mongol khans continued to flirt with the idea of joining with European Christian powers against a common Muslim foe.

In 1287 Arghun, il-khan of Persia (r. 1284–1291), a nephew and subordinate of the Great Khan, Kubilai (r. 1260–1294), sent a Nestorian Christian monk,* Rabban (Master) Sauma (ca. 1230–1294) to the West, bearing letters for the pope, the kings of France and England, and the emperor of Constantinople, in which the Mongol prince offered to become a Christian in return for an alliance against the Muslims of Syria-Palestine. Arghun died before he or anyone else could act on the proposal, and in 1295 his successor embraced Islam, thereby ending any hope of a Mongol-European crusade in the Holy Land. Arghun's overtures, however, set in motion a remarkable adventure for one Franciscan missionary.

In response to Rabban Sauma's appearance in Rome in 1289, Pope Nicholas IV dispatched a Franciscan friar,* John of Monte Corvino (1247–ca. 1328), to the Mongols with letters for Arghun and other khans farther to the east, including the khan of khans, Kubilai. Friar John had only just returned to Rome, after having served as a missionary in Armenia and Mongol-controlled Persia between about 1280 and 1289. Apparently, his report so impressed Pope Nicholas that the pope ordered John to return immediately to the Middle East and then to travel on to the Great Khan in northern China.

In 1291 John was in Tauris (modern Tabriz), Arghun's capital, but the il-khan died in March of that year, and between May and July of the same year, the last crusader strongholds in the Holy Land fell to Muslim forces. Having nothing further to accomplish in Persia, John set out for the court of the Great Khan in China. Civil war among the Mongols delayed Friar John's journey across Central Asia and resulted in a detour to India, from where Friar John sent back to Rome a detailed report on India's native Christian communities. Due to this delay, John arrived at the Mongol capital of Khanbaliq (modern Beijing) in northern China in 1295, a year after Kubilai's death. Making the best of his situation, John decided to remain in China as a missionary.

In the course of his long stay in China, Friar John wrote two letters to his fellow Franciscans back home. In response, Pope Clement V appointed him archbishop* of Khanbaliq in 1307 and dispatched several assistant missionaries. The new archbishop remained at his post until his death around 1328, and Pope Benedict XII subsequently sent a replacement. Notwithstanding this effort, the Roman Catholic mission in China barely limped along. When the Mongols finally were expelled from China by the native Ming Dynasty in 1368, European missionary activity in China ended and would not be revived until the coming of the Jesuits in the sixteenth century.

The following document is one of the letters that Friar John sent to the West from China. In it, he relates his success working with the late King Kerguz, or George, leader of the Ongut Turks, whose family had intermarried with that of Chinggis Khan.

QUESTIONS FOR ANALYSIS

1. What problems did Friar John encounter?
2. How was Friar John able to gain most of his converts, and from which group(s) does he seem to have won most of them, the Turkic Nestorian Christians, the non-Christian Mongols, or the Chinese? What do you conclude from your answers?
3. What does John's letter suggest about Mongol attitudes and policy toward Christians?
4. What does this letter allow us to infer about European-Chinese contacts in the late thirteenth and early fourteenth centuries?
5. What picture does John draw of the Mongol empire? How, if at all, has it changed since the mid thirteenth century?
6. How, if at all, have Mongol-European relations changed since the mid thirteenth century?
7. Review Urban's sermon at Clermont (source 72). In what ways, if at all, does John of Monte Corvino's letter reflect a different European view of the world?

I, Friar John of Monte Corvino, of the order of Minor Friars, departed from Tauris, a city of the Persians, in the year of the Lord 1291, and proceeded to India. And I remained in the country of India, wherein stands the church of St. Thomas the Apostle,[1] for thirteen months, and in that region baptized* in different places about one hundred persons. The companion of my journey was Friar Nicholas of Pistoia, of the order of Preachers, who died there, and was buried in the aforesaid church.

I proceeded on my further journey and made my way to Cathay,[2] the realm of the emperor of the Tatars[3] who is called the Grand Khan. To him I presented the letter of our lord the pope, and invited him to adopt the Catholic faith of our Lord Jesus Christ, but he had grown too old in idolatry. However he bestows many kindnesses upon the Christians, and these two years past I am abiding with him.

The Nestorians, a certain body who profess to bear the Christian name, but who deviate sadly from the Christian religion, have grown so powerful in those parts that they will not allow a

---

[1]Missionaries (according to tradition, led by St. Thomas the Apostle*) had apparently established a small Christian community on India's western coast in the late first century. In John of Monte Corvino's day, these St. Thomas Christians held Nestorian beliefs (see note 4).

[2]Northern China. So called because of the Khitan people, who established a kingdom centered on Beijing from 916 to 1125.
[3]Timur Khan (r. 1294–1307).

Christian of another ritual to have ever so small a chapel, or to publish any doctrine different from their own.[4]

To these regions there never came anyone of the apostles, nor yet of the disciples.[5] And so the aforesaid Nestorians, either directly or through others whom they bribed, have brought on me the sharpest of persecutions. For they got up stories that I was not sent by our lord the pope, but was a great spy and impostor; and after a while they produced false witnesses who declared that there was indeed an envoy sent with presents of immense value for the emperor, but that I had murdered him in India and stolen what he had in charge. And these intrigues and calumnies went on for some five years. And thus it came to pass that many a time I was dragged before the judgment seat with ignominy and threats of death. At last, by God's providence, the emperor, through the confessions of a certain individual, came to know my innocence and the malice of my adversaries; and he banished them with their wives and children.

In this mission I abode alone and without any associate for eleven years, but it is now going on for two years since I was joined by Friar Arnold, a German of the province* of Cologne.[6]

I have built a church in the city of Khanbaliq, in which the king has his chief residence. This I completed six years ago; and I have built a belltower to it, and put three bells in it. I have baptized there, as well as I can estimate, up to this time some 6,000 persons; and if those charges against me of which I have spoken had not been made, I should have baptized more than 30,000. And I am often still engaged in baptizing.

Also I have gradually bought one hundred and fifty boys, the children of pagan parents, and of ages varying from seven to eleven, who had never learned any religion. These boys I have baptized, and I have taught them Greek and Latin after our manner. Also I have written out psalters for them, with thirty hymnaries and two breviaries.[7] By help of these, eleven of the boys already know our service, and form a choir and take their weekly turn of duty as they do in convents, whether I am there or not. Many of the boys are also employed in writing out psalters and other things suitable. His Majesty the emperor moreover delights much to hear them chanting. I have the bells rung at all the canonical hours,* and with my congregation of babes and sucklings I perform divine service, and the chanting we do by ear because I have no service book with the notes.

A certain king of this part of the world, by name George, belonging to the sect of Nestorian Christians, and of the illustrious family of that great king who was called Prester John of India,[8] in the first year of my arrival here attached himself to me, and being converted by me to the truth of the Catholic faith, took the lesser orders,[9] and when I celebrated mass* he used to attend me wearing his royal robes. Certain others of the Nestorians on this account accused him of apostasy, but he brought over a great part of his people with him to the true Catholic faith, and built a church on a scale of royal magnificence in honor of our God, of the Holy Trinity,*

---

[4]Nestorians believed in a clear distinction between the divine and human natures of Jesus and rejected, therefore, the Byzantine and Roman belief that Mary was *Theotokos,* or "the Mother of God." Once a great Asian Church but largely destroyed in the fourteenth century by the armies of Timur the Lame, the Nestorian Church survives today as the *Assyrian Church.* Its members can be found in Iraq, Iran, other areas of Southwest Asia, and in the United States of America.

[5]In other words, Christianity was not introduced into China until after the Apostolic Age of the first and second centuries A.D.

[6]He dated the thirteen-year mission from 1291. See the letter's date.

[7]Various prayer books.

[8]When premodern Europeans used the term *India,* or *the Indies,* they usually meant Farther Asia and did not specifically refer to the subcontinent of India.

[9]He was admitted to the four minor clerical* orders below those of priest,* deacon,* and subdeacon.*

and of our lord the pope, giving it the name of the *Roman Church.*

This King George six years ago departed to the Lord a true Christian, leaving as his heir a son scarcely out of the cradle, and who is now nine years old. And after King George's death his brothers, perfidious followers of the errors of Nestorius,[10] perverted again all those whom he had brought over to the church, and carried them back to their original schismatical creed. And being all alone, and not able to leave his Majesty the khan, I could not go to visit the above-mentioned church, which is twenty days' journey distant.

Yet, if I could but get some good fellow-workers to help me, I trust in God that all this might be retrieved, for I still possess the grant which was made in our favor by the late King George before mentioned. So I say again that if it had not been for the slanderous charges which I have spoken of, the harvest reaped by this time would have been great!

Indeed if I had had but two or three comrades to aid me 'tis possible that the emperor khan would have been baptized by this time! I ask then for such brethren to come, if any are willing to come, such I mean as will make it their great business to lead exemplary lives. . . .

As for the road hither I may tell you that the way through the land of the Goths[11] subject to the emperor of the Northern Tatars, is the shortest and safest; and by it the friars might come, along with the letter-carriers, in five or six months. The other route again is very long and very dangerous, involving two sea-voyages; the first of which is about as long as that from Acre

to the province of Provence,[12] whilst the second is as long as from Acre to England. And it is possible that it might take more than two years to accomplish the journey that way.[13] But, on the other hand, the first-mentioned route has not been open for a considerable time, on account of wars that have been going on.

It is twelve years since I have had any news of the papal* court, or of our order, or of the state of affairs generally in the West. Two years ago indeed there came hither a certain Lombard . . . surgeon, who spread abroad in these parts the most incredible blasphemies about the court of Rome and our order[14] and the state of things in the West, and on this account I exceedingly desire to obtain true intelligence. I pray the brethren whom this letter may reach to do their possible to bring its contents to the knowledge of our lord the pope and the cardinals,* and the agents of the order at the court of Rome. . . .

I have myself grown old and grey, more with toil and trouble than with years; for I am not more than fifty-eight. I have got a competent knowledge of the language and character which is most generally used by the Tatars. And I have already translated into that language and character the New Testament and the psalter, and have caused them to be written out in the fairest penmanship they have; and so by writing, reading, and preaching, I bear open and public testimony to the Law of Christ. And I had been in treaty with the late King George, if he had lived, to translate the whole Latin ritual, that it might be sung throughout the whole extent of his territory; and while he was alive I used to celebrate mass in his church, according to the Latin ritual,

---

[10]An early fifth-century patriarch* of Constantinople who was deposed in 431.

[11]He probably means the Alans, a Christian, Iranian people who dwelt on the northern shores of the Black Sea. Undoubtedly, he is telling them to take the overland route across the steppes.

[12]From Israel to Mediterranean France. Acre was a major crusader port, which fell to Islam in May 1291.

[13]The sea route would involve sailing down either the Red Sea or, more likely, the Persian Gulf into the Indian Ocean and from there, across to India, then to Southeast Asia, and finally northward to a southern Chinese port.

[14]There was a bitter conflict between Pope Boniface VIII and a radical, splinter sect known as the *Spiritual Franciscans.*

reading in the before-mentioned language and character the words of both the preface and the canon.[15]

And the son of the king before-mentioned is called after my name, John; and I hope in God that he will walk in his father's steps.

As far as I ever saw or heard tell, I do not believe that any king or prince in the world can be compared to his majesty the khan in respect of the extent of his dominions, the vastness of their population, or the amount of his wealth. Here I stop.

Dated at the city of Khanbaliq in the kingdom of Cathay, in the year of the Lord 1305, and on the 8th day of January.

---

[15]The preface of the mass is a series of opening prayers; the canon,* or core, of the mass consists of the offertory, consecration, and communion. In other words, he celebrated the Latin rite mass in the language of King George's people.

Part Three

▼▼▼

Crisis, Retrenchment,
Recovery, and a
New World: A.D. *1300–1500*

The two centuries that constitute the Late Middle Ages present vivid contrasts. The fourteenth century was characterized by spectacular catastrophes, which seemed to threaten to destroy European civilization, whereas the fifteenth century saw Europe emerge from these crises and set itself along a road to recovery that resulted in its becoming one of the major players in global history during the sixteenth century. How can we describe this two-hundred-year period: as medieval Europe's age of senescence or as the Renaissance? As the following two chapters illustrate, each of these descriptions fails to define adequately this complex era.

Chapter 12

▼▼▼

The Fourteenth Century: Catastrophe and Creativity

If the period around 1050 to 1300 was an age of advancement on numerous fronts, the fourteenth century was an age of adversity brought on by numerous crises that, to many Europeans, cumulatively presaged the end of the world. The world, as they knew it, did not end, but it was changing. Much of that change was for the worse, but certainly not all of it. Once again, Europeans exhibited a great capacity for resilience in the face of disaster and creativity in the midst of breakdown.

A change in climatic patterns around 1300 brought colder, wetter weather to Europe, which, in turn, resulted in disastrous floods, crop failures, and recurrent, widespread instances of famine. Long-distance trade routes that had opened up and expanded in the three preceding centuries began to close down in the fourteenth century, due to several factors: the loss of Europe's last crusader strongholds on the coast of Southwest Asia in 1291; the rising power of the Ottoman Turks, who by the end of the century essentially controlled the Balkans; the breakup of the trans–Eurasian Mongol Empire by midcentury; and the destructive fury of Timur the Lame's conquests during the last decades of the century, which disrupted the southern land routes running from China to the Mediterranean. Chronic warfare also bedeviled Europe throughout the century. Italy and Germany witnessed numerous conflicts among competing cities, factions, and dynasties, and in 1337 Edward III of England and Philip VI of France initiated the Hundred Years' War. Peasant rebellions shook France, England, and Catalonia, and increasing urban-class tension was dramatically underscored by the revolt of

Florence's working poor, the *Ciompi*, in 1378. At the other end of the economic scale, Europe's three greatest international banking houses — the Acciaiuoli, the Bardi, and the Peruzzi of Florence — collapsed in the 1340s due to bad debts; Europe would have to wait for a century for another banking house of comparable size to emerge. In the arena of religion, the Roman papacy* lost tremendous prestige in the course of the century, due first to its prolonged residence at Avignon and then, more seriously, to the Great Schism, which began in 1378. As the clergy* came under increasing scrutiny and criticism, new spiritual and theological movements, which ranged from orthodox* forms of mysticism to new heresies,* presented challenges to the Church's authority.

Each of these crises was significant, but none matched the horror and devastation occasioned by a bacterial *epidemic* that swept westward from China in the mid fourteenth century. Not only did the arrival of this new killing disease exacerbate all of the other crises that beset Europe, it also had a profound impact on the collective psyche of Western civilization. A mood of preoccupation with death and decay pervaded much of European visual art, letters, and thought during the latter part of the fourteenth century.

At the same time, Europeans exhibited tremendous powers of endurance in the face of these crises and even proved capable of significant creativity in many areas. The fourteenth century, after all, was the age in which the English House of Commons took shape and the Hanseatic League became a full-fledged political entity. In the arts, it was the age of such literary giants as Dante, Petrarch, Boccaccio, Langland, and Chaucer and such revolutionary painter artists as Giotto, Martini, and Lorenzetti. So far as thought was concerned, the century saw several Parisian thinkers break with Aristotelian physics, thereby anticipating the Scientific Revolution of the seventeenth century. For all of its fourteenth-century ills, Europe was not on the brink of collapse.

▼▼▼

Natural Disasters and Their Consequences

Despite wars, regional famines, and local epidemics, Europe's population steadily increased throughout most of the High Middle Ages, multiplying by a factor of about 2.5 between A.D. 1000 and 1300. This population growth was largely due to several centuries of favorable weather and the adoption of a variety of farming innovations that combined to raise crop production substantially. Average life expectancy was still low by modern standards, but reasonably abundant food supplies translated into a high birthrate, which more than compensated for a high deathrate. Notwithstanding these facts, late-thirteenth-century Europe was probably overpopulated relative to its ability to feed itself consistently well. The fact that the demographic growth curve was flattening out, and even declining in certain areas, before 1300 indicates that Europe had momentarily reached, or even exceeded, the limit of its ability to exploit its soil and water. Should the climate change for the worse and remain so for a substantial period of time, Europe would be in serious trouble.

Toward 1300 Europe did experience a long-term change in climatic patterns, whereby the weather became colder and wetter. Herring, a major protein staple, migrated out of the Baltic Sea, which froze over on several occasions. Moreover, grain rotted in fields, and some crops could no longer be raised successfully in certain marginal areas. Much of Norway could no longer grow wheat, and grapes now failed to mature in England. Widespread famine followed, with its first major onslaught occurring between 1315 and 1317.

Europe could have conceivably weathered this crisis in reasonably good order and with few, if any, long-term effects, but a now ill-nourished, weakened society was devastated toward midcentury when a bacterial infection, known as the *plague,* swept across the trade routes of Asia and entered Europe by way of the Mediterranean. The result was a phenomenon that later generations referred to as the *Black Death.* In its two major forms, bubonic and pneumonic, the plague ravaged Europe between 1347 and 1350 and then became endemic, returning in four additional waves before the century was over. No subsequent outbreak, however, was as devastating as the first onslaught of the plague, which carried away at least one-third and maybe closer to one-half of Europe's total population in less than three years.

Needless to say, this sudden, massive die-off had a profound effect on the physical and psychic state of European civilization, as the following two documents illustrate.

Explaining and Responding to Catastrophe

▼▼▼

79 ▼ Jean de Venette, CHRONICLE

Jean de Venette (ca. 1307–1368) — priest,* master of theology at the University of Paris, and head of the French province* of the order of Carmelite Friars* — composed a graphic account of French history, covering the years 1340 to 1368, in which he concentrated on the disasters that seemed to characterize his age. Of peasant origin himself, he displayed genuine concern for the sufferings of France's lower classes, who bore such a disproportionate amount of the pain in that society. The following selections deal with the famine of 1315–1317, the onslaught of the Black Death in France, and some of the human responses to the latter catastrophe.

QUESTIONS FOR ANALYSIS

1. How does Venette attempt to understand and explain the dual disasters of famine and plague? What does your answer suggest about Europe's ability to cope with the crisis?

2. Compare the consequences that the plague had for Europe's Jewish population with the impact of the First Crusade on European Jews (Chapter 11, source 74). What conclusions follow from this comparison?

3. Compare the Jewish response to this crisis with that of the Rhineland Jews in 1096. What do you conclude?

4. What does the flagellant movement suggest about the psychological effects of the plague? Compare it with the age's persecution of the Jews. Were they connected in any way? Explain your answer.

5. What does the attitude of the masters of theology at Paris, the pope, and Venette toward the flagellants suggest?

6. According to Venette, what were the most serious consequences of the plague? What does this tell us about the man and the purpose behind his history?

7. What is the general tone of this history, and what does it suggest about the fourteenth century?

Let anyone who wishes to be reminded of most of the noteworthy events which happened in the kingdom of France from 1340 on read this present work in which I, a friar at Paris, have written them down briefly, in great measure as I have seen and heard them. I shall begin with some hitherto unknown prognostications or prophecies which have come to hand. What they mean is not altogether known. Whether they speak truth or not I do not say but leave to the decision of the reader. This is one such. A priest of the diocese* of Tours, freed in A.D. 1309 from the hands of the Saracens, who had held him captive for the space of thirteen years and three months, was saying mass* in Bethlehem where the Lord was born. While he was praying for all Christian people . . . there appeared to him letters of gold written in this wise:

> In the year of the Lord 1315, on the fifteenth day of the month of March, shall begin so great a famine on earth that the people of low degree shall strive and struggle against the

mighty and rich of this world. Also the wreath of the mightiest boxer shall fall to the ground very quickly afterwards. Also its flowers and its branches shall be broken and crushed. Also a noble and free city shall be seized and taken by slaves. Also strangers shall dwell there. Also the Church shall totter and the line of Saint Peter shall be execrated. Also the blood of many shall be poured out on the ground. Also a red cross shall appear and shall be lifted up. Therefore, good Christians, watch.

These are the words of this vision, but what they mean is not known.

Yet you must know that I, at the age of seven or eight, saw this great and mighty famine begin the very year foretold, 1315. It was so severe in France that most of the population died of hunger and want. And this famine lasted two years and more, for it began in 1315 and ceased in 1318. . . . Now, as I promised, I come to some of the noteworthy events, though not to all, which took place in the kingdom of France, and to a few which took place elsewhere, about A.D. 1340 and thereafter. I shall narrate them truthfully, as I saw them or heard about them. . . .

In A.D. 1348, the people of France and of almost the whole world were struck by a blow other than war. For in addition to the famine which I described in the beginning and to the wars which I described in the course of this narrative, pestilence and its attendant tribulations appeared again in various parts of the world. In the month of August, 1348, after Vespers[1] when the sun was beginning to set, a big and very bright star appeared above Paris, toward the west. It did not seem, as stars usually do, to be very high above our hemisphere, but rather near. As the sun set and night came on, this star did not seem to me or to many other friars who were watching it to move from one place. At length, when night had come, this big star, to the amazement of all of us who were watching, broke into many different rays and, as it shed these rays over Paris toward the east, totally disappeared and was completely annihilated. Whether it was a comet or not, whether it was composed of airy exhalations and was finally resolved into vapor, I leave to the decision of astronomers. It is, however, possible that it was a presage of the amazing pestilence to come, which, in fact, followed very shortly in Paris and throughout France and elsewhere, as I shall tell. All this year and the next, the mortality of men and women, of the young even more than of the old, in Paris and in the kingdom of France, and also, it is said, in other parts of the world, was so great that it was almost impossible to bury the dead. People lay ill little more than two or three days and died suddenly, as it were in full health. He who was well one day was dead the next and being carried to his grave.

Swellings appeared suddenly in the armpit or in the groin[2] — in many cases both — and they were infallible signs of death. This sickness, or pestilence, was called an epidemic by the doctors. Nothing like the great numbers who died in the years 1348 and 1349 has been heard of or seen or read of in times past. This plague and disease came from . . . association and contagion, for if a well man visited the sick he only rarely evaded the risk of death.[3] Wherefore in many towns timid priests withdrew, leaving the exercise of their ministry to the regular clergy* who were more daring. In many places not two out of twenty remained alive. So high was the mortality at the Hôtel-Dieu in Paris that for a long time, more than five hundred dead were carried daily with great devotion in carts to the cemetery of the Holy Innocents in Paris for burial.[4] A very great number of the saintly sisters of the Hôtel-Dieu who, not fearing to die, nursed the sick in all sweetness and humility, with no thought of honor, a number too often renewed by death, rest in peace with Christ, as we may piously believe. . . .

Some said that this pestilence was caused by infection of the air and waters, since there was at this time no famine nor lack of food supplies, but on the contrary great abundance. As a result of this theory of infected water and air as the source of the plague the Jews were suddenly and violently charged with infecting wells and water and corrupting the air. The whole world rose up against them cruelly on this account. In Germany and other parts of the world where Jews lived,[5] they were massacred and slaughtered by Christians, and many thousands were burned everywhere, indiscriminately. The unshaken, if fatuous, constancy of the [Jewish] men and their

---

[1]The sixth of the seven daily canonical hours,* it took place in the late afternoon or early evening and signaled the end of work.
[2]These swellings, or *buboes,* give the bubonic form of the plague its name.
[3]The high contagion rate is associated with the pneumonic form of the plague, which can be transmitted by airborne bacteria that travel from one set of lungs to another.

[4]Historians believe that "the House of God," Paris's largest hospital, was constructed to care for about five hundred people. If historians are correct, either the hospital was overcrowded and had a high turnover rate of patients or Venette exaggerates here.
[5]France had expelled and then readmitted its Jews on several occasions. The most recent expulsion had begun in 1306, but the Jews were allowed to return in 1315.

wives was remarkable. For mothers hurled their children first into the fire that they might not be baptized* and then leaped in after them to burn with their husbands and children. It is said that many bad Christians were found who in a like manner put poison into wells. But in truth, such poisonings, . . . [if] . . . they actually were perpetrated, could not have caused so great a plague nor have infected so many people. There were other causes; for example, the will of God and the corrupt humors and evil inherent in air and earth.[6] Perhaps the poisonings, if they actually took place in some localities, reinforced these causes. The plague lasted in France for the greater part of the years 1348 and 1349 and then ceased. Many country villages and many houses in good towns remained empty and deserted.

After the cessation of the epidemic, pestilence, or plague, the men and women who survived married each other. There was no sterility among the women, but on the contrary fertility beyond the ordinary. Pregnant women were seen on every side. Many twins were born and even three children at once.[7] But the most surprising fact is that children born after the plague, when they became of an age for teeth, had only twenty or twenty-two teeth, though before that time men commonly had thirty-two in their upper and lower jaws together. What this diminution in the number of teeth signified I wonder greatly, unless it be a new era resulting from the destruction of one human generation by the plague and its replacement by another. But woe is me! the world was not changed for the better but for the worse by this renewal of population. For men were more avaricious and grasping than before,

even though they had far greater possessions. They were more covetous and disturbed each other more frequently with suits, brawls, disputes, and pleas. Nor by the mortality resulting from this terrible plague inflicted by God was peace between kings and lords established. On the contrary, the enemies of the king of France and of the Church were stronger and wickeder than before and stirred up wars on sea and on land. Greater evils than before populated everywhere in the world. And this fact was very remarkable. Although there was an abundance of all goods, yet everything was twice as dear, whether utensils, foods, or merchandise, hired helpers or peasants and serfs.* The only exception was landed property and houses, of which there is a glut even today. Charity began to cool, and iniquity with ignorance and sin to abound, for few could be found in the good towns and castles who knew how or were willing to instruct children in the rudiments of grammar. . . .

In the year 1349, while the plague was still active and spreading from town to town, men in Germany, Flanders, Hainaut, and Lorraine[8] uprose and began a new sect on their own authority. Stripped to the waist, they gathered in large groups and bands and marched in procession through the crossroads and squares of cities and good towns. There they formed circles and beat upon their backs with weighted scourges, rejoicing as they did so in loud voices and singing hymns suitable to their rite and newly composed for it. Thus for thirty-three days[9] they marched through many towns doing their penance and affording a great spectacle to the wondering people. They flogged their shoulders and arms

---

[6]Until the triumph of the germ theory in the late nineteenth century, one widely held explanation for disease was that it originated from *miasma,* the poisonous fumes arising from swamps and other putrefying matter.

[7]If Venette is correct about a dramatic postplague birthrate, it was temporary. The later plague of 1363 is usually referred to as the *Plague of Children* because of a similar, short-lived phenomenon. Europe's general population did not begin to recover in any meaningful way until the sixteenth century, and then it suffered setbacks from seventeenth-century outbreaks of the plague.

[8]Regions in modern Belgium, northwest Germany, eastern France, and Luxembourg.

[9]Medieval Christians believed Jesus had lived on earth for thirty-three years.

with scourges tipped with iron points so zealously as to draw blood. But they did not come to Paris nor to any part of France, for they were forbidden to do so by the king of France, who did not want them. He acted on the advice of the masters of theology of the University of Paris, who said that this new sect had been formed contrary to the will of God, to the rites of Holy Mother Church, and to the salvation of all their souls. That indeed this was and is true appeared shortly. For Pope Clement VI was fully informed concerning this fatuous new rite by the masters of Paris through emissaries reverently sent to him and, on the grounds that it had been damnably formed, contrary to law, he forbade the Flagellants under threat of excommunication* to practice in the future the public penance which they had so presumptuously undertaken. His prohibition was just, for the Flagellants, supported by certain fatuous priests and monks,* were enunciating doctrines and opinions which were beyond measure evil, erroneous, and fallacious. For example, they said that their blood thus drawn by the scourge and poured out was mingled with the blood of Christ. Their many errors showed how little they knew of the Catholic faith. Wherefore, as they had begun fatuously of themselves and not of God, so in a short time they were reduced to nothing. On being warned, they desisted and humbly received absolution and penance at the hands of their prelates* as the pope's representatives. Many honorable women and devout matrons, it must be added, had done this penance with scourges, marching and singing through towns and churches like the men, but after a little like the others they desisted.

The Effects of the Plague in England
▼▼▼
80 ▼ *Henry Knighton, CHRONICLE*

England's abundant plague-era records indicate that the island kingdom suffered grievously during the eighteen months of the disease's initial onslaught. Modern estimates of human losses in England range between forty and fifty-five percent of a total population of anywhere from four to five million people. Two centuries later, England's population was still about a half million below what it had been on the eve of the arrival of the Black Death.

One of the best sources for the economic and social effects of the plague on English society is the chronicle* of Henry Knighton, an Augustinian canon* of St. Mary's Abbey* in Leicester. The fourth and final book of Henry's chronicle of English history covers the period from 1337 to 1366, presumably the year of his death, and displays a fine eye for detail. The following selection begins in 1348, the year the plague entered the British Isles.

QUESTIONS FOR ANALYSIS

1. According to Knighton, what immediate impact did the plague have on commodity prices? Can you think of any reasons for this change in value, other than the one that he supplies?

2. Did commodity prices remain stable after their initial reaction to the epidemic? How do you explain what happened?
3. What immediate impact did the plague have on wages? Why?
4. How did the Crown attempt to counter the effect on wages? How successful was that policy?
5. Can you think of any other reasons why the king might have fined those who paid excessive wages?
6. What impact, according to Knighton, did the plague have on the English Church?
7. What effect did the plague seem to have on England's manorial system?
8. Based on this account, what appear to have been the major short- and long-term effects of the Black Death on English society?
9. Venette (source 79) also deals with some of the economic and social effects of the plague. Does his testimony support or contradict Knighton's account? Can you reconcile these two sources? What conclusions can you draw after having studied both sources?

Then that most grievous plague penetrated the coastal region of England through Southampton[1] and came to Bristol. Those seized by the disease — almost the entire population of the town — were dying off as though struck by sudden death, for few lingered in their beds more than three days or two days or for even half a day. Raging death would burst out all around a town within its second day of arrival. At Leicester, in the little parish* of Saint Leonard, more than 380 died; in Holy Cross parish, more than 400; in the parish of Saint Margaret in Leicester, 700. And so in each parish, they died in huge numbers. Then the bishop* of Lincoln sent word throughout his whole diocese,* giving general power to each and every priest,* regular clerics* as well as seculars,* to hear confessions* and also to give absolution, with full and total episcopal* authority, for all sins, except those involving cases of debt. In such cases, the person ought first to make restitution while he lived, if he could, but certainly, others should do it for him from his property after his death.[2] Likewise, the pope granted full remission of all sins to anyone in danger of death, the absolution to be given one time only, and he conceded this license to last until the following Easter. Each person could choose whomever he wished as a confessor.*

During that same year, there was a great outbreak of pestilence among sheep everywhere throughout the kingdom, to such a degree that in one locality more than 5,000 sheep died in a single pasture, and their corpses so stank that neither beast nor bird would touch them. And the price of everything was cheap because of the fear of death. For there were truly few people who cared for riches or anything else. A person could purchase a horse, which earlier had been valued at forty shillings,[3] for half a mark,[4] a large fat ox for four shillings, a cow for twelvepence, a

---

[1]Other witnesses claimed that Bristol was the plague's first port of entry. The difference hardly matters.

[2]Any priest, not just one's parish priest or some friar* who had a special license to minister to the people of the area, could hear and absolve all sins without condition, except those for which restitution was required. In those cases, restitution or at least the intention of restitution was required before absolution could be given.

[3]Or two pounds sterling. Twenty shillings, or two hundred forty silver pennies, equaled one pound. Twelvepence made one shilling.

[4]A mark was a standard of weight that equaled approximately eight ounces. Because the pound sterling weighed twelve ounces, the English mark was two-thirds of a pound sterling, or thirteen shillings, fourpence. A half mark was six shillings, eightpence (or eighty pence). The price of eighty pence is one-sixth of forty shillings.

heifer for sixpence, a fat sheep for fourpence, a ewe for threepence, a lamb for twopence, a large pig for fivepence, a stone[5] of wool for ninepence. And sheep and cattle wandered unchecked through fields and among the crops, and there was no one to drive them away or to round them up. Rather, for lack of supervision, animals perished in uncountable numbers throughout every region, dying in out-of-the-way ditches and hedgerows. Because there was such a shortage of serfs[*] and laborers, there was no one available who knew what needed to be done. For no memory existed of such a severe and inexorable mortality since the age of Vortigern, king of the Britons, in whose time, as Bede testifies in his book on the history of the Angles, the living did not suffice to bury the dead.[6] In the following autumn, it was not possible to hire a single reaper for a wage lower than eightpence and food or a single mower for less than twelvepence and food. Because of this, many crops rotted in the fields for lack of harvesters, but in the year of the plague, as mentioned above in reference to other matters, there was such an abundance of every sort of grain that no one cared about it. . . .

Master Thomas Bradwardine was consecrated as archbishop[*] of Canterbury by the pope, and when he returned to England, he went to London, and within two days, he was dead. He was renowned above all other clerics[*] in all Christendom, especially in theology but likewise in other liberal studies. At that time, there was such a scarcity of priests everywhere that many churches were widowed and had no divine offices,[7] masses,[*] matins, vespers, sacraments,[*] or sacramentals.[8]

A person could scarcely secure a single chaplain to minister to any church for less than ten pounds or ten marks,[9] and whereas before the plague, when there had been an abundance of priests, one could secure a chaplain for four or five marks, or for two marks with board, in this time, there was scarcely anyone who wanted to accept a vicarage for twenty pounds or twenty marks.[10] Within a short period of time, however, a huge multitude of men whose wives had died in the plague rushed into holy orders. Of these, many were illiterate and were almost purely laymen, and even if they could read, they could not understand what they read.[11]

Ox hides went for a trifle, about twelvepence each; shoes went for about ten-, twelve-, or fourteenpence; a pair of boots went for about three or four shillings. Meanwhile the king sent word into each county of the kingdom that reapers and other laborers could not take more than customary wages, under the prescribed statutory penalty, and he renewed the statute regarding this matter.[12] The laborers, however, were so arrogant and contrary minded that they did not heed the king's order; rather, if anyone desired to hire them, he had to pay what they wanted. One either lost his fruits and crops, or, as they wished, he pandered to the arrogant, greedy desires of the laborers. When it was brought to the king's attention that people were not obeying his statute but were giving higher wages to their laborers, he levied heavy fines on abbots,[*] priors,[*] great and lesser knights, and on others, from both the higher and lower ranks, throughout the kingdom. From some he took a hundred shillings,

---

[5]A somewhat variable weight for dry goods that equaled about fourteen pounds.

[6]Vortigern ruled in the latter half of the fifth century. For Bede, see Chapter 4, source 22.

[7]The prayers offered throughout the day, such as morning matins and evening vespers. Also known as the canonical hours.[*]

[8]An item, such as holy water or candles, blessed by a priest but which a layperson may carry away for private devotional use.

[9]This is confusing. Knighton seems to equate a *mark* with a *pound,* but a mark was two-thirds of a pound (see note 4).

[10]See note 9.

[11]Knighton's point of reference is that true clerics read and were able to communicate in Latin; laypeople generally knew little or no Latin, even though they might be literate in a vernacular language.

[12]On June 18, 1349, King Edward III published an ordinance forbidding laborers from receiving wages higher than those paid in 1346. On February 9, 1351, the king's Parliament passed the Statute of Laborers, which reaffirmed the earlier ordinance and gave it greater precision by establishing a schedule of wages for different occupations; any laborer who received a higher wage had to pay a fine equal to twice the wage received.

from others forty shillings, from others twenty shillings, from each according to what he could pay. And he took twenty shillings from each farm throughout the kingdom, raising not less than a fifteenth from this fine.[13] Finally, the king ordered numerous laborers arrested and imprisoned. Many of these ran away and fled to the forests and woodlands for a while. Those who were captured were severely fined, and most swore that they would not take daily wages that were greater than the standard established by ancient custom, and so they were freed from incarceration. The same was done for other, more skilled workers in the boroughs and villages. . . .

In the wake of the aforementioned plague, many large and small buildings fell into ruin and collapsed to the ground in every city, borough, and village, for lack of inhabitants. Likewise, many villages and hamlets were deserted, with not one home left in them, because all who had lived therein were dead. In all likelihood, many of these villages would never again be inhabited. In the following winter, there was such a shortage of serfs for all areas of activity that, as was popularly believed, there could have scarcely been in earlier times a shortage of similar magnitude.

Beasts and all the farm animals that a person possessed wandered about without a shepherd, and all of a person's possessions were without a guardian. As a consequence, all necessities became so expensive that something that in earlier times had been valued at a single penny now at this time cost four- or fivepence. Moreover, given the reality of a shortage of serfs and a scarcity of commodities, the kingdom's magnates and other, lesser lords who had tenants remitted a portion of the rent, lest their tenants leave. Some remitted half the rent, some more and some less; some remitted it for two years, some for three, and some for one, according to what they could negotiate with their tenants. Likewise, those who received customary labor service throughout the entire year from tenants born into that situation[14] had to release them and remit such labor obligations. They either had to excuse them totally or, under easier terms, to set a small rent, out of fear that otherwise their houses would be excessively and irreparably damaged and the land everywhere be left totally uncultivated. All foodstuffs and all other necessities became exceedingly high priced.

---

[13]The *fifteenth* was theoretically the amount equal to fifteen percent of the value of all the moveable goods within a community that it would pay to the king, with parliamentary approval, in special times of royal need. In fact, the fifteenth tended to be a negotiated lump sum that equaled less than fifteen percent of the actual value of moveable goods. According to Knighton, Edward's fines amounted to no less than what a nationwide assessment of a fifteenth would bring in.

[14]That is, from serfs, as opposed to free tenants who paid rent but usually owed no labor service.

▼▼▼

Schism, Rebellion, and War

During the fourteenth century, the forces of disharmony and separation became quite evident and, at times, seemed to threaten not just the stability but the very existence of European Christian civilization.

The Roman papacy,* which represented the ideal of Christendom united under the guidance of God's deputy on earth, increasingly came under criticism. Criticism of perceived papal excesses had deep roots in the twelfth and thirteenth centuries, but during the fourteenth century, it began to reach new proportions, as orthodox* reformers and heretics* alike called to account popes who seemed, to many individuals, to be subverting the message of the Gospels.*

Warfare, a cause of human misery in every age, certainly appears to have reached alarming levels of frequency and intensity during this century. Most dramatically, the monarchs of France and England became embroiled in the *Hundred Years' War,* a series of destructive campaigns fought on French soil and in the waters of the English Channel. Equally fierce conflicts ravaged the lands of Germany and Italy, where the supporters of competing factions shed one another's blood. Increasingly violent class tensions beset Europe's cities, and in the countryside, peasant rebellions shook France, England, and Catalonia. Disasters of human origin exacerbated the devastating effects of the disasters of nature.

The Babylonian Captivity and the Great Schism

▼▼▼

81 ▼ Saint Catherine of Siena, LETTERS

Many scandals rocked the late-medieval papacy, but none were more disastrous for its image than the so-called Babylonian Captivity and the Great Schism that followed upon its heels. Between 1305 and 1377 seven consecutive French popes resided outside of Italy, and from 1309 onward the papal* court was at Avignon on the Rhone, where a massive palace arose. The popes at Avignon were not evil men; most were quite pious and, moreover, were conscientious in their attempts to rule well. During this era, however, the papacy gained the reputation, no matter how poorly deserved, of being a tool of French royal policies, because even though Avignon was not part of the kingdom of France, it was located in a region that was under French royal influence. The Avignon papacy also gained the reputation, undoubtedly better deserved, of presiding over a highly bureaucratic and venal papal establishment that had moved away from the simplicity of the Gospel ideal. The Italian poet (and disappointed office seeker) Petrarch petulantly characterized midcentury Avignon as *the Babylon of the West,* thereby providing an image for this era that has persisted to our own day.

In 1377 Pope Gregory XI returned the papal court to Rome and died the following year. His successor, Urban VI (r. 1378–1389), the first Italian pope in over seventy years, proved to be a disastrous choice and soon alienated a substantial percentage of the largely French College of Cardinals.* The dissident cardinals declared Urban's election invalid and elected another pope, a Frenchman who assumed the title Clement VII (r. 1378–1394); along with their pope, these cardinals returned to Avignon, leaving Urban and his supporters in Rome. For the next three and a half decades, the Church had two rival popes, each with his own papal court and subordinate clergy,* and European Christendom was divided over the issue of who was the legitimate pope.

One of the major figures in the closing years of the Babylonian Captivity and the opening stages of the Great Schism was St. Catherine of Siena (ca. 1347–

1380), an Italian mystic who was associated with the Dominican Order. Despite her humble origins, lack of advanced education, and youth, Catherine had a large following of devoted spiritual disciples, including many churchmen. In 1376 she traveled to Avignon at the request of the city of Florence, in the hope of making peace between the Florentines and the pope. There, she made a profound impact on Pope Gregory XI and was instrumental in his decision to return the papal court to Rome. When the Great Schism broke out in 1378, Pope Urban VI called Catherine to Rome to work for his cause. Despite deteriorating health, the saint remained in Rome until her death, tirelessly pleading the pope's case.

The following letters, addressed to Pope Gregory XI and Queen Joanna I of Naples, reveal Catherine's passionate involvement in the affairs of Western Christendom. The first letter, dictated in her native Tuscan dialect in March 1376, was sent to the pope as Catherine was preparing to travel to Avignon. The letter to Queen Joanna (r. 1343–1381), one of the age's most gifted rulers, dates to August 1379. In it, St. Catherine upbraids the queen for having abandoned the cause of Pope Urban.

Joanna originally supported Clement VII but shifted to Urban, due to a pro-Urban rebellion in Naples; she later returned to Clement's camp when it became expedient to do so. The queen's machinations ultimately failed to save her, however. Charles of Durazzo, whom Urban crowned as king of Naples in June 1381, captured Naples and deposed and imprisoned Joanna during that same summer. The following year, Joanna was murdered.

QUESTIONS FOR ANALYSIS

1. According to Catherine's letter to the pope, what ills beset Christendom, and what were their causes?
2. According to Catherine, what three things must the pope do in order to reform Christendom? What does her proposed program of reform suggest about Western Christendom in the age of the Babylonian Captivity?
3. According to Catherine, how seriously had Queen Joanna erred in espousing Clement VII's cause, and what would be the consequences of the queen's act?
4. Assuming that the partisans of Clement VII were equally as sincere and passionate in defense of his claim to the papacy, what impact do you think the Great Schism had on Western Europe?
5. What tone does Catherine assume in her letter to Pope Gregory? In her letter to Queen Joanna?
6. By what authority does St. Catherine presume to instruct the pope and the queen?
7. What do the two letters allow you to infer about St. Catherine's view of the papacy?
8. What do the letters allow you to infer about St. Catherine's image of contemporary Christendom and her place within it?

To: Gregory XI

Most holy, sweet and dearest father in Christ sweet Jesus,

Your wretched and unworthy daughter Catherine, servant and slave of the servants of Jesus Christ,[1] writes to you in His precious blood. With desire I have desired to see in you such fullness of divine grace that you may thereby be the means and the instrument for bringing peace to the whole world. And so I urge you, dearest father, to exercise the power and authority that are yours with all diligence and a most earnest desire for peace, the honor of God and the salvation of souls. And if you say to me, father: "The world is so very torn and troubled. How can *I* bring about peace?," I answer, on behalf of Christ crucified, "You need to exercise your power in three main areas: first, in the garden which is the Church let you (who are in charge) pull out all the stinking flowers, full of filth and greed and swollen with pride" — that is, all the bad shepherds and rulers who are poisoning and polluting the garden. O please, dear father gardener, use your power. Dig up those flowers. Throw them out where they can no longer wield authority. Compel them to learn how to govern themselves by a good and holy life. Plant fragrant flowers in the garden for us: shepherds and rulers who will be true servants of Jesus Christ crucified, concerned only for the honor of God and the salvation of souls, men who will be true fathers of the poor.

Alas, what a spectacle! To see the very men who should be mirrors of voluntary poverty, humble lambs distributing the Church's wealth to the poor, more involved in the empty pleasures, pomp and power of the world than if they belonged to it a thousand times over! Indeed, many laypeople put them to shame by their good and holy lives. It really looks as if the supreme eternal Goodness is compelling us by force to do

what we have not done through love; is allowing the Bride's[2] luxuries and power to be taken from her, as if to show that He wills holy Church to go back to being poor, meek and humble, as in those blessed early days when her one concern was the honor of God and the salvation of souls, spiritual and not temporal things. Ever since she has attended more to the temporal than to the spiritual, things have gone from bad to worse.[3] So you see, God in His supreme justice is allowing her to suffer and be persecuted.

But take heart, father, and have no fear, whatever happens or may happen, for God is doing this to make the Church perfect once more; to ensure that lambs will once again graze in this garden instead of wolves who devour the honor due to God by stealing it and appropriating it to themselves. Take heart in Christ sweet Jesus, for I trust that His help, the fullness of divine grace, will soon support and sustain you. If you act as I have said, you will come from war to great peace, from persecution to great unity not by human means but by the practice of virtue — and so prevail over the devils we see — wicked men — and the ones we don't, though they are ever on the watch.

But remember, sweet father, that you would be unlikely to achieve this unless you also do the other two things that make up the three — namely your return,[4] and then that you raise the standard of the most holy cross.[5] Your holy desire must not falter whatever you may see or hear in the way of scandal, or cities in revolt. Rather, let such things be as fuel on the fire of your holy desire to accomplish these things. In any case, do not postpone your coming. Pay no heed to the Devil; he knows he stands to lose and is doing his utmost to put obstacles in your way and rob you of what is yours, by making you lose love and charity and preventing your coming. I tell you, father in Christ Jesus, to come, soon,

---

[1]Here, Catherine plays on the papal title *servant (or slave) of the servants (slaves) of God.* See Chapter 4, source 20, note 12.

[2]The Bride of Christ, or the Church.

[3]An allusion to the fact that the papacy had essentially lost control over its Italian possessions, due to antipapal rebellions.

[4]To Rome.

[5]Of a crusade against the Turks.

like a meek lamb. Respond to the Holy Spirit*
who is calling you. Come, come, come, I say, and
do not wait for time which does not wait for you.
Then you will do as the Lamb who was slain did,
whose vicar you are. Unarmed He destroyed our
enemies, for He came as a meek lamb, the virtue
of love being His only weapon, His one aim being the protection of spiritual things and the
restoring of grace to man who had lost it through
sin.

Alas, sweet father, with such gentleness I beg
you, nay I say to you from Christ crucified, to
come and overthrow our enemies. Put no faith
in the Devil's counselors who may try to block
your good and holy resolution. Show the manli-
ness I expect from you — no more cowardice!
Answer God's call to you to come and take possession of the place of the glorious shepherd Saint
Peter, whose vicar you still are, and then to raise
the standard of the holy cross for, as by the cross
we were delivered (as *Pavoloccio*[6] said) so when
this standard — which I see as the solace and
refuge of Christians — is raised, we shall be delivered from war, disputes and iniquities and the
infidel people from their infidelity. In this way
you will come, and then you will see holy Church
reformed through the appointment of good pastors; you will restore to her the color of glowing
charity she has lost — so much blood has been
sucked out of her by wicked gluttons that she
has gone pale all over. But take courage and come,
father. Do not keep the servants of God waiting
any longer, for they are in torment with their
desire. And I, poor wretch, can wait no longer.
Though alive, I feel I am dying of anguish, when
I see God so vilified. But do not abandon peaceful measures because of what has happened in
Bologna,[7] just come, for I tell you that these raging wolves will put their heads in your lap as
meek as lambs and will beg for mercy.

Father, I will say no more. I beg you to grant
an audience and to listen to what Fra Raimondo[8]

and those with him have to say, for they come
from Christ crucified and from me;[9] they are true
servants of God and sons of holy Church. Pardon my own ignorance, father, and in your gracious kindness forgive me for the love and sorrow
that make me speak. Grant me your blessing.

Abide in the sweet and holy love of God. Sweet
Jesus. Jesus, Love.

▾ ▾ ▾

To: Queen Joanna I of Naples.

Dearest and respected mother,
("Dear" you will be to me when I see you being
a [real] daughter, duly subject and obedient to
holy Church, and "respected" in that I shall pay
you all due respect once you have turned away
from the darkness of heresy to follow the light.)

I, Catherine, slave of the servants of Jesus
Christ, write to you in his precious blood, desiring to see in you that true knowledge of yourself
and your Creator which is necessary for our salvation, for from this blessed knowledge every
virtue springs. . . .

Sweetest mother, I yearn to see *you* grounded
in this truth, which you will follow if you abide
in self-knowledge, but not otherwise. That is why
I said I longed to see you know yourself. To this
truth I invite you, that you may know it and so
love it: the truth that God created you for eternal life. Let yourself dwell on the humble Lamb,
for He has revealed this truth to you in His blood;
for this it was shed and given to us as our ransom; [for this] it was poured into the body of
holy Church. What does this Truth promise to
one who loves it? That the price of the Blood
will bring it eternal life, through a good confession,* together with contrition and satisfaction.
It promises, too, that every good deed will be
rewarded and every sin punished, thus instilling
into us a holy fear and love by leading us to fear
the sin as we fear the punishment.

---

[6]"Dear little Paul" — a Tuscan nickname for St. Paul.
[7]The city of Bologna had recently rebelled against the pope.
[8]A Dominican priest* who officially served as Catherine's
spiritual advisor but who, like all of Catherine's circle, de-
ferred to her as his spiritual mother.

[9]She sent them on ahead of her, and the letter serves as
their credentials.

Alas, dearest mother, you know that the truth cannot lie. Then why choose to go against it? By going against the truth of holy Church and of Pope Urban VI, you are going against God's truth and losing the fruit of Christ's blood, since it is on this truth that holy Church is founded. Alas, if you are not concerned for your own salvation, show some concern for the peoples entrusted to you, the subjects you have ruled with such diligence and in such peace for so long. Yet now, because you have gone against this truth, you see them at loggerheads, the curse of division setting them at war among themselves, killing one another like animals. Alas, how can you endure to see them torn apart on your account, white rose against red,[10] the truth against a lie, and your heart not burst? Alas, my wretched soul! Do you not see that they were all created by the spotless [white] rose of the eternal will of God and recreated in grace by the glowing red rose of the blood of Christ, which cleansed us from our sin in holy baptism,* brought us together as Christians and made us all one in the garden of holy Church? Reflect that they were cleansed and given these glorious roses, not by you or by anyone else, but by our Holy Mother Church alone, through the Supreme Pontiff,* Pope Urban VI, who holds the keys of the Blood. How, then, can your soul allow you even to want to take from them something that you cannot give them? And do you not see how cruel you are to yourself? Through their wickedness and lack of unity, you are undermining your own position. Moreover, you will have to account to God for the souls that are perishing because of you. What account can you give? A very bad one. So we shall make a very poor showing before the supreme Judge at the moment of death, which will be upon us any moment.

Alas, if this does not move you, at the very least ought you not be moved by the shame you have incurred before the world? Much more so now, after your conversion, than before. This lat-est fault is much more serious and displeasing to God and to creatures than the earlier one. After the first one you had acknowledged the truth and confessed your guilt; like a daughter, you had seemed to profess your willingness to return to the mercy and loving-kindness of your Father. Yet after all this, you have behaved even worse than before, either because you were not being sincere and were putting on an act, or because Justice has willed that I should do penance anew for my own old sins, so long persisted in; the penance, that is, of not meriting to see you feed peacefully at the breast of holy Church, who was there waiting to feed you, and to be fed by you — she feeding you with grace in the blood of the Lamb and you helping her with your support. For you saw how widowed she — the Church of Rome, seat and center of our faith — had become without her husband, and we without our father. Now that she has got him back again, she was looking to you to be a pillar supporting her husband, a shield ready to ward off the blows from him, and hit back at those who seek to wrest him from her. Oh, our ingratitude! Not only is he your father by his dignity, but your son, too,[11] so it is very cruel of you to reverse things [and to present us] with the spectacle of a daughter quarrelling with her own father, a mother with her own son. This grieves me so deeply that I can carry no greater cross in this life. When I think of the letter I received from you, in which you confessed that Pope Urban was truly supreme father and pontiff, and said that you wished to obey him! Yet now I find the opposite. Alas! Round off your confession, for the love of God! What is needed for confession, as I said, is to confess the truth with contrition of heart, and to make satisfaction. Make satisfaction, then, by rendering your debt of obedience, since you have confessed that he is the vicar of Christ on earth. Obey, and so receive the fruit of grace and placate God's wrath towards you. What has happened to the truth normally

---

[10]Urban's coat of arms contained six red roses; possibly, his enemies chose the white rose as their symbol. If so, Catherine's imagery needs some fixing.

[11]A Neapolitan by birth, Pope Urban had been one of Queen Joanna's subjects when he was still Bartholomew Prignani.

found in the mouth of a queen, which is usually, which must be, gospel? Nothing that she promises rightly and according to God must ever be taken back. And I see and have proof that you made a promise; that you said you were willing to obey the supreme pontiff, yet now you are doing the opposite, in word and in deed. I am appalled and unbearably grieved to see the eye of your understanding so darkened by the self-love induced by the devil's illusions and evil counsel that you care nothing about your own damnation, the ruination of your people in soul and body, your own physical fate, or your reputation before the world.

Sweetest mother, for the love of Christ crucified, be sweet, and not now bitter, to me. Come back to your senses a little; sleep on no longer in such a slumber, but rouse yourself in the little time you have left. Don't wait for time which does not wait for you. With true knowledge, know yourself and the great goodness of God who *has* waited for you; who, in His great mercy, has not taken time from you in your darkened state. With the desire [we spoke of] embrace virtue, put on truth and return to your father, humbled by true knowledge. You will find mercy and kindness in His Holiness, for He is a compassionate father who desires the life of His child. For the love of Christ crucified, do not lie on in death of soul, lest this shameful and wretched disgrace live on after your death — for bodily death is at your heels, yours and everyone else's,

but more especially at the heels of those whose youth is already behind them.[12] No one, however great or powerful, has power or might enough to fend off death. It is a sentence passed on us the moment we are conceived in the womb, and one from which none can escape. And we are not animals! Once dead, an animal is no more. But *we* are rational creatures, created to the image and likeness of God, so that when the body dies, the soul, in its being, does not, though it certainly dies to grace, through sin, if one dies in mortal sin. So let sheer necessity drive you; be merciful, not cruel, to your own self. Respond to God who calls to you with his clemency and compassion, and don't be slow to respond. Do so resolutely, lest you should have addressed to you those harsh words: "You did not think of me during your life, so I do not think of you at your death" — that is, you did not respond when I called to you while you still had time; now time for you is past, and you have no other way out.

I am relying on the infinite goodness of God to give you the grace to force yourself to respond with great eagerness and prompt obedience to holy Church and to Pope Urban VI. God will not despise all the many prayers and tears that have been and are being poured out by His servants for your salvation. Be grateful and appreciative for such a gift, that the spring of filial piety may well up within you. I will say no more.

Abide in the sweet and holy love of God. Sweet Jesus. Jesus, Love.

---

[12]Queen Joanna was in her fifties, having been born around 1326.

A New Challenger to the Church's Authority
▼▼▼

82 ▾ *John Wyclif,* CONCERNING THE POPE

Orthodox* reformers were not the only critics of the late-fourteenth-century papacy's* performance. The Oxford scholar and priest* John Wyclif (ca. 1330–1384) rose to public prominence in 1371 for his assault on the Church's claim that its property was inviolate from all use, tax, and seizure by the state, even in times of emergency. From this beginning, Wyclif went on to develop a theory of dominion that included the proposition that lay rulers could rightfully deprive sinful clerics* of their ecclesiastical* holdings because their sins made them unworthy of exercising any legitimate authority. Wyclif's increasingly radical ideas came to the notice of Pope Gregory XI, who in 1377 issued a list of eighteen erroneous propositions attributed to Wyclif and ordered his arrest and examination. Various attempts to condemn Wyclif in England initially failed, largely due to the protection afforded him by such royal patrons as Queen Joan, mother of King Richard II. Thus protected, Wyclif continued to write voluminously, producing theological treatises that increasingly deviated from the teachings of the Roman Church. Among his conclusions was the *doctrine of election and predestination* — the belief that God predestines every human for either salvation (the *elect*) or damnation. Based on this theological premise, Wyclif drew a sharp distinction between the invisible Church of the elect and the visible, earthly Church of Rome, which was mired in corruption. In this and many other ways, Wyclif anticipated the theological teachings of the sixteenth-century Protestant reformers. Finally, in 1382, an English church council* condemned twenty-four of Wyclif's opinions and forced some of his followers to recant them. Wyclif, however, was neither excommunicated* nor removed from his clerical office. He continued writing, despite failing health, and died of a stroke on December 31, 1384.

Even before his death, Wyclif's followers popularized his ideas (which he originally presented in rather dry, academic Latin treatises) by producing English digests of his most important works. Wyclif possibly had a hand in producing some of these English tracts, which were read and used by a group of wandering lay preachers known as *Lollards*. Although the Crown eventually suppressed heretical* Lollardy during the fifteenth century, Wyclif's ideas traveled to Central Europe, where they had a significant impact on the thought of Jan Hus (1370–1415), the Bohemian reformer. Through Hus's writings, some of Wyclif's ideas eventually came to the notice of Martin Luther.

The following document is an excerpt from the Middle English pamphlet *Concerning the Pope,* a simplified reworking of some of the points made in Wyclif's learned work *Concerning the Pope's Power* of late 1379. In order to avoid confusion, the editor has rendered the text into modern English.

QUESTIONS FOR ANALYSIS

1. Can you find any internal evidence that allows us to assign an approximate date to this document?
2. Why do we conclude that this work was aimed at a general audience?
3. What does the author think of the Great Schism?
4. What failings does the author find in the popes?
5. Which points do you think would strike the intended audience as especially telling? Why?
6. What, if anything, is heretical about this tract? What points might an orthodox reformer agree with? In addressing this question, you might find

it helpful to review Chapter 7, sources 40–43, and Chapter 10, sources 65–66.

7. How, if at all, does this tract reflect the fourteenth century's mood of crisis?

Note how God shows love for His Church through the schism that has recently befallen the papacy. Our faith teaches us through the words of Saint Paul that all good things happen to those of God's children who fear Him, and so Christians should heed them. The first book of God's law relates how God threatened the fiend when He said: "I shall create an enmity between you and the woman and between your seed and her seed, and she shall totally crush your head."[1] And so some people conclude that the holy prayers that the Church made to Christ and His mother[2] moved Him to send this grace down to sever the head of Antichrist,[3] so that his falsity might be better known. And it seems to them that the pope is Antichrist on earth, because he is the opposite of Christ in life and lore.

Christ was a very poor man from His birth to His death and forswore worldly riches and begging,[4] in accord with the state of primal innocence,[5] but Antichrist, in contrast to this, from the time that he is made pope to the time of his death, covets worldly wealth and tries in many shrewd ways to gain riches. Christ was a most meek man and urged that we learn from Him, but people say that the pope is the proudest man on earth, and he makes lords kiss his feet,[6] whereas Christ washed His apostles' feet.[7] Christ was a most unpretentious man in life, deeds, and

words. People say that this pope is not like Christ in this way, for whereas Christ went on foot to cities and little towns alike, they say this pope desires to live in a castle in a grand manner. Whereas Christ came to John the Baptist to be baptized* by him,[8] the pope summons people to come to him wherever he might be, yea, as though Christ Himself, and not he the pope, had summoned them to Him. Christ embraced young and poor in token of his humility; people say that the pope desires to embrace worldly prestige and not good people for the sake of God, lest he dishonor himself. Christ was busy preaching the Gospel,* and not for worldly prestige or for profit; people say that the pope allows this, but he would gladly make laws to which he gives more prestige and sanction than Christ's law. Christ so loved His flock that He laid down his life for them and suffered sharp pain and death in order to bring them to bliss. People say that the pope so loves the prestige of this world that he grants people absolution that guarantees a straight path to Heaven[9] so that they might perform acts that redound to his honor. And so this foolishness could be the cause of the death, in body and soul, of many thousands of people. And how does he follow Christ in this way? Christ was so patient and suffered wrongs so well that He prayed for His enemies and taught His

---

[1]The Bible, Genesis, 3:15. The woman is Eve and the reference is to the hatred that Eve's descendants would have for snakes, which were often worshipped as divinities in the ancient Near East but which Judaism treated as unclean and loathsome creatures. Medieval Christians regarded this as a prophecy of the coming of Mary, the New Eve, whose Son would destroy the devil's power.

[2]Despite his growing heterodoxy,* Wyclif maintained a deep devotion to Mary, although he excoriated those aspects of her cult that seemed to him to border on idolatry.

[3]The pseudo-Christ, who would emerge toward the end of time as the final and greatest incarnation of evil on earth.

[4]Apparently, an oblique attack on the mendicant friars,* who claimed to follow a life of Apostolic Poverty in imitation of Jesus and his apostles* (Chapter 7, source 41). Wyclif despised the friars.

[5]The presumed innocence of Adam and Eve before the Fall.

[6]A long-standing tradition. For the papal* perspective, see the *Dictatus Papae,* Chapter 10, source 65.

[7]The Gospel of John, 13:4–11.

[8]The Gospel of Matthew, 3:13–17; the Gospel of Mark, 1:9–11; the Gospel of Luke, 3:21–22.

[9]A reference to the Roman Church's indulgences,* which had become increasingly systematized and popular during the twelfth and thirteenth centuries.

apostles not to take vengeance.[10] People say that the pope of Rome wishes to be avenged in every way, by killing and by damning and by other painful means that he devises. Christ taught people to live well by the example of His own life and by His words, for He did what He taught and taught in a manner that was consonant with His actions. People say that the pope acts contrary to this. His life is not an example of how other people should live, for no one should live like him, inasmuch as he acts in a manner that accords to his high state. In every deed and word, Christ sought the glory of God and suffered many assaults on His manhood for this goal; people say that the pope, to the contrary, seeks his own glory in every way, yea, even if it means the loss of the worship of God. And so he manufactures many groundless gabblings.

If these and similar accusations are true of the pope of Rome, he is the very Antichrist and not Christ's vicar on earth.

---

[10]The Gospel of Matthew, 5:38–48; the Gospel of Luke, 6:27–36.

The Hundred Years' War and the English Peasant Rebellion
▼▼▼

83 ▼ Jean de Froissart, *CHRONICLES OF FRANCE, ENGLAND, AND NEIGHBORING COUNTRIES*

Europe's earliest historians wrote in Latin, as befit their clerical* status, and Latin continued to be the language of choice of most clerical historians, such as Henry Knighton (source 80), throughout the Middle Ages. Early in the thirteenth century, however, two French crusader-soldiers, Geoffrey de Villehardouin and Robert de Clari, independent of one another, composed eyewitness accounts of the Fourth Crusade in their native tongue, thereby initiating a tradition among a handful of French historians of writing history in vernacular prose, a practice that Jean de Joinville continued so brilliantly a century later (Chapter 10, source 64). The earliest French-language histories revolved around the later crusades, adventures in which French knighthood played such a prominent part. For much of the fourteenth and fifteenth centuries, however, the series of campaigns fought between the English and French, known as the *Hundred Years' War* (1337–1452), captivated the attention of most French chroniclers.*

The greatest of the French-language chroniclers of the Hundred Years' War was Jean Froissart (ca. 1337–after 1404): cleric, courtier, writer of romances, and poet. Froissart sprang from the merchant class of Flanders but attached himself to the nobility of England and France and shared the chivalric values of his patrons. As he noted, he wrote history "to encourage all valorous hearts and to show them honorable examples." Beginning his task around 1370, Froissart composed a chronicle in four books that spanned the period 1325 to 1400 and centered on the battles waged by the flower of European chivalry. The first book covered the history of his age to 1377 and heavily borrowed from *The True Chronicles* of Jean le Bel of Liege for events up to 1361. Thereafter, Froissart depended on his own observations and research, traveling widely to interview participants and view documents.

The first excerpt describes the Battle of Poitiers of 1356, in which the forces of the prince of Wales, Edward of England, defeated King John of France. The second excerpt, from Book II, deals with the English Peasants' Rebellion of 1381.

QUESTIONS FOR ANALYSIS

1. The English victory at Poitiers stunned people throughout Europe. Even the English thought it a miracle. Does this account suggest any factors that were key to the victory? How so?
2. Compare the actions of the English archers and men-at-arms with the scene of King John's capture. What does your answer suggest about fourteenth-century combat?
3. Consider how Prince Edward treats two enemies: Robert de Duras and King John. What do his actions suggest?
4. "Fourteenth-century English and French nobles exhibited both a growing sense of national identity and a strong residual sense of class loyalty that transcended ethnic and regional boundaries." Comment on this quotation, given the evidence provided by the first excerpt.
5. According to Froissart, why were the English peasants disaffected?
6. Consider Froissart's testimony in light of what Knighton tells us (source 80). How do the two sources portray the state of the English peasantry in the second half of the fourteenth century?
7. John Ball was a priest.* Some scholars have seen a connection between Wyclif's ideas (source 82) and those espoused by Ball. How strong does this putative connection seem to you?
8. Consider the peasants' relationship with the citizens of London. What role(s) did the Londoners play, and what do their actions suggest about the nature of this rebellion?
9. Consider the people and places that the rebels focused on in their attacks. Does a pattern emerge? If so, what does it suggest?
10. How and why was King Richard able to defeat the rebellion, and what conclusions do you draw from that victory?

The prince and his army . . . marched forward, burning and destroying the country in their approach to Anjou and Touraine. The French troops had taken up their quarters in a plain before the city of Poitiers, and it was reported to Edward by a detachment of his own men, that they were in immense numbers. "God help us," said Edward, "we must now consider which will be the best manner to fight them most advantageously." This night the English quartered in a very strong position, not far from the enemy, among vineyards and hedges.

The next day was Sunday, and early in the morning after he had heard mass* and received communion, the king of France, who was very impatient for battle, ordered his whole army to prepare. Upon this the trumpet sounded, and every one mounted his horse, and made for that part of the plain where the king's banner was planted. There were to be seen all the nobility of France richly dressed in brilliant armor, with banners and pennons gaily displayed; for no knight or squire,* for fear of dishonor, dared to remain behind. . . .

As soon as the cardinal's* negotiations were ended,[1] the prince of Wales thus addressed his army: "Now, my gallant fellows, what though we be a small number compared with our enemies, do not be cast down; victory does not always follow numbers; it is the Almighty who bestows it. I entreat you to exert yourselves and to combat manfully, for if it please God and St. George[2] you shall see me this day act like a true knight." The whole army of the prince, including every one, did not amount to 8,000; while the French, counting all sorts of persons, were upwards of 60,000 combatants, among whom were more than 3,000 knights; however, the English were in high spirits. . . .

The engagement now began on both sides; and the battalion of the [French] marshals was advancing before those who were intended to break the battalion of the [English] archers, and had entered the lane, where the hedges on both sides were lined by the archers, who, as soon as they saw them fairly entered, began shooting in such excellent manner from each side of the hedge, that the horses smarting under the pain of the wounds made by their bearded arrows would not advance, but turned about, and by their unruliness threw their riders, and caused the greatest confusion, so that the battalion of the marshals could never approach that of the prince; how-

ever, there were some knights and squires so well mounted, that by the strength of their horses they passed through and broke the hedge; but even these, in spite of their efforts, could not get up to the prince's battalion. . . .

The battalion of the marshals was soon after put to rout by the arrows of the archers, and the assistance of the men-at-arms, who rushed among them as they were struck down, and seized and slew them at their pleasure. . . .

To say the truth, the English archers were of infinite service to their army, for they shot so thickly and so well, that the French did not know which way to turn themselves to avoid their arrows. . . . In that part the battle was very hot, and greatly crowded; many a one was unhorsed, and you must know that whenever any one fell, he had but little chance of getting up again. As the prince[3] was thus advancing upon his enemies, followed by his division, and upon the point of charging them, he perceived the Lord Robert de Duras lying dead near a small bush on his right hand, with his banner beside him, and ten or twelve of his people, upon which he ordered two of his squires and three archers to place the body upon a shield, and carry it to Poitiers, and present it from him to the cardinal of Périgord, saying, "I salute him by that token." . . .

The English archers shot so well that none cared to come within reach of their arrows, and they put to death many who could not ransom themselves.[4] . . .

King John, on his part, proved himself a good knight; indeed, if a fourth of his people had behaved as well, the day would have been his own. Those also who were more immediately about him, acquitted themselves to the best of their power, and were either slain or taken prisoners. Scarcely any attempted to escape. . . . During the whole engagement the Lord de Chargny, who was near the king, and carried the royal banner,

---

[1]Cardinal Talleyrand de Périgord, who unsuccessfully attempted to prevent bloodshed through mediation.
[2]A legendary warrior-saint who served as patron saint of England.

[3]Edward.
[4]If a captive could pay a hefty ransom, it made no sense to kill him.

fought most bravely; the English and Gascons,[5] however, poured so fast upon the king's division, that they broke through the ranks by force, and in the confusion the Lord de Chargny was slain, with the banner of France in his hand. There was now much eagerness manifested to take the king; and those who were nearest to him, and knew him, cried out, "Surrender yourself, surrender yourself, or you are a dead man." In this part of the field was a young knight from St. Omer, engaged in the service of the king of England, whose name was Denys de Morbeque; for three years he had attached himself to the English, on account of having been banished from France in his younger days for a murder committed during an affray at St. Omer. Now it fortunately happened for this knight, that he was at the time near to the king of France, to whom he said in good French, "Sire, sire, surrender yourself." The king, who found himself very disagreeably situated, turning to him asked, "To whom shall I surrender myself? Where is my cousin, the prince of Wales?[6] if I could see him I would speak to him." "Sire," replied Sir Denys, "he is not here; but surrender yourself to me, and I will lead you to him." "Who are you?" said the king. "Sire, I am Denys de Morbeque, a knight from Artois; but I serve the king of England because I cannot belong to France, having forfeited all I possessed there." The king then gave him his right-hand glove, and said, "I surrender myself to you." . . .

▷ Once it is clear that his army has carried the day, Prince Edward begins to wonder what has happened to King John and dispatches the earl of Warwick and Lord Reginald Cobham to search for the French king.

The two barons immediately mounting their horses left the prince, and made for a small hillock that they might look about them; from this position they perceived a crowd of men-at-arms on foot, advancing very slowly. The king of France was in the midst of them, and in great danger, for the English and Gascons had taken him from Sir Denys de Morbeque, and were disputing who should have him; some bawling out, "It is I that have got him;" "No, no," replied others, "we have him." The king, to escape from this perilous situation, said, "Gentlemen, gentlemen, I pray you to conduct me and my son, in a courteous manner, to my cousin the prince, and do not make so great a riot about my capture, for I am a great lord, and I can make all sufficiently rich." These words, and others which fell from the king, appeased them a little; but the disputes were always beginning again, and the men did not move a step without rioting. When the two barons saw this troop of people they descended from the hillock, and sticking spurs into their horses, made up to them. On their arrival they asked what was the matter, and were informed that the king of France had been made prisoner, and that upwards of ten knights and squires challenged him at the same time as belonging to each of them. The two barons then pushed through the crowd by main force, and ordered all to draw aside. They commanded in the name of the prince, and under pain of instant death, that every one should keep his distance, and none approach unless ordered so to do. All then retreated behind the king, and the two barons, dismounting, advanced to the royal prisoner with profound reverence, and conducted him in a peaceable manner to the prince of Wales. . . .

Lord James Audley had not long left the prince's presence, when the earl of Warwick and Lord Reginald Cobham entered the pavilion and presented the king of France to him. The prince made a very low obeisance to the king, and gave him all the comfort as he was able. He ordered wine and spices to be brought, which, as a mark

---

[5]Prince Edward's father, King Edward III of England, was also duke of Gascony, a province in southwest France; consequently, many Gascons served in his army.

[6]King Philip III of France was Prince Edward's great-great-grandfather and King John's great-grandfather.

of his great affection, he presented to the king himself.

Thus was this battle won, as you have heard related, on the plains of Maupertuis, two leagues from the city of Poitiers, on the 19th day of September, 1356. The victory brought much wealth to the English, for there were large quantities of gold and silver plate, and rich jewels in the French camp. Indeed, the loss on the part of the French was very great; besides the king, his son Lord Philip, seventeen earls, and others who were taken prisoners, it is reported that five or six thousand were left dead on the field. When evening came the prince of Wales entertained his royal prisoner at supper with marked attention. The next day the English left Poitiers and advanced to Bordeaux,[7] where they passed the winter in feasting and merriment. In England, when the news arrived of the battle of Poitiers, and of the defeat of the French, there were great rejoicings, solemn thanksgivings were offered up in all the churches, and bonfires made in every town and village. . . .

When winter was over and the season was sufficiently advanced for traveling, the prince made preparations for quitting Bordeaux, and for conducting the French king and his principal prisoners to England, leaving behind him several of his own knights to guard the cities and towns which he had taken. After a long and tedious voyage he and his retinue, together with the captured monarch, arrived at Sandwich, disembarked, and proceeded to Canterbury. When the king of England was informed of this, he gave orders to the citizens of London to make such preparations as were suitable for the reception of so mighty a person as the king of France.

The prince and his royal charge remained one day at Canterbury, where they made their offerings to the shrine of St. Thomas, and the next morning proceeded to Rochester, the third day to Dartford, and the fourth to London, where they were received with much honor and distinction. The king of France, as he rode through London, was mounted on a white steed, with very rich furniture, and the prince of Wales on a little black hackney by his side. The palace of the Savoy was first appropriated to the French king's use; but soon after his arrival he was removed to Windsor Castle, where he was treated with the greatest possible attention, and hunting, hawking, and other amusements were provided for him.

▼ ▼ ▼

There happened great commotions among the lower orders in England, by which that country was nearly ruined. In order that this disastrous rebellion may serve as an example to mankind, I will speak of all that was done from the information I had at the time. It is customary in England, as well as in several other countries, for the nobility to have great privileges over the commonalty; that is to say, the lower orders are bound by law to plough the lands of the gentry, to harvest their grain, to carry it home to the barn, to thrash and winnow it; they are also bound to harvest and carry home the hay. All these services the prelates* and the gentlemen exact of their inferiors; and in the counties of Kent, Essex, Sussex, and Bedford, these services are more oppressive than in other parts of the kingdom. In consequence of this, evil people living in these districts began to murmur, saying, that in the beginning of the world there were no slaves, and that no one ought to be treated as such, unless he had committed treason against his lord, as Lucifer[8] did against God; but they had done no such thing, for they were neither angels nor spirits, but men formed after the same likeness as these lords who treated them as beasts. This they would bear no longer; they were determined to be free, and if they labored or did any work, they would be paid for it. A crazy priest in the county of Kent, called John Ball, who for his absurd preaching had thrice been confined in prison by

<hr>

[7]The capital of Gascony.

[8]The rebellious angel who became the Devil.

the archbishop* of Canterbury, was greatly instrumental in exciting these rebellious ideas. Every Sunday after mass, as the people were coming out of church, this John Ball was accustomed to assemble a crowd around him in the marketplace and preach to them. On such occasions he would say, "My good friends, matters cannot go on well in England until all things shall be in common; when there shall be neither vassals* nor lords; when the lords shall be no more masters than ourselves. How ill they behave to us! For what reason do they thus hold us in bondage? Are we not all descended from the same parents, Adam and Eve? And what can they show, or what reason can they give, why they should be more masters than ourselves? They are clothed in velvet and rich stuffs, ornamented with ermine and other furs, while we are forced to wear poor clothing. They have wines, spices, and fine bread, while we have only rye and the refuse of the straw; and when we drink it must be water. They have handsome seats and manors, while we must brave the wind and rain in our labors in the field; and it is by our labor they have wherewith to support their pomp. We are called slaves,[9] and if we do not perform our service we are beaten, and we have no sovereign to whom we can complain or who would be willing to hear us. Let us go to the king[10] and remonstrate with him; he is young, and from him we may obtain a favorable answer, and if not we must ourselves seek to amend our condition."

With such language as this did John Ball harangue the people of his village every Sunday after mass. The archbishop, on being informed of it, had him arrested and imprisoned for two or three months by way of punishment; but the moment he was out of prison, he returned to his former course. Many in the city of London, envious of the rich and noble, having heard of John Ball's preaching, said among themselves that the country was badly governed, and that the nobility had seized upon all the gold and silver. These wicked Londoners, therefore, began to assemble in parties, and to show signs of rebellion; they also invited all those who held like opinions in the adjoining counties to come to London, telling them that they would find the town open to them and the commonalty of the same way of thinking as themselves, and that they would so press the king that there should no longer be a slave in England.

By this means the men of Kent, Essex, Sussex, Bedford, and the adjoining counties, in number about 60,000, were brought to London, under command of Wat Tyler, Jack Straw, and John Ball. This Wat Tyler, who was chief of the three, had been a tiler of houses — a bad man and a great enemy to the nobility. When these wicked people first began their disturbances, all London, with the exception of those who favored them, was much alarmed. The mayor and rich citizens assembled in council and debated whether they should shut the gate and refuse to admit them; however, upon mature reflection they determined not to do so, as they might run the risk of having the suburbs burned. The gates of the city were therefore thrown open, and the rabble entered and lodged as they pleased. True it is that full two-thirds of these people knew neither what they wanted, nor for what purpose they had come together; they followed one another like sheep. . . .

In order that gentlemen and others may take example and learn to correct such wicked rebels, I will most amply detail how the whole business was conducted. On the Monday preceding the feast of the Holy Sacrament* in the year 1381, these people sallied forth from their homes to come to London, intending, as they said, to remonstrate with the king, and to demand their freedom. At Canterbury, they met John Ball, Wat Tyler, and Jack Straw. On entering this city they were well feasted by the inhabitants, who were all of the same way of thinking as themselves; and having held a council there, resolved to proceed on their march to London. They also sent emissaries across the Thames into Essex, Suffolk,

---

[9]More precisely, they were serfs.*

[10]King Richard II (r. 1377–1399).

and Bedford, to press the people of those parts to do the same, in order that the city might be quite surrounded. It was the intention of the leaders of this rabble that all the different parties should be collected on the feast of the Holy Sacrament on the day following. At Canterbury the rebels entered the Church of St. Thomas, where they did much damage; they also pillaged the apartments of the archbishop. . . . After this they plundered the abbey* of St. Vincent, and then, leaving Canterbury, took the road toward Rochester. As they passed they collected people from the villages right and left, and on they went like a tempest, destroying all the houses belonging to attorneys, the king's agents, and the archbishop, which came in their way. . . .

On Friday morning the rebels, who lodged in the square of St. Catherine's, before the Tower,[11] began to make themselves ready. They shouted much and said, that if the king would not come out to them, they would attack the Tower, stone it, and slay all who were within. The king, alarmed at these menaces, resolved to speak with the rabble; he therefore sent orders for them to retire to a handsome meadow at Mile-end, where, in the summer time, people go to amuse themselves, at the same time signifying that he would meet them there and grant their demands. Proclamation to this effect was made in the king's name, and thither, accordingly, the commonalty of the different villages began to march; many, however, did not care to go, but stayed behind in London, being more desirous of the riches of the nobles and the plunder of the city. Indeed, covetousness and the desire of plunder was the principal cause of these disturbances, as the rebels showed very plainly. When the gates of the Tower were thrown open, and the king, attended by his two brothers and other nobles, had passed through, Wat Tyler, Jack Straw, and John Ball, with upward of 400 others, rushed in by force, and running from chamber to chamber, found the archbishop of Canterbury, by name Simon, a valiant and wise man, whom the rascals seized

and beheaded. The prior* of St. John's suffered the same fate, and likewise a Franciscan friar,* a doctor of medicine, who was attached to the duke of Lancaster, also a sergeant-at-arms whose name was John Laige.

The heads of these four persons the rebels fixed on long spikes and had them carried before them through the streets of London; and when they had made sufficient mockery of them, they caused them to be placed on London Bridge, as if they had been traitors to their king and country. . . .

▷ King Richard meets the rebels outside London.

The king showed great courage, and on his arrival at the appointed spot instantly advanced into the midst of the assembled multitude, saying in a most pleasing manner, "My good people, I am your king and your lord, what is it you want? What do you wish to say to me?" Those who heard him made answer, "We wish you to make us free for ever. We wish to be no longer called slaves, nor held in bondage." The king replied, "I grant your wish; now therefore return to your homes, and let two or three from each village be left behind, to whom I will order letters to be given with my seal, fully granting every demand you have made: and in order that you may be the more satisfied, I will direct that my banners be sent to every stewardship, castlewick, and corporation." . . .

Thus did this great assembly break up. The king instantly employed upwards of thirty secretaries, who drew up the letters as fast as they could, and when they were sealed and delivered to them, the people departed to their own counties. The principal mischief, however, remained behind: I mean Wat Tyler, Jack Straw, and John Ball, who declared, that though the people were satisfied, they were by no means so, and with them were about 30,000 also of the same mind. These all continued in the city without any wish

---

[11]The Tower of London, which was a royal residence.

to receive the letters or the king's seal, but did all they could to throw the town into such confusion, that the lords and rich citizens might be murdered and their houses pillaged and destroyed. The Londoners suspected this, and kept themselves at home, well armed and prepared to defend their property. . . .

At the same time that a party of these wicked people in London burnt the palace of the Savoy, the church and house of St. John's, and the hospital of the Templars, there were collected numerous bodies of men from Lincolnshire, Norfolk, and Suffolk, who, according to the orders they had received, were marching towards London. On their road they stopped near Norwich, and forced every one whom they met to join them. . . .

This day all the rabble again assembled under Wat Tyler, Jack Straw, and John Ball, at a place called Smithfield, where every Friday the horse-market is kept. There were present about 20,000, and many more were in the city, breakfasting, and drinking Rhenish wine and Malmsey Madeira in the taverns, . . . without paying for anything; and happy was he who could give them good cheer to satisfy them. Those who collected in Smithfield had with them the king's banner, which had been given to them the preceding evening; and the wretches, notwithstanding this, wanted to pillage the city, their leaders saying, that hitherto they had done nothing. "The pardon which the king has granted will be of no use to us; but if we be of the same mind, we shall pillage this rich and powerful town of London before those from Essex, Suffolk, Cambridge, . . . Lincoln, York, and Durham shall arrive; for they are on their road. . . . Let us, then, be beforehand in plundering the wealth of the city; for if we wait for their arrival, they will wrest it from us." To this opinion all had agreed, when the king, attended by 60 horses, appeared in sight; he was at the time not thinking of the rabble, but had intended to continue his ride, without coming into London; however, when he arrived before the abbey of St. Bartholomew, which is in Smithfield, and saw the crowd of people, he

stopped, saying that he would ascertain what they wanted, and endeavor to appease them. Wat Tyler, seeing the king and his party, said to his men, "Here is the king, I will go and speak with him; do you not stir until I give you a signal." He then made a motion with his hand, and added, "When you shall see me make this signal, then step forward, and kill every one except the king; but hurt him not, for he is young, and we can do what we please with him; carrying him with us through England, we shall be lords of the whole country, without any opposition." . . .

▷   Wat Tyler approaches the king and begins negotiating with him. In the midst of this parlay, the mayor of London strikes Tyler down, and one of the king's squires finishes him off with a sword.

When the rebels found that their leader was dead, they drew up in a sort of battle array, each man having his bow bent before him. The king at this time certainly hazarded much, though it turned out most fortunately for him; for as soon as Tyler was on the ground, he left his attendants, giving orders that no one should follow him, and riding up to the rebels, who were advancing to revenge their leader's death, said, "Gentlemen, what are you about: you shall have me for your captain: I am your king, remain peaceable." The greater part, on hearing these words, were quite ashamed, and those among them who were inclined for peace began to slip away; the riotous ones, however, kept their ground. The king returned to his lords, and consulted with them what next should be done. Their advice was to make for the fields; but the mayor said, that to retreat would be of no avail. "It is quite proper to act as we have done; and I reckon we shall very soon receive assistance from our good friends in London."

While things were in this state, several persons ran to London, crying out, "They are killing the king and our mayor;" upon which alarm, all those of the king's party sallied out towards Smithfield, in number about seven or eight thousand. . . . These all drew up opposite to the rebels, who had with them the king's banner, and showed as if they intended to maintain their ground by offering combat. . . .

As soon as Sir Robert Knolles arrived at Smithfield, his advice was immediately to fall upon the insurgents, and slay them; but King Richard would not consent to this. "You shall first go to them," he said, "and demand my banner; we shall then see how they will behave; for I am determined to have this by fair means or foul." The new knights were accordingly sent forward, and on approaching the rebels made signs to them not to shoot, as they wished to speak with them; and when within hearing, said, "Now attend; the king orders you to send back his banners; and if you do so, we trust he will have mercy upon you." The banners, upon this, were given up directly, and brought to the king. It was then ordered, under pain of death, that all those who had obtained the king's letters should deliver them up. Some did so, but not all; and the king on receiving them had them torn in pieces in their presence. You must know that from the time the king's banners were surrendered, these fellows kept no order; but the greater part, throwing their bows upon the ground, took to their heels and returned to London. Sir Robert Knolles was very angry that the rebels were not attacked at once and all slain; however, the king would not consent to it, saying, that he would have ample revenge without doing so.

When the rabble had dispersed, the king and his lords, to their great joy, returned in good array to London. . . .

John Ball and Jack Straw were found hidden in an old ruin, where they had secreted themselves, thinking to steal away when things were quiet; but this they were prevented doing, for their own men betrayed them. With this capture the king and his barons were much pleased, and had their heads cut off, as was that of Tyler, and fixed on London Bridge, in place of those whom these wretches themselves had put there.

News of this total defeat of the rebels in London was sent throughout the neighboring counties, in order that all those who were on their way to London might hear of it; and as soon as they did so, they instantly returned to their homes, without daring to advance farther. . . .

After the death of Tyler, Jack Straw, John Ball, and several others, the people being somewhat appeased, the king resolved to visit his bailiwicks, castlewicks, and stewardships, in order to punish the principal insurgents, and to recover the letters of pardon which had been forced from him, as well as to settle other matters tending to the peace of the realm. By a secret summons he assembled 500 spears and as many archers, and with them took the road to Kent, in which quarter the rebellion had first broken out. The first place he stopped at was a village called Comprinke; here he ordered the mayor, and all the men of the village, to be called, with whom one of his council remonstrated, telling them how much they had erred, and that because this mischief, which had nearly proved the ruin of England, must have had some advisers, it was better that the ringleaders should suffer than the whole; his majesty, therefore, demanded, under pain of incurring his displeasure for ever, that those should be pointed out who had been most culpable. When the people heard this, and saw that the innocent might escape by pointing out the guilty, they looked at each other, and said: "My lord, here is one by whom this town was excited." Immediately the person alluded to was taken and hanged, as were seven others. The letters-patent, which had been granted, were demanded back, and given up to the king's officer, who tore them in pieces, saying, "We command, in the king's name, all you who are here assembled to depart every one to his own home in peace; that you never more rebel against the king or against his ministers. By the punishment which has been inflicted your former deeds are pardoned." The people with one voice exclaimed, "God bless the king and his good council." In the same manner they acted in many other places in Kent, and, indeed, throughout England, so that upwards of 1,500 were beheaded or hanged.

▼▼▼

Social Commentary

Perhaps the fact that Europeans could still laugh at themselves in the midst of the many crises that beset them is proof positive of the basic resiliency of four-teenth-century society. As the following two sources illustrate, insightful com-mentary on the many ways that individuals and classes deviated from society's ideals and highest standards could be and often was presented with a wry smile, rather than a worried frown.

Disorder in the Court
▼▼▼

84 ▼ Franco Sacchetti, *THREE HUNDRED NOVELLAS*

John of Viterbo explained how government in an Italian commune functioned in theory (Chapter 8, source 50), but only a satirist could do justice to the human comedy that was an ever-present reality in the busy law courts of Italy's cities. Franco Sacchetti (ca. 1332–1400), a citizen of Florence who rose high in that city's public offices, is most remembered today not for his active political life but for his collection of *novellas* (or, if one prefers the Italian plural, *novelle*). The novella, the most distinctive literary genre of fourteenth-century Italy, was essentially a secular* variation of the colorful *exemplum,* or moral anecdote, that popular preachers used in their sermons (Chapter 7, source 39). Written not in Latin but in the vernacular dialects of Italy, these short stories attest the vigorous, literate lay culture of late-medieval Italian cities. Their humor and language are often crude, but in their very lack of polish, novellas offer invaluable insights into the modes of expression and thought of ordinary fourteenth-century urban Italians.

Giovanni Boccaccio (1314–1375) of Florence, whose *Decameron* was and is the most justly celebrated of all novella collections, defined and popularized the genre, and his influence on those who followed, including Sacchetti, was profound. The *Decameron*'s one hundred novellas were held together by an overarching theme — a group of young urbanites, fleeing the Black Death in Florence, amuse them-selves in their rural hideaway by telling stories. In theory, each story had an edi-fying moral lesson, but in reality, its primary purpose was entertainment, often with a bawdy flavor.

Sacchetti borrowed the setting of a flight from a plague-stricken city as the background for his own collection of novellas and freely acknowledged his debt to Boccaccio. At the same time, his *Three Hundred Novellas* (of which 223 are extant) is quite distinctive in content, inasmuch as its author drew heavily on his own political experiences and wide travels. Its tone is also distinctive. The lan-guage is less artful than Boccacio's and thereby more authentically common. If Boccaccio is a fine glass of Chianti classico, then Sacchetti is a tumbler of raw

Tuscan table wine. The richly humorous characterizations are also very much Sacchetti's own, as is the social criticism, which he aimed at city government, clerical* corruption, and the pretensions of the privileged classes. True to the genre, however, Sacchetti wanted, above all else, to tell entertaining stories based on the humorous side of daily life in Tuscany.

In this novella, the author takes dead aim at the legal profession, which flourished and proliferated in urban Italy's highly litigious environment. By the end of the story, none of the characters comes off looking good — which was, in all likelihood, exactly what Sacchetti's readers demanded from a story about lawyers.

QUESTIONS FOR ANALYSIS

1. On the basis of this story, describe the different levels of Florence's legal profession and explain the functions of each.
2. What does the courtroom scene tell us about fourteenth-century Florentine judicial procedure?
3. What stereotypes does Sacchetti employ in drawing each of his characters? Be specific in your answers. What, for example, are Ser Bonavere's most notable characteristics? What might these various stereotypes suggest about popular images of lawyers and judges?
4. One modern scholar has written that this story communicates a sense of lost confidence in the system. Do you agree or disagree? Why?

Once, in the neighborhood of Santo Brancazio,[1] Florence, there was a notary[2] named Ser[3] Bonavere. He was a big, coarse man, quite jaundiced — practically yellow skinned[4] — and badly built, as if he had been hewn with a pickaxe. He was an ever-eager petitioner, and right or wrong, he never ceased to dispute. And it was his custom that he never had an inkwell or pen or ink in the pen-case he carried. And if, while going through the street, he was asked to draft a contract, he would search his pen-case and say that through forgetfulness he had left the inkwell and pen at home, and on that account, he said, they should go to the grocer and pick up a reed and folio of paper.

Now it happened that a rich man from those parts was nearing death after a long illness and wished to make a will, and his relatives feared he might die before he could do this. With one of them at the window, they spied Ser Bonavere making his way through the street. They called out that he should come up and meet them halfway on the stairs, and they said he had been sent by God to make this much-needed will. Ser Bonavere searched the pen-case and said that he did not have his inkwell. He said that he would

---

[1]Each neighborhood, or *popolo,* was identified by its parish* church — here, Santo Brancazio.
[2]A professional who specialized in drawing up private and public documents according to established formulas that gave the documents legal validity.
[3]An honorific title of respect, used especially for notaries and priests.*

[4]According to fourteenth-century medical theory (as inherited from the Ancient Greeks), yellowish skin was indicative of a bilious, or irascible, temper, due to an overabundance of yellow bile in the system.

go for it at once, and so he went. When he got home, he took great pains for a good hour to find the inkwell and a pen. The others, who wished that the good man who was dying should make his will, saw how long Ser Bonavere stayed away. Fearing that the sick man might *not* die, they quickly sent for Ser Nigi da Santo Donato and had him make the will.

Finally Ser Bonavere left his house, after having spent a good deal of time softening the wick of his inkwell,[5] and arrived to draw up the will. But he was told that he had taken so long that they had had Ser Nigi do it. Greatly humiliated, he turned back. And lamenting sorely to himself over the loss that seemed to have befallen him, he thought for the longest time about actually supplying himself with ink and folios and pens and a quill-case, so that a similar misfortune could not interfere with his plans again. And when he reached the grocer's shop, he bought a gathering of folios, which he bound up tight and tossed into his pen-case; and he bought a phial with its chamber full of ink and hung it from his belt; and he bought not one pen, but a bundle of pens, and one enormous pen, big enough to last a large brigade for a full day, and he hung it from his side in a leather spice-pouch. And so furnished, he said: "Now we'll see if I'm ready to draw up a will like Ser Nigi!"

With Ser Bonavere so well furnished in this manner, it happened that he went to the *Palazzo del Podestà*[6] that same day to give an exception[7] to a *collaterale*[8] of the podesta, who came from Monte di Falco. This judge, an elderly man, wore a biretta[9] encircled with whole squirrel-skins, and

was clad in red cloth. He was sitting at the bench when the aforementioned Ser Bonavere showed up with the packet at his side and with the folio of the exception in hand, and having plunged through the huge throng that was there, he arrived and stood before the judge. The advocate[10] of the other party was Messer[11] Cristofano de' Ricci, and the proctor[12] was Ser Giovanni Fantoni. When they caught sight of Ser Bonavere with the exception, they thrust their way through the crowd and, dividing the ranks, came before the judge. And as they squeezed up against the judge, Messer Cristofano said: "This exception is just a case of pissing into the wind! We're going to fight this one out with hatchets!"

And as they bumped up against one another, the phial of ink was broken, and the greater part of the ink went over the long hooded garment of the judge, and some splashed onto that of the advocate. When the judge saw this, he lifted the hem and, marveling to himself, he began to look around. He shouted to the servants to lock the door of the palazzo, so that the source of this fearful occurrence could be found. Seeing and hearing all this, Ser Bonavere lowered his hand; and when he searched for the phial, he found it all broken, with a lot of ink still on it. He quickly slipped between the men and departed with God. The judge, still stained almost from head to toe, and Messer Cristofano, covered with splashes, looked at one another, and, as if they had taken leave of their senses, some looked at one and some looked at the other. The judge stared at the ceiling vaults, as if the ink had come from above, and then he turned to the walls. And failing to

---

[5]The inkwell had bristles that functioned as a wick to draw up ink from a reservoir below.

[6]The public building where the city's podesta (Chapter 8, source 50) exercised his authority.

[7]A legal instrument presented to contest the jurisdictional competence of a judge.

[8] A professional judge who ran the court of the podesta.

[9]A stiff, square, ceremonial hat of office.

[10]A legal professional who pleaded and presented cases in court.

[11]An honorific title that implied high rank or social status, rather than simply professional status (as *Ser*). Because Cristofano came from the aristocratic Ricci clan, he was accorded the more dignified *Messer.*

[12]A legal professional who represented a private citizen in a suit by composing and filing on the client's behalf all necessary documents. Unlike the *advocate,* whose principal expertise was in courtroom oral argument, the *proctor* was a highly trained expert who crafted all of the legal paperwork.

see where such a thing could have come from, he turned toward the bench, looking above it. Then, bowing his head, he looked under it. Then, climbing the steps of the bench, he examined each step in turn. At last, having seen everything, he began to rub himself all over, as if he were going quite out of his mind.

Messer Cristofano and Ser Giovanni, having a bit more of their wits about them, said: "Oh, *Messer lo Collaterale,* don't touch it; leave it to dry." Others said: "That robe is ruined." Others said: "It looks like one of those gloomy dark things they used to wear."[13]

And with each one looking and speaking in this manner, the judge grew suspicious. Facing them, he said: "And do you know who has done this thing that has humiliated me?" Someone gave one explanation and someone else another, so that the judge, now practically beside himself, told his bailiff to have the neighborhood public sanitation officer draw up an official complaint on the matter. And the bailiff, very nearly laughing, said: "And against whom shall he draw it up? It all happened to you, and you do not even know who did it! It would be better if you were to see that from now on no one brings ink to the bench. As for your robe, which you've made black to the feet, just cut it here; that would make it shorter. Who cares if you end up looking like a middle-rank soldier?"

Hearing these arguments, the judge, mocked from essentially every side, followed through with what the bailiff had said to him and remained completely baffled by the affair. And for a good two months at the bench, he watched everyone who came there, certain that ink would continually be thrown at him. From what he cut from the feet of his robe he made socks and gloves, as best he could. Messer Cristofano, on

his part, cut off the armbands, and lifting the strips, he shut his mouth in astonishment. And Ser Giovanni Fantoni, who was with him, said: "By Christ's Gospel,* that's a great wonder!"

And so most people forgot it in the morning, except that Ser Bonavere had no more than one pair of white gloves, and these, when he found himself at home, he discovered to be all covered with ink, so that they looked like a boy's abacus table. Those involved washed themselves and cleaned up the ink as best they could, but the best remedy was in resigning themselves to the whole business.

It would have been better had the said Ser Bonavere not been a notary, but since he was, he should have gone out prepared and equipped with the tools of his craft, just like his colleagues. Had he done so, he would have drawn up the will, which would have been quite profitable for him. He would not have ruined the judge's robe, nor that of Messer Cristofano, nor would he have driven the judge and the others who were there crazy, and he would not have spilled ink on his own tunic and gloves, which he ended up throwing out for a really quite lousy reason. And in the end, he would not have had the expense of the broken phial or the ink that was in it, though it could have been worse. For if that judge had known about him, he would have had to mend the ruined robes, and perhaps he would have had to do worse.

And so it remains, as the saying goes: "In a hundred years and in a hundred months, water returns to its place of origin." And so it went against Ser Bonavere who, having gone dry and without ink for a very long time, then set so much of it at his side that he painted the podesta's court with it.

---

[13]Many people responded to the crisis of the Black Death by wearing colorful, ostentatious, and even provocative clothing as a way of affirming life. Sacchetti, who composed these novellas between around 1388 and 1395, probably refers here to somber pre–Black Death styles.

Fourteenth-Century English Society
▼▼▼
85 ▼ Geoffrey Chaucer, THE CANTERBURY TALES

Like Sacchetti, his Italian contemporary, Geoffrey Chaucer (ca. 1342–1400) was a man of public affairs whose lasting fame rests on his literary, not on his political, achievements. Also like Sacchetti, Chaucer was a sharp-eyed social satirist whose art was influenced by Giovanni Boccaccio but who was much more than a mere imitator.

Chaucer was born in London, the son of a prosperous wine merchant. After obtaining a rudimentary classical education at one of London's leading schools, Chaucer served as a page in the household of the countess of Ulster, where he learned courtly manners and probably continued his education under a tutor. In 1359 Chaucer campaigned with the army of Edward III in France, where he was captured. King Edward himself, who held Chaucer in high regard, paid a substantial portion of the young man's ransom in 1360, and thereafter Chaucer rose rapidly in the king's service. Twice while serving on royal business, Chaucer visited Italy, where he probably had an opportunity to acquaint himself firsthand with the writings of Boccaccio. Chaucer certainly read Italian, as well as French and Latin, and was a prodigious reader with an extraordinary memory. During these years as a trusted servant of King Edward, Chaucer also began to compose a variety of literary pieces in his native English.

In 1386 Chaucer suddenly was relieved of his many offices when the duke of Gloucester, the person who momentarily controlled the young King Richard II, placed his own people in these posts. Although Chaucer's career and fortunes were later revived, at this juncture he found himself with a three-year period of enforced retirement. This ultimately proved to be a blessing, insofar as it provided him with the leisure to begin organizing his masterpiece, *The Canterbury Tales.*

The Canterbury Tales is framed around the device that a group of about thirty pilgrims,* who have joined to travel to the shrine of St. Thomas at Canterbury, will entertain one another by telling stories — two each on the way to Canterbury and two each on the return trip. Chaucer never completed this immense project, apparently tiring of it, but what he did leave behind is, for all of its flaws, one of the great works of European literature.

As we have already seen, collections of stories were common in the fourteenth century, and as was true of most of the creators of these collections, Chaucer borrowed the majority of his stories quite unabashedly from ancient and modern writers. Collectively, *The Canterbury Tales* show the wide range of wares in fourteenth-century Europe's storehouse of imagination and experience. Chaucer's special genius was not in creating the tales that he chose to tell; it lay, rather, in his delineation of character, as he used the tales and their tellers to shed light on many different aspects of English society in his day.

The following selection, which is translated into modern English from the original Middle English verse, comes from the General Prologue, in which Chaucer introduces his readers to some of the memorable characters who will journey to Canterbury.

QUESTIONS FOR ANALYSIS

1. What do the knight's campaigns suggest about late-fourteenth-century crusading?
2. Compare the knight and the squire.* Aside from their generational differences, what other message does Chaucer seemingly want to convey in his juxtaposition of the portraits of these two men? In addressing this issue, you might want to review the relevant sources in Chapters 8, 9, and 11, as well as Froissart (source 83).
3. Consider the yeoman. What seems to be Chaucer's message regarding this individual? Does a rereading of Froissart (source 83) shed any light on what Chaucer is doing here?
4. Consider Madame Eglantine and the monk.* How well do they conform to the Rule of Saint Benedict (Chapter 4, source 17)? Consider Friar Hubert. How well does he conform to the Franciscan ideal (Chapter 7, source 41)? Who of the three is the most sympathetic, or likeable, character? Who is the least sympathetic? What does Chaucer seem to be saying in presenting these three portraits? Explain your answers.
5. What do your answers to question 4 suggest about late-fourteenth-century stereotypes of nuns,* monks, and friars?*
6. Consider the parson, especially given Chaucer's portraits of the three other church figures. What is Chaucer trying to tell us here?
7. Some scholars claim to find Lollard sympathies in Chaucer's work; others find him quite orthodox* in his Catholic beliefs and attitudes. Consider these excerpts from the Prologue in light of sources 82 and 83. What do you conclude? Why?
8. What does Chaucer's portrait of the merchant suggest about the interests and activities of this class and the attitudes of nonmerchants toward the mercantile class? (Do not forget that Chaucer's father was a merchant.)
9. The Wife of Bath is one of Chaucer's most unforgettable characters. How does he present her? Compare her with Madame Eglantine. What do you infer from Chaucer's portraits of these two women?
10. Consider the knight, the merchant, and the Wife of Bath. What do their interests suggest about fourteenth-century travel?
11. All things considered, what do these nine people allow us to conclude about late-fourteenth-century English society? Explain your answer.
12. Reconsider your answer to question 8 of source 80 (Knighton), based on the evidence that Chaucer provides.

There with us was a KNIGHT, a worthy man
Who, from the very first time he began
To ride about, loved honor, chivalry,
The spirit of giving, truth and courtesy.
He was a valiant warrior for his lord;
No man had ridden farther with the sword
Through Christendom and lands of heathen
        creeds,[1]
And always he was praised for worthy deeds.
He helped win Alexandria in the East,
And often sat at table's head to feast
With knights of all the nations when in
        Prussia.
In Lithuania as well as Russia
No other noble Christian fought so well.
When Algaciras in Granada fell,
When Ayas and Attalia were won,
This Knight was there. Hard riding he had
        done
At Benmarin. Along the Great Sea coast
He'd made his strikes with many a noble host.
His mortal battles numbered then fifteen,
And for our faith he'd fought at Tramissene
Three tournaments and always killed his foe.
This worthy Knight was ally, briefly so,
Of the lord of Palathia (in work

Performed against a fellow heathen Turk).
He found the highest favor in all eyes,
A valiant warrior who was also wise
And in deportment meek as any maid.
He never spoke unkindly, never played
The villain's part, but always did the right.
He truly was a perfect, gentle knight.
But now to tell of his array, he had
Good horses but he wasn't richly clad;
His fustian[2] tunic was a rusty sight
Where he had worn his hauberk, for the
        Knight
Was just back from an expedition when
His pilgrimage he hastened to begin.
    There with him was his son, a youthful
        SQUIRE,
A lover and knight bachelor[3] to admire.
His locks were curled as if set by a press.
His age was twenty years or so, I guess.
In stature he was of an average height
And blest with great agility and might.
He'd ridden for a time with cavalry
In Flanders and Artois and Picardy,[4]
Performing well in such a little space
In hopes of standing in his lady's grace.
He was embroidered like a flowerbed

Source: From *The Canterbury Tales,* trans. Ronald L. Ecker and Eugene J. Crook, Hodge & Braddock, Publishers, 1933. Reprinted with permission.

[1]The knight's campaigns include the following: In addition to the Hundred Years' War ("a valiant warrior for his lord"), he participated in the ill-fated crusade to capture Jerusalem by way of Alexandria in Egypt that Peter I of Lusignan, king of Cyprus, led in 1365. He rode with the Teutonic Knights, a German crusading military order, against pagan Prussians and Lithuanians in the Baltic and against Eastern Orthodox Christians in Russia. In Spain he participated in the capture of Algeciras in 1344, by which King Alfonso XI of Castile secured Gibraltar, thereby cutting off from North Africa the kingdom of Granada, the last Muslim state in Iberia. He participated in raids on Muslim coastal towns in North Africa and accompanied Peter of Lusignan when the king captured Antalya (Attalia) on the coast of Turkey in 1361 and raided Ayas in Armenia in 1367. He fought in Algeria at Tremessen and even briefly served under the Turkish governor of Palatye (Palathia) in Anatolia.* All of these expeditions attracted crusaders from all over Europe, and a number of fourteenth-century English knights (such as Henry Grosmont, duke of Lancaster)

participated in multiple crusades from Granada to Prussia to the eastern Mediterranean. In fact, Henry of Derby, the future King Henry IV of England, led a raid into Lithuania in 1391.
[2]A coarse, sturdy cloth of cotton and flax.
[3]A young knight-in-training in the service of an older, more experienced knight.
[4]Areas in the kingdom of France where various battles of the Hundred Years' War were fought.

Or meadow, full of flowers white and red.
He sang or else he fluted all the day;
He was as fresh as is the month of May.
His gown was short, his sleeves were long and
    wide.
And well upon a horse the lad could ride;
Good verse and songs he had composed, and he
Could joust and dance, drew well, wrote
    gracefully.
At night he'd love so hotly, without fail,
He slept no more than does a nightingale.
He was a courteous, humble lad and able,
And carved meat for his father at the table.

    Now he had brought one servant by his side,
A Yeoman[5] — with no more he chose to ride.
This Yeoman wore a coat and hood of green.
He had a sheaf of arrows, bright and keen,
Beneath his belt positioned handily —
He tended to his gear most yeomanly,
His arrow feathers never drooped too low —
And in his hand he bore a mighty bow.
His head was closely cropped, his face was
    brown.
The fellow knew his woodcraft up and down.
He wore a bracer[6] on his arm to wield
His bolts. By one side were his sword and
    shield,
And on the other, mounted at the hip,
A dagger sharply pointed at the tip.
A Christopher[7] of silver sheen was worn
Upon his breast; a green strap held his horn.
He must have been a forester, I guess.

    There also was a Nun, a Prioress,[8]
Her smile a very simple one and coy.
Her greatest oath was only "By Saint Loy!"
Called Madam Eglantine, this Nun excelled
At singing when church services were held,
Intoning through her nose melodiously.
And she could speak in French quite fluently,

After the school of Stratford-at-the-Bow
(The French of Paris wasn't hers to know).
Of table manners she had learnt it all,
For from her lips she'd let no morsel fall
Nor deeply in her sauce her fingers wet;
She'd lift her food so well she'd never get
A single drop or crumb upon her breast.
At courtesy she really did her best.
Her upper lip she wiped so very clean
That not one bit of grease was ever seen
Upon her drinking cup. She was discreet
And never reached unseemly for the meat.
And certainly she was good company,
So pleasant and so amiable, while she
Would in her mien[9] take pains to imitate
The ways of court, the dignity of state,
That all might praise her for her worthiness.
To tell you of her moral consciousness,
Her charity was so great that to see
A little mouse caught in a trap would be
Enough to make her cry, if dead or bleeding.
She had some little dogs that she was feeding
With roasted meat or milk and fine white
    bread;
And sorely she would weep if one were dead
Or if someone should smite it with a stick.
She was all tender heart right to the quick.
Her pleated wimple was of seemly class,
She had a well-formed nose, eyes gray as glass,
A little mouth, one that was soft and red.
And it's for sure she had a fair forehead —
It must have been a handbreadth wide, I own,
For hardly was the lady undergrown.
The beauty of her cloak I hadn't missed.
She wore a rosary[10] around her wrist
Made out of coral beads all colored green,
And from it hung a brooch of golden sheen
On which there was an *A* crowned with a
    wreath,

---

[5]A free farmer.
[6]An archer's arm guard.
[7]A medal of St. Christopher, patron of travelers.
[8]Depending on the size of her convent, she would either be second-in-charge at an abbey,* under an abbess,* or the head of a smaller house known as a *priory.* Considering her retinue, she seems to be in charge of a priory.

[9]Manner, or bearing.
[10]A collection of stringed beads used as an aid to prayer.

With *Amor vincit omnia*[11] beneath.
 She brought along another NUN, to be
Her chaplain, and her PRIEST,* who made it
  three.
 A MONK there was, a fine outrider of
Monastic* lands, with venery his love;
A manly man, to be an abbot* able.
He had some dainty horses in the stable,
And when he rode, his bridle might you hear
Go jingling in the whistling wind as clear
And loud as might you hear the chapel bell
Where this lord not too often kept his cell.[12]
Because Saint Maurus[13] and Saint Benedict[14]
Had rules he thought were old and rather
  strict,
This mounted Monk let old things pass away
So that the modern world might have its day.
That text he valued less than a plucked hen
Which says that hunters are not holy men,
Or that a monk ignoring rules and order
Is like a flapping fish out of the water
(That is to say, a monk out of his cloister).
He held that text not worth a single oyster,
And his opinion, I declared, was good.
Why should he study till he's mad? Why
  should
He pore through books day after day indoors,
Or labor with his hands at all the chores
That Austin[15] bids? How shall the world be
  served?
Let such works be to Austin then reserved!
And so he was a pricker and aright;
Greyhounds he had as swift as birds in flight,
For tracking and the hunting of the hare
Were all his pleasure, no cost would he spare.
His sleeves, I saw, were fur-lined at the hand
With gray fur of the finest in the land,

And fastening his hood beneath his chin
There was a golden, finely crafted pin,
A love-knot in the greater end for class.
His head was bald and shinier than glass.
His face was shiny, too, as if anointed.
He was a husky lord, one well appointed.
His eyes were bright, rolled in his head and
  glowed
Just like the coals beneath a pot. He rode
In supple boots, his horse in great estate.
Now certainly he was a fine prelate,*
He wasn't pale like some poor wasted ghost.
Fat swan he loved the best of any roast.
His palfrey[16] was as brown as is a berry.
 A FRIAR there was, a wanton one and merry,
Who begged within a certain limit.[17] None
In all four orders[18] was a better one
At idle talk, or speaking with a flair.
And many a marriage he'd arranged for fair
And youthful women, paying all he could.
He was a pillar of his brotherhood.
Well loved he was, a most familiar Friar
To many franklins[19] living in his shire[20]
And to the worthy women of the town;
For he could hear confessions* and played
  down
The parish* priest. To shrive[21] in every quarter
He had been given license by his order.
He'd sweetly listen to confession, then
As pleasantly absolve one of his sin.
He easily gave penance when he knew
Some nice gift he'd receive when he was
  through.
For when to a poor order something's given,
It is a sign the man is truly shriven.
If someone gave, the Friar made it clear,
He knew the man's repentance was sincere.

---

[11]"Love conquers all."
[12]A monk's private room.
[13]A sixth-century disciple of St. Benedict.
[14]St. Benedict, the formulator of the Rule that governed most Western monks (see Chapter 4, source 17).
[15]St. Augustine of Hippo (Chapter 1, source 4). St. Augustine's instructions to his clergy* at Hippo, on whom he imposed a semimonastic life, were later regarded as a rule for canons regular.*
[16]A riding horse.

[17]His begging was limited to a specific region.
[18]The four orders of begging friars — Franciscans, Dominicans, Carmelites, and the Austin Friars.
[19]Country gentlemen of nonnoble birth who held extensive property.
[20]A county, or administrative district.
[21]Forgive sins.

For many men are so hard of the heart
They cannot weep, though grievous be the
    smart;
Instead of tears and prayers, they might
    therefore
Give silver to the friars who are poor.
He kept his cape all packed with pins and
    knives
That he would give away to pretty wives.
At merriment he surely wasn't middling;
He sang quite well and also did some fiddling,
And took the prize with all his balladry.
His neck was white as any fleur-de-lis,
His strength like any wrestler's of renown.
He knew the taverns well in every town,
Each hosteler and barmaid, moreso than
He knew the leper and the beggarman.
For anyone as worthy as the Friar
Had faculties that called for something higher
Than dealing with those sick with leprosy.
It wasn't dignified, nor could it be
Of profit, to be dealing with the poor,
What with the rich and merchants at the store.
Above all where some profit might arise
Was where he'd be, in courteous, humble
    guise.
No man had greater virtue than did he,
The finest beggar in the friary.
(He paid a fee for his exclusive right:
No brethren might invade his begging site.)
And though a widow shoeless had to go,
So pleasant was his *"In principio"*[22]
He'd have a farthing[23] when he went away.
He gained much more than what he had to
    pay,
And he could be as wanton as a pup.
He'd arbitrate on days to settle up
In law disputes, not like a cloisterer
Dressed in a threadbare cope[24] as students
    were,
But rather like a master or a pope.

He wore a double-worsted semicope
As rounded as a church bell newly pressed.
He lisped somewhat when he was at his best,
To make his English sweet upon his tongue.
And when he fiddled and his songs were sung,
His eyes would twinkle in his head as might
The stars themselves on any frosty night
Now Hubert was this worthy Friar's name.

    A MERCHANT with a forked beard also came,
Dressed in a motley.[25] Tall and proud he sat
Upon his horse. A Flemish beaver hat
He wore, and boots most elegantly wrought.
He spoke with pomp on everything he
    thought,
And boasted of the earnings he'd collected.
He felt the trade route had to be protected
Twixt Middleburgh and Orwell by the sea.[26]
He speculated in French currency.
He used his wits so well, with such finesse,
That no one guessed the man's indebtedness,
So dignified he was at managing
All of his bargains and his borrowing.
He was a worthy fellow all the same;
To tell the truth, I do not know his name. . . .
    From near the town of BATH a good WIFE
    came;
She was a little deaf, which was a shame.
She was a clothier, so excellent
Her work surpassed that of Ypres and Ghent.[27]
When parish wives their gifts would forward
    bring,
None dared precede her to the offering —
And if they did, her wrath would surely be
So mighty she'd lose all her charity.
The kerchiefs all were of the finest texture
(And must have weighed ten pounds, that's no
    conjecture)
That every Sunday she had on her head.
The fine hose that she wore were scarlet red
And tightly laced, she had a nice new pair
Of shoes. Her face was ruddy, bold and fair.

---

[22]"In the beginning." The opening words of the Bible's Book of Genesis, as well as the Gospel of St. John and, presumably, the opening lines of the friar's sermon.
[23]A coin worth one-fourth of an English penny.

[24]An outer robe.
[25]A bright, multicolored garment.
[26]A sea lane in the English Channel.
[27]Two cities in Flanders noted for their textile production.

She was a worthy woman all her life:
At church door with five men she'd been a
    wife,
Not counting all the company of her youth.
(No need to treat that now, but it's the truth.)
She'd journeyed to Jerusalem three times;
Strange rivers she had crossed in foreign
    climes;
She'd been to Rome and also to Boulogne,
To Galicia for Saint James and to Cologne,[28]
And she knew much of wandering by the way.
She had the lover's gap-teeth, I must say.
With ease upon an ambling horse she sat,
Well wimpled, while upon her head her hat
Was broad as any buckler to be found.
About her ample hips a mantle wound,
And on her feet the spurs she wore were sharp.
In fellowship she well could laugh and carp.
Of remedies of love she had good notions,
For of that art's old dance she knew the
    motions.

    There was a good man of religion, too,
A Parson of a certain township who
Was poor, but rich in holy thought and work.
He also was a learned man, a clerk;
The Christian gospel* he would truly preach,
Devoutly his parishioners to teach.
Benign he was, in diligence a wonder,
And patient in adversity, as under
Such he'd proven many times. And loath
He was to get his tithes* by threatening oath;
For he would rather give, without a doubt,
To all the poor parishioners about
From his own substance and the offerings.
Sufficiency he found in little things.
His parish wide, with houses wide asunder,
He'd never fail in either rain or thunder,
Though sick or vexed, to make his visitations

With those remote, regardless of their stations.
On foot he traveled, in his hand a stave.
This fine example to his sheep he gave:
He always did good works before he taught
    them.
His words were from the gospel as he caught
    them,
And this good saying he would add thereto:
"If gold should rust, then what will iron do?"
For if a priest be foul in whom we trust,
No wonder that the ignorant goes to rust.
And it's a shame (as every priest should keep
In mind), a dirty shepherd and clean sheep.
For every priest should an example give,
By his own cleanness, how his sheep should
    live.
He never set his benefice* for hire,[29]
To leave his sheep encumbered in the mire
While he ran off to London and Saint Paul's
To seek a chantry, singing in the stalls,[30]
Or be supported by a guild.[31] Instead
He dwelt at home, and he securely led
His fold, so that the wolf might never harry.
He was a shepherd and no mercenary.
A holy, virtuous man he was, and right
In showing to the sinner no despite.
His speech was never haughty or indignant,
He was a teacher modest and benignant;
To draw folks heavenward to life forever,
By good example, was his great endeavor.
But if some person were too obstinate,
Whether he be of high or low estate,
He would be sharply chided on the spot.
A better priest, I wager, there is not.
He didn't look for pomp or reverence
Nor feign a too self-righteous moral sense;
What Christ and his apostles* had to tell
He taught, and he would follow it as well.

---

[28]All were popular pilgrimage sites. The church of St. James of Compostella in northwest Spain, for example, was believed to shelter the body of the Apostle James, and Cologne on the Rhine claimed to have the relics* of the Three Magi.
[29]He was not guilty of hiring a deputy, or *vicar,* to tend his church, pocketing the difference between his church's income, or benefice, and the pittance he paid the vicar.

[30]A good living could be earned by chanting masses* for the souls of the wealthy dead, who had left bequests for this service.
[31]Serving as chaplain to a religious confraternity, or *guild,* which would pay him handsomely.

The Study of Nature

Europe's fascination with nature, which we saw expressed in Giselbertus's *Eve* and the sculptures of Strasbourg cathedral* (Chapter 9, sources 56–58), was fed by the massive influx of Latin translations of Greek and Arabic scientific texts from the late eleventh century onward. Of these, the most influential were the works of the fourth-century B.C. philosopher and scientist Aristotle. Thanks to their Greek and Arabic teachers, European students of natural philosophy came to acquire, in the course of the twelfth and thirteenth centuries, the conviction that nature operates in an orderly fashion and, by studying that order, one can gain insight into the mysteries of God's universe.

During the fourteenth century, the natural mysteries that most involved scientifically minded scholars and even educated laypeople were in the arenas of geography, anthropolgy, astronomy, and mechanical physics. The first source illustrates the geographic and anthropological facts and fictions that educated fourteenth-century Europeans accepted as a reasonable and true picture of the world. The second source illustrates how, in the area of mechanical physics, several important fourteenth-century scholars challenged the scientific work and theories of Aristotle.

"People Can Encircle the Entire World"
▼▼▼
86 ▼ *John Mandeville, TRAVELS*

If we wish to discover how literate Europeans of the Late Middle Ages viewed the world beyond their subcontinent, we can do no better than to turn to the pages of Sir John Mandeville's *Travels.* First appearing in Europe between 1356 and 1366, Mandeville's book purported to be the firsthand account of an English knight's adventures in the East between 1322 and 1356, in which he supposedly served both the sultan of Egypt and the Mongol khan of China. In fact, the work is a fictional *tour de force* by a gifted author who masked his identity behind the pen name *John Mandeville* and whose expeditions were largely to European libraries, where he discovered quite a few travel books from which he borrowed liberally. Some evidence suggests that Mandeville (or whatever his name was) traveled to the eastern Mediterranean, but he seems to have gone no farther east. The basic outline of Sir John's vividly described travels to the Indies and Cathay is plagiarized from the genuine travel account of the Franciscan missionary Odoric of Pordenone (ca. 1265–1331), who spent thirty-five years in Russia and Asia, including three years as an assistant to Archbishop* John of Monte Corvino in Khanbalik (Chapter 11, source 78). Mandeville amplified Friar* Odoric's rather sparse story by adding fables and tales from many other authors, by giving free rein to his own fertile imagination and sardonic wit, and by spicing his story with an impressive array of geographic and astronomical theories, many of them based on borrowed Arabic science.

No matter its overall lack of authenticity as a traveler's tale, Mandeville's *Travels,* written originally in French, was widely circulated and translated into every major European language by 1400, becoming late-medieval Europe's most popular travelogue in an age noted for its fascination with long-distance travel. Even Christopher Columbus consulted Mandeville's account prior to his epic voyage. Although Sir John did not travel to most of the regions he claimed to have visited, his work is historically important because it illustrates the manner in which Europeans of the fourteenth and fifteenth centuries viewed lands and peoples beyond their frontiers. Indeed, in many ways, Mandeville was instrumental in shaping that vision.

In the first selection, Sir John deals with the shape and size of the earth. Most people today are unaware that the notion that medieval European scholars believed the world was flat is a modern myth, created, tongue in cheek, by nineteenth-century American writer and humorist Washington Irving. In the second selection, Mandeville shares his putative firsthand knowledge of the wondrous land of Prester John, the mythic Christian emperor whom we saw in Joinville's biography of St. Louis of France (Chapter 11, source 77).

As you read both selections, keep in mind that the author often uses his descriptions of the exotic peoples and places he supposedly encountered as a way of subtly pointing out the shortcomings of his own Christian Europe.

QUESTIONS FOR ANALYSIS

1. Can you find in this source any roots of the Western notion of the *noble savage?* If so, identify them.
2. What was John's view of the world? Be specific.
3. What do these stories suggest about the author's attitudes toward alien customs and the world beyond Europe?
4. Based on what you read in Mandeville, what would a late-medieval person expect to find in the lands of the East?
5. How does Mandeville's Prester John differ from the one described by Joinville? What might explain the differences?
6. Many societies cherish a myth of a promised redeemer, or hero-to-come. How and why had the Christian West created in the mythic Prester John a person who represented the fulfillment of some of their deepest wishes?
7. In what ways, if at all, does Sir John use these stories to point out the shortcomings of his own society?
8. Do you see in these stories any echoes of other fourteenth-century social criticisms? If so, what?

From India, people go by the ocean sea by way of many islands and different countries, which it would be tedious for me to relate. Fifty-two days' journey from that land there is another large country called Lamary [Sumatra]. That land is extremely hot, so that the custom there is for men and women to walk about totally naked, and they scorn foreigners who wear clothes. They say that God created Adam and Eve naked, and no person, therefore, should be ashamed to appear as God made him, because nothing that comes from nature's bounty is foul. They also say that people who wear clothes are from another world, or else they are people who do not believe in God. They say that they believe in God who created the world and made Adam and Eve and everything else. Here, they do not marry wives, since all the women are common to all men and no woman forsakes any man. They say that it is sinful to refuse any man, for God so commanded it of Adam and Eve and all who followed when he said: "Increase and multiply and fill the earth."[1] Therefore, no man in that country may say: "This is my wife." No woman may say: "This is my husband." When they bear children, the women present them to whatever man they wish of those with whom they have had sexual relations. So also all land is held in common. What one man holds one year, another has another year, and everyone takes that portion which he desires. Also all the produce of the soil is held in common. This is true for grains and other goods, as well. Nothing is held in private; nothing is locked up, and every person there takes what he wants without anyone saying "no." Each is as rich as the other.

There is, however, in that country an evil custom. They eat human flesh more happily than any other meat, this despite the fact that the land abounds in meats, fish, grains, gold, silver, and every other commodity. Merchants go there, bringing with them children to sell to the people of that country, and they purchase the children. If they are plump, they eat them immediately. If they are lean, they feed them until they fatten up, and then they eat them. They say this is the best and sweetest flesh in all the world.

In that land, and in many others beyond it, no one can see the Transmontane Star, known as the Star of the Sea, which is immoveable and stands in the north and is called the Lode Star.[2] They see, rather, another star, its opposite, which stands in the south and is called the Antarctic Star. Just as sailors here get their bearings and steer by the Lode Star, so sailors beyond those parts steer by the southern star, which we cannot see. So our northern star, which we call the Lode Star, cannot be seen there. This is proof that the earth and sea are round in shape and form. For portions of the heavens that are seen in one country do not appear in another. . . . I can prove that point by what I have observed, for I have been in parts of Brabant[3] and seen, by means of an astrolabe, that the Transmontane Star is 53 degrees in elevation. In Germany and Bohemia, it is 58 degrees; and farther north, it is 62 degrees and some minutes high. I personally have measured it with an astrolabe. Understand that opposite the Transmontane Star is the other known as the Antarctic Star, as I have said. These two stars never move, and around them, all the heavens revolve, just like a wheel about an axle. So those two stars divide the heavens into two equal parts, with as much above [the equator] as below. . . .

I say with certainty that people can encircle the entire world, below the equator as well as above,[4] and return to their homelands, provided they have good company, a ship, and health. And all along the way, one would find people, lands, and islands. . . . For you know well that those people who live right under the Antarctic Star are directly underneath, feet against feet, of those

---

[1]The Bible, Genesis 1:22.
[2]Polaris, or the North Star, which guides mariners.
[3]A region between modern Belgium and the Netherlands.

[4]Here Mandeville was refuting a notion, accepted by classical Greco-Roman geographers, that the *antipodes,* or lands south of the equator, were uninhabitable due to their extreme heat.

who dwell directly under the Transmontane Star,[5] just as we and those who dwell under us[6] are feet to feet. For every part of the sea and the land has its opposite, which balances it, and it is both habitable and traversable. . . . So people who travel to India and the foreign isles girdle the roundness of the earth and the seas, passing under our countries in this hemisphere.

Something I heard about as a youth has occurred to me often. A worthy man from our country departed some time ago to see the world. And so he passed through India and the islands beyond India, which number more than 5,000.[7] He traveled so far by sea and land and had so girdled the globe over the period of so many seasons that he found an island where he heard his own language being spoken. . . . He marveled at this, not knowing what to make of it. I conclude he had traveled so far by land and sea that he had encircled the entire globe, circumnavigating to the very frontier of his homeland. Had he traveled only a bit farther, he would have come to his own home. But he turned back, returning along the route by which he had come. And so he spent a great deal of painful labor, as he acknowledged when he returned home much later. For afterward he went to Norway, where a storm carried him to an island. While on that island he discovered it was the island where earlier he had heard his own language spoken.[8] . . .

That could well be true, even though it might seem to simple-minded persons of no learning that people cannot travel on the underside of the world without falling off toward the heavens. That, however, is not possible, unless it is true that we also are liable to fall toward heaven from where we are on the earth. For whatever part of the earth people inhabit, above or below [the equator], it always seems to them that they are in a more proper position than any other folk. And so it is right that just as it seems to us that they are under us, so it seems to them that we are beneath them. For if a person could fall from the earth into the heavens, it is more reasonable to assume that the earth and sea, which are more vast and of greater weight, should fall into the heavens. But that is impossible. . . .

Although it is possible for a person to circumnavigate the world, nonetheless, out of a 1,000 persons, one might possibly return home. For given the magnitude of the earth and the sea, a 1,000 people could venture forth and follow a 1,000 different routes. This being so, no person could plot a perfect route toward the place from where he left. He could only reach it by accident or the grace of God. For the earth is very large and is some 20,425 miles in circumference, according to the opinion of wise astronomers from the past, whose words I am not going to contradict, even though it seems to me, with my limited understanding and with all due respect, that it is larger.[9]

▾ ▾ ▾

This emperor, Prester John, commands a very large region and has many noble cities and fair towns in his realm, as well as many islands large and broad. For this land of India is divided into islands due to the great rivers that flow out of Paradise, dividing the land into many parts.[10] He also has many islands in the sea. . . . This Prester John has many kings and islands and many different peoples of various cultures subject to him. And this land is fertile and wealthy, but not as wealthy as the land of the Great Khan. For merchants do not as commonly travel there to purchase merchandise as they do to the land

---

[5]In other words, the South Pole is 180 degrees south of (or under) the North Pole.

[6]The place directly opposite on the globe.

[7]The islands of Southeast Asia.

[8]This story, especially in light of the passage that follows, seems to claim that the Englishman traveled south to India and the islands of Southeast Asia and then continued south across the South Pole and up the far side of the globe across the North Pole to Scandinavia; he then returned home by retracing his steps.

[9]Actually, it is closer to 25,000 miles.

[10]According to John, four rivers flow out of the Terrestrial Paradise, from which Adam and Eve were expelled and which lies far to the east of Prester John's country. These rivers — the Ganges, Nile, Tigris, and Euphrates — divide the major lands of the earth.

of the Great Khan, for it is too far to travel to. Moreover, people can find in that other region, the Island of Cathay,[11] every manner of commodity that people need — gold, cloth, silk, spices, and every sort of precious item. Consequently, even though commodities are less expensive in Prester John's island, nonetheless people dread the long voyage and the great sea-perils in that region. . . . Although one must travel by sea and land eleven or twelve months from Genoa or Venice before arriving in Cathay, the land of Prester John lies many more days of dreadful journey away. . . .

The Emperor Prester John always marries the daughter of the Great Khan, and the Great Khan likewise marries Prester John's daughter.[12] For they are the two greatest lords under heaven.

In Prester John's land there are many different things and many precious gems of such magnitude that people make vessels, such as platters, dishes, and cups, out of them. There are many other marvels there, so many, in fact, that it would be tiresome and too lengthy to put them down in a book, . . . but I shall tell you some part.

This Emperor Prester John is Christian, as is a great part of his country, as well. Yet they do not share all the articles of our faith. They believe fully in God, in the Son, and in the Holy Spirit.* They are quite devout and faithful to one another, and they do not quarrel or practice fraud and deceit.

He has subject to him 72 provinces, and in every province there is a king. And these kings have kings under them, and all are tributaries to Prester John. And he has in his lordships many marvels. In his country is a sea that people call the Gravelly Sea.[13] It is all gravel and sand, without a drop of water, and it ebbs and flows in great waves, as other seas do, and never rests at any time. No one can cross that sea by ship or any

other craft, and, therefore, no one knows what land lies beyond that sea. Although it has no water, people find in it and on its banks plenty of good fish of a shape and size such as are found nowhere else, but they are tasty and delicious to eat. Three days journey from that sea are great mountains, out of which flows a great river that originates in Paradise. And it is full of precious stones, without a drop of water. . . . Beyond that river, rising toward the deserts, is a great gravel plain set between the mountains. On that plain everyday at sunrise small trees begin to grow, and they grow until midday, bearing fruit. No one dares, however, to eat the fruit, for it is like a deceptive phantom. After midday, the trees decrease and reenter the earth, so that by sun set they are no longer to be seen. And they do this every day. And that is a great marvel. In that desert are many wild people who are hideous to look at, for they are horned and do not speak but only grunt like pigs. . . .

When Emperor Prester John goes into battle against any other lord, he has no banners borne before him. Rather, he has three crosses of fine gold, which are massive and very tall and encrusted with precious stones.[14] Each cross is set in a richly adorned chariot. To guard each cross, there is a detail of 10,000 mounted men at arms and 100,000 men on foot, . . . and this number is in addition to the main body of troops. . . . When he rides out in peacetime with a private entourage, he has borne before him only one wooden cross, unpainted and lacking gold, silver, or gems, as a remembrance that Jesus Christ suffered death on a wooden cross. He also has borne before him a golden platter filled with earth, in token of the fact that his nobility, might, and flesh will all turn to earth. He also has borne before him a silver vessel full of great nuggets of gold and precious gems, as a token of his lordship, nobility, and might.

---

[11]Northern China.

[12]This particular version of the Prester John myth seems to be a somewhat distorted reflection of the fact that many Mongol khans had Nestorian Christian wives. See Chapter 11, source 78, for further information on the Nestorian Turks of Inner Asia.

[13]Apparently, a garbled reference to the Gobi (Gravel) Desert of Central Asia.

[14]Keep in mind that *crusade* means "to bear a cross."

Does the Earth Revolve on Its Axis?

▼▼▼

87 ▾ *Nicholas Oresme,* *ON THE BOOK OF THE HEAVENS AND THE WORLD OF ARISTOTLE*

Europe's most advanced work in physics in the thirteenth and fourteenth centuries took place within the Arts faculties of the West's two premier universities — Oxford and Paris. The two leading physicists from Paris were Jean Buridan (ca. 1295–1358) and his student Nicholas Oresme (ca. 1320–1382). Both raised significant questions about the validity of some of Europe's received Greco-Arabic science. Working within the framework of scholastic disputation, a method of logical analysis that Peter Abelard and Thomas Aquinas had championed (Chapter 9, sources 53–54), Buridan and Oresme were bold enough to question the authority of Aristotle on certain points.

Aristotle had presented convincing arguments in support of the conclusion that the earth is stationary, and this was the unanimous medieval opinion, although a handful of scholars thought it worthwhile to explore, at least as an academic exercise, the ramifications of a theory that postulated an earth that rotates daily on its axis. The arguments that Buridan and, more fully, Oresme raised anticipated, by several centuries, some of the sixteenth- and seventeenth-century scientific breakthroughs of Nicholas Copernicus and Galileo Galilei. Unlike Copernicus and Galileo, however, Oresme backed away from the implications of his arguments, and in the end he apparently rejected the idea of the earth's daily rotation.

The next selection comes from Oresme's commentary on Aristotle's *On the Heavens and the World,* which the Parisian master composed in French in 1377. In it he addresses the argument that had led Buridan to abandon the theory that the earth could rotate daily. Buridan accepted the objection that if the earth did rotate, an arrow shot directly overhead on a windless day should fall forward, somewhere to the west, rather than come straight down, as invariably happens.

As you read Oresme's arguments and conclusions, keep in mind that he was a theologian and a churchman, as well as a student of natural philosophy. He received his advanced degree in theology at Paris in the mid 1350s and served as chaplain to King Charles V while working on this treatise. The year following its completion, he was elevated to the bishopric* of Lisieux. It is possible that Oresme composed his commentary for theological, as well as cosmological, reasons? Or are his closing remarks truly indicative of his state of mind? Was he, perhaps, engaging in a bit of irony?

QUESTIONS FOR ANALYSIS

1. What objections from sense experience does Oresme raise against the theory of the earth's diurnal (daily) rotation? How does he answer them?

2. How does Oresme regard sense experience as a tool for scientific investigation? What does your answer say about his scientific methods and vision?

3. What arguments from common sense does Oresme raise against the notion of a diurnal rotation of the heavens, and how does he answer or refute each? Why, for example, would current astronomic charts be unaffected if the earth revolves on its axis?

4. What do Oresme's answers to all of the common-sense and scientific objections suggest about his knowledge of the physics of motion and his approach to science?

5. What do his answers to the scriptural objections suggest about his view of the language and imagery of the Bible?

6. What argument does Oresme raise in support of the theory of the earth's daily rotation? What does it suggest about his cosmological vision?

7. After taking us through this exercise, Oresme rejects the theory of the earth's daily rotation. What are his professed reasons? Do they strike you as sincere? Defend your answer.

1. It seems to me, subject to correction, that one could support well and give luster to the . . . opinion . . . that the earth, and not the heavens, is moved with a daily movement. Firstly, I wish to state that one could not demonstrate the contrary by any experience. Secondly I will show that the contrary cannot be demonstrated by reasoning. And thirdly, I will put forth reasons in support of it [i.e., the diurnal rotation of the earth].

2. As for the first point, one experience commonly cited in support of the daily motion of the heaven is the following: We see with our senses the sun and moon and many stars rise and set from day to day, and some stars turn around the arctic pole. This could not be except by the movement of the heavens. . . . Thus the argument runs, the heaven is moved with a diurnal movement. Another experience cited is this: if the earth is so moved, it makes a complete turn in a single natural day. Therefore, we and the trees and the houses are moved toward the east very swiftly, and so it should seem to us that the air and the wind blow continuously and very strongly from the east. . . . But the contrary appears by experience. The third experience is that which Ptolemy advances: if a person were on a ship moving rapidly eastward and an arrow were

shot directly upward, it ought not to fall on the ship but a good distance westward away from the ship. Similarly, if the earth is moved so very swiftly in turning from west to east, and it has been posited that one throws a stone directly above, then it ought to fall, not on the place from which it left, but rather a good distance to the west. But in fact the contrary is apparent. It seems to me that by using what I shall say regarding these experiences, one could respond to all the other experiences which might be adduced in this matter. . . .

3. I make the supposition that local motion can be sensibly perceived only in so far as one may perceive one body to be differently disposed with respect to another. In support of this I give the following illustration: If a person is in one ship called *a* which is moved very carefully, i.e., without pitching or rolling — either rapidly or slowly — and this person sees nothing except another ship called *b*, which is moved in every respect in the same manner as *a* in which he is situated, I say that it will seem to this person that neither ship is moving. And if *a* is at rest and *b* is moved, it will appear and seem to him that *b* is moved. On the other hand, if *a* is moved and *b* at rest, it will appear to him as before that *a* is at rest and that *b* is moved. And thus, if *a*

were at rest for an hour and *b* were moved, and then immediately in the following hour the situation were reversed, namely, that *a* were moved and *b* were at rest, this person on *a* could not perceive this mutation or change. Rather it would continually seem to him that *b* was moved; and this is apparent by experience. The reason for this is because these two bodies, *a* and *b,* are continually changing their dispositions with respect to each other in the same manner throughout when *a* is moved and *b* is at rest as they were conversely when *b* is moved and *a* is at rest. . . . I say, then, that if the upper of the two parts of the universe mentioned above should today move with a diurnal movement, just as it is, and the lower part should not, and tomorrow the contrary should prevail, namely that the lower should be moved with a diurnal movement while the upper should not, we could not perceive this change in any way, but everything would seem to be the same today and tomorrow. It would seem to us continually that the part where we are situated was at rest and that the other part was always moved, just as it seems to a person who is in a moving ship that the trees outside are moved. Similarly, if a person were in the heavens and it were posited that they were moved with a diurnal movement, and furthermore that this man who is transported with the heaven could see the earth clearly and distinctly and its mountains, valleys, rivers, towns, and chateaux, it would seem to him that the earth was moved with a diurnal movement, just as it seems to us who are on the earth that the heavens move. Similarly, if the earth and not the heavens were moved with a diurnal movement, it would seem to us that the earth was at rest and the heavens were moved. This can be imagined easily by anyone with good intelligence. From this reasoning is evident the response to the first experience, since one could say that the sun and the stars appear thus to set and rise and the heavens to turn as the result of the movement of the earth and its elements where we are situated.

4. To the second experience, according to this opinion, the response is this: Not only is the earth so moved diurnally, but with it the water and the air, as was said, in such a way that the water and the lower air are moved differently than they are by winds and other causes. It is like this situation: If air were enclosed in a moving ship, it would seem to the person situated in this air that it was not moved.

5. To the third experience, which seems more effective, i.e., the experience concerning the arrow or stone projected upward, etc., one would say that the arrow is trajected upwards and simultaneously with this trajection it is moved eastward very swiftly with the air through which it passes and with all the mass of the lower part of the universe mentioned above, it all being moved with a diurnal movement. For this reason the arrow returns to the place on the earth from which it left. This appears possible by analogy: if a person were on a ship moving toward the east very swiftly without his being aware of the movement, and he drew his hand downward, describing a straight line against the mast of the ship, it would seem to him that his hand was moved with rectilinear movement only. According to this opinion of the diurnal rotation of the earth, it seems to us in the same way that the arrow descends or ascends in a straight line. . . .

6. As to the second point relative to the rational demonstration of the diurnal movement of the heavens, I first note the following: It seems to me that this rational demonstration proceeds from these arguments which follow and to which I shall respond in such a fashion that, using the same reasoning, one could respond to all other arguments pertaining to it. . . .

Again, if the heavens were not moved with diurnal movement, all astronomy would be false and a great part of natural philosophy where one supposes throughout this movement of the heavens.

Also, this seems to be against the Holy Scripture which says: "The sun riseth, and goeth down, and returneth to his place: and there rising again, maketh his round by the south, and turneth again to the north; the spirit goeth forward surveying all places round about, and returneth to his circuits."[1] And so it is written of the earth that God made it immobile: "For God created the orb of the earth, which will not be moved."[2]

Also, the Scriptures say that the sun was halted in the time of Joshua.[3] . . . If the earth were moved and not the heavens, as was said, such an arrestment would have been a returning. . . . And this is against what the Scriptures state. . . .

7. To the . . . argument, where it is said that if the heavens would not make a rotation from day to day, all astronomy would be false, etc., I answer this is not so because all aspects, conjunctions, oppositions, constellations, figures, and influences of the heavens would be completely just as they are, as is evident clearly from what was said in response to the first experience. The tables of the movements and all other books would be just as true as they are. . . .

8. To the . . . argument concerning the Holy Scripture which says that the sun revolves, etc., one would say of it that it is in this part simply conforming to the manner of common human speech, just as is done in several places, e.g., where it is written that God is "repentant" and that he is "angry" and "pacified" and other such things which are not just as they sound. Also appropriate to our question, we read that God covers the heavens with clouds — "who covereth the heavens with clouds"[4] — and yet in reality the heavens cover the clouds. Thus one would say that according to appearances the heavens and not the earth are moved with a diurnal motion, while in actuality the contrary is true. . . . To the . . . [other] argument, one would answer in just about the same way, that according to appearances in the time of Joshua the sun was arrested, . . . but actually the earth was arrested in the time of Joshua. . . . This latter opinion supporting the diurnal rotation of the earth seems to be more reasonable than the former, as we shall make clear later.

As to the third main point of this gloss, I wish to put forth persuasions or reasons by which it would appear that the earth is moved as was indicated. . . .

9. Again, all philosophers say that something done by several or largescale operations which can be done by less or smaller operations is done for nought. And Aristotle says in the eighth chapter [actually the fourth chapter] of the first book that God and Nature do not do anything for nought. But if it is so that the heavens are moved with a diurnal movement, it becomes necessary to posit in the principal bodies of the world and in the heavens two contrary kinds of movement, one of an east-to-west kind and others of the opposite kind, as has been said often. With this theory of the diurnal movement of the heavens it becomes necessary to posit an excessively great speed. This will become clear to one who considers thoughtfully the height or distance of the heaven, its magnitude, and that of its circuit; for if such a circuit is completed in one day, one could not imagine nor conceive of how the swiftness of the heaven is so marvelously and excessively great. It is so unthinkable and inestimable. Since all the effects which we see can be accomplished, and all the appearances saved, by substituting for this diurnal movement of the heavens a small operation, i.e., the diurnal movement of the earth, which is very small in comparison with the heavens, and since this can be done without making the number of necessary operations so diverse and outrageously great, it follows that if the heaven rather than the earth is moved then God and Nature would have made and ordained things for nought. But this is not fitting, as was said. . . .

10. It is apparent, then, how one cannot demonstrate by any experience whatever that the heavens are moved with daily movement, because, regardless of whether it has been posited that the heavens and not the earth are so moved or that the earth and not the heavens is moved, if an observer is in the heavens and he sees the earth clearly, it [the earth] would seem to be

---

moved. The sight is not deceived in this, because it senses or sees nothing except that there is movement. But if it is relative to any such body, this judgment is made by the senses from inside that body. . . . Afterwards it was demonstrated how it cannot be concluded by reasoning that the heavens are so moved. Thirdly, reasons have been put forth in support of the contrary position, namely that the heavens are not so moved. Yet, nevertheless, everyone holds, and I believe, that they [the heavens], and not the earth, are so moved, for "God created the orb of the earth, which will not be moved," notwithstanding the arguments to the contrary. This is because they are "persuasions" which do not make the conclusions evident. But having considered everything which has been said, one could by this believe that the earth and not the heavens is so moved, and there is no evidence to the contrary. Nevertheless, this seems prima facie as much, or more, against natural reason as are all or several articles of our faith. Thus, that which I have said by way of diversion in this manner can be valuable to refute and check those who would impugn our faith by argument.

Chapter 13

▼▼▼

The Fifteenth Century: An Age of Rebirth?

The advent of the fifteenth century did not signal the end of Europe's troubles. The Hundred Years' War continued for a half century more, and after it ended, France and England continued to experience internal dynastic struggles. The eventual end of the papal* schism in 1417 was followed by a constitutional crisis known as the *Conciliar Movement,* and the institutional Church continued to exhibit a systemic inability to meet the rising demand for reform; the plague continued to reappear periodically, but with less virulence than in the mid fourteenth century; and the Ottoman Turks continued to press vigorously against Western Christendom throughout the 1400s and beyond. To many fifteenth-century Europeans, the world seemed bleak and the future, unpromising.

Despite real reasons for pessimism, however, Europe had weathered another age of adversity and was ready to expand along both new and traditional lines. The term *Renaissance* is misleading as a descriptive tag for fifteenth-century Europe, but certainly, Europe underwent a general revival in this century. Great bankers, such as the Medici of Florence, the Fuggers of Augsburg, and Jacques Coeur of Bourges, as well as countless small merchants and artisans, combined to drive Europe's economic turnaround. In the area of statecraft, the monarchs of England, France, Portugal, Aragon, and Castile had, by 1500, created kingdoms that were more stable and centralized than they had been for ages. Military innovations — primarily cannons, new infantry tactics, and royal standing armies — combined to reduce the traditional dominance of mounted feudal* knights. Revived interest in Greco-Roman antiquity provided many intellectuals and artists with a sense of renewal and rediscovery, which they expressed in many different forms. New emphasis on Ciceronian political ideals and Roman Stoicism influenced trends in political and social philosophy. Interest in Platonic and Neoplatonic Greek thought provided new inspiration to philosophical studies and had a similarly fruitful influence on arts and letters, especially in Italy. Indeed, so far as the visual arts were concerned, Europe truly experienced a fifteenth-century transformation.

Above all else, Europe's fifteenth-century ventures into the waters of the Atlantic provided new horizons and new areas for expansion. Portuguese mariners sailed along the west and then east coast of Africa until, finally, with the help of an Arab geographer, Vasco da Gama sailed into the port of Calicut in 1498, thereby opening the rich lands of the Indian Ocean to direct European contact on a scale never before seen. In a similar attempt to reach the Indies directly by water, Christopher Columbus stumbled across the Americas, thereby setting into motion a series of explorations and conquests that would transform both Amerindian and European societies and prove to be a major turning point in the history of the entire human family.

▼▼▼

The Late-Medieval Church and Christian Society

The Roman Catholic Church was a major force in the fifteenth century, but in some respects, the Church and Christian society seemed to be on two divergent paths. Popular religiosity burned intensely in late-medieval Europe, but the institutions of the Church seemed, to many people, less relevant in the 1400s than they had been in earlier centuries. To be sure, the Church continued to attract many pious idealists who became clerics* and sought to reform society in traditional ways. At the same time, however, lay piety of every variety became an increasingly important phenomenon as the fifteenth century grew older — a sure sign of the clergy's* growing loss of prestige and power.

The decrease in clerical authority in the midst of a wave of deep popular spirituality was due to many factors. Certainly, the Church's inability or unwillingness to cleanse its own house was a key element. Rather than addressing the issue of ecclesiastical* reform in any meaningful manner, popes and general councils* spent the greater part of the century bickering over the question of who had ultimate authority over the Church — the pope or an ecumenical council.* The hard-won victory of the papacy* over *conciliarism* marked the end of any effort at churchwide reform, at least for the fifteenth century. Another equally important factor was simply the rising importance of the common layperson's voice. The Church, in concert with the emperor, could silence a single critic, the Bohemian priest* Jan

Hus, by burning him at the stake as a heretic* in 1415. It could not, however, stamp out the legions of his outraged lay followers, the so-called Hussites, who successfully resisted five Catholic crusading armies and forced the emperor and the Church to acknowledge an essentially independent Hussite Church in Bohemia by 1436.

The Hussites' success was due, in part, to the Conciliar Controversy, which hamstrung the Church and also resulted in the Council of Basle's recognizing the more moderate wing of the Hussites in 1433, as the council jockeyed with the papacy for power. The first set of documents that follows sheds light on the issues involved in the Conciliar Movement and suggests how the controversy could have so engaged the attention and energies of so many high-ranking clerics.

The second source, which describes the drummer of Niklashausen's short-lived protest movement, demonstrates that not every lay attack on church authority ended as successfully as the Hussite rebellion. In fact, the Hussites were unique in their success. As the incident of the drummer of Niklashausen suggests, however, the Hussites were not alone in their expression of social and religious discontent and in the violence that emerged from their challenge to church authority.

Conciliarism in Victory and Defeat

▼▼▼

88 ▼ *The Council of Constance, HAEC SANCTA and FREQUENS, and Pope Pius II, EXECRABILIS*

The Council of Constance (1414–1417), convened at the insistence of emperor-elect Sigismund and on the dubious authority of Pope John XXIII (r. 1410–1415), finally solved the problem of the Great Schism by deposing two popes, persuading a third to abdicate, and electing Martin V (r. 1417–1431) as sole pope. The council* was able to act so decisively because it was dominated by reformers who accepted the theory that the Church was a constitutional monarchy in which the pope's powers were limited by a general council, which alone represented the universal Church. Therefore, only a general council possessed the full authority that Christ had bestowed upon the Church. In order to assure the victory of their vision, the conciliarists at Constance pushed through a constitutional statute on April 6, 1415, known as *Haec Sancta* (also known as *Sacrosancta*), which unambiguously laid out the essence of conciliar doctrine. In order to control the papacy and guide the Church, general councils had to meet on a frequent basis; for this reason, the Council of Constance also promulgated the canon* *Frequens,* which stipulated the frequency of future church councils.

Needless to say, popes found conciliar theory to be totally unacceptable, and by midcentury, they managed to destroy the movement, largely through good luck, the ineptitude of subsequent fifteenth-century councils, and the support that a number of European princes and monarchs gave the papacy, in return for wide-sweeping powers over their national and regional churches. When Pope Pius II

(r. 1458–1464) published *Execrabilis,* his official condemnation of conciliarism, in 1459, the movement had already been essentially dead for a decade. The papacy's victory was not total, however. Popes were so frightened of the specter of rebellious councils that they put off calling a new general council to institute church reforms. There would be no fifteenth-century counterpart to the Fourth Lateran Council (Chapter 7, source 42). Moreover, although the papacy had preserved its theoretical *plenitudo potestatis* (fullness of power) over the Church and many of its ecclesiastical perquisites and sources of wealth, the heyday of papal moral authority had passed. A fitting symbol of that fact was the death scene of Pius II, who passed away at Ancona in Italy while vainly waiting for a crusade against the Ottoman Turks that he called but which never materialized.

QUESTIONS FOR ANALYSIS

1. According to *Haec Sancta,* on what does the council base its authority?
2. According to the decree, what are a council's duties and powers?
3. What theories underlie *Frequens?*
4. What specific procedure does the canon establish?
5. Can you spot any possible weaknesses in this procedure that could potentially play into the hands of anticonciliarists? Explain your answer.
6. Precisely what does Pius II prohibit?
7. Suppose another crisis arises in the Church. How, according to Pius's decree, will it be settled? Are there any potential dangers in that procedure? Again, explain your answer.

In the name of the Holy and Indivisible Trinity, of the Father, Son, and Holy Spirit.* Amen.*

This holy[1] synod* of Constance, constituting a general council for the extirpation of the present schism and the union and reformation of the Church of God in head and members, legitimately assembled in the Holy Spirit, to the praise of omnipotent God, in order that it may the more easily, safely, effectively, and freely bring about the union and reformation of the Church of God, hereby determines, decrees, ordains, and declares what follows:

It first declares that this same council, legitimately assembled in the Holy Spirit, forming a general council and representing the Catholic Church militant,[2] has its power immediately from Christ, and every one, whatever his position or rank, even if it be the papal dignity itself, is bound to obey it in all those things which pertain to the faith, to the healing of the schism, and to the general reformation of the Church of God in head and members.

It further declares that any one, whatever his position, station, or rank, even if it be the papal, who shall contumaciously refuse to obey the mandates, decrees, ordinances, or instructions

---

[1] *Haec sancta* (this holy). Normally, the opening words of a decree become its title.

[2] All living members of the Church who are still fighting sin and the Devil in the world. The other two portions of the Church are the *Church Suffering* (dead members being purged of their guilt in purgatory*) and the *Church Triumphant* (those in Heaven).

which have been, or shall be, issued by this holy council, or by any other general council legitimately summoned, which concern, or in any way relate to, the above-mentioned objects, shall, unless he repudiate his conduct, be subjected to condign penance and be suitably punished, having recourse, if necessary, to the resources of the law.

▾ ▾ ▾

A frequent celebration of general councils is a special means for cultivating the field of the Lord and effecting the destruction of briars, thorns, and thistles, to wit, heresies,* errors, and schism, and of bringing forth a most abundant harvest. The neglect to summon these fosters and develops all these evils, as may be plainly seen from a recollection of the past and a consideration of existing conditions. Therefore, by a perpetual edict, we sanction, decree, establish, and ordain that general councils shall be celebrated in the following manner, so that the next one shall follow the close of this present council at the end of five years. The second shall follow the close of that, at the end of seven years, and councils shall thereafter be celebrated every ten years in such places as the pope shall be required to designate and assign, with the consent and approbation of the council, one month before the close of the council in question, or which, in his absence, the council itself shall designate. Thus, with a certain continuity, a council will always be either in session, or be expected at the expiration of a definite time.

This term may, however, be shortened on account of emergencies, by the supreme pontiff,[3] with the counsel of his brethren, the cardinals* of the holy Roman Church, but it may not be hereafter lengthened. The place, moreover, designated for the future council may not be altered without evident necessity. If, however, some complication shall arise, in view of which such a change shall seem necessary, as, for example, a state of siege, a war, a pest, or other obstacles, it shall be permissible for the supreme pontiff,* with the consent and subscription of his said brethren, or two thirds of them, to select another appropriate place near the first, which must be within the same country, unless such obstacles, or similar ones, shall exist throughout the whole nation. In that case, the council may be summoned to some appropriate neighboring place, within the bounds of another nation. To this the prelates,* and others, who are wont to be summoned to a council, must betake themselves as if that place had been designated from the first. Such change of place, or shortening of the period, the supreme pontiff is required legitimately and solemnly to publish and announce one year before the expiration of the term fixed, that the said persons may be able to come together, for the celebration of the council, within the term specified.

▾ ▾ ▾

The execrable and hitherto unknown abuse has grown up in our day, that certain persons, imbued with the spirit of rebellion, and not from a desire to secure a better judgment, but to escape the punishment of some offence which they have committed, presume to appeal from the pope to a future council, in spite of the fact that the pope is the vicar of Jesus Christ and to him, in the person of St. Peter, the following was said: "Feed my sheep" and "Whatsoever thou shalt bind on earth shall be bound in heaven."[4] Wishing therefore to expel this pestiferous poison from the church of Christ and to care for the salvation of the flock entrusted to us, and to remove every cause of offence from the fold of our Savior, with the advice and consent of our brothers, the cardinals of the holy Roman church, and of all the prelates, and of those who have been trained in the canon* and civil law,* who are at our court, and with our own sure knowledge, we condemn all such appeals and prohibit them as erroneous and detestable.

---

[3]The pope.

[4]See Innocent III's *Solitae* (Chapter 10, source 66).

Beating the Drum of Unrest
▼▼▼

89 ▼ *Georg Widman,* CHRONICLE

Between 1544 and 1550 Georg Widman recorded in his *Chronicle** the story of
Hans Böhm (ca. 1450–1476), known as *Hansel the Drummer* (or the *Piper*) *of
Niklashausen,* a village in Franconia in western Germany. Böhm, who earned his
sobriquet by entertaining fellow peasants with a kettledrum and bagpipe, initiated a short-lived but quite large social-religious protest in March 1476.

QUESTIONS FOR ANALYSIS

1. Whatever did Böhm mean by his preaching against pointed shoes, slashed
   sleeves, and long hair, and what possible connection did that have with the
   rest of his message? What does your answer suggest about Böhm's world
   view?
2. By what authority did Böhm claim to preach? What implications are
   contained in that claim?
3. Why do you think Böhm preached against priests?*
4. How were Böhm and his message received by the masses? What do you
   conclude from your answer?
5. What do you make of the story of the pig sticker and his wife?
6. Compare Böhm's message and proposed program of reform with that of the
   leaders of the English Peasants' Rebellion of 1381 (Chapter 12, source 83).
   What conclusions do you reach?
7. Compare the fate of Böhm and his followers with that of John Ball, Wat
   Tyler, and their followers. What do you conclude?
8. Compare the tone of Widman's account with that of Froissart's account of
   the English Peasants' Rebellion. What do you conclude?

In the year of our Lord 1476 there came to the
village of Niklashausen in the county of
Wertheim on the Tauber River a cowherd and
drum player who preached violently against the
government and the clergy,* also against pointed
shoes, slashed sleeves, and long hair. He also
claimed that water, pasture, and wood ought to
be held in common by all and that tolls and escort payments should be abolished. The whole
country, he said, was mired in sin and wantonness, and, unless our people were ready to do
penance and change their wicked ways, God
would let all Germany go to destruction. This

vision, he said, was revealed to him by the Virgin Mary, who appeared in a radiant light one
Saturday night as he sat guarding his cattle. It
was the Virgin, he said, who commanded him to
preach.

Thus it came to pass that great numbers of
people went to Niklashausen to pray in the
church of Our Lady there. All Germany seemed
to be in commotion. Stable boys ran from their
horses, taking away the bridles. Reapers left their
reaping, carrying their scythes. Women ceased
haying, coming with their rakes. Wives left husbands, husbands wives. As it happened, the grape

harvest had been excellent and abundant, and wine was cheap that year. Taverns were set up in the fields and on the roads about Niklashausen to ply the pilgrims* with food and drink. At night the pilgrims slept in village teams and in the open fields, men and women helter skelter and some improper goings-on, you may be sure.

So great was the crush that the drummer, who was then staying in a farm house, stuck his head out of a window in the roof so that the crowd might see him and hear him preach. And some say that a Franciscan friar* was seen standing at his back, prompting him as he spoke.[1] When his sermon had ended, the pilgrims began to bewail their sins though it may be that it was really the drink in them causing their misery. They cut the long points off their shoes (pointed shoes being then in fashion) and trimmed their hair, and it seemed as though a dozen carts would not suffice to haul away the hair and shoes being discarded that day, to say nothing of embroidered kerchiefs, robes, doublets,[2] and other female and male adornments. Many men and women took off all their clothes and left them in the church, going away naked except for their shifts. Before they had traveled a mile from Niklashausen, however, with the noise and the wine abating in their heads, they began to regret having abandoned their clothing. And an incredible amount of money was donated by these pilgrims, also wax and wax candles stuck like hedgehogs with coins of neighboring cities and regions.

The drummer wore on his head a kind of cap with tufts on it. A few among the people who could reach him tore these tufts from his cap, believing them to have the power to cure ills and ease pain. Women in labor swore that application of one of these tufts to the belly guaranteed a safe delivery. Wherever the drummer went, people touched his hands and his staff, thinking these to be capable of wonderful cures.

There were also some who sought their own advantage in the simple folk's faith in miraculous signs. These attempted to make money out of the general excitement. For instance, in the valley of the Fischach there dwelled a pig sticker and his wife, both of whom liked to drink. Though the woman was in perfect health, her husband bound her with a rope to his horse as if she were lame and unable to walk a step. In this way they rode to Niklashausen, where the man begged the milling crowd to fall silent so that he might explain the cause of his pilgrimage. From all around they came running to hear the news. He announced that his wife had for years been lame in all her limbs, and no medicine could help her. Then one night she had heard a voice bidding her go to Niklashausen and pledge to the church of Our Lady there a gift of as many pounds of wax as she weighed herself. If she were to do so, the voice said, she would be cured. The woman replied to the voice, "I cannot make this vow because I have not the means to buy such a quantity of wax." But the voice instructed her to proceed with the vow and go on to Niklashausen, where a great crowd of pilgrims, seeing a miracle performed on her, would help her toward the purchase of the wax. "And now, dear wife," said the man, turning to the woman, "if the Holy Mother of God has really made you well, leap from your horse and go into the church to offer thanks to the Virgin." Saying this, he pulled the loop of the rope, and his wife jumped off the horse and ran into the church. Then the pig sticker removed his hat and begged the crowd to help with contributions for the wax which he had promised to buy. They were poor devils, he said, and without the aid of others would not be able to keep their vows. And everyone present tossed a coin into the hat until it was full. Thus the pig sticker and his wife returned to their home and had plenty of money for wine.

This drummer preached so vehemently against the priests that the pilgrims of Niklashausen made up a special song, which they chanted along with their other hymns. It went:

---

[1]The Italian Franciscan preacher St. John Capestrano had made a great impact on Germany in the early 1450s, and apparently Böhm was inspired by him.

[2]A tight-fitting jacket.

God in Heaven, on you we call,
    Kyrie eleison,[3]
Help us seize our priests and kill them all,
    Kyrie eleison.

One Saturday the drummer announced to the public that all who wished to honor and support Our Lady should assemble in Niklashausen on the following Saturday and bring their weapons. Upon their arrival he would tell them what Our Lady had in mind for them to do. Hearing rumors of this gathering, the bishop* of Würzburg, Rudolf von Scherenberg, suspecting that trouble was likely to come of it and afraid of the misuse such rebellious peasants would make of the Gospel,* decided not to wait until the following Saturday. He ordered armed retainers to go at once to Niklashausen to arrest the drummer and his chief henchmen and take them to Würzburg to be thrown into prison. On the appointed Saturday great crowds converged on Niklashausen. When they learned that the drummer, whom they called "Our Lady's Emissary," had been put in chains, they started at once for Würzburg, brandishing clubs, sticks, banners, candles — anything that came to hand — and intending to ask the bishop for the release of "Our Lady's Emissary." They planned to say to the bishop that if he refused their request, his prison tower would fall of its own accord and "Our Lady's Emissary" would go forth from it unhurt.

As they approached Our Lady's Mountain,[4] they were stopped by a troop of armed men from the city, who questioned them about their intentions. They said that they wished only to have "Our Lady's Emissary" released to them. If this were not done, they declared themselves prepared to besiege the prison and remove him by force. While the soldiers sought to calm the rabid populace, some in the mob attacked them with clubs and other weapons, an action which so infuriated the soldiers that they struck back, leaving many a bloody head. As the mob advanced to Our Lady's Mountain, the bishop ordered cannons to be aimed from the ramparts and fired to kill. The bishop's councillors, however, felt pity for the poor wretches and saw to it that the cannons were pointed safely above the heads of the crowd. But this seemed only to increase the stubbornness of the mob. They said, "Our Lady will protect us from harm. You cannot hurt us." Hearing these words, the soldiers charged the crowd, killing and wounding many, for they wished to teach them a lesson about the harm that could be done to them. Many people were captured; in Würzburg the towers and dungeons were filled to overflowing. Later, however, most were pardoned. Only the drummer and two or three others were burned at the stake,[5] and their ashes thrown into the Main River so that no superstitious cult might be made of them. All the same, a few of the faithful succeeded one night in digging up some soil from the spot where the drummer had been burned. They carried this to their homes and treasured it as a sacred relic.*

---

[3]"Lord have mercy," a Greek invocation that is part of the ceremony of the Latin mass.*

[4]The *Frauenberg,* a rocky hill across the Main River, on which the bishop of Würzburg had his residence.
[5]On July 19, 1476.

▼▼▼

Joan of Arc: Saint or Witch?

The nineteenth-century American historian Henry Adams noted: "The study of history is useful to the historian by teaching him his ignorance of women; and the mass of this ignorance crushes one who is familiar enough with what are called historical sources to realize how few women have ever been known. The woman who is known only through a man is known wrong." The following two sources underscore the essential truth of Adams's insight in markedly different ways. Modern historical scholarship has made significant strides in reversing the gender bias of historiography that Adams bewailed a century ago and discovering the all-too-often overlooked historical voices of women. One medieval woman whom we hear clearly and loudly today is Christine de Pisan, the author of the first selection. The second selection is the product of the pen of a German churchman, Johann Nider. Had Adams read Nider's work, he undoubtedly would have placed the churchman within that teeming battalion of male writers whom he accused of gross ignorance when it came to the concerns and actions of women.

In the following sources both Pisan and Nider deal with one of the fifteenth century's most extraordinary and controversial individuals, Joan of Arc (ca. 1412–1431), a French heroine who almost single-handedly rallied France around King Charles VII (r. 1422–1461) and destroyed the myth of English invincibility during the latter stages of the Hundred Years' War, thereby setting the stage for France's eventual recovery and victory. Joan, known as the *Maid of Orléans* because of her success in raising the siege of that city in May 1429, led the weak-willed Charles to Rheims in July, where he was finally crowned king, thereby preserving his family's hold on a crown claimed by England's kings.

After these initial successes, Joan's fortunes took a turn for the worse. Taken prisoner in 1430, this pious teen-age woman, who claimed divine guidance, was tried for witchcraft. Her condemnation was essential to the English; without it they would have to admit that they were fighting a saint sent by God. Found guilty by an ecclesiastical* tribunal that was under the thumb of the English, Joan was executed by burning in 1431. Despite her death, the English were beginning to lose the war, in large part because of Joan's installation of Charles VII as anointed king and the inspiration that she had given the king's armies.

Joan of Arc, Blessed Heroine of France
▼▼▼
90 ▼ Christine de Pisan, DITIÉ DE JEHANNE D'ARC

In 1429 Christine de Pisan, the most widely read and respected female writer of her century and arguably France's greatest late-medieval author, composed the *Ditié de Jehanne d'Arc* (*The Song of Joan of Arc*). This was the first poem, in any language, written about Joan and the last work from the pen of this great poet. Completed on July 31, 1429, it was crafted at a moment when Joan was at the height of her success. She had lifted the siege of Orléans and triumphantly escorted Charles VII to Rheims, where he was crowned king. It seemed as though her army would soon liberate Paris and defeat totally the Anglo-Burgundian forces, which had so recently seemed to be on the brink of total victory in a war that had devastated France and its people. To Pisan, this turn of events could only be a miracle and a sign of God's love for France, her adopted homeland.

Christine de Pisan (or Pizan) was born in Venice around 1364 but moved to France in 1368 to join her father, who had accepted a position as astrologer and physician at the court of King Charles V. In 1379, when fifteen years of age, Pisan married a man ten years her senior and bore three children. Upon her husband's sudden death in 1389, she found herself in desperate financial straits and turned to writing in order to support herself, her children, her widowed mother, and a niece.

Although a female professional writer was a novelty in fifteenth-century Europe, Christine de Pisan succeeded brilliantly. After producing a large body of commissioned poems, which established her reputation as a French writer of distinction, she turned to topics of her own choice and produced over fifteen longer works in prose and poetry that addressed such topics as religion, morality, history, royal biography, chivalry, warfare, statecraft, contemporary misogyny, and feminine education. These last two issues were the focus of several of her most celebrated works, most notably *The Book of the City of Ladies* of 1405, which proved to be her age's most eloquent defense of women against the slurs of their detractors.

In 1418, when Burgundian forces occupied Paris, thereby forcing the Dauphin Charles, son and presumptive heir of Charles VI (r. 1380–1422), to flee, Pisan sought refuge in a female monastic* convent. A strong partisan of the Valois royal family since her childhood at the court of Charles V, Pisan chose life in a nunnery* rather than life under the Burgundians. Eleven years after her forced retirement and silence, she broke out in poetic song for one last time to celebrate the miracle that was taking place in her old age. We hear no more of Christine de Pisan after this poem; apparently she died in 1430, before Joan's execution.

QUESTIONS FOR ANALYSIS

1. What was the nature and depth of Pisan's feelings for France and its royal house? For example, why does she believe that God has a special solicitude for France? What did she believe France and its kings would accomplish?
2. What does this poem allow us to infer about the level of French national feeling during the latter stages of the Hundred Years' War?
3. According to Pisan, Joan had both national and universal missions. What were they? What do these presumed missions suggest about Pisan's values and world view?
4. At her trial, Joan was accused of having dishonored her sex. How does Pisan anticipate and answer such a charge? How does Pisan see Joan and interpret her deeds? In answering this question, take into account the images and allusions that Pisan uses to describe Joan.
5. Some scholars have seen a feminist theme running through this poem. Do you see one? If so, what is it?
6. Are there any other major themes in this poem? If so, what are they?
7. Compare Froissart's vision of the Hundred Years' War (Chapter 12, source 83) with Pisan's. What are the differences, and how do you explain them?
8. Compare this poem with Urban II's speech at Clermont (Chapter 11, source 72). What conclusions do you draw from your comparative analysis?

9. "The *Ditié* is a mish-mash of old and new sentiments." Whatever could this commentator mean? Do you agree or disagree? Why?

I   I, Christine, who have wept for eleven years in a walled abbey* where I have lived ever since Charles (how strange this is!) the king's son — dare I say it? — fled in haste from Paris, I who have lived enclosed there on account of the treachery, now, for the first time, begin to laugh. . . .

III   In 1429 the sun began to shine again. It brings back the good, new season which had not really been seen for a long time — and because of that many people had lived out their lives in sorrow; I myself am one of them. But I no longer grieve over anything, now that I can see what I desire. . . .

V   The reason is that the rejected child of the rightful king of France, who has long suffered many a great misfortune and who now approaches, rose up as if towards prime, coming as a crowned king in might and majesty, wearing spurs of gold.

VI   Now let us greet our king! Welcome to him on his return! Overjoyed at the sight of his noble array, let us all, both great and small, step forward to greet him joyously — and let no one hold back — praising God, who has kept him safe, and shouting "Noël!" in a loud voice. . . .

X   Did anyone, then, see anything quite so extraordinary come to pass (something that is well worth noting and remembering in every region), namely, that France (about whom it was said she had been cast down) should see her fortunes change, by divine command, from evil to such great good,

XI   as the result, indeed, of such a miracle that, if the matter were not so well-known and crystal-clear in every aspect, nobody would ever believe it? It is a fact well worth remembering that God should nevertheless have wished (and this is the truth!) to bestow such great blessings on France, through a young virgin.

XII   And what honor for the French crown, this proof of divine intervention! For all the blessings which God bestows upon it demonstrate how much He favors it and that He finds more faith in the Royal House than anywhere else; as far as it is concerned, I read (and there is nothing new in this) that the Lilies of France[1] never erred in matters of faith.

XIII   And you Charles, king of France, seventh of that noble name, who have been involved in such a great war before things turned out at all well for you, now, thanks be to God, see your honor exalted by the Maid who has laid low your enemies beneath your standard (and this *is* new!)

XIV   in a short time; for it was believed quite impossible that you should ever recover your country which you were on the point of losing. Now it is manifestly yours for, no matter who may have done you harm, you have recovered it! And all this has been brought about by the intelligence of the Maid who, God be thanked, has played her part in this matter!

XV   And I firmly believe that God would never have bestowed such grace upon you if it were not ordained by Him that you should, in the course of time, accomplish and bring to completion some great and solemn task; I believe too that He has destined you to be the author of very great deeds.

XVI   For there will be a king of France called Charles, son of Charles, who will be supreme ruler over all kings. Prophecies have given him the

---

[1]The *fleur-de-lis,* or lily, was the emblem of the French royal house.

name of "The Flying Stag," and many a deed will be accomplished by this conqueror (God has called him to this task) and in the end he will be emperor.[2] . . .

XIX   And how will you ever be able to thank God enough, serve and fear Him in all your deeds (for He has led you from such great adversity to peace and raised up the whole of France from such ruin) when His most holy providence made you worthy of such signal honor? . . .

XXI   And you, blessed Maid, are you to be forgotten, given that God honored you so much that you untied the rope which held France so tightly bound? Could one ever praise you enough for having bestowed peace on this land humiliated by war?

XXII   Blessed be He who created you, Joan, who were born at a propitious hour! Maiden sent from God, into whom the Holy Spirit* poured His great grace, in whom [i.e. the Holy Spirit] there was[3] and is an abundance of noble gifts, never did Providence refuse you any request. Who can ever begin to repay you?

XXIII   And what more can be said of any other person or of the great deeds of the past? Moses, upon whom God in His bounty bestowed many a blessing and virtue, miraculously and indefatigably led God's people out of Egypt. In the same way, blessed Maid, you have led us out of evil!

XXIV   When we take your person into account, you who are a young maiden, to whom God gives the strength and power to be the champion who casts the rebels down and feeds France with the sweet, nourishing milk of peace,[4] here indeed is something quite extraordinary!

XXV   For if God performed such a great number of miracles through Joshua[5] who conquered many a place and cast down many an enemy, he, Joshua, was a strong and powerful *man*. But, after all, a *woman* — a simple shepherdess — braver than any man ever was in Rome! As far as God is concerned, this was easily accomplished.

XXVI   But as for us, we never heard tell of such an extraordinary marvel, for the prowess of all the great men of the past cannot be compared to this woman's whose concern it is to cast out our enemies. This is God's doing: it is He who guides her and who has given her a heart greater than that of any man.

XXVII   Much is made of Gideon,[6] who was a simple workman, and it was God, so the story tells, who made him fight; nobody could stand firm before him and he conquered everything. But whatever guidance God gave [him], it is clear that He never performed so striking a miracle as He does for this woman.

XXVIII   I have heard of Esther, Judith and Deborah,[7] who were women of great worth, through whom God delivered His people from oppression, and I have heard of many other worthy women as well, champions every one, through them He performed many miracles, but He has accomplished more through this Maid.

XXIX   She was miraculously sent by divine command and conducted by the angel of the Lord to the king, in order to help him. Her achieve-

---

[2]Known as the *Second Charlemagne* prophecy, it was popularly believed since at least the fourteenth century that a king of France would arise who would surpass all of Europe's kings and become emperor.

[3]Compare this with opening lines of the popular prayer known as the *Ave Maria* (Hail, Mary): "Hail, Mary, full of grace, the Lord is with you. Blessed are you among women."

[4]This brings to mind one of the West's most popular artistic images of the Virgin Mary: the nursing mother, feeding Jesus.

[5]Moses's lieutenant and successor, who led the Israelites into the Promised Land.

[6]One of Israel's judges, or war lords, he led the Israelites in defending their holdings in the Promised Land against the attacks of the Midianites.

[7]Esther and Judith are, respectively, the heroines and central characters of the books of Esther and Judith, two of the several apocryphal books of the Hebrew Bible. The apocrypha are not part of the thirty-nine canonical* books of the Hebrew Tanakh (known as the *Old Testament* to Christians), but the medieval Church revered them as authoritative. Deborah was a prophetess who lived a generation before Gideon (note 6). See the Bible, the Book of Judges, 4–5.

ment is no illusion for she was carefully put to the test in council (in short, a thing is proved by its effect)

XXX and well examined, before people were prepared to believe her; before it became common knowledge that God had sent her to the king, she was brought before clerks* and wise men so that they could find out if she was telling the truth. But it was found in history-records that she was destined to accomplish her mission.[8] . . .

XXXIII Oh, how clear this was at the siege of Orléans where her power was first made manifest! It is my belief that no miracle was ever more evident, for God so came to the help of His people that our enemies were unable to help each other any more than would dead dogs. It was there that they were captured and put to death.

XXXIV Oh! What honor for the female sex! It is perfectly obvious that God has special regard for it when all these wretched people who destroyed the whole kingdom — now recovered and made safe by a woman, something that 5000 *men* could not have done — and the traitors [have been] exterminated. Before the event they would scarcely have believed this possible.

XXXV A little girl of sixteen (isn't this something quite supernatural?) who does not even notice the weight of the arms she bears — indeed her whole upbringing seems to have prepared her for this, so strong and resolute is she! And her enemies go fleeing before her, not one of them can stand up to her. She does all this in full view of everyone,

XXXVI and drives her enemies out of France, recapturing castles and towns. Never did anyone see greater strength, even in hundreds or thousands of men! And she is the supreme captain of our brave and able men. Neither Hector nor Achilles[9] had such strength! This is God's doing: it is He who leads her.

XXXVII And you trusty men-at-arms who carry out the task and prove yourselves to be good and loyal, one must certainly make mention of you (you will be praised in every nation!) and not fail to speak of you and your valor in preference to everything else,

XXXVIII you who, in pain and suffering, expose life and limb in defence of what is right and dare to risk confronting every danger. Be constant, for this, I promise, will win you glory and praise in Heaven. For whoever fights for justice wins a place in Paradise — this I do venture to say.

XXXIX And so, you English, draw in your horns for you will never capture any good game! Don't attempt any foolish enterprise in France! You have been check-mated. A short time ago, when you looked so fierce, you had no inkling that this would be so; but you were not yet treading the path upon which God casts down the proud.

XL You thought you had already conquered France and that she must remain yours. Things have turned out otherwise, you treacherous lot! Go and beat your drums elsewhere, unless you want to taste death, like your companions, whom wolves may well devour, for their bodies lie dead amidst the furrows!

XLI And know that she will cast down the English for good, for this is God's will: He hears the prayer of the good whom they wanted to harm! The blood of those who are dead and have no hope of being brought back to life again cries out against them. God will tolerate this no longer — He has decided, rather, to condemn them as evil.

XLII She will restore harmony in Christendom and the Church. She will destroy the unbelievers people talk about, and the heretics* and their vile ways, for this is the substance of a prophecy

---

[8]A reference to a number of popular prophecies that are more specifically alluded to in section XXXI, which is not included here.

[9]Respectively, the leading warriors of the Trojans and the Argives (Greeks) in the Trojan War.

that has been made. Nor will she have mercy on any place which treats faith in God with disrespect.

XLIII   She will destroy the Saracens, by conquering the Holy Land. She will lead Charles there, whom God preserve! Before he dies he will make such a journey. He is the one who is to conquer it. It is there that she is to end her days and that both of them are to win glory. It is there that the whole enterprise will be brought to completion.

XLIV   Therefore, in preference to all the brave men of times past, this woman must wear the crown, for her deeds show clearly enough already that God bestows more courage upon her than upon all those men about whom people speak. And she has not yet accomplished her whole mission! I believe that God bestows her here below so that peace may be brought about through her deeds.

XLV   And yet destroying the English race is not her main concern for her aspirations lie more elsewhere: it is her concern to ensure the survival of the Faith. As for the English, whether it be a matter for joy or sorrow, they are done for. In days to come scorn will be heaped on them. They have been cast down!

XLVI   And all you base rebels who have joined them,[10] you can see now that it would have been better for you to have gone forwards rather than backwards as you did, thereby becoming the serfs* of the English. Beware that more does not befall you (for you have been tolerated long enough!), and remember what the outcome will be!

XLVII   Oh, all you blind people, can't you detect God's hand in this? If you can't, you are truly stupid for how else could the Maid who strikes you all down dead have been sent to us? — And you don't have sufficient strength! Do you want to fight against God?

---

[10]Here, she addresses the Burgundians and the Gascons, who were allied with the English forces.

Joan of Arc and Other Female Rebels
▼▼▼
91 ▼ *Johann Nider, FORMICARIUS*

Europe's witch hunt, which witnessed the executions and murders of possibly tens of thousands of accused witches and sorcerers, was largely a sixteenth- and seventeenth-century phenomenon, reaching its peak of intensity between 1560 and 1680 in both Catholic and Protestant lands. Indeed, it was not until the fifteenth century, when Europe was still in the throes of its "crisis of the Late Middle Ages," that the fervor of witch hunters began to make a substantial impression on Western society.

In both the popular imagination and the teachings of theologians, witchcraft was any formal alliance with the Devil. By virtue of this pact with Satan, the witch or warlock (a male witch) learned to harness the powers of the demonic forces, thereby making her or him a major danger to society. Therefore, in the eyes of many, cutting out such dangerous tumors from the body of Christian Europe became a necessary act of self-survival.

Although Europe did not become obsessed with rooting out witches until the 1500s, the previous century had its zealous witch hunters and several highly publicized witch trials and executions. The most famous execution of the fifteenth century was that of Joan of Arc, who was executed as a witch essentially for political and not religious reasons.

The next selection comes from the pages of the *Formicarius* of Johann Nider (ca. 1380–1438). The work's curious title literally means "ant hill" but is best translated as "a hive of activity" — a reference to the fact that it is a lengthy collection of anecdotes and dialogues relating to the religious life of fifteenth-century Europe. Nider, a priest* and member of the Dominican Order, was a professor of theology at the University of Vienna and an active preacher against the Hussites in the region around Prague. A lifelong foe of heresy* and every other form of what he perceived as devilish error, Nider included long discourses on contemporary diabolical activities in the *Formicarius,* which he completed only shortly before his death. In the following excerpt, Nider uses a stylized dialogue between himself and a fictional pupil to relate the story of Joan of Arc.

QUESTIONS FOR ANALYSIS

1. On what grounds was Joan of Arc judged to be a witch?
2. What about Joan particularly offended Nider?
3. What qualities did all four so-called witches share?
4. Why were they perceived as threats to society? How so?
5. Two of these four witches escaped execution. How did they manage that, and what do you infer from the means they used to do so?
6. Consider Nider's final comments about women in light of sources 23 (Chapter 4), 38 and 39 (Chapter 7), and 56 (Chapter 9). It has been said that Christian clerics* tended to portray women as either saints or seductresses. On the basis of the evidence, what do you think of this judgment?
7. Compare the four women in Nider's story with Chaucer's women (Chapter 12, source 85). Are they portrayed differently? If so, to what do you ascribe those differences?
8. Compose either Pisan's commentary on Nider's description of Joan of Arc or Nider's commentary on Pisan's poem.

PUPIL: In your opinion, have some good people been deceived by sorceresses and witches in our own day?

MASTER: I suspend judgment concerning the truth of the story that follows, but I will tell you what is related by public rumor and report. We have in our days the distinguished professor of divinity, Brother Heinrich Kaltyseren, Inquisitor of Heretical* Activity.[1] As he told me himself, last year, while performing his inquisitorial office in Cologne,[2] he discovered in the region a certain young woman who always went around in male clothing, bore weapons, and wore the type of degenerate garments that are favored by courtiers.[3] She danced with men and was so given

---

[1]See Chapter 7, source 43.
[2]A German city on the Rhine River.

[3]Tight-fitting doublets and hose. See source 89.

to feasting and drinking that she seemed to over-step totally the boundaries of her sex, which she did not conceal. Because the bishopric of Trier[4] was, at that time, gravely beset by two rivals contending for the office of bishop* (as, unfortunately is also the case today), she boasted that she could and would set one of the claimants on the throne, just as Maid Joan, of whom I will presently speak, had done shortly before with King Charles of France, by confirming him in his royal office. In fact, this woman claimed to be that same Joan, raised from the dead by God! One day, when she had come into Cologne with the youthful count of Württemberg, who protected and favored her, and there, in the presence of the nobility, had performed marvels that seemed magical, she was at last diligently scrutinized and publicly cited by the aforesaid inquisitor, in order that she might be formally examined. She was said to have cut a napkin into pieces and suddenly have restored it whole in the sight of the people; to have thrown a glass against the wall, thereby breaking it, and to have repaired it in a moment; and to have shown many similar idle devices. The wretched woman, however, would not obey the Church's commands. The count protected her from arrest and sneaked her out of Cologne. In this way, she escaped the inquisitor's hands but did not elude the sentence of excommunication.* Bound by this curse, she left Germany for France, where she married a knight, in order to protect herself from ecclesiastical* penalty and the sword [of secular* punishment].[5] Then a priest, or rather pimp, seduced this witch with talk of love. Finally, she ran away with him and went to Metz,[6] where she lived as his concubine and openly showed everyone by what spirit she was led.

Moreover, there was in France, within the past ten years, a maid named Joan, about whom I have already spoken, who was distinguished, so it was thought, for her prophetic spirit and the power of her miracles. She always wore men's clothes, and none of the arguments of the learned doctors[7] convinced her to put them aside and to content herself with feminine dress, even though she openly professed her womanhood and virginity. She said: "I have been sent by God in these masculine garments, that serve as a token of future victory, to preach by both word and attire, to help Charles, the true king of France, and to set Charles firmly upon his throne, from which the king of England and the duke of Burgundy are striving to chase him." At that time, those two men were allied and were oppressing France grievously with war and carnage.[8] Joan, therefore, rode constantly around like a knight with her lord, predicted many successes to come, was present in the field at some victories, and performed many other wonders that elicited a sense of marvel not only in France but in every realm in Christendom. Finally, this Joan reached such a level of presumption that, before France had yet recovered, she was already sending threatening letters to the Bohemians, among whom there were a host of heretics.[9] From that period onward, both lay people and clerics began to have doubts about the spirit that ruled her, wondering whether it was diabolical or divine. Then certain learned men wrote treatises concerning her, in which they expressed not only diverse but even adverse opinions concerning the Maid. Then following that, after she had given Charles tremendous assistance and had confirmed his hold on the throne for some years, by God's will, as it

---

[4]A German city on the Mosel River.

[5]Church and state generally worked in harmony in attempting to extirpate heresy and witchcraft. The Church's inquisitors tried and condemned heretics and similar nonconformists, but it was secular governments who punished and executed them.

[6]A city in eastern France, not too far from Joan of Arc's home region.

[7]Of theology and canon law.*

[8]King Henry VI (r. 1422–1461) of England claimed to be the rightful monarch of France (actually, the claim was made for him because he was an infant), and in this period, the English crown was allied with the duke of Burgundy against Charles VII.

[9]The Hussites. Nider refers here to a famous fifteenth-century letter that was incorrectly ascribed to Joan's authorship. However, see what Pisan writes about Joan's crusading intentions, which the Maid of Orléans apparently did harbor and express.

is believed, she was captured in battle by the English[10] and cast into prison. Large numbers of masters of both canon and civil law* were summoned, and she was examined for many days. As I have heard from Master Nicholas Midi, Master of Theology, who represented the University of Paris, she finally confessed that she had a personal angel from God. Based on many conjectures and proofs, and the opinion of the most learned men, this "angel" was judged to be an evil spirit. Consequently, this spirit made her a sorceress. For this reason, they permitted her to be burned at the stake by the common executioner. . . .

At this same time, two women sprang up near Paris, publicly preaching that God had sent them to aid Maid Joan, and, as I heard from the lips of the aforesaid Master Nicholas, they were immediately arrested as witches or sorcerers by the Inquisitor for France, examined by many doctors of theology, and found at last to have been deceived by the ravings of an evil spirit. When, therefore, one of these women perceived she had been misled by an angel of Satan, she followed the advice of her masters, abandoned that which she had begun, and, as was her duty, immediately renounced her error. The other one, however, remained obstinate and was burned.

PUPIL: I cannot marvel enough how the frail sex can dare to rush into such presumptuous matters.

MASTER: These matters are marvelous to simple folk like you, but they are not rare in the eyes of wise men. For there are three things in nature that, if they transgress the limits of their own condition, whether by diminution or excess, attain to the highest pinnacles of goodness and evil. They are the tongue, the cleric, and woman. All are commonly the best of all, as long as they are guided by a good spirit, but the worst of all, if guided by an evil spirit.

---

[10]Actually, she was captured by the Burgundians and later turned over to the English.

▼▼▼

New Secular Rulers

Contradictions were inherent in the culture of late-medieval Europe, and possibly nothing illustrates that society's internal tensions more than its ability to juxtapose intense, widespread religiosity and deep spirituality with its growing secularization.* In 1324 Marsilio of Padua (ca. 1275–1342) proclaimed in his treatise *The Defender of the Peace* that the secular state, not the Church, was the superior authority in Christian society. Moreover, although all power emanated from the community, it was the secular ruler, whom the community designated to lead it, who exercised supreme power over both Church and state. Marsilio of Padua's ideas were radical and not widely accepted in his age. Indeed, he lost his university post at Paris and was declared an excommunicated* heretic* by Pope John XXII. Nevertheless, Marsilio's ideas described not simply a theory but an emerging reality — the fact that states and their rulers were becoming laws unto themselves, answerable to no external authorities, the pope included. In other words, the laws of the state received their sanction solely from the will of the sovereign and not from any absolute system of moral precepts, as interpreted by an institutional priesthood.*

By the end of the fifteenth century, a number of strong states had emerged, ruled by vigorous sovereigns who willingly accepted no limitations upon their power. The monarchs of England, France, Aragon, Castile, and Portugal managed to carve out fairly large realms, which they subjected to extensive royal authority. In Italy and the so-called Holy Roman Empire, where central authority was a myth, a number of local princes managed to create smaller, equally independent secular states, which they ruled with a sovereign authority that rivaled that of the great monarchs of Europe.

The following sources present character sketches of two of late-fifteenth-century Europe's most interesting New Rulers, King Louis XI of France and Lorenzo the Magnificent of Florence.

Louis XI: A Character Sketch

▼▼▼

92 ▼ *Philippe de Commynes, MEMOIRS*

Philippe de Commynes (ca. 1447–1511) has earned the reputation as France's last great medieval historian and its first modern political observer, a judgment that says as much about the futility of trying to distinguish sharply between *medieval* and *modern* as it does about the transitional nature of the late fifteenth and early sixteenth centuries.

Born into the nobility of Flanders, Commynes entered into the service of Charles the Rash, duke of Burgundy, but in 1472 he shifted allegiance to King Louis XI (r. 1461–1483), Charles the Rash's mortal enemy. Commynes quickly became one of the king's most valued counsellors, possibly the most valued. His crowning achievement was advising the king how best to manipulate the events that led to the downfall and death of Charles the Rash in 1476. From 1477 on, Commynes seems to have played a less important role in the councils of Louis XI, but he continued to serve his monarch faithfully, including traveling as a diplomat to the court of Lorenzo de' Medici in Florence (source 93). Following King Louis's death in 1483, Commynes fell afoul of the regents of the young Charles VIII (r. 1483–1498) and found himself imprisoned for several years and then exiled to one of his estates in disgrace in 1489. In this period of enforced quiet, which extended to 1491, Commynes began his *Memoirs* and composed its first six books, all of which deal with the reign of Louis XI.

By 1491 Commynes had regained partial royal favor, and although he served Charles VIII on several diplomatic missions in Italy, he never again had the influence he had enjoyed under Louis XI. Pensioned off by King Louis XII (r. 1498–1515), Commynes died in 1511, largely out of touch with the royal court. Commynes's career as a statesman ended badly, but long before his death, he revised his *Memoirs* and added two additional books, carrying his story down to 1498. He left the work behind to serve as his memorial and public justification.

More than a narrative, Commynes's story contains lengthy didactic passages addressed to anyone who wishes to learn the craft of effective government by studying the examples of recent history. By adding these passages, Commynes transformed his work into a mirror, or handbook, for princes — a popular late-medieval genre. In the first excerpt, which appears early in Book 1, the author digresses on the virtues and vices of his late sovereign, King Louis IX. In the second excerpt, which comes toward the end of Book 6, Commynes describes Louis's death and sums up the man and his reign.

QUESTIONS FOR ANALYSIS

1. Can you find any possible autobiographical allusions in the first excerpt? If they are autobiographical, what do they suggest about Commynes's relationship with King Louis and his attitude toward that monarch?
2. Does Commynes excuse away or remain silent about any of King Louis's less admirable qualities or actions? What do you conclude from your answer?
3. According to Commynes, what personal qualities contributed to Louis's success as a ruler?
4. According to Commynes, what were Louis's weaknesses, and how, if at all, did he attempt to mitigate them?
5. Compare Commynes's treatment of Louis XI with Joinville's description of Louis IX (Chapter 10, source 64) and Froissart's description of the Battle of Poitiers (Chapter 12, source 83). Which strike you as more significant, the differences or the similarities? What conclusions do you draw from your analysis?
6. How do you think Commynes would have judged kings Louis IX and John the Good?
7. Based on your answers to questions 3, 4, 5, and 6, construct a picture of Commynes's ideal ruler.
8. "Commynes's values and world view were transitional — both medieval and early modern yet not fully either." Please evaluate the merits of this statement.

I have entered upon this discourse because I have seen many deceptions in this world and many servants set against their masters. I have seen that haughty princes and lords who seldom listen to their servants are more often deceived than those who are humble and listen gladly. And of all those whom I have ever known, the wisest in extricating himself from a tricky situation in an adverse time was our master, King Louis XI, and he was the humblest in word and attire and one who ever worked to win over a man who could serve him or do him harm. He was never put off by being refused once by a man whom he was at-tempting to win but continued in his endeavors, promising grandiosely and giving actual money and offices which he knew would please him. Those whom he had expelled and banished in time of peace and prosperity he would repurchase dearly when he had need of them. He made use of them and did not hold any grudge against them for past deeds.

He was by nature a friend of men of middling estate and enemy of all the great who were able to do without him. No man ever lent his ear so readily to others nor inquired about so many things as he did nor wanted to know so many men. For truthfully, he knew all the powerful and influential men in England, Spain, Portugal, Italy, the lordships of the duke of Burgundy and in Brittany, as well as he knew his own subjects. And these manners and qualities which he had, which I have just mentioned, saved his crown for him, seeing the enemies which he had acquired at his accession to the kingdom.[1]

But above all his great generosity has served him because wisely as he conducted himself in adversity, as soon as he thought he was safe, on the other hand, even if it was only a truce, he would begin to upset men by petty ways which served him ill and he was scarcely able to endure peace. He spoke lightly of men both in their presence and in their absence, except of those whom he feared, who were legion, for he was somewhat fearful by nature. When, indeed, by his manner of speaking, he had harmed himself or suspected that he had and he wished to repair the damage, he spoke these words to the person concerned, "I'm well aware that my tongue has caused me great damage, but sometimes it has brought me much pleasure. Nevertheless it is right that I should make amends." And he never used these words without recompensing the person to whom he was speaking and that he did in no small way.

Yet God grants a great favor to a prince when he recognizes good and evil and especially when the good exceeds the evil as in the case of our master. For in my opinion, it was the hardship which he experienced in his youth, when he was a fugitive from his father and fled to Duke Philip of Burgundy with whom he lived for six years,[2] that stood him in good stead because he was constrained to humor those of whom he had need.

Adversity taught him this lesson which was no mean thing. When he found himself powerful and a crowned king, he first of all thought only of revenge but soon this caused him injury and he felt quite as much repentance. He set right this folly and error by winning back those whom he had wronged, as you will hear later. If he had only had the education of other lords whom I have seen brought up in this kingdom, I do not believe that he could have recovered again. For they were only brought up to make fools of themselves in dress and speech. They have no knowledge of letters, not a single wise man is found in their company, they have governors to whom one speaks about their business, not to them, and these latter dispose of all their business. Such lords, who have not thirteen *livres* in rents,[3] puff themselves up and say, "Speak to my men," thinking that by these words they imitate the very great. I have often seen their servants make their own profit, giving their masters to understand that they were fools. And so if by chance one of them regains control of his own affairs and wants to find out what belongs to him, it is so late that it scarcely matters, because it is necessary to realize that all famous men, who have achieved great things, began very young and their success springs from their education or from God's grace.

▼ ▼ ▼

He continued to say sensible things and his illness lasted, as I said, from Monday to Saturday evening. For this reason I want to draw a comparison between the ills and anguish which he caused many others to suffer and those which he

---

[1]A reference to the situation that led to the War of the Public Weal (Good), 1464–1465, in which a league of princes — including Philip the Good, duke of Burgundy, and King Louis's brother, Charles, duke of Berry — rose in rebellion against Louis's government. The young Philippe de Commynes served as a squire* in the forces of Charles, count of Charolois, the son of Duke Philip and the future Duke Charles the Rash. Inasmuch as Duke Philip was Commynes's godfather, it was natural that Commynes should join the side of the rebels.

[2]Following the collapse in 1456 of one of his conspiracies against his father, Charles VII (r. 1422–1461), Prince Louis found sanctuary at the court of Philip the Good, the king's bitter enemy. Louis remained at the Burgundian court until his father's death and his own accession to the throne.
[3]An exceedingly small sum for annual rents.

suffered himself before dying, for I trust that they have borne him to paradise and will make up part of his time in purgatory.* And if they were not so severe or long as those he inflicted on others he had a different and a greater office in this world than they did and had never been subject to anyone, but had always been obeyed so that it seemed that Europe had been created only in order to obey him. For this reason the little that he did suffer against his will and custom was more difficult for him to bear. . . .

In a previous paragraph I started to make a comparison between the sufferings which he inflicted on certain people, and several of those who lived under his rule and in his obedience, with those similar ones he suffered before he died (and if these were not so severe or long, as I said in that paragraph, they were very considerable in view of his temper which demanded more strict obedience than any other prince of his time. This obedience he received; so that the least word of opposition to his will constituted a very serious punishment for him to bear). I have mentioned how his impending death was announced to him with so little discretion. But some five or six months previously the king was very suspicious of everybody, particularly all those who were fit to exercise authority. He was afraid of his son and had him kept under strict watch. No one could see him or speak to him except with the king's permission. In the end he was even frightened of his daughter and son-in-law, the present duke of Bourbon. He wanted to know who entered Plessis[4] with them and, finally, he broke up a council which the duke of Bourbon was holding there on his orders. When his son-in-law and the count of Dunois returned from conducting the embassy, which had come to the marriage of the king,[5] his son, and the queen at Amboise, and they came back to Plessis and brought many people in with them, the king, who had the gates heavily guarded, was in a gallery overlooking the court. He called one of the captains of his guard and ordered him to go and touch the followers of these lords to see if they were wearing brigandines[6] under their clothes and to do this while talking to them and without appearing to do it. Just see! If he had made many men live in fear and suspicion under him, how amply he was repaid! Whom could he trust when he was suspicious of his own son, daughter and son-in-law! I say this not only about him but about all lords who desire to be feared; they are never aware of revenge until they are old and then, as a penance, they fear everybody. What torment it was for this king to have such fears and passions! . . .

It is true that the king, our master, had dreadful prisons made, including cages, some of iron and others of wood, fitted with iron bars inside and out and with terrible locks, about eight feet wide and a foot higher than a man. The original inventor of such prisons was the bishop* of Verdun. He was immediately put in the first of them to be made where he spent fourteen years. Many others have cursed him since, myself included, because I did eight months in one of them during the reign of the present king.[7] Previously the king had obtained horrible shackles from the Germans. These were very heavy and terrible and were put on the feet, with one ring on each foot, and were very difficult to open, like a collar, having a thick, heavy chain with a huge iron ball on the end, much heavier than it need or ought to have been. They were called the king's daughters. Yet I have seen many well-born prisoners wearing them on their feet; they have since been released and enjoyed great honor and happiness and even received great benefits from him. . . .

But this is not our main concern, and to return to that it must be said that, as in his time these evil and various types of prison were invented, so before he died he found himself in similar or even greater fear than those he had

---

[4]The royal residence at Plessis-les-Tours.
[5]The current king, Charles VIII.

[6]Shirts of canvas and metal plates, which would deflect a dagger.
[7]Charles VIII.

imprisoned in them. This I hold to be a matter of great favor for him and part of his time in purgatory. And I mention it to show that there is no one, whatever his rank, who does not suffer either privately or in public, particularly if he has made others suffer.

Towards the end of his life the king had his castle at Plessis-les-Tours entirely surrounded by iron bars in the form of a thick grille. At the four corners of the house were placed the four large, strong, pierced, iron sentry boxes. The grille rested against the wall on one side and on the edge of the moat on the other, for it had a flat bottom and steep sides. He had many iron spikes fastened into the wall, each with three or four points and they were placed very close to one another. Furthermore he ordered ten crossbowmen from each of the sentry boxes to stay in the moat to shoot at those who approached before the gate was open. He wanted them to lie in the moat and withdraw to the iron sentry boxes when necessary.

He clearly understood that this fortification would not be strong enough to withstand a large number of men or an army but that did not worry him. He was simply afraid that one lord or a handful might attempt to take the place by night, partly in collusion with those inside and partly by force, and that they would take away his authority and force him to live like an insane man unfit to govern. The gate of Plessis did not open before eight o'clock in the morning, nor was the drawbridge lowered. Then the officers entered the castle and the captains of the guards placed the normal gatekeepers at their post and ordered pickets of archers, either to the gate or around the courtyard, as if it were a closely guarded frontier post. No one entered except by a wicket-gate, nor without the king's knowledge, unless they were stewards of the household or people of this type who were not going into his presence. Is it possible to keep a king, in suitable state, in closer imprisonment than he kept

himself? The cages where he had held other people were some eight feet square and he, who was such a king, had a small court of the castle in which to walk about. Even then he hardly went into it but stayed in the gallery, not leaving it except to go into rooms. He went to Mass* without going through that courtyard. Who would want to deny that the king was suffering when he shut himself up and had himself guarded, when he was afraid of his children and all his closest relatives, when he changed and removed his servants and those he had patronized from day to day, when they owed all their wealth and honor to him, and when he dared not trust any of them but shut himself up with such strange chains and barricades? It is true that the castle was larger than a common prison but he was greater than any common prisoner. One could say that others have been more suspicious than he but this was not in my time nor were they, perhaps, such wise kings with such loyal subjects. They were probably cruel tyrants anyway. But the king never harmed anybody unless he had offended him.

I have not said these things merely to record the suspicious nature of our king but to show the patience which he displayed in his sufferings, which were similar to those he had inflicted on others. I consider that it was Our Lord's punishment of him in this world so that he would have less in the next, both with regard to the things I have mentioned and to his illness which were great and sorrowful burdens to him. He feared them a great deal before they came upon him. I mentioned them too, in order that those who follow him might have a little more pity on the people and be less keen to punish than he was, although I do not want to blame him nor say that I have ever seen a better prince. It is true that he oppressed his subjects but he would not allow anyone else, whether a friend or a stranger, to do so.

Lorenzo de' Medici: A Character Sketch
▼▼▼

93 ▼ *Francesco Guicciardini,* *THE HISTORY OF FLORENCE*

Messer Francesco Guicciardini (1483–1540) had a lucrative law practice in his native Florence, but unlike Sacchetti's comic lawyers (Chapter 12, source 84), he possessed wit and intelligence. Like many of his contemporary doctors of law, Guicciardini was politically ambitious and immersed himself in the rough world of Florentine civic life. In 1508–1509, in the midst of his early career, Guicciardini composed a history of Florence that traces the fortunes of this Tuscan city from 1378 to 1509, where the story ends abruptly — in midsentence. Unlike his masterpiece, *The History of Italy,* which he continued to polish and rework until his death, Guicciardini never returned to update or complete his initial foray into Florentine history, although he later composed a second work entitled *Florentine Affairs,* which covers much of the same ground.

The History of Florence, written in the Tuscan dialect and without rhetorical flourishes, has all of the flaws and strengths of a youthful work composed in the heat of the moment. Above all else, it is pervaded by the attitude that history is a human-driven process that conforms to certain discoverable laws.

In the following excerpt, Guicciardini describes and evaluates the life of Lorenzo de' Medici (1449–1492), known as *the Magnificent.* Lorenzo was the grandson of Cosimo de' Medici, the head of a prosperous banking family who had achieved control over Florence in 1434 and maintained it down to his death in 1464. Under Cosimo's subtle but effective one-man rule, Florence reached a level of political and social stability that it had not known for quite awhile. Lorenzo inherited his family's mantle in 1469 and controlled the city for the next twenty-three years — a period that is often regarded as the high-water point of Florentine cultural creativity. Like his grandfather, Lorenzo controlled the republic of Florence indirectly through his well-placed partisans. The Florentines were not deceived by the charade, but most seem to have cheerfully acquiesced in an arrangement that brought prosperity and glory to their city.

Guicciardini was only nine years old when Lorenzo died in 1492, so he did not write from intimate personal knowledge. What he presents is largely a portrait of Lorenzo as remembered a decade and a half after his death. In light of the evils that befell Florence with the collapse of Medici fortunes in 1492, there was a tendency only a few years later to look back with longing to the era of Lorenzo the Magnificent as a golden age.

QUESTIONS FOR ANALYSIS

1. What does Guicciardini mean when he states that Lorenzo had "all those signs and evidence of virtue that are connected with civic life"?

2. What does Guicciardini mean when he refers to Lorenzo as a *universal man?*

3. The house of Medici initially rose to prominence in Florence because of its successful and far-flung banking interests. How did Lorenzo compromise that base of Medici power?

4. Guicciardini states that Lorenzo "desired glory and excellence more than any man." How did Lorenzo manifest that desire, and how did his quest for glory differ from that of the heroes of Froissart's account (Chapter 12, source 83) or Chrétien's de Troyes's Erec (Chapter 9, source 60)? What conclusions follow from your answers?

5. Did Lorenzo share any characteristics with Louis XI? If so, what were they, and were they significant? If significant, what might they suggest about these so-called New Rulers and their states?

6. Do you find any significant differences between Lorenzo and Louis XI? If so, how do you explain them?

7. Imagine that you have been commissioned to write a manual for late-fifteenth-century princes and monarchs. Based on sources 92 and 93, what advice would you include? Why?

The city enjoyed perfect peace. The citizens in power were united and close, and their regime was so powerful that no one dared oppose it. Every day, the people were treated to shows, feasts, and novelties; provisions abounded in the city, and all the trades prospered. Genius and ability flourished, for all men of arts, letters, and ability were welcomed and honored. At home, the city enjoyed complete peace and quiet; and abroad, the highest glory and reputation, . . . and it had become virtually the fulcrum of all Italy. Just then something happened that reversed everything, throwing not only the city but all Italy into confusion. In the year 1491, Lorenzo suffered a long illness which the doctors at first had judged to be of little importance. Perhaps they did not treat it with all the diligence they should have, for it continued and got worse. At any rate, on the [eighth] day of April, 1492, he departed this life. . . .

Lorenzo de' Medici was forty-three years of age when he died, and had ruled the city for twenty-three years. When his father Piero died in '69 he was only twenty — quite young, and somewhat under the tutelage of Messer Tommaso Soderini and some other elder statesmen. But within a very short time he gained strength and acquired reputation, and was able to rule the city as he wished. . . . Until his death, he ruled the city and controlled it as completely as if he had been its tyrant.[1] Because the greatness of this man was extraordinary and never equalled in Florence, and because his fame was very widespread both before and after his death, I do not think it will be out of place — in fact it may be very useful — if I describe in detail his manner and character. I do not, to be sure, know these things from experience, for when he died I was a little boy. But I do have them from authentic sources and from people worthy of faith; so that, unless I am deceived, what I am about to write is the pure truth.

Lorenzo was a man of many outstanding virtues. He also had several vices, some of them natural, some the products of necessity. He had so much authority that the city, one might say, was not free in his time; and yet it abounded in

---

[1]Meant here in the original sense of the Greek term: "one who governs without restriction of law or constitution." It does not necessarily mean a harsh or brutal ruler.

all the glories and happiness there can possibly be in a city that is free in name, but in fact tyrannized by one of its citizens. Assuredly, some of the things he did may be criticized. But his deeds were so outstanding and so great that they are far more admirable when they are studied than when they are heard, for through no fault of his, but rather because of the age and because of the custom of the time, they do not include those feats of arms and that military art and discipline which brought so much fame to the ancients. We will not read of a brilliant defense of a city, a notable capture of some stronghold, strategy in battle, or victory over his enemies. His accomplishments do not shine with the splendor of arms. But we will indeed find in him all those signs and evidence of virtue that are connected with civic life. No one, not even his enemies or those who maligned him, can deny that his was a great and singular mind. To deny it would be folly, for it is clearly proved by the fact that he ruled the city for twenty-three years, always increasing its power and glory. It is especially clear if we remember that Florence is very free in its speech and full of very scheming and restless minds. Moreover, the Florentine dominion is very small, incapable of satisfying all citizens with its offices, so that to satisfy a small part others must necessarily be excluded. His greatness is also attested by the friendship and credit he enjoyed among many princes both in Italy and beyond. . . . All this was due to nothing other than his ability to deal very skillfully and perceptively with these princes. Among

those who heard him, his greatness is attested by his very witty and perspicacious public and private speeches, through which he acquired great reputation at many times and in many places. . . . It is attested by the letters he dictated, so full of genius that one could hardly wish for more. And these accomplishments seemed all the more attractive for being accompanied by great eloquence and very elegant diction.

His judgment was sound and wise, but not of a quality comparable to his intellect. He committed several rash actions: there was the war against Volterra, in which, by trying to deprive the Volterrans of their alum mines, he forced them to rebel,[2] igniting a fire that could have turned Italy upside down, though as a matter of fact all came out well in the end.[3] After the events of '78 there might not have been a war if he had been more gentle with the pope and the king.[4] But his insistence on acting out fully the part of the injured party, and his unwillingness to minimize the offense, may well have caused that war, which put him and the city in such great danger. His trip to Naples was considered too bold and too hurried a decision, for he put himself into the hands of a king who was unreliable, completely faithless, and very much his enemy. The fact that both he and the city needed peace very badly might be used to excuse him; but still some people thought he could have brought it about just as easily by remaining in Florence, with greater security and with no less advantage.[5]

He desired glory and excellence more than any man, but he can be criticized for having carried

---

[2]In 1472.

[3]Volterra was captured and sacked in 1473.

[4]The Pazzi Conspiracy of 1478 was an attempt to rid Florence of Medici control through assassination. Spearheaded by the Pazzi family, it led to the death of Lorenzo's beloved brother Giuliano and Lorenzo's own wounding and narrow escape. The people of Florence rallied to Lorenzo's side, and in the riot that ensued, the archbishop* of Pisa, who was one of the plotters, was hanged. Pope Sixtus IV, who hated the Medici, declared everyone connected with the archbishop's death excommunicated* and placed Florence under *interdict* (a sentence forbidding celebration of mass* and administration of most sacraments*). King Ferrante of Naples seized the opportunity to invade Florentine territory as a papal* champion.

[5]In a bold move, Lorenzo went personally to Naples in December 1479 and secured a peace with King Ferrante. This effectively stripped Pope Sixtus of support, and in December 1481 the Florentines made their peace with the pope.

this desire even into unimportant matters. In versifying, in games, and in other pursuits he got very angry with anyone who equalled or imitated him. The desire was too strong in important matters too. He wanted to equal and compete with all the princes of Italy in everything, which displeased Signor Ludovico[6] a great deal. On the whole, though, his ambition was praiseworthy and brought him glory and fame everywhere, even outside Italy, for it caused him to strive to make the Florence of his time stand out above all other Italian cities in all arts and skills. He had a university founded in Pisa, principally for the study of letters. When people adduced many reasons to show that it could not have as many students as Padua or Pavia, he said he would be satisfied to have more faculty members than the others. In his time, all the most excellent and most famous men in Italy taught there and received very high salaries, for he avoided neither expense nor labor to get them. In Florence, the study of the humanities flourished under Messer Agnolo Poliziano, Greek under Messer Demetrio [Chalcondylas] and then under [Constantine] Lascaris, philosophy and art under Marsilio Ficino, Giorgio Benigno, Count Pico della Mirandola, and other excellent men. Lorenzo showed the same favor to poetry in the vernacular, to music, architecture, painting, sculpture, and to all the arts of mind and hand, so that the city overflowed with all these exquisite things. And these arts flourished all the more because Lorenzo, a universal man, could pass judgment and distinguish among men, so that they competed with one another to please him. Furthermore, there was his infinite liberality, which provided all talented men with livelihoods and with all the instruments necessary for their work. To give an example: when he decided to establish a Greek library, he sent the very learned Lascaris all the way to Greece to look for good ancient books.

The same liberality preserved his fame and his friendship with princes in Italy and abroad; for

he omitted no form of magnificence — no matter how costly — that might enable him to keep the favor of the powerful. The result was that at Lyons, Milan, Bruges, and other places where he had business interests, his magnificence and his gifts caused his expenses to multiply, whereas his profits diminished because his affairs were governed by men of little ability. . . .

Lorenzo was by nature very haughty. Not only did he not want anyone to contradict him, he wanted people to understand him almost intuitively, so that in important matters his words would be few and vague. In ordinary conversation he was very facetious and pleasant. In his home life he was modest rather than sumptuous, except for the banquets, at which he very lavishly honored many noble foreigners who came to Florence. He was very libidinous, completely carnal, and persistent in his love affairs, which lasted many years. Many thought that this so weakened his body that it caused him to die quite young. . . .

Some people considered him naturally cruel and vindictive on account of the severity he showed in the case of the Pazzi, imprisoning the innocent youths and forbidding the girls to marry even after so much blood had been shed. Nevertheless, that event was so bitter for him that his extraordinary resentment is not surprising. Moreover, we see that after he had been softened by time, he allowed the girls to marry and was satisfied to see the young Pazzi set free, to go and live outside the territory. We can see too from his other dealings that he was neither cruel nor bloodthirsty. His gravest and most troublesome fault was his suspiciousness. It was caused perhaps not so much by nature as by the recognition that he had to keep a republic subjugated, and that whatever had to be done needed to be done through the magistrates and according to the statutes of the city, with the appearance and external forms of liberty. At the beginning of his career, then, when he was starting to gain strength, he strove to keep down as much as pos-

---

[6]The duke of Milan — a rival prince.

sible those citizens whose nobility, wealth, power, or reputation he thought would cause them to be highly esteemed. If these men were of a family or background in which the state could have confidence, they were liberally bestowed with magistracies in the city, embassies, commissaries, and other such honors. But since he did not trust them, he chose as officials of the candidacy lists and taxes, privy to his most intimate secrets, men whom he had raised to reputation, men who would have had no power whatever without his support. . . .

This same suspiciousness made him see to it that powerful families did not become related through marriage. Indeed, he tried to pair people off in such a way that they would not give him cause to worry. At times, to avoid the marriages he feared, he would force some young man of quality to marry a woman who would normally have been unacceptable. Things came to such a pass that none except unimportant marriages were contracted without his participation and permission. This same distrust caused him to place a permanent chancellor in Rome, Naples, and Milan, to ensure that the ambassadors there would never depart from his wishes. The chancellor, a salaried public official, was to be at the service of the resident ambassador, but in direct touch with Lorenzo to keep him informed about what was going on. I do not want to label mis-

trust the fact that he moved about with a large number of armed guards, to whom he showed great favor, giving some of them hospitals and holy places; for the Pazzi conspiracy had caused that. Nevertheless, it was not the sort of thing typical of a republic and of a private citizen, but rather of a tyrant and a subjected city. In fact, we must conclude that under him the city was not free, even though it could not have had a better tyrant or a more pleasant one. His natural inclinations and goodness gave birth to an infinite number of good results; the exigencies of tyranny brought with them several evils, but these were moderate and never exceeded the limits of necessity. Very few abuses were the results of wilfulness or free intention. Although the men who were held down were glad he died, the men in power and even those who were sometimes offended by him were very sad, for they did not know where this change would lead. He was mourned by the populace and by the lower classes, who had constantly enjoyed abundance, pleasures, entertainments, and many feasts in his time. His death deeply grieved all those in Italy who excelled in letters, painting, sculpture, and similar arts, for they had either received highly paid commissions from him, or else they were held in all the greater esteem by other princes, who feared that if they stopped treating them well they would go to Lorenzo.

▼▼▼

The Arts

Guicciardini was not exaggerating when he stated that all of the arts flourished in Florence under the generous patronage of Lorenzo the Magnificent. In addition to his interest in classical scholarship, especially the study of Platonic philosophy as taught by Marsilio Ficino, Lorenzo was a talented poet and generously patronized poets at his court. In the fields of architecture, sculpture, and painting, the Medici family showed its favor to such geniuses as Brunelleschi, Alberti, Donatello, Fra Angelico, Botticelli, and the young Michelangelo. Medicean Florence was truly the center of one of the West's most significant periods of creativity in the arts.

As the first source indicates, one of *Quattrocento* (fifteenth-century) Florence's greatest glories was that it was the nursery for a literary-intellectual movement known as *Renaissance Humanism.* Fifteenth-century Humanism was rooted in the cult of Greco-Roman classical studies, and its devotees adopted a vigorous educational program predicated on the assumption that classical forms, standards, and models were the surest guides to proper human expression and behavior. Although developed first in Italy, Renaissance Humanism crossed the Alps and deeply influenced Northern Europe's literary and artistic circles by the end of the fifteenth century.

In the first selection, we will look at the thought of Leonardo Bruni, one of Florence's early champions of the study of the humane arts. In the second source, which juxtaposes two pieces of visual art, we shall see how the Gothic North created brilliant works of sculpture and painting that combined deep piety with a fast-developing humanistic fascination for naturalistic expression, especially in regard to the human body.

What Studies Befit a Lady Humanist?
▼▼▼

94 ▼ *Leonardo Bruni,*
ON THE STUDY OF LITERATURE

Leonardo Bruni (1370–1444), sometimes called *Leonardo Aretino,* after his native town of Arezzo, was the central figure of Florentine Humanism in the first half of the fifteenth century. Bruni moved to Florence as a young man, where he became an expert in Latin and Greek literature. After spending ten years as a secretary at the papal* court, he returned to Florence, never to leave it again. In 1427 he attained the high civic office of chancellor of Florence, a post he held until his death. In addition to his political activities, Bruni was an avid collector of ancient manuscripts, an editor and translator of classical Greek and Latin texts, and a prolific writer on a wide variety of topics. His *History of the Florentine People,* which traced the history of his adopted city from antiquity to 1404, deeply influenced many subsequent historians of Florence, including Guicciardini (source 93).

The following selection comes from an essay that Bruni composed around 1424 and dedicated to Lady Battista Malatesta of Montefeltro (ca. 1384–1447), a famous female scholar and wife of the lord of Pesaro. Bruni presented his essay in the form of a personal letter but intended it for general circulation.

QUESTIONS FOR ANALYSIS

1. Describe the topic, theme, and tone of this essay. Why do you think Bruni composed it?
2. According to Bruni, what subjects of study are inappropriate for a woman? Why? What subjects are appropriate? Why? What conclusions do you draw from these answers?

3. Compose a commentary on this letter by Christine de Pisan (source 90).
4. The visual arts were reaching levels of brilliance at this time in Italy. What place does Bruni accord the visual arts in his humanistic program? What about science and mathematics? What place does he accord them? What do your answers suggest about fifteenth-century Humanism?
5. What is Bruni's overall humanistic program, and what is its underlying philosophy?
6. Fifteenth-century Florentine Humanism has been characterized as secular.* On the basis of this essay, does that characterization seem appropriate? Why or why not?

I feel myself constrained, dear lady, by many successive reports of your wonderful virtues to write to you in commendation of the perfect development of those innate powers of which I have heard so much that is excellent, or, if that is too much, at least to urge you, through these literary efforts of mine, to bring them to such a perfection. There is, indeed, no lack of examples of women renowned for their letters and their eloquence that I could mention to exhort you to excellence. Cornelia, the daughter of Scipio, wrote letters in the most elegant of styles, which letters survived for many centuries after her death.[1] The poetical works of Sappho were held in the highest honor among the Greeks for their unique eloquence and literary skill.[2] Then, too, there was Aspasia, a learned lady of the time of Socrates, who was outstanding in eloquence and literature, and from whom even so great a philosopher as Socrates did not blush to admit he had learned certain things.[3] I could mention still others, but let these three stand sufficient as examples of the most renowned women. Be encouraged and elevated by their excellence! It is not fitting that such understanding and intellectual power as you possess were given you in vain, not fitting that you should be satisfied with mediocrity; such gifts expect and encourage the highest excellence. And your glory will be all the brighter, for those other women flourished in ages when there was an abundance of learned persons whose very number decreases the estimation in which we must hold them, while you live in these times when learning has so far decayed that it is regarded as positively miraculous to meet a learned man, let alone a woman. By learning, however, I do not mean that confused and vulgar sort such as is possessed by those who nowadays profess theology,[4] but a legitimate and liberal kind which joins literary skill with factual knowledge, a learning Lactantius possessed, and Augustine, and Jerome,[5] all of whom were finished men of letters as well as great theologians. It is shameful, by contrast, how very little modern theologians know of letters.

But I digress. Let me rather pursue our discourse, not for you to be instructed by me (for of that I imagine you have no need), but simply for

---

[1] Born around 190 B.C., she was the daughter of Scipio Africanus, a war hero, and mother of two political reformers, the Gracchi brothers.

[2] Sometimes called *the tenth muse,* Sappho of Lesbos, who flourished in the late seventh and early sixth century B.C., was classical Greece's greatest love poet.

[3] Aspasia was a fifth-century B.C. Athenian woman of extraordinary accomplishment and genius who held a literary-philosophical salon in her house. Socrates (ca. 469–399 B.C.) is considered to be Greece's first great moral philosopher.

[4] Those people who have received their doctorates in theology from universities that Bruni considers to be intellectually and spiritually sterile, particularly the schools of Northern Europe.

[5] Three fourth- and fifth-century Christian moralists and writers. All three were Latin rhetoricians,* as well as Christian apologists. For Lactantius, see Chapter 1, source 1; for Augustine, see source 4.

you to understand my views on the subject of literary study.

The person aiming at the kind of excellence which I am calling you to needs first, I think, to acquire no slender or common, but a wide and exact, even *recherché* familiarity with literature. Without this basis, no one can build himself any high or splendid thing. The one who lacks knowledge of literature will neither understand sufficiently the writings of the learned, nor will he be able, if he should himself attempt to write, to avoid making a laughingstock of himself. To attain this knowledge, elementary instruction has its place, but much more important is our own effort and study. . . .

The most important rule of study is to see to it that we study only those works that are written by the best and most approved authors, and avoid the crude and ignorant writings which only ruin and degrade our natural abilities. The reading of clumsy and corrupt writers imbues the reader with their own vices, and infests his mind with a similar corruption. Study is, so to speak, the pabulum of the mind by which the intellect is trained and nourished. For this reason, just as gastronomes are careful in the choice of what they put in their stomachs, so those who wish to preserve purity of taste will only allow certain reading to enter their minds.

This then will be our first study: to read only the best and most approved authors. Our second will be to bring to this reading a keen critical sense. The reader must study the reasons why the words are placed as they are, and the meaning and force of each element of the sentence, the smaller as well as the larger; he must thoroughly understand the force of the several particles whose idiom and usage he will copy from the authors he reads.

Hence a woman who enjoys sacred literature and who wished to observe stylistic propriety will take up Augustine and Jerome and any authors she finds similar to them. . . . But the greatest of all those who have ever written of the Christian religion, the one who excels them all with his brilliance and richness of expression, is Lactantius Firmianus, without doubt the most eloquent of all Christian authors, and the one whose eloquence and technique are best able to nourish and educate the type of ability I am considering. . . . A woman, on the other hand, who enjoys secular literature will choose Cicero, a man — Good God! — so eloquent! so rich in expression! so polished! so unique in every *genus* of glory![6] Next will be Vergil, the delight and ornament of our literature,[7] then Livy and Sallust[8] and the other poets and writers in their order. With them she will train and strengthen her taste, and she will be careful, when she is obliged to say or write something, to use no word she has not first met in one of these authors. . . .

Having said that genuine learning was a combination of literary skill and factual knowledge, we have set forth our view of what literary skill is. Let us now, therefore, say something about knowledge. Here again I have in mind someone whose intellect shows the greatest promise, who despises no branch of learning, who holds all the world as her province, who, in a word, burns marvellously with a desire for knowledge and understanding. An ardent and well-motivated person like this needs, I think, to be applauded and spurred on in some directions, while in others she must be discouraged and held back. Disciplines there are, of whose rudiments some knowledge is fitting, yet whereof to obtain the mastery is a thing by no means glorious. In geometry and arithmetic,[9] for example, if she waste a great deal of time worrying their subtle obscurities, I should seize her and tear her away from them. I should do the same in astrology, and even, perhaps, in the art of rhetoric.* I say this with

---

[6]Cicero (106–43 B.C.) was a Roman politician, orator, and essayist.

[7]Vergil (70–19 B.C.) was Rome's greatest poet and the writer most admired by medieval European students of Latin literature.

[8]Two first-century B.C. Roman historians.

[9]Along with astrology and music, arithmetic and geometry comprised the quantitative portion of the Seven Liberal Arts.*

some hesitation, since if any living men have labored in this art, I would profess myself to be of their number. But there are many things here to be taken into account, the first of which is the person whom I am addressing. For why should the subtleties of the *status,* the *epicheiremata,* the *krinomena,*[10] and a thousand other rhetorical conundrums consume the powers of a woman, who never sees the forum?[11] That art of delivery, which the Greeks call *hypocrisis* and we *pronunciatio,* and which Demosthenes[12] said was the first, the second, and the third most important acquirement of the orator, so far is that from being the concern of a woman that if she should gesture energetically with her arms as she spoke and shout with violent emphasis, she would probably be thought mad and put under restraint. The contests of the forum, like those of warfare and battle, are the sphere of men. Hers is not the task of learning to speak for and against witnesses, for and against torture, for and against reputation; she will not practice the commonplaces, the syllogisms, the sly anticipation of an opponent's arguments. She will, in a word, leave the rough-and-tumble of the forum entirely to men.

When, then, do I encourage her, when do I spur her on? Just when she devotes herself to divinity and moral philosophy. It is there I would beg her to spread her wings, there apply her mind, there spend her vigils. It will be worth our while to dwell on this in some detail. First, let the Christian woman desire for herself a knowledge of sacred letters. What better advice could I give? Let her search much, weigh much, acquire much in this branch of study. But let her fondness be for the older authors. The moderns, if they are good men, she will honor and revere, but she should pay scant attention to their writings. A woman of literature will find no instruction in them that is not in St. Augustine, and

St. Augustine, moreover, unlike them, has the diction of an educated person, and one well worth attending to.

Nor would I have her rest content with a knowledge of sacred literature; let her broaden her interests into the secular studies as well. Let her know what the most excellent minds among the philosophers have taught about moral philosophy, what their doctrines are concerning continence, temperance, modesty, justice, courage, liberality. She should understand their beliefs about happiness: whether virtue is in itself sufficient for happiness, or whether torture, poverty, exile, or prison can affect it. Whether, when such misfortunes befall the blessed, they are made miserable thereby, or whether they simply take away happiness without inducing actual misery. Whether human felicity consists in pleasure and the absence of pain, as Epicurus would have it, or in moral worth, as Zeno believed, or in the exercise of virtue, which was Aristotle's view.[13] Believe me, such subjects as these are beautiful and intellectually rewarding. They are valuable not only for the guidance they give in life, but they also supply us with a marvelous stock of knowledge which can be used in every variety of oral and written expression.

These two subjects, then, divinity and moral philosophy, will be her most important goals, the *raisons d'être* of her studies. Other subjects will be related to them in proportion as they contribute to them or to their embellishment. . . .

To the aforesaid subjects there should first be joined, in my view, a knowledge of history, which is a subject no scholar should neglect. It is a fit and seemly thing to be familiar with the origins and progress of one's own nation, and with the deeds in peace and in war of great kings and free peoples. Knowledge of the past gives guidance

---

[10]Technical terms in rhetoric.
[11]The place of public, political debate.
[12]A fourth-century B.C. Greek orator.

[13]All were fourth-century B.C. Greek philosophers. Zeno (332–262 B.C.) was the founder of Stoicism; Epicurus (341–270 B.C.) was the founder of Epicureanism; and Aristotle (384–322 B.C.) was the most admired Greek philosopher in the West during the twelfth and thirteenth centuries and Bruni's favorite thinker.

to our counsels and our practical judgment, and the consequences of similar undertakings [in the past] will encourage or deter us according to our circumstances in the present. History, moreover, is the most commodious source of that stock of examples of outstanding conduct with which it is fitting frequently to embellish our conversation. Then, too, some of the outstanding historians are distinguished and polished writers as well, and so make valuable reading for literary purposes: Livy, I mean, and Sallust and Tacitus, . . . and especially Julius Caesar, who described his own deeds with the greatest ease and elegance in his *Commentaries*.[14] These, then, the woman of high promise will go on to acquire, the more so as they make pleasant reading. For here there are no subtleties to be unravelled, no knotty *quaestiones*[15] to be untied; only narrations of facts that are easy to grasp, and, once grasped (at least by an outstanding mind such as I am considering), will never be forgotten.

I would further urge her not to neglect the orators. Where else is virtue praised with such passion, and vice condemned with such ferocity? It is the orators who teach us to praise the good deed and to hate the bad; it is they who teach us how to soothe, encourage, stimulate, or deter. All these things the philosophers do, it is true, but in some special way anger, mercy and the arousal and pacification of the mind are completely within the power of the orator. Then, too, those figures of speech and thought, which like stars or torches illuminate our diction and give it distinction, are the proper tools of the orator which we borrow from them when we speak or write, and turn to our use as the occasion demands. In sum, all the richness, power, and polish in our expression, its lifeblood, as it were, we derive from the orators.

The poets, too, I would have her read and understand. This is a knowledge . . . which all great men have possessed. . . . The poets have many wise and useful things to say about life and how it should be lived; in them are to be found the principles and causes of nature and birth — the seeds as it were, of all teachings — by their antiquity and their reputation for wisdom they possess a high authority, by their elegance they have acquired a splendor and a distinction, by their nobility and liberality they have so far made themselves a worthy study for free men, that he who knows them not seems to be something of a rustic. . . .

The wisest of the ancients tell us that the divine mind dwells in the poets, and that they are called *vates*[16] because they speak not so much of their own accord as through a divine inspiration, in a kind of higher mental state. Though here Vergil appeals to the authority of the Cumaean Sibyl,[17] who, as Lactantius shows, had predicted the advent of Christ.[18] The Sibyl then did prophesy Christ's coming, but did not clearly reveal the time when He would come; but Vergil, born many ages after the Sibyl, recognized that that time was now come and announced in wonder and amazement "the new offspring sent from Heaven." And still some say we should not read the poets, that we should never taste a branch of literature that I might with exact truth pronounce divine! Such persons are most often those who, having no training in polite learning themselves, in consequence neither understand nor value in literature any excellent thing. My view of the matter is that poetical knowledge is of primary importance in our education, alike for its utility, as aforesaid — that wide and various acquaintance we get with facts — and for the brilliance of its language. . . . For the moment,

---

[14]Julius Caesar (100–44 B.C.) composed a self-serving history of his military campaigns in Gaul.

[15]The conundrums debated by theologians and lawyers in the universities.

[16]A word that means both *poet* and *prophet*.

[17]A famous female oracle of Cumae, in Greek Sicily.

[18]In the fourth of his ten *Eclogues* (or more correctly, *Bucolic Poems*), which he composed between 42 and 38 B.C., a time of vicious civil war in the late Roman Republic, Vergil writes that his hopes for future peace lie in a child, perhaps yet to be born. Later Christian writers interpreted this as an unconscious, God-inspired prophecy of the birth of Jesus.

this only would I have be understood: that it is to poetry, more than to any other branch of letters, that nature attracts us; that it possesses utility, pleasure, and nobility; and that that man who has no knowledge of it can by no means be said to be liberally educated.

I have, I realize, gone on about poetry rather more than I had at first intended; once started, it is more difficult to control the multitude of ideas that seem to come thronging around of their own accord than to mind what it is one should be saying. But I was the more inclined to do so as I am aware that a prince of your house, if he should happen to hear of this discourse of mine, will be the first to object to it.[19] He is, to be sure, a man of the noblest birth and outstanding for the number and greatness of his virtues, but a stubborn fellow in debate, who is reluctant to abandon a position once taken. So having sometime declared that we should not read the poets, he pursues his error even unto death. . . . "I am a Christian," my critic says; "their mores are not mine." As though honor and moral seriousness were something different then from what they are now! As though the same and even worse cannot be found in the Holy Scriptures! Do we not find there depicted Samson's wild lusts, when he put his mighty head in a wench's lap and was shorn of his strength-giving hair?[20] Is this not poetical? And is this not shameful? I pass over in silence the shocking crime of Lot's daughters, the detestable filthiness of the Sodomites,[21] two circumstances that I, praiser of poets though I be, can hardly suffer myself to relate. Why speak of David's passion for Bathsheba, his crime against Uriah,[22] Solomon's fratricide and his flock of concubines?[23] All of these stories are wicked, obscene, and disgusting, yet do we say that the Bible is not therefore to be read? Surely not. Then neither are the poets to be rejected because of

the occasional reference to human pleasures. For my part, whenever I read Vergil's account of the *affaire* of Dido and Aeneas,[24] I am so lost in admiration of his poetical genius that I scarcely attend to the thing itself, knowing it to be a fiction. Other poetical fictions affect me the same way. My concupiscence is not aroused, since I know the circumstances to be fictional and allegorical in intent. When I read the Scriptures, on the contrary, knowing the facts to be true, I suffer temptation. But I don't insist; I am perfectly willing to abandon a little of my ground, especially given that I am addressing a woman. I admit that, just as there are distinctions between nobles and commoners, so too among the poets there are certain grades of respectability. If somewhere a comic poet has made his theme too explicit, if a satirist excoriates vice a little too frankly, let her avert her gaze and not read them. For these are the plebian poets. The aristocrats of poesy, Vergil, I mean, and Seneca and Statius[25] and the others of their sort, must be read if she is not to do without the greatest ornaments of literature. And without them, she may not hope for glory.

In sum, then, the excellence I speak of comes only from a wide and various knowledge. It is needful to read and comprehend a great deal, and to bestow great pains on the philosophers, the poets, the orators and historians and all the other writers. For thus comes that full and sufficient knowledge we need to appear eloquent, well-rounded, refined, and widely cultivated. Needed too is a well-developed and respectable literary skill of our own. For the two together reinforce each other and are mutually beneficial. Literary skill without knowledge is useless and sterile; and knowledge, however extensive, fades into the shadows without the glorious lamp of literature. Of what advantage is it to know many fine things

---

[19]Carlo Malatesta (d. 1429), the ruler of Rimini.
[20]The Bible, the Book of Judges, 16:4–21.
[21]Genesis, 19:1–38.
[22]2 Samuel, 11:1–27.
[23]1 Kings, 2:13–25 and 11:1–8.

[24]The love affair between Queen Dido of Carthage and Aeneas, the Trojan prince who became the progenitor of the Romans. The story appears in Vergil's *Aeneid*.
[25]Both were first-century A.D. men of letters.

if one has neither the ability to talk of them with distinction or write of them with praise? And so, literary skill and factual knowledge are in a manner of speaking wedded to each other. It was the two joined together that advanced the glory and fame of those ancients whose memory we venerate. . . .

To conclude: the intellect that aspires to the best, I maintain, must be in this way doubly educated, and it is for the sake of acquiring these two knowledges that we mass up our reading; yet we must also take stock of the time at our disposal, devoting ourselves only to the most important and the most useful subjects, and not wasting time with the obscure and profitless. It is religion and moral philosophy that ought to be our particular studies, I think, and the rest studied in relation to them as their handmaids, in proportion as they aid or illustrate their meaning; and it is with this in mind that we must fix upon the poets, orators and other writers. In literary study care should be taken to employ noble precepts and long and perceptive observation, and never to read any but the best and most approved books.

Such are my opinions about the study of literature, though if you hold different views, I shall willingly yield to you. For I do not write as master to pupil (I should not presume so much), but simply as one of the crowd of your admirers, who want to unite my convictions with yours and, as they say, cheer the runner on to victory. Farewell.

Visions of Death and Life
▼▼▼

95 ▼ *Anonymous,*
VANITY: ALLEGORY ON THE
TRANSITORINESS OF LIFE, and
Martin Schongauer,
THE ADORATION OF THE SHEPHERDS

Northern European painters and sculptors of the Late Middle Ages brought Gothic naturalism (Chapter 9, sources 57 and 58) to new heights of technical artistry. Simultaneously, they stressed the narrative qualities of visual art, probably under the influence of Europe's many popular vernacular prose genres. The two works shown here, each an excellent example of fifteenth-century northern religious art at its best, illustrate both of those elements and, when juxtaposed, reveal the dual vision of that ambiguous century. The first piece, a small ivory figurine by an unknown French sculptor, dates from around 1450 and is entitled *Vanity: Allegory on the Transitoriness of Life.* As you study this allegorical sculpture, keep in mind that the primary meaning of the Latin word *vanitas* is "emptiness." "Excessive pride" or "conceit" is a secondary meaning. The second work of art, *The Adoration of the Shepherds,* was painted by the Alsatian German artist Martin Schongauer (ca. 1450–1491) between 1475 and 1480 and originally served as the central panel in an altarpiece for a private home.

QUESTIONS FOR ANALYSIS

1. What can we infer about the age and status of the woman in the French sculpture? Whom or what does she represent?
2. Consider the skeleton. What does it represent, and what is it saying to the woman by its posture and gestures? What choices do you think the woman is contemplating?
3. What is the story and message of this work of art?
4. Compare this female nude with Giselbertus's *Eve* (Chapter 9, source 56). What conclusions do you reach?
5. Compare the Virgin Mary, Joseph, her husband, and the shepherds in Schongauer's nativity scene with the woman and the skeleton in the French sculpture. What are the similarities? The differences? Which are more significant? Why?
6. What is the story and message of Schongauer's work?
7. Compare Schongauer's work with Strasbourg Cathedral's *Dormition of the Virgin* (Chapter 9, source 58). What conclusions do you draw from that comparative analysis?
8. How, if at all, do the French ivory and Schongauer's painting represent two complementary visions of life?
9. How, if at all, do either or both masterpieces seem to share the humanistic spirit that is evident in Bruni's letter to Lady Battista Malatesta?

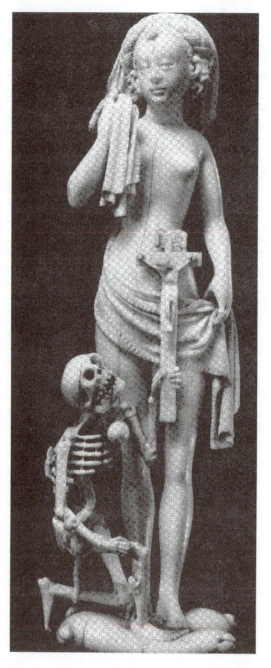

Vanity: Allegory on the Transitoriness of Life

The Adoration of the Shepherds

▼▼▼

New Geographic Horizons

The loss of the West's last crusader strongholds in Southwest Asia in the last decade of the thirteenth century, the onslaught of the Eurasianwide pandemic of the Black Death, massive economic depression that affected lands and peoples throughout Eurasia, the breakup of the Mongol Empire around the middle of the fourteenth century, the disruption of the ancient Silk Road routes of Inner Asia by the armies of the Turkish conqueror Timur the Lame (Tamerlane) between 1369 and 1405, the increasing xenophobia of China's Ming Dynasty (r. 1368–1644), and the successes of the Ottoman Turks, who swept through Anatolia* and the Balkans, finally capturing Constantinople in 1453 — all combined to block effectively by 1400 Western Europe's direct access to East Asia by way of the overland routes that had opened up in the thirteenth century (Chapter 11, source 78).

To be sure, there was still a trickle of Western contact with Central, South, and East Asia in the early and mid fifteenth century. Venetians held Tana at the mouth of Ukraine's Sea of Azov until at least the mid fifteenth century, and Caffa in the Black Sea's Crimean Peninsula remained a Genoese base for farther inland trade until Turks conquered it in 1475. A handful of European merchants and adventurers even managed to reach the waters of the Indian Ocean. Niccolo Conti of Venice left home for Syria in 1419 but wound up traveling to India, Ceylon, Sumatra, Java, Burma, Malaya, and finally back to the Holy Land by way of the Indian Ocean and Red Sea, arriving back in Venice in 1444. Nevertheless, the heady days of regular mercantile and missionary contact with the fabled land of Cathay, as exemplified by the well-known adventures of the Venetian Marco Polo (ca. 1253–1324), were now at an end — at least for the moment.

Not realizing that the Mongols no longer ruled China, Europeans dreamed of re-establishing contact with the Great Khan, whom Marco Polo had served for seventeen years, and even possibly reuniting with the khan in a final crusade to push back Islam and to recover Jerusalem. With the land routes now blocked, it fell to the kingdoms of Iberia that had ports on the Atlantic to attempt contact by way of the ocean. The results of their attempts proved quite extraordinary. During the last decade of the fifteenth century, Spain supported an enterprise that resulted in the European discovery of the Americas, and Portugal pushed into the Indian Ocean by way of Africa and also stumbled across Brazil in 1500.

When these late-fifteenth-century adventurers sailed out into the Atlantic and Indian Oceans, they expected to find fabulous lands and exotic peoples. Although they failed to find many of the wonders that their books and legends had prepared them for, the marvels they did discover were no less astounding.

The Marvels of Nature
▼▼▼

96 ▼ Johann Bämler,
WONDROUS FOUNTAINS AND PEOPLES

Here we see a woodcut from Conrad of Megenburg's *Book of Nature,* which the Augsburg printer Johann Bämler printed in 1475, more than a century after the work's composition, and subsequently reissued five times before 1499. Conrad (ca. 1309–1374), a scholar and churchman, composed his work in German around 1350, freely adapting it from the thirteenth-century Latin encyclopedia *On the Nature of Things,* by the Dominican friar* Thomas of Cantimpré (ca. 1201–1271). Compiled between about 1228 and 1244 from Hebrew, Greek, Latin, and Arabic sources, Thomas of Cantimpré's work was a massive compendium of all that was known and believed about natural phenomena and the properties of nature's creatures. The work was immensely popular and quite influential in the Arts faculties of Europe's universities, especially at Paris, where Conrad of Megenberg taught between 1334 and 1342. Conrad's adaptation of this one-hundred-year-old classic potentially made the subject of natural history available to those Germans who could read their native tongue but not Latin. Bämler's six printings of the book more than a century later made that possibility a reality, as the new European printing press enabled the Augsburg printer to produce hundreds of copies of the work.

At the very end of his book, Megenberg takes up the topics of marvelous streams of water and fantastic people. The former include a fountain in mythical Arcadia, from which pregnant women drink in order to prevent miscarriage, and springs that flow with hot water, which has been heated by passing through sulpher and chaulk. To illustrate some of these wonders of nature, Bämler included a hand-colored woodcut print. Following the regulations of the guild of printers to which he belonged, Bämler personally drew, carved, and colored all of his woodcuts.

QUESTIONS FOR ANALYSIS

1. Describe each scene, person, and item. What, for example, is the woman doing at the top-center of the page? What sort of marvelous individuals parade across the page? Two hints: (1) The items that are springing out of the top of the fountain in the upper-righthand corner are colored red; (2) In his text, Megenberg writes that in certain regions, especially Burgundy, women develop goiters the size of pumpkins that hang down to their navels.
2. Why do you think nine of these individuals are naked?
3. What is the overall message of this illustration, and what does it suggest about late-medieval Europe's vision of the world?
4. Compare this source with what Mandeville (Chapter 12, source 86) tells us about the faraway world of South and East Asia. Which strike you as more significant, the similarities or dissimilarities? What conclusions follow from your answer?

Woodcut from Book of Nature

"With the Royal Standard Unfurled"

▼▼▼

97 ▼ *Christopher Columbus,*
A LETTER CONCERNING RECENTLY
DISCOVERED ISLANDS

The marriage in 1469 of Isabella, future queen of Castile-León (r. 1474–1504), with Ferdinand, heir to the kingdom of Aragon (r. 1482–1516), promised the potential fusion of the Iberian peninsula's two largest and most prosperous kingdoms into a single bloc, and when they succeeded to their respective realms, that promise was realized. With their conquest of Granada, the last independent Muslim enclave in Iberia, on January 2, 1492, Isabella I and Ferdinand V, "the Catholic Monarchs" (as the papacy* entitled them), had laid the basis for a new state that would dominate European affairs for the next century. Indeed, sixteenth-century Spain was one of the richest and most powerful empires in the entire world, by virtue of its far-flung overseas colonies, especially those in the Americas.

Spain's emergence as the dominant power in the Americas is forever associated with the name of a single mariner — Christopher Columbus (1451–1506). Sponsored by the "king and queen of the Spains," as he styled them, this Genoese sea captain sailed westward into the Atlantic, seeking a new route to the empires of East Asia described by John Mandeville (Chapter 12, source 86), Marco Polo, and others, whose books of travels Columbus had avidly read and digested. On October 12, 1492, his fleet of three ships dropped anchor at a small Bahamian island, which Columbus claimed for Spain, naming it *San Salvador.* The fleet then sailed to the larger islands of Cuba, which he named *Juana,* and Hispaniola (where the modern nations of Haiti and the Dominican Republic are located), which he named *Española.*

After exploring these two main islands and establishing the post of Navidad del Señor on Española, Columbus departed for Spain in January 1493. On his way home, the admiral prepared a preliminary account of his expedition to the "Indies" for Luis de Santángel, a counselor to King Ferdinand and one of Columbus's more enthusiastic supporters. In composing the letter, Columbus borrowed heavily from his official ship's log, often lifting passages verbatim. When he landed in Lisbon, Portugal, in early March, Columbus dispatched the letter overland, expecting it to precede him to the Spanish royal court in faraway Barcelona, where Santángel would communicate its contents to the two monarchs. The admiral was not disappointed. His triumphal reception at the court in April was proof that the letter had served its purpose.

As you analyze the document, consider several facts. The admiral was returning with only two of his vessels. He had lost his flagship, the *Santa María,* when it was wrecked on a reef off present-day Haiti on Christmas Day. Also, many of Columbus's facts and figures reflect more his enthusiasm than dispassionate analysis. For instance, his estimate of the dimensions of the two main islands he explored grossly exaggerates their sizes, and his optimistic report of the wide availability of such riches as gold, spices, cotton, and mastic was not borne out by subsequent explorations and colonization. Although he obtained items of gold and received plenty of reports of nearby gold mines, the metal was rare in the islands. Moreover, the only indigenous spice proved to be the fiery chili pepper, the wild cotton was excellent but not plentiful, and mastic, an eastern Mediterranean aromatic gum, was not native to the Caribbean.

QUESTIONS FOR ANALYSIS

1. How does Columbus indicate that these lands are worth the careful attention of the Spanish monarchs?
2. What does Columbus's description of the physical attributes of the islands suggest about some of the motives for his voyage?
3. Often the eyes only see what the mind prepares them to see. What evidence is there that Columbus saw what he wanted to see and discovered what he expected to discover? In other words, how had his environment prepared Columbus to see and interpret what he encountered in the Caribbean?
4. What evidence suggests that Columbus's letter was a carefully crafted piece of self-promotion by a person determined to prove he had reached the Indies?
5. Notwithstanding the obvious self-promotion, is there any evidence that Columbus also attempted to present an objective and fairly accurate account of what he had seen and experienced? In other words, to what extent, if at all, can we trust his account?
6. What do the admiral's admitted actions regarding the natives and the ways in which he describes these people allow us to conclude about his attitudes toward these "Indians" and his plans for them?
7. What does this letter tell us about the culture of the Tainos on the eve of European expansion into their world? Does Columbus tell us anything about these people that doesn't seem to ring totally true? What do you infer from your answer to that latter question?

Sir, as I know that you will be pleased at the great victory with which Our Lord has crowned my voyage, I write this to you, from which you will learn how in thirty-three days, I passed from the Canary Islands to the Indies with the fleet which the most illustrious king and queen, our sovereigns, gave to me. And there I found very many islands filled with people[1] innumerable, and of them all I have taken possession for their highnesses, by proclamation made and with the royal standard unfurled, and no opposition was offered to me. To the first island which I found, I gave the name *San Salvador,*[2] in remembrance of the Divine Majesty, Who has marvelously be-

---

[1]The Tainos, a tribal branch of the Arawak language family. Arawak speakers inhabited an area from the Amazon River to the Caribbean.

[2]The Holy Savior — Jesus Christ.

stowed all this; the Indians call it "Guanahani." To the second, I gave the name *Isla de Santa Maria de Concepción;*[3] to the third, *Fernandina;* to the fourth, *Isabella;* to the fifth, *Isla Juana,*[4] and so to each one I gave a new name.

When I reached Juana, I followed its coast to the westward, and I found it to be so extensive that I thought that it must be the mainland, the province of Catayo.[5] And since there were neither towns nor villages on the seashore, but only small hamlets, with the people of which I could not have speech, because they all fled immediately, I went forward on the same course, thinking that I should not fail to find great cities and towns. And, at the end of many leagues,[6] seeing that there was no change and that the coast was bearing me northwards, which I wished to avoid, since winter was already beginning and I proposed to make from it to the south, and as moreover the wind was carrying me forward, I determined not to wait for a change in the weather and retraced my path as far as a certain harbor known to me. And from that point, I sent two men inland to learn if there were a king or great cities. They traveled three days' journey and found an infinity of small hamlets and people without number, but nothing of importance. For this reason, they returned.

I understood sufficiently from other Indians, whom I had already taken,[7] that this land was nothing but an island. And therefore I followed its coast eastwards for one hundred and seven leagues to the point where it ended. And from that cape, I saw another island, distant eighteen leagues from the former, to the east, to which I at once gave the name "Española." And I went there and followed its northern coast, as I had in the case of Juana, to the eastward for one hundred and eighty-eight great leagues in a straight line. This island and all the others are very fertile to a limitless degree, and this island is extremely so. In it there are many harbors on the coast of the sea, beyond comparison with others which I know in Christendom, and many rivers, good and large, which is marvelous. Its lands are high, and there are in it very many sierras and very lofty mountains, beyond comparison with the island of Teneriffe.[8] All are most beautiful, of a thousand shapes, and all are accessible and filled with trees of a thousand kinds and tall, and they seem to touch the sky. And I am told that they never lose their foliage, as I can understand, for I saw them as green and as lovely as they are in Spain in May, and some of them were flowering, some bearing fruit, and some in another stage, according to their nature. And the nightingale was singing and other birds of a thousand kinds in the month of November there where I went. There are six or eight kinds of palm, which are a wonder to behold on account of their beautiful variety, but so are the other trees and fruits and plants. In it are marvelous pine groves, and there are very large tracts of cultivatable lands, and there is honey, and there are birds of many kinds and fruits in great diversity. In the interior are mines of metals, and the population is without number. Española is a marvel.

The sierras and mountains, the plains and arable lands and pastures, are so lovely and rich for planting and sowing, for breeding cattle of every kind, for building towns and villages. The harbors of the sea here are such as cannot be believed to exist unless they have been seen, and so with the rivers, many and great, and good waters, the majority of which contain gold. In the trees and fruits and plants, there is a great difference from those of Juana. In this island, there are many spices and great mines of gold and of other metals.

---

[3]Holy Mary of the Immaculate Conception — the Virgin Mary, whom Catholics believe was so sinless that she was conceived without the stain of Original Sin (the sin of Adam and Eve) on her soul.
[4]Named for Prince Juan, heir apparent of Castile.
[5]The Spanish term for *Cathay,* or China.

[6]A league is three miles.
[7]Columbus took seven Tainos on board at San Salvador to instruct them in Spanish and use them as guides and interpreters.
[8]One of the Canary Islands.

The people of this island, and of all the other islands which I have found and of which I have information, all go naked, men and women, as their mothers bore them,[9] although some women cover a single place with the leaf of a plant or with a net of cotton which they make for the purpose. They have no iron or steel or weapons, nor are they fitted to use them, not because they are not well built men and of handsome stature, but because they are very marvelously timorous. They have no other arms than weapons made of canes, cut in seeding time, to the ends of which they fix a small sharpened stick. And they do not dare to make use of these, for many times it has happened that I have sent ashore two or three men to some town to have speech, and countless people have come out to them, and as soon as they have seen my men approaching they have fled, even a father not waiting for his son. And this, not because ill has been done to anyone; on the contrary, at every point where I have been and have been able to have speech, I have given to them of all that I had, such as cloth and many other things, without receiving anything for it; but so they are, incurably timid. It is true that, after they have been reassured and have lost their fear, they are so guileless and so generous with all they possess, that no one would believe it who has not seen it. They never refuse anything which they possess, if it be asked of them; on the contrary, they invite anyone to share it, and display as much love as if they would give their hearts, and whether the thing be of value or whether it be of small price, at once with whatever trifle of whatever kind it may be that is given to them,

with that they are content.[10] I forbade that they should be given things so worthless as fragments of broken crockery and scraps of broken glass, and ends of straps, although when they were able to get them, they fancied that they possessed the best jewel in the world. So it was found that a sailor for a strap received gold to the weight of two and a half *castellanos*,[11] and others much more for other things which were worth much less. As for new *blancas*,[12] for them they would give everything which they had, although it might be two or three *castellanos'* weight of gold or an *arroba*[13] or two of spun cotton. . . . They took even the pieces of the broken hoops of the wine barrels and, like savages, gave what they had, so that it seemed to me to be wrong and I forbade it. And I gave a thousand handsome good things, which I had brought, in order that they might conceive affection, and more than that, might become Christians and be inclined to the love and service of their highnesses and of the whole Castilian nation, and strive to aid us and to give us of the things which they have in abundance and which are necessary to us. And they do not know any creed and are not idolaters;[14] only they all believe that power and good are in the heavens, and they are very firmly convinced that I, with these ships and men, came from the heavens, and in this belief they everywhere received me, after they had overcome their fear. And this does not come because they are ignorant; on the contrary, they are of a very acute intelligence and are men who navigate all those seas, so that it is amazing how good an account they give of everything, but it is because they have never seen

---

[9]See Mandeville (Chapter 12, source 86) and Bämler (source 96). In his widely popular account of his late-thirteenth-century travels in Asia, which Columbus read and annotated, Marco Polo also described a number of islanders in South Asia who went naked.

[10]Compare this to Mandeville's testimony regarding the people of Sumatra.

[11]A gold coin of considerable value that bore the seal of Castile.

[12]The smallest and least valuable Spanish coin, it was worth about one-sixtieth of a castellano. Composed of billon, a mixture of copper and silver, it had a whitish hue; hence, the name *blanca*, or "white."

[13]The equivalent of about sixteen skeins, or balls, of spun textile.

[14]Normally, the term *idolater* means anyone who worships idols, or sacred statues, but it is uncertain exactly what Columbus means here. The Tainos worshipped a variety of deities and spirits known as *cemis*, whom they represented in stone statues and other hand-crafted images, also known as *cemis*. It is hard to imagine Columbus's not having seen carved cemis, which filled the Tainos' villages. To compound the problem of what Columbus meant by their not being idolaters, consider the penultimate paragraph of this letter, where the admiral refers to idolaters who will be enslaved.

people clothed or ships of such a kind.

And as soon as I arrived in the Indies, in the first island which I found, I took by force some of them, in order that they might learn and give me information of that which there is in those parts, and so it was that they soon understood us, and we them, either by speech or signs, and they have been very serviceable. I still take them with me, and they are always assured that I come from Heaven, for all the intercourse which they have had with me; and they were the first to announce this wherever I went, and the others went running from house to house and to the neighbouring towns, with loud cries of, "Come! Come to see the people from Heaven!" So all, men and women alike, when their minds were set at rest concerning us, came, so that not one, great or small, remained behind, and all brought something to eat and drink, which they gave with extraordinary affection. In all the island, they have very many canoes, like rowing *fustas,*[15] some larger, some smaller, and some are larger than a *fusta* of eighteen benches. They are not so broad, because they are made of a single log of wood, but a *fusta* would not keep up with them in rowing, since their speed is a thing incredible. And in these they navigate among all those islands, which are innumerable, and carry their goods. One of these canoes I have seen with seventy and eighty men in her, and each one with his oar.

In all these islands, I saw no great diversity in the appearance of the people or in their manners and language. On the contrary, they all understand one another,[16] which is a very curious thing, on account of which I hope that their highnesses

will determine upon their conversion to our holy faith, towards which they are very inclined.

I have already said how I have gone one hundred and seven leagues in a straight line from west to east along the seashore of the island Juana, and as a result of that voyage, I can say that this island is larger than England and Scotland together, for, beyond these one hundred and seven leagues, there remain to the westward two provinces to which I have not gone. One of these provinces they call "Avan,"[17] and there the people are born with tails;[18] and these provinces cannot have a length of less than fifty or sixty leagues, as I could understand from those Indians whom I have and who know all the islands.

The other, Española, has a circumference greater than all Spain, from Colibre, by the seacoast, to Fuenterabia in Vizcaya, since I voyaged along one side one hundred and eighty-eight great leagues in a straight line from west to east. It is a land to be desired and, seen, it is never to be left. And in it, although of all I have taken possession for their highnesses and all are more richly endowed than I know how, or am able, to say, and I hold them all for their highnesses, so that they may dispose of them as, and as absolutely as, of the kingdoms of Castile, in this Española, in the situation most convenient and in the best position for the mines of gold and for all intercourse as well with the mainland here as with that there, belonging to the Grand Khan, where will be great trade and gain. I have taken possession of a large town, to which I gave the name *Villa de Navidad,*[19] and in it I have made fortifications and a fort, which now will by this

---

[15]A small oared boat, often having one or two masts.

[16]This is not totally accurate. Columbus's Taino interpreters knew only a little of the language of the Ciguayos, whom the admiral encountered on Española in January 1493 (note 25).

[17]Which the Spaniards transformed into *La Habana,* or *Havana.*

[18]Marco Polo reported the existence of tailed humans (possibly orangutans) in the islands of Southeast Asia. In his description of the various fantastic peoples who supposedly inhabited the islands of Southeast Asia, John Mandeville listed hairy persons who walked on all fours and climbed trees.

[19]The village of the Nativity (of the Lord). The destruction of the *Santa Maria* off the coast of Española on Christmas Day (Navidad del Señor) forced Columbus to leave behind thirty-nine sailors at the garrison that he named after the day of the incident.

time be entirely finished, and I have left in it sufficient men for such a purpose with arms and artillery and provisions for more than a year, and a *fusta,* and one, a master of all seacraft, to build others, and great friendship with the king of that land, so much so, that he was proud to call me, and to treat me as, a brother. And even if he were to change his attitude to one of hostility towards these men, he and his do not know what arms are and they go naked, as I have already said, and are the most timorous people that there are in the world, so that the men whom I have left there alone would suffice to destroy all that land, and the island is without danger for their persons, if they know how to govern themselves.[20]

In all these islands, it seems to me that all men are content with one woman, and to their chief or king they give as many as twenty.[21] It appears to me that the women work more than the men. And I have not been able to learn if they hold private property; what seemed to me to appear was that, in that which one had, all took a share, especially of eatable things.[22]

In these islands I have so far found no human monstrosities, as many expected,[23] but on the contrary the whole population is very well-formed, nor are they negroes as in Guinea,[24] but their hair is flowing, and they are not born where there is intense force in the rays of the sun; it is true that the sun has there great power, although it is distant from the equinoctial line twenty-six degrees. In these islands, where there are high mountains, the cold was severe this winter, but they endure it, being used to it and with the help of meats which they eat with many and extremely hot spices. As I have found no monsters, so I have had no report of any, except in an island "Quaris," the second at the coming into the Indies, which is inhabited by a people who are regarded in all the islands as very fierce and who eat human flesh. They have many canoes with which they range through all the islands of India and pillage and take as much as they can.[25] They are no more malformed than the others, except that they have the custom of wearing their hair long like women, and they use bows and arrows of the same cane stems, with a small piece of wood at the end, owing to lack of iron which they do not possess. They are ferocious among these other people who are cowardly to an excessive degree, but I make no more account of them than of the rest. These are those who have intercourse with the women of "Matinino," which is the first island met on the way from Spain to the Indies, in which there is not a man. The women engage in no feminine occupation, but use bows and arrows of cane, like those already mentioned, and they arm and protect themselves with plates of copper, of which they have much.[26]

[20]When Columbus returned in November 1493, he discovered the entire garrison had been killed by the native inhabitants in reaction to abuses. Columbus's actions prior to departing for Europe, such as his staging a mock battle, suggest that he was uneasy about leaving these men behind and wanted to impress the Tainos with a display of Spanish firepower and fighting skills.

[21]Generally, only chiefs could afford large numbers of wives because of the substantial bride prices that were paid, in goods or services, to a woman's family. Notwithstanding, many commoners could and did have two or three wives.

[22]See note 10.

[23]Consider these words in the context of sources 86 (Chapter 12) and source 96.

[24]Sub-Saharan West Africa.

[25]The Caribs, who shortly before the arrival of Columbus began to displace the Arawak peoples of the Lesser Antilles, the archipelago to the east and south of Hispaniola. Sixteenth-century Spanish writers unanimously agreed that the Caribs were fierce warriors and cannibalistic. On Janu-ary 13, 1453, Columbus and his men had a short skirmish on Española with some previously unknown natives, whom the admiral incorrectly assumed were Caribs. They were actually Ciguayos, who were less peaceful than the Tainos.

[26]This same account appears in Columbus's log. Father Ramón Pane, who composed an ethnographic study of Taino culture during Columbus's second voyage of 1493–1494, also related in great detail the legend of the island of Matinino, where only women resided. The story, as reported by Pane, however, contains no hint that these were warlike women. Apparently, Columbus took this Taino legend and combined it with stories of the female Amazon warriors of Greco-Roman legend. Mandeville had also written of the land of Amazonia, populated totally by warrior women, and Marco Polo described two Asian islands: one inhabited solely by women; another, exclusively by men. See also Bämler, source 96. There is no evidence that this female society reported by Columbus and Pane ever existed in the Caribbean.

In another island, which they assure me is larger than Española, the people have no hair.[27] In it, there is gold incalculable, and from it and from the other islands, I bring with me Indians as evidence.[28]

In conclusion, to speak only of that which has been accomplished on this voyage, which was so hasty, their highnesses can see that I will give them as much gold as they may need, if their highnesses will render me very slight assistance; moreover, spice and cotton, as much as their highnesses shall command; and mastic,[29] as much as they shall order to be shipped and which, up to now, has been found only in Greece, in the island of Chios,[30] and the Seignory[31] sells it for what it pleases; and aloe wood, as much as they shall order to be shipped, and slaves, as many as they shall order to be shipped and who will be from the idolaters.[32] And I believe that I have found rhubarb and cinamon,[33] and I shall find a thousand other things of value, which the people whom I have left there will have discovered, for I have not delayed at any point, so far as the wind allowed me to sail, except in the town of Navidad, in order to leave it secured and well established, and in truth, I should have done much more, if the ships had served me, as reason demanded.

This is enough . . . and the eternal God, our Lord, Who gives to all those who walk in His way triumph over things which appear to be impossible, and this was notably one; for, although men have talked or have written of these lands, all was conjectural, without suggestion of ocular evidence, but amounted only to this, that those who heard for the most part listened and judged it to be rather a fable than as having any vestige of truth. So that, since Our Redeemer[34] has given this victory to our most illustrious king and queen, and to their renowned kingdoms, in so great a matter, for this all Christendom ought to feel delight and make great feasts and give solemn thanks to the Holy Trinity* with many solemn prayers for the great exaltation which they shall have, in the turning of so many people to our holy faith, and afterwards for temporal benefits, for not only Spain but all Christians will have hence refreshment and gain.

This in accordance with that which has been accomplished, thus briefly.

Done in the caravel, off the Canary Islands, on the fifteenth of February, in the year one thousand four hundred and ninety-three.

At your orders.   El Almirante.

---

[27]John Mandeville described people with little body hair, and Marco Polo told of Buddhist monks* whose heads and faces were shaved. See also the two-headed person in Bämler's woodcut.

[28]Columbus brought seven Tainos back to Spain, where they were baptized,* with King Ferdinand and Prince Juan acting as godparents. One remained at the Spanish court, where he died, and the others returned with Columbus on his second voyage in 1493.

[29]Columbus and his men wrongly identified a native gumbo-limbo tree, which does contain an aromatic resin, with the rare mastic tree, whose costly resin was a profitable trade item for Genoa (note 31).

[30]An island in the eastern Mediterranean.

[31]The ruling body of Genoa, an Italian city-state. Chios was a possession of Genoa, whose merchants controlled the mastic trade.

[32]Church law forbade the enslavement of Christians, except in the most exceptional circumstances.

[33]Actually, when members of the crew showed Columbus what they thought were aloe, mastic, and cinnamon, the admiral accepted the aloe and mastic as genuine but rejected the supposed cinnamon. One of his lieutenants reported seeing rhubarb while on a scouting expedition.

[34]Jesus Christ.

Glossary

abbey. *See* abbot.

abbot (*female:* **abbess**). From the Hebrew *abba* (father); the head of a large monastery,* known as an *abbey* (*see also* monk, nun, and prior).

Anatolia. The eastern Mediterranean peninsula in which modern Asiatic Turkey is located.

apostles. With the exception of St. Paul, the apostles had been Jesus of Nazareth's closest friends and followers. Following Jesus' death and what Christians believe to be his resurrection and ascension into Heaven, the apostles served as the Church's first leaders and missionaries. Paul joined this coterie sometime in the 40s, believing he had been called personally to his apostolate by the resurrected Jesus.

Apostolic See. The see,* or diocese,* of the Apostle* Peter, the person whom the Roman Church believes was chosen by Jesus to lead the Church; hence, the bishopric* of Rome, or the papacy* (*see also* pope).

archbishop. A bishop* who governs a province,* or archdiocese,* and has jurisdiction over other bishops within that province; these subordinate bishops are known as *suffragan* bishops. Archbishops are also known as *metropolitans*, because their cathedrals* are often located in metropolises, or major cities.

archdiocese. *See* archbishop, diocese, and province.

baptism. The sacrament* that initiates a person into the Christian community. The act of pouring water over the person and invoking the Holy Trinity* is believed to remove the stain of Original Sin (the sin of Adam and Eve) from the person's soul, thereby giving the baptized person his or her first gift of divine grace and the opportunity for salvation.

benefice. Essentially an ecclesiastical* term meaning a cleric's* source of income; often land and its attached rents (*see also* prebend). In the feudal* world, the term was sometimes used as a synonym for fief.*

bishop. The chief priest* of an administrative district known as a diocese.* He is in charge of the church and all of its people, clerical* and lay, in his diocese.

canon. A Greek word that means "standard of measurement." It has many different ecclesiastical* meanings; four of the most common are (1) a church law, especially the decree of an ecumenical council;* (2) a clerical* member of a chapter* of canons serving some administrative, teaching, or priestly* function in a cathedral* church (*see also* canon regular); (3) an authoritative list, such as *the canon of officially recognized biblical books;* and (4) the main part of the mass,* in which the Eucharist* is offered, consecrated, and consumed in communion.

canon law. The law of the Church.

canon regular. A member of a religious community bound by a quasi-monastic* rule and vows (*see also* regular clerics) but serving secular* clerical* functions, such as in a cathedral's* chapter* of canons.* Most cathedral canons, however, were *not* regular clerics.*

canoness. A woman who lives in a religious community under a rule but who is not bound by perpetual, or lifelong, vows.

canonical hours. Also known as the *Divine Office,* or simply the *Office,* and the *Opus Dei* (God's Work); the seven periods of prayer and reflection that mark the day. The canonical hours began as a monastic* convention but were soon adopted by the secular clergy.* In a monastic community, the Divine Office is sung and recited by the entire assembled community. The hours are Matins, Prime, Terce, Sext, None, Vespers, and Compline. Daytime is divided into twelve equal *hours.* Thus, Prime (the first hour) is celebrated at daybreak, whereas Matins is prayed well before dawn; Sext (the sixth hour) is the noon office, and None (the ninth hour) is celebrated at a point equidistant between noon and nightfall. Compline, the day's last office, takes place at sunset.

cardinal. Originally, cardinals were clerics* who performed special ceremonial and administrative tasks in Rome. At the highest level stood the cardinal bishops.* Next came the cardinal priests,* who ranked one step higher in the clerical order than cardinal deacons.* They, in turn, outranked cardinal subdeacons.* In the reign of Pope Leo IX (r. 1049–1054), the cardinalate was transformed into a college, or body, of close papal* advisors.

cathedral. From the Latin *cathedra* (seat); the church in which a bishop* or archbishop* resides and from which he rules.

cenobite. A monk* or nun* who lives in a convent, or religious house, under the rule of a superior (*see also* abbey, abbot, monastery, and prior).

chapter. (1) The daily meeting of a monastic* community, where a portion of a chapter of *The Rule of St. Benedict* is read aloud and the affairs of the monastery are discussed; (2) the community of canons* who serve as administrators in a cathedral* church.

chronicle. A narrative account of notable events, usually presented in strict chronological sequence. Chronicles are essentially catalogues of facts presented in a straightforward manner and normally lack the analysis found in more developed histories.

civil law. Based on the sixth-century *Body of Civil Law* of Emperor Justinian (r. 527–565); the West's primary body of recovered Roman law.

Church Fathers. *See* Fathers of the Church.

clergy. The class of clerics.*

cleric. A person who serves the Church in a ministerial office. The Roman Church has seven clerical offices, or ranks. The highest is priest,* followed by deacon* and subdeacon.* The term *clerk* is an archaic variant (*see also* clerics, regular, and clerics, secular).

clerics, regular. Clerics,* such as friars,* monks,* and canons regular,* who take solemn perpetual vows to live in regulated religious communities according to a specific rule (*regula* in Latin), as opposed to secular clerics.*

clerics, secular. Clerics* who serve in the world (*see also* secular*), as opposed to belonging to a cloistered or semicloistered community of regular clerics.* Parish* and diocesan* clergy,* such as canons,* are normally secular clerics.

confession. The sacrament* in which a person contritely tells his or her sins to a priest* and receives absolution and a penance. The penance can be remitted by an indulgence.*

confessor. (1) A person who, by his or her life and actions, heroically confesses, or gives witness to, the faith; (2) a priest* who listens to and absolves the sins of a penitent in confession.*

council. A meeting (also known as a synod*) of church leaders, in which decisions regarding doctrine, conduct, and ecclesiastical* administration are decided. These decisions become law (*see also* canon law*), especially when such councils are so large as to be ecumenical councils.*

deacon. A Greek word meaning "minister" or "administrator"; a special assistant to a bishop* who performs such tasks as preaching and dispensing alms to the community's needy. The early Church also had *deaconesses,* older women who performed a variety of important administrative and ceremonial tasks. For males, the *diaconate* is the clerical* rank just below that of priest.*

dialectic. One of the Seven Liberal Arts,* it is the art of critical reasoning and argumentation based on analysis of the meanings of words and the veracity of arguments and conclusions.

diocese. The region ruled by a bishop.*

Divine Office. *See* canonical hours.

ecclesiastical. Anything having to do with the Church (*ecclesia* in Latin).

ecumenical council. A council,* or meeting, that represents the universal Church, in which church leaders gather to decide issues that concern all of Christendom. The doctrinal decisions of these councils are considered infallible, because it is believed that the entire Church, under the guidance of the Holy Spirit,* can never err.

episcopal. Anything that relates to a bishop* or his office; for example, episcopal authority (from the Greek word *episcopos,* which means "overseer").

Eucharist. Derived from the Greek, "to bestow grace"; believed by Roman Catholic and Eastern Orthodox* Christians to be the actual body and blood of Jesus, which is received under the appearance of bread and wine at the mass* (*see also* canon and sacrament).

evangelical. Preaching or teaching centered on the Christian New Testament and especially the Gospels.*

Evangelist. (1) One of the authors of the four Gospels;* (2) a person who preaches the Gospel, or Good News, of Christianity.

excommunication. A sentence of exclusion from the community and protection of the Church. It was believed that "outside of the Church there is no salvation."

Fathers of the Church. Early church writers whose theological and devotional works were considered especially authoritative. The fours major Fathers of the Western Church were Saints Ambrose, Augustine, Jerome, and Gregory the Great.

fealty. The sworn faithfulness of a vassal* to a feudal* lord.

feudalism. A military and political system based on the service of a warrior, known as a vassal,* to a lord. In return for such service, the vassal received a fief.*

fief. One of the major reasons a person became a vassal* was to receive a fief (*feudum* in Latin, hence the term *feudal*) as payment for services rendered. A fief could be any source of income, but as time went on, it more often than not consisted of lands and offices.

friars. *See* mendicant friars.

Gospel(s). Literally, "the Good News"; the four biblical accounts of the teachings of Jesus ascribed to the Evangelists:* Matthew, Mark, Luke, and John.

Hellenistic. An amalgamation of classical Greek (Hellenic) and Near Eastern cultural elements that took shape in the wake of Alexander the Great's conquests of the late fourth century B.C.

Byzantium was arguably the last Hellenistic civilization.

heresy. A religious belief that is at variance with established dogma. Heresy is a cause for excommunication* (*see also* heterodoxy).

heretic. A person whose religious beliefs deviate from the doctrine of the established Church.

heterodoxy. From the Greek, "different thought"; heretical* thought or teaching, which, therefore, does not agree with the teaching of the Church (*see also* orthodoxy).

Holy Spirit. The third person of the Holy Trinity.*

Holy Trinity. *See* Trinity, Holy.

indulgence. The remission of punishment for sins already forgiven at confession;* normally this punishment must be paid either on earth while living or in purgatory* after death. The Roman Church, however, grants partial and plenary (full) indulgences for such *good works* as going on pilgrimage,* contributing money to such activities as crusades and the building of churches, and performing certain prescribed religious rituals.

mass. The central religious ceremony of the Roman Church, at which the Eucharist* is consecrated and consumed in commemoration of Jesus' sacrifice on the cross.

mendicant friars. Literally, "begging brothers." In the early thirteenth century, four orders of friars emerged: the Order of Friars Minor, or Franciscans; the Order of Preachers, or Dominicans; the Carmelite Friars; and the Augustinian, or Austin, Friars. Although they were regular clerics,* friars, unlike monks,* did not cloister themselves away from the world. Their chief mission was to serve the spiritual needs of urban people. The religious houses in which friars live are known as *convents,* rather than monasteries.*

metropolitan. *See* archbishop.

monastery. The house, or community, in which monks* or nuns* reside. Large monasteries are called *abbeys** and are ruled by abbots* or abbesses.* Smaller monasteries are ruled by priors* or prioresses* and are known as *priories.* Monasteries, especially those of women, are sometimes called *convents.*

monk. A man who has chosen to take lifelong, or perpetual, religious vows and to live in a community that separates itself from the world (*see also* cenobite, monastery, and nun).

mosaic. A picture, often a mural (wall decoration), composed of small pieces of tile, stone, metal, and semiprecious stones.

nun. A woman who lives a cloistered life in a religious house (often termed a *convent*); the female counterpart to a monk* (*see also* abbot, canoness, cenobite, monastery, and prior).

Opus Dei. *See* canonical hours.

orthodoxy. Literally, "right thinking"; refers to correct religious dogma, as opposed to heterodoxy,* or heresy.*

papacy. *See* pope.

papal. *See* pope.

parish. The lowest level of that portion of the Church served by the secular clergy.* Each parish is served by a priest,* who administers the sacraments* to the laity and is subject to the authority of the local bishop.*

patriarch. Literally, "ruling father"; a term of honor accorded certain archbishops* of exceptionally important sees,* such as Rome, Constantinople, Alexandria, Antioch, and Jerusalem. Taken together, these five patriarchs are often referred to as the *Pentarchy* (the five rulers).

pilgrim. A person who undertakes a penitential journey, or *pilgrimage,* to a relic* site or other sacred place.

pontiff. A high priest.* As a title, *pontiff* is reserved for archbishops,* bishops,* and popes.* The pope claims the special titles *Roman Pontiff* and *Supreme Pontiff.*

pope. From the Latin *papa* (father); a title normally reserved for the bishop* of Rome. Hence, the *papacy,* or the *papal* office, means the see* of Rome (*see also* Apostolic See, pontiff, and prelate).

prebend. A cleric's* source of income (*see also* benefice).

prelate. A Latin term that means "one set before"; a prelate is a high-ranking cleric,* such as a bishop* or abbot,* whose office brings with it supervision over a substantial number of other clerics. The pope* claims the title *Supreme Prelate.*

priest. A cleric* who has the power to celebrate mass* and to act as a confessor* for persons seeking absolution of their sins. In essence, priests dispense the Church's sacraments.* Bishops* (and therefore archbishops*) are chief priests, with the power to ordain other priests. Monks* and friars* can be priests, but they can also be *lay brothers,* who have no priestly powers. Deacons* are not priests.

primate. The chief archbishop* of a major region or country; for example, the archbishop of Canterbury is the primate of England. The pope* claims the title *Primate of the Church.*

prior (*female:* **prioress**). Either the second-in-charge of an abbey* (*see also* abbot), or the head of a small monastery* known as a *priory.*

province. In ecclesiastical* usage: (1) the region ruled by an archbishop;* (2) a large, often kingdomwide administrative division used by various orders of regular clergy,* especially the mendicant friars.*

purgatory. The place where the souls of good people who do not quite deserve Heaven go after death to be purged of the remaining traces of guilt and sin before entry into Paradise. The Roman Church developed the concept of purgatory during the twelfth century (*see also* indulgence).

regular clerics. *See* clerics, regular.

relic. Literally, "something left behind"; any object associated with Jesus or a saint. In the case of a saint, a relic is often a body part that is kept and venerated after the person's death because it is believed to transmit the holiness and sacred power of that person. In the medieval era, relics were generally believed to have healing powers.

rhetoric. One of the Seven Liberal Arts;* the study of the elements of language, literature, and oratory.

sacraments. The seven key rites, or ceremonies, administered by a priest,* a bishop,* and in some cases a deacon*: baptism,* confession,* holy Eucharist,* confirmation, holy orders, marriage, and the last blessing (before death). The Roman and Byzantine Churches consider each to be an essential vehicle of grace instituted by Jesus himself.

secular. Things that pertain to the world (*saeculum* in Latin).

secular clerics. *See* clerics, secular.

see. Also known as a *seat,* or a cathedral* seat; literally, the throne on which a bishop* sits in his cathedral church. In its broader sense, it is a bishop's church and the city and region over which he rules. A synonym is *diocese.*

serf. A semifree tenant farmer who is bound to the soil.

Seven Liberal Arts. The seven areas of study inherited from late-Roman antiquity. Grammar, rhetoric,* and dialectic* form the *trivium* (the confluence of three roads), or the literary and persuasive portion. Arithmetic, geometry, music, and astronomy form the *quadrivium* (the crossroads where four roads meet), or the quantitative portion.

simony. The sin of buying or selling anything that is sacred, especially the sacraments* or a priestly* office. It receives its name from the magician Simon Magus, who offered money to Saints Peter and John for the power to confer the Holy Spirit:* the Bible, Acts of the Apostles, 8:9–24.

subdeacon. A cleric* who ranks just below and assists a deacon.*

squire. A young noble attendant of a knight who served as a knight-in-training; also known as a *knight bachelor.*

Supreme Pontiff. The pope (*see also* pontiff).

synod. Usually, a local church council* convened by a bishop* or archbishop.* Synods can be called *councils,* and even ecumenical councils* can be called *synods.*

tithe. The tax paid for upkeep of a church; theoretically, one tenth of all produce or income, but it tended to be less.

Trinity, Holy. Christians believe that God is three co-eternal, co-equal, distinct, and separate divine persons in one indivisible divine essence: God the Father, the Creator; God the Son, the Redeemer (who became the fully human and fully divine Jesus of Nazareth); and God the Holy Spirit,* the Sanctifier and Illuminator, who dispenses grace and divine wisdom to God's people.

vassal. Literally, "one who serves"; he served his lord as a feudal* warrior and enjoyed, in return, a variety of political, social, and economic benefits, including a fief.*

Sources

Part One ▾ The Collapse of Roman Unity and the Emergence of Three Successor Civilizations: A.D. 100–1050

Chapter 1

Source 1: From J. L. Creed, ed., Lactantius, *De mortibus persecutorum* (Oxford: Clarendon Press, 1984), pp. 10–12, trans. Alfred J. Andrea. **Source 2:** From Pharr, Clyde, trans., *The Theodosian Code and Novels and the Sirmondian Constitutions* (pp. 115–117, 155–156, 174, 176, 178, 181, 230, 232–233, 342–344, 351, 363, 390–391, 407–408, 413, passim). Copyright © 1952 by Princeton University Press. Renewed by Ray Pharr 1980. Published by Princeton University Press. Reprinted by permission of Princeton University Press. **Source 3:** Adapted from Arthur C. McGiffert, trans., in *A Select Library of Nicene and Post-Nicene Fathers,* 14 vols. (Second series; Christian Literature Company, 1890), vol. 1, pp. 349–350, 369–370, 386–387. **Source 4:** From Marcus Dodds, trans., in *A Select Library of Nicene and Post-Nicene Fathers,* 14 vols. (First series; Christian Literature Company, 1887), vol. 2, pp. 411–413. **Source 5:** *The Redeemer,* Museo Arcivescovile, Ravenna, Italy. Photograph by Alinari/Art Resource, NY.

Chapter 2

Source 6: Adapted from A. J. Church and W. J. Brodribb, trans., *The Agricola and Germany* (London: Macmillan, 1885), pp. 87–107, passim. **Source 7:** From Katherine Fischer Drew, trans., *The Law of the Salian Franks* (Philadelphia: University of Pennsylvania Press, 1991), pp. 65, 77–80, 82–84, 86, 92–94, 104–106, 116–117, 122, passim. Reprinted with permission. **Source 8:** Adapted from Thomas Hodgkin, trans., *The Letters of Cassiodorus* (London: Henry Frowde, 1886), pp. 131, 198–199, 157–158, 206, 160, 174, 186–187, 251, 219, 321–322. **Source 9:** From Ernest Brehaut, trans., *History of the Franks,* Columbia Records of Civilization Series (New York: Columbia University Press), pp. 1, 36–48, passim. **Source 10: p. 71,** *The Barberini Ivory,* The Louvre, Paris, France. Photograph by Giraudon/Art Resource, NY. **p. 72,** *Christ in Majesty,* Museo del Duomo, Cividale, Italy. Photo courtesy of Museo del Duomo.

Chapter 3

Source 11: pp. 76–77, Reprinted with permission of Pocket Books, a Division of Simon & Schuster, from Procopius: *History of the Wars and Other Selections,* edited by Averil Cameron (The Great Histories Series, H. R. Trevor-Roper, Series Editor), pp. 333–335. Copyright © 1967 by Washington Square Press, Inc. (With an additional portion translated from the Greek by Alfred J. Andrea.) **pp. 77–81,** Excerpted from Procopius, *Secret History,* trans. Ri-chard Atwater, pp. 67–68, 70–71, 89–94, passim. Copyright © 1961 by The University of Michigan Press. Reprinted with permission. **Source 12:** Excerpts from A. E. R. Boak (trans.), "The Book of the Prefect," in *Journal of Economic and Business History,* 1 (Cambridge, Massachusetts: Presidents and Fellows of Harvard College, 1929), pp. 605, 613–614. **Source 13:** Pages 43–48 from *Fourteen Byzantine Rulers,* by Michael Psellus, translated by E. R. A. Sewter (Penguin Classics, 1966), copyright © E. R. A. Sewter 1966. Reproduced by permission of Penguin Books Ltd. **Source 14:** From Arthur J. Arberry (trans.), *The Koran Interpreted,* 2 Vols. (vol. 1, pp. 73–77, 79–83, 85, passim). Copyright © 1955 by George Allen and Unwin Ltd. Reprinted with permission. **Source 15:** From T. W. Arnold, trans., *The Preaching of Islam,* 2nd ed. (London, 1913), pp. 57–59. **Source 16:** Selected excerpts from *Islam: From the Prophet Muhammad to the Capture of Constantinople,* Volume II (pp. 27–30), by Bernard Lewis, Ed. & Trans. Copyright © 1974 by Bernard Lewis. Reprinted by permission of HarperCollins Publishers, Inc.

Chapter 4

Source 17: From *The Rule of St. Benedict,* in Gregory Arroyo, ed., *Sancti Benedicti Regula Monasteriorum* (Silos, 1947), pp. 10–15, 45–50, 53, 58–60, 96–97, trans. Alfred J. Andrea. **Source 18:** From James Harvey Robinson, *Readings in European History,* 2 vols. (Boston: Ginn, 1904), vol. 1, pp. 90–92. **Source 19:** Reprinted with the permission of Simon & Schuster from *The Crisis of Church and State 1050–1300,* by Brian Tierney (pp. 13–15). Copyright © 1964 by Prentice-Hall, Inc., Renewed 1992 by Brian Tierney. **Source 20:** Select letters of Gregory I, trans. Alfred J. Andrea. **Source 21:** From Oliver J. Thatcher and Edgar H. McNeal, trans., *A Source Book for Mediaeval History* (New York: Charles Scribner's Sons, 1905), pp. 96–100. **Source 22:** Adapted from J. A. Giles, trans., *Bede's Ecclesiastical History of England* (London: George Bell and Sons, 1903), pp. 76–82. **Source 23:** From *Vita Liuthirgae Virginis,* trans. Linda Breuer Gray, in "Mighty in Appropriate Ways: Liutbirg, A Ninth-Century Life," M.A. Thesis, The University of Vermont (1994), pp. 15–29, 32–33, 46–47, 49, passim. Reprinted with permission.

Chapter 5

Source 24: From *The Life of Charlemagne,* trans. S. E. Turner (New York: Harper and Bros., 1880), pp. 26–28, 50–66, 69, passim. **Source 25:** From D. C. Munro, trans., *University of Pennsylvania Translations and Reprints* (Philadelphia: University of Pennsylvania, 1900), vol. 6, no. 5, pp. 12–14; Oliver J. Thatcher and Edgar H. McNeal, trans., *A Source Book for Mediaeval History* (New York: Charles Scribner's Sons, 1905), p. 107; and Munro, *Translations,* vol. 6, no. 5, pp. 11–12. **Source 26:** From D. C. Munro, trans., *University of Pennsylvania Translations and Reprints* (Philadelphia: University of Pennsylvania, 1900), vol. 6, no. 5, pp. 2–5, 16–27. **Source 27:** Lateran mosaic, S. Giovanni in Laterano, Rome, Italy. Photograph by Alinari/Art Resource, NY. **Source 28:** Excerpted from Bernhard Walter Scholz (trans.), *Carolingian Chronicles: Royal Frankish Annals and Nithard's Histories* (pp. 129–133, 166–168, 174). Copyright © 1970 by The University of Michigan Press. Reprinted with permission. **Source 29:** From *Reginonis Chronicon* in MGH, SS, 1:598–601, trans. Alfred J. Andrea.

Chapter 6

Source 30: From Gerard Sitwell, *St. Odo of Cluny . . . Life of St. Gerald* (London: Sheed & Ward, 1958), pp. 94–101, 111–116, passim. **Source 31:** From Frederic A. Ogg, trans., *A Source Book of Medieval History* (New York: American Book Company, 1907), pp. 220–221. **Source 32:** From Oliver J. Thatcher and Edgar H. McNeal, trans., *A Source Book for Mediaeval History* (New York: Charles Scribner's Sons, 1905), pp. 412–416. **Source 33:** Adapted from Frederic A. Ogg, trans., *A Source Book of Medieval History* (New York: American Book Company, 1908), pp. 191–194. **Source 34:** From F. A. Wright (trans.), *The Works of Liudprand of Cremona* (New York: E. P. Dutton, 1930), pp. 215–218, 220–223, 226–229, passim. Reprinted with permission of Routledge. **Source 35:** Adapted from Oliver J. Thatcher and Edgar H. McNeal, trans., *A Source Book for Mediaeval History* (New York: Charles Scribner's Sons, 1905), pp. 119–121. **Source 36:** From Christopher St. John (trans.), *The Plays of Roswitha* (London: Chatto & Windus, 1923), pp. 131–137, 140–147. **Source 37:** Selected excerpts from *Christianity through the Thirteenth Century,* by Marshall Baldwin (pp. 217–222). Copyright © 1970 by Marshall W. Baldwin. Reprinted by permission of HarperCollins Publishers, Inc.

Part Two ▾ The High Middle Ages: European Efflorescence and Expansion: A.D. 1050–1300

Chapter 7

Source 38: From S. J. Eales, *The Life and Works of St. Bernard of Clairvaux,* 4 vols. (London, 1896), vol. 3, pp. 298–301, 315–316. **Source 39: pp. 207–208,** From James Harvey Robinson, *Readings in European History,* 2 vols. (Boston: Ginn, 1904), vol. 1, pp. 357–358. **p. 208,** From Thomas F. Crane, ed., *The Exempla . . . of Jacques de Vitry* (1890; New York: Burt Franklin, 1971 reprint), pp. 92–93, trans. Alfred J. Andrea. **Source 40:** From *Heresies of the High Middle Ages,* by Walter L. Wakefield and Austin P. Evans (pp. 209–210). Copyright © 1969 by Columbia University Press. Reprinted with permission of the publisher. **Source 41:** Adapted from Paschal Robinson, trans., *The Writings of Saint Francis of Assisi* (Philadelphia: Dolphin Press, 1906), pp. 81–86. **Source 42:** From Norman P. Tanner, S.J. (ed. &

trans.), *Decrees of the Ecumenical Councils,* 2 volumes (vol. 1, pp. 233–237, 240, 242–245, 248, 263–267, passim). Copyright © 1990 by Georgetown University Press. Reprinted by permission. **Source 43:** From Henry Charles Lea, *A History of the Inquisition of the Middle Ages,* 3 vols. (New York: Harper and Brothers, 1887), vol. 1, pp. 411–414.

Chapter 8

Source 44: From Oliver J. Thatcher and Edgar H. McNeal, trans., *A Source Book for Mediaeval History* (New York: Charles Scribner's Sons, 1905), pp. 553–562, passim. **Source 45:** From Oliver J. Thatcher and Edgar H. McNeal, trans., *A Source Book for Mediaeval History* (New York: Charles Scribner's Sons, 1905), pp. 572–573. **Source 46:** From Kohl, Benjamin G., and Smith, Alison Andrews (Editors), *Major Problems in the History of the Italian Renaissance,* First Edition (pp. 75–76). Copyright © 1995 by D. C. Heath. Reprinted by permission of Houghton Mifflin Company. **Source 47:** *The Song of Roland,* trans. Alfred J. Andrea. **Source 48:** Excerpted from Douglas, David C., and Greenaway, George W. (eds.), *English Historical Documents,* Vol. 2 (pp. 937–940, 942–943). Copyright © 1953 by Eyre and Spottiswoode. Reprinted with the permission of Cambridge University Press. **Source 49:** From E. P. Cheney, trans., *University of Pennsylvania Translations and Reprints* (Philadelphia: University of Pennsylvania, 1897), vol. 2, no. 1, pp. 12–17. **Source 50:** From A. Gandenzi, ed., *Bibliotheca Juridica Medii Aevi,* 3 vols. (Bologna, 1888–1901), vol. 3, pp. 218–219, 228–229, 260, trans. Alfred J. Andrea. **Source 51:** From Oliver J. Thatcher and Edgar H. McNeal, trans., *A Source Book for Mediaeval History* (New York: Charles Scribner's Sons, 1905), pp. 577–578. **Source 52:** Reprinted by permission of James F. Powers.

Chapter 9

Source 53: Excerpted from Brian Tierney, Donald Kagan, and L. Pearce Williams, *Great Issues in Western Civilization,* Second Edition (vol. 1, pp. 412–414). Copyright © 1972 by Random House. Reprinted with permission of The McGraw-Hill Companies. **Source 54:** From *The Summa Contra Gentiles of Saint Thomas Aquinas, Literally Translated by the English Dominican Fathers from the Latest Leonine Edition,* 4 vols. (London: Burns, Oates, & Washbourne Ltd., 1924), vol. 1, pp. 4–7, 14–15. Reprinted by permission of Burns & Oates. **Source 55:** From *University Life and Records in the Middle Ages,* by Lynn Thorndike (pp. 85–86). Copyright © 1944 by Columbia University Press. Reprinted with permission of the publisher. **Source 56: Top,** *Eve,* by Giselbertus, Musée Rolin, Autun, France. Photograph by Giraudon/Art Resource, NY. **Bottom,** *A Gallo-Roman Relief,* Musée des Beaux Arts, Beaune, France. Photograph courtesy of Musée des Beaux Arts. **Source 57: p. 278,** *Notre Dame la Brune,* Abbey Church of St. Philbert, Tournus, France. Photograph by Alfred J. Andrea. **p. 279, Left,** *Ecclesia* and *Synagoga,* Musée de l'Oeuvre Notre-Dame, Strasbourg, France. Photographs by Giraudon/Art Resource,

NY. **Source 58:** Top, *Dormition Typanum,* Strasbourg Cathedral, Strasbourg, France. Photograph by Foto Marburg/Art Resource, NY. **Bottom,** *Dormition Fresco,* Monastery Church, Ohrid, Macedonia. Photograph by Erich Lessing/Art Resource, NY. **Source 59:** pp. 285–287, "The Confession of Golias," by George Whicher, from *The Golliard Poets* (pp. 107–117). Copyright © 1949 by New Directions Publishing Corp. Reprinted by permission of New Directions Publishing Corp. **pp. 287–288,** "The Canticle of the Creatures," from Benan Fahy, O.F.M. (trans.), *The Writings of St. Francis of Assisi* (pp. 130–131). Copyright © 1963 by the Franciscan Herald Press. Used by permission of Franciscan Press. **pp. 288–289,** "Dies Irae," from Franklin Johnson, trans., in Eveline Warner Brainerd, ed., *Great Hymns of the Middle Ages* (New York: Century, 1909), pp. 104–107. **Source 60:** From Chrétien de Troyes, *Arthurian Romances,* trans. W. W. Comfort (London: Dent, 1914), pp. 28–34. **Source 61:** From *Evangelium Secundum Marcas Argenti,* in Paul Lehmann, ed., *Die Parodie im Mittelalter* (Stuttgart: Anton Hiersemann, 1963), pp. 183–184, trans. Alfred J. Andrea.

Chapter 10

Source 62: *The Gospel Book of Monte Cassino,* The Vatican, Rome, Italy. Photograph courtesy of the Vatican Library. **Source 63:** From William Stubbs, *A Translation of Such Documents As Are Untranslated in Mr. Stubbs' Collection from the Earliest Times to the Conclusion of Edward the First's Reign* (Oxford: E. B. Gardner et al., 1873), pp. 143–146. **Source 64:** From Frank T. Marzials, trans., *Memoirs of the Crusades* (London: Dent, 1908), pp. 148–151, 219–220, 231–232, 311–315. **Source 65:** From Oliver J. Thatcher and Edgar H. McNeal, trans., *A Source Book for Mediaeval History* (New York: Charles Scribner's Sons, 1905), pp. 136–138, 151–152, 155–156, 165–166. (The translation of the "Concordat of Worms" has been modified by Alfred J. Andrea based on his reading of the Latin text in the MGH, Leges, 2:75–76.) **Source 66:** From *Gesta Innocentii III,* in David R. Gress-Wright, ed., *The* Gesta Innocentii III: *Text, Introduction, and Commentary,* Ph.D. Dissertation, Bryn Mawr (1981), pp. 103–109, trans. Alfred J. Andrea. **Source 67:** Reprinted with the permission of Simon & Schuster from *The Crisis of Church and State 1050–1300,* by Brian Tierney (pp. 207–210, passim). Copyright © 1964 by Prentice-Hall, Inc., Renewed 1992 by Brian Tierney. **Source 68:** Reprinted by permission of Joseph F. O'Callaghan, trans., from the following: Julio González, *Alfonso IX,* 2 vols. (Madrid, 1945), vol. 2, pp. 23–26, no. 11; Georg Gross, "Las Cortes de 1252. Ordenamiento otorgado al Consejo de Burgos en las Cortes celebradas en Sevilla el 12 de Octubre de 1252 (según el original)," *Boletín de la Real Academia de la Historia,* 182 (1985), pp. 95–114; *Cortes de los antiguos reinos de Aragón y Valencia y Principado de Cataluña,* ed. Real Academia de la Historia, 25 vols. (Madrid, 1896–1919), vol. 1, pp. 140–153. **Source 69:** From E. P. Cheney, trans., *University of Pennsylvania Translations and Reprints* (Philadelphia: University of Pennsylvania, 1897), vol. 1, no. 6, pp. 6–16. **Source 70:** From Oliver J. Thatcher and Edgar H. McNeal, trans., *A Source Book for Mediaeval History* (New York: Charles Scribner's Sons, 1905), pp. 238–240. **Source 71:** From E. P. Cheney, trans., *University of Pennsylvania Translations and Reprints* (Philadelphia: University of Pennsylvania, 1897), vol. 1, no. 6, pp. 33–35.

Chapter 11

Source 72: From Oliver J. Thatcher and Edgar H. McNeal, trans., *A Source Book for Mediaeval History* (New York: Charles Scribner's Sons, 1905), pp. 514–521. **Source 73:** Manuscript miniature illumination of the *Estoire d' Eracles,* a continuation of William of Tyre's *Historia Iherosolimitana.* Photograph courtesy of The Walters Art Gallery, Baltimore, Maryland. **Source 74:** Excerpts from Shlomo Eidelberg (trans. and ed.), *The Jews and the Crusaders: The Hebrew Chronicles of the First and Second Crusades* (pp. 21–22, 25–26, 30–32, 35, passim). Copyright © 1977 by The University of Wisconsin Press. Reprinted with permission of Shlomo Eidelberg. **Source 75:** From Philip K. Hitti (trans.), *The Memoirs of an Arab-Syrian Gentleman* (Beirut: Khayat, 1964), pp. 161, 163–164, 167–170. **Source 76:** From *Hystoria Constantinopolitana,* trans. Alfred J. Andrea. **Source 77:** From Frank T. Marzials, trans., *Memoirs of the Crusades* (London: Dent, 1908), pp. 253–259. **Source 78:** From Henry Yule, ed. and trans., *Cathay and the Way Thither,* 2nd ed., rev. by H. Cordier (London: Hakluyt, 1913–1916), pp. 45–51.

Part Three ▾ Crisis, Retrenchment, Recovery, and a New World: A.D. 1300–1500

Chapter 12

Source 79: From *Chronicle of Jean de Venette,* edited by Richard A. Newhall, translated by Jean Birdsall (pp. 31–32, 48–52, passim). Copyright © 1953 by Columbia University Press. Reprinted with permission of the publisher. **Source 80:** J. R. Lumby, ed., *Chronicon Henrici Knighton vel Cnitthon Monachi Leycestrensis,* 2 vols. (Rolls Series, vols. 91–92, 1889 and 1895), vol. 2, pp. 61–65, trans. Alfred J. Andrea. **Source 81:** Excerpted from Kenelm Foster and Mary John Ronayne (eds.), *I, Catherine: Selected Writings of St. Catherine of Siena* (pp. 107–110, 255–260, passim). Copyright © 1980 by Collins Publishers. Reprinted with permission of HarperCollins Publishers Limited. **Source 82:** Herbert E. Winn, ed., *Wycliff: Select English Writings* (Oxford: Oxford University Press, 1929), pp. 70–72, trans. Alfred J. Andrea. **Source 83:** From Thomas Johnes, trans., *Chronicles of England, France, and Spain and the Adjoining Countries,* rev. ed. (New York: Colonial Press, 1901), pp. 51–65, 211–230, passim. **Source 84:** From Blake Beattie, trans., *Il Trecentonovelle,* ed. Antonio Lanza (Florence, 1984), pp. 362–365 (novella CLXIII). Reprinted by permission of Blake Beattie. **Source 85:** From *The Canterbury Tales,* trans. Ronald L. Ecker and Eugene J. Crook, Hodge & Braddock, Publishers, 1993. Reprinted with permission. **Source 86:** From fourteenth-century Middle English translation in the Cotton Manuscript of the British Museum, printed 1725, Chapters 20 and 30, trans. Alfred J. Andrea. **Source 87:** From Clagett, Marshall. *The Science of Mechanics in the Middle Ages* (pp. 70–72). © 1961. r1987. (Madison: The University of Wisconsin Press.) Reprinted by permission of The University of Wisconsin Press.

Chapter 13

Source 88: From James Harvey Robinson, *Readings in European History,* 2 vols. (Boston: Ginn, 1904), vol. 1, pp. 511–513; and Oliver J. Thatcher and Edgar H. McNeal, trans., *A Source Book for Mediaeval History* (New York: Charles Scribner's Sons, 1905), p. 332. **Source 89:** From Gerald Strauss, Ed. & Trans., *Manifestations of Discontent in Germany on the Eve of the Reformation* (Bloomington, Indiana: Indiana University Press, 1971), pp. 218–222. Reprinted with permission of Indiana University Press. **Source 90:** From Christine de Pisan, *Ditié de Jeanne d'Arc,* ed. and trans. by Angus J. Kennedy and Kenneth Varty (Oxford: Society for the Study of Mediaeval Languages and Literature, 1977), pp. 41–48, passim. Reprinted with permission of Angus J. Kennedy and Kenneth Varty. **Source 91:** From Johann Nider, *Formicarius* (Douaii, 1602), p. 385, trans. Alfred J.

Andrea. **Source 92:** Pages 98–100, 402, 404–408 from *Memoirs,* by Philippe de Commynes, translated by Michael Jones (Penguin Classics, 1972). Copyright © Michael Jones, 1972. Reproduced by permission of Penguin Books Ltd. **Source 93:** Excerpts from *The History of Florence* (pp. 69–76, passim), by Francesco Guicciardini, translated by Mario Domandi. Copyright © 1970 by Mario Domandi. Reprinted by permission of HarperCollins Publishers, Inc. **Source 94:** From Gordon Griffiths, James Hankins, and David Thompson, trans. & eds., *The Humanism of Leonardo Bruni,* Medieval & Renaissance Texts Series, Vol. 46, pp. 240–251, passim. Copyright © 1987 by The Renaissance Society of America. Reprinted with permission. **Source 95:** p. 462, *Vanity: Allegory on the Transitoriness of Life,* Bayerisches Nationalmuseum, Munich, Germany. Photograph courtesy of Bayerisches Nationalmuseum. p. 463, *The Adoration of the Shepherds,* by Martin Schongauer, from Gemäeldegalerie, Staatlichen Museen, Berlin, Germany. Photograph by Foto Marburg/Art Resource, NY. **Source 96:** "The Marvels of Nature," woodcut from *Das Buch der Natur,* by Konrad von Megenberg (Augsburg: Johann Bämler, 1481), Rosenwald Collection of Rare Books, the Library of Congress, Washington, DC. Photograph courtesy of the Library of Congress. **Source 97:** From Cecil Jane, ed. and trans., *Select Documents Illustrating the Four Voyages of Columbus,* 2 vols. (London: Hakluyt Society, 1930–1933), vol. 1, pp. 2–18.